Complexity, Endogenous Money and Macroeconomic Theory

Complexity, Endogenous Money and Macroeconomic Theory

Essays in Honour of Basil J. Moore

Edited by

Mark Setterfield

Professor of Economics, Trinity College, Hartford, USA and Associate Member, Cambridge Centre for Economic and Public Policy, Cambridge University, UK

Edward Elgar
Cheltenham, UK • Northampton, MA, USA

Published by
Edward Elgar Publishing Limited
Glensanda House
Montpellier Parade
Cheltenham
Glos GL50 1UA
UK

Edward Elgar Publishing, Inc.
136 West Street
Suite 202
Northampton
Massachusetts 01060
USA

A catalogue record for this book
is available from the British Library

Library of Congress Cataloguing-in-Publication Data
Complexity, endogenous money and macroeconomic theory : essays in honour of Basil J. Moore / edited by Mark Setterfield.
p. cm.
1. Macroeconomics. 2. Econometrics. 3. Money. 4. Endogenous growth (Economics) I. Setterfield, Mark, 1967– II. Moore, Basil J.

HB172.5.C645 2006
339—dc22 2005056792

ISBN-13: 978 1 84376 987 3
ISBN-10: 1 84376 987 5

Printed and bound in Great Britain by MPG Books Ltd, Bodmin, Cornwall

Contents

PART V UNEMPLOYMENT, INFLATION AND THE DETERMINATION OF AGGREGATE INCOME

List of contributors

Philip Arestis, Cambridge University, Cambridge, UK
John Cornwall, Dalhousie University, Halifax, Canada
Wendy Cornwall, Mount Saint Vincent University, Halifax, Canada
Jerry Courvisanos, University of Ballarat, Ballarat, Australia
Paul Davidson, New School For Social Research, New York, USA
Richard Day, University of Southern California, Los Angeles, USA
Giuseppe Fontana, University of Leeds, Leeds, UK
Mathew Forstater, University of Missouri, Kansas City, USA
Claude Gnos, Université de Bourgogne, Dijon, France
Wynne Godley, Cambridge University, Cambridge, UK
Charles Goodhart, London School of Economics, London, UK
G.C. Harcourt, Jesus College, Cambridge, UK
Arne Heise, University of Hamburg, Hamburg, Germany
Peter Howells, University of the West of England, Bristol, UK
Steve Keen, University of Western Sydney, Sydney, Australia
Marc Lavoie, University of Ottawa, Ottawa, Canada
Chris Niggle, University of Redlands, Redlands, USA
Colin Richardson, University of Abertay, Dundee, Scotland
Louis-Philippe Rochon, Laurentian University, Sudbury, Canada
Colin Rogers, University of Adelaide, Adelaide, Australia
J. Barkley Rosser, Jr., James Madison University, Harrisonburg, USA
Claudio Sardoni, University of Rome 'La Sapienza', Rome, Italy
Malcolm Sawyer, University of Leeds, Leeds, UK
Mark Setterfield, Trinity College, Hartford, USA
Otto Steiger, Universität Bremen, Bremen, Germany
L. Randall Wray, University of Missouri, Kansas City, USA

Foreword

I much enjoyed my first ever trip to South Africa to take part in the conference in January 2004 in honour of Basil Moore's 'retirement', just as I enjoyed the conference itself (even though I teased Basil that the conference in the first week of our visit was the stick, while the safari/coach tour in the second week was the carrot). So it is a great privilege for me to write a Foreword to the splendid volume that has resulted from the conference. That the chapters in the volume cover such a wide range of important, often fundamental, topics is a proper tribute to Basil's influence and contributions over his working life (thanks be, still in full swing, as is his tennis game).

Basil is primarily known in the literature for his pioneering writings on the concept and role of endogenous money in the functioning of modern advanced capitalist economies. His 1988 book, *Horizontalists and Verticalists: The Macroeconomics of Credit Money* (Cambridge University Press), already has the status of a classic and *Shaking the Invisible Hand: Complexity, Endogenous Money and Exogenous Interest Rates* (Palgrave Macmillan) – the *magnum opus* that he worked on for over 20 years, and which has recently been published – may well jockey with the 1988 book for a similar position. But, important as these contributions have been, Basil has influenced many other topics, sometimes by his innovative thinking, sometimes by being the irritant that has led other oysters to create pearls of their own. Especially is this true of his highly individual approach to the true meaning of the Keynes–Kahn–Meade multiplier concept and also to the validity of Keynes's concept of effective demand as presented in *The General Theory*. Basil has made us think anew about our understanding of the natures of saving and investment, their relationship to each other, to the concept of an under-employment rest state, and also of the relationship of the macroeconomic income and expenditure accounts, balance sheets and funds statements to the behavioral relationships originally developed by Keynes and his followers. To sometimes disagree with Basil's arguments is not at all to detract from the great stimulus he has provided for fundamental rethinks of basic, central, core concepts and relationships.

His contributions also dovetail into the existing developments of recent years associated with complexity theory and its applications to economic processes. These links and developments are well reflected in the volume.

Basil has also always stressed the need to understand the nature of monetary and other institutions, their historical development, and their roles in the workings of modern economies. These themes, too, are well represented in chapters in the volume.

Altogether we have much rich fare expertly brought together by our patient editor, Mark Setterfield. The volume is a fitting tribute to a serious, gifted scholar who has not only brought enlightenment to us, his devoted friends and colleagues, but also much fun and hospitality besides. I hope I have whetted appetites enough for readers immediately to wish to taste and see what follows.

G.C. Harcourt
Jesus College, Cambridge
August 2005

Preface

This book is a Festschrift for Basil J. Moore, formerly Professor of Economics at Wesleyan University, USA and currently Professor Extraordinary of Economics at the University of Stellenbosch, South Africa. It comprises a selection of papers that were originally presented at a conference in Professor Moore's honour held at the University of Stellenbosch in January 2004, together with several specially invited papers by authors with whom Professor Moore has had a particularly close association during his career.

The conference in Stellenbosch would have proved impossible to organize without the invaluable assistance of Subithra Moodley-Moore. Many thanks, Sibs, for all your help! Thanks are also due to Sasha and Tara for their work (not to mention their cheerfulness and patience) during the conference itself, to the staffs of the D'Ouwe Werf Hotel, the Stellenbosch Hotel and the University of Stellenbosch – and in particular, Archie September – for their hospitality, and to Cathy Raymond of Vintage Cape Tours for marshalling some spectacular scenery!

Manuscript completion was made possible by a grant from the Office of the Dean of Faculty at Trinity College. Last, but by no means least, I would like to thank Adrienne Quinn for her patient and tireless assistance with the editing of the final manuscript.

Mark Setterfield
Trinity College, Connecticut
September 2005

Acknowledgements

The publishers wish to thank the following who have kindly given permission for the use of copyright material.

Every effort has been made to trace all the copyright holders but if any have been inadvertently overlooked the publishers will be pleased to make the necessary arrangements at the first opportunity.

A tribute to Basil J. Moore and an introduction to *Complexity, Endogenous Money and Macroeconomic Theory*

Mark Setterfield

During a long and distinguished academic career, spent largely at Wesleyan University in Connecticut (but during which he has maintained a long-standing association with the University of Stellenbosch in South Africa, where he is now Professor Extraordinary of Economics), Basil Moore has made numerous important contributions to macroeconomics and monetary economics. One indication of his considerable impact as a scholar can be found in Bodenhorn's (2003) recent study of scholarship at elite liberal arts colleges, wherein Moore is ranked fifth in terms of total citations amongst all Full Professors at the top 50 liberal arts colleges in the USA. His books and articles cover a broad range of topics, including the accounting relationship between aggregate saving and investment, the destabilizing effects of wage and price flexibility and the case for the abolition of exchange rates – to name the subject matter of but three of his recent publications. Most notably, Moore is renowned for his contributions to monetary economics and, in particular, as the progenitor of the 'horizontalist' analysis of endogenous money. According to the horizontalist view, the volume of credit – and, by extension, the size of the money supply – is driven by the demand for bank loans by creditworthy borrowers, a demand that, given the price charged by the central bank for borrowing reserves, is accommodated by commercial banks at a fixed interest rate of their own making. Moore's horizontalism is perhaps best exemplified by his pioneering 1988 book *Horizontalists and Verticalists: The Macroeconomics of Credit Money* (Cambridge University Press). Several of the debates initiated by this book – including those concerning the precise ways in which the financial sector and the money supply respond to the growth of nominal income, and whether or not these responses are accompanied by increases in interest rates – are still in progress.

Always skeptical of the usefulness of equilibrium analysis, Moore has, more recently, embraced complexity theory and the insights of contemporary contributions to macroeconometrics that have highlighted the seeming ubiquity of unit roots in macroeconomic time series. His desire to integrate the visions of complexity analysis and modern time series macroeconometrics into macroeconomic and monetary theory is part of an ongoing effort to reconcile economic analysis with the flux of history and, in the process, to understand macroeconomics as an evolving, path-dependent process. The fruits of this synthesis can be found in his recently published – and eagerly anticipated – book, *Shaking the Invisible Hand: Complexity, Endogenous Money and Exogenous Interest Rates* (2006).

Apart from publishing a large number of influential books and articles, Moore has held visiting positions at universities around the world, including Yale, Stanford, Cambridge and both the University of British Columbia and Simon Fraser University in his native Canada. He has also acted as a consultant for governments and government agencies in the US, Morocco and Malaysia. What these various facts and accomplishments do not reveal, however, is perhaps the single most laudable feature of Moore's career: the spirit of openness and inquiry that characterizes his scholarship. His continual and ongoing efforts to engage and persuade those with whom his views differ, whilst simultaneously subjecting his work to maximum exposure to critical scrutiny by his peers, are typical of a scholar whose interests and motivations lie purely in the development and advancement of ideas, and are a model of enlightened scholarly activity.

The purpose of this book is to celebrate Basil Moore's career and, in particular, his interests in and contributions to monetary theory, macroeconomics, and complexity analysis. It features 21 essays by internationally renowned authors writing from a Post Keynesian perspective. The structure of the volume borrows from the contents of Moore's own (and aforementioned) book, *Shaking the Invisible Hand: Complexity, Endogenous Money and Exogenous Interest Rates* (2006), by emphasizing five distinct but interrelated themes: basic economic concepts, tools and methodology; complexity, uncertainty and path dependence; the macroeconomics of endogenous money; the macroeconomics of exogenous interest rates; and unemployment, inflation and the determination of aggregate income. A separate section of the Festschrift is devoted to each of these themes. In this way, it is hoped that the resulting book is truly representative of the interests and contributions of the honoree, making it a book that is both *for* Professor Moore and one that is *about his work* – work that continues to raise questions about economic methodology, the workings of the macroeconomy and the proper conduct of monetary policy that inspire his students and colleagues, and that are of paramount importance to professional economists and policy makers alike.

ECONOMIC CONCEPTS, TOOLS AND METHODOLOGY

Part I of the book features two chapters that discuss basic economic concepts, tools and methodology. The premise of Claude Gnos's chapter is that accounting identities – contrary to popular belief – make important contributions to economic knowledge. This he demonstrates with respect to three key debates in macroeconomics, concerning the endogeneity of money, the relationship between saving and investment, and the status of the expenditure multiplier.

Addressing the first of these debates, Gnos first highlights the different interpretations accorded to the relationship between credit money and bank deposits by Basil Moore on one hand, and the circuitist school on the other. He then shows how these differences can be resolved by appropriate analysis of the process of monetary exchange using the principles of double-entry bookkeeping.

Gnos then turns to the relationship between saving and investment and the question as to whether or not it is ever meaningful to think of the amounts of aggregate investment and saving as being unequal. Using double-entry bookkeeping, he shows that there exists an important distinction between investment in circulating capital and investment in fixed capital and that on this basis, it is possible to reconcile the idea that saving and investment are identical with the notion that the amounts of saving and investment may be unequal.

Finally, Gnos analyzes the multiplier process and its purported role in equating planned saving and investment through the gradual adjustment of income. Gnos argues that the appropriate treatment of saving and investment through double-entry bookkeeping supports Moore's view (see, for example, Moore, 1994) that the multiplier relationship does not arise as a result of successive adjustments in income gradually equating saving and investment, as traditionally conceived.

Steve Keen begins his chapter by noting with approval Basil Moore's concern that economic outcomes are properly viewed as resulting from processes in real time (rather than timeless equilibration mechanisms), of which money is an intrinsic and essential feature (rather than an afterthought in what would otherwise function equally well as a barter system). Anticipating many of the sentiments of the chapters in the second part of the book, Keen argues that this 'process view' in which 'money matters' has made gains in recent years, as economics has become increasingly influenced by concepts from complexity theory. But he cautions that the 'timeless barter' view of the economy has an unfortunate habit of reasserting itself – sometimes in places where it might be least expected. Keen illustrates this latter point with reference to the work of the circuitist school and, in particular, Graziani (1989). Ostensibly committed to the process view in which money matters, Keen shows how, by degrees, Graziani misses opportunities to model the economy as an evolving dynamic process and instead slips back into a timeless equilibrium analysis in which money is irrelevant.

Keen goes on to argue that in order to avoid lapses of this nature without giving up hope of formal modelling, non-neoclassical economists sympathetic to the process view of the economy must begin to adopt methods of analysis developed in engineering, physics and computing, disciplines that have never suffered the fetish with equilibrium analysis that is characteristic of mainstream economics. He illustrates this point by drawing attention to the value of systems engineering software and of direct numerical solutions to differential equations as means of identifying and solving flaws in Graziani's circuitist model and illustrating the workings of Goodwin's (1967) predator–prey growth cycle model.

COMPLEXITY, UNCERTAINTY AND PATH DEPENDENCE

The second part of the book comprises several chapters on the theory and application of the concepts of complexity, uncertainty and path dependence. Richard Day begins with an exploration of the development of complexity theory in the physical sciences and its capacity to illuminate the workings of the social realm. Day first establishes that the basic theory of economic decision making is ripe for the application of complexity analysis – as long as the former is understood as describing purposive, deliberative behavior by contemplative agents, and not as a theory of instantaneous global optimization incorporating rational expectations in an environment of perfect information. Day argues that his preferred process view of economic behavior has a long tradition in economics – it is evident in the work of Cournot, Walras and Marshall – and has been kept alive ever since in the work of, for example, Simon, Winter and various macroeconomists inspired by the work of Keynes.

The problem that remains is to describe how economic systems populated by such contemplative decision makers function as a whole – the 'disequilibrium existence problem' as Day calls it. The secret, he suggests, lies in the analysis of stock-flow mechanisms inherent in such processes as inventory adjustment and fluctuations in the accumulation of monetary assets and liabilities. Ultimately, he envisages such analysis as giving rise to a process view of the economy in which markets and banks constitute adjustment processes, intermediating the out-of-equilibrium behavior of households, firms and governments.

The basic argument developed by J. Barkley Rosser, Jr. is that complexity theory provides a foundation for Post Keynesian economics and, in particular, for the concept of fundamental uncertainty that is central to Post Keynesianism. Rosser begins with a 'big tent' definition of complexity that embraces the 'four C's': cybernetics, catastrophe theory, chaos theory and 'small tent' complexity. He then shows how complexity analysis so-defined can help articulate and/or provide foundations for many of the most important concerns of the three 'strands' of Post Keynesianism (the fundamentalist Keynesian, neo-Ricardian and Kaleckian strands) originally identified by Hamouda and Harcourt (1988). Rosser also shows how complexity can complement and undergird ideas associated with Post Keynesianism that are not, in and of themselves, Post Keynesian in origin – such as hysteresis and evolutionary economics. Finally, Rosser considers the relationship between complexity and two of the central tenets of Basil Moore's macroeconomics: the claim that there is no useful role for equilibrium in economic analysis; and the notion that economic systems are open and evolutionary. Rosser argues that both of these tenets are *consistent with* complexity analysis, but expresses ambivalence as to whether or not they are *necessarily implied by* such analysis.

In the first of two more applied chapters, Jerry Courvisanos and Colin Richardson use complexity theory as a basis for modelling a Post Keynesian theory of the cycle, according to which fluctuations in investment expenditures both: (a) drive the demand-led aggregate fluctuations of the economy; and (b) cause fluctuations in the 'susceptibility' of the investment process, by affecting the illiquidity of firms and hence their exposure to the pitfalls of fundamental uncertainty. The latter process, it is argued, has feedback effects on the volume of investment spending itself that can eventually bring upswings and downswings in economic activity to an end.

Courvisanos and Richardson first outline the concept of investment susceptibility and its role as a 'filter' in the investment decision between the objective determinants of investment (including profitability, firms' gearing ratios and the rate of capacity utilization) and actual investment spending by firms. The authors next construct a formal model of investment-driven growth, demonstrating by means of numerical analysis that any departure of this model from its steady state results in endogenously generated and self-perpetuating growth cycles. It is then shown that introducing susceptibility into the investment function increases the economy's 'corridors of viability' – that is, the range within which real output can fluctuate without these fluctuations becoming explosive or chaotic. Since this increases the model's plausibility as a representation of the reality it is intended to imitate, Courvisanos and Richardson argue that their analysis lends support to the Post Keynesian view that the investment process is susceptible as a result of its exposure to fundamental uncertainty. They conclude by highlighting the policy implications of their analysis, which include the recommendation that public authorities seek to deliberately narrow the economy's 'corridor of viability' in an effort to limit the amplitude of the business cycle.

Mark Setterfield's chapter serves as a precursor to some of the themes explored in detail in Parts III and IV, but its principal focus is the importance of modelling in path-dependent terms, and the possibility of approaching and shedding light on an old debate in monetary economics (horizontalism versus structuralism) by examining it through the lens of the 'history versus equilibrium' debate in macrodynamics. The chapter first develops a 'shifting equilibrium' model of effective demand which describes aggregate economic activity as an evolutionary sequence of outcomes arising from the recursive interaction of short- and long-term expectations. It is shown that in the context of this model, changes in the financial fragility of the non-bank private sector coupled with the possibility of commercial banks making discretionary responses to these changes together give rise to a dynamic credit supply schedule that is path dependent. In particular, the shape of this 'Moorian' credit supply schedule cannot be identified as either horizontal or upward sloping *a priori*, but may turn out to be either in practice. It is argued that the Moorian credit supply schedule is an important step towards narrowing the differences between horizontalism and structuralism, and that it also helps to make sense of the claim that the horizontal credit supply schedule is not a special case.

THE MACROECONOMICS OF ENDOGENOUS MONEY

Part III is devoted to discussion of perhaps the single most important idea with which Basil Moore's work is associated: the theory of endogenous money. Paul Davidson begins with a discussion that focuses on the fundamental debate as to whether changes in the money supply are properly regarded as an exogenous cause of changes in nominal income (as, for example, in monetarism) or an endogenous effect of changes in nominal income (as argued by Moore and as is now widely accepted by central bankers and in most modern macroeconomics). Davidson seeks to clarify this debate by distinguishing between the *interest elasticity* and the *stability* of the money supply function. He argues that a necessary condition for the monetarist view of money as an exogenous cause is that the money supply function be perfectly interest inelastic. Basil Moore's horizontalism – which posits a perfectly interest *elastic* money supply function – establishes that money is an endogenous effect precisely by virtue of its departure from the necessary elasticity condition implicit in the monetarist position.

Davidson then goes on to argue that a money supply function that is at least somewhat interest elastic is, in fact, essential to the income generating process in a monetary production economy, in which entrepreneurs must contract ahead for factor services and must also pay factors for their services before output has been produced, goods sold, sales revenues raised and profits realized. In this environment, an elastic supply of money is essential in order to finance expansions in economic activity before the additional income that will accrue from such expansions has been generated.

Davidson concludes by warning that accommodating the finance-demands of the private sector, whilst essential to the expansion of real income, can also succeed in accommodating competing claims on a *fixed* real income, thus facilitating inflation. The problem, he argues, is that the banking sector (including the central bank) cannot clearly distinguish between *which* process – inflation or real expansion – they are being asked to finance. Hence the use of monetary policy to control inflation always risks limiting real expansion to rates that are below potential.

While rejecting the notion of an exogenous money supply, Otto Steiger's chapter questions whether the money supply is *completely* endogenous, arguing that central banks retain some power to exogenously control the quantity of money in circulation. The fundamental premise of Steiger's argument is that in order to borrow from the central bank, commercial banks must both (a) promise to pay interest, and (b) provide good security. The latter requirement, he argues, is frequently overlooked in contemporary discussions of central banking, but has a crucial bearing on the endogeneity of money. This is because a central bank's capacity to create its own money is limited by the extent of its accumulated capital. Central banks cannot, Steiger argues, create unlimited quantities of central bank money without threatening their own solvency. By setting a limit on the capacity of the central bank to create high-powered money, the central bank's capital, by extension, sets a limit on the extent to which the money supply can be considered endogenous. Steiger proceeds to illustrate this theory of the less-than-completely-endogenous money supply with reference to the monetary policy operations of the Eurosystem (the European Central Bank and the various national central banks of the European Monetary Union member nations).

Written by a self-professed, unreconstructed horizontalist, the purpose of the chapter by Louis-Philippe Rochon is to defend and further develop several specific features of the horizontalist theory of the endogenous supply of credit money. Rochon begins by revisiting the structuralism versus horizontalism debate and, in particular, the claims that both commercial banks and central banks play an entirely passive role in the money creation process in horizontalism. Rochon rejects these claims, arguing in the first instance that horizontalists only ever claimed that commercial banks meet the demand for loans (at any given rate of interest) from *creditworthy* borrowers. Commercial banks are thus *active* in the money creation process, both determining and applying the standards of creditworthiness. As regards the central bank, Rochon argues that full and automatic 'accommodationism' is *not* an accurate description of the horizontalist position – although such behaviour ought to be regarded as the *general* case, since: (a) maintaining the liquidity of both individual banks and the banking sector as a whole is paramount amongst central bank functions; and (b) departures from full accommodationism will change interest rates, an important but relatively infrequent purpose of central bank behavior.

Having re-established these first principles of horizontalism, Rochon then turns to the task of further developing the horizontalist theory of credit supply. He argues that any such further development must focus on the evolution of the fundamental constraint on borrowers that is created by the assessment of their creditworthiness. This, in turn, is influenced by both 'microuncertainty' (uncertainty about the future prospects of individual borrowers) and 'macrouncertainty' (uncertainty about the future prospects of the economy as a whole). Rochon argues that fluctuations in macrouncertainty influence banks' lending standards (and hence the 'threshold' criteria that define a creditworthy borrower), whereas differences in microuncertainty influence the interest rates that different creditworthy borrowers are charged. These principles furnish a Post Keynesian theory of credit rationing in an environment in which there is no literal scarcity of credit.

Peter Howells begins by demonstrating that 'we are all endogenous money theorists now', and suggests that for some time the only real debate in the endogenous money literature has concerned refinements of the basic theory. The rest of his chapter is then devoted to discussion of one such refinement, concerning the question as to who *holds* the money that is endogenously generated by the loan creation process.

Howells accepts the horizontalist argument that commercial banks supply loans at a given rate of interest in response to the demand for loans from creditworthy borrowers. His concern, however, is that this horizontalist view of money creation provides no account of why, following an endogenous expansion of the money supply, there will be a corresponding increase in the *quantity of money demanded*: someone must be willing to hold additional, loan-induced deposits in order to restore monetary equilibrium at the new, higher quantity of money in circulation. Howells rejects Moore's convenience lending explanation of why the additional money created is always willingly held, arguing that the willingness of the public to always *accept* money in the first instance does not preclude the possibility that they will subsequently seek to alter the amount of money they hold in accordance with their portfolio preferences. Some further adjustments in prices and/or quantities must occur, Howells, argues, in order to reconcile the demand for money with the available supply.

Howells then shows that, in the current environment, the most obvious mechanism for reconciling money demand with an endogenous money supply is the capacity of the private sector to 'destroy' money through the repayment of outstanding debt. This mechanism was first proposed by Kaldor and Trevithick (1981), but Howells shows that it has only recently been rendered truly plausible by the amount of unsecured lending to households, which has increased so greatly as to ensure that most households (as well as firms) now carry debt that permits discretionary repayment at no cost. An important lesson of this analysis, then, is the profound sensitivity of monetary *theory* to the institutions and practices of the monetary sector itself.

An important principle of the modern Chartalist view of endogenous money associated with authors such as Wray (1998) is the concept of 'tax-driven money' (TDM) – the idea that the state's ability to levy taxes and dictate the form in which these taxes are payable determines what circulates as money. The purpose of Mathew Forstater's chapter is to document hitherto unrecognized instances of this TDM view in the history of economic thought, economic history and the practice of economic policy making.

Forstater shows that there is clear recognition of the TDM principle in the works of Smith, Say, Mill and Marx, arguing that the latter recognized tax liabilities as being instrumental in the emergence of wage labor. Further evidence of the acceptance of the TDM view is found in the works of progenitors of neoclassical economics such as Jevons and Wicksteed, twentieth-century authors such as Abba Lerner (whose 1946 entry on 'Money' in the *Encyclopaedia Britannica* is infused with Chartalist principles and contains a concise explanation of the TDM principle) and even contemporary general equilibrium theory.

Forstater goes on to show that the cowrie currency that emerged in West Africa in the late thirteenth/early fourteenth century was TDM and not, as conventional wisdom would have it, a 'primitive' money, before demonstrating that the TDM principle was clearly understood by early US economic policy makers. He concludes by lamenting the fact that seemingly the only literature in which there is no discussion of TDM is modern economics textbooks!

Philip Arestis and Malcolm Sawyer's chapter explores the nature and policy implications of endogenous money in both 'new consensus' macroeconomics and Post Keynesian economics. They begin by discussing the new consensus model and highlighting some of its main features: acceptance of the natural rate hypothesis; characterization of inflation as a purely demand-pull phenomenon; and emphasis on the interest rate as the instrument of monetary policy (as a result of which the quantity of money in circulation is rendered an endogenous 'residual', determined by the demand for money). The authors then critically examine the potential for using monetary policy to stabilize output at its 'natural' level in this model – the key role assigned to monetary policy in new consensus macroeconomics. Using plausible values for the responsiveness of aggregate demand to changes in interest rates, Arestis and Sawyer show that correcting a once over but permanent deviation of output from its natural value would require implausibly large changes in the real interest rate.

Arestis and Sawyer then outline an alternative, Post Keynesian macro model, in which output and employment do not automatically gravitate towards supply-determined, natural levels, inflation can emanate from cost-push sources, and money is endogenous by virtue of the very workings of the financial sector in a monetary-production economy (as a result of which manipulation of the interest rate charged for bank reserves emerges as the only plausible instrument of monetary policy). The authors show that this model has important implications for monetary policy, suggesting that the latter be conducted along lines that differ markedly from those associated with new consensus macroeconomics. In particular, the Post Keynesian model requires that the *objective* of monetary policy change to take account of its potentially lasting effects on real variables and also suggests the periodic need for credit control policies.

The chapter by Claudio Sardoni examines the impact of the information and communication technology (ICT) revolution on the financial sector. In particular, Sardoni investigates two questions central to the future conduct of monetary policy: will the ICT revolution give rise to new payment and clearing systems that impair the ability of central banks to conduct monetary policy; and will the ICT revolution ultimately render markets sufficiently close to the ideal of perfect competition to eliminate the need for monetary policy?

Sardoni concurs that ICTs could very well give rise to parallel payment and clearing systems that operate independently of the central bank. However, he argues that such developments will not undermine the capacity of the central bank to influence the economy as long as the central bank's liability remains the economy's unit of account. Whilst it is possible in principle to envisage a situation in which the central bank's liability is displaced as unit of account, Sardoni argues that the obstacles to this are formidable – not least because the state itself can influence the process by, for example, continuing to demand payment of taxes in the form of 'traditional money' denominated in terms of the central bank's liability.

Sardoni next turns to the claim that, by improving the flow of information, ICTs may cause actual economies to converge towards the ideal of perfect competition, rendering obsolete the need for monetary policy interventions. But Sardoni argues that whilst ICTs might improve the flow of information about the present and past, they can do nothing to remedy the paucity of information about the *future* that is the crux of the pervasive problem of fundamental uncertainty. In this sense, ICTs do not present a radical change in the way that capitalist economies operate and do not, therefore, provide any basis for believing that the need for monetary policy interventions will eventually be eliminated as the diffusion of ICTs continues. Indeed, to the extent that the increased flow of information about the past and present gives rise to ever more *speculative* activity in asset markets, ICTs may even give rise to the need for a more active monetary policy designed to redress financial instability and safeguard the steady advance of the economy's income-generating process.

Marc Lavoie and Wynne Godley's contribution is part of a larger project that aims to create a stock-flow consistent Post Keynesian analysis of the interactions between money, credit, production, income and wealth. The particular focus of this chapter is the modelling of the banking sector within this larger project.

Lavoie and Godley begin by emphasizing that a crucial role of the banking sector in a Post Keynesian world is to provide a *buffer* to households and firms when (as is usually the case) expectations are disappointed. This is accomplished by providing access to previously accumulated deposits and/or through the issuance of loans.

The authors next construct simple stock-flow consistent Post Keynesian models of asset-based and overdraft financial systems, drawing attention to the fact that, in either system, the central bank supplies reserves of high-powered money to commercial banks on demand as part of an endogenous money creation process. Utilizing simulation techniques, they then demonstrate that an increase in the compulsory reserve ratio – contrary to conventional wisdom – will not reduce the money supply, although it will lead to an increase in deposit and lending rates if banks operate with a target banking liquidity ratio (measured as the ratio of Treasury bills to deposits) motivated by liquidity preference. Lavoie and Godley then discuss various extensions to their basic models of the banking sector, designed to make the latter more realistic. They conclude by noting that their ultimate aim is not to create a canonical Post Keynesian model of the banking sector, but rather to pave the way for future research into stock-flow consistent macro models that help to draw attention to the substantially different outcomes to which the Post Keynesian conception of the banking sector gives rise, as compared to the results associated with the orthodox neoclassical theory of the banking sector.

THE MACROECONOMICS OF EXOGENOUS INTEREST RATES

In addition to emphasizing the endogeneity of the quantity of money in circulation, a second major theme of horizontalism as originally articulated by Moore (1988) is the exogeneity of the interest rate. Each of the three chapters in Part IV is focused on this horizontalist theme of external manipulation of the interest rate by the central bank.

The expressed purpose of L. Randall Wray's chapter is to consider four interrelated questions: what does it mean to say that the interest rate is exogenous; which interest rate(s) is (are) exogenous; how does exogeneity of the interest rate arise in the first place; and what are the implications of exogenous interest rates for Keynes's theory of liquidity preference and Minsky's financial instability hypothesis?

Wray adopts the convention of defining an exogenous interest rate as one that is set by government policy. The overnight, inter-bank lending rate is exogenous in this sense, he argues, but whether or not 'retail' rates should be similarly regarded as exogenous depends on the behavior of the markup applied to the overnight rate by banks. The point, however, is that there is room for debate about the latter without this obscuring the more fundamental claim that central banks accommodate the demand for reserves from central banks 'horizontally' at an interest rate of their own making.

Wray next investigates the circumstances under which interest rates are rendered exogenous, arguing that exogeneity is an institutional (and hence historically specific) phenomenon, rather than a logical necessity. In particular, he identifies the exchange rate regime as a key determinant of interest rate exogeneity/endogeneity, arguing that in a fixed exchange rate regime, the commercial bank is obliged to adjust the interest rate in response to the demands of international financial markets in order to protect the exchange rate peg, rendering the interest rate endogenous.

Finally, Wray shows that there is no conflict between contemporary Post Keynesian monetary theory on one hand, and either Keynes's liquidity preference theory of asset prices or Minsky's financial instability hypothesis on the other – both of which are shown to apply in a horizontalist environment of endogenous money and exogenous interest rates.

Colin Rogers begins his chapter by noting that mainstream monetary theory has abandoned the assumption of an exogenous money supply and now explicitly regards the interest rate as the instrument of monetary policy. The question that he then poses is: do these developments signal the conversion of the mainstream to the type of monetary analysis advocated by Basil Moore in *Horizontalists and Verticalists*?

Rogers first reviews Moore's monetary analysis, noting that whilst endogenous money and exogenous interest rates are features of this analysis, so, too, are the propositions that the monetary and real sectors of the economy are inextricably entwined, and that money is non-neutral in the long run. In short, endogenous money and exogenous interest rates (horizontalism) *alone* are not sufficient to capture the full substance of Moore's monetary analysis.

Rogers then shows that the macroeconomics of the 'new horizontalists' in mainstream theory falls far short of Moore's monetary macroeconomics. The mainstream has adopted horizontalism merely as a practical solution to the problem that any assumption to the effect that central banks manipulate an exogenous money supply is patently unrealistic. Meanwhile, the 'new horizontalists' retain the pre-Keynesian notions that there exists a dichotomy between the real and nominal sectors of the economy, and that money is neutral (at least in the long run) – propositions that are antithetical to Moore's analysis. Rogers concludes, however, that whilst the emergence of the 'new horizontalists' by no means represents the conversion of the mainstream – nor even does justice – to Moore's monetary macroeconomics, it may have created a moment in the development of macroeconomics that is particularly suited to highlighting the claims of Post Keynesian macroeconomics, including the interdependence of the monetary and real sectors and the long run non-neutrality of money.

The chapter by Charles Goodhart starts with a conundrum. Observation of the actual pattern of interest rate changes by the Bank of England's Monetary Policy Committee (MPC) is strongly suggestive of a policy of gradualism, as a result of which the interest rate is adjusted slowly over an interval of time in order to return inflation to its target level. But neither Goodhart's recollections of the decision making of the MPC (of which he was a member from 1997 to 2000) nor econometric evidence relating changes in interest rates to the forecasted discrepancy between actual and target inflation support the view that the Bank of England is consciously committed to gradualism. Goodhart's purpose is to explore and provide an explanation for this conundrum.

He begins by reviewing the arguments in favour of gradualism, concluding that there are reasons why central bankers might prudently adopt such a policy. But this does not resolve the conundrum identified above: why do UK interest rates appear to reflect gradualism despite the fact that this is not the expressed policy of the MPC? One reason is related to the Bank of England's forecasting methods which in and of themselves, Goodhart shows, are likely to result in some autocorrelation in interest rate changes. Evidence provides some support for this explanation, but also suggests that it acts as only a sporadic influence on the course of UK interest rates.

A second explanation is that the Bank's forecasts are characterized by systematically autocorrelated errors, so that whilst policy at any point in time is intended to react fully to forecasted deviations of inflation from its target rate (or of output from its 'natural' level), subsequent, autocorrelated adjustments in interest rates are frequently (indeed, usually) necessary in response to autocorrelated errors in the Bank's forecasts themselves. Goodhart shows that there is strong empirical support for the view that inflation and (in particular) output forecasts are subject to autocorrelated errors, and that observed interest rate changes are a response to these errors. Hence, according to Goodhart, interest rate policy in the UK is *de facto* gradualist, largely as a result of the MPC's responses to the Bank of England's own forecast errors.

UNEMPLOYMENT, INFLATION AND THE DETERMINATION OF AGGREGATE INCOME

Part V contains four chapters that focus on macroeconomic theory and policy. In the first of these, Arne Heise develops a formal model of a credit-based economy designed to reflect several important features of Post Keynesian macro theory (including fundamental uncertainty, the central role of money, and the implications of these first two features for the interaction of financial markets, the goods market and the labor market). By using this model to analyze the interactions between the central bank and the private sector, Heise examines the possibility of pursuing 'hydraulic' demand-management policies based on the manipulation of interest rates by the central bank. An important result that emerges from this exercise is that the effects of monetary policy on the economy are asymmetric, thanks to an asymmetry in the model's price dynamics and hence in the response of inflation expectations to monetary policy. In short, restrictive monetary policy always succeeds in depressing real economic activity in a conventional fashion, but expansionary monetary policy may or may not succeed in reflating the real economy. The resulting uncertainty over the effects of expansionary monetary policy precludes the possibility of 'hydraulic' demand-management in which the central bank acts to 'fine tune' the economy, although, as Heise points out, this does not mean that there is no role for monetary policy. On the contrary, the creation of institutions that reduce uncertainty and instability coupled with 'coarse tuning' remain legitimate policy goals, he argues.

Giuseppe Fontana's chapter is concerned with the teaching of macroeconomics and, in particular, the successful incorporation of the Post Keynesian theory of endogenous money into a teachable macroeconomic model. Whilst acknowledging that the exogenous money hypothesis has been abandoned in other work aimed at undergraduates (for example, Romer, 2000), Fontana's ambition is to transcend what he identifies as the crude empiricism of the 'new consensus' and develop a teachable macro model embodying endogenous money that provides students with a more sound theoretical appreciation of the roles and interaction of the banking and non-financial sectors in the income-generating process.

Fontana focuses on the traditional aggregate demand schedule drawn in price/quantity space. He shows how a familiar downward-sloping aggregate demand schedule can be rationalized by postulating: (a) that at least some components of aggregate expenditures are interest sensitive; (b) that commercial banks act as 'producers of credit' to finance private expenditures, pricing their output at a mark-up over the 'wholesale' interest rate at which they borrow from the central bank; and (c) that the central bank follows a monetary policy rule according to which it adjusts the wholesale interest rate in response to the price level. Combination of these postulates results in the familiar inverse relationship between price and aggregate output that characterizes the conventional aggregate demand schedule.

Fontana goes on to show that this model can also be used to discuss Post Keynesian hypotheses such as the instability of aggregate demand in response to expectations formed under uncertainty. He concludes by arguing that the chief virtue of his model, aside from its 'teachability', is that it eschews the exogenous money hypothesis and incorporates from the start a view of the money supply as being endogenous. In this way, and without abandoning simple and potentially useful pedagogical tools such as the downward-sloping aggregate demand curve, the model provides a vehicle for establishing endogenous money as a fundamental principle of macroeconomics in even the earliest of undergraduate course work.

Chris Niggle identifies three competing approaches in contemporary macroeconomics: New Classical Economics (NCE), based on the notion of an inherently self-regulating economy characterized by steady growth and requiring minimal government intervention; Institutionalist-Post-Keynesian Economics (IPKE), in which the economy is characterized by chronic unemployment and instability problems and an uneven growth process requiring systematic government intervention; and a New

Keynesian, 'New Consensus' Macroeconomics (NCM), in which occasional episodes of instability require periodic government intervention and government policy can affect the endogenous growth rate. Niggle argues that both IPKE and NCM can be understood as reactions against NCE, but that these two approaches are otherwise fundamentally different, with IPKE constituting the more radical departure from the strictures of NCE.

Niggle shows that NCM retains certain critical features of NCE (such as its emphasis on individualistic microfoundations and the concept of a supply-determined, natural rate of unemployment), but rejects others. Hence the price mechanism is conceived as sclerotic, so that aggregate demand shocks regularly affect quantities (of output and employment) and policy intervention is required to accelerate the otherwise sluggish adjustment of the economy to these shocks. Moreover, monetary policy is understood to be conducted via the manipulation of interest rates with the quantity of money in circulation determined as an endogenous residual (although as in the NCE, monetary policy is privileged over fiscal policy and the sole focus of macro policy is the abatement of inflation – an inevitable consequence of NCM's adherence to natural rate doctrine). Finally, NCM conceives a role for state intervention in the growth process, via manipulation of the supply-side determinants (such as education or R&D activity) of the endogenous growth rate.

In contrast, Niggle characterizes IPKE as a radical critique of NCE. It involves a wholly different conception of the economy, in which decision makers face fundamental uncertainty (rather than just probabilistic risk), giving rise to a different theory of money. Aggregate output and employment are demand-determined: supply does not automatically create its own demand, so there is no natural rate of unemployment. In this environment, the price mechanism is potentially destabilizing, not simply sclerotic. Such barriers as do exist to downward wage and price flexibility may be beneficial, rather than impediments to macroeconomic adjustment. Finally, although IPKE shares with NCM an emphasis on interest rates as the key instrument of monetary policy, this results from a theory of endogenous money in which credit-creation is an essential feature of a monetary-production economy. Moreover, monetary policy is not privileged over fiscal policy: via their impact on aggregate demand, both are understood to impact macro performance in both the short and long run, the latter being characterized by a growth process that is demand-led.

In the final chapter, John and Wendy Cornwall contemplate a future for Keynesian macroeconomics, demonstrating how short-run Keynesian macro principles can be extended and embellished to permit analyses of the medium and long runs.

Cornwall and Cornwall distance their own brand of Keynesianism from New Keynesian Economics. Foremost amongst the authors' criticisms of the latter is their observation that, with its emphasis on self-correcting, short-run disturbances around a supply-determined steady state expansion path, New Keynesianism provides no explanation for the lengthy, medium-run 'episodes' of better or worse macroeconomic performance that have characterized actual capitalist economies during the twentieth century. The Cornwalls then set about developing a medium- and long-run Keynesian analysis that *is* consistent with the stylized facts of the past century. Working in the context of a demand-constrained macro model (which does not automatically revert to a supply-determined equilibrium), they contend that the demand for expansionary macro policies (based on the distribution of political power) coupled with the willingness to supply expansionary policies (based on the inflation costs of any given rate of unemployment) are the ultimate determinants of aggregate demand and hence macro outcomes within any given episode of capitalist macro performance. These outcomes are then allowed to have feedback effects on the structural determinants of the demand for and supply of expansionary policies, setting up a model in which the recursive interaction of the demand for and supply of expansionary policies on one hand, and macroeconomic outcomes on the other, creates a long run that is an evolutionary sequence of medium-run episodes of macro performance.

Finally, Cornwall and Cornwall demonstrate the explanatory value of their model by explaining macro outcomes during both the Golden Age (1948–73) and the subsequent Age of Decline (post 1973) in terms of the distribution of political power and the inflation costs of any given rate of unemployment. The particular configuration of the structural determinants of the demand for and supply of expansionary policies during the Age of Decline – and hence macro outcomes during this episode – is shown to have been induced by macro outcomes during the Golden Age. The authors conclude, in a fitting finale to the volume that Basil Moore himself would no doubt appreciate, that the future of Keynesian macroeconomics – indeed, the future of macroeconomics *writ large* – must involve rejection of all vestiges of supply-determined equilibrium analysis and a willingness to better explain the key stylized facts of capitalist macroeconomic performance.

REFERENCES

Bodenhorn, H. (2003) 'Economic Scholarship at Elite Liberal Arts Colleges: A Citation Analysis with Rankings', *Journal of Economic Education*, Fall, 341–59.
Goodwin, R.M. (1967) 'A Growth Cycle', in C.H. Feinstein (ed.), *Socialism, Capitalism and Economic Growth*, Cambridge: Cambridge University Press,

54–8. Reprinted in R.M. Goodwin (1982), *Essays in Dynamic Economics*, London: Macmillan.

Graziani, A. (1989) 'The Theory of the Monetary Circuit', *Thames Papers in Political Economy*, Spring, 1–26. Reprinted in M. Musella and C. Panico (eds) (1995), *The Money Supply in the Economic Process*, Aldershot, UK and Brookfield, USA: Edward Elgar.

Hamouda, O.F. and G.C. Harcourt (1988) 'Post Keynesianism: From Criticism to Coherence', *Bulletin of Economic Research*, 40, 1–33.

Kaldor, N. and J. Trevithick (1981) 'A Keynesian Perspective on Money', *Lloyds Bank Review*, January.

Moore, B.J. (1988) *Horizontalists and Verticalists: The Macroeconomics of Credit Money*, Cambridge: Cambridge University Press.

Moore, B.J. (1994) 'The Demise of the Keynesian Multiplier: A Reply to Cottrell', *Journal of Post Keynesian Economics*, 17, 121–33.

Moore, B.J. (2006) *Shaking the Invisible Hand: Complexity, Endogenous Money and Exogenous Interest Rates*, London: Palgrave Macmillan.

Romer, D. (2000) 'Keynesian Macroeconomics without the *LM* Curve', *Journal of Economic Perspectives*, 14, 149–69.

Wray, L.R. (1998) *Understanding Modern Money*, Cheltenham, UK and Northampton, MA, USA: Edward Elgar.

PART I

Economic concepts, tools and methodology

1. Accounting identities: more than just bookkeeping conventions

Claude Gnos

INTRODUCTION

Economists usually view accounting identities as mere bookkeeping conventions yielding no interesting information as to how the economy actually works. No doubt one of Moore's many contributions to economics is to have shown that accounting identities do matter. Namely, allowing for them adds something important to economic knowledge. This chapter emphasizes the relevance of Moore's methodology with reference to the creation of bank money and the role of money and banks.

The following section confirms Moore's argument that bookkeeping is central to the endogeneity of money. It is because bank money is both a liability and an asset with no existence outside banks' balance sheets that the endogeneity thesis is valid. The next section hammers this point home while showing that the identity of banks' assets and liabilities is key to a better understanding of the nature and role of money and bank intermediation in economic transactions. The following section further refers to bookkeeping and the ensuing I-S identity in examining the role of money and credit in the financing of production. The next section goes on to examine the meaning of the I-S identity, especially with reference to Keynes's concept of demand deficiency and his theory of the investment multiplier. The final section concludes.

THE IDENTITY OF BANKS' ASSETS AND LIABILITIES IS CENTRAL TO THE ENDOGENEITY OF MONEY

In his 1988 book, Moore contrasts bank money with commodity money. The former is generated by demand for credit and thus cannot be supplied independently of demand: 'Since the supply of credit money is furnished by the extension of credit, the supply schedule is no longer independent of demand' (p. 13). Not so when money is metallic (or even fiat):

> . . . its supply can be meaningfully regarded as independent of the demand for it. The stock existing at any moment can be regarded as largely given, or at least exogenously determined. Major changes in supply come in from 'outside' – for example, with new gold discoveries or with balance-of-payments surpluses. (Moore, 1988, p. 10)

Commodity money is a net asset; its existence does not presuppose that someone has borrowed it: 'Because commodity money is a material thing rather than a financial claim, it is an asset to its holder but a liability to no one. Thus, the quantity of commodity money in existence denotes nothing about the outstanding volume of credit' (Moore, 1988, p. 13). Its quantity may be considered as given or exogenously determined with regard to the needs of the economy and as playing a causal role in economic phenomena: 'The view of money as a causal factor was central to the original formulation of the quantity theory by Locke and Hume, when money depended on a country's stocks of gold and silver' (p. 5).

By contrast, credit money does not exist if it is not borrowed by someone. This of course means that the demand for credit plays a crucial role in determining the quantity of money banks supply. Cause and effect are reversed: wages and prices (for a given level of employment and output) are determinants of the quantity of money in the economy. Bank money is demanded with regard to the wages and prices that have to be paid. However, it is the very existence of money that is at stake: bank money does not exist except in the form of double entries in banks' books. That is why it cannot be supplied independently of the demand for it. When created, it exists in the form of an asset and a liability for the public (deposits holders and borrowers) as well.

With reference to Heinsohn and Steiger (1983), and to Polanyi (1944), Wray (1990) has questioned the relevance of the supposed historical succession from commodity money to credit money which Moore describes. Wray argues that historically money has never been primarily a physical device used to facilitate exchanges but a unit of account used to calculate debts arising with the creation of private property and, by extension, a debt used to settle purchases or other debts. So, '[c]redit money was the first form of money' (Wray, 1990, p. 54). I shall not expand on this point here since it does not challenge the legitimacy of Moore's views on bank money. In fact, Wray's argument extends the historical range of the endogeneity thesis.

How are we to explain that, in our world of credit money, monetarist writers have endorsed the exogenous view of money? Moore reminds us that Friedman (1956, 1959, 1969) saw no point in inquiring into the nature of money: for the leader of Monetarism, money is whatever category of assets provides the best results in econometric tests of the demand for money. But '[u]nfortunately for this view, econometric tests do not give clear, unambiguous, and durable results' (Moore, 1988, p. 7), so that '[t]he time is ripe for re-examining the age-old question of the nature of money' (p. 7). The flaw of econometric tests is a relevant argument but Moore makes an even more telling criticism: Friedman's view actually begs the question because it takes for granted that money is an asset which may be supplied independently of the demand for it.

> The very basis of the quantity theory is something so elementary that it is almost never discussed, reflectively considered, or even noticed: the assumption that *there exists an independent supply function for money*. (Moore, 1988, p. 7, original emphasis)

Many Post Keynesian writers have emphasized that the endogenous money thesis is usually supported by the way banks act in modern economies: 'It turns out that very few countries function or have functioned according to the high powered money fantasy' (Lavoie, 1993, p. 4). But, of course, this is not a conclusive point; what is prevalent is the bookkeeping nature of bank money. As Moore puts it, the endogeneity of money may as well be concealed by banks' practice, 'because the banking system operates under rules imposed upon it by the monetary authorities' (Moore, 1988, p. 14). For the same reason, the more or less accommodating attitude of commercial and central banks vis-à-vis the public's demand is not conclusive either: 'In fact, because of the nature of money as debt, it is endogenous irrespective of whether the central bank accommodates the reserve needs of commercial banks' (Rochon, 2001, p. 40). All in all, we thus have initial confirmation that accounting identities provide true information with regard to the real world.

THE IDENTITY OF BANKS' ASSETS AND LIABILITIES AS A KEY TO UNDERSTANDING THE NATURE AND ROLE OF MONEY AND BANK INTERMEDIATION

We turn now to the precise meaning of the simultaneous assets and liabilities arising from credit granted by banks. Post Keynesians, and some Circuitists as well, usually ascribe the status of money to banks' liabilities (deposits). Credit, they argue, stands on the assets side of banks' balance sheets. In their view, banks create deposits which they lend to borrowers, with the borrowers using them as a means of payment. This definition of money has the advantage, as Chick puts it, of conforming to common usage:

> To Post Keynesians, money is bank liabilities, that is, deposits (cash is irrelevant here). This, it should be emphazised, conforms to the definition used by central banks and international statistical agencies. The hallmark of this money is its liquidity or general acceptability, as a means of payment, or as a unit of account for debt contracts. Bank liabilities are to be sharply distinguished from bank credit, the advances which count as bank assets, even though bank credit is used to effect payments and is responsible for the creation of bank deposits. (Chick, 2000, p. 130)

Moore does not explicitly question this description of things. He explains at length in his book that credit money finances deficit spending by economic units (consumers and firms): the money created enables them, in any period, to spend more than they earn.[1] However, his constant reference to double-entry bookkeeping raises an ambiguity which deserves close attention. We can well imagine that banks supply money, in the form of deposits, to consumers and firms who spend more than they earn in the current period. So, consumers and firms would benefit from credit unilaterally supplied by banks. But at the same time Moore argues that deposits are a source of finance for banks, matching the credit they grant to borrowers. Depositors are creditors of banks and 'ultimately the creditors of bank borrowers' (p. 20); banks are thus 'simply one type of financial intermediary' (p. 20). Why should payees grant credit to banks, in the form of what Moore calls 'convenience lending'? Are they not duly paid in money, that is, by means of deposits? Double-entry bookkeeping, which denotes the equality of sources and applications of funds, actually questions the distinction usually made between credit and money entries which supposedly feature, respectively, on the assets side and on the liabilities side of banks balance sheets. Deposits actually feature credit granted by depositors.

To explain the difficulty further, let us quote Moore once more:

> Nonbank intermediaries play the brokerage role of making the cash surpluses of some groups available to finance the cash deficit of other groups. In contrast bank intermediaries *create* credit and money, as well as perform this brokerage role. (Moore, 1988, p. 295, original emphasis)

Money creation allows banks to play a brokerage role. This statement is a cornerstone of the analysis of credit money worked out by Moore: money is made up of bank deposits through which, according to the author, depositors give credit to borrowers. But what do depositors lend to borrowers? When nonbank intermediaries play this role, cash surpluses of some economic agents are lent to deficit-spenders to finance their purchases. The meaning of these cash surpluses is examined below; what matters here is that assets and liabilities resulting from brokerage are clearly distinct from the cash that is lent. By contrast, when banks enter the picture, the answer is less obvious since cash cannot be distinguished from assets resulting from brokerage: depositors allegedly lend cash that, according to the proposed interpretation, is made up of assets (that is, banks' liabilities) recording that same loan. The coherence of the whole analysis is in question, and an alternative interpretation of banks' balance sheets is needed.

To look into this matter, I propose first to refer to some Circuitist writers, A. Parguez and M. Seccareccia (2000), who maintain that credit money is made up of debts which banks issue upon themselves *ex nihilo* to finance loans. So, money is defined as a claim to money (an IOU) which banks do not need to meet: the claim is allegedly full-blown money borrowed by economic agents who, thus, are able to buy real resources and labor. This interpretation of banks' balance sheets is consistent with a view deeply rooted in the history of economic thought, which Schumpeter wittily summed up: 'you cannot ride on a claim to a horse, but you can pay with a claim to money' (Schumpeter, 1954, p. 321).

A crucial consequence of money creation, in this view, is that banks are the actual source of credit available to borrowers until they are able to sell goods in their turn. Contrary to usual financial assets, credit money is not supposed to constitute a claim to anything lent by the bearer and due to him: money and claims to money are supposedly one and the same thing. Thus, Parguez and Seccareccia may explicitly deny that credit might be financed, through banks, by depositors: 'it would be wrong to conceive holders of bank liability as bank creditors' (Parguez and Seccareccia, 2000, pp. 105–6). This statement, both authors acknowledge, runs counter to Moore's own views.

Is this latter interpretation actually relevant? The process of bookkeeping, which is undoubtedly relevant since we are dealing with bank money, acts as an important constraint here: the double-entry principle does not allow banks to extend credit to borrowers without gaining an equivalent credit from depositors. This is an inference Keynes already made in the *General Theory*:

> The prevalence of the idea that saving and investment, taken in their straightforward sense, can differ from one another, is to be explained, I think, by an optical illusion due to regarding an individual depositor's relation to his bank as being a one-sided transaction, instead of seeing it as the two-sided transaction which it actually is. It is supposed that a depositor and his bank can somehow contrive between them to perform an operation by which savings can disappear into the banking system so that they are lost to investment, or, contrariwise, that the banking system can make it possible for investment to occur, to which no saving corresponds. (Keynes, 1936, p. 81)

How are we to sort things out? I think that there is some discrepancy between the common interpretation of monetary transactions and their actual accounting features. On the common interpretation, sellers of goods earn money (be it a mere claim to money) which they later spend on goods. As shown above, the difficulty we are examining arises because accounting tells us that sellers do not merely receive money but grant credit to banks and, through them, to borrowers (that is, deficit-spenders). I would suggest that we go further in referring to accounting. Closer scrutiny shows that accounting does not support the common interpretation. Double-entry bookkeeping does not, actually, record the supposed exchange of goods for money. It records sales of goods in the form of the monetary proceeds which sales generate and, as a counterpart, the use that the recipient makes of these proceeds. This is one of the features Moore highlights in his book. He argues that the same money (which constitutes the sellers' income) is not simply accumulated but is spent on financial assets, including bank deposits; surplus sellers are surplus spenders too:

> In any period all economic units who have experienced a net accumulation of money balances must necessarily have been surplus spenders by an identical amount in that period. Such surplus spending need not have been planned or in any sense volitional. It follows most simply from the accounting definition of saving as income not consumed, or as the net accumulation of financial assets . . . . (Moore, 1988, p. 296)

Why is this so? Income is saved in the form of financial assets which have to be purchased. This latter assertion is obvious when savers buy assets supplied by nonbank agents but it holds as well, although implicitly, when income holders obtain bank deposits. In a footnote, Moore confirms this point with reference to double-entry bookkeeping: 'This follows simply from the principles of double-entry bookkeeping. Credit money is a financial asset. Deficit spending must be financed by the sale of a financial asset. Surplus spending similarly implies the purchase of a financial asset' (Moore, 1988, p. 299, footnote 15).

It should be noted too that Keynes had already come to the same conclusion when discussing the bilateral character of monetary transactions in the *General Theory*: '. . . no one can save without acquiring an asset, whether it be cash or a debt or capital-goods' (Keynes, 1936, p. 81).

All in all, we again come to the conclusion that, far from resulting in truisms, bookkeeping provides true information about the world we live in. Insofar as bank money is concerned, we have to discard the common interpretation of monetary transactions, whereby goods are exchanged for money. Instead, it appears that the sale of goods generates monetary proceeds (sellers' income) which recipients simultaneously 'spend' on bank deposits by which they grant credit to banks and, in the final analysis, to purchasers. This is so because sellers are simultaneously credited with the money they earn and debited with it. The ambiguity we have been examining is then easy to clear up. We may, as Moore suggests, part with the traditional notion of money as a stock,[2] and consider monetary flows separately from the financial assets which bank deposits actually are. More precisely, we may argue with Schmitt (1984), who also grounds his analysis of bank money in bookkeeping, that any payment performed by a bank defines a circular flow of money, the bank, as well as the payer and the payee, being simultaneously credited and debited with a given amount of money units.[3] This is why, to do its business, the bank needs not call up some specific good or asset, deemed money, as the supposed counterpart to its commitments. Indeed, Keynes himself highlighted this point at the time he was preparing his plan for an international clearing union: the banking principle simply consists in 'the necessary equality of credits and debits' (Keynes, 1942, p. 171). From this he notably concluded, in opposition to the generally accepted view, that the possession of capital by banks is not a prerequisite for money creation. To perform payments, banks have to make use of a pure unit of account allowing them to credit and debit their accounts. Payments are effective, nonetheless, because they result in the formation of assets and debts that tie sellers and buyers through banks. What is the object of these assets and debts? Moore emphasizes that, fundamentally, each economic unit pays for its purchases in goods. What we learn from the necessary equality of credits and debits is that the intermediation of money does not run counter to this statement. Resulting in the formation of deposits, monetary payments run into a financial intermediation whereby sellers give credit to buyers who are thus allowed to postpone their own sales of goods. *Stricto sensu*, money comprises only units of account with which banks simultaneously debit and credit their accounts. It may in no way be identified with bank deposits, which are financial assets.

MONEY FLOWS, THE I-S IDENTITY AND THE FINANCING OF PRODUCTION

In articles published in 1937 Keynes highlighted the role of money and credit in financing production. He explained that entrepreneurs considering investing in new production have to secure a 'financial provision' which they will use to meet their spending on production costs. As a result, when they spend the finance they have obtained, firms become indebted to banks or to the public while the latter hold bank deposits, that is savings. Keynes insists that this 'finance motive' fuels demand for money which is distinct from demand for credit in the sense of saving. These developments confirm the distinction between money and deposits, and the role of money and credit discussed above.

Let us quote Keynes at some length:

> But 'finance' has nothing to do with saving. At the 'financial' stage of the proceedings no net saving has taken place on anyone's part, just as there has been no net investment. 'Finance' and 'commitments to finance' are mere credit and debit book entries, which allow entrepreneurs to go ahead with assurance.
>
> It is possible, then, that confusion has arisen between credit in the senses of 'finance', credit in the sense of 'bank loans' and credit in the sense of 'saving'. I have not attempted to deal here with the second. It should be observed that a confusion between the first and the last would be one between a flow and a stock. Credit, in the sense of 'finance', looks after a flow of investment. It is a revolving fund which can be used over and over again. It does not absorb or exhaust any resources . . . Each new net investment has new net saving attached to it. The saving can be used once only. It relates to the net addition to the stock of actual assets. (Keynes, 1937a, p. 209)

> . . . 'finance' is essentially a revolving fund. It employs no savings. It is, for the community as a whole, only a book-keeping transaction. As soon as it is 'used' in the sense of being expended, the lack of liquidity is automatically made good and the readiness to become temporarily unliquid is available to be used over again. Finance covering the interregnum is, to use a phrase employed by bankers in a more limited context, necessarily 'self-liquidating' for the community taken as a whole at the end of the interim period. (Keynes, 1937b, p. 219)

As pointed out by Cardim de Carvalho (2002, p. 80), this analysis has 'become the source of apparently unending controversies'. Due to space constraints, I cannot expand here on these controversies. Instead, I propose to comment on the quoted passages with reference to the distinction between money and deposits signaled in the preceding section.

Actually, the distinction between money and deposits is explicitly used by Keynes. As already observed, the finance motive feeds a demand for money which is distinct from the demand for saving. For Keynes, finance 'may be provided either by the new issue market or the banks' (Keynes, 1937a, p. 208). Considering both possibilities will help us understand the bearing of the distinction between money and deposits, and also the notion of the revolving fund of finance used by Keynes.

As Keynes emphasizes, banks and the new issue market alike provide a service designed to bridge the gap 'between the time when the decision to invest is taken and the time when the correlative investment and saving actually occur' (p. 208). What does this service consist of? Let us first consider the reference to banks, and more specifically to overdraft facilities provided by banks. The notion of overdraft facilities is explicit enough: it is a commitment by banks to pay for the expenses incurred by their customers, that is, here, by firms. However, as soon as firms actually draw on the facilities they were provided with, deposits are formed which consist in an amount of saving attached to the investment made. When does money proper intervene then? The only possibility left, as I argued in the preceding section, is that money intervenes in the flows involved in payments. Before payments take place there are only overdraft facilities; afterwards there are deposits, that is, savings. To transform overdraft facilities into deposits, banks have to simultaneously credit and debit firms and factors of production with units of account. This is where money and monetary flows come in.

Let us now consider the finance provided by the market. At first sight, one might think that market issues take up bank deposits, that is saving, supplied by the public. But this is not Keynes's understanding: 'the market's commitments will be in excess of actual saving to date' (p. 208). In this way, Keynes rightly means that when purchasing a debt issued by firms, the public does not surrender its saving but simply converts it into illiquid assets. Does not the public, however, transfer bank deposits to the firms which in turn transfer them to their creditors? Double-entry bookkeeping provides a straightforward answer. To purchase firms' debts, the public draws on its bank deposits, meaning that the latter are cancelled correspondingly. Simultaneously, firms are credited with sums of money they employ in constituting new deposits with banks. Subsequently, when firms pay production costs, their deposits with banks are cancelled and new deposits are created to the benefit of their creditors, just as they are created when the finance provision is provided by banks instead of the market. The only difference in comparison with the latter case is that firms become indebted to the public instead of the banks. And the current amount of deposits in the economy remains constant since the new deposits are matched by the cancellation of an equal amount of pre-existent deposits. Moreover, it should be noticed that the deposits firms obtain when selling debts to the public play the same role as overdraft facilities considered above: they denote drawing rights on the banks. This is actually what makes bank deposits special compared with other financial assets: they are liquid, that is, their holders may draw on them when they wish, so asking banks to make payments on their behalf. In the last section, we considered the brokerage role of nonbank intermediaries which lent surplus cash balances of some economic agents to deficit-spenders. These cash balances amount to the drawing rights on banks we are now referring to.

We may conclude, then, that money is definitely distinct from deposits. When asking for money in order to pay for production costs, firms do not ask for deposits *per se* but for the possibility to draw on banks, that is, to ask the latter to make payments on their behalf. Moreover, the reference to the new issue market bears out the idea of a revolving fund used by Keynes: as soon as new deposits are formed, the entire operation of financing may be resumed, provided deposit holders are ready to part with them and so convert their savings into illiquid assets. When firms resort to bank overdrafts, the conclusion is the same: liquidity is created which may be available for further payments.

THE I-S IDENTITY, KEYNES'S CONCEPT OF DEMAND DEFICIENCY AND HIS THEORY OF THE INVESTMENT MULTIPLIER

As soon as it is acknowledged that investment in new production gives rise to an equivalent amount of savings, a further difficulty arises. Namely, the identity of saving (S) and investment (I), defined in this way, apparently contradicts Keynes's theory of employment whereby saving may be in excess of investment. Again due to space constraints I cannot expand on an issue that has given rise to a wide debate in the literature. Instead let me make a suggestion directly related to the above analysis of the finance motive.

I believe that a distinction should be kept in mind as regards investment, depending on whether it refers to the payment of factor costs or to the purchase of capital goods. The reference to bookkeeping confirms that spending on factor costs met by entrepreneurs when committed in new production defines an investment matched by an equal amount of saving. This means that firms invest in the production of goods which are the actual subject matter of the financial intermediation performed by banks when paying for factor cost. Benefiting from a credit from factors through banks, firms retain control of the goods that are in the course of manufacture or stocked in their stores until they can sell them on the market. The payment of factor cost is specific in that it defines incomes which are saved in the form of bank deposits until they are spent on goods. As Keynes puts it:

> . . . if the banking system chooses to make the finance available and the investment projected by the new issues actually takes place, the appropriate level of incomes will be generated out of which there will necessarily remain over an amount of saving exactly sufficient to take care of the investment. (Keynes, 1937a, p. 210)

On the contrary, the purchase of capital goods exhausts pre-existent saving, even when it is financed from overdraft facilities. To test this argument, suppose that capital goods were produced by firm F1, which finances the payment of its factor cost from bank overdraft facilities. As a result, F1 is indebted to the bank while the factors it employed hold deposits with the bank (for simplicity, we may suppose that there is only one bank in the economy). As stated above, this financial relationship between F1 and deposit holders defined through the bank, is backed by the goods produced by F1. Suppose now that, at a second stage, firm F2 buys the goods produced by F1. If F2 finances its purchase from bank overdraft facilities, it becomes indebted to the bank. Simultaneously, F1 becomes a creditor of the bank, and is then able to settle its debt with the bank. Finally, the bank's balance sheets show F2, which is indebted to the bank, and the factors employed by F1, who still hold the deposits formed when they were paid. The goods produced by F1 having been sold, the credit relationship (through the bank) between F2 and the factors employed by F1 may not be backed by these goods. Although the factors employed by F1 have maintained their deposits with the bank, their deposits no longer represent a saved part of the current income (output) available in the economy. Through the bank, deposit holders have henceforth become creditors of F2 and may lay claim to goods which this firm is going to produce.

We may infer, then, that the inequality of investment and saving at the core of Keynes's theory of unemployment does not relate to the payment of factor cost and the resulting formation of incomes, but on the contrary to the spending of savings on capital goods. As Keynes puts it:

> The outline of our theory can be expressed as follows. When employment increases, aggregate real income is increased. The psychology of the community is such that when aggregate real income is increased aggregate consumption is increased, but not by so much as income. Hence employers would make a loss if the whole of the increased employment were to be devoted to satisfying the increased demand for immediate consumption. Thus, to justify any given amount of employment there must be an amount of current investment sufficient to absorb the excess of total output over what the community chooses to consume when employment is at a given level. For unless there is this amount of investment, the receipts of the entrepreneurs will be less than is required to induce them to offer the given amount of employment. (Keynes, 1936, p. 27)

The identity and the inequality of saving and investment are not contradictory inasmuch as they relate to separate stages of the circuit featured by the payment of factors' incomes by firms and the correlated spending of incomes on the purchase of the goods produced. On the contrary, the identity conditions the definition of a possible inequality. It is because the payment of factor costs represents an investment by firms, which they have to finance from credit, that firms meet actual losses when the goods produced are not bought. The demand deficiency underpinning Keynes's theory of unemployment is not simply a gap between supply and demand (as it would be in neoclassical theory) but a gap between solvent demand, as defined by the income formed, and the actual spending of incomes on consumption and investment goods. Once more, we have a confirmation that the accounting identity of investment and saving is far from a mere truism yielding no interesting information as to how the economy works.

Another controversial issue relates to the Keynesian multiplier. The identity of saving and investment appears to refute 'the Keynesian notion that the level of income adjusts to bring planned saving and planned investment . . . into equality by a "multiplier" process' (Moore, 1988, p. 309). Elsewhere (Gnos, forthcoming), I have argued that Moore's argument is perfectly right with regard to the standard interpretation of the Keynesian multiplier, whereby an increment in investment is supposed to induce purchases of consumption goods generating a succession of incomes and purchases until planned saving equals the initial increment in investment. This supposed multiplier expansion path is at variance with the characteristics of bank money, which cannot finance investment without simultaneously generating an equivalent saving attached to it. It is also at variance with Keynes's analysis of the 'finance motive' whereby the financing of any new production does not rely on pre-existent resources. I have also argued, however, that Keynes's conception of the multiplier cannot be reduced to the standard interpretation of it, and deserves fuller reappraisal.

In the *General Theory*, Keynes defines the multiplier within a framework characterized by the principle of effective demand which, in fact, dismisses the very notion of a chain of events by which the spending of incomes would form further incomes until I and S become equal. According to the principle of effective demand, entrepreneurs determine employment on the basis of the proceeds of sales they are expecting, which are dependent on the volume of employment they pay for. The determination of current output and income (Y_1) is subject to the principle of effective demand, just as the determination of the output of the year before (Y_0) was. This is a point that Moore has already made against the proponents of the standard multiplier theory: 'The situation at Y_1 is, from the viewpoint of the expected future change in income, no different from that at Y_0' (Moore, 1994, p. 131). Then, in Keynes's words, the multiplier is logical, it 'holds good continuously, without time-lag, at all moments of time' (Keynes, 1936, p. 115). It is not dependent on any supposed succession of incomes through time. It corresponds to the fact that an increase in investment allows entrepreneurs to expect an increase in demand for consumption goods, which, proportionally to the marginal propensity to consume, is dependent on the extra incomes formed in the production of capital goods and in the production of the increased quantity of consumption goods entrepreneurs are to decide upon. It is true, however, that Keynes concedes that 'the consequences of an expansion in the capital-goods industries . . . take gradual effect, subject to time-lag and only after an interval' (pp. 122–3). This latter statement may have spoken in favor of the existence of the expansion path described by the standard theory. Nonetheless, Keynes argues his genuine theory of the multiplier is in no way challenged by the fact that the increase in investment may take gradual effect. This is so because such a gradual effect is simply to be explained by the fact that the entrepreneurs are unlikely to be able to foresee in full what the increased demand for consumption goods will be:

> The discussion has been carried on, so far, on the basis of a change in aggregate investment which has been foreseen sufficiently in advance for the consumption industries to advance *pari passu* with the capital-goods industries . . . . In general, however, we have to take account of the case where the initiative comes from an increase in the output of the capital-goods industries which was not fully foreseen. (Keynes, 1936, p. 122)

The principle of effective demand, which is central to the multiplier, holds good whether changes in demand are accurately foreseen or not. Hence Keynes's conclusion: 'The fact that an unforeseen change only exercises its full effect on employment over a period of time . . . does not in any way, affect the significance of the theory of the multiplier as set forth in this chapter . . .' (Keynes, 1936, p. 124).

Moreover, and this is crucial in the present discussion, this theory in no way runs counter to the I-S identity. Spending incomes formed in the production of capital goods on consumption goods means that an equal amount of incomes formed in the production of consumption goods is simultaneously saved. This is so because, as stated above, incomes are cancelled only when spent on goods. When incomes formed in the production of capital goods are spent on consumption goods, an equal amount of incomes formed in the production of consumption goods is precluded from being spent on the latter goods. It is saved, and cannot be spent except on investment goods in the place of the other incomes.

CONCLUSION

This chapter confirms the validity of Moore's insistence on bookkeeping in his examination of the way a monetary economy works. We have been able to confirm the role Moore assigns to bookkeeping in asserting the endogeneity of money and in questioning the standard interpretation of Keynes's investment multiplier. The identity of banks' assets and liabilities prevents us from seeing money as an asset which could be supplied independently of the demand for it. The I-S identity following from the bookkeeping nature of money undoubtedly runs counter to the standard interpretation of the multiplier whereby an increment in investment would induce purchases of consumption goods, generating a succession of incomes and purchases until saving is equated to the initial increment in investment.

Also, we have undertaken to apply Moore's method to issues he did not examine in full, and that to some extent Keynes himself had already considered with reference to bookkeeping. These issues concern the distinction between flows and stocks, and the role of money and banks in economic transactions, especially in the financing of production. Our main conclusion is that we have to take seriously the fact that bookkeeping records sales of goods (or services) in the form of monetary proceeds and, as a counterpart, the use that recipients make of these proceeds. Payments are flows that banks effect in crediting and debiting accounts with sums of money defined in pure units of account, and that result in the building up of stocks, debts and deposits, that is, financial liabilities and assets, with which sellers extend credit to buyers through banks. This invalidates the common view that goods exchange for money assets (bank deposits). Bookkeeping and the ensuing identity of saving and investment are then confirmed as cornerstones of economics in its quest to explain the characteristics of the real world. By way of further illustration of this point, we have shown that neither Keynes's theory of unemployment nor his genuine theory of the multiplier (as opposed to the standard interpretation of it) runs counter to the I-S identity but on the contrary is tied in with it.

NOTES

1. 'In all monetary economies it is possible for individual economic agents *to spend more than they earn in any period*, that is, to receive more goods and services than they give in exchange . . .' (Moore, 1988, p. 294; emphasis added).
2. 'A central message of this book is that the conventional conception of the "money stock" has become anachronistic' (Moore, 1988, p. 371).
3. Cf. also Rossi (2001).

REFERENCES

Chick, V. (2000) 'Money and the Effective Demand', in John Smithin (ed.), *What is Money?*, London and New York: Routledge, 124–38.

de Carvalho, F.J.C. (2002) 'On Keynes's Concept of the Revolving Fund of Finance', in P. Arestis, M. Desai and S. Dow, *Money, Macroeconomics and Keynes, Essays in Honour of Victoria Chick*, Cheltenham, UK and Northampton, MA, USA: Edward Elgar, 1, 79–90.

Friedman, M. (1956) *Studies in the Quantity Theory of Money*, Chicago: University of Chicago Press.

Friedman, M. (1959) 'The Demand for Money: Some Theoretical and Empirical Results', *Journal of Political Economy*, 67, August, 327–51.
Friedman, M. (1969) *The Optimum Quantity of Money and Other Essays*, Chicago: Aldine.
Gnos, C. (forthcoming) 'The Multiplier, the Principle of Effective Demand and the Finance Motive: A Single Coherent Framework', in C. Gnos and L.P. Rochon (eds), *The Keynesian Multiplier*, London and New York: Routledge.
Heinsohn, G. and O. Steiger (1983) 'Private Property, Debts and Interest or: The Origin of Money and the Rise and Fall of Monetary Economics', mimeo, University of Naples (Italy) and University of Bremen.
Keynes, J.M. (1936) *The General Theory of Employment, Interest and Money*, London: Macmillan.
Keynes, J.M. (1937a) 'Alternative Theories of the Rate of Interest', *The Economic Journal*, reprinted in D. Moggridge (ed.) (1973), *The Collected Writings of John Maynard Keynes*, Volume XIV, London: Macmillan, 201–15.
Keynes, J.M. (1937b) 'The "Ex Ante" Theory of the Rate of Interest', *The Economic Journal*, reprinted in D. Moggridge (ed.) (1973), *The Collected Writings of John Maynard Keynes*, Volume XIV, London: Macmillan, 215–23.
Keynes, J.M. (1942) 'Proposals for an International Clearing Union', in D. Moggridge (ed.) (1980), *The Collected Writings of John Maynard Keynes*, Volume XXV, London: Macmillan, 168–95.
Lavoie, M. (1993) 'A Post-Classical View of Money, Interest, Growth and Distribution', in G. Mongiovi and C. Rühl (eds), *Macroeconomic Theory: Diversity and Convergence*, Aldershot, UK and Brookfield, USA: Edward Elgar.
Moore, B. (1988) *Horizontalists and Verticalists: The Macroeconomics of Credit Money*, New York: Cambridge University Press.
Moore, B. (1994) 'The Demise of the Keynesian Multiplier: a Reply to Cottrell', *Journal of Post Keynesian Economics*, 17, 121–33.
Moore, B. (2001) 'Some Reflections on Endogenous Money', in L.P. Rochon and M. Vernengo (eds), *Credit, Interest Rates and the Open Economy*, Cheltenham, UK and Northampton, MA, USA: Edward Elgar, 11–30.
Parguez, A. and M. Seccareccia (2000) 'The Credit Theory of Money: The Monetary Circuit Approach', in John Smithin (ed.), *What is Money?*, London and New York: Routledge, 101–23.
Polanyi, K. (1944) *The Great Transformation: The Political and Economic Origins of Our Time*, New York: Farrar & Rinehart.
Rochon, L.P. (2001) 'Horizontalism: Setting the Record Straight', in L.P. Rochon and M. Vernengo (eds), *Credit, Interest Rates and the Open Economy*, Cheltenham, UK and Northampton, MA, USA: Edward Elgar, 31–65.
Rossi, S. (2001) *Money and Inflation, A New Macroeconomic Analysis*, Cheltenham, UK and Northampton, MA, USA: Edward Elgar.
Schumpeter, J.A. (1954) *History of Economic Analysis*, New York: Oxford University Press.
Schmitt, B. (1984) *Inflation, chômage et malformations du capital*, Albeuve and Paris: Castella et Economica.
Wray, L.R. (1990) *Money and Credit in Capitalist Economies: The Endogenous Money Approach*, Aldershot, UK and Brookfield, USA: Edward Elgar.

2. The need and some methods for dynamic modelling in Post Keynesian economics

Steve Keen

Basil Moore states in 'Money and Interest Rates in a Monetary Theory of Production' that:

> Macroeconomic behaviour cannot be usefully modelled as the simultaneous solution of a set of Walrasian general equilibrium equations, where all exchanges occur simultaneously, all coordination problems are resolved by assuming perfect and complete markets, and all agents are omnisciently rational. In this vision of what is in effect a perfect barter economy, money can have no role. (Moore, 1998, p. 341)

He continues optimistically that 'There appears at last to be a growing consensus in the profession that the timeless perfect barter paradigm must be rejected'.

Perhaps; certainly there is now a substantial subset of the discipline affected by concepts from complexity theory,[1] and there are even welcome interlopers from physics ('econophysicists') to whom thinking in process terms is second nature. Frequently, however, the timeless perfect barter paradigm enters by stealth through the back door of economists' continuing obsession with equilibrium, and reliance upon simultaneous equations – even when their verbal vision is clearly incompatible with the inherent timelessness of both concepts.

One striking illustration of this is provided by a key paper from a school of non-neoclassical economics that has otherwise made almost as significant a contribution to the analysis of endogenous money as has Basil: the European 'Circuitist' School. Starting from an a-priori discussion of what money must be, this School has developed a vision of capitalism in which money is not the '$n+1^{\text{th}}$ commodity' tacked onto an n-good barter economy, but an essential component of a monetary capitalist system. As Graziani puts it,

> The starting point of the theory of the circuit, is that a true monetary economy is inconsistent with the presence of a commodity money. A commodity money

> is by definition a kind of money that any producer can produce for himself. But an economy using as money a commodity coming out of a regular process of production, cannot be distinguished from a *barter economy*. A true monetary economy *must therefore be using a token money*, which is nowadays a paper currency. (Graziani, 1989, p. 3)

He then specifies two additional key conditions needed 'In order for money to exist':

> b) money has to be accepted *as a means of final settlement* of the transaction (otherwise it would be credit and not money);
> c) money must not grant privileges of seigniorage to any agent making a payment. (Graziani, 1989, p. 3)

From this he derives the insight that 'any monetary payment must therefore be a triangular transaction, involving at least three agents, the payer, the payee, and the bank':

> The only way to satisfy those three conditions is to have payments made by means of *promises of a third agent*, the typical third agent being nowadays a bank . . . Once the payment is made, no debt and credit relationships are left between the two agents. But one of them is now a creditor of the bank, while the second is a debtor of the same bank. (Graziani, 1989, p. 3; all emphases in original)

This perspective clearly delineates a monetary vision of capitalism from the neoclassical barter paradigm. In the neoclassical world, transactions are two-sided two commodity barter exchanges: person A gives person B units of commodity X in return for units of commodity Y (see Figure 2.1). Calling one of these 'the money commodity' does not alter the essentially barter personality of the transaction.

In a monetary world, transactions are three-sided, single commodity, financial exchanges: person A gives person B units of commodity X, in return for person B requesting the bank Z (and the bank agreeing) to debit Y currency units from B's account and credit A's account with the same amount (see Figure 2.2).[2]

The financial aspects of a credit system become integral to capitalism from this Circuitist perspective: money is quintessentially credit money, with the bank in Figure 2.2 granting $300 of credit to agent B, and B in turn incurring a debt obligation to the bank of this amount with its concomitant interest payment commitments, etc. (though as it happens this aspect of the credit system is not adequately incorporated in Graziani's model). Banks are thus an essential component of capitalism, and cannot be treated simply as a particular type of firm, as Graziani emphasizes:

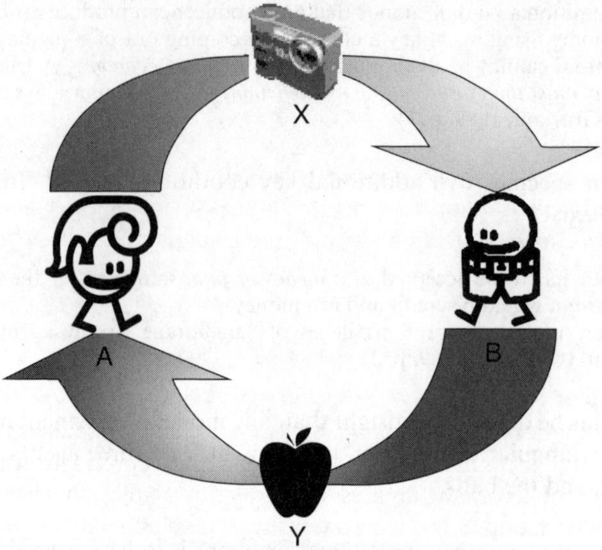

Figure 2.1 Neoclassical exchange

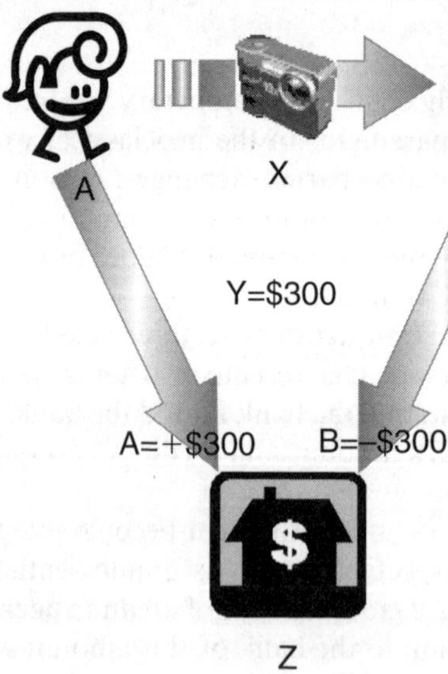

Figure 2.2 Monetary exchange

> Since in a monetary economy money payments necessarily go through a third agent, the third agent being one that specialises in the activity of producing means of payment (in modern times a bank), *banks and firms must be considered as two distinct kinds of agents* . . . In any model of a monetary economy, *banks and firms cannot be aggregated into one single sector*. (Graziani, 1989, p. 4; emphasis in original)

Graziani next attempts to develop a model of the production process as a monetary circuit, starting from this firm grounding in a monetary view of capitalism.

GOING ASTRAY

Graziani's model of the production process begins with banks deciding to grant 'credit to firms in order to enable them to start production' (Graziani, 1989, p. 4).[3] This credit creates money, and enables the firms to hire workers. Workers then receive wages, which they either spend upon products produced by the firm(s), deposit in banking accounts, or use to purchase securities issued by the firms.

The latter two activities enable the firms to extinguish their obligations to the banking sector, and once they do so Graziani alleges that 'the money initially created is destroyed' (Graziani, 1989, p. 5).[4] Graziani then makes a deduction which should have been the foundation of a dynamic model of the circuit: that if workers spent their salaries instantly, money would be destroyed virtually as soon as it was created and would therefore effectively not exist. As a result, 'An assumption is therefore required for the existence of a money stock, namely that wage-earners spend their money incomes gradually over time' (Graziani, 1989, p. 6).[5]

Graziani discusses this assumption as if it is something which is on the surface indefensible.[6] But it is simply a statement of reality: wage-earners *do* spend their money incomes gradually over time. Wages are paid at a defined frequency (say once every two weeks), and workers then dissipate those funds on commodity and other expenditures at something approaching the same frequency.[7]

The most general way to model workers' money balances is that the rate of change of the part of the money stock held by workers M_W is a positive function of inflows F_i and a negative function of outflows F_o:

$$\frac{d}{dt}M_W = F_i - F_o \tag{2.1}$$

If we omit the (at this stage of modelling) unnecessary complication of workers purchasing securities issued by firms, the simplest dynamic way to model the Circuitist insight – that the level of the money stock in existence depends in part on the gradual rather than instantaneous expenditure of wages – is that outflows are a linear function of the time lag between workers' receipt of wages and their expenditure of those incomes. Expressing this time lag as $1/\tau$ (the reason for this inverse form will become evident shortly), the verbal model given by Graziani with a single injection of funds M_0 (rather than a flow, so that the F_i term disappears) reduces to

$$\frac{dM_w}{dt} = -\frac{1}{\tau} \cdot M_W \tag{2.2}$$

The symbolic solution to this equation is $M_W(t) = M_0 \cdot e^{-\frac{1}{\tau}}$. Workers' share of the money stock will therefore decay exponentially from an initial injection of M_0 dollars, as shown in Figure 2.3. If we set $\tau = \frac{1}{2}$, the tangent to this curve at $t = 0$ cuts the time axis at ½ of a time unit (a week), which indicates that τ is the time lag in workers' expenditure of income (Andresen, 1998) shows using theorems from systems engineering that this function is quite a valid approximation for a large number of individuals who do not particularly transact with each other). Thus with a time lag of half a week, workers spend their money stock down to almost zero after two weeks.

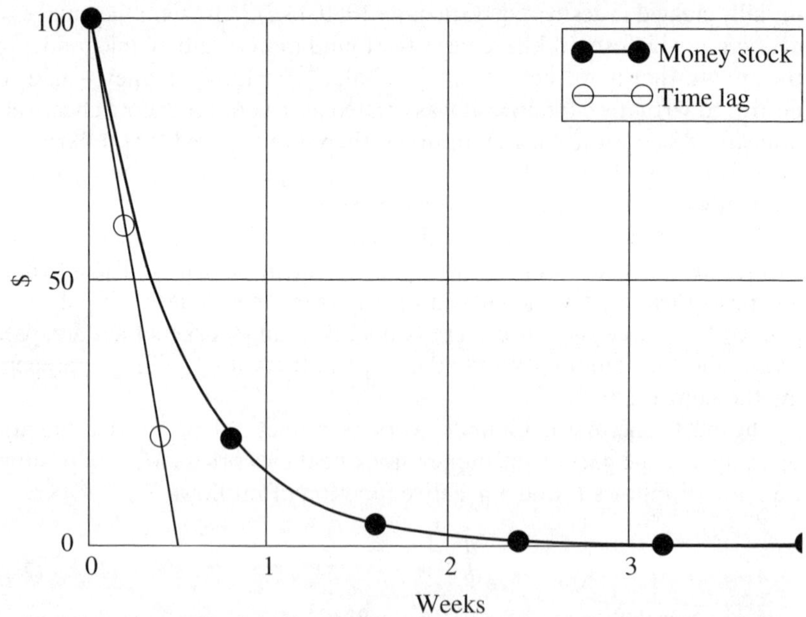

Figure 2.3 Exponential decay of money stock with a time lag in spending

This could and should have been the basis for a dynamic model of the monetary circuit; unfortunately it was not. For the sake of this commentary, the importance of equation (2.2) arises from Graziani's description of it as 'a necessary assumption, if we do not want the velocity of circulation to become infinite and money to disappear altogether from the system' (Graziani, 1989, p. 6). Therefore neither τ nor dM_w/dt can be zero in Graziani's simple model of a once-only injection, since if they are then the money stock no longer exists.

After some further discussion, Graziani attempts to derive some general principles for price formation, the rate of profit, etc., from a simultaneous equation statement of the equality of output and demand:

$$\pi Np = cwN + ciB + \pi bNp \tag{2.3}$$

where π is worker productivity, N total employment, p the price level, c the consumption propensity of wage earners (and s the corresponding propensity to save), w the money wage rate, i the rate of interest paid on bonds, B the value of bonds issued by firms, and b the proportion of output purchased by firms (ignored earlier on by Graziani but introduced here). With some manipulations he derives p as

$$p = \frac{1-s}{1-b}\left(\frac{w}{\pi} + \frac{iB}{\pi N}\right) \tag{2.4}$$

on which he makes the following observations:

> a) the level of money prices does not depend on the quantity of money. In fact, the quantity of money does not even appear in the equation for the price level. The money stock, being a totally endogenous variable, cannot enter into the determination of the price level;
> b) the level of money prices depends instead on the savings and investment propensities (s and b), as well as on the level of money costs;
> c) any change in the level of money prices will induce a corresponding change in the money stock, if the velocity of circulation is taken as constant. (Graziani, 1989, p. 14)

There is just one problem with this analysis and these observations: since they are derived from a simultaneous equation, they apply only in equilibrium when dM_W/dt and all other rates of change $(\frac{d}{dt}p, \frac{d}{dt}N, \ldots)$ are zero. But from Graziani's own prior observation, in this situation the money stock is zero and money has 'disappear[ed] altogether from the system'. How then could money play any role in price determination, etc., if in this state it does not exist?

THE EQUILIBRIUM CRINGE

The root of Graziani's conversion of an excellent verbal analysis into a faulty mathematical one is the equilibrium cringe that still afflicts non-neoclassical economics – as opposed to the equilibrium fetish that defines neoclassicism. Because we have for so long been schooled in an equilibrium manner of thinking, this often unconsciously enters non-neoclassical research, especially when an attempt is made to move from verbal to symbolic analysis – and even when that verbal analysis has established that the concepts we wish to model are incompatible with equilibrium.

I call this a cringe because it very akin to the 'cultural cringe' that often afflicts residents of a non-mainstream culture – audiences regard the home-grown product as inherently inferior to the Hollywood offering, when Hollywood's commercial dominance is often the product of sheer economies of scale rather than innate quality (the analogy with economics is obvious). Likewise equilibrium: even as non-orthodox economists, we tend to believe that equilibrium is the only valid state, that whatever we hypothesize must apply 'in equilibrium' to be truly significant.

The reality is precisely the opposite: the economy has never been and will never be 'in equilibrium' (and as Joan Robinson once observed, if ever it was, how would we know?). The economy is dynamic and evolutionary. The concept of equilibrium is anathema to the latter, and while equilibria can be defined for dynamic models, in the most interesting such models the equilibria are unstable and therefore define conditions which will *never* apply, either in the model or the reality it purports to represent. To be truly important, the hypotheses we develop must apply *out of equilibrium*. That is the real test of economic significance.

This attitude is commonplace outside economics, and second nature to those interlopers from physics who are now making their presence felt on the fringes of our discipline. To these researchers, models are only valid if they apply *out* of equilibrium. To quote from a recent paper:

> To physicists, given the dynamics of real economic interactions and the many social and political forces that impinge on economic interactions, the argument that actual trades occur in equilibrium and are market clearing appears strange. We expect that trades will usually be out-of-equilibrium, that is, price will differ from value, and the existence of fluctuating levels of stocks of all kinds of unsold goods is manifest proof that real prices are not 'market clearing'. (Scafetta et al., 2004)

Clearly this is how Graziani began, with the insight about workers' expenditures. But then the equilibrium cringe took over, both in these simultaneous equations and in Graziani's commentaries upon them:

It should be noticed that the preceding equality may seem as being in the nature of an *equilibrium* condition in a perfectly competitive market; if $s = b, \ldots$ profits are zero, as in a perfectly competitive *equilibrium*; '*Equilibrium*' prevails if firms, by selling commodities and by issuing securities, get back the whole of the money they have initially spent and that they now owe to the banks. Whenever the money cost of production along with the existing quantity of money (and therefore the debt of firms towards banks) are constant, firms are in '*equilibrium*'; Circuit theory, as we know, defines the money stock as a debt of firms towards the banks. The consequence of such a definition is that, as soon as money balances exceed their *equilibrium* level, firms will reduce their debt, therefore destroying money by the same amount. (Graziani, 1989, various; emphases added)

THE DYNAMIC ALTERNATIVES

Once the equilibrium cringe is abandoned, so too necessarily are simultaneous equations. What then are the alternatives?

One, perhaps, is nothing at all. Certainly there are some non-neoclassicals who make the proposition, in varying degrees, that modelling itself must be abandoned. Paul Davidson, for one, makes the claim that economic reality is subject to fundamental uncertainty and is non-ergodic, and therefore deterministic dynamic models cannot be applicable in economics.[8]

There are two flaws in this perspective. The first is Davidson's own approach to modelling, which employs static Marshallian techniques. If his objection is taken to its logical conclusion, then deterministic static models are also ruled out: certainly deterministic static analysis has more formal limitations on its applicability than deterministic dynamic analysis.

The second and more constructive problem is that this perspective displays a lack of appreciation of the interplay between deterministic nonlinear dynamics and sensitivity to initial conditions. Davidson defines an ergodic system as one in which 'future events are always reliably predictable by using a probability analysis of past and current outcomes' (Davidson, 1994, p. 89). By this definition, a deterministic nonlinear model can be non-ergodic: if such a model generates chaotic outcomes,[9] then after a certain period of time, its future course becomes unpredictable given anything less than *infinite* precision in the statement of its initial conditions.

Ott (1993) puts this very well with the example of the Henon attractor. He considers two simulations with the initial conditions differing by a factor of 10^{-14}, a minute difference statistically. Yet even though the model is deterministic, it is not 'ergodic' as defined by Davidson since the system cannot be predicted for more than 45 iterations, and doubling this predictive range to 90 iterations requires an impossible level of increase in the accuracy of measurement of the initial conditions:

> Suppose that we wish to predict to a longer time, say, twice as long, i.e., to $n \sim 90$. Then we must improve the accuracy of our initial measurement from 10^{-14} to 10^{-28}. That is, we must improve our accuracy by a tremendous amount, namely 14 orders of magnitude! . . . chaos may make prediction past a certain time . . . impossible in a practical sense. (Ott, 1993, p. 18)

This property of chaotic systems (now more commonly called complex systems) could be termed 'endogenous fundamental uncertainty'. It is therefore not true that all deterministic models are 'ergodic' (again, as defined by Davidson). Deterministic *linear* models are certainly ergodic – especially so static ones! – but deterministic *nonlinear* models can generate 'non-ergodic' outcomes.

It could be argued that this form of uncertainty is epistemological rather than fundamental, since it rests on the impossibility of economic observers knowing the state of the world to a necessary level of accuracy: achieve that level of accuracy, and the world-view shifts from non-ergodic to ergodic. However, this underestimates just how enormous is the impact of this epistemological uncertainty, and yet how easily this level of uncertainty is generated in real world data. The Henon attractor is a simple iterated map with only two variables and two parameters, which is nothing compared to the complexity of an economy. Yet even with a complete model of the Henon process, its future cannot be predicted beyond a very finite horizon. Even if a true 'complex systems model of the economy' could be constructed, its dimensional complexity would mean that the information needed to turn the model from 'non-ergodic' to 'ergodic' for any meaningful time-frame would exceed the information-storage capacity of the universe. This is a rather fundamental form of 'epistemological' uncertainty!

It can also coexist with Keynes's 'we simply do not know' uncertainty of the future, while still making it feasible to provide a deterministic model of our economic insights. The key models of Post Keynesian economics are themselves deterministic – though normally stated verbally – and are often also implicitly or explicitly evolutionary. Minsky's financial instability hypothesis, for example, envisages a cycle of rising debt leading to a debt-deflationary crisis (in the absence of a government sector) or perpetual cycles (with a government sector). The evolutionary aspects to this model – such as changes in attitudes to financial risk and changes in financial institutions since 'stability is destabilizing' – cannot be captured with a dynamic model, but the essence of this verbal model is reproducible with a dynamic model alone (Keen, 2000). However such behavior cannot be reproduced using a static equilibrium framework, since in equilibrium the apposite question is 'Crisis? What crisis?'. Dynamic models are in that sense closer to evolutionary models than static models are to evolutionary ones, and Post Keynesian reasoning should begin not with inappropriate static thinking but with at least approximately correct dynamic analysis.

Economists – even, in general, Post Keynesian ones – therefore have a lot of both learning and unlearning to do. Fortunately, there are many sources of help. Dynamic modelling has been developed dramatically by professions which were never afflicted with the equilibrium fetish: engineering, mathematics, physics, computing. I will outline two here – direct numerical solutions of differential equations, and systems engineering software – and use them to identify several errors in the Circuitist framework. Finally I will use them to illustrate Goodwin's (1967) predator–prey growth cycle model.

A Circuitist Model as a Flowchart

Systems engineering programs (such as Matlab's *Simulink* or Mathsoft's *Vissim*) employ the *GUI* 'graphical user interface' concept of a flowchart to display systems of differential equations as feedback systems. Rather than attempting symbolic solutions – which are impossible anyway with third-order or higher continuous time nonlinear systems – these programs simulate models numerically. These numerical techniques are extensions of the Laplace method for solving differential equations by transforming them into polynomials in powers of a variable typically denoted as s (consequently these programs use the symbol $1/s$ to indicate integration).

Since these programs use integration rather than differentiation,[10] the first step in converting a model from equation to flowchart form is to 'integrate both sides' of a differential equation. The simple differential equation for workers' money stock $dM_W/dt = -\frac{1}{\tau} \cdot M_W$ thus becomes $M_W(t) = M_0 + \int_0^t -\frac{1}{\tau} \cdot M_W \cdot ds$, and the integral is evaluated numerically. Figure 2.4 shows the flowchart representation of the equation. The operations of addition (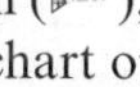), multiplication (), integration and so on are performed by flowchart operators, as shown. Reading the flowchart from left to right, the time lag *Tau* (τ) is set at 0.5 weeks; this is then negated and inverted to give us the equivalent of $-1/\tau$ in the equation. This is multiplied by workers' money stock M_w and integrated (this is equivalent to $\int_0^t -\frac{1}{\tau} \cdot M_W \cdot ds$), added to the initial injection of money from the wage ($100 million), so that the output of the model is the money stock M_w time t (which varies continuously from zero to two weeks in this simulation).

One deficiency in Graziani's paper – the failure to explicitly account for interest accruing on deposits and debts – can easily be corrected in this model. If wages are paid directly into workers' bank accounts, and an interest rate of r_d (set at 2 per cent p.a. in Figure 2.5) is paid on deposits, then the rate of change of workers' money stock becomes

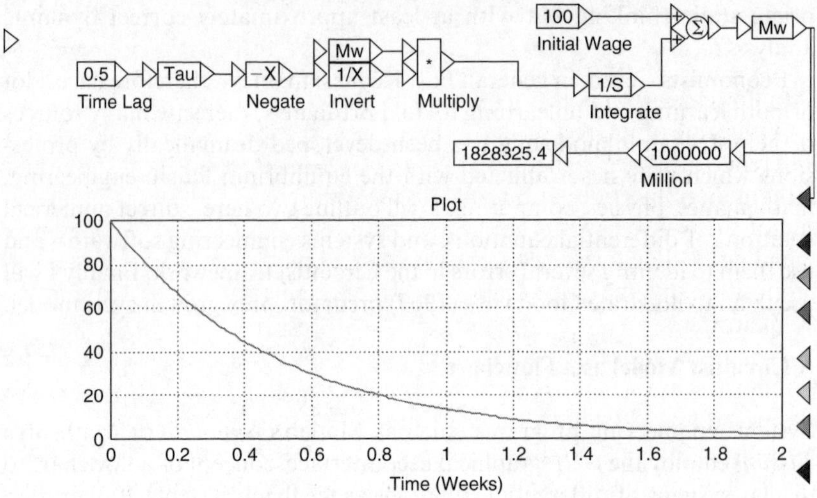

Figure 2.4 Exponential decay of money stock in flowchart format

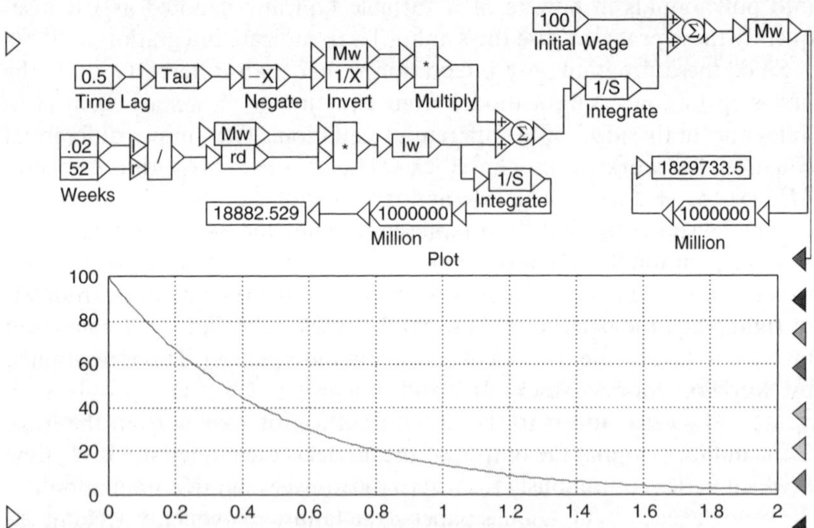

Figure 2.5 Workers money stock adjusted for interest paid

$$\frac{dM_w}{dt} = -\frac{1}{\tau} \cdot M_W + r_d \cdot M_W \qquad (2.5)$$

In flowchart format this results in the model shown in Figure 2.5.

With a rate of interest on deposits of 2 per cent p.a., this makes a $18,823 difference to workers' incomes over the two-week period from the initial $100 million injection, and results in an additional $1,408 existing at the end of the two weeks (the rest of the additional income goes on increased spending). While this is not a huge numerical difference, it contradicts the proposition that the money supply will be extinguished once workers spend all their wages.

This partial model provides a foundation for a complete rendition of the Circuitist schema, and it points out another flaw in their analysis: the absence of any explicit treatment of the relationship between the borrowed working capital and production.

The flow of funds out of workers' accounts is simultaneously (in this model without securities or workers' saving propensities) a flow into capitalists' bank accounts. At the same time, the initial wage payment to workers is matched by a *negative* entry in capitalists' accounts (representing the initial debt of capitalists to banks), and capitalists pay interest (at a higher rate) on their outstanding debt. Specifying the rate of interest on loans as r_l, and capitalists' *negative* bank balance as M_C, the simplest expression for the rate of change of capitalists' bank accounts is:

$$\frac{d}{dt}M_C = r_l \cdot M_C + \frac{1}{\tau} \cdot M_W + r_d \cdot M_W \qquad (2.6)^{11}$$

M_C is negative in this equation because the initial loan from banks to capitalists appears as a 'negative deposit' in capitalist bank accounts. With Graziani's assumption that this loan is then paid directly and immediately to workers by capitalists, this initial negative is balanced in a double-entry bookkeeping sense by the instantaneous depositing of the *positive* equivalent amount in workers' bank accounts (so that $M_W(0) = -M_C(0) > 0$).

Figure 2.6 renders this as a flowchart. The top half of the diagram defines W_{Fo} as the outflow of funds from workers' accounts; the second half is the analog to equation (2.6).

To complete the model, we need to explicitly record the activity of bankers. In this model, they make a profit on the spread between the (low rate) interest payments made to workers and the (high rate) interest charged to capitalists. Presuming that bankers then spend part of this profit on consumption and accumulate the rest, we get the relations shown in Figure 2.7.

The top part of the diagram consolidates the banks' interest charging and paying activities. The first component shows the interest payments to workers

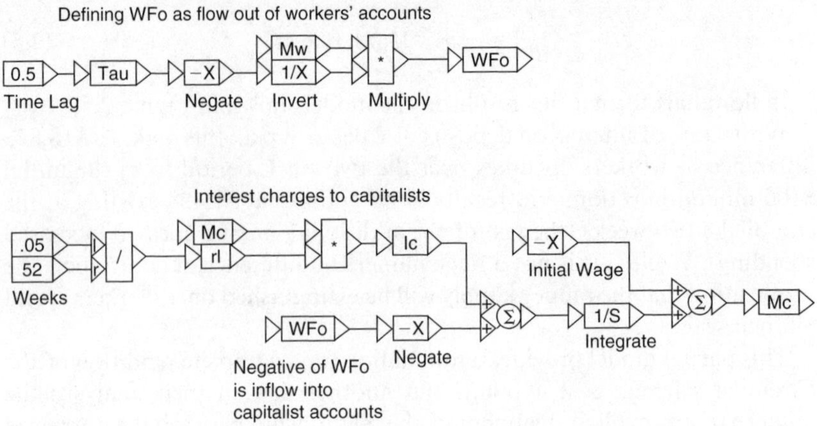

Figure 2.6 Capitalist accounts linked to debt repayment and workers' expenditure

and the second component shows the interest charges to capitalists. Both these are negated to show their impact on the gross profit position of bankers, and the third component of the top plot shows the overall flow of profits to bankers. The bottom half of the diagram then shows an apportionment of this gross banking profit between accumulation and consumption, with B_{pc} representing the bankers' propensity to consume. Consumption expenditure by bankers of course becomes a positive flow into the bank accounts of capitalists, which requires the negation of the inputs again.

With the addition of this component, the model is closed at this basic level, and the overall model can be simulated – with its results pointing out another flaw in the Circuitist logic, but also showing the way to solve the problem indicated. Figure 2.8 shows the submodel for capitalists' accounts, and shows that at the end of the circuit as described by Graziani, capitalists are in net deficit.

By the end of the two weeks, workers have a net financial position of \$1.83 million (see Figure 2.5), and banks have accumulated roughly \$25,500 (Figure 2.7). But capitalists are out of pocket by \$1.85 million! Who'd be a capitalist?

The answer, simply, is anyone who doesn't simply pay all the money he/she borrows to the workers! The dilemma of 'how do capitalists repay their debt?' is solved in part by realizing that what capitalists borrow from banks in the first instance in this model is working capital, which is used to finance production that generates a physical surplus that in turn is priced by capitalists to generate a monetary surplus. In this model as it stands, all

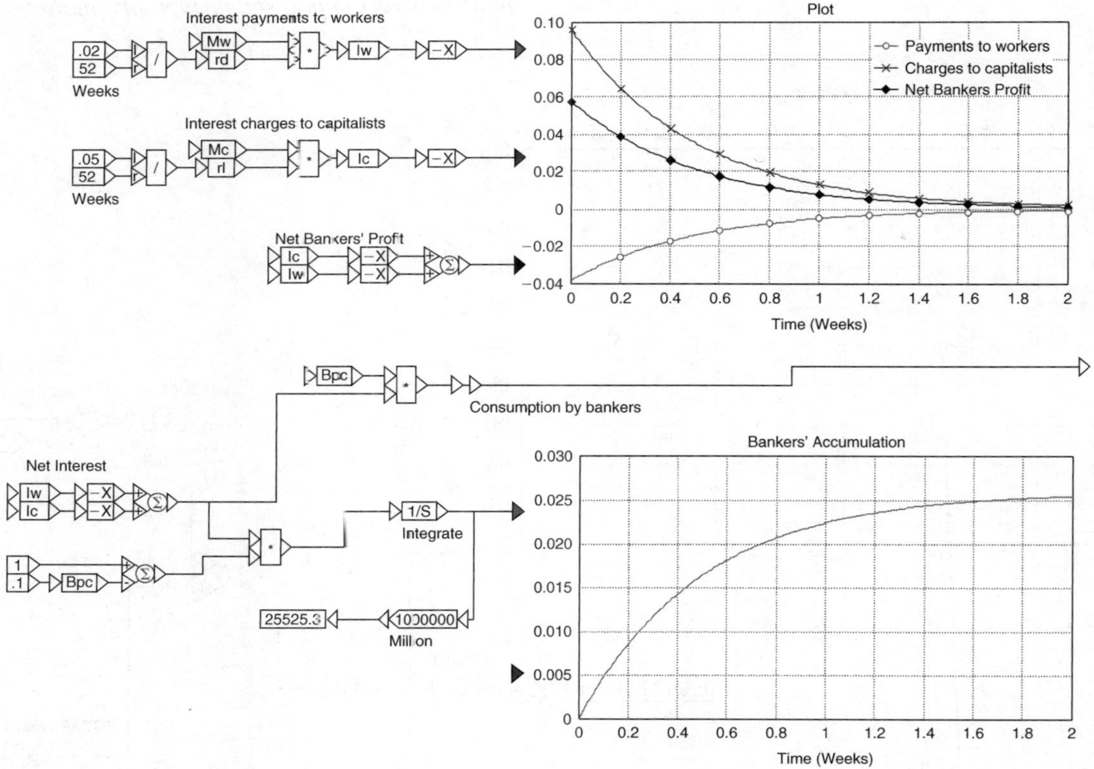

Figure 2.7 *Bankers' expenditure and accumulation*

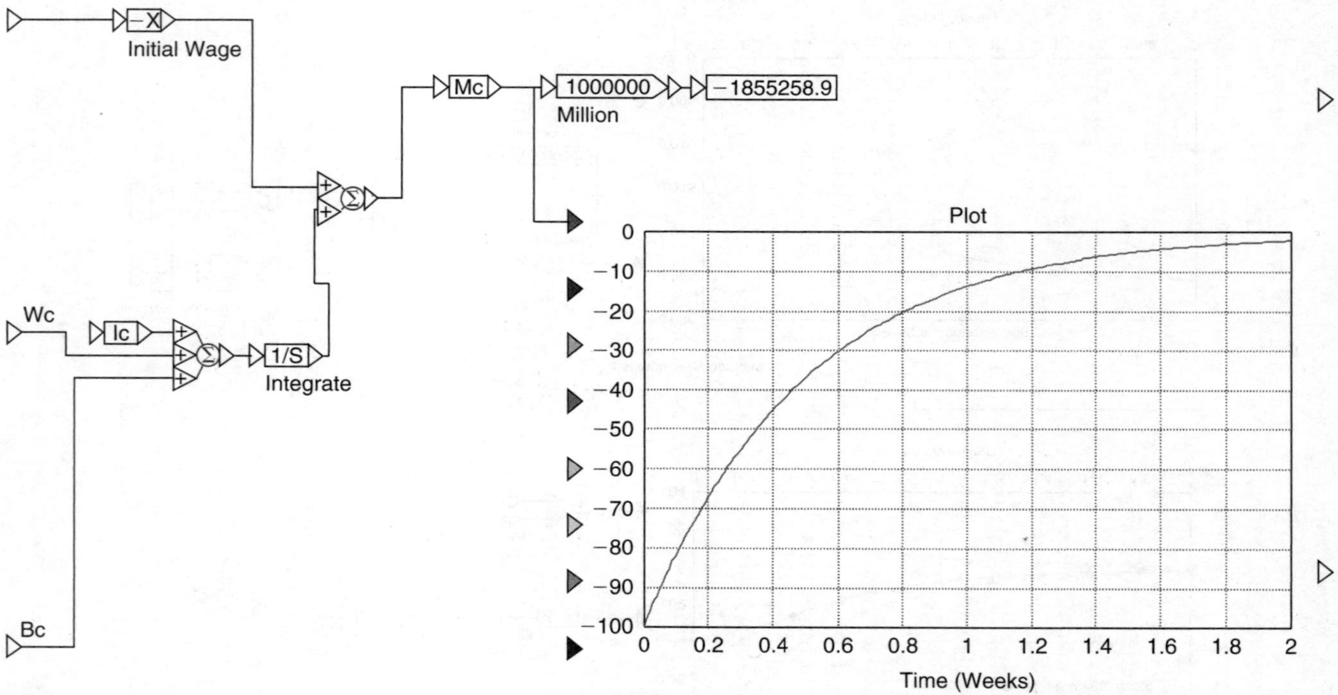

Figure 2.8 Capitalist financial position in Graziani circuit

that capitalists do is borrow money, hand it over to the workers, and then pay the loan back with interest.

To model the use of this borrowing as working capital, two accounts for capitalists are required – one with a positive balance containing the initial loan from banks and used to finance production, the other with an initially equivalent negative balance subject to interest charges. Andresen (2006) shows, contrary to Fontana (2000), that an initial injection of working capital can enable an indefinite circulation process (given appropriate interest rates, income shares, etc.) without the need for further injections of credit (though these do in practice occur, of course).

Intuitively, it would seem that (contrary to Graziani's simultaneous equation analysis), the amount of money in circulation *would* be an argument (or at least an influence) in setting the price level, allied to expressions for the rate of turnover of working capital relative to the rate of surplus production and the velocity of circulation of money. With the model properly closed, a rate of achieved profit could be determined and (given an investment function) a flow of new demand for debt could be generated.

Substantial extensions to the Circuitist framework would be needed, including replacing the time lag rendition of workers' expenditure with a time-dependent purchase of commodities function, production relations, income distribution dynamics, capitalist consumption and investment demand functions, a price formation model, and so on. Such modelling extensions exceed the purpose of this chapter and are the subject of future research. I hope, however, that the exercise thus far indicates both the necessity and the value of expressing any Post Keynesian model in dynamic terms. In what follows I show how this is done with the established Goodwin growth cycle model, using the modern computing tools outlined above.

Goodwin's Model

As is well known, Goodwin's model reduces to a set of two coupled differential equations in ω (workers' share of output W/Y) and λ (the rate of employment L/N):

$$\frac{d\omega}{dt} = \omega \times (P(\lambda) - \alpha)$$

$$\frac{d\lambda}{dt} = \lambda \times \left(\frac{1-\omega}{v} - \alpha - \beta\right) \tag{2.7}$$

where $P(\lambda)$ is a Phillips curve relation between the rate of employment and the rate of change of wages, α is the rate of technological change, v is the accelerator K/Y, and β is the rate of population growth. When Goodwin first derived this model, he sketched its properties using a novel four-sector graph (and employing a linear Phillips curve). Now such a model can easily be numerically simulated in any one of a number of commercial and freeware mathematics programs.

Using my personal favourite of the commercial packages (Mathcad), it is now possible to derive a dynamic model and then simulate it using exactly standard mathematical notation.

A functional form is also needed for the Phillips curve; I use a generalized exponential that takes as arguments the minimum asymptote m, an (x,y) coordinate pair, and the slope s of the function at that point: $P(\lambda, x, y, s, m) = (y - m) \cdot e^{\frac{s}{y-m}\cdot(\lambda - x)} - m$. With the parameters $x = 0.96$, $y = 0$, $s = 2$, $m = -0.04$, the real wage will be constant at an unemployment rate of 4 per cent, increase 2 per cent for a 1 per cent increase in employment at that level, and fall by no more than 4 per cent p.a.

The model is then simulated using the 'Odesolve' and the resulting numerical simulation graphed (see Figure 2.9) – and the numerical data can be further analysed.

There is no intrinsic limit to the number of differential equations that can be coupled and simulated using these technologies, and therefore no need to limit dimensionality in order to make a model analytically tractable, as in Jarsulic (1989). My published extensions to Goodwin's model to include Minsky's financial instability hypothesis add another three variables (debt, net government subsidies and a price index), while Chiarella and Flaschel (using their own proprietary software) have modelled up to eighteen dimensional systems (see Chiarella and Flaschel, 2000).

However, this approach does have the drawback that a reduced form has to be derived from initial causal relations. This is time consuming, and can result in the underlying causal model being 'lost' in the complexity of derivations. The closed form shown above expresses this model in terms of the two system states $\lambda = L/N$ and $\omega = W/Y$. However, this model can be rendered in its original form using systems engineering software.

Expressing Goodwin's model in causal form, the model starts with an investment-driven perspective specified in terms of aggregate output and capital. In the following equations causation works from right to left:

- Investment determines the rate of change of capital stock: $d/dt(K) = I$
- Capital stock determines output, given the accelerator v: $Y = K/v$
- Output determines how many workers need to be hired, given labor productivity a that grows at α per cent p.a.: $L = Y/a$
- The number of workers hired determines the employment rate λ, given the population level that grows at β per cent p.a.: $\lambda = L/N$

Given

$$\frac{d}{dt}\omega(t) = \omega(t)\cdot\left(P\left(\lambda(t), 96\%, 0, 2, -4\%\right) - \alpha\right) \qquad \omega(0) = 80\%$$

$$\frac{d}{dt}\lambda(t) = \lambda(t)\cdot\left(\frac{1-\omega(t)}{v} - \alpha - \beta\right) \qquad \lambda(0) = 95\%$$

$$\begin{pmatrix}\omega\\ \lambda\end{pmatrix} := \text{Odesolve}\left[\begin{pmatrix}\omega\\ \lambda\end{pmatrix}, t, 20, 1000\right]$$

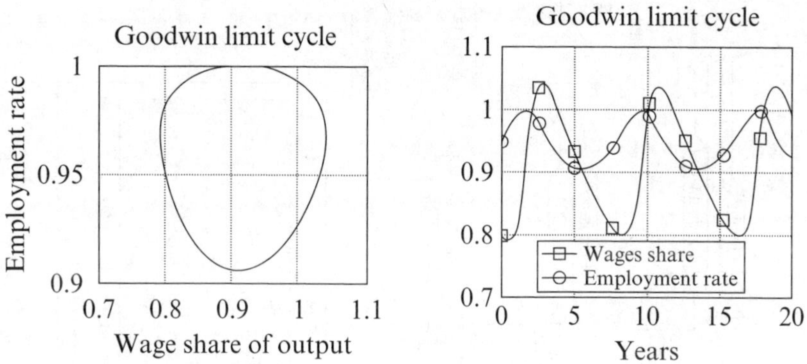

Figure 2.9 Simulating Goodwin's growth cycle in Mathcad

- The employment rate determines the change in real wages w: $\frac{1}{w}\frac{d}{dt}w = P(\lambda)$
- Output minus real wages determines profit Π: $\Pi = Y - w \cdot L$
- All profits are invested: $I = \Pi$

Figures 2.10 and 2.11 show this model in Vissim form; it is a relatively simple matter to choose any part of the diagram as a starting point and follow the causal loop. Figure 2.10 shows all the blocks at one level while Figure 2.11 applies grouping to reduce the diagram clutter.

As meritorious as Goodwin's original model was, this is still a 'toy' model, both in terms of its own complexity, and the level of complexity that can be modelled in this software. Since few economists are aware of this technology, there are few representative (in the non-neoclassical sense!) economics models; but the engineering world abounds with complex simulations of real world systems that are modelled in this software before being

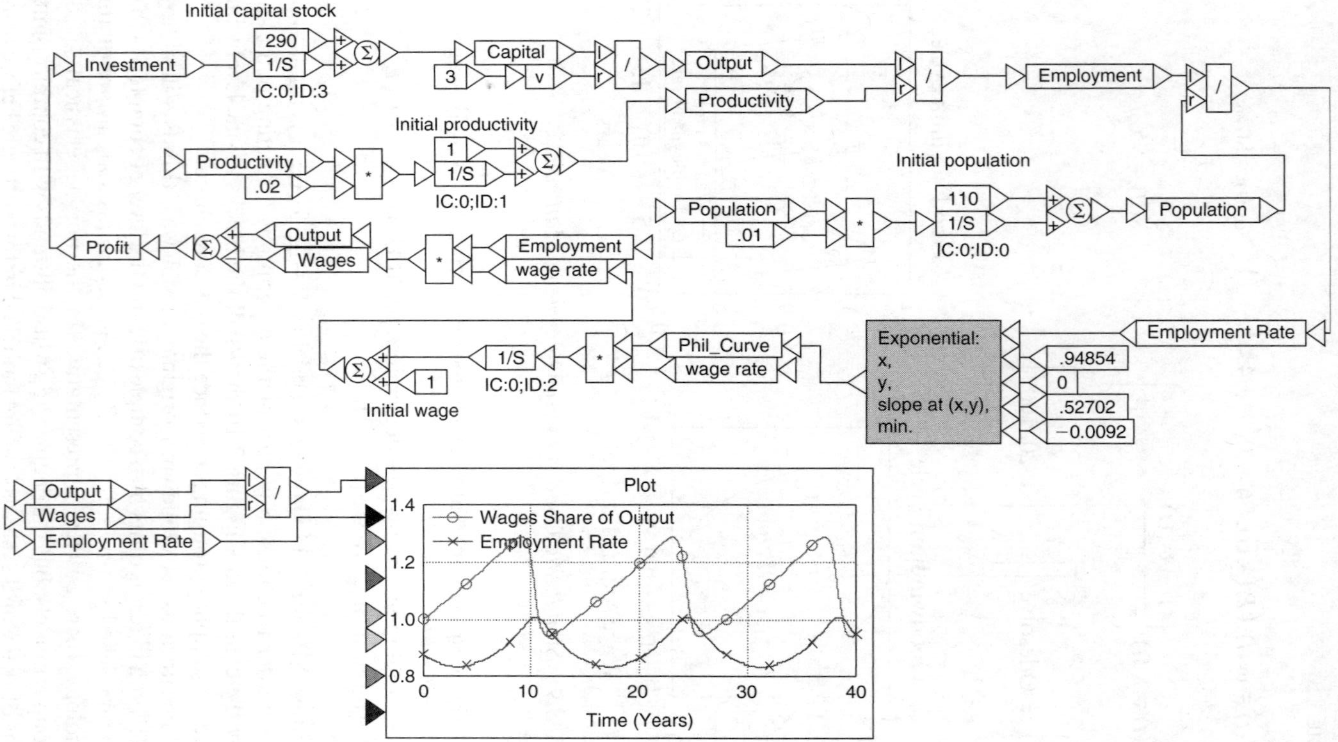

Figure 2.10 Goodwin model in Vissim without compound blocks

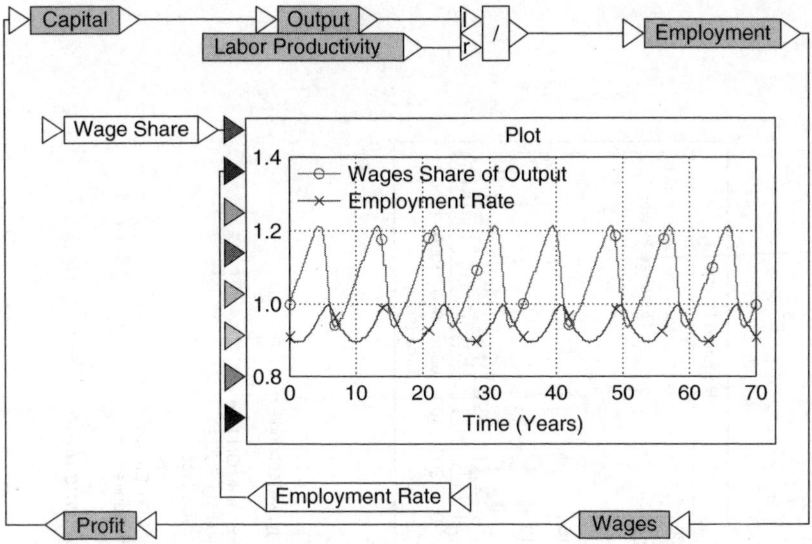

Figure 2.11 Goodwin model in Vissim with compound blocks

implemented in actual designs (Figure 2.12 shows part of an automotive engineering model).

Graziani (and the Circuitist School in general, with its ambition to model the monetary circuit) should have expressed the circuit in dynamic tools and implemented a model of this class. That he did not speaks volumes for the extent to which non-neoclassical economists have yet to break free of the equilibrium cringe, and the extent to which economists in general are isolated from developments in applied sciences that have made the modelling of complex dynamic processes commonplace.

COMMANDMENTS AGAINST THE CRINGE

Equilibrium thinking dominates neoclassical economics because it is in the nature of a religious belief: capitalism necessarily leads to the best of all possible worlds, and in that world we live in Pareto optimality (if not in actual harmony). It dominates non-neoclassical economic analysis because habit has inculcated it to such a degree that we are not aware of the religious gesture that is the Sign of the (Marshallian or Walrasian) Cross.

This demi-religious blindspot tempts me to suggest a set of commandments for the non-neoclassical, to break away from this cringe and finally

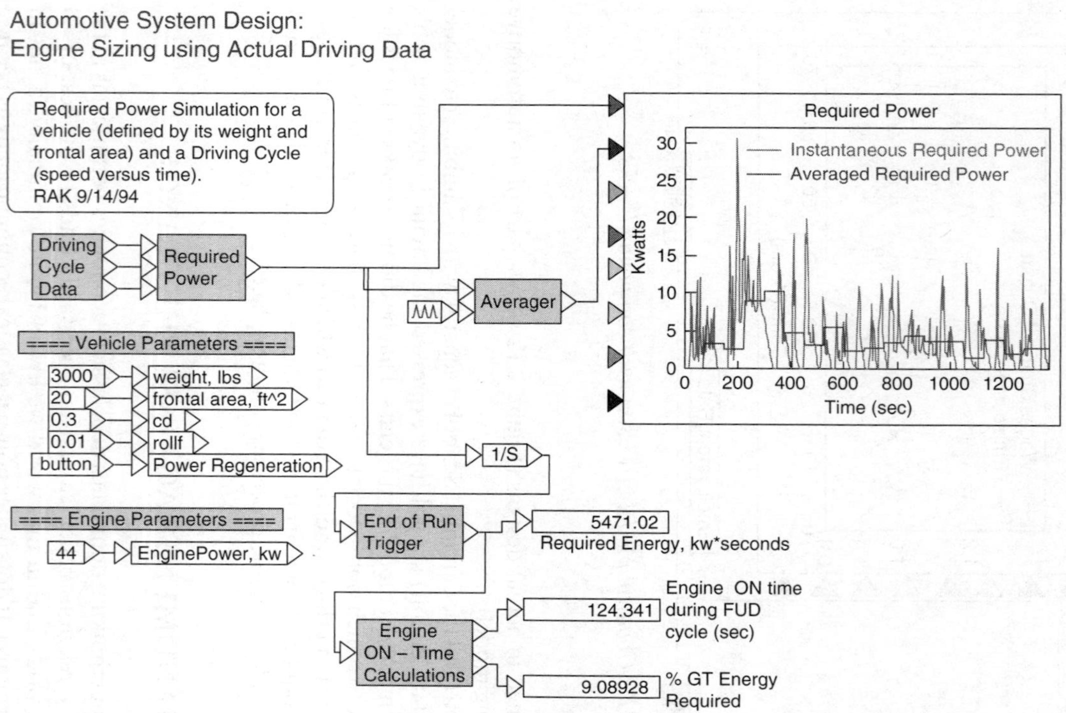

Figure 2.12 Vissim simulation to estimate required engine power from driving data

start to develop an analytic approach to economics which is as rich as the verbal analyses that characterize the non-neoclassical greats (from Marx, Veblen and Schumpeter to today's Galbraith, Moore and the late Hyman Minsky):

1. Thou shalt not make the Sign of the (Marshallian) Cross;
2. Thou shalt not use simultaneous equations;
3. Thou shalt express all economic relationships in terms of time and causal relations;
4. Thou shalt learn differential equations from mathematics, and dynamic methods from engineering and sciences;
5. Thou shalt strive to develop evolutionary modelling techniques, no matter how hard this may be.

Of course, commandments alone do not an alternative theory of economics make. But they may at least remind us of the need to break from that old time equilibrium religion.

NOTES

1. Carl Chiarella and his collaborators are the most advanced here; see Chiarella and Flaschel (2000).
2. The use of a money token is equivalent but has confused economists, and the Circuitists' emphasis upon a pure credit economy where all monetary exchanges are bank account transfers puts the focus upon the true nature of money.
3. There are problems even at this stage, since Graziani ignores inter-firm transfers on the grounds that they are 'internal transactions [so that] no further monetary payment is required' (p. 4). This effectively treats exchange between firms as a barter activity, which violates the Circuitist perspective on exchange under capitalism being three-sided However it could be argued that at this stage the model is of a single-commodity single-firm system, which could later be generalized to a multi-commodity multi-firm analysis. Graziani's extended discussion under 'The demand for finance' implies this interpretation.
4. This point is challenged by Andresen (2006).
5. Further errors arise prior to this important insight. Graziani argues that 'If the expenditure of wage-earners equals the whole of their wages, no matter whether they spend money on the commodities market or on the financial market, firms get back the whole of their expenditure and they are able to repay fully their debt to the banks' (Graziani, 1989, p. 5). This ignores the interest obligations incurred by the firms' debt to the banks.
6. 'This may well seem an assumption of irrational behaviour, if no uncertainty is present. It is however a necessary assumption, if we do not want the velocity of circulation to become infinite and money to disappear altogether from the system' (p. 6).
7. Spending all of wages instantaneously would itself be 'irrational' – since workers rather than firms would then have to incur the storage costs for the commodities needed over the next two weeks.
8. This perspective has been expressed more in exchanges on PKT (the 'Post-Keynesian Thought' discussion group, now defunct) than in published papers, where he directs his critique – justifiably – at neoclassical modelling. See http://archives.econ.utah.edu/archives/pkt/

9. Colloquially, this applies when the paths the system follows from two initial conditions that are arbitrarily close to each other diverge exponentially. Technically, the dominant Lyapunov exponent for the model exceeds zero.
10. These packages do include differentiation operators, but integration is normally used because it is an inherently more stable numerical operation. Z-transforms are used for discrete time systems. *Mathcad* and the like work directly with differential equations.
11. The negative entry for interest on workers' accounts here is an artefact of the convention used here that capitalist accounts are negative (reflecting the debt to banks). This convention has been dispensed with in subsequent modelling, which has also derived a fully functional Circuitist model (see Keen and Chapman, forthcoming) that solves the 'dilemma' of how capitalists can borrow money, repay it with interest, and make a profit.

REFERENCES

Anderson, E.S. and M. Valente (2002) *Artificial Economic Evolution*, Aalborg University, Denmark: Danish Research Unit for Industrial Economics.

Andresen, T. (1998) 'The Macroeconomy as a Network of Money-Flow Transfer Functions', *Modeling, Identification and Control*, 19, 207–23.

Andresen, T. (2006) 'A Critique of a Post Keynesian Model of Hoarding, and an Alternative Model', *Journal of Economic Behavior and Organization* (forthcoming).

Blatt, J.M. (1983) *Dynamic Economic Systems*, Armonk: M.E. Sharpe.

Chiarella, C. and P. Flaschel (2000) *The Dynamics of Keynesian Monetary Growth*, Cambridge: Cambridge University Press.

Davidson, P. (1994) *Post-Keynesian Macroeconomic Theory*, Aldershot, UK and Brookfield, USA: Edward Elgar.

Fontana, G. (2000) 'Post Keynesians and Circuitists on Money and Uncertainty: An Attempt at Generality', *Journal of Post Keynesian Economics*, 23, 27–48.

Goodwin, R.M. (1967) 'A Growth Cycle', in C.H. Feinstein (ed.), *Socialism, Capitalism and Economic Growth*, Cambridge: Cambridge University Press, 54–8. Reprinted in R.M. Goodwin (1982), *Essays in Dynamic Economics*, London: Macmillan.

Graziani, A. (1989) 'The Theory of the Monetary Circuit', *Thames Papers in Political Economy*, Spring, 1–26. Reprinted in M. Musella and C. Panico (eds) (1995), *The Money Supply in the Economic Process*, Aldershot, UK and Brookfield, USA: Edward Elgar.

Jarsulic, M. (1989) 'Endogenous Credit and Endogenous Business Cycles', *Journal of Post Keynesian Economics*, 12, 35–48.

Keen, S. (1995) 'Finance and Economic Breakdown: Modelling Minsky's Financial Instability Hypothesis', *Journal of Post Keynesian Economics*, 17, 607–35.

Keen, S. (1999) 'The Nonlinear Dynamics of Debt Deflation', *Complexity International*, Volume 6: http://journal-ci.csse.monash.edu.au/ci/vol06/keen/keen.html.

Keen, S. (2000) 'The Nonlinear Economics of Debt Deflation', in W. Barnett, C. Chiarella, S. Keen, R. Marks and H. Schnabl (eds), *Commerce, Complexity and Evolution*, New York: Cambridge University Press, 83–110.

Keen, S. (2003) 'Standing on the Toes of Pygmies: Why Econophysics Must be Careful of the Economic Foundations on which it Builds', *Physica A*, 324, 108–16.

Keen, S. (2004) 'Improbable, Incorrect or Impossible: The Persuasive but Flawed Mathematics of Microeconomics', in E. Fullbrook (ed.), *Student's Guide to What's Wrong with Economics*, London: Routledge, 209–22.

Keen, S. and B. Chapman (forthcoming) 'Hic Rhodus, Hic Salta! Profit in a Dynamic Model of the Monetary Circuit', Storia del Pensiero Economico.

Marshall, A. (1920) *Principles of Economics*, 8th edition, London: Macmillan.

Moore, B. (1998) 'Money and Interest Rates in a Monetary Theory of Production', in R.J. Rotheim (ed.), *New Keynesian Economics/Post Keynesian Alternatives*, London: Routledge.

Ott, E. (1993) *Chaos in Dynamical Systems*, New York: Cambridge University Press.

Scafetta, N., S. Picozzi and B.J. West (2004) 'An Out-of-Equilibrium Model of the Distributions of Wealth', *Quantitative Finance*, 4, 353–64.

PART II

Complexity, uncertainty and path dependence

3. The complex problem of modelling economic complexity

Richard Day

Complexity: a group of interrelated or entangled relationships.
The New Shorter Oxford English Dictionary (1993)

. . . history . . . where everything is in a state of flux, of perpetual transition and combinations . . .
Jacob Burckhardt, *Reflections on History* (1979)[1]

SOME SCIENTIFIC BACKGROUND

Theoretical science generates testable, logical (mathematical) systems of thought that explain or comprehend observations and empirical data that themselves only reflect some properties of some realm of experience. Progress began to occur rapidly when stable, repetitive patterns were discovered such as the motion of stellar bodies which could be carefully observed and their distances, masses, and velocities measured, and such as the ratios in which various pure substances interacted to form different compound substances.

At the basis of all such efforts is an elemental faculty of the brain, one that enables the mind to discriminate, to discern the differences and similarities of things and happenings, in the former case just recalled, between complex and simple motions isolated by telescopic observations, in the latter, between simple and complex interactions isolated in test-tubes. In general, this fundamental faculty permits classification of the manifold complexity of individual things and events into categories relatively small in number with measurable, quantifiable, or qualitatively discernible attributes.

It was the brilliant insight of Newton to show how a quantifiable index of matter in motion, the mass of objects, could play a central role in explaining and predicting the behavior of macro physical objects – as long as one wanted only to explain their positions relative to one another and not all the things going on inside or immediately around them. So the earth, moon, sun, and other planets become mass points. There never has been a more radical simplification of experience than that! But the single number, used to characterize an infinitely complex object like the earth, is not a contradiction of experience. It is not the earth but *of* the earth, an abstract representation of a quantifiable, emergent macro property – and useful: among other things, men landed on the moon.

For a long time the principle of cause and effect that is central to the kind of theories just exemplified seemed to be wholly inappropriate for understanding complex patterns and irregular trajectories of physical, biological, and cultural events. The nineteenth century, however, began to contribute analytical advances that greatly extended the applicability of the kind of mathematics already in use to explain regular relationships and predictable events. Among the advances, one attributed to Poincaré, is the discovery that the nonlinear equations of mechanics could generate nonperiodic, random-like trajectories. It was a crucial step in the development of chaotic dynamics which isolated the conditions that imply irregular, essentially unpredictable behavior and showed how to characterize it with the tools of probability theory. These developments provided the foundation for modelling the complex dynamics that arise in many fields where the nonlinear causal relationships involved are already known and derivable from standard theoretical constructs. A rather different development that had a somewhat earlier origin was the finding that the average location of independently and dynamically interacting but constrained objects could be characterized by stable probability distributions, even though their individual trajectories could not be followed.

Together, chaotic dynamics and statistical mechanics provide potential templates for models of variables in any domain whose behavior is governed by nonlinear, interacting causal forces and characterized by nonperiodic, highly irregular, essentially unpredictable behavior beyond a few periods into the future.

Although widely applied now, including extensively in economics, the theories recalled so far originated in physical science. A second, more general, analytically less tractable category of dynamical concepts had long been recognized. Eighteenth century explorers and scientists had already provided the classificatory foundations for geological and biological theories of transformation. Then in the next century a comprehensive theory of evolution in the biological world was set forth by Darwin and Wallace based on variation and selection.[2]

Even broader ideas of structural transformation and evolution were emerging from speculation about ecological and archeological observations and the study of written records and histories produced in the ancient world. Differing production technologies and forms of socio-political organization and their development from one into another could be discerned. Adam Smith, later exponents of the German Historical School, and subsequent researches in archeology, as for example described in V. Gordon Childe's (1951) *Man Makes Himself*, explained how economic life passed through stages of successively advancing development.[3]

Ancient historians were well aware of the development of peoples and their periods of growth and decay. The widespread revival of Greek and Roman literature led inescapably to the idea of civilization's rise and fall already enshrined in masterful prose by Edward Gibbon in just the same year that Adam Smith's own masterpiece appeared.

These broad descriptive works describe and explain technological, economic, political, and cultural evolution but for the most part lack the mathematical precision of the physical sciences. The possibility, however, that a first-rate scientific mind could construct a rigorous conceptual system that clarifies and helps understand human history was produced in Carol Quigley's (1979) *Evolution of Civilizations*. In any case, human experience as the object of inquiry poses a unique problem for the development of scientific theory, one that convinces many that a science of human cultural evolution is an oxymoron. In common parlance, that problem is 'mind over matter'.

MIND OVER MATTER: ON RATIONALITY AND EQUILIBRIUM

Philosophers, scientists, and mystics have argued over the issue: Can the human mind change matter or energy? Most people do not ask the question. They just live their lives, move themselves about, fabricate things with their hands, or control the use of a machine or instrument that transforms a part of the material world. Obviously, therefore, the question makes sense only if it is about the world in its ultimately elemental aspects of material and energy. If it is about human action, the mind *is* elemental. Thus, is it not true that all the dynamics of agriculture and industry are initiated by the force of human thought? Is it not true that humans even cause atoms to be split and can guide electrons along pre-designed and constricted pathways?

Somehow, out of the matter and energy that make up a brain emerge thoughts that live in a realm of mind that cannot be seen, that can only be communicated imperfectly, but that move men and mountains. It is the discerning, analyzing, and problem solving rational mind we are now talking about. It is this aspect of mind that brings us to economics.

Formalizing their predecessors' verbally expressed theories of economic systems and behavior, Cournot and later Walras constructed the mathematical theories of production, consumption, exchange, and competition based on an idealized disentanglement of two of the basic components of a market economy, the Consumer or Household and the Producer or Business Firm. The general mathematical conditions required to demonstrate the existence and properties of equilibrium were provided many decades later by Wald, von Neumann, Arrow, Debreu, Dorfman, Samuelson, and Solow. The first empirical implementation (still more radically simplified compared to the pure theory) was the inter-industry economics of Leontief.

Iconoclasts of the present era, in our eagerness to gain attention for an explicitly dynamic, adaptive, evolutionary point of view, tirelessly point out the deficiencies of *that* new classical school: its dependence primarily on statics, its exclusion of common attributes of economizing behavior such as imitation, trial and error search, learning by doing, and so on. What we often forget is that this general equilibrium theory is a theory of complexity based on mind over matter, not on the random encounters of thoughtless objects, but on the choices of thinking consumers and producers. These theoretical, thinking, heterogeneous agents, an arbitrary number of them (none necessarily alike) exercise the rational capacity of the mind to set the flow of commodities in motion. The general equilibrium theorists showed how – in principle – a system of prices could coordinate the implied flow of goods and services among the arbitrarily many heterogeneous individual decision-makers.

Of course, that is not good enough. We must have a theory that goes beyond the equilibrium property, that directly confronts the more fundamental problem of existence: how to model the mechanisms that mimic the dynamic process of coordination *out of equilibrium*. Before touching on a few contributions to this objective, let me make an important point about the logical content of the neoclassical concept of equilibrium among heterogeneous, rational agents. The rationality is based on the same faculty of discrimination that permits scientific thought. We discriminate among things and actions and compare their desirability according to some kind of attribute or set of attributes, and order those alternatives, picking one among those highest (best or optimal) in the order. The mathematical theorist gives the set of alternatives being considered and the ordering of elements of that set symbolic representations amenable to a logical characterization and further analytical investigation. The exact conditions that permit feasible exchanges among all the individuals so that the agents are able to execute what they consider to be their best choices is the theoretical problem Walras formed and his followers solved.

Agents in this theory need *not* be assumed to have perfect knowledge of all possible alternatives. It need only be assumed that they recognize distinct well-ordered opportunities. For this reason, in a competitive equilibrium so defined, Pareto-superior choices could exist if only the agents knew more. Contrastingly, for a *social* welfare equilibrium, total knowledge of *all* possible alternatives would be required. But aside from that requirement, in pure logic the theory is *not* about perfect knowledge or unbounded rationality!

If neoclassical economics – interpreted correctly – is not about perfect knowledge or unbounded rationality, what is it about? It is about perfect coordination. It identifies those conditions on the alternatives and orderings for which a price system exists – in principle – that could – if it prevailed – permit perfect decentralized coordination: agents only know their *own* minds – to the extent that they know it – and among perceived feasible alternatives choose one they prefer. If they base their choice on equilibrium prices, they all get to carry out their chosen actions.

Thoughtful economists understand the questions begged by this theory of perfect coordination among boundedly rational minds: Where do the perfectly coordinating prices come from? Supposing they are found, what do agents do until they appear? And, once the dust settles, wouldn't the agents, those with any mammal's curiosity, observe something not noticed before, and learn something from the choices made?

The simplest way to deal with these questions is to call them 'some other kind of economics' and ignore them all together, instead – in contradiction of the boundedly rational foundations of the theory – endowing agents with equilibrium knowledge and call it 'rational expectations'. Now there is an oxymoron!

The more complicated way to deal with the problems not yet solved is to acknowledge their existence and do something about them. That brings us to consider some steps in the right direction.

STEPS IN THE RIGHT DIRECTION

First, we should remember that the seminal founders of neoclassical economics, themselves, initiated steps in this direction: Cournot with his adaptive or recursive best response strategies as a model of competition in oligopolistic markets; Walras with his consumers' and producers' tâtonnement mechanism with prices adjusting to demand/supply disequilibrium and quantities adjusting to profit disequilibrium; Marshall, more or less analogously, with his quasi-rent theory of investment and marginal adjustment of consumer choices at their present operating point.

Some readers may be surprised that these steps had already been taken well over a century ago and may wonder why no one has told you about them. All of us should wonder why these early disequilibrium theories of market dynamics are not being exposed to graduate students today.

Quite distinct from the neoclassical microeconomics and the messoeconomic, interindustry economics of Leontief was the construction of a macroeconomics theory on an abstract basis as daring as Newton's, namely Keynes' equations of aggregate consumption, investment, government spending, demand, output and income, all represented by statistical indexes constructed from various observational data, but like Newton's mass, not observable themselves. At about the same time, Tinbergen constructed the first macroeconometric model of a national economy, encompassing more detail than did Keynes but still basing the statistical estimates on more or less highly aggregated variables. A decade later the Klein–Goldberger model initiated a worldwide explosion of research in macroeconometric models. This general approach came to form a separate sub-discipline just as optimal growth theory has done in more recent decades. But out-of-equilibrium macro – still being extended in substantial works – has been defamed on grounds that it is ad hoc. Rather, it is a tractable approach for modelling out-of-equilibrium behavior. Modern investigators are continuing to improve on the approach. (I think here, for example, of recent studies by Flaschel et al., 1997 and Chiarella et al., 2000). The frequent criticism that Keynesian macro theory does not have a micro foundation is also mistaken. Indeed, Morishima (1994) provided a quite explicit micro foundation of macro based on an elaborate extension of general equilibrium theory.

At the other extreme, Simon and his then young colleagues, March and Cyert, began a serious reconstruction of microeconomics from an adaptive out-of-equilibrium point of view. Simon's original work (1983) and his later collaboration with March (March and Simon, 1958) was concerned with the internal structure of decision-making and administration in large business and government organizations. Cyert and March (1992) elaborated these ideas in an explicit attempt to model and simulate the adaptive microeconomic processes on computers. A more formal effort to develop an adaptive theory of business behavior was that of Modigliani and Cohen (1963) who focused on the formulation of expectations and partial adjustment mechanisms.

Hard on the heels of these works came two studies, each attempting to build a coherent dynamic out-of-equilibrium theory. Forgive me if I mention my own work at this point, the first applied, empirical version of which was published in 1963. This recursive programming or adaptive economizing approach is a more general and explicitly behavioral restatement of Cournot and Walras' models of recursively optimizing agents who adapt to disequilibrium signals. Agents form alternative possibilities subject to technical constraints and choose a best alternative on the basis of adaptively adjusted price expectations and updated resource constraints – and here is introduced a specific behavioral element – they choose in the neighborhood of their current operating point. This neighborhood is their *zone of flexible response* or ZFR. In the specific form implemented in empirical work, the ZFR expands in the direction of a successful past choice and contracts in the direction of less successful past choices. Behavior then follows a local economizing, learning-by-doing sequence of adjustments to experience as it unfolds.

In all of this early work, I represented choice alternatives as processes which allow one to represent families of distinct technological activities, follow their paths of adoption and abandonment and to derive the implied demands for labor and other resources. These applied studies and the basic ideas on which they are based, together with some broad inferences about economic development in general, are described in a recent Cambridge University Press volume, *The Divergent Dynamics of Economic Growth* (2004).

Sidney Winter's (1964) dissertation, 'Economic "Natural" Selection and the Theory of the Firm', in the *Yale Economic Essays*, advanced the Simon–March–Cyert behavioral viewpoint in an evolutionary framework built on the real primitives of decision-making in complex organizations: rules, strategies, or routines. The fundamental selection process driving businesses in his system is the innovation, adoption, and abandonment of alternative rules and procedures or routines, the work subsequently elaborated and developed in collaboration with Nelson, culminating in their influential book in 1982, *An Evolutionary Theory of Economic Change*, which marks a true milestone in the development of the discipline.

Clearly, any selection among alternatives involving an explicit comparison according to an ordering criterion is an example of the economic principle of rationality, the simplest being a choice between two objects such as two apples, between two or more alternative production activities as in my RP (recursive programming) models, or between two routines that could be carried out to accomplish some task within a complex production or administrative process, as in Nelson and Winter.

Moreover, all operational optimizing models of any complexity require algorithms for their solution which consist of sequences of simple computational routines that involve at each step a locally improving direction of search according to an explicit criterion. In my terms they constitute recursive programming systems based on local search within prescribed zones of flexible response. In this way, we find our way back to a foundation in neoclassical theory based on rational choice.

We are not developing 'some other kind of theory' but extending the theory of our intellectual fathers in the same direction as their own faltering steps, but, hopefully, well beyond. And it *is* possible to derive analytical results: the condition under which trajectories exist and their dynamic properties such as their multiple phase switching (evolutionary) character and possible non-convergence, periodic, chaotic, or convergent properties. To derive such properties, one must construct models that simplify the approach with one, or at least a very small number of variables, or one must formulate the model abstractly as in the Day–Kennedy paper (1970), or as Nelson and Winter did more concretely in their 'Economic Growth as a Pure Selection Process', Chapter 10 in their 1982 book.

I also want to remind the reader of a very early collection of papers, *Adaptive Economic Models* (Day and Groves, 1975), based on a 1974 conference at the University of Wisconsin's Mathematics Research Center, which made significant advances in outlining the methodological underpinnings of the adaptive evolutionary approach and in exemplifying various aspects of the theory in specific theoretical and empirical models. Alan Kirman's paper in that volume, 'Learning by Firms about Demand Conditions', illustrated an especially important insight: (i) what can potentially be learned depends on how you learn; and (ii) a learning procedure may converge when there is still more to be learned if only the way one is learning could be suitably reconstituted. As Kirman (1975, p. 138) put it, 'the firm . . . may develop an inaccurate picture of the world which nevertheless generates exactly the information it does in fact observe. The firm may well be satisfied with this situation and there is little evidence to suggest that such unjustified complacency is uncommon.'

DISEQUILIBRIUM EXISTENCE

Most of what has been reviewed in the previous section is concerned with how agents behave out-of-equilibrium given that they have and find feasible opportunities. Yet to be dealt with is the disequilibrium existence problem. How does an agent get along in a world it does not fully understand, when it is influenced by other agents whose actions it does not control, when one may find it difficult to 'fit in', and when one's existence can be threatened by unpredictable physical or financial disasters?

Indeed, how does any living thing survive the vicissitudes of its life? The answer is immediately available on every hand, just by observing the living systems around us, especially our own. The physician, Cannon, in an exceptionally readable book, *The Wisdom of the Body* (1963), articulated the solution precisely in physiological terms: the stock/flow mechanisms in living beings that store the various fats, proteins, and carbohydrates in various forms throughout the organism, retaining quantities sufficient for all but the most extreme and prolonged demands, replenishing them at more or less regular intervals as they are drawn down. Cannon coined the term 'homeostasis' for these mechanisms. He also suggested explicitly that such homeostatic mechanisms operate within economic systems, and, where they do not, troubles can arise that might be overcome by introducing them. The stocks maintained in economic homeostasis are inventories of goods in process, goods in transit, goods in warehouses and stores, and goods maintained in household cupboards, pantries, and refrigerators. Building on papers by D.H. Robertson and Eric Lundberg, Lloyd Metzler showed how, at the macroeconomic level, the stock/flow inventory mechanisms led to fluctuations, which, given certain stability properties on the marginal propensity to consume and invest, are bound within limits, just as physiological balances adjust within limits consistent with survival.

The study of such stock/flow mechanisms at the micro level took place in the literature on inventory control, but as far as I know has never been incorporated into general economic interdependence theory. Metzler himself emphasized the mathematical difficulties of further complications. But progress might be made by adapting the Bourboki–Arrow–Debreu-like level of abstraction, an obvious task, it seems to me, that should be undertaken.

But that will not be enough to solve the disequilibrium existence problem. Monetary economies run on financial assets and debts, which define intended future flows of monetary payments. The creation of such assets and debts by means of bank credit has played a crucial role in the development of market economies and in the nonperiodic incidence of prosperity and depression.

The flow of income payments that the stock of debts is supposed to generate is based on expectations that may not be realized. When such failures become widespread and sufficiently grave to produce widespread bankruptcy, homeostasis is threatened. Economy-wide breakdowns can occur. The nonperiodic incidence of alternating prosperity and recession has led to further innovation in the use of debt instruments. Hence, the refinancing of consumer and business debt, with central banks relaxing or restricting the requirements for credit expansion, and with ad hoc government loans and grants as saviors of last resort.

My old friend, John Burr Williams, wrote in an unpublished manuscript that, 'To leave money out of a book on the private enterprise market economy was like leaving blood out of a book on physiology'. It was Keynes' most important contribution to have devised a way to introduce that financial blood into economics at the macroeconomic level. In spite of some brave efforts to overcome this lacuna at the microeconomic level and despite the flourishing development of the field of finance at the general disequilibrium level, the task remains, for there is no area of economic theory so badly in need of development as the disequilibrium dynamics of financial stocks and flows. It is precisely here that the contributions of Basil Moore, summarized and extended in some of the chapters in this volume, are so welcome.

I have not mentioned in these remarks the creative faculty of mind responsible for generating the design for things that did not exist before and scenarios of action one has never previously experienced. Nor have I touched on the social aspect of mind that leads people to cohere in groups, to believe in similar thoughts, to follow a leader, and to adhere to the dictates of some kind of group mentality. But perhaps the basic problem of disequilibrium existence has to be solved first. My impression is that many of us go out of our way to avoid that task, becoming intrigued with all manner of mathematics, models, and mechanisms only peripherally related to the task of explaining how governments and central banks interact with the private household and business sectors.

Of course, there is the view that market systems must inevitably self-destruct. Believers in this point of view argue that the best course of action is to help them do so and get it over with. Evidently, experiments carried out in the last century with that intent proved unpleasant. They produced long, miserable interludes in the general process of economic evolution. I would rather continue our basic mission, that of focusing on how democratic market systems work, how market institutions and banks use out-of-equilibrium stock/flow intermediation and adjustment processes to maintain viability for the system of interacting households, firms, government institutions. In the process of this research we might then identify policies that improve the stability and distributional properties of the system as a whole.

NOTES

1. Published in German posthumously in 1905. Burckhardt died in 1897. Translated by M.D. HoHinger in 1943. See Burckhardt (1979).
2. For a beautifully insightful survey into the development of physical and biological sciences, see Toulmin and Goodfield (1961, 1962).
3. For a brief survey of the German Historical School, see Schumpeter (1954, pp. 808–82).

REFERENCES

Burckhardt, J. (1979) *Reflections on History*, Indianapolis: Liberty Classics.
Cannon, W. (1963) *The Wisdom of the Body*, New York: W.W. Norton and Co.
Chiarella, C., P. Flaschel, G. Groh and W. Semmler (2000) *Disequilibrium Growth and Labor Market Dynamics*, Berlin: Springer-Verlag.

Childe, V.G. (1951) *Man Makes Himself*, New York: The New American Library of World Literature, Inc. Originally published in 1931.

Cyert, R. and J. March (1992) *A Behavioral Theory of the Firm*, 2nd edition, Cambridge, MA: Basil Blackwell.

Day, R. (1963) *Recursive Programming and Production Response*, Amsterdam: North-Holland Publishing Co.

Day, R. (1994) *Complex Economic Dynamics, Volume I, An Introduction to Dynamical Systems and Market Mechanisms*, Cambridge, MA: The MIT Press.

Day, R. (2000) *Complex Economic Dynamics, Volume II, An Introduction to Macroeconomic Dynamics*, Cambridge, MA: The MIT Press.

Day, R. (2004) *The Divergent Dynamics of Economic Growth*, New York: Cambridge University Press.

Day, R. and T. Groves (1975) *Adaptive Economics Models*, New York: Academic Press.

Day, R. and P. Kennedy (1970) 'Recursive Decision Systems: An Existence Analysis', *Econometrica*, 38, 666–81.

Flaschel, P., R. Franke and W. Semmler (1997) *Dynamic Macroeconomics: Instability, Fluctuations and Growth in Monetary Economics*, Cambridge, MA: The MIT Press.

Kirman, A. (1975) 'Learning by Firms about Demand Conditions', in R. Day and T. Groves (eds), *Adaptive Economic Models*, New York: Academic Press.

March, J. and H. Simon (1958) *Organizations*, New York: John Wiley and Sons, Inc.

Metzler, L. (1941) 'The Nature and Stability of Inventory Cycles', *Review of Economic Statistics*, 23, 100–129.

Modigliani, F. and K.J. Cohen (1963) *The Role of Anticipations and Plans in Economic Behavior*, Urbana: University of Illinois.

Morishima, M. (1994) *Dynamic Economic Theory*, Cambridge: Cambridge University Press.

Nelson, R. and S. Winter (1982) *An Evolutionary Theory of Economic Change*, Cambridge, MA: Harvard University Press.

Quigley, C. (1979) *The Evolution of Civilizations*, Indianapolis: Liberty Press.

Schumpeter, J. (1954) *History of Economic Analysis*, New York: Oxford University Press.

Simon, H. (1983) *Reason in Human Affairs*, Stanford: Stanford University Press.

Toulmin, S. and J. Goodfield (1961) *The Fabric of the Heavens*, Chicago: University of Chicago Press.

Toulmin, S. and J. Goodfield (1962) *The Architecture of Matter*, Chicago: University of Chicago Press.

Winter, S. (1964) 'Economic "Natural" Selection and the Theory of the Firm', *Yale Economic Essays*, New Haven: Yale University Press.

4. Complex dynamics and Post Keynesian economics

J. Barkley Rosser, Jr.[1]

INTRODUCTION

The nature of the relationship between complex dynamics and Post Keynesian economics[2] (PKE) has been a controversial matter for some time. Some argue that it is a distraction that leads innocent Post Keynesians into 'classical sin'. Davidson (1994, 1996) argues that core Post Keynesian (PK) ideas such as that insufficient aggregate demand arises from fundamental uncertainty in a monetary economy do not depend on nonlinearity or complexity, that these core concepts are axiomatically and ontologically true, and that the inability of agents to forecast well in dynamically complex situations reflects mere epistemological problems of insufficient computational abilities. Thus complex dynamics is merely a classical stalking horse.

This writer (Rosser, 1990, 1998, 2001) disagrees with the argument presented above and its relatives (Mirowski, 1990; Carrier, 1993). Dynamic complexity provides a foundation for fundamental uncertainty in Keynesian and PK models, and this applies to most of the various sub-branches of PKE besides Davidson's 'fundamentalist' or 'Keynes-Post Keynesian'[3] approach.

The argument will be considered regarding three subdivisions of Post Keynesianism as identified by Hamouda and Harcourt (1988): the aforementioned fundamentalist Keynesianism, Sraffian (or neo-Ricardian), and Kaleckian (or Kaleckian-Robinsonian).[4] Following King (2002, chap. 10), I admit to being more in sympathy with those he describes as 'synthesizers' than with the more partisan sectarians of these approaches.[5] I shall describe how each sub-branch has been analyzed using ideas of complex dynamics, and I suggest that this common element should be kept in mind by those who do hold to any of the more sharply held positions in this debate. I shall also discuss PK approaches that are not so easily labeled, notably the hysteresis and evolutionary approaches. I shall discuss the question of equilibrium versus disequilibrium and methodological issues relating to open versus closed systems.

Of the schools of PKE, Basil J. Moore has been identified with the fundamentalist Keynesian school, based on his role as perhaps the most influential developer and advocate of the idea of endogenous money (Moore, 1988). Along with the idea of fundamental uncertainty, the fundamentalist Keynesian school is also often viewed as stressing the role of money in the economy more than the Sraffian or Kaleckian schools. However, Moore has increasingly stressed the role of complexity in various forms as intrinsically linked with the process of endogenous money formation and the uncertainties of economic dynamics, openly disagreeing with Davidson on this issue on the PKT Internet list[6] and elsewhere. He argues that all this implies the need for non-equilibrium and open-system approaches in his recent book, *Shaking the Invisible Hand: Complexity, Endogenous Money and Exogenous Interest Rates*.

DEFINING COMPLEX DYNAMICS

Elsewhere (Rosser, 1999a) I have discussed defining complex dynamics for applications in economics. Richard Day (1994) argues that a system is dynamically complex if due to endogenous reasons it fails to converge to a point, a limit cycle,[7] or a smooth explosion or implosion. Such systems can generate endogenous discontinuities in system variables. Nonlinearity[8] somewhere in the system is a necessary but not sufficient condition for such endogenous dynamics in an economy, with simple exponential growth models showing how nonlinear dynamics may not be complex as defined above.

For Post Keynesians the endogenous nature of fluctuations is important, as the new classical school explains macroeconomic fluctuations as due to exogenous stochastic shocks describable by a probability function implicitly known by agents with rational expectations. Such fluctuations may be both equilibrium and Pareto optimal, thus abrogating any argument for sustained policy intervention. The reality of complex dynamics undermines this view on two grounds, first that the presence of complex endogenous dynamics means that the economy is not necessarily self-stabilizing or optimal, and second that such dynamics undermine the assumption of rational expectations. Chaotic dynamics imply sensitive dependence on initial conditions (Rosser, 1996), or the 'butterfly effect', the idea that a butterfly flapping its wings in Brazil could set off hurricanes in the United States (Lorenz, 1993). Recognition of this led one prominent new classical economist to modify his views (Sargent, 1993).

While the physicist Seth Lloyd has accumulated about 45 different definitions of 'complex system' from many different disciplines (Horgan,

1997, p. 303, footnote 11), most of these have not been used in economics. Some emphasize difficulty for computability or length of algorithms, used occasionally in economics (Albin, 1982; Albin with Foley, 1998; Leijonhufvud, 1993; Stodder, 1997). Another definition with some resonance with standard Sraffian models is 'structural' and focuses on the 'complicatedness' of patterns of intersectoral connections and institutional relations in the economy (Pryor, 1995; Stodder, 1995). Some argue that complexity implies a new philosophical perspective on how humanity relates to nature and the world, indeed on how each individual does so, replacing formal deduction with inductive or abductive methods as analysts seek to understand an ever-changing and evolving complex reality.

In Rosser (1999a) I identified the first definition above as 'broad tent complexity', seen as consisting of four sub-types, the 'four C's', *cybernetics, catastrophe theory, chaos theory,* and *'narrow tent complexity'*. The first was developed by Norbert Wiener (1961) and has had relatively limited application in economics, with Forrester (1977) being an important example.[9] Catastrophe theory was developed by René Thom (1972), with Christopher Zeeman's (1974) model of stock market crashes and Hal Varian's (1979) model of endogenous business cycles based on an arguably Post Keynesian model of Kaldor (1940) providing economic applications. Chaos theory had numerous developers in mathematics and physics, with Robert May (1976) first suggesting applications in economics, and David Rand (1978) the first to take him up on it.[10] 'Small tent complexity' emphasizes models of heterogeneous interacting agents, often using computer simulations, with Thomas Schelling's (1971) model of urban racial segregation and Hans Föllmer's (1974) statistical mechanics model being early examples. Horgan argues that these were all fads that have risen and deservedly fallen, but I argue that they represent a cumulative intellectual development that is now reaching fruition[11] and that allows PK ideas to broadly enter mainstream economics, which is undergoing profound changes that are leading it into uncharted areas (Colander et al., 2004).

COMPLEX DYNAMICS AND THE SCHOOLS OF POST KEYNESIAN ECONOMICS

Fundamentalist Keynesianism or Keynes-Post Keynesianism

The central argument of this sub-branch of PK thought emphasizes the foundational role of fundamental uncertainty based on Keynes's own ideas, hence the adjective 'fundamentalist'. This was a profoundly important idea for Keynes, while it was less so for Sraffa and Kalecki. It first

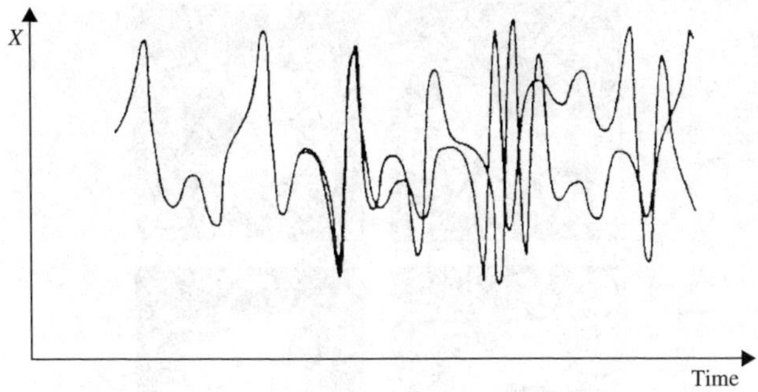

Figure 4.1 Butterfly effect

appears in Keynes's (1921) *Treatise on Probability*[12] and is brought to center stage in chapter 12 of his (1936) *General Theory*, where it is seen as the foundation for animal spirits driving macroeconomic fluctuations.

When the neo-Keynesian-classical synthesis was dominant, the crucial PK figure to emphasize uncertainty in Keynesian analysis was G.L.S. Shackle (1955).[13] Among those influenced by Shackle were Brian Loasby (1976), John Hicks (1979) and especially Paul Davidson (1978, 1982–3), who would emphasize that uncertainty explains how holding money can bring about involuntary unemployment and also how it undermines rational expectations.[14] That uncertainty underlies the demand for money has been further developed by Moore (1988) and by Runde (1994). Davidson (1996) does not believe that complexity theory enhances these arguments.

Complex dynamics enter into the analysis of Keynesian uncertainty in at least two ways. Complex dynamics provide an independent source of how such fundamental uncertainty and uncertainty, as discussed by Keynes in chapter 12 of the *General Theory*, can lead to speculative bubbles in asset markets. These can lead to financial fragility (Minsky, 1972) and follow a variety of complex dynamics (Day and Huang, 1990; Keen, 1995, 1997; Rosser, 2000a, chaps. 4–5).

If a system exhibits chaotic dynamics, it is subject to sensitive dependence on initial conditions, arguably the most important defining characteristic of chaotic dynamics.[15] If a small change in an initial condition or a parameter value can lead quite rapidly to substantially different behavior in a system, this disrupts the learning mechanisms that underpin rational expectations (Rosser, 1996). Figure 4.1 shows the original example of sensitive dependence discovered by Edward Lorenz (1963) for a three equation model of climate. The bifurcation point occurred after simulating the system and restarting a second simulation part way through to get

Source: From Peitgen et al. (1992).

Figure 4.2 Basins of attraction with frontal boundaries, three magnets

coffee. The different path arose from round-off error at the sixth decimal place.

Another possible source of deep uncertainty in economic systems due to complex dynamics is the possibility of fractal basin boundaries, first found for economics by Hans-Walter Lorenz (1992) in the arguably PK model of Kaldor (1940). With fractal basin boundaries there are multiple equilibria, and the basins of attraction for each of the equilibria are entwined with each other so that their boundaries may become arbitrarily close to each other. There may not be chaotic dynamics, but the system can jump discontinuously from one basin of attraction to another from nearly infinitesimal changes, thus rendering the possibility of forming rational expectations impossible. Figure 4.2, from Peitgen et al. (1992), shows the basins and their boundaries for a system in which a metal ball on a string is suspended over three magnets.

How uncertainty can lead to speculative dynamics that imply complex dynamics and financial fragility is that a source of uncertainty is our inability to know what other people are thinking (Carabelli, 1988; Davis, 1993; Arestis, 1996; Koppl and Rosser, 2002). This can lead to group dynamics as analyzed by Keynes for the beauty contest, where each party tries to guess the average state of expectation of the other parties. When different people have different views about each other's expectations the results can be dynamically complex, even when some of the parties may actually possess rational expectations. This is the problem of heterogeneous expectations identified with the 'narrow tent complexity' view.

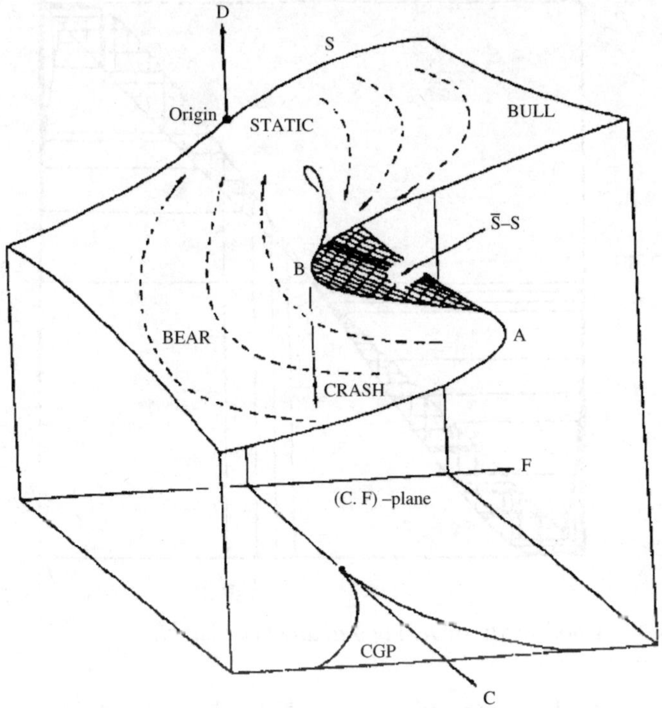

Figure 4.3 Zeeman stock market crash model

A basic example is the first model using catastrophe theory in economics (Zeeman, 1974) of stock market dynamics in a world of 'fundamentalist investors' (with something like rational expectations) and 'chartist' investors who chase trends. The balance between these two groups varies as outcomes in the market vary. As long as the fundamentalists dominate the market there is a unique equilibrium and the market is stable. However, when the chartists dominate there may be multiple equilibria, unstable speculative bubbles, and eventual market crashes. Figure 4.3 presents a cusp catastrophe model developed by Zeeman where the vertical axis is the rate of change of prices in the market, the F axis represents the demand by fundamentalists, and the C axis represents the demand by chartists. When a crash happens the proportion of investors shifts back towards dominance by the fundamentalists until a new outbreak of speculation appears. Such dynamics very much reflect arguments made by Keynes and by Hyman Minsky.

A similar model can also generate chaotic dynamics, or 'chaotic bubbles' (Day and Weihong Huang, 1990). They add a third set of agents, market

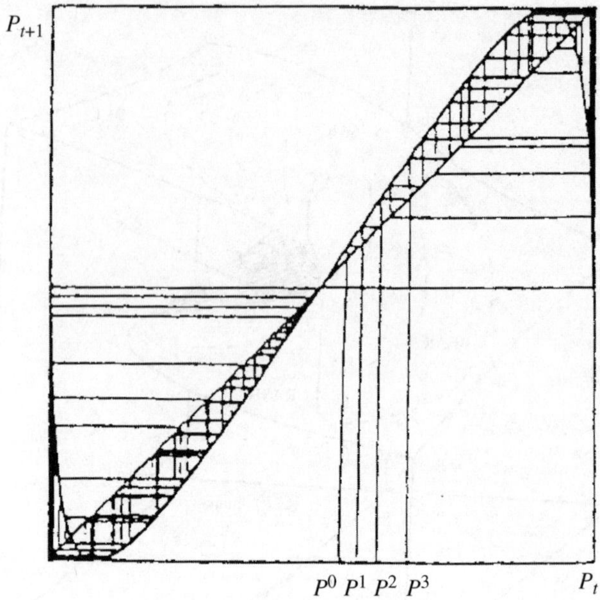

Figure 4.4 Chaotically switching bull and bear bubbles

makers to the basic Zeeman model of fundamentalists and chartists ('sheep' in Day and Huang). Figure 4.4 shows the time pattern for such a model when the destabilizing 'sheep' are dominant, with their actions generating chaotic dynamics. The market oscillates between chaotically rising bull markets and chaotically declining bear markets.

Brock and Hommes (1997, 1998) show a larger range of complex dynamics arising from models in which agents switch back and forth between costly strategies that are more stabilizing and less expensive strategies that may be destabilizing. A model with many different agents following an evolving set of competing strategies has been studied by Arthur et al. (1997), its essential dynamics resembling those already described. If a majority of the agents pursue stabilizing strategies the market is stable, but as a majority moves towards strategies that resemble trend chasing the market destabilizes and behaves in a complex and erratic manner.

Even without financial speculation, there is a large literature showing how money itself can lead to chaotic dynamics within more or less Keynesian models. Many of these models are less fundamentalist Keynesian in nature than Kaleckian (Foley, 1987; Delli Gatti et al., 1993, Semmler and Sieveking, 1993; Chiarella and Flaschel, 2000), or Minskian (Keen, 1995, 1997).

Sraffianism or Neo-Ricardianism

As discussed by Geoff Harcourt (1972), the Sraffian or neo-Ricardian subbranch emerged out of the Cambridge controversies in the theory of capital, initially over the implications of the possibility of the reswitching of techniques and the associated possibility of capital reversal.[16] Although associates of Keynes had vetted problems with aggregating capital for some time (Robinson, 1954), the key publication was Piero Sraffa's (1960) *Production of Commodities by Means of Commodities* after a 35-year gestation period, which really crystallized the debate. This book was the foundational document for the broader Sraffian approach (Kurz and Salvadori, 1995). For many younger economists in the 1960s this capital controversy provided a critique of standard neoclassical theory, and many observers, including Harcourt, have seen it as a crucial stage in the evolution of PK thought. Thus it is frustrating for many that this theoretical victory by the Sraffians had so little impact on mainstream economics and that there emerged the deep divide between the fundamentalist Keynesians and the Sraffians.

A major source of this divide has been the Sraffians emphasizing comparisons between long-run steady states, while Keynes dismissed long-run equilibrium ('In the long run we are all dead.') The first warning shot of this divide came with Joan Robinson's (1974) attack on the concept of equilibrium more broadly when she contrasted it with history, or the contrast between 'logical' and 'historical' time. Such models also tend to ignore uncertainty and the role of money. Indeed, they often abstract from any dynamic analysis at all, with some exceptions, notably Luigi Pasinetti (1993).

Nevertheless, one can find seeds of complex dynamics hiding within Sraffian models, especially those relating to the capital controversies. The possibility that discontinuity lies hidden beneath apparent continuity was a deep implication coming from some of the models, with Pasinetti (1969) probably the first to recognize this, arguing that 'continuity in the variation of techniques as the rate of profit changes, does not imply continuity in the variation of the values of capital goods per man and of net outputs per man', a point also emphasized by Donald Harris (1973).

Some economists (Yeager, 1976) argued that the existence of continuous substitutability in production functions was sufficient to eliminate the Sraffian paradoxes of capital theory such as reswitching. However, Rosser (1978) provides an example of such continuous substitution that nevertheless exhibits reswitching.[17] Figure 4.5 shows such an 'eccentric reswitching' example, the axes showing wage and profit rates, and the outer envelope of the wage-profit curves for each technique is the wage-profit frontier.

Somewhat less Sraffian, allowing for an optimal adjustment process in this model, Rosser (1983) considers movement from one equilibrium state

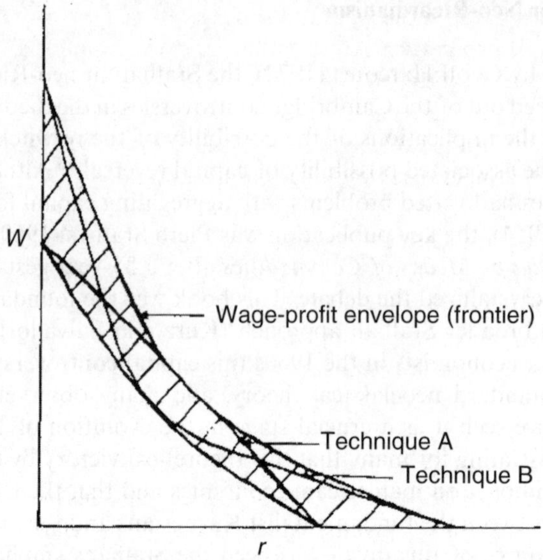

Figure 4.5 Eccentric reswitching case

to another when the rate of population growth varies continuously.[18] A discontinuity in the profit rate can emerge at a particular point, when the system jumps from one half of the wage-profit frontier to the other. Rosser (1983; 2000a, chap. 8) shows that this can be analyzed with a cusp catastrophe framework. Day and Walter (1989) show the possibility for 'historical reswitching' in dynamic models of technological change over very long time horizons with chaotic dynamics. Thus, Sraffian models contain the possibility of complex dynamics, although in order to observe such possibilities one must move beyond the Sraffian framework of only considering comparisons between long-run steady states.

Kaleckianism

Michal Kalecki has been regarded (Robinson, 1966; Feiwel, 1975; Sawyer, 1985; King, 1996) as providing a more solid foundation for a unified PKE analysis than Keynes or Sraffa. Although lacking as sophisticated an analysis of financial markets and such philosophical conundra as fundamental uncertainty as Keynes, he has a microfoundation based on the degree of monopoly and a mathematical model of fluctuations (1935, 1937, 1939), later combined with growth (1971), and more clearly recognizes the roots of this analysis in Marx's study of the surplus value realization problem. Unlike the Sraffians he abjures long-run equilibria and argues that economic dynamics consist of a series of short-run equilibria simply strung together, emerging out of each other. Any possible long-run equilibrium is rendered irrelevant by the traverse, that the movement toward an equilibrium also moves it. In the more recent controversies among Post Keynesians, the Kaleckians have seemed the centrist synthesizers between the more sharply conflicting fundamentalist Keynesians and Sraffians.

Kalecki's focus upon microfoundations is of less interest to us here because it did not lead to any models involving complex dynamics.[19] However, his analysis of macroeconomic fluctuations played a profoundly innovative and seminal role and laid the groundwork for a large literature in complex dynamics, even though he did not study such models himself.

Although somewhat incomplete and flawed (and only a partial translation of an earlier model formulated in Polish), the crucial breakthrough in English was Kalecki's 1935 paper in *Econometrica*, 'A Macrodynamic Theory of Business Cycles', which would be refined and improved in later versions in 1937 and 1939. At the core of this theory is his investment model, a nonlinear function of profits, which in turn are related to aggregate output. Shifts of this function with the capital stock can generate cyclical fluctuations. Another model that relies on a nonlinear investment function directly related to the level of output that shifts in a similar manner to Kalecki's was developed by Nicholas Kaldor (1940), and it is from this variation, particularly a version due to Chang and Smyth (1971), that a large modern literature showing the possibility of multiple varieties of complex dynamics arose. Figure 4.6 shows the nonlinear investment function from Kaldor's model, which has a more Keynesian equilibrium associated with an equality of savings and investment. As the investment function shifts up and down with business cycles discontinuities can emerge, a result shown within a catastrophe theory context by Varian (1979).

What is involved in such models is a mechanism somewhat similar to the investment accelerator, known to generate cyclical fluctuations since Aftalion (1913). Harrod (1936) combined it with Kahn's multiplier (1931) to provide a model that generated fluctuations. Paul Samuelson (1939) suggested that the consumption function of the multiplier-accelerator model might be nonlinear,[20] but then Hicks (1950) and Richard Goodwin (1951) proposed nonlinear accelerators to give nonlinear investment functions within such models. Strotz et al. (1953) first discovered chaotic dynamics while studying Goodwin's model, without realizing what they had discovered. Among those studying chaotic and other complex dynamics arising from Hicks's formulation have included Blatt (1983), Hommes (1991), and Puu (2003).

The alternative strand derived from Kalecki and Kaldor has generated an even more subtle variety of complex dynamics models. After the Varian model, others found chaotic dynamics arising from this model as well,

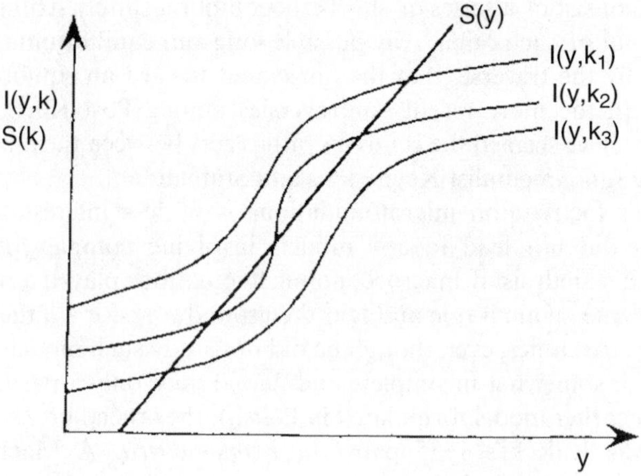

Figure 4.6 Shifting nonlinear investment function

notably Dana and Malgrange (1984), Hermann (1985), and Lorenz (1987a). A later study by Lorenz (1992) would be the first to observe fractal basin boundaries in an economic model. It was also the first paper in economics to demonstrate the possibility of non-chaotic strange attractors and of transient chaotic dynamics.

The original Kalecki model of the 1930s had a greater emphasis on class struggle entering the profit equation that ultimately drove investment. Although not taken from Kalecki, Goodwin's (1967) predator–prey model of class struggle in a cyclical growth model has a Marxist element. Variations of this model were shown to be able to generate chaotic dynamics by Pohjola (1981), Lorenz (1987b), Skott (1989), Goodwin (1990), Jarsulic (1994), and Chiarella and Flaschel (2000). Soliman (1997) showed that it could also generate models with fractal basin boundaries. Thus, even if few of these studies were directly of Kalecki's own models, his basic ideas have played a very important role in the general evolution of models of complex macroeconomic dynamics.[21]

Hysteresis and Evolutionary Models

Derived from the Greek *hysterein*, meaning 'to be behind', hysteresis is one of many economic concepts derived from physics (Ewing, 1881), its original use referring to how a magnetized ferric metal does not return to its unmagnetized state after the magnetic force is removed from it. In economics it has come to mean that the impact of an exogenous shock persists in the system in some way, even after the shock ceases. There are many interpretations, definitions and applications of this (Mitchell, 1993), but we are interested in those that assume a nonlinear source, implying multiple equilibria, with the possibility of catastrophic dynamics. Arguing that the physics concept is relevant to Post Keynesian analysis, especially of the persistence of unemployment after negative demand shocks, has been Rod Cross (1987, 1993), although Davidson (1993) has criticized this approach as being another classical model pretending to be Keynesian.

Others advocating the hysteresis approach in PK models (Setterfield, 1993, 1997; Katzner, 1993, 1999) invoke Joan Robinson's (1962, 1974) distinction between logical and historical time, arguing that the path of history puts one into the zone of one kind of equilibrium or another. Setterfield also invokes the cumulative causation arguments of Kaldor (1972) and the path-dependence arguments of Paul David (1985) and Brian Arthur (1994), with these implying possibilities of technological lock-ins, potentially of an unfavorable nature. Setterfield (1997) uses such arguments to explain the relative economic decline of Great Britain after 1900.[22] French Regulation School adherent Frédéric Lordon (1997) combines such arguments to analyze larger regimes of technological change and growth, arguably more a Schumpeterian evolutionary view.

Puu (1989) presents a business cycle model that combines catastrophic hysteresis effects with chaotic dynamics (or *chaotic hysteresis*), a variation of the Hicks–Goodwin nonlinear accelerator model in which the investment function is cubic and thus exhibits non-monotonicity. For particular parameter values the model follows the dynamics exhibited in Figure 4.7, where the horizontal axis is national income and the vertical axis is the rate of change of national income. Puu (2003) has since shown that this model can also generate fractal basin boundaries.

A more recent addition to PK approaches is evolution, with Cornwall and Cornwall (2001) affirming it, although it is arguably distant from more traditional Keynesian and Post Keynesian approaches. One factor in this development is the opening to the institutionalists, perhaps due to the apparent melting away of the Sraffians. Traditionally the old institutionalists have emphasized evolution, as symbolized by the Assocation for Evolutionary Economics, reflecting the influence of Thorstein Veblen (1898), with Geoffrey Hodgson (1993) important recently. The emphasis on hysteresis and path dependence, especially as derived from the Robinsonian emphasis on historical rather than logical time, furthers this also, fitting with the complex dynamics view of Basil Moore (2006) that disavows an equilibrium perspective and posits emergent order that does not go in any particular direction, but simply evolves.

Finally, Schumpeterian models of technological change have been merged with models of cyclical fluctuations combining various nonlinear business

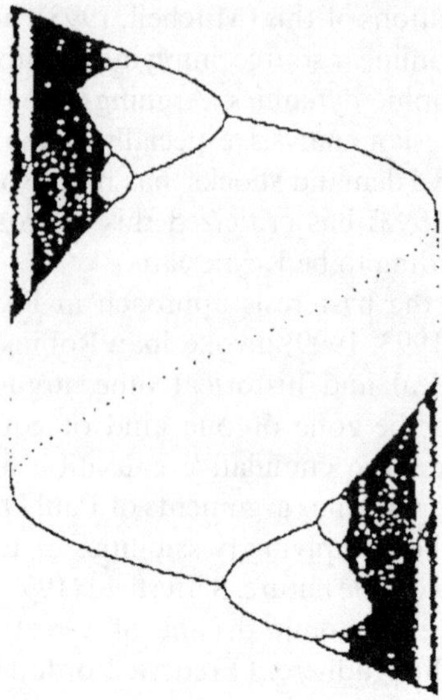

Figure 4.7 Chaotic hysteresis in Puu nonlinear accelerator model

cycle models discussed above, with such a view broadly consistent with a Kaleckian perspective. Those considering chaotic dynamics in connection with such models include Goodwin (1986), Henkin and Polterovich (1991), Mosekilde et al. (1993), Silverberg and Lehnert (1996), and Rosser and Rosser (1997). Day and Walter (1989) combine Schumpeterian technological change with Malthusian population dynamics in a model that can exhibit chaotic dynamics in shorter periods and 'historical reswitching' between technologies in longer periods, as shown in Figure 4.8 with the horizontal axis being time and the vertical being output. This model was inspired by an effort to understand the nature of the collapse of the Mayan civilization.

SOME METHODOLOGICAL CONSIDERATIONS: WHERE DO WE GO FROM HERE?

Let us consider two linked questions posed by Moore's views on the implications of complex dynamics for PKE, one his view that complex dynamics obviate any usefulness of the equilibrium concept, the other that complex dynamics imply that economic systems are ultimately open and evolutionary. These are reasonable and consistent conclusions, even if not the only ones possible.

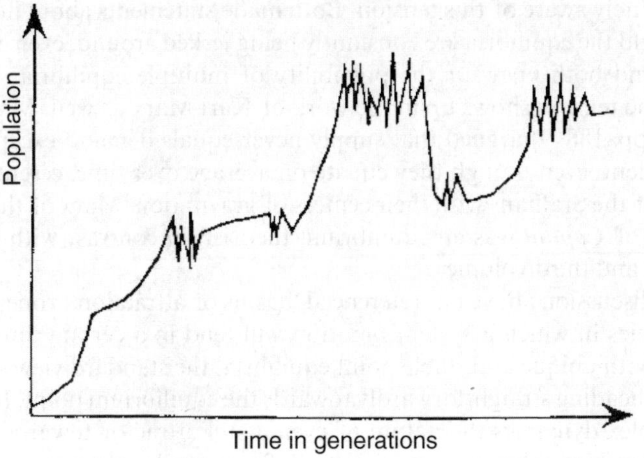

Source: From Day and Walter (1989).

Figure 4.8 Long-run Day–Walter dynamics with chaos and historical reswitching

Regarding equilibrium, an important point is Joan Robinson's argument regarding historical versus logical time, the view being that equilibrium is a construct of the latter and thus ultimately irrelevant in the real world of the former, a view shared with the more radical Austrians and also profoundly derived from the arguments of Shackle (1974). Such a view is also favored by some Kaleckians, especially those who argue that the problem of the traverse implies that equilibrium is meaningless, even though Kalecki's models always had at least temporary equilibria in them.[23] Those pursuing such perspectives tend to criticize the Sraffians and their emphasis upon the role of long-run steady states as 'centers of gravitation'.

While financial markets exhibit rather trivial temporary equilibria and equilibria can be easily obtained in some auctions, many markets are rarely, if ever, in equilibrium. The issue becomes whether it is more useful to consider their dynamics as reflecting out-of-equilibrium adjustments determined by their position (and motion) relative to the (possibly moving) equilibrium state, or to view the motion of the equilibria as so great or rapid or chaotic or endogenous as to render the concept useless. Furthermore, there are the problems of possible multiple equilibria or non-existence of equilibrium at all.

I think we shall never know for sure. That we rarely observe equilibrium does not mean that equilibrium does not exist. The older theorists of equilibrium, including Walras (1900, p. 370) and Marshall (1920, p. 346), were acutely aware of this tension. Both made statements about how in the real world the equilibria are constantly being jerked around, even endogenously, and both knew of the possibility of multiple equilibria. Furthermore, the tension shows up in the work of Karl Marx as well. Marx (1967 [1894], pp. 188–9) argued that supply never equals demand except briefly by accident, even though they equate on average over time, essentially the vision of the Sraffians with their centers of gravitation. Marx of the second volume of *Capital* was an equilibrium theorist, in contrast with Marx of the first and third volumes.[24]

The discussion above has referenced 'basins of attraction', zones of variable values in which a system's motion will tend in a certain direction or other. With unique and stable point equilibria, the standard view sees such motion heading straightforwardly towards the equilibrium point. However, in complex dynamics the nature of even a still attractor towards which a system tends may be very complex itself, for example, 'strange', possessing a fractal shape, implying a complex dynamic, even chaotic, in equilibrium. Furthermore, the convergence to the attractor may also be complex. Thus the concept of equilibrium itself may be quite messy.

Finally, in Moore's view open complex systems are associated with the non-existence of any equilibrium and the tendency for economies to evolve in a self-organizing manner with no particular direction. The idea of open systems came from dialectics (Bogdanov, 1912–22), general systems theory (von Bertalanffy, 1962), and more recent critical realist arguments (Lawson, 1997; Dow, 1999). This view will probably be increasingly influential among Post Keynesian economists.

A point of potential contradiction involves the question of exogenous versus endogenous models. One of the strongest links between complex dynamics and PK views has been the idea of endogenous macroeconomic fluctuations. Moore would argue that this represents non-ergodic self-organization, contrasted with the ergodic fluctuations due to exogenous shocks of the new classical model. The odd contradiction is that the latter model is arguably more 'open' than the former, driven by forces outside itself, which may in turn behave non-ergodically. The endogenous system is in a sense 'closed', even if it evolves spontaneously in an endogenous and non-ergodic manner.[25]

CONCLUSIONS

Much of the development of complex dynamics in economics has been based on PK models. Complex dynamics models generate key ideas of PKE such as non-ergodicity and fundamental uncertainty. Thus PKE and complex economics dynamics theory have coevolved. Indeed, complex dynamics may even offer a reconciliation between the Sraffian and other schools of PK thought. To the extent that Sraffians are willing to allow that short-run dynamics around centers of gravitation may be irregular or chaotic or complex in other ways, much as Henri Poincaré (1890) first discovered chaotic dynamics while studying gravitational dynamics for three body systems (and the 'tumbling' asteroid Hyperion appears to have a chaotic orbit), then the door to a possible reconciliation among Post Keynesians may not be closed.

NOTES

1. The author wishes to thank Geoff Harcourt and Mark Setterfield for useful and thoughtful remarks. The usual caveat holds.
2. It is well known that there has been much controversy regarding the spelling of this term, with 'post-Keynesian' and 'Post Keynesian' both often used. I follow John E. King's *A History of Post Keynesian Economics since 1936* (2002) and *The Elgar Companion to Post Keynesian Economics* (2003) as justification, with this usage seemingly more widespread recently. Harcourt personally reports that Joan Robinson was using the term 'post-Keynesian' as early as the late 1950s.
3. The term 'fundamentalist Keynesianism' is due to Coddington (1976). Not particularly liking that, Davidson (1994) introduced 'Keynes-Post Keynesianism' as an alternative.
4. For earlier versions of this trifurcation see Harcourt (1976, 1981).
5. King argues that Joan Robinson (1971) was the first synthesizer, although she later turned against the Sraffian approach, if not against Sraffa himself. He identifies more recent synthesizers as Peter Reynolds (1987), Philip Arestis (1992), Marc Lavoie (1992), Thomas Palley (1996), and Heinrich Bortis (1997), with Edward Nell (1998) also arguably qualifying. King sees the Kaleckian sub-branch as more open to synthesis than the other two, with the fundamentalists and the Sraffians engaging in the sharpest of conflicts at the Trieste summer conferences in the 1980s (Kregel, 1983; Garegnani, 1983). A sign that many no longer consider the Sraffians to be Post Keynesians is their exclusion from *A New Guide to Post Keynesian Economics* (Holt and Pressman, 2001), with some replacing them with the Institutionalists (Arestis et al., 1999).
6. The archives of the PKT list are at http://archives.econ.utah.edu/archives/pkt/index.htm.
7. Some Keynesian observers would include convergence to limit cycles as part of complex dynamics. This is sufficient for endogenous macroeconomic cycles implying the need for government intervention to stabilize the economy.
8. Davidson argues that the core Keynesian ideas will hold in linear models as long as non-ergodicity and thus fundamental uncertainty is assumed to hold axiomatically and ontologically, thus implying that the complexity view is insufficiently general. However, nonlinear systems may generate fundamental uncertainty even when they are ergodic, as for example in cases of chaotic dynamics, hence rendering this argument about generality undetermined (Rosser, 1998).
9. Some of Forrester's followers at the MIT Sloan School of Management have arguably been involved in all four of the C's, notably John Sterman (Mosekilde et al., 1993).
10. The first demonstration of possible chaotic dynamics in economics was by Strotz et al. (1953) in studying Goodwin's (1951) arguably Post Keynesian nonlinear accelerator model. However, they did not understand mathematically what they had discovered when they discovered it.

11. See Rosser (2000a, chap. 2) for discussion of these issues, and Rosser (2004) for a collection of crucial papers. Puu (2003) provides coverage of variations such as multidimensional chaos models and forms of non-chaotic dynamics that also generate extreme difficulty for agents to form rational expectations, such as those with fractal basin boundaries.
12. O'Donnell (1990) and Runde (1990) discuss the philosophical foundations of Keynes's statistical methodology that underlies his view of fundamental uncertainty. Keynes's treatise was originally written in the first decade of the twentieth century.
13. Shackle has been the Post Keynesian most admired by the Austrians, many of whom also emphasize the importance of uncertainty in economic analysis (O'Driscoll and Rizzo, 1985). Hayek (1967) was an independent and early enthusiast of complexity theory, arguing that largely laissez-faire economies would self-organize in a desirable manner.
14. Coddington (1982) argues that such a great emphasis on the inevitability of fundamental uncertainty that cannot be quantified implies a policy-less 'nihilism'. Davidson (1994) responds by citing Shackle (1955) regarding 'cruciality'. For non-crucial decisions people fall back on conventions and rule of thumb behaviors that are often somewhat predictable.
15. There is much debate regarding how to define chaotic dynamics (Rosser, 2000a, chap. 2), but all parties to this debate agree that sensitive dependence on initial conditions is a necessary condition for its existence.
16. For an overview of developments since 1972, see Ahmad (1991) and Cohen and Harcourt (2003).
17. Garegnani (1970) initially presented a somewhat similar example, his paper's publication delayed for a decade.
18. This raises the problem of the *traverse*, much studied by PK economists (Halevi and Kriesler, 1992; Lavoie, 1992) since first analyzed by Hicks (1965). In the case of this model it is not as serious due to the continuous variation of states, at least up to the point of discontinuity.
19. While Kalecki's degree of monopoly approach did not lead to complex dynamics models, there is a large literature on complex dynamics in oligopoly models (Rosser, 2002). The first self-conscious model of chaotic dynamics was Rand's (1978) model of duopoly dynamics. Interestingly, Joan Robinson's (1933) recognition of possible non-monotonic marginal revenue curves eventually led to models of chaotic monopoly dynamics (Puu, 1995).
20. Gabisch (1984) would show that the Samuelson model could generate chaotic dynamics, and Nusse and Hommes (1990) showed that these could be non-ergodically chaotic.
21. See Rosser (2000a, chap. 7) for a more complete review.
22. Arestis and Skott (1993) have found hysteresis effects empirically in the more recent UK economy, and Fischer and Jammernegg (1986) found them empirically for inflation in the US economy in the 1970s, within a catastrophe theory context.
23. It is not just Kalecki, but Keynes himself, most Post Keynesians, and most mainstream Keynesians who rely on equilibrium analysis. Kaldor (1934), emphasizing increasing returns, was an early exception, although he also produced models that involved equilibrium conditions.
24. See Rosser (1999b, 2000b) for further discussion of these matters. John Bellamy Foster (2000) examines Marx's doctoral dissertation on Epicurus and the 'swerve' as an evolutionary ecological concept, even as Marx later advocated the idea of labor values as 'centers of gravitation'.
25. There is an old saw that the only truly exogenous force in the economy is the sun.

REFERENCES

Aftalion, A. (1913) *Les Crises Périodiques de Surproduction, Vols. I–II*, Paris: Rivière.

Ahmad, S. (1991) *Capital in Economic Theory: Neoclassical, Cambridge, and Chaos*, Aldershot, UK and Brookfield, USA: Edward Elgar.

Albin, P.S. (1982) 'The Metalogic of Economic Prediction', *Mathematical Social Sciences*, 3, 329–58.

Albin, P.S. with D.K. Foley (1998) *Barriers and Bounds to Rationality: Essays on Economic Complexity and Dynamics in Interactive Systems*, Princeton: Princeton University Press.

Arestis, P. (1992) *The Post Keynesian Approach to Economics: An Alternative Analysis of Economic Theory and Policy*, Aldershot, UK and Brookfield, USA: Edward Elgar.

Arestis, P. (1996) 'Post-Keynesian Economics: Towards Coherence', *Cambridge Journal of Economics*, 20, 111–35.

Arestis, P., S.P. Dunn and M. Sawyer (1999) 'Post Keynesian Economics and its Critics', *Journal of Post Keynesian Economics*, 21, 527–49.

Arestis, P. and P. Skott (1993) 'Conflict, Wage Determination, and Hysteresis in U.K. Wage Determination', *Journal of Post Keynesian Economics*, 15, 365–86.

Arthur, W.B. (1994) *Increasing Returns and Path Dependence in the Economy*, Ann Arbor: University of Michigan Press.

Arthur, W.B., J.H. Holland, B. LeBaron, R. Palmer and P. Tayler (1997) 'Asset Pricing under Endogenous Expectations in an Artificial Stock Market', in W.B. Arthur, D.A. Lane and S.N. Durlauf (eds), *The Economy as an Evolving Complex System II*, Reading: Addison-Wesley, 15–44.

Blatt, J.M. (1983) *Dynamic Economic Systems: A Post-Keynesian Approach*, Armonk: M.E. Sharpe.

Bogdanov, A.A. (1912–22) *Vseobshcina Organizatsionnaia Nauka: Tektologia* [The Universal Science of Organization: Tektology], *Vols. 1–3*, St Petersburg and Moscow: Izdatelstvo A.I. Grbschebina.

Bortis, H. (1997) *Institutions, Behaviour and Economic Theory: A Contribution to Classical-Keynesian Political Economy*, Cambridge: Cambridge University Press.

Brock, W.A. and C.H. Hommes (1997) 'A Rational Route to Randomness', *Econometrica*, 65, 1059–95.

Brock, W.A. and C.H. Hommes (1998) 'Heterogeneous Beliefs and Routes to Chaos in a Simple Asset Pricing Model', *Journal of Economic Dynamics and Control*, 22, 1235–74.

Carabelli, A. (1988) *On Keynes's Method*, London: Macmillan.

Carrier, D. (1993) 'Will Chaos Kill the Auctioneer?' *Review of Political Economy*, 5, 299–320.

Chang, W.W. and D.J. Smyth (1971) 'The Existence and Persistence of Cycles in a Nonlinear Model: Kaldor's 1940 Model Re-examined', *Review of Economic Studies*, 38, 37–44.

Chiarella, C. and P. Flaschel (2000) *The Dynamics of Keynesian Monetary Growth: Macrofoundations*, Cambridge: Cambridge University Press.

Coddington, A. (1976) 'Keynesian Economics: The Search for First Principles', *Journal of Economic Literature*, 14, 1258–73.

Coddington, A. (1982) 'Deficient Foresight: a Troubling Theme in Keynesian Economics', *American Economic Review*, 72, 480–87.

Cohen, A.J. and G.C. Harcourt (2003) 'Whatever Happened to the Cambridge Capital Theory Controversies?' *Journal of Economic Perspectives*, 17(1), 199–214.

Colander, D., R.P.F. Holt and J.B. Rosser, Jr. (2004) *The Changing Face of Economics: Conversations with Cutting Edge Economists*, Ann Arbor: University of Michigan Press.

Cornwall, J. and W. Cornwall (2001) *Capitalist Development in the Twentieth Century: An Evolutionary-Keynesian Analysis*, Cambridge: Cambridge University Press.

Cross, R.B. (1987) 'Hysteresis and Instability in the Natural Rate of Unemployment', *Scandinavian Journal of Economics*, 89, 71–89.

Cross, R.B. (1993) 'On the foundations of Hysteresis in Economic Systems', *Economics and Philosophy*, 9, 53–74.

Dana, R.A. and P. Malgrange (1984) 'The Dynamics of a Discrete Version of a Growth Model', in J.P. Ancot (ed.), *Analyzing the Structure of Economic Models*, Boston: Martinus Nijhoff, 115–42.

David, P. (1985) 'Clio and the Economics of QWERTY', *American Economic Review, Papers and Proceedings*, 75, 332–7.

Davidson, P. (1978) *Money and the Real World*, 2nd edition, London: Macmillan.

Davidson, P. (1982–3) 'Rational Expectations: A Fallacious Foundation for Studying Crucial Decision-making Processes', *Journal of Post Keynesian Economics*, 5, 182–97.

Davidson, P. (1993) 'The Elephant and the Butterfly: Or Hysteresis and Post Keynesian Economics', *Journal of Post Keynesian Economics*, 15, 309–22.

Davidson, P. (1994) *Post Keynesian Macroeconomic Theory*, Aldershot, UK and Brookfield, USA: Edward Elgar.

Davidson, P. (1996) 'Reality and Economic Theory', *Journal of Post Keynesian Economics*, 18, 479–508.

Davis, J.B. (1993) *Keynes's Philosophical Development*, Cambridge: Cambridge University Press.

Day, R.H. (1994) *Complex Economic Dynamics: An Introduction to Dynamical Systems and Market Mechanism, Volume I*, Cambridge, MA: MIT Press.

Day, R.H. and W. Huang (1990) 'Bulls, Bears, and Market Sheep', *Journal of Economic Behavior and Organization*, 14, 299–329.

Day, R.H. and J.L. Walter (1989) 'Economic Growth in the Very Long Run: On The Multiple Interaction of Population, Technology, and Social Infrastructure', in W.A. Barnett, J. Geweke and K. Shell (eds), *Economic Complexity: Chaos, Sunspots, Bubbles, and Nonlinearity*, Cambridge: Cambridge University Press, 253–89.

Delli Gatti, D., M. Gallegatti and L. Gardini (1993) 'Investment Confidence, Corporate Debt and Income Fluctuations', *Journal of Economic Behavior and Organization*, 22, 161–88.

Dow, S.C. (1999) 'Post Keynesianism and Critical Realism: What are the Connections?' *Journal of Post Keynesian Economics*, 22, 15–34.

Ewing, J.A. (1881) 'On the Production of Transient Electric Charge in Iron and Steel Conductors by Twisting Them when Magnetised or by Magnetising Them when Twisted', *Proceedings of the Royal Society of London*, 33, 21–3.

Feiwel, G.R. (1975) *The Intellectual Capital of Michal Kalecki: A Study in Economic Theory and Policy*, Knoxville: University of Tennessee Press.

Fischer, E.O. and W. Jammernegg (1986) 'Empirical Investigation of a Catastrophe Theory Extension of the Phillips Curve', *Review of Economics and Statistics*, 68, 9–17.

Foley, D.K. (1987), 'Liquidity-Profit Rate Cycles in a Capitalist of Economy', *Journal of Economic Behaviour and Organization*, 8, 363–77.

Föllmer, H. (1974) 'Random Economies with Many Interacting Agents', *Journal of Mathematical Economics*, 1, 51–62.

Forrester, J.W. (1977) 'Growth Cycles', *De Economist*, 125, 525–43.

Foster, J.B. (2000) *Marx's Ecology: Materialism and Nature*, New York: Monthly Review Press.

Gabisch, G. (1984) 'Nonlinear Models of Business Cycle Theory', in G. Hammer and D. Pallaschke (eds), *Selected Topics in Operations Research and Mathematical Economics*, Berlin: Springer-Verlag, 205–22.

Garegnani, P. (1970) 'Heterogeneous Capital, the Production Function and the Theory of Distribution', *Review of Economic Studies*, 37, 407–36.

Garegnani, P. (1983) 'Two Routes to Effective Demand', in J.A. Kregel (ed.), *Distribution, Effective Demand and International Relations*, London: Macmillan, 69–80.

Goodwin, R.M. (1951) 'The Nonlinear Accelerator and the Persistence of Business Cycles', *Econometrica*, 19, 1–17.

Goodwin, R.M. (1967) 'A Growth Cycle', in C.H. Feinstein (ed.), *Socialism, Capitalism, and Economic Growth: Essays Presented to Maurice Dobb*, Cambridge: Cambridge University Press, 54–8.

Goodwin, R.M. (1986) 'The Economy as an Evolutionary Pulsator', *Journal of Economic Behavior and Organization*, 7, 341–9.

Goodwin, R.M. (1990) *Chaotic Economic Dynamics*, Oxford: Oxford University Press.

Halevi, J. and P. Kriesler (1992) 'An Introduction to the Traverse in Economic Theory', in J. Halevi, D. Laibman and E.J. Nell (eds), *Beyond the Steady State: A Revival of Growth Theory*, Basingstoke: Macmillan, 225–34.

Hamouda, O.F. and G.C. Harcourt (1988) 'Post Keynesianism: From Criticism to Coherence', *Bulletin of Economic Research*, 40, 1–33.

Harcourt, G.C. (1972) *Some Cambridge Controversies in the Theory of Capital*, Cambridge: Cambridge University Press.

Harcourt, G.C. (1976) 'The Cambridge Controversies: Old Ways and New Horizons – or Dead End?' *Oxford Economic Papers*, 28, 25–65.

Harcourt, G.C. (1981) 'Marshall, Sraffa, and Keynes: Incompatible Bedfellows?' in C. Sardoni (ed.), *On Political Economists and Modern Political Economy: Selected Essays of G.C. Harcourt*, London: Routledge, 250–64.

Harris, D.J. (1973) 'Capital, Distribution, and the Aggregate Production Function', *American Economic Review*, 63, 100–113.

Harrod, R.F. (1936) *The Trade Cycle*, Oxford: Clarendon Press.

Hayek, F.A. (1967) 'The Theory of Complex Phenomena', in F.A. Hayek, *Studies in Philosophy, Politics, and Economics*, London, Routledge & Kegan Paul, 22–42.

Henkin, G.M. and V.M. Polterovich (1991) 'Schumpeterian Dynamics as a Nonlinear Wave Model', *Journal of Mathematical Economics*, 20, 551–90.

Hermann, R. (1985) 'Stability and Chaos in a Kaldor-type Model', Department of Economics Discussion Paper No. 22, University of Göttingen.

Hicks, J.R. (1950) *A Contribution the Theory of the Trade Cycle*, Oxford: Oxford University Press.

Hicks, J.R. (1965) *Capital and Growth*, Oxford: Oxford University Press.

Hicks, J.R. (1979) *Causality in Economics*, New York: Basic Books.

Hodgson, G.M. (1993) *Economics and Evolution: Bringing Life Back into Economics*, Ann Arbor: University of Michigan Press.

Holt, R.P.F. and S. Pressman (eds) (2001) *A New Guide to Post Keynesian Economics*, London: Routledge.

Hommes, C.H. (1991) *Chaotic Dynamics in Economic Models: Some Simple Case-Studies*, Groningen: Wolters-Noordhoff.

Horgan, J. (1997) *The End of Science: Facing the Limits of Scientific Knowledge in the Twilight of the Scientific Age*, paperback edition, New York: Broadway Books.

Jarsulic, M. (1994) 'Continuous-time Dynamical Models with Distributed Lags', in W. Semmler (ed.), *Business Cycles: Theory and Empirical Methods*, Boston: Kluwer Academic, 145–61.

Kahn, R.F. (1931) 'The Relation of Home Investment to Unemployment', *The Economic Journal*, 41, 173–98.

Kaldor, N. (1934) 'A Note on the Determinateness of Equilibrium', *Review of Economic Studies*, 1, 122–36.

Kaldor, N. (1940) 'A Model of the Trade Cycle', *The Economic Journal*, 50, 78–92.

Kaldor, N. (1972) 'The Irrelevance of Equilibrium Economics', *The Economic Journal*, 82, 1237–55.

Kalecki, M. (1935) 'A Macrodynamic Theory of Business Cycles', *Econometrica*, 3, 327–44.

Kalecki, M. (1937) 'A Theory of the Business Cycle', *Review of Economic Studies*, 4, 77–97.

Kalecki, M. (1939) *Essays in the Theory of Economic Fluctuations*, London: Allen & Unwin.

Kalecki, M. (1971) *Selected Essays on the Dynamics of the Capitalist Economy*, Cambridge: Cambridge University Press.

Katzner, D.W. (1993) 'Some Notes on the Role of History and the Definition of Hysteresis and Related Concepts in Economic Analysis', *Journal of Post Keynesian Economics*, 15, 323–45.

Katzner, D.W. (1999) 'Hysteresis and the Modeling of Economic Phenomena', *Review of Political Economy*, 11, 171–81.

Keen, S. (1995) 'Finance and Economic Breakdown: Modeling Minsky', *Journal of Post Keynesian Economics*, 17, 607–35.

Keen, S. (1997) 'From Stochastics to Complexity in Models of Economic Instability', *Nonlinear Dynamics, Psychology, and Life Sciences*, 1, 151–72.

Keynes, J.M. (1921) *Treatise on Probability*, London: Macmillan.

Keynes, J.M. (1936) *The General Theory of Employment, Interest and Money*, London: Macmillan.

King, J.E. (ed.) (1996) *An Alternative Macroeconomic Theory: The Kaleckian Model and Post-Keynesian Economics*, Boston: Kluwer Academic.

King, J.E. (2002) *A History of Post Keynesian Economics since 1936*, Cheltenham, UK and Northampton, MA, USA: Edward Elgar.

King, J.E. (ed.) (2003) *The Elgar Companion to Post Keynesian Economics*, Cheltenham, UK and Northampton, MA, USA: Edward Elgar.

Koppl, R. and J.B. Rosser, Jr. (2002) 'All that I have to Say has Already Crossed your Mind', *Metroeconomica*, 53, 339–60.

Kregel, J.A. (1983) 'Effective Demand: Origins and Development of the Notion', in J.A. Kregel (ed.), *Distribution, Effective Demand and International Relations*, London: Macmillan, 50–68.

Kurz, H.D. and N. Salvadori (1995) *Theory of Production: A Long Period Analysis*, Cambridge: Cambridge University Press.

Lavoie, M. (1992) *Foundations of Post-Keynesian Economic Analysis*, Aldershot, UK and Brookfield, USA: Edward Elgar.

Lawson, T. (1997) *Economics and Reality*, London: Routledge.
Leijonhufvud, A. (1993) 'Towards a Not-too-rational Macroeconomics', *Southern Economic Journal*, 60, 1–13.
Loasby, B.J. (1976) *Choice, Complexity and Ignorance*, Cambridge: Cambridge University Press.
Lordon, F. (1997) 'Endogenous Structural Change and Crisis in a Multiple Time-scales Growth Model', *Journal of Evolutionary Economics*, 7, 1–21.
Lorenz, E.N. (1963) 'Deterministic Non-periodic Flow', *Journal of Atmospheric Science*, 20, 130–41.
Lorenz, E.N. (1993) *The Essence of Chaos*, Seattle: University of Washington Press.
Lorenz, H.W. (1987a) 'Strange Attractors in a Multisector Business Cycle Model', *Journal of Economic Behavior and Organization*, 8, 379–411.
Lorenz, H.W. (1987b) 'Goodwin's Nonlinear Accelerator and Chaotic Motion', *Zeitschrift für Nationalökonomie*, 47, 413–18.
Lorenz, H.W. (1992) 'Multiple Attractors, Complex Basin Boundaries, and Transient Motion in Deterministic Economic Systems', in G. Feichtinger (ed.), *Dynamic Economic Models and Optimal Control*, Amsterdam: North-Holland, 411–30.
Marshall, A. (1920) *Principles of Economics*, 8th edition, London: Macmillan.
Marx, K. (1967) *Capital: A Critique of Political Economy, Vol. III: The Process of Capitalist Production as a Whole*, New York: International Publishers, originally in German, 1894.
May, R.M. (1976) 'Simple Mathematical Models with Very Complicated Dynamics', *Nature*, 261, 459–67.
Minsky, H.P. (1972) 'Financial Instability Revisited: The Economics of Disaster', *Reappraisal of the Federal Reserve Discount Mechanism*, 3, 97–136.
Mirowski, P. (1990) 'From Mandelbrot to Chaos in Economic Theory', *Southern Economic Journal*, 57, 289–307.
Mitchell, W.F. (1993) 'Testing for Unit Roots and Persistence in OECD Unemployment Rates', *Applied Economics*, 25, 1489–501.
Moore, B.J. (1988) *Horizontalists and Verticalists: The Macroeconomics of Credit Money*, Cambridge: Cambridge University Press.
Moore, B.J. (2006) *Shaking the Invisible Hand: Complexity, Endogenous Money and Exogenous Interest Rates*, London: Palgrave Macmillan.
Mosekilde, E., E.R. Larsen, J.D. Sterman and J.S. Thomsen (1993) 'Mode Locking and Nonlinear Entrainment of Macroeconomic Cycles', in R.H. Day and P. Chen (eds), *Nonlinear Dynamics & Evolutionary Economics*, Oxford: Oxford University Press, 58–83.
Nell, E.J. (1998) *The General Theory of Transformational Growth*, New York: Cambridge University Press.
Nusse, H.E. and C.H. Hommes (1990) 'Resolution of Chaos with Applications to a Modified Samuelson Model', *Journal of Economic Dynamics and Control*, 14, 1–19.
O'Donnell, R.M. (1990) 'Keynes on Mathematics: Philosophical Foundations and Economic Applications', *Cambridge Journal of Economics*, 14, 29–47.
O'Driscoll, G.P. and M.J. Rizzo (1985) *The Economics of Time and Ignorance*, New York: Blackwell.
Palley, T.I. (1996) *Post Keynesian Economics: Debt, Distribution and the Macro Economy*, London: Macmillan.
Pasinetti, L.L. (1969) 'Switches of Technique and the Rate of Return in Capital Theory', *Quarterly Journal of Economics*, 74, 508–31.

Pasinetti, L.L. (1993) *Structural Economic Dynamics: A Theory of the Economic Consequences of Human Learning*, Cambridge: Cambridge University Press.
Peitgen, H.O., H. Jürgens and D. Saupe (1992) *Chaos and Fractals: New Frontiers of Science*, New York: Springer-Verlag.
Pohjola, M.T. (1981) 'Stable, Cyclic and Chaotic Growth: The Dynamics of a Discrete Time Version of Goodwin's Growth Cycle Model', *Zeitschrift für Nationalökonomie*, 41, 27–38.
Poincaré, H. (1890) 'Sur les équations de la dynamique et le probléme de trois corps', *Acta Mathematica*, 13, 1–270.
Pryor, F.L. (1995) *Economic Evolution and Structure: The Impact of Complexity on the U.S. Economic System*, New York: Cambridge University Press.
Puu, T. (1989) *Nonlinear Economic Dynamics*, Heidelberg: Springer-Verlag.
Puu, T. (1995) 'The Chaotic Monopolist', *Chaos, Solitons & Fractals*, 5, 35–44.
Puu, T. (2003) *Attractors, Bifurcations, and Chaos: Nonlinear Phenomena in Economics*, 2nd Édition, Heidelberg: Springer-Verlag.
Rand, D. (1978) 'Exotic Phenomena in Games and Duopoly Models', *Journal of Mathematical Economics*, 5, 173–84.
Reynolds, P.J. (1987) *Political Economy: A Synthesis of Kaleckian and Post Keynesian Economics*, Brighton: Wheatsheaf.
Robinson, J. (1933) *The Economics of Imperfect Competition*, London: Macmillan.
Robinson, J. (1954) 'The Production Function and the Theory of Capital', *Review of Economic Studies*, 21, 81–106.
Robinson, J. (1962) *Economic Philosophy*, Harmondsworth: Penguin.
Robinson, J. (1966) 'Kalecki and Keynes', in *Economic Dynamics and Planning: Essays in Honour of Michal Kalecki*, Oxford: Pergamon, 335–41.
Robinson, J. (1971) *Economic Heresies: Some Old Fashioned Questions in Economic Theory*, London: Macmillan.
Robinson, J. (1974) *History Versus Equilibrium*, Thames Papers in Political Economy, London: Thames Polytechnic.
Rosser, J.B, Jr. (1978) 'Continuity and Capital-Reversal: Comment', *Economic Inquiry*, 16, 143–6.
Rosser, J.B., Jr. (1983) 'Reswitching as a Cusp Catastrophe', *Journal of Economic Theory*, 31, 182–93.
Rosser, J.B., Jr. (1990) 'Chaos Theory and the New Keynesian Economics', *The Manchester School of Economic and Social Studies*, 58, 265–91.
Rosser, J.B., Jr. (1996) 'Chaos Theory and Rationality in Economics', in L.D. Kiel and E. Elliott (eds), *Chaos Theory in the Social Sciences: Foundations and Applications*, Ann Arbor: University of Michigan Press, 199–213.
Rosser, J.B., Jr. (1998) 'Complex Dynamics in New Keynesian and Post Keynesian Models', in R.J. Rotheim (ed.), *New Keynesian Economics/Post Keynesian Alternatives*, London: Routledge, 288–302.
Rosser, J.B., Jr. (1999a) 'On the Complexities of Complex Economic Dynamics', *Journal of Economic Perspectives*, 13, 169–92.
Rosser, J.B., Jr. (1999b) 'The Prehistory of Chaotic Economic Dynamics', in M.R. Sertel (ed.), *Contemporary Economic Issues, Volume 4: Economic Behaviour and Design*, IEA Conference Volume 124, London: Macmillan, 207–24.
Rosser, J.B., Jr. (2000a) *From Catastrophe to Chaos: A General Theory of Economic Discontinuities, Volume I: Mathematics, Microeconomics, Macroeconomics, and Finance*, 2nd edition, Boston: Kluwer Academic, 1st edition, one volume, 1991.

Rosser, J.B., Jr. (2000b) 'Aspects of Dialectics and Non-linear Dynamics', *Cambridge Journal of Economics*, 24, 311–24.

Rosser, J.B., Jr. (2001) 'Alternative Keynesian and Post Keynesian Perspectives on Uncertainty and Expectations', *Journal of Post Keynesian Economics*, 23, 545–66.

Rosser, J.B., Jr. (2002) 'The Development of Complex Oligopoly Dynamics and Theory', in T. Puu and I. Sushko (eds), *Oligopoly Dynamics: Models and Tools*, Heidelberg: Springer-Verlag, 15–29.

Rosser, J.B., Jr. (ed.) (2004) *Complexity in Economics, Volumes I–III*, Cheltenham, UK and Northampton, MA, USA: Edward Elgar.

Rosser, J.B., Jr. and M.V. Rosser (1997) 'Schumpeterian Evolutionary Dynamics and the Collapse of Soviet-bloc Socialism', *Review of Political Economy*, 9, 211–23.

Runde, J. (1990) 'Keynesian Uncertainty and the Weight of Arguments', *Economics and Philosophy*, 6, 275–92.

Runde, J. (1994) 'Keynesian Uncertainty and Liquidity Preference', *Cambridge Journal of Economics*, 18, 129–44.

Samuelson, P.A. (1939) 'A Synthesis of the Principle of Acceleration and the Multiplier', *Journal of Political Economy*, 47, 786–97.

Sargent, T.J. (1993) *Bounded Rationality in Macroeconomics*, Oxford: Clarendon Press.

Sawyer, M.C. (1985) *The Economics of Michal Kalecki*, London: Macmillan.

Schelling, T.C. (1971) 'Dynamic Models of Segregation', *Journal of Mathematical Sociology*, 1, 143–86.

Semmler, W. and M. Sieveking (1993) 'Nonlinear Liquidity Growth Dynamics with Corridor Stability', *Journal of Economic Behavior and Organization*, 22, 189–208.

Setterfield, M. (1993) 'Towards a Long-run Theory of Effective Demand: Modeling Macroeconomic Systems with Hysteresis', *Journal of Post Keynesian Economics*, 15, 347–64.

Setterfield, M. (1997) *Rapid Growth and Relative Decline: Modelling Macroeconomic Dynamics with Hysteresis*, London: Macmillan.

Shackle, G.L.S. (1955) *Uncertainty in Economics and Other Reflections*, Cambridge: Cambridge University Press.

Shackle, G.L.S. (1974) *Keynesian Kaleidics: The Evolution of a General Political Economy*, Edinburgh: Edinburgh University Press.

Silverberg, G. and D. Lehnert (1996) 'Evolutionary Chaos: Growth Fluctuations in a Schumpeterian Model of Creative Destruction', in W.A. Barnett, A.P. Kirman and M. Salmon (eds), *Nonlinear Dynamics and Economics: Proceedings of the Tenth International Symposium in Economic Theory and Econometrics*, Cambridge: Cambridge University Press, 45–74.

Skott, P. (1989) *Conflict and Effective Demand in Economic Growth*, Cambridge: Cambridge University Press.

Soliman, A.S. (1997) 'Assessing the Effect of Shock Policies in Nonlinear Macroeconomic Dynamic Systems using Fractal Boundaries in Parameter Space', *Chaos, Solitons & Fractals*, 8, 909–15.

Sraffa, P. (1960) *Production of Commodities by Means of Commodities: Prelude to a Critique of Economic Theory*, Cambridge: Cambridge University Press.

Stodder, J.P. (1995) 'The Evolution of Complexity in Primitive Economies: Theory', *Journal of Comparative Economics*, 20, 1–31.

Stodder, J.P. (1997) 'Complexity Aversion: Simplification in the Herrnstein and Allais Behaviors', *Eastern Economic Journal*, 23, 1–16.

Strotz, R.H., J.C. McAnulty and J.B. Naines, Jr. (1953) 'Goodwin's Nonlinear Theory of the Business Cycle: An Electro-analog Solution', *Econometrica*, 21, 390–411.
Thom, R. (1972) *Stabilité Structurelle et Morphogenèse: Essai d'une Théorie Générales des Modèles*, New York: Benjamin, English translation, 1975.
Varian, H.R. (1979) 'Catastrophe Theory and the Business Cycle', *Economic Inquiry*, 17, 14–28.
Veblen, T. (1898) 'Why is Economics Not an Evolutionary Science?' *Quarterly Journal of Economics*, 12, 373–92.
von Bertalanffy, L. (1962) *General Systems Theory*, New York: George Braziller.
Walras, L. (1900) *Éléments d'Économie Politique Pure*, 4th edition, Lausanne: F. Rouge, English translation, 1926.
Wiener, N. (1961) *Cybernetics: Or Control and Communication in the Animal and the Machine*, 2nd edition, Cambridge, MA: MIT Press.
Yeager, L.B. (1976) 'Toward Understanding some Paradoxes in Capital Theory', *Economic Inquiry*, 14, 313-46.
Zeeman, E.C. (1974) 'On the Unstable Behavior of the Stock Exchanges', *Journal of Mathematical Economics*, 1, 39–44.

5. Corridor of viability: complexity analysis for enterprise and investment

Jerry Courvisanos and Colin Richardson[1]

COMPLEXITY AND INVESTMENT

Basil Moore has driven a spear into the mainstream ('verticalist') view of the stock of money as a supply-based instrument of monetary policy. He has done this by identifying behavior within the banking system as being determined by endogenous demand-based processes of deposit creation (the 'horizontalist' view). Similarly, this chapter takes the perspective that the mainstream view of investment in capital goods with its supply-based focus is untenable and instead identifies investment with decision-making behavior determined by endogenous demand-based processes of profit generation. This challenges the mainstream account of 'optimal' investment allocation policy being determined using specific supply-based criteria like the real interest rate in an ergodic world of rational expectations.[2]

Since the early 1990s, investment theory has made significant progress by examining critically the issue of investment decision-making under uncertainty. The mainstream, led by Avinash Dixit and Robert Pindyck, has developed an optimal decision-making model incorporating the 'value of waiting' in the investment decision function to avoid downside risk in revenues over the uncertain future, while sacrificing profit flow by postponing viable investment projects (Dixit, 1992, p. 110; see also Dixit and Pindyck, 1994). Their approach reflects the neo-classical agenda of breaking down the economic system into optimal decision-making actions that tend towards some equilibrium, even if it is '. . . the equilibrium of an industry as an organic process over time' in this *investment under uncertainty* analysis (Dixit, 1992, p. 121). Using this approach, all investment decisions under uncertainty can be decomposed into their elements to derive an optimal balance between the decision to invest and waiting for more information. This closes the information system at any point in time. Then, the optimal balance (or equilibrium) can 'organically' alter in a series of comparative static changes over logical (ahistorical) time.

An alternative *investment under uncertainty* analysis has developed where the information system is always open and decision-making has to begin on the basis that there is no optimal balance. Thus, Post Keynesians attempt to handle non-ergodic (or open and unknowable) fundamental uncertainty as an epistemic instability of beliefs, reinforced and magnified by institutional features in financial markets and technological change (Runde, 1991, pp. 142–3). A behavioral motivation to decision-making underlies economic instability, resulting in a non-equilibrium open system based on historical-time dynamic processes with cumulative causation and accompanying path dependence in the system's evolution. The investment decision-making dynamics in this approach originate with the work of Michal Kalecki on investment cycles and increasing risk, in which profits derived from effective demand provide both ability and incentive to invest (Kalecki, 1939). Kaleckian foundations deliver an investment cycle of corporate instability due to entrepreneurial uncertainty built into conventions and rules that are sensitive to information about the unknown future *and* evolutionary processes of technological innovation. Courvisanos (1996) synthesizes this alternative analysis by identifying susceptibility of investment as the sensitivity factor; a brief outline of his approach is set out in the next section.

The original 1996 work on susceptibility of investment was qualitative research conducted via the case study method from a critical realist perspective (see Lawson, 1997). This chapter uses the complexity approach, applying numerical analysis to investment behavior and deriving the associated policy implications. Basil Moore introduced one of the authors to complexity as being appropriate for research into susceptibility, and in an attempt to do what he suggested the following incorporates the science of complexity into the Post Keynesian *investment under uncertainty* analysis.[3] This should help identify the complex underlying forces that explain volatile surface behavior in investment spending and its impact on the economy.

Complexity as a concept is congruent with investment cycle analysis. This approach recognizes an open system which overall ('macroscopically') creates and dissolves patterns over time, whereas the neo-classical approach involves reducing a closed system into its individual parts. The science of complexity allows investigation of open systems in which '. . . the collective behaviour of many basic but interacting units' evolves over time, with self-organization and adaptation (Coveney and Highfield, 1995, p. 7). This fits into the evolutionary and cumulative causation aspects of the investment cycle. As such the analysis here is situated in the integration of the

Kaleckian and evolutionary models of complexity outlined by Rosser in Chapter 4 of this volume.

Only with the recent increase in the power of computers have complexity issues been able to be grasped and manipulated. 'The science of complexity is intricately entwined with and crucially dependent on computer technology' (Coveney and Highfield, 1995, p. 15). This chapter presents two computer-based nonlinear dynamic models of a simple corn-credit economy with clearly identified behavioral specifications and a watertight set of accounting identities. The economy is simulated over 100 years by an Excel computer program and the results interpreted. One model cannot handle *excessive* investment instability but the other can, thanks to a built-in kaleidic mechanism based on investment susceptibility. These models and the difference between their results provide support for the Post Keynesian view of investment under uncertainty.

UNCERTAINTY AND SUSCEPTIBILITY

There are two principal sources of uncertainty in investment decision-making. The first is based on the sensitivity that entrepreneurs have to altered information and related imagination that drives innovation.[4] The second is concerned with evolutionary change and the accompanying technical and market uncertainties arising from such discontinuities.[5] Courvisanos (1996) shows how both these sources of uncertainty can be accommodated within the framework of Kalecki's investment cycle theory. Essentially entrepreneurs attempt to preserve stability in an uncertain world by forming a view on the state of confidence in long-term expectations based on past knowledge, then incorporate this into conventions and rules on business practice. This includes the use of mark-up pricing, discounted cash flow analysis, payback periods, and gearing (debt:equity or debt:assets) ratios. The susceptibility of these long-term expectations to change creates instability in investment decision-making (O'Donnell, 1989, p. 262), with the frequency and extent of such changes being an empirical matter.

The concept of investment susceptibility '. . . refers to the psychological tension felt by entrepreneurs in relation to their fragile confidence about a particular investment decision, given the level of investment orders already committed' (Courvisanos, 1996, p. 116). Such 'fragile confidence' is manifested through three observable objective elements of the investment orders decision – profits, increasing risk (based on gearing ratios) and capacity utilization. At a given level of investment orders, a rise in investment commitments engenders increased susceptibility, whereas a fall causes susceptibility to decrease. This reduces the risk and exposure to uncertainty that is the cause of tension. A reduction in susceptibility allows for the possibility of a rise in investment orders which again, in turn, increases the level of susceptibility.

In all cycles, the explanation of turning points is crucial. Courvisanos (1996) identifies the turning points in susceptibility cycles that occur when entrepreneurs' susceptibility is such that current conventions used for investment decision-making are rejected, leading to structural breaks in the pattern of investment behavior. This occurs after the point of inflection on the expansion phase of the business cycle, usually associated with boom conditions.[6] From this point, the three observable Kaleckian elements can be detected building up tension as investment orders are increased. In these boom conditions, continued expansion of investment generates cumulative tension with reduction in profit increments, higher gearing ratios and, finally, lower utilization rates. It manifests itself as an inclination to decrease investment commitments and/or postpone investment plans. As tension increases, ultimately some factor (seasonal, secular or random) or combination of such factors leads to postponement or reduction of investment commitments. This releases tension, reduces susceptibility and the cycle starts its contractionary phase, reflected in decreasing investment orders.

The process is not symmetrical at the upper and lower turning points of the susceptibility cycle. At the lower turning point, it is a situation of increased resilience on the part of more spirited entrepreneurs that will induce greater risk-taking and lead to higher levels of current and future investment commitments. This will lead to rising profit increments, relatively low gearing ratios and rising utilization rates.

The investment susceptibility cycle model can be formalized in an investment order function that provides the objective reflection of susceptibility:

$$I_t = f(R_{t-1}, \Delta R_t, g_{t-1}, cu_{t-1}) \tag{5.1}$$

where I_t is the level of aggregate investment orders in the current period; R_{t-1} = the previous period level of profits; ΔR_t = the actual increment in profit levels; g_{t-1} = the previous period gearing ratio; and cu_{t-1} = the previous period capacity utilization. The peak of susceptibility is reached when I_t is at its maximum value. At this point the contradictory pulls on profits, risk and capacity utilization create enough susceptibility tension for investment orders to turn down. The trough of susceptibility is reached when I_t is at a minimum value.

Complexity is evident in the way that susceptibility operates in the investment decision-making processes that unfold through a great many independent agents interacting with each other so that physical capital is created within the economy. The '. . . very richness of these interactions allows the system as a whole to undergo *spontaneous self-organization*' (Waldrop, 1992, p. 11; original emphasis). This means that through a myriad of investment decisions, the economy develops its own organic reproduction system that is continually adapting to the environment within which the investment processes occur. Actively, all organizations in the system – businesses, governments, non-profit sector – constantly reorganize their investment spending by reordering, postponing, modifying, suspending, and scrapping capital stock. All these adaptations are responses to profitability, gearing and utilization signals that are sifted through the susceptibility pressures that emerge over time.

The time pattern of investment spending which results is not a neoclassical equilibrium tendency towards some stable nirvana, nor is it some weirdly unpredictable gyration into chaos. There is a coherence to investment historically evident in the capitalist system by the semi-regularity of investment cycles recognized and noted by writers from Marx ([1867] 1954), through Schumpeter (1939) and on to Zarnowitz (1973). Coherence is not equilibrium; the only 'balance' that emerges in investment cycles is at the edge of chaos, where 'the components of a system never quite lock into place, and yet never dissolve into turbulence, either' (Waldrop, 1992, p. 12). Susceptibility is the behavioral tension variable that defines a 'corridor of viability' within which investment moves. Since investment is the major driver of business cycles, investment plays a central role in the type and extent of instability in a capitalist economy (Hansen, 1964, p. 122). Goodwin (1987, p. 125) identifies changing investment confidence as the 'endogenous generator of irregularity'.

Empirical evidence to support the susceptibility hypothesis has been provided in two studies to date. Courvisanos (1996, pp. 190–216) identifies long-term patterns of cyclical investment from numerous case studies of investment behavior in different capitalist economies, across vastly different industries and over long periods of time. Laramie *et al.* (2004) conduct an econometric test on the susceptibility thesis using UK quarterly data for the period 1980 (Q1) to 1996 (Q3). This is an OLS estimate of the investment *decisions* function specified in equation (5.1) above. These decisions are measured by investment orders and not by the standard approach of testing investment *expenditure* functions. The independent variables in equation (5.1) that are all included in the test function represent objective reflections of susceptibility. The authors note the behavioral aspect of this test by stating: '[I]t is only recently that uncertainty has been formally introduced into Kaleckian theory via Courvisanos' concept of susceptibility' (p. 160). Their conclusion is: 'Our econometric results provide support for an objective Kaleckian formulation of the concept of susceptibility' (p. 160). They subject the final 1968 version of Kalecki's own investment equation to the same econometric test and find the results are much weaker than the investment-susceptibility version.

In the next two sections, computer simulation exercises are performed to provide a dynamic example of complexity science in operation. The results identify susceptibility as the behavioral variable that controls the corridor of viability within which investment expenditures cycle. This has policy implications that are dramatically different to the current neo-liberal and previous Keynesian approaches, and these are outlined in the final section.

THE SIMULATION MODEL WITHOUT SUSCEPTIBILITY

In this section, a dynamic, nonlinear and recursive circulating capital model based on Richardson (2002, 2004) is constructed, solved for the stationary state, then used to generate a steady state of growth, before seeding an endogenous business cycle – one whose peaks and troughs recur over 100 years of simulated historical time. Our purpose is to establish a baseline model.

The next section incorporates 'susceptibility' into the model's investment function to see whether this will ameliorate a problem which plagued it, namely too narrow a 'corridor of viability', outside of which the economy was prone to collapse. The investment function is expressed in physical terms, with sacks of seedcorn being retained (investment orders) after each end-of-year harvest, then almost immediately sown (investment expenditure) as the new crop year opens.

The lack of any fixed capital equipment has two implications. On the one hand, there is no way innovation and the influence of capacity utilization on susceptibility can be incorporated. On the other, the debt:equity ratio – here expressed as the debt:assets ratio – may appear 'unreasonably low' because debt is only ever incurred to finance (on average) one week of the economy's annual wage bill, and not any fixed capital formation. However, a low debt:assets ratio cannot be construed as a low-risk ratio in such a lightly monetized economy.

Corn models occupy an important place in the history of economic thought and this competitive capitalist 'corn-credit model' is a synthesis of work by a line of theorists stretching from William Petty to Basil Moore. The economy operates in a region of uniformly fertile and well-watered flat land, so there need be no Ricardian diminishing returns to more intensive cultivation and the Marshallian 'extensive margin' contracts and expands as seedcorn-driven cycles ebb, flow and propagate.

The workforce (η_t fieldhands) – and, with it, the population – initially is constant, but then is made to grow at 1 per cent per annum. Each 31 December, capitalist farmers decide the flow of 'seedcorn' (Qi_t sacks p.a.), then store the balance of that year's harvest as the economy's flow of 'foodcorn' (Qs_t sacks p.a.) – after holding back a flow of 'farmcorn' (π_t sacks p.a.) to feed their own families over the coming year. Also initially constant, farmcorn later is made to grow at the workforce/population rate.

The farmers rule off their account books and compute two significant measures: the profit they earned (R_t dollars p.a.) and the profit rate they realized (r_t per cent p.a.) during the year ended 31 December. For analytical clarity, they are assumed to entertain 'static expectations' that next year's expected return on capital (re_{t+1} per cent p.a.) will equal this year's realized profit rate.

On 1 January – the very next day – the now-lagged seedcorn flow (Qi_{t-1}) becomes the economy's opening stock of seedcorn, which then is sown by those employed to raise the new year's crop. Likewise, Qs_{t-1} becomes the opening stock of foodcorn available for sale to consumers at weekly markets while the new crop is being tended. Furthermore, π_{t-1} becomes the opening stock of farmcorn.

Seedcorn yield (θ sacks harvested per sack planted) and the opening stock of circulating capital (the Qi_{t-1} sacks of seedcorn) between them determine the volume of corn to be harvested (Q_t sacks p.a.). In turn, this fixes the level of employment at L_t fieldhands (whose average productivity is α sacks/fieldhand p.a.), drawn from the economy's workforce.

Segue now from the corn aspect to the credit aspect. The richest farmers also act as the economy's bankers. It is they who hold the largest stocks of seedcorn and foodcorn *qua* collateral, meaning that the paper credits they issue are universally trusted. Fieldhands' fortnightly wages, together with all profit and interest incomes, are calculated and paid in a money of account. These 'dollars' enter circulation when credit is extended fortnightly by the bankers, thus enabling farmers to meet each of their 26 forthcoming payrolls. After each weekly foodcorn market, farmers return their sales proceeds to the bankers that extinguish, on average, half their outstanding debts.

In this economy there is no way that supply and demand can determine the price of money, that is, the interest rate on loans of working capital. There is no Friedmanian helicopter; the only way money can get into the system is by bankers extending their trusted credits to farmers. This 'demand-determined and credit-created' money enters the economy via the endogenous money supply process identified by Basil Moore (1988). If there is no demand for money, none can be created by those having the power to supply, a power which is based on trust and, ultimately, on the collateral held by a minority of banker/farmers by virtue of their possessing the economy's largest stocks of valuable seedcorn and foodcorn. The interest rate (i_t per cent p.a.) is determined by the demand for credit, in line with Kalecki's 'principle of increasing risk' (see Kalecki, 1939).

Each 1 January, farmers approach bankers, proposing fortnightly schedules for borrowing W_t dollars p.a. to finance their payrolls. Bankers know that, on average, farmers will be carrying a debt of $D_t = W_t/\mu$ dollars, where $\mu = 52 = [2 \times 26]$ since half the credits drawn down as each fortnight opens will remain outstanding. Bankers next consider the lender's risk they will bear by agreeing to extend credit, so they view the farmers' latest balance sheets and inspect their debt:assets ratio $d_t = D_t/K_{t-1}$ (the denominator being the value of last year's seedcorn plus average foodcorn capital on hand), then determine how this ratio has changed since the previous year. If its growth rate $gd_t = [(d_t/d_{t-1}) - 1]$ per cent p.a. is greater (less) than zero, the bankers will raise (lower) last year's market interest rate. On the other hand, if there has been no change in the debt:assets ratio, lender's risk is unchanged; bankers are content to leave i_t per cent p.a. at its existing level.

The money wage rate (w_t dollars/fieldhand p.a.) will be higher than last year's if this year's 'employment ratio' exceeds unity (i.e. if $e = [L_t/\eta_t] > 1$) and lower if **e** is less than one, implying that involuntary unemployment occurs. The phenomenon of 'overfull employment' (**e** > 1) can be validated in two ways: (a) the stock of labour (η_t) is defined as a 'normal' workforce, hence the participation rate may rise while the excess demand for labour persists or (b) employees work 'normal' hours, hence the notional excess of L_t over η_t fieldhands manifests as hours of paid overtime, spread in some equitable manner over the economy's workforce. In the collective bargaining sessions held each 1 January, farmers and fieldhands also factor in last year's inflation rate $gp_{t-1} = [(p_{t-1}/p_{t-2}) - 1]$ per cent p.a., where $p_t = P_t/P_0$ is the corn price index. Given that they hold static expectations, all participants believe inflation will continue at the same rate throughout year t. If growth of the price level is positive (negative), money wages will rise (fall); if zero, there will be no change, *ceteris paribus*.

Annually, all wage (W_t dollars p.a.) and interest (J_t dollars p.a.) money income is spent on foodcorn released from the farmers' granaries onto the weekly markets and all of their profit income (R_t dollars p.a.) is saved. These assumptions allow one to state a necessary, sufficient, simple and elegant relationship for determining to what level the average money price of foodcorn (P_t dollars/sack) must float.

The seven structural-form equations of the corn-credit model are:

Corn Produced	$Q_t = \theta\, Qi_{t-1}$	sacks p.a.	(5A)
Seedcorn	$Qi_t = (1 + \phi\, z_t)\, Qi_{t-1}$	sacks p.a.	(5B)

Employment	$L_t = Q_t/\alpha$	fieldhands	(5C)
Profit Rate	$r_t = R_t/K_t$	percent p.a.	(5D)
Corn Price	$P_t = (W_t + J_t)/Qs_{t-1}$	\$/sack	(5E)
Money Wage	$w_t = w_{t-1} + \varepsilon\,(e_t - 1) + \rho\, gp_{t-1}$	\$/fieldhand p.a.	(5F)
Interest Rate	$i_t = i_{t-1} + \lambda\, gd_t$	percent p.a.	(5G)

The corn price equation (5E) originates in the Kalecki-influenced economic growth and income distribution models of Robinson (1956) and Harcourt (1963). It expresses the fact that, during the series of weekly markets, all stored foodcorn (Qs_{t-1} sacks) is sold to the workers and interest recipients in exchange for all the money they earn. Logically, then, the farmers must receive back as the overall average corn price (P_t dollars/sack) all of their current wage and interest outlays in return for most of last year's crop, that is, that part not retained by them for investment (Qi_{t-1} sacks) and their own household consumption (π_{t-1} sacks). The Robinson–Harcourt price equation is fully consistent with 'Kalecki's dictum' concerning the direct dependence of capitalists' profits upon their own investment and consumption outlays.

The structural-form equation (5B) determining the volume of seedcorn is crucial. The corresponding reduced form (see equations (5A′) through (5G′) in the Appendix) shows that farmers' aggregate investment decisions drive the evolution of all other economic variables, including profit incomes that are saved rather than spent on consumption. (Farmer households are sustained by farmcorn retained from the previous year's harvest.) In proper Keynesian fashion, the flow of dollar saving accommodates itself to the flow of dollar investment outlays, both *ex post* and *ex ante*, every year along the corn-credit economy's range of possible growth paths.

In turn, seedcorn is itself driven by the time-series of profitability gaps between the expected (= latest realized, under static expectations) and the required rates of return on capital stock, in a process of circular and cumulative causation. This target or required or normal profit rate (n_t per cent p.a.) is the opportunity cost of capital and has two components (market interest rate plus risk premium φ per cent p.a.), as shown in identity (6) below.

A behavioral parameter – the constant 'reaction coefficient' (ϕ) – determines the rate of seedcorn capital accumulation as a fraction of the economy's profitability gap, and this gives rise to the positive feedback, cumulative causation and path dependence that sustains the endogenous business cycle (and its trajectory) as it weaves and wends its way through simulated historical time.

The right-hand sides of the seven structural-form equations (5A to 5G) would be very long and look extremely messy, were it not for the 15 identities defined below:

Wage Bill	$W_t = w_t L_t$	dollars p.a.	(1)
Seedcorn Capital	$Ka_t = P_t Qi_{t-1}$	dollars	(2)
Foodcorn Capital	$Kb_t = P_t Qs_{t-1}/\kappa$	dollars	(3)
Capital Stock	$K_t = Ka_t + Kb_t$	dollars	(4)
Profit	$R_t = P_t Q_t - W_t - Ka_t - J_t$	dollars p.a.	(5)
Normal Profit Rate	$n_t = i_t + \varphi$	per cent p.a.	(6)
Profitability Gap	$z_t = r_t - n_t$	per cent p.a.	(7)
Foodcorn	$Qs_t = Q_t - Qi_t - \psi$	sacks p.a.	(8)
Price Level	$p_t = P_t/P_0$	ratio	(9)
Inflation Rate	$gp_t = (p_t/p_{t-1}) - 1$	per cent p.a.	(10)
Employment Rate	$e_t = L_t/\eta$	ratio	(11)
Average Debt	$D_t = W_t/\mu$	dollars	(12)
Debt:Assets Ratio	$d_t = D_t/K_{t-1}$	ratio	(13)
D:A Ratio Growth Rate	$gd_t = (d_t/d_{t-1}) - 1$	per cent p.a.	(14)
Interest Bill	$J_t = i_t D_t$	dollars p.a.	(15)

Note that $\kappa = 2$ in identity (3) because farmers' granaries, averaged over the entire year, will be half full of lagged foodcorn. This volume of corn, as with lagged seedcorn in identity (2), is only valued at the end of year t because that is when farmers calculate the annual overall average price (P_t dollars/sack) they received at the series of weekly competitive foodcorn markets.

In this structural-form equation/identity system, there are seven unknown variables to be determined, but only six independent equations are available. Equation (5D) is not independent, but a mere identity defining the realized profit rate: $r_t = R_t/K_t$ per cent p.a. Therefore, the model is under-determined since it has one too many unknowns than independent equations to fix the values of these dependent variables.

In line with usual practice, the simulation model is made just-determined by reducing its number of unknowns. However, this system is dynamic and recursive (historical time), rather than merely simultaneous (logical time). In principle, one simply sets the profitability gap identity to zero ($z = [r - n] = 0$ per cent p.a.), then solves the model. But to enforce the stationary-state condition, there is need to employ a procedure commonly used in numerical analysis. A standard optimizing algorithm ('Solver') is used to juggle some of the model's parameters until the realized profit rate (r_t per cent p.a.) achieves strict equality with the normal profit rate (n_t per cent p.a.) during every year of the century.

Having realized the equation/identity system as a spreadsheet, the model is solved numerically for a century-long stationary state. All it needs to commence its progress through 100 years of simulated historical time (starting in year 1) are three initial values in year 0, viz. Qi_0 = 40,000 sacks, w_0 = \$200/fieldhand p.a. and i_0 = 4 per cent p.a.

In any stationary state, the economy simply replicates itself year after year, with all its variables plotting as horizontal or 'flatline' graphs. However, just below the tranquil surface lurks a witches' brew of potential dynamics. The reduced-form equations are extraordinarily complex, with Qi_{t-1}^2 (and even higher powers) helping drive seedcorn, the corn price and the interest rate. Different initial conditions or model parameters can trigger cycles, runaway growth, even collapse.

Next, a smooth exponential growth path or steady state[7] is generated by forcing two formerly constant parameters (workforce and farmcorn) to grow at the exponential rate of 1 per cent p.a. The cauldron of underlying dynamics is always on the point of seething, as demonstrated below once the cyclical growth process is ignited. In any steady state, the economy simply expands at the same rate annually, with most of its variables plotting as exponential or 'growthline' graphs. All ratio variables are constant in the steady state, including positive-valued prices, wage rates, profit and interest rates, and zero-valued unemployment and inflation rates. Effectively, steady states are stationary states in proportions; this handy mathematical fact allows neo-classical 'growth' theorists to pass off their static, timeless analyses as 'dynamic'.

Finally, an endogenous business cycle is kicked into life by a once-for-all 'crop misallocation event', which frees up all the dynamic forces. Five years out from the base year, on 31 December, fieldhands mistakenly carry part of what the farmers had earmarked as seedcorn into the granaries instead of the barns. So, the next day (as year 6 opens) a smaller crop than is consistent with maintaining the ongoing steady state is sown. As a concomitant, during that year a larger volume of lagged foodcorn – one that is inconsistent with Golden Age continuance – will be released for sale onto the weekly foodcorn markets, depressing the dollar price of corn and its realized profitability. This precipitates a sudden economic downswing, the opening salvo in an endogenous, genuinely dynamic, historical-time process that converts smooth growth into cyclical growth as shown in Figure 5.1.

As one might expect, Figure 5.1 shows that the largest-amplitude cycles afflict the economy's key realized profit aggregate (R_t). As this represents the dollar residual of all revenues after every expense has been deducted, no other variable is the final resultant of so many (and often contradictory) economic, financial and social forces while, at the same time, constituting

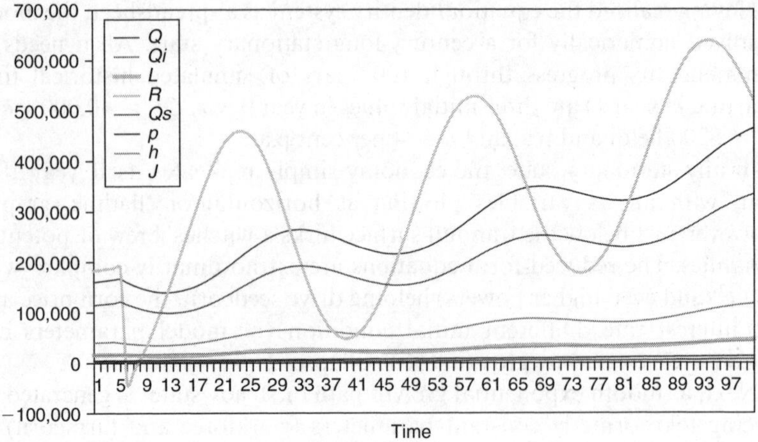

Figure 5.1 Cyclical state of growth – model without susceptibility

a key element in the investor calculations that set those same forces in motion at the turn of each simulated year.

As in the real world, there are no more flatlines and growthlines – although an upward trajectory is apparent. Certainly, the underlying supply-side 1 per cent p.a. expansion in the workforce and volume of farm-corn plays its part. However, the economy's growth (and business cycle) is actually being *determined* by the behavior of one demand-side variable (seedcorn), as shown in the Appendix. This, in turn, is being determined by the time series of changing profitability gaps, which signal farmers to raise, lower or maintain their previous level of investment. When they do, this of course feeds back onto their own profitability in a Myrdalian process of circular and cumulative causation, which can take the economy on a roller-coaster ride. Capitalists are the benefactors and victims of their own macroeconomic investment-profitability nexus.

Despite the surface plausibility of the 'cyclical state of growth' displayed in Figure 5.1, there is an important limitation of the complexity model generating these time-series plots. As identified in Richardson (2002, p. 242), '. . . the corn-credit economy suffers a catastrophic collapse if the reaction coefficient constant is set outside its own range of viability'. Recall from structural-form equation (5B) above that it is the constant reaction coefficient ($\phi = 0.5962$) which links the profitability gap with the volume of seedcorn. Numerical analysis experiments have established that there exists a 'corridor of viability' within which the economy's real gross product neither cycles up towards infinity nor down towards zero. The baseline corn-credit economy is only viable when the reaction coefficient is confined within the limits $0 \leq \phi \leq 0.6558$. Can the introduction of susceptibility raise this upper limit and make the model economy more viable?

THE SIMULATION MODEL WITH SUSCEPTIBILITY

The corn-credit economy, even in its first incarnation, is not a bloodless, mechanistic contraption: human agency is paramount. Its reaction coefficient represents an 'average of individual behaviors'; that is, not all entrepreneurs react by (say) increasing their own volume of seedcorn last year by precisely 5.962 per cent whenever they calculate that their realized profit rate exceeded their opportunity cost of capital by 10 percentage points. The $0 \leq \phi \leq 0.6558$ reaction coefficient is the limit to this 'measure of central tendency' that establishes a corridor of viability for cyclical activity without chaos. Adding 'susceptibility' gets closer to the actual behavior of capitalist entrepreneurs who, while always willing to take risks, nonetheless do keep a 'weather eye' on their exposure to potential financial ruin from a 'higher than normal' debt:assets ratio.

The susceptibility hypothesis of Courvisanos (1996) is a behavioral theory; it 'humanizes' the mechanistic investment theories of Michal Kalecki. Of the four determinants of investment orders in Courvisanos (1996), two of them – total profit (R_{t-1}) and profit increment (ΔR_t) – already are covered in equation (5B) above, via the presence of equation (5D) for the realized profit rate ($r_t = R_t/K_t$ per cent p.a.) on its right-hand side, courtesy of identities (6) and (7). Capacity utilization cannot be incorporated, but the gearing ratio (here expressed as the debt:assets ratio, d_t) can be incorporated via a new, susceptibility-based equation for seedcorn investment.

This gearing ratio (d_t) is included by changing one constant (ϕ) into a variable (ϕ_t). Phi remains the 'reaction coefficient' because it still governs how entrepreneurs alter seedcorn depending on the value of the principal explanator of their investment behavior: the profitability gap. Now, however, the reaction coefficient varies with two of the three susceptibility determinants. The place of phi has been taken by an identical concept called the 'profit susceptibility constant' ($\sigma 1$). If seedcorn was not influenced by the gearing ratio then $\phi_t = \sigma 1$ would prevail.

According to Courvisanos (1996), however, d_t does influence investment, hence the need to introduce two extra concepts: the 'debt susceptibility constant' ($\sigma 2$) and d_0 as a 'normal' or 'acceptable' gearing ratio for farmers, this base-year, opening or initial value being consistent with tranquil stationary and steady states of growth.

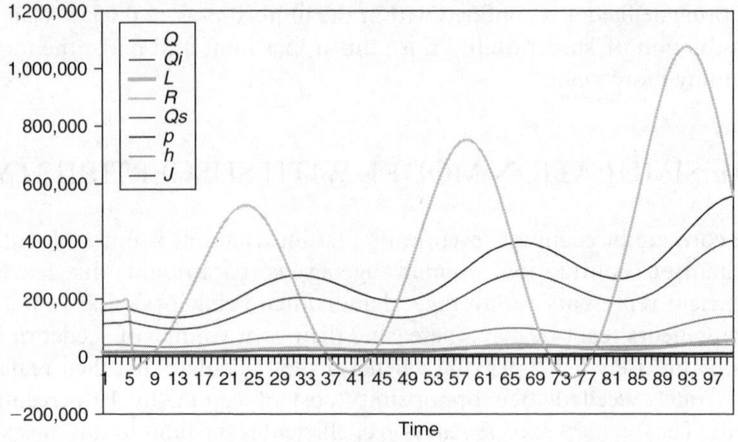

Figure 5.2 Cyclical state of growth – model with susceptibility

Here, then, is the equation for the new reaction coefficient, which now varies with the ratio of the normal to the actual gearing ratio:

$$\phi_t = \sigma 1 \times [d_0/(\sigma 2 \times d_t)].$$

Equivalently, this can be recast as

$$\phi_\tau = (\sigma 1 \times d_0)/(\sigma 2 \times d_t). \quad (5H)$$

When equation (5H) is inserted into the baseline model without susceptibility and the new parameters are set to

$$\sigma 1 = 0.6758$$

(that is, deliberately greater than the $\phi = 0.6558$ value, above which the previous model collapses) and to

$$\sigma 2 = 1.1$$

(that is, an arbitrary value), the graph shown in Figure 5.1 now looks like Figure 5.2.

One can see that the simulation model with susceptibility remains viable, due to its having a variable reaction coefficient whose value (when it was a constant) never could be set above its own upper viability limit of 0.6558.

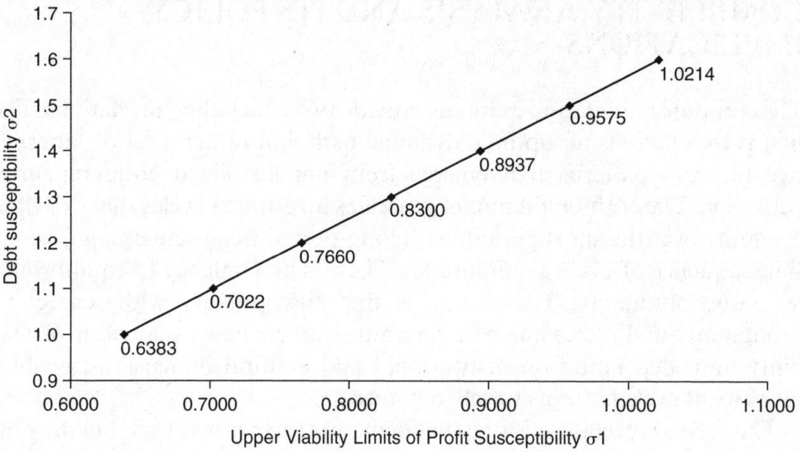

Figure 5.3 Upper limits of the corn-credit economy's viability: model with susceptibility

The closely related profit susceptibility constant which replaced it was deliberately set higher at 0.6758 and, in fact, a numerical analysis experiment has verified that it could even have gone as high as 0.7022 before the corn-credit economy became unviable. Clearly the influence of debt susceptibility has ameliorated (though not completely solved) the problem identified in Richardson (2002).

From equation (5H) – and the above result – a linear trade-off exists between the two susceptibility constants. Figure 5.3 shows that as the farmers' susceptibility to debt ($\sigma 2$) increases, so their susceptibility to profit ($\sigma 1$) can rise without destroying their economy's viability. However this rising of $\sigma 2$ (representing 'fear of debt') which ameliorates ever-higher $\sigma 1$ (representing 'greed for profit') has important public policy implications outlined below.

It remains to be shown whether incorporating 'Utilization Susceptibility' will expand the corn-credit economy's corridor of viability beyond the present model's limits. Adding a measure of capacity utilization to the right-hand side of equation (5H) – together with a new utilization susceptibility constant ($\sigma 3$) – would settle the question. However, this presupposes a massive expansion of the corn-credit model to introduce stocks and flows of fixed capital equipment, together with invention and innovation. In Courvisanos and Richardson (2003), the authors have begun moving in that direction and plan to incorporate all aspects of susceptibility: profitability, gearing ratio and capacity utilization.

COMPLEXITY ANALYSIS AND ITS POLICY IMPLICATIONS

The computer simulation exercises provide two concluding revelations. The first is that there is no optimal dynamic path, but rather a set of 'alternative futures': patterns that emerge from unconstrained entrepreneurial behaviors. The corn-credit model generates investment cycles that drive the economy over the short period, with long-period trends emerging from its time sequence of cyclical amplitudes. There is no tendency to equilibrium, let alone optimality. The second is that susceptibility with respect to profitability and increasing risk determines an economy's corridor of viability and, depending on institutional and cultural dimensions, enables investment cycle patterns to self-organize.

The second revelation is one that demands further research, building on the conclusions from the first revelation. As a starting point, some broad public and private sector policy implications can be suggested.

Public Policy Implications

Planning and regulatory public agencies should recognize the role that susceptibility can play in keeping the corridor of viability narrow enough to ensure there are no major inflation bubbles and deep recessions, originating from large amplitudes in business cycles driven by excessive investment instability. This is the first major aim of macroeconomic policy. The 'irrational exuberance' experienced in major capitalist economies of the late 1980s and the late 1990s (particularly the USA) are both examples where $\sigma 1$ was increasing at an alarming rate, with financial institutions adopting lending policies that enticed corporations to lower their 'fear of debt' (or $\sigma 2$) on the back of unsustainably rising share prices. This type of behavior stretches susceptibility outside the corridor of viability, with drastic consequences that could be ameliorated by public regulation.

There must, however, be sufficient instability in the investment cycle to engender creative imagination through profitable and productive innovations. This will also have a 'release valve effect' so that catastrophic outside-the-corridor exuberance does not occur. Adolph Lowe's work on 'Instrumental Analysis' provides the framework to construct such a policy regime (see Forstater, 1999). Lowe expressed the desire for investment to be 'regularised' by public policy rather than 'stabilised' (Lowe, 1954, p. 318). This forms the second major aim of macroeconomic policy, ensuring that the evolution of the economy be consistent with cyclical growth paths that are developed through Instrumental Analysis.

Private Policy Implications

Corporations need to adopt strategic innovation and investment policies to cope with the uncertainty that arises from investment susceptibility and take advantage of the susceptibility of competing firms. Successful introduction of major innovations through new technology systems '. . . make [s] the economy less vulnerable to depression' (Schmidt, 1954, p. 342) due to the amelioration of susceptibility. This approach can begin by applying the firm resource-based analysis of Penrose (1959) to the recent literature on strategic innovation by writers like Peter Drucker, Michael Porter and Zoltan Acs.

Equitable market reform and the dynamics of strategic innovation are but two implications of complexity analysis using the susceptibility concept. There is a vast new landscape of complexity science that needs to be used in a Post Keynesian world and the explorations in this chapter are but a small step in this direction.

NOTES

1. The authors would like to express their gratitude to the editor for helpful comments that have clarified important points in this chapter.
2. See Baddeley (2003) for a critical exposition of mainstream neo-classical investment theory and an outline of the alternative Post Keynesian investment analyses.
3. For an exposition of Basil Moore's views on complex economic dynamics, see Moore (1999).
4. Shackle (1970, p. 111) describes how entrepreneurs make future-oriented investment decisions in the context of their imagination of 'what *can* happen' rather than 'what *will* happen'. The nonlinear dynamic model by Courvisanos and Richardson (2003) features innovation and fixed capital accumulation, so this chapter concentrates on susceptibility with respect to investment in circulating capital only.
5. Freeman (1982, pp. 149–52) outlines the technical and market uncertainties that emerge from innovation. The degree of this innovative uncertainty depends on the level of change involved in the innovation process.
6. Prior to this point of inflection high up on the S-shaped cyclical upswing, increasing investment leads to higher capacity utilization as generally acknowledged in Post Keynesian models.
7. The particular steady state generated is Joan Robinson's famous 'Golden Age' of high investment, good profits, full employment, remunerative wages and zero inflation. She also mentioned that this name was adopted because of its strong associations with Greek mythology. See Robinson (1964).

REFERENCES

Baddeley, M. (2003) *Investment Theories and Analysis*, Basingstoke, UK and New York, US: Palgrave Macmillan.

Courvisanos, J. (1996) *Investment Cycles in Capitalist Economies: A Kaleckian Behavioural Contribution*, Cheltenham, UK and Brookfield, USA: Edward Elgar.
Courvisanos, J. and C. Richardson (2003) 'A Nonlinear Dynamic Model of Innovation and Capital Accumulation: A Post-Keynesian, Neo-Austrian and Evolutionary Approach', presented at the International Confederation of Associations for Pluralism in Economics (ICAPE) Conference, University of Missouri, Kansas City, 5–7 June.
Coveney, P. and R. Highfield (1995) *Frontiers of Complexity: The Search for Order in a Chaotic World*, New York: Fawcett Columbine.
Dixit, A. (1992), 'Investment and Hysteresis', *Journal of Economic Perspectives*, 6(1), Winter, 107–32.
Dixit, A. and R. Pindyck (1994) *Investment under Uncertainty*, Princeton: Princeton University Press.
Forstater, M. (1999) 'Working Backwards: Instrumental Analysis as a Policy Discovery Procedure', *Review of Political Economy*, 11(1), 5–18.
Freeman, C. (1982) *The Economics of Industrial Innovation*, 2nd edition, London: Frances Pinter.
Goodwin, R. (1987) 'Macrodynamics', in R. Goodwin and L. Punzo, *The Dynamics of a Capitalist Economy: A Multi-sectoral Approach*, Cambridge: Polity Press, 1–160.
Hansen, A. (1964) *Business Cycles and National Income*, expanded edition, London: Allen & Unwin.
Harcourt, G.C. (1963) 'A Critique of Mr. Kaldor's Model of Income Distribution and Growth', *Australian Economic Papers*, 1(1), 20–26.
Kalecki, M. (1939) *Essays in the Theory of Economic Fluctuations*, London: Allen & Unwin. Reprinted in J. Osiatyński (ed.) (1990), *Collected Works of Michal Kalecki, Volume I: Capitalism – Business Cycles and Full Employment*, Oxford: Clarendon Press, 233–318.
Laramie, A., D. Mair and A. Miller (2004) 'Kalecki's Investment Theory Reconsidered', in Z. Sadowski and A. Szeworski (eds), *Kalecki's Economics Today*, London: Routledge, 143–61.
Lawson, T. (1997) *Critical Realism*, London: Macmillan.
Lowe, A. (1954), 'Comment', in National Bureau of Economic Research, *Regularization of Business Investment*, Princeton: Princeton University Press, 318.
Marx, K. (1867) *Capital: A Critique of Political Economy, Volume I*, reprinted (1954), Moscow: Progress Publishers.
Moore, B.J. (1988) 'The Endogenous Money Supply', *Journal of Post Keynesian Economics*, 10(3), Spring, 479–87.
Moore, B.J. (1999) 'Economics and Complexity', in M. Setterfield (ed.), *Growth, Employment and Inflation: Essays in Honour of John Cornwall*, London: Macmillan and New York: St Martin's Press, 41–56.
O'Donnell, R.M. (1989) *Keynes: Philosophy, Economics and Politics*, London: Macmillan.
Penrose, E. (1959) *The Theory of the Growth of the Firm*, Oxford: Basil Blackwell.
Richardson, C.L. (2002) 'The Traverses of a Post-Keynesian Model of a Corn-Credit Economy', Unpublished Ph.D. Thesis, Hobart: University of Tasmania.
Richardson, C.L. (2004) 'The Corn-Credit Economy', paper presented to the Scottish Economic Society Conference, March 2004, Perth, Scotland.
Robinson, J. (1956) *The Accumulation of Capital*, London: Macmillan.

Robinson, J. (1964) *Essays in the Theory of Economic Growth*, London: Macmillan.
Runde, J. (1991) 'Keynesian Uncertainty and the Instability of Beliefs', *Review of Political Economy*, 3(2), 125–45.
Schmidt, E. (1954) 'Promoting Steadier Output and Sales', in National Bureau of Economic Research, *Regularization of Business Investment*, Princeton: Princeton University Press, 319–68.
Schumpeter, J. (1939) *Business Cycles; A Theoretical, Historical and Statistical Analysis of the Capitalist Process*, 2 vols, New York: McGraw-Hill.
Shackle, G.L.S. (1970) *Expectations, Enterprise and Profit: The Theory of the Firm*, London: Allen & Unwin.
Waldrop, M. (1992) *Complexity: The Emerging Science at the Edge of Order and Chaos*, New York: Simon & Schuster.
Zarnowitz, V. (1973) 'Recent Work on Business Cycles in Historical Perspective: A Review of Theories and Evidence', *Journal of Economic Literature*, 23, June, 523–80.

APPENDIX: REDUCED FORM OF THE MODEL WITHOUT SUSCEPTIBILITY

Corn Produced	$Q = \theta Qio$	sacks p.a.	(5A′)
Seedcorn	$Qi = [1 - \phi\{io - \delta - [(\theta - 1)Qio - Qso]/(Qio + Qso/\kappa) + \varepsilon\delta\theta^2 Qio^2/\eta\lambda^2\mu doKo + \delta\theta(wo - \varepsilon + \rho gpo)Qio/\lambda\mu doKo - \varphi\}]\, Qio$	sacks p.a.	(5B′)
Employment	$L = \theta Qio/\lambda$	fieldhands	(5C′)
Realized Profit Rate	$r = ((\theta - 1)Qio - Qso)/[(Qio + Qso)/\kappa]$	per cent p.a.	(5D′)
Corn Price	$P = [\theta Qio\{\varepsilon\theta Qio + \eta\lambda(wo - \varepsilon + \rho gpo)\}\, \{\varepsilon\delta\theta^2 Qio^2 + \eta\lambda^2\mu(io - \delta + \mu)doKo + \eta\lambda\delta\theta(wo - \varepsilon + \rho gpo)Qio\}]/\eta^2\lambda^4\mu^2 doKoQso$	dollars/sack	(5E′)
Money Wage	$w = wo + \varepsilon(\theta Qio/\lambda\eta - 1) + \rho gpo$	\$/worker p.a.	(5F′)
Interest Rate	$i = [\varepsilon\delta\theta^2 Qio^2 + \eta\lambda^2\mu(io - \delta)doKo + \eta\lambda\delta\theta(wo - \varepsilon + \rho gpo)Qio]/\eta\lambda^2\mu doKo$	per cent p.a.	(5G′)

The Wolfram Research program suite Mathematica was used to derive this reduced form of the model without susceptibility.

Time subscripts have been omitted for improved readability, with the letter '*o*' in lower case indicating a 'one-year lagged' variable, for example, Qi_t is now simply Qi, while Qi_{t-1} is now Qio.

Please note that lagged seedcorn (Qio) appears on the right-hand side of all seven reduced-form equations.

6. Effective demand and endogenous money in a path-dependent economy: towards a 'Moorian' credit supply curve – and a reconciliation between horizontalists and structuralists?

Mark Setterfield[1]

INTRODUCTION

This chapter builds on three of the central themes in Basil Moore's macroeconomics: the absence of a fixed point towards which the economy automatically and inevitably tends; the importance of the credit-creation process, through which the money supply expands endogenously in order to finance the growth of nominal income; and the notion that aggregate economic activity is demand determined. It does so by modelling the level of economic activity in the short run as an evolutionary sequence of outcomes arising from the debt-financed expansion of autonomous demand, in the context of a 'shifting equilibrium' model of effective demand.[2]

The resulting model sheds light on a fourth important theme in Basil Moore's macroeconomics – the shape of the credit supply schedule. As is well known, this theme has become the topic of a vexed debate between horizontalists and structuralists. The model developed in this chapter is based on an essentially horizontalist conception of the credit supply process. But it is shown that, under certain circumstances, it is possible to recover from the model a credit supply schedule that is an upward-sloping step function. This credit supply schedule can be derived only *ex post*, however, as the product of a precise historical sequence of changes in aggregate income and commercial banks' discretionary responses to these changes. Indeed, the resulting credit supply schedule need not be upward-sloping at all. As a result, it is suggested that an important step towards reconciling horizontalism and structuralism – or at least narrowing the differences between these competing strands of Post Keynesian monetary theory – involves regarding as misguided any attempt to theorise *the* credit supply schedule as either upward-sloping or horizontal on an *a priori* basis. Instead, we can only be sure that *a* credit supply schedule – what is ultimately described as a dynamic or 'Moorian' credit supply schedule – that may be either horizontal or an upward-sloping step function, will emerge as a path-dependent product of the recursive interaction of the financial and industrial/household sectors over the course of the cycle.

The remainder of the chapter is organized as follows. In the next section, the model of effective demand on which the chapter is based is outlined. The third section postulates changes in the financial fragility of the non-bank private sector as nominal income expands, and examines the possible responses of commercial banks to these changes. The implications of commercial bank behavior for the shape of the credit supply schedule are investigated in the fourth section. Finally, the fifth section offers some conclusions.

A 'SHIFTING EQUILIBRIUM' MODEL OF EFFECTIVE DEMAND

The Determination of Nominal Income

The basic model of effective demand on which this chapter is based can be stated as follows:

$$Z_t = kWN_t \tag{6.1}$$

$$kWN_t = Y^e \tag{6.2}$$

$$D_t = E_t + a_t \tag{6.3}$$

$$E_t = \gamma Z_t, \quad 0 < \gamma < 1 \tag{6.4}$$

$$a_t = \phi A_t, \quad 0 < \phi < 1 \tag{6.5}$$

$$A_t = A(r_t, e(\alpha_t)), \quad A_r < 0, A_e > 0, e' > 0 \tag{6.6}$$

$$Z_t \equiv D_t \tag{6.7}$$

where Z is the value of aggregate supply, k is a constant, W is the (given) nominal wage, N is the level of employment, Y^e denotes firms' short-run expectations of nominal income, D is the value of aggregate demand, E denotes endogenous components of aggregate demand, a is realized autonomous spending, A denotes planned autonomous spending, r is the commercial interest rate, α represents the state of long-run expectations

(SOLE) and ϕ is the proportion of the notional demand for credit that commercial banks are willing to satisfy and hence render effective. Equations (6.1) and (6.2) describe aggregate supply as a function of firms' short-run expectations, while in equation (6.3), aggregate demand is described as the sum of endogenous and realized autonomous components of expenditure. Equation (6.4) is the endogenous expenditure function, while equation (6.6) describes *planned* autonomous spending as a function of the commercial rate of interest and a shift parameter that depends on the SOLE. It is assumed that all autonomous spending is financed by the creation of new credit, so that planned autonomous spending is equivalent to the notional demand for credit, and realized autonomous spending is equivalent to the effective demand for credit. Hence equation (6.5) which, given the definition of ϕ, describes the relationship between planned and realized autonomous spending. Finally, equation (6.7) implies that the realized value of nominal income is always determined on the demand side. In other words, even if short-run expectations are disappointed in any given period (so that $Y_t^e = Z_t \neq D_t$), aggregate supply adjusts to aggregate demand within the period via inventory and/or price adjustments (so that within any given period, $Z_t \equiv D_t$ *ex post*). This is consistent with the methodology of open systems modelling on which subsequent sections of this chapter are based, in which 'behavior that is seen as occurring simultaneously in each period must be uniquely resolved in some way in a closed submodel valid only at that moment while, at the same time, the overall model itself necessarily remains open to allow for the unforeseen novelty that the future hides' (Katzner, 1998, p. 266). The sense in which the model that is being developed here remains open will be made clear in what follows.

Combining (6.1), (6.4), (6.5), (6.6) and (6.3), we find that:

$$D_t = \gamma kWN_t + \phi A(r_t, e(\alpha_t)) \tag{6.8}$$

The determination of nominal income at any point in time by means of equations (6.1), (6.2), (6.7) and (6.8) is summarized in Figure 6.1, where Y_0^e has been arbitrarily chosen to conform to the case where short-run expectations are disappointed such that $Y_0^e = Z_0 < D_0 = Y_0$ in some initial period 0 (as a result of which the model is not in the equilibrium depicted at (N^*, Y^*) in Figure 6.1).

The Financial Sector

The behavior of the financial sector is described as follows:

$$a = \phi A(r_t, e(\alpha_t)) \tag{6.9}$$

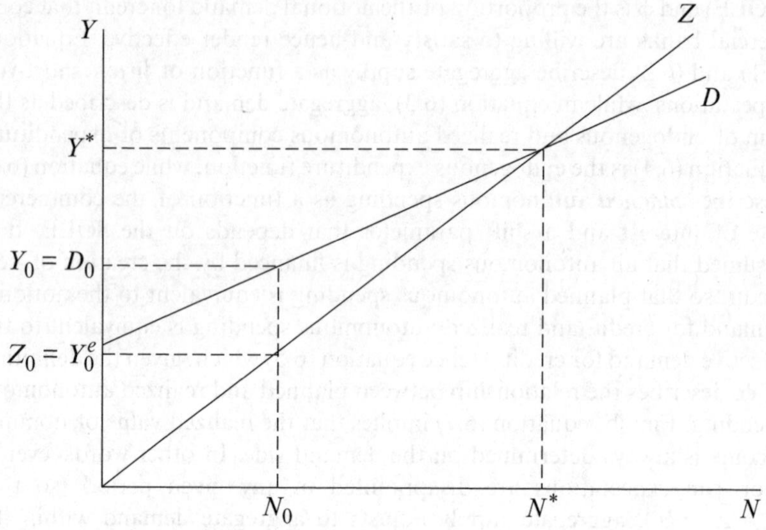

Figure 6.1 The determination of nominal income when short-run expectations are disappointed

$$r_t = (1 + \tau)\delta_t \tag{6.10}$$

$$\delta_t = \overline{\delta} \tag{6.11}$$

where τ is the commercial bank mark-up (initially taken as given), δ is the central bank discount rate and all other variables are as previously defined. As discussed above, equation (6.9) (which results from a combination of (6.5) and (6.6)) constitutes the effective demand for credit. Meanwhile, substituting (6.11) into (6.10) yields:

$$r_t = \overline{r} = (1 + \tau)\overline{\delta} \tag{6.12}$$

which is the (horizontal) credit supply schedule. Since the values of both ϕ and τ are taken as given in (6.9) and (6.12), it is evident that the model of the financial sector developed here is one of 'pure accommodationism', in which the behavior of the financial sector is altogether unaffected by the income-generating process described in the previous sub-section.[3]

Expectations

The basic model is completed by a description of how short-run expectations and the SOLE are determined. Short-run expectations are described as follows:

$$Y_t^e = Y^e(D_{t-1}, \beta) \tag{6.13}$$

where β denotes subjective influences on short-run expectations and all other variables are as previously defined. For the sake of simplicity, we assume $Y_D^e = 1$ and $Y_\beta^e = 0$, so that short-run expectations can be described according to the simple adaptive rule:[4]

$$Y_t^e = D_{t-1} \tag{6.14}$$

Meanwhile, revision of the SOLE is described by the following reaction function:

$$\alpha_t = f_t(D_{t-1}, Z_{t-1}) = \begin{cases} \alpha_{t-1} + \varepsilon_t & \text{if } D_{t-1} - Z_{t-1} \geq c \\ \alpha_{t-1} & \text{if } |D_{t-1} - Z_{t-1}| < c \\ \alpha_{t-1} - \varepsilon_t & \text{if } D_{t-1} - Z_{t-1} \leq -c \end{cases} \tag{6.15}$$

where $\varepsilon_t \sim (\mu_{\varepsilon t}, \sigma^2_{\varepsilon t})$, $\varepsilon_t > 0\ \forall t$ and c is a constant. Equation (6.15) describes the process by which the SOLE is revised in response to the disappointment of short-run expectations.[5] The variable ε is drawn from a distribution with time-dependent moments, in which the mean, μ, represents the modal or *conventional* response to any disappointment of short-run expectations exceeding the magnitude c.[6] The variance σ^2 is non-zero, denoting that conventional behaviors are not absolutely binding. In other words, it is possible for decision-makers to deviate from conventional behavior without this deviance undermining the convention on which their behavior is routinely based.

It is expected that the value μ will be relatively enduring (that is, it may remain constant for a number of consecutive periods), but that it is ultimately subject to change over time. Moreover, by hypothesis, this process of change is not amenable to description in terms of a structurally stable equation of motion, or as the result of a draw from a distribution of conventions with time-invariant moments. These assumptions are consistent with the idea that the system we are modelling is an *open* system, in which choice can produce novelty and the future is fundamentally uncertain, in the sense that it is not possible for decision-makers to know all possible future outcomes and/or their probabilities of occurrence.[7]

Shifting Equilibrium

If we now combine equation (6.8) with (6.2), (6.12) and (6.14), we arrive at:

$$D_t = \gamma D_{t-1} + \phi A(\bar{r}, e(\alpha_t)) \tag{6.16}$$

or:

$$D_t = \gamma^t D_0 + \phi \sum_{i=1}^{t} \gamma^{t-i} A(\bar{r}, e(\alpha_i)) \tag{6.17}$$

Given equation (6.7), equations (6.15) and (6.17) suffice to describe a shifting equilibrium model of effective demand, in which short-run expectations are generally disappointed and the SOLE is non-constant and influenced by the disappointment of short-run expectations. In this model, aggregate economic activity can be thought of as an evolutionary sequence of outcomes arising from the recursive interaction of short- and long-term expectations. Note that the potential time paths of the resulting model of shifting equilibrium will 'consist of sequences of realized points whose components . . . [cannot] be predicted in advance of their realization . . . [since they] cannot generally be characterized in advance by single equations or sets of equations because the equations themselves are not stable across time' (Katzner, 1998, p. 374). But this does not make the model nihilistic – certain general properties of its potential time paths can be inferred. To see this, suppose that the situation in Figure 6.1 is such that $D_0 - Z_0 = k_0 \geq c$. Under these conditions, we will have $\alpha_1 = \alpha_0 + \varepsilon_1 > \alpha_0$ by (6.15). It is clear from equation (6.8) that this will cause an increase in aggregate demand, shifting the aggregate demand schedule in Figure 6.1 upwards. Meanwhile, equations (6.1), (6.2) and (6.14) ensure that there will be a simultaneous increase in the aggregate quantity supplied, moving the economy along the aggregate supply schedule in Figure 6.1. As a result of these adjustments, the economy will experience the aggregate outcomes depicted in Figure 6.2. Note that, as depicted in Figure 6.2, the economy is not simply converging towards a fixed-point equilibrium. Instead, the conditions and hence the position of equilibrium (which in period 1 is found at (N^{**}, Y^{**}) in Figure 6.2) are being redefined by the very adjustments of the economy towards it – hence the notion of a 'shifting equilibrium' model of effective demand.

In order to further examine the time path of the economy, we need to know whether or not the new disequilibrium outcome depicted in Figure 6.2 is such that:

$$D_1 - Z_1 \geq c = (D_0 - Z_0) - k_0 + c$$

or:

$$\Delta D_1 - \Delta Z_1 \geq -(k_0 - c)$$

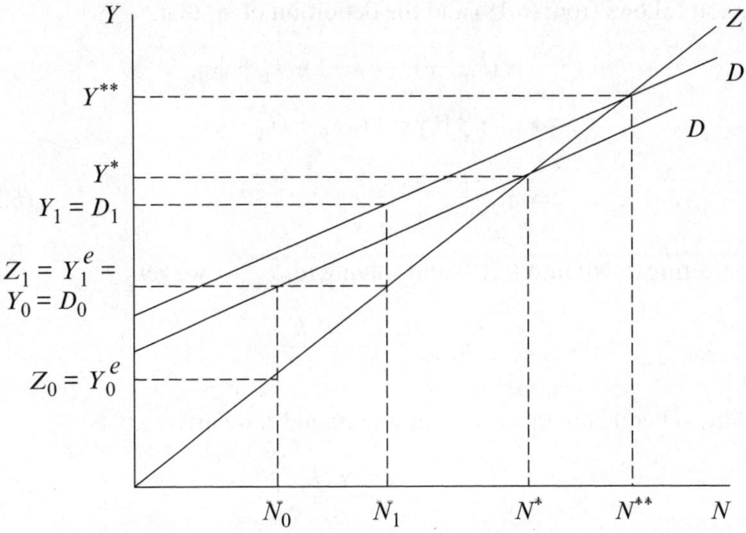

Figure 6.2 The shifting equilibrium model of effective demand

Given (6.1), it follows from (6.8) that:

$$\Delta D_1 = \gamma(Z_1 - Z_0) + \phi \,.\, A_e \,.\, e' \,.\, \varepsilon_1$$

where $A_c \,.\, e' = \delta A/\delta\alpha$ and $d\alpha_1 = \varepsilon_1$ by hypothesis. Since $Z_1 = D_0$ by combination of (6.1), (6.2) and (6.14) and $D_0 - Z_0 = k_0$ by hypothesis, we can write:

$$\Delta Z_1 = D_0 - Z_0 = k_0$$

Combining these results, it follows that:

$$\Delta D_1 - \Delta Z_1 = (\gamma - 1) \,.\, k_0 + \phi \,.\, A_e \,.\, e' \,.\, \varepsilon_1 \qquad (6.18)$$

Now define the variable η_1 as:

$$\eta_1 = A_e \,.\, e' \,.\, \varepsilon_{1\,\min} \qquad (6.19)$$

where η_1 represents the minimum change in planned autonomous spending necessary to satisfy the condition $D_1 - Z_1 \geq c$. Since this latter condition can be rewritten as $\Delta D_1 - \Delta Z_1 \geq -(k_0 - c)$ as demonstrated above, it follows from (6.18) and the definition of η_1 that:

$$- (k_0 - c) = (\gamma - 1) \,.\, k_0 + \phi\eta_1$$

$$\Rightarrow \eta_1 - \frac{1}{\phi}[(\gamma - 1) \,.\, k_0 + (k_0 - c)]$$

$$\Rightarrow \eta_1 = \frac{c - \gamma \,.\, k_0}{\phi} \tag{6.20}$$

Substituting (6.20) into (6.19) and solving for $\varepsilon_{1\ \min}$, we get:

$$\varepsilon_{1\ \min} = \frac{c - \gamma \,.\, k_0}{\phi \,.\, A_e \,.\, e'}$$

Finally, generalizing this result for any period t, we arrive at:

$$\varepsilon_{t\ \min} = \frac{c - \gamma \,.\, k_{t-1}}{\phi \,.\, A_e \,.\, e'} \tag{6.21}$$

Note that the value of $\varepsilon_{t\ \min}$ in (6.21) is path dependent – it is defined in terms of the exogenous givens c, γ, ϕ, A_e and e^l, *and* the *historical* given k_{t-1}, which is a product of the prior adjustment path of the economy. Utilizing (6.21), we can conclude that self-reinforcing tendencies in nominal income will emerge and persist if $|D_0 - Z_0| \geq c$ initially, and the following conditions apply:

$$\varepsilon_t \geq \frac{c - \gamma \,.\, k_{t-1}}{\phi \,.\, A_e \,.\, e'} = \varepsilon_{t\ \min} \quad \forall t \geq 1 \tag{6.22}$$

Under these conditions, the economy is in a perpetual state of motion of the type depicted in Figure 6.2, simultaneously chasing and changing the position of a stationary state equilibrium that it never 'gets into'. This results from the fact that movement towards the stationary state redefines the conditions and hence position of this equilibrium, pushing it further away from the current level of income even as the latter ostensibly adjusts towards its equilibrium value.

FINANCIAL FRAGILITY AND THE RESPONSE OF COMMERCIAL BANKS

As previously intimated, the model developed thus far embodies 'pure accommodationism', according to which financial sector behavior is unaffected by the cumulative expansions (or contractions) of nominal income that it helps to facilitate through the debt financing of autonomous spending by households and firms. But suppose that we now define the variable F to denote an index of the non-bank private sector's financial fragility.[8] Suppose further that:

$$F_t = g_t(D_{t-1}), \quad g_t' > 0 \tag{6.23}$$

that is, that F is increasing in nominal income,[9] and:

$$F_t^* = h_t(D_{t-1}), \quad g_t' > h_t' > 0 \tag{6.24}$$

where F_t^* is the maximum value of F_t that is acceptable to commercial banks at any point in time.

In other words, we assume that commercial banks' tolerance of non-bank private sector financial fragility is *also* increasing in nominal income, but at a slower rate. This is designed to capture a fundamental asymmetry between households and firms on one hand, and commercial banks on the other. Hence the future earnings of firms, for example, are innately dependent on investments in long-term projects subject to fundamental uncertainty, whereas banks can earn income through means other than financing the acquisition of industrial capital. As a result, a difference between the conventions or *cultures* of the non-bank and banking sectors is postulated, according to which the latter is assumed to be more inclined towards a culture of prudence than the former, where a greater acceptance of exposure to uncertainty is likely to prevail. Another way of putting this is as follows: the financial sector is assumed to have an intrinsically higher *liquidity preference* than the non-financial sector.[10]

Equations (6.23) and (6.24) are illustrated in Figure 6.3, wherein the functions $g_t(.)$ and $h_t(.)$ have been linearized for ease of exposition. The simple but important point that emerges from Figure 6.3 is that as nominal income expands, we eventually reach a level of income at which the financial fragility of the non-bank private sector is unacceptable to commercial banks (at least at the current rate of interest).

How might these developments modify commercial banks' behavior? The following commercial bank reaction function mimics the structure of the SOLE reaction function introduced earlier:

$$\tau_t = \tau_t(F_t, F_t^*) = \begin{cases} \tau_{t-1} + \nu_t & \text{if } F_t > F_{t-1} \wedge F_t > F_t^* \\ \tau_{t-1} - \nu_t & \text{if } F_t < F_{t-1} \wedge F_t < F_t^* \\ \tau_{t-1} & \text{otherwise} \end{cases} \tag{6.25}$$

where $\nu_t \sim (\mu_{\nu t}, \sigma^2_{\nu t})$, $\nu_t \geq 0\ \forall t$. According to equation (6.25), commercial banks will increase (decrease) their mark-ups over time, in a manner that

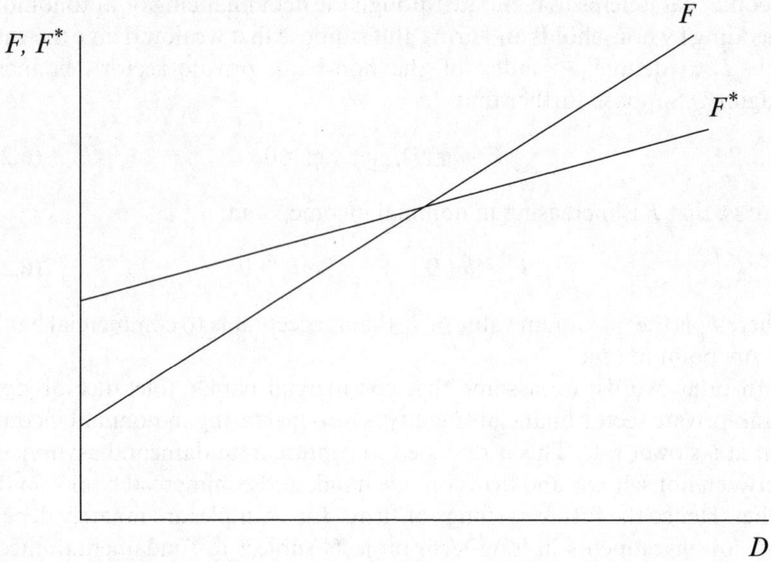

Figure 6.3 The relationships between F, F and D*

involves discretionary choice, if private sector financial fragility is increasing (decreasing) *and* exceeds (is less than) the maximum level acceptable to commercial banks in the current period.[11]

IMPLICATIONS FOR THE EVOLUTION OF NOMINAL INCOME AND THE SHAPE OF THE CREDIT SUPPLY CURVE

We can now consider the behavior of our model of effective demand as modified by the introduction of the commercial bank reaction function described in (6.25). The reduced form of the basic model can now be written as:

$$D_t = \gamma D_{t-1} + \phi \,.\, A(r_t, e(\alpha_t)) \tag{6.16a}$$

or:

$$D_t = \gamma^t D_0 + \phi \,.\, \sum_{i=1}^{t} \gamma^{t-i} \,.\, A(r_i, e(\alpha_i)) \tag{6.17a}$$

where $r_t = (1 + \tau_t)\bar{\delta}$. Given equation (6.7), equation (6.17a), together with the behavior of F and F^* as described in (6.23) and (6.24) and the reaction functions in equations (6.15) and (6.25), now suffices to describe the evolution of nominal income in accordance with the principles of a shifting equilibrium model of effective demand.

Suppose, then, that $F_0^* < F_0$ and $D_0 - Z_0 \geq c$ initially, and that subsequently:

$$\varepsilon_t \geq \frac{c - \gamma \,.\, k_{t-1}}{\phi \,.\, A_e \,.\, e'} \quad \forall t = 1, \ldots, n-1$$

In other words, the economy is in the midst of a cumulative expansion in nominal income. Suppose, further, that whereas:

$$g_{n-1}(D_{n-2}) = F_{n-1} < F_{n-1}^* = h_{n-1}(D_{n-2})$$

we have:

$$g_n(D_{n-1}) = F_n > F_n^* = h_n(D_{n-1})$$

in some period n. Note that what this implies is that in period n, both of the criteria for a potential increase in the mark-up, τ, as described in equation (6.25), are satisfied. Hence in this period, the economy will be influenced by an improvement in the SOLE (which, *ceteris paribus*, will raise planned autonomous spending) and a potential increase in commercial banks' mark-ups over the discount rate. If $\nu > 0$ so that mark-ups do rise, this will reduce planned autonomous spending, *ceteris paribus*. The question that then arises is, under what conditions would we observe:

$$\begin{aligned} &D_n - Z_n \geq c \\ &\Rightarrow \Delta D_n - \Delta Z_n \geq -(k_{n-1} - c) \end{aligned}$$

that is, the conditions necessary for continuation of the current expansion, and under what conditions would we observe:

$$\begin{aligned} &D_n - Z_n \leq -c \\ &\Rightarrow \Delta D_n - \Delta Z_n \leq -(k_{n-1} + c) \end{aligned}$$

that is, the conditions necessary for the onset of a contraction?

Setterfield (2004) shows that there exists a value $\nu_{n\ \min}$ – that is, a minimum increase in the mark-up, τ – that is consistent with the conditions necessary for the onset of a contraction, but that there also exists a $\nu_{n\ \max}$ –

that is, a maximum increase in the mark-up, τ – that is consistent with the conditions necessary for continuation of the current expansion, given by:

$$v_{n\,\max} = \frac{c - \gamma k_{n-1} - \phi \,.\, A_e \,.\, e' \,.\, \varepsilon_n}{\phi \,.\, A_r \,.\, \delta} \tag{6.26}$$

In other words, $v_t \leq v_{t\,\max}$ for $t \geq n$ will result in a continuation of the current expansion, but this will be accompanied by progressive monetary tightening (that is, increases in τ and hence ever higher commercial interest rates) to the extent that we also observe $v_t > 0$. Let us now focus on this second scenario (where $0 \leq v_t \leq v_{t\,\max}$) and its implications for the shape of the credit supply schedule.

An enduring debate in Post Keynesian monetary theory concerns the precise nature of the endogenous money supply. Are changes in interest rates caused exclusively by changes in the discount rate by a central bank that is generally accommodating, or is the central bank non-accommodating, and do commercial banks adjust interest rates autonomously (that is, independently of changes in the discount rate)? The way in which these questions are answered can lead to differing conceptions of the credit supply schedule as either horizontal or upward sloping.

The following propositions can be identified with structuralist contributions to this debate:[12]

1. the financial structure of the private sector changes in the course of a boom
2. commercial banks react to this by changing commercial interest rates independently of changes in the discount rate
3. the credit supply schedule is therefore upward sloping in interest rate-quantity of credit space.

Horizontalists, meanwhile, are typically portrayed as questioning the first two of these propositions, with the result that the third is denied. But closer inspection reveals that what horizontalists seek to deny is the *inevitability* of increases in private sector financial fragility and/or increasing concern about this state of affairs on the part of lenders during the course of a boom, not the *possibility* of these events (see, for example, Lavoie, 1996, pp. 285–90).[13] On this reading, the horizontalist objection to the third proposition above seems to have as much to do with the 'history versus equilibrium' debate as it does with the niceties of monetary theory. Specifically, the third proposition can be understood as objectionable because it postulates something akin to a long-run equilibrium construct. The notion that the credit supply schedule can be conceived as upward sloping *a priori* involves postulating mechanical (and therefore predictable) changes in the financial structure of the non-bank private sector and similarly mechanical (and predictable) responses of the financial sector to these changes. This, in turn, involves a level of determinism that seems at odds with the open-systems ontology of fundamental uncertainty that is central to Post Keynesianism. Reinterpreting the horizontalist versus structuralist debate in terms of the history versus equilibrium debate in this fashion certainly seems to be in keeping with Moore's (1988, p. 265) comment that the long-run money supply function should be regarded as undefined *a priori*.

What, if any, contribution to this suggested reinterpretation of the horizontalist versus structuralist debate is made by the shifting equilibrium model of effective demand developed earlier? The value of the model in this context is that it is possible to recover from it credit supply schedules that are neither structuralist nor horizontalist in the traditional, stylized sense, but are instead 'Moorian' in the sense that their precise shape remains undefined *a priori*. To see this, consider the example of the sort of credit supply schedule that can emerge from the model developed earlier in Figure 6.4.[14] Note that Figure 6.4 is drawn so as to correspond to the conditions observed during a cumulative expansion of nominal income accompanied by progressive monetary tightening. In other words, Figure 6.4 depicts the case where $D_t - Z_t \geq c\ \forall t$ and $0 < v_t \leq v_{max}\ \forall t \geq n$. Note also that, in keeping with our earlier assumptions about the financing of autonomous spending, $Q_t \equiv a_t$ denotes the quantity of new credit money created in any period t. Finally, Figure 6.4 assumes for simplicity the absence of any monetary reflux: each new effective demand for credit creates a corresponding net addition to the outstanding stock of credit in existence.

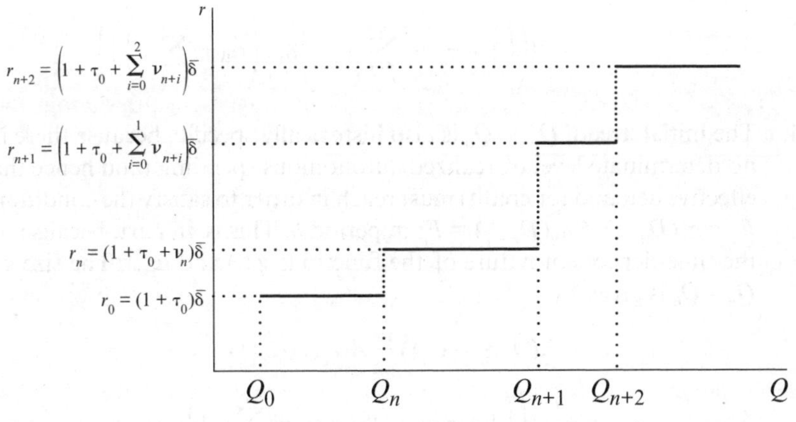

Figure 6.4 The 'Moorian' credit supply schedule: an example

The following remarks about the credit supply schedule depicted in Figure 6.4 are pertinent to the debate between structuralists and horizontalists and the claim that this schedule is Moorian:

1. Each point on the credit supply schedule in Figure 6.4 represents a point in historical time, at which a quantity of credit Q_t has been created to meet the total (effective) demand for credit $a_t = \phi \,.\, A(r_t, e(\alpha_t))$ in that period. Figure 6.4 is therefore drawn strictly *ex post* – it is not an *ex ante* description of what credit supply conditions *will be* in the future, but rather a description of *what they have been* in the recent past and *what they are* in the present. The credit supply schedule is, therefore, a historical construct. This claim is borne out by the observations that follow.
2. The size of each 'step' in Figure 6.4 is given by $\nu_t \,.\, \bar{\delta}$, $t \geq n$ and the slope of the credit supply schedule (were it to be linearized) at any point in time $t \geq n$ will depend on $\Sigma_{i=0}^{t-n}\nu_{n+i}$.[15] As is obvious, each of these magnitudes is historically specific. What is less obvious from Figure 6.4 but equally important to emphasize is that since $\nu_t = 0$ is consistent with the reaction function in (6.25), we may observe $\Sigma_{i=0}^{t-n}\nu_{n+i} = 0$, in which case the credit supply schedule will be *horizontal* up to period t.[16]
3. Each of the 'treads' $Q_t - Q_{t-1}$ $\forall t > n$ in Figure 6.4 is historically specific, given by:

$$a_t - a_{t-1} = \phi(A(r_t, e(\alpha_t)) - A(r_{t-1}, e(\alpha_{t-1})))$$

$$= \phi\left(A\left(\left(1 + \tau_0 + \sum_{i=0}^{t-n} \nu_{n+i}\right)\bar{\delta},\, e\left(\alpha_0 + \sum_{i=1}^{t} \varepsilon_i\right)\right)\right.$$

$$\left.- A\left(\left(1 + \tau_0 + \sum_{i=0}^{t-n-1} \nu_{n+i}\right)\bar{\delta},\, e\left(\alpha_0 + \sum_{i=1}^{t-1} \varepsilon_i\right)\right)\right)$$

4. The initial 'tread' $Q_n - Q_0$ is also historically specific, because there is no determinate level of realized autonomous spending (and hence the effective demand for credit) must reach in order to satisfy the condition $F_n = g_n(D_{n-1}) > h_n(D_{n-1}) = F_n^*$ in period n. This is, in part, because of the time-dependent nature of the functions $g_t(.)$ and $h_t(.)$. The size of $Q_n - Q_0$ is given by:

$$a_n - a_0 = \phi(A(r_n, e(\alpha_n)) - A(r_0, e(\alpha_0)))$$

$$= \phi\left(A\left(\left(1 + \tau_0 + \nu_n\right)\bar{\delta},\, e\left(\alpha_0 + \sum_{i=1}^{n} \varepsilon_i\right)\right)\right)$$

$$- A((1+\tau_0)\overline{\delta}, e(\alpha_0)))$$

Note, however, that, even if the functions $g(.)$ and $h(.)$ are *not* time-dependent (as, for example, in Figure 6.4), both the length of calendar time, n, that it takes for there to be an initial departure from the interest rate r_0, and the precise quantity of credit created when this occurs (Q_n) remain indeterminate – but are strictly inversely related to one another. To see this, suppose that:

$$F_1 = g(D_0) < h(D_0) = F_1^*$$

and define $\overline{D} > D_0$ as the smallest possible value of D necessary to satisfy:

$$\overline{F} = g(\overline{D}) > h(\overline{D}) = \overline{F}^*$$

Now suppose that:

$$D_n = E_n + a_n = \overline{D}$$
$$\Rightarrow D_n = \gamma D_{n-1} + \phi \,.\, A(r_0, e((\alpha_n)) = \overline{D}$$

Under the conditions of a cumulative expansion in nominal income (under which conditions Figure 6.4 is drawn), D_n is, of course, increasing in n,[17] so that γD_{n-1} is also increasing in n. It follows that:

$$\phi \,.\, A(r_0, e(\alpha_n)) - a_n = Q_n - \overline{D} - \gamma D_{n-1}$$

is *decreasing* in n, given that $\overline{D}$ is fixed.

The intuition behind this result is straightforward. Because income and hence endogenous components of aggregate demand are increasing over time, and because $\overline{D}$ is a fixed magnitude, the longer (in calendar time) that the economy takes to reach $\overline{D}$, the more of this target level of income will be accounted for by endogenously generated expenditures and the less by autonomous expenditures. And since autonomous expenditures are responsible for credit creation, it follows that the larger is n, the smaller will be the value of Q_n relative to Q_0 in Figure 6.4.

What is the significance of these remarks for the debate between structuralists and horizontalists? What has been shown above is that, assuming that there *are* changes in the financial structure of the private sector in the course of a boom (the first of the three structuralist propositions identified earlier), commercial banks *may* react to this by changing their mark-ups and the credit supply schedule *may* be an upward-sloping step function, independently of central bank interventions. But if this schedule is not horizontalist, neither is it structuralist: the credit supply schedule in Figure 6.4 is, instead, 'Moorian'. It is a historical artefact that can be derived only *ex post*, as the product of a particular historical sequence of changes in aggregate income. As has been explicitly demonstrated above, *every* aspect of the credit supply schedule depicted in Figure 6.4 is path dependent including its slope, which may, in fact, be horizontal. What all this suggests is a basis for moving towards some reconciliation between horizontalists and structuralists by reinterpreting the differences between these schools in terms of the history versus equilibrium debate. As explicitly demonstrated in the context of a shifting equilibrium model of effective demand, this allows us to conceive the credit supply schedule as an inherently dynamic construct that is neither strictly horizontal nor upward sloping in the traditional sense, but is instead Moorian – that is, *either* upward sloping *or* horizontal, but with a precise slope that is undefined *a priori*.

A second significant feature of the preceding analysis is its bearing on the idea that a horizontal credit supply schedule is a special case (geometry alone dictating that there can be only one horizontal schedule, but a plethora of upward-sloping schedules of varying slopes). As the analysis above has shown, at any point in time, we have a given interest rate (determined at the start of the period) and the amount of credit created will then depend on both the notional demand for credit at this interest rate coupled with the willingness of banks to issue credit to would-be borrowers. Putting all this together, far from its being a special case, the *only conceivable* credit supply schedule is a horizontal line passing through the prevailing rate of interest. But this is not to suggest that the economy can 'move along' this horizontal schedule from period to period. On the contrary, in order to study what happens over time, we need the Moorian credit supply schedule derived above. And as shown above, this can be either horizontal or an upward-sloping step function.[18]

CONCLUSION

This chapter develops a shifting equilibrium model of effective demand, in which the state of long-run expectations is non-constant and responds to the disappointment of short-run expectations, and the level of economic activity can be thought of as an evolutionary sequence of outcomes arising from the recursive interaction of short- and long-term expectations. The notion that the financial fragility of the private sector varies directly with nominal income is then entertained, and the *possibility* that commercial banks react to increased financial fragility by changing their mark-ups is allowed for. It is shown that implicit in this model is a credit supply schedule that emerges from an initially strict horizontalist conception of credit supply conditions, which is then modified by the *possibility* of commercial banks' discretionary responses to changes in the financial structure of the private sector. This credit supply schedule may be either horizontal or upward sloping, but cannot be drawn as either *ex ante*. Rather, it is a path-dependent, historical artefact, derivable only *ex post* as the product of a particular historical sequence of changes in nominal income. There is, therefore, an important distinction between the credit supply schedule at a point in time (which is always horizontal) and the *dynamic* or Moorian credit supply schedule, the shape of which is undefined in principle but which may be, in practice, either horizontal or upward sloping. This suggests the possibility of a reconciliation between structuralist and horizontalist theories of the endogenous money supply,[19] based on recognition of the fact that the shape of the dynamic or 'Moorian' credit supply schedule is undefined *a priori*, and is therefore neither horizontal nor upward sloping in principle. It may be either in practice, depending on the precise sequence of changes in aggregate income that actually materializes, the impact this has on the financial structure of the private sector, and the reaction of the financial sector to these changes.

NOTES

1. I would like to thank, without implicating, Marc Lavoie and Otto Steiger for their comments on an earlier draft of this chapter.
2. See Kregel (1976), Davidson (1978), Davidson and Kregel (1980), Dutt (1991–2) and Setterfield (1999, 2000, 2004) for precursors of the path-dependent model of effective demand developed here.

   The term 'evolution' has become so over-worked in economics as to have been rendered almost meaningless. In the context of this chapter, a system is described as 'evolutionary' if it experiences endogenously generated structural change characterized by novelty. It will become clear in what follows that the model developed in this chapter is evolutionary in the sense of this definition of the term.
3. Pure accommodationism is defined here in terms of the response of the financial sector to changes in economic activity. Specifically, there are no feedbacks from aggregate activity to financial sector policy, as captured by the values of ϕ, τ and δ (see also Palley, 1996, pp. 586–9). It must be remembered that because $\phi < 1$, this is not equivalent to suggesting that commercial banks are willing to grant any and all loan requests. Pure accommodationism is, then, perfectly consistent with the observation that some loan applicants find their requests for credit denied (see also Lavoie, 1996, pp. 283–5).
4. See Setterfield (1999, p. 487) for discussion of this short-run expectations adjustment rule and Katzner (1998, p. 406) for discussion of alternatives.
5. Note that α denotes the SOLE of both firms *and* households. The hypothesis in (6.15) is that whilst firms revise their SOLE as a direct response to the disappointment of short-run sales revenue expectations implicit in $D \neq Z$, households do so as a result of the changes in realized nominal income and employment opportunities that arise as a consequence of these same conditions (on which, see below). The possibility of there being a difference in the lag structure of the response of α to $D \neq Z$ as between households and firms is overlooked for the sake of simplicity.

6. Note that the distribution of ε must be symmetric about μ in order to render the mean and mode of this distribution equivalent.

   The magnitude of c can also be thought of as a convention which, although relatively enduring, is susceptible to change over time. The model developed here abstracts from this possibility.
7. See Setterfield (2000) for further discussion.

   Choice that involves novelty and which cannot, therefore, be reduced to description in terms of a foreclosed (deterministic or stochastic) decision-making algorithm can be defined as *discretionary* or *effective* choice.
8. For example, F might measure the leverage ratios of households and firms, their debt to income ratios and/or the proportion of their liabilities that can be classified as either speculative or Ponzi finance schemes (Minsky, 1978).
9. This is a controversial proposition within the rubric of Post Keynesian monetary theory. We will return to discuss this controversy in greater detail in the following section.
10. As Lavoie (1996) remarks, in a monetary-production economy that is subject to fundamental uncertainty:

    > agents might simply be looking for safe assets rather than unsafe ones, or for clearly defined short-term assets rather than long-term assets the return [on] which is uncertain. Briefly put, a generalised liquidity preference theory tells us to what extent the various agents in the economy are ready to become illiquid and to abandon liquid assets, as can be found in Keynes's *Treatise On Money*. (Lavoie, 1996, p.293)

    What is being postulated above, then, is that agents in the financial sector are inclined to be more averse to illiquid positions (that is, to have a higher liquidity preference) than those in the industrial and household sectors.
11. As will be discussed below, the dynamic or 'Moorian' credit supply schedule that results from adding the commercial bank reaction function in (6.25) to the shifting equilibrium model of effective demand developed earlier may, in fact, be horizontal, even though (6.25) invites the possibility of commercial banks changing their mark-ups in the course of a cumulative expansion of nominal income. It should be noted that commercial banks' responses to the evolution of F and F^* may involve their acting on ϕ rather than τ – that is, changing the proportion of notional loan demands that they deem credit-worthy and hence are willing to render effective, rather than changing their mark-ups (on which see Rochon's discussion of banks' reactions to macro uncertainty in this volume, and Setterfield (2004)). In this case, the Moorian credit supply schedule will *always* be horizontal. The reaction function in (6.25) is thus adopted here to allow for the *possibility* that the Moorian credit supply schedule may be non-horizontal.
12. The term 'structuralism' is used here to denote the proposition that the liability structure of the private sector (industrial and financial) changes over the course of the cycle, and that this may affect commercial interest rates. This is rather broader than the conventional usage, in which structuralism is associated with the following propositions: the central bank may refuse to accommodate commercial banks' demands for reserves, commercial banks will therefore resort to liability management in order to increase their lending, and commercial interest rates will rise as a result. See Pollin (1991) and Lavoie (1996, pp. 281–2).
13. Horizontalists argue that the non-bank private sector *need not* (rather than *cannot*) become increasingly financially fragile in the course of a boom, and that lenders *need not* (rather than *cannot*) reach a point where they become concerned about this increasing fragility (to the extent that it materializes). In the model developed here, both increasing financial fragility and the eventual concern of lenders with this fragility *are* inevitable, because of the assumptions made about F and F^*. This suggests that the model is best thought of as capturing what may happen *if* financial fragility and lenders' concern with this fragility do, indeed, emerge in the course of a boom – a possibility that, as noted above, is not rejected by horizontalists.
14. As remarked by Lavoie (1996, p. 278), since endogenous money theory argues that the total money supply is credit driven, it makes most sense to examine credit supply

schedules when discussing debates over the nature of money creation in Post Keynesian monetary theory.

15. It will also depend on the length of the 'treads' in Figure 6.4, of course, on which see points 3 and 4.
16. In terms of equation (6.25), and given $\mu_v > 0$, this might be associated with commercial banks' use of discretion in the setting of τ to 'test the waters' during the course of an expansion. This is, perhaps, most likely to happen if there is a sense that old conventional responses to the increased indebtedness of the non-bank private sector (as captured by the functional form of $h_t(.)$ and the value of μ_v) are outdated.

    Of course, the credit supply schedule may also be horizontal during the course of a boom if a turning point is reached prior to period n due to an exogenous shock.
17. This is easily demonstrated. Given that:

    $$D_0 = \gamma Z_0 + \phi \,.\, A(r_0, e(\alpha_0))$$

    and:

    $$D_1 = \gamma D_0 + \phi \,.\, A(r_0, e(\alpha_0 + \varepsilon_1))$$

    and since $D_0 > Z_0$ and $\varepsilon_1 > 0$ by hypothesis, it follows that $D_1 > D_0$. The claim that, *ceteris paribus*, $D_t > D_{t-1}$ $\forall t$ given that $\varepsilon_t \geq \varepsilon_{t\,\min}$ $\forall t$ follows by induction.
18. Support for these arguments can be found in Wray's contribution to this volume, when he succinctly states (p. 275):

    > If I dared to venture into the horizontalist-structuralist debate, I would note that structuralists (wrongly) sought to refute a horizontal loan supply curve on the argument that over an expansion interest rates tend to rise because mark-ups rise as perceived risks grow. However, Moore's horizontal loan supply curve is at a point in time, while theirs is a plot of interest rates over time. Moore's horizontalism is not inconsistent with a rising mark-up over time as risks in the economy increase, and the structuralist concern with innovation and evolution of practice can be incorporated within Moore's framework.
19. See also the conclusions reached by Lavoie (1996) and Palley (1996).

REFERENCES

Arestis, P. (1996) 'Post Keynesian Economics: Towards Coherence', *Cambridge Journal of Economics*, 20, 111–36.

Arestis, P., S.P. Dunn and M. Sawyer (1999) 'Post Keynesian Economics and its Critics', *Journal of Post Keynesian Economics*, 21, 527–49.

Davidson, P. (1978) *Money and the Real World*, 2nd edition, New York: Wiley.

Davidson, P. (1991) *Controversies in Post Keynesian Economics*, Aldershot, UK and Brookfield, USA: Edward Elgar.

Davidson, P. (1992) 'Would Keynes be a New Keynesian?', *Eastern Economic Journal*, 18, 449–63.

Davidson, P. and J. Kregel (1980) 'Keynes's Paradigm: A Theoretical Framework for Monetary Analysis', in E.J. Nell (ed.), *Growth, Profits and Prosperity*, Cambridge: Cambridge University Press.

Deaton, A. (1992) *Understanding Consumption*, Cambridge: Cambridge University Press.

Dutt, A.K. (1991–2) 'Expectations and Equilibrium: Implications for Keynes, the Neo-Ricardian Keynesians and the Post Keynesians', *Journal of Post Keynesian Economics*, 14, 205–24.

Katzner, D.W. (1998) *Time, Ignorance and Uncertainty in Economic Models*, Ann Arbor: University of Michigan Press.

Kregel, J. (1976) 'Economic Methodology in the Face of Uncertainty: The Modelling Methods of Keynes and the Post Keynesians', *Economic Journal*, 86, 209–25.

Lavoie, M. (1992) *Foundations of Post-Keynesian Economic Analysis*, Aldershot, UK and Brookfield, USA: Edward Elgar.

Lavoie, M. (1996) 'Horizontalism, Structuralism, Liquidity Preference and the Principle of Increasing Risk', *Scottish Journal of Political Economy*, 43, 275–300.

Minsky, H. (1978) 'The Financial Fragility Hypothesis: A Restatement', *Thames Papers in Political Economy*, London: Thames Polytechnic.

Moore, B. (1988) *Horizontalists and Verticalists: The Macroeconomics of Credit Money*, Cambridge: Cambridge University Press.

Palley, T.I. (1994) 'Debt, Aggregate Demand, and the Business Cycle: An Analysis in the Spirit of Kaldor and Minsky', *Journal of Post Keynesian Economics*, 16, 371–90.

Palley, T.I. (1996) 'Accommodationism versus Structuralism: Time for an Accommodation', *Journal of Post Keynesian Economics*, 18, 585–94.

Pollin, R. (1991) 'Two Theories of Money Supply Endogeneity: Some Empirical Evidence', *Journal of Post Keynesian Economics*, 13, 366–96.

Setterfield, M. (1999) 'Expectations, Path Dependence and Effective Demand: A Macroeconomic Model along Keynesian Lines', *Journal of Post Keynesian Economics*, 21, 479–501.

Setterfield, M. (2000) 'Expectations, Endogenous Money and the Business Cycle: An Exercise in Open Systems Modelling', *Journal of Post Keynesian Economics*, 23, 77–105.

Setterfield, M. (2004) 'Financial Fragility, Effective Demand and the Business Cycle', *Review of Political Economy*, 16, 207–23.

Solow, R. (1994) 'Perspectives on Growth Theory', *Journal of Economic Perspectives*, 8, 45–54.

Taylor, L. and S.A. O'Connell (1985) 'A Minsky Crisis', *Quarterly Journal of Economics*, 100, 871–85.

PART III

The macroeconomics of endogenous money

7. Exogenous versus endogenous money: the conceptual foundations

Paul Davidson

Basil Moore's name will always be associated with bringing the concept of endogenous money to the attention of economists in the last decades of the twentieth century.

Under the influence of Milton Friedman's Monetarist arguments where money was dropped on the economic system via a helicopter, until the mid 1980s, mainstream economists, central bankers, and Wall Street pundits invoked the exogenous money concept in discussing the cause of inflation. With his 1983 article 'Unpacking the Post Keynesian Black Box: Bank Lending and the Money Supply', Moore defied this conventional wisdom and became an outspoken champion of applying an endogenous money supply concept to real world monetary economic analysis. Although mainstream professional economists have not given explicit recognition to Moore's important contribution, it is fair to say that central bankers in the twenty-first century have discarded the exogenous money supply concept and instead explicitly developed monetary policies that are more compatible with Moore's endogenous supply concept. Basil Moore deserves a niche in the Economist's Hall of Fame for wresting central bank policy from the dead hand of Friedman's Monetarist analysis.

A RECURRING THEME

A recurring theme in the long evolution of monetary theory is the dispute whether exogenous changes in (bank) money supplies play a causal part in influencing the price level and/or economic activity, or whether variations in the observed money supply are an endogenous effect of changes in economic activity necessary to overcome the obstacles of barter in an interdependent developed production economy organized by entrepreneurial firms. The view of money as an exogenous cause of inflation represents a Currency School legacy, descending from Lord Overstone and the charter revision of the Bank of England in the 1840s. Money, viewed as an effect, constituted the core of the 'real bills' Banking Principle doctrine espoused at the time of William Tooke. Precursors abound as Marget's (1938) careful documentation reveals.

In the last decades of the twentieth century, this Currency School cause versus Banking School effect controversy evolved into a dispute between: (1) the Monetarists, who argued that the quantity of money supplied is (should be) exogenous and therefore a cause of inflation, and that by controlling money supply changes one controls the rate of inflation; and (2) the Post Keynesians, who, following Keynes (1973, pp. 222–3), believe that in a good monetary system, changes in the quantity of money supply should be endogenous, that is, central bankers should develop institutions that ensure that the money supply is responsive to changes in the demand for liquidity.

This cause versus effect of the money supply question became intertwined with the terms exogenous versus endogenous. If the money supply is strictly exogenous, as Monetarist theory requires, then to the extent that changes in the quantity of money are, in the mind of the analyst, associated with changes in the price level, money can only play (by definition) a causal role in the process of price inflation. If the money supply is endogenous or an effect, on the other hand, then anti-inflation policies aimed at restricting the growth of the money supply are effective only if they limit changes in aggregate effective demand sufficiently to create slack markets that reduce the rent-seeking ability of owners of the factors of production in an unregulated market place. In an endogenous monetary system, policies to deliberately limit growth in money incomes of factor owners relative to factor productivity increases, that is, incomes policies, is the effective tool for fighting inflation without suffering the pains of recession and depression. Accordingly, the theoretical issue of whether money supplies are exogenous or endogenous has important implications for the cause versus effect role of monetary policy in a modern market-oriented production economy.

Unfortunately, the conceptual basis of the terms exogenous and endogenous has not been clearly defined. The participants in the discussion of exogenous versus endogenous money have often conflated two different concepts of the money supply function, namely (a) the magnitude of the interest elasticity of the money supply function and (b) the independence (stability) of the money supply function vis-à-vis shifts in the money demand function.

Under the Monetarist approach, money is exogenous if, and only if, the quantity of money supplied by the banking system is perfectly inelastic with respect to alternative possible interest rates. Consequently, observed changes in the money supply must be the result of shifts in the money supply function over time. These shifts are the result of deliberate central bank policy rules and actions independent of the market rate of interest on debt securities. Thus (by hypothesis), change in the measured money supply must be the cause of some economic event; it cannot be the result (effect).

If, on the other hand, the quantity of money supplied in the system is less than perfectly inelastic – but not perfectly elastic – then this implies that central bankers will partially accommodate changes in the public's demand for liquidity as it affects the market rate of interest even if the money supply function itself is stable over time in the sense that the money supply function is independent of any changes in the demand function for liquidity. Accordingly, in this case, observed changes in the quantity of money outstanding are the result of central bankers' responses to changes in interest rates due to shifts in the demand for money function. But should such increases in the quantity of money, occurring as interest rates are rising, be considered exogenous changes in the money supply, or should they be considered endogenous variations in the money supply as changes in interest rates are partly accommodated?

If the money supply is not perfectly elastic, as long as the money supply function does not shift in response to shifts in the demand for money function, then the supply function is independent of demand. In such a case, any changes in the observed money supply must always be an endogenous effect of the shift in demand. In other words, any change in the observed quantity of money must be considered endogenous if the money supply function is presumed stable over time.

Every elementary economics principles textbook stresses the importance of distinguishing between a change in the quantity supplied (or demanded), that is, a movement along a supply (or demand) curve, and a change in supply (or demand), that is, a shift in a supply (demand) curve. Most economic principles instructors warn of the horrible semantic confusion that can result unless one clearly differentiates between a change in supply and a change in the quantity supplied. Unfortunately, most of the literature on exogenous versus endogenous money does not draw this distinction.

In Moore's 1988 book *Horizontalists and Verticalists*, Verticalists are those whose analysis assumes a perfectly inelastic money supply function that shifts only as the result of deliberate central bank policy. Friedman's Monetarist approach as well as the neoclassical synthesis IS-LM framework basically invoke the Verticalist view. In such a world, any (shift) in the demand function for money plays up against the perfectly inelastic or vertical supply function so that the rate of interest changes sufficiently to offset any change in the demand for money.

Contrary to some obvious facts, orthodox economists in the last half of the 20th century assumed this Verticalist case governed real world economic systems. Since Monetarists also assumed that a free market would automatically assure full employment, and therefore that gross domestic product (GDP) can grow over time only if the labor force increases and/or productivity per worker rises over time, Monetarists therefore argued for a monetary growth 'rule' requiring an independent time rate of growth of the money supply in step with long-run productivity and labor force trends.

On the other hand, Neoclassical Synthesis Keynesians and New Keynesians assume there is no automatic market mechanism that produces full employment in the short run. Although these mainstream Keynesians assume an exogenous money supply system, they are willing to permit central bankers to use their discretion as to when they exogenously increase the money supply as long as the economy is, in the short run, at less than full employment. After all, even if the money supply is not increased, these Keynesians argue, exogenous fiscal policy changes could always increase aggregate effective demand sufficiently to generate full employment, *even if interest rates rose as the expansion towards full employment occurred.*

Since both Monetarists and mainstream Keynesians assume an exogenous money supply concept, the Monetarist versus mainstream Keynesian argument as to whether an exogenous fiscal policy should be invoked in order to achieve full employment becomes a question of whether the 'crowding out effect' of rising interest rates depresses investment spending sufficiently to offset any expansionary fiscal spending effect.

Unlike the Monetarists and mainstream Keynesians, Horizontalists, according to Moore, believe that, at any moment in time, central banks set the basic rate of interest and then completely accommodate all demands for money from the banking system at that rate of interest. For Moore's Horizontalists, the money supply function is perfectly elastic (horizontal) at the interest rate exogenously set by the central bank. As long as the central bankers do not change their exogenously determined rate of interest, changes in the observed quantity of money in circulation are the results of changes in the demand for money playing against this fully accommodating money supply banking system.

Clearly, between the onset of the Second World War and the 1951 Treasury-Federal Reserve Accord, the Federal Reserve pursued a Horizontalist (accommodating) approach to monetary policy. This permitted the United States to fight and win the Second World War at the cost of a 2 to 3 per cent rate of interest even when the Federal deficit in the war years approached 40 to 50 per cent of the national income and the outstanding federal debt grew to more than 120 per cent of the US gross domestic product.

THE INDEPENDENT (STABILITY) MONEY SUPPLY FUNCTION CONCEPT

In Moore's dichotomization of all monetary analysis into the Verticalists' perfectly inelastic money supply function and the Horizontalists' perfectly elastic supply function, there is no room for the central bankers to be partly accommodating to changes in the demand for money. In both the extreme Verticalist and Horizontalist views, the exogenity versus endogenity issue relies on assuming a time stability of the money supply function, until the central bank takes deliberate action to either: (a) directly exogenously change the money supply (in the Verticalist view); or (b) exogenously change the rate of interest (in the Horizontalist view). In both the Verticalist and Horizontalist theoretical systems, central bankers always have the option of shifting the money supply function – but depending on which view is being espoused, use different tools to shift the money supply function.

The question then becomes: what are the factors that will lead the central bank to shift the money supply function and how, once they decide to shift the function, do they accomplish this change in the money supply function? For Verticalists, whether they be of the Monetarist or Mainstream Keynesian persuasion, central bankers alter the money supply through some form of open market operation, whereby they buy (sell) government securities from the public (or the banks). This results in their creating (destroying) exogenous money directly when they buy (sell) bonds from (to) the public, or indirectly when purchases (sales) from (to) bank portfolios increase (decrease) banks' reserves and thereby encourage banks to alter the size of their loan portfolios. Since engaging in open market operations requires the 'desk' at the central bank to actively enter the bond market as a buyer (or seller), Verticalists identify such actions as exogenous.

For Horizontalists, central bankers set some basic interest rate (for example, the federal funds rate) at which they will make loans to member banks. In this monetary policy operation, discretion is left to each individual bank to initiate the making of a loan from the central bank if the private sector bank needs additional reserves to expand credit to its customers. Accordingly, in the Horizontalist analysis, the central bank permits the money supply to change endogenously as actions of the private banks in the system reflect the behavior of their customers' demand for loans.

THE MONEY SUPPLY PROCESS REVISITED

Ever since the 1970s, Post Keynesians have been warning orthodox economic theorists that they have not properly depicted the money supply process (for example, Davidson and Weintraub, 1973; Davidson, 1978). Keynes's general theory (1936, ch. 17) argued that an 'essential property' of money (and all other liquid assets) is a zero (or negligible) elasticity of production. This elasticity property means that money does not grow on trees and therefore cannot be harvested by private sector entrepreneurs hiring workers to pluck money from the money orchard. Consequently, if one is to specify properly how observed changes in the supply of money come about, one must focus on the relevant banking institutions and operations which bring money into (or remove money from) the system. In the real world, Keynes reminded us at the very beginning of the *Treatise on Money* (1930, vol. 1, p. 3), money 'comes into existence along with debts, which are contracts for deferred payment and . . . offers of contracts for sale or purchase', that is, the supply of money, and debt and production-offer contracts are intimately and inevitably related. For Keynes, money does not enter the system like manna from heaven, nor is it dropped from the sky via a Friedmanian helicopter, nor is it produced by the application of labor to the harvesting of money trees. For Keynes and Post Keynesians, the supply of money in a modern economy can increase only via two distinct money supply processes – both of which are related to contracts. One supply process is associated with exogenous money and the other with endogenous money.

THE INCOME FINANCE PROCESS AND ENDOGENOUS MONEY

In the income finance money supply process, an increased desire to buy more reproducible goods in each accounting period – the finance motive (Keynes, 1973, pp. 215–23; Davidson, 1978) – induces individuals, firms, governments, and foreigners to enter into additional debt contracts with the banking system. If these contracts are accepted by the banking system without any active intervention by the central bank, then the money supply elasticity cannot be perfectly inelastic. The additional debts of banks are issued and used to pay for the additional offer contracts of producers and workers expanding the flow of produced goods during the period. In this process, a change in the production flow process induces a change in the quantity of money supplied. In the income-generating finance process, the quantity of money supplied is always endogenous. Additional private debt financing contracts can, on a system-wide basis, only be accepted by the private sector banking system if there is an active accommodation by the central bank via its 'real bills' function. The assumed money supply function permits an accommodating expansion of the money supply as central bankers do their job.

In the income-generating finance process, any exogenous planned increase in aggregate effective demand for goods provokes an increased entrepreneurial demand for money which induces bankers to increase the supply of money. As long as banks are willing and able to make additional bank-debt contracts available under the rules of the game (and, of course, it is in the self-interest of bankers to do so), the money supply will respond endogenously to changes in aggregate effective demand. This increase in the measured money supply is used to finance additional orders for producible goods. Depending on the various supply elasticities of the various industries stimulated, increases in real incomes and prices will rise along with the endogenous increase in the money supply.

THE PORTFOLIO CHANGE PROCESS AND EXOGENOUS MONEY

An alternative process for changing the money supply observed in the economy can be labeled the portfolio change process. In this process the central bank initiates the observed change in the money supply by going into the open market and directly buying existing liquid assets, at a price the seller finds acceptable, from either the general public or from the banking system. If the purchased assets were held by the general public, then the immediate effect would be to increase the public's holding of bank deposits (money) in their portfolios. If the assets are bought directly from the banks then the effect is to increase the reserves of the banking system which, it is hoped, will stimulate the banks to make additional loans to the general public. In the portfolio money supply, the initial cause of a change in the money supply is an explicit *ceteris paribus* policy decision on the part of the Monetary Authority to shift the supply function of money at any given rate of interest. Accordingly, the portfolio change money supply process always involves an exogenous change in the money supply function.

In the portfolio change process, the banks and/or public are induced to alter the composition of money versus other liquid assets in their portfolios. This 'independent' increase in the money supply function due to open market operations *initiated* by the central bank will increase the demand for produced goods only via the usual Keynesian effect of lowering the financing costs of purchasing the products of industry.

FINANCE – REAL VERSUS INFLATION BILLS

The income-generating finance process demonstrates that the financial system holds the key to facilitating the transition of an entrepreneurial economy from a lower to a higher level of economic activity. Long duration, mass production processes must be planned ahead if they are to be efficiently organized in non-slave and/or non-cooperative economies. Entrepreneurs require the institution of long duration forward money contracts to ensure the cooperation of owners of factor inputs in delivering *on time* factor services and materials according to the production schedule. Since these entrepreneurial contractual commitments require monetary payments (cash outflows) to factor owners before the product is sold and sales revenues (cash inflows) are received, entrepreneurs must be assured that they can obtain sufficient money finance to meet these production cash outflow commitments. Any inability to obtain sufficient financial commitments today prevents entrepreneurs from initiating production activities, no matter how profitable these productive processes are expected to be at a later date when the product is finally sold.

In an entrepreneurial system of organizing production, economic growth requires a banking system that will provide an 'elastic currency' so that the expanding needs of trade can be readily financed. This is the essence of the foundation of the 'real bills doctrine'. In the absence of a financial system which can provide such an endogenous money system, an entrepreneurial, market-oriented, monetary-production economy will find that its best made plans for expansion will be stymied.

Unfortunately, the same banking system which provides a mechanism for the endogenous expansion of the money supply to meet the real needs of trade (the real bills doctrine) cannot normally distinguish between increased entrepreneurial requirements to finance larger payrolls due to (a) increased employment (at a given money wage) associated with greater production flow and (b) higher money pay per unit of labor (or other factor service) effort (after adjusting for changes in labor productivity), that is, higher efficiency wages or unit money costs of production. Consequently, any banking system designed to provide a financial environment that eases the transition from a lower to a higher level of employment and output is also capable of supporting inflationary forces due to economic, social and political demands from various groups for higher money income to obtain, *ceteris paribus*, a greater share of any aggregate output flow. In other words, any financial structure that is appropriately designed to provide an endogenous money supply under the real bills doctrine is simultaneously capable of creating a permissive environment for wage or profit inflation. In a healthy banking system, the needs of trade can be subverted to create an elastic currency of 'inflation bills' rather than 'real bills'. Any deliberate monetary policy aimed at restricting the banking system's ability to issue 'inflation bills' will therefore concurrently limit the banking system's ability to supply sufficient real bills to maintain as rapid real economic expansion as the economy's resources permit.

Keynes (1930, vol. 2, pp. 219–20) noted that 'Credit is the pavement along which production travels, and bankers if they know their duty, would provide the transport facilities to just the extent that is required in order that the productive powers of the community can be employed to their full capacity'. This real bills view is encapsulated in Basil Moore's argument regarding the importance of endogenous money in economic growth. Moore deserves kudos for forcing central bankers and mainstream economists to focus on the real world monetary problems of the twenty-first century.

REFERENCES

Davidson, P. (1967) 'Keynes's Finance Motive', *Oxford Economic Papers*, 17. Reprinted in L. Davidson (ed.) (1990), *Money and Employment, The Collected Writings of Paul Davidson, vol. 1*, London: Macmillan, 11–31.

Davidson, P. and S. Weintraub (1973) 'Money as Cause and Effect', *Economic Journal*, 83. Reprinted in L. Davidson (ed.) (1990) *Money and Employment, The Collected Writings of Paul Davidson, vol. 1*, London: Macmillan, 152–69.

Davidson, P. (1978) 'Why Money Matters: Lessons from a Half-Century of Monetary Theory', *Journal of Post Keynesian Economics*, 1, 46–70.

Keynes, J.M. (1930) *A Treatise on Money*, London: Macmillan.

Keynes, J.M. (1936) *The General Theory of Employment, Interest and Money*, New York: Harcourt Brace.

Keynes, J.M. (1973) 'The Ex Ante Theory of the Rate of Interest', *Economic Journal*, 47. Reprinted in D. Moggridge (ed.) *The Collected Writings of John Maynard Keynes, vol. 14*, London: Macmillan.

Marget, A. (1938) *The Theory of Prices*, New York: Prentice-Hall.

Moore, B.J. (1983) 'Unpacking the Post Keynesian Black Box: Bank Lending and the Money Supply', *Journal of Post Keynesian Economics*, 5(4), 537–56.

Moore, B.J. (1988) *Horizontalists and Verticalists: the Macroeconomics of Credit Money*, Cambridge, MA: MIT Press.

8. The endogeneity of money and the Eurosystem: a contribution to the theory of central banking[1]

Otto Steiger

> While a central bank can extend emergency loans for unlimited amounts, *its capacity to absorb losses is limited* (up to the size of its capital).
>
> Dirk Schoenmaker (2000, p. 222; emphasis added)

IS THE MONEY SUPPLY FUNCTION CLEARLY HORIZONTAL?

In his book of 1988 on *Horizontalists and Verticalists*, which should become the fundamental text for the endogenous theory of money, Basil Moore argues that the money supply in modern economies is *not* under the control of central banks, even if the most important one, the Federal Reserve System, '*purports* to control quantitatively the amount of banking system reserve borrowing' in the US. 'Central banks typically supply cash reserves *automatically on demand* at the minimum lending rate. In such cases *the money supply function is clearly horizontal*' at this rate (Moore, 1998, pp. 111 f.; second and third emphasis added).

While I agree with Moore that the supply of central bank money is not exogenously determined by the central bank, I wonder, however, whether it is determined completely by the demand of its counterparties. Rather, I suggest that the central bank has *some* exogenous power to control the *quantity* of its supply by *rationing* or *queuing*. More importantly, the central bank is *forced* to do so! The central bank cannot merely exist as an automat responding to the wishes of the commercial banks. The following section discusses in more detail why the central bank has to restrict its supply by emphasizing some neglected fundamentals of central banking. The next section demonstrates how the supply of central bank money can be controlled by looking at the monetary policy operations of the Eurosystem. The final section offers some conclusions on how to revise the horizontal money supply function.

THE CAUSE FOR RESTRICTING THE SUPPLY OF CENTRAL BANK MONEY, OR: SOME NEGLECTED FUNDAMENTALS OF CENTRAL BANKING

A two-tiered banking system consists of a central bank, with a monopoly on issuing *banknotes* in credit contracts with its counterparties the commercial banks. The latter can obtain these notes only by pledging *good securities* and promising *interest*, while the former for its note issue has – *in addition* to the collateral of its counterparties – to dispose of its *own capital*. Since it is *property* that is at the core of any good security and own capital, such a banking system can only function in property-based societies (Heinsohn and Steiger, 1996, 2000a, 2006b and forthcoming).[2]

The central bank must not accept as underlying assets in such a contract any debt instruments issued by its counterparty, or by any other entity with which the counterparty has close links. Commercial bank *A*, for example, will only be accepted at the trading desk of the central bank with securities bought from a private company *B*, or another entity like the government,[3] but not with its own paper, or that of a company *C* in which it holds a stake, even if these titles should prove to be highly marketable. The meaning of this rule is that debt titles delivered to a central bank have to be guaranteed by *A*, and not by the issuer of the titles. Thus, genuine central bank money always has to be a *creditor's*, and not a *debtor's* money.

In the classical texts on central banking, these prerequisites of genuine money were not fully understood. However, the founding fathers of the theory of central banking, Henry Thornton (1802) and Walter Bagehot (1873), always tied the creation of money to good securities, even in the case of a liquidity crisis. The former was the first to conceive of a lender of last resort. In his discussion of the financial crisis of 1793 in England, Thornton observed that the country banks ceased to give out their notes because the public refused to accept them, instead demanding Bank of England notes. Therefore he proposed two rules: 'First, . . . the Bank of England . . . should be disposed to extend its discounts in a greater degree than heretofore . . . . Secondly, the country bankers should be taught . . . to provide themselves with a larger quantity of that *property* which is quickly convertible in Bank of England notes' (Thornton, 1802, p. 188; emphasis added).

To merely focus on interest, as is common practice in modern texts on central banking, would never have entered the minds of Thornton and Bagehot. The latter's rationale for the central bank as the lender of last resort is far from merely providing liquidity by whatever means. Unwaveringly, he emphasized two rules: 'First. That these loans should only be made at a very high rate of interest. . . . Secondly. That at this rate these advances should be made at all *good* banking securities and as largely as the public ask for them' (Bagehot, 1873, p. 197; emphasis added).

Ralph Hawtrey (1932) was also well aware that the lender of last resort responsibility must never be interpreted in a way that allows business banks to obtain cash without pledging prime property titles. 'The essential duty of the central bank as the lender of last resort . . . cannot mean that it should lend to *any* bank that needs cash, regardless of the borrowing bank's behaviour or circumstances. Neither a commercial concern nor a public institution could undertake to supply cash to insolvent borrowers' (Hawtrey, 1932, p. 126).

All three authors emphasized the necessity of good securities because they understood that the principles of banking apply to a private bank of issue no less than to any other bank. They were beautifully set out already in 1767 by James Steuart in what can be regarded as mercantilism's most important treatise. Steuart was also the first to explain *why* good securities are necessary. 'Many, who are unacquainted with the nature of banks [of issue], have a difficulty to comprehend how they should ever be at a *loss* for money, as they have a mint of their own, which requires nothing but paper and ink to create millions. But if they consider the principles of banking, they will find that every note issued for value consumed in place of value received and preserved, is neither more or less, than a partial spending either of their *capital*, or profits on the bank'. Therefore, he emphasized 'that banks [of issue] give credit upon nothing but the *best* securities' (Steuart, 1767, vol. II, pp. 151 f. and 603; emphasis added).

Thornton and Bagehot were no less concerned than Steuart about the dangers in the business of issuing money. 'Banknotes emitted without obtaining value in return . . . are [a] great source both of *loss and danger* to a banking company' (Thornton, 1802, p. 244; emphasis added). By accepting '*bad* bills or *bad* securities . . . the Bank [of issue] will ultimately *lose*' (Bagehot, 1873, p. 198; emphasis added).[4] Hawtrey, too, had no difficulty in seeing the central bank's common commercial woes. 'A commercial concern in particular cannot afford to take *risks* out of proportion to its *own capital*' (1932, p. 126; emphasis added).

The balance sheet of a central bank, like that of any other business in the monetary economy, has to consist not only of assets and liabilities but also of a surplus of the former over the latter. With this net worth or own capital, it safeguards itself against the threat of bankruptcy. Only a few central banking theorists in our times, most notably David Folkerts-Landau, Peter Garber, Charles Goodhart, and Dirk Schoenmaker, have understood this old wisdom. 'In any credit operation that it undertakes in the lender-of-last-resort role, a central bank will incur the credit risk and potential *losses*, associated with the claims it acquires when expanding its liabilities to supply credit' (Folkerts-Landau and Garbert, 1992, p. 99; emphasis added). Therefore, 'a LOLR [lender of last resort] loan by a CB [central bank] is like any other loan, in that it may be repaid (plus interest) or alternatively will be subject to *default* and some potential loss', and independently whether the central bank is private or 'becomes explicitly a public sector body' (Goodhart, 1999, p. 233; emphasis added; and see our opening quote of Schoenmaker, 2000, p. 222).

It was because economists had forgotten this insight that dubious recommendations, most prominently by Paul Krugman, were made in recent years to the Bank of Japan to salvage the deflation-ridden Japanese economy by engaging in large-scale purchase of long-term government debt. The idea that such a policy will lift bond prices and lower short-term interest rates and, thereby, trigger an upswing, does not take into account that this could bankrupt the Bank. The more this policy succeeds in dispelling deflation and the more the economy prospers, the higher long-term interest rates will be. But their increase means, of course, a decrease in the prices of the bonds held by the Bank of Japan. 'If the Bank held only 10 per cent of the long-term government bonds outstanding and interest rates rose by two percentage points, the resulting losses would *wipe out the institution's entire capital and reserves*' (Lerrick, 2001, p. 13; emphasis added). As underlined by Goodhart (1999, p. 233; emphasis added), the independent capacity of the Bank of Japan for action remains 'in some large part, though not entirely, *bounded by its capital*'.

Notwithstanding these fundamentals of central banking, the view of the omnipotence of the central bank is maintained by modern monetary economists, most prominently Anna Schwartz. 'The only institution that had the resources to provide . . . loans in a [liquidity] crisis is the central bank, which could create high-powered money *without limit*, and hence was the lender of last resort' (2002, p. 450; emphasis added). How can such a view be explained? A closer look at modern textbooks reveals that most central banking theorists have never looked in detail at the balance sheet of a central bank, in particular never asked why the central monetary institution, like any other bank or company in the monetary economy, must have the item 'capital' on its liability side.

In Paul Krugman and Maurice Obstfeld's classical text on *International Economics* (2003, pp. 486 f.), for example, no capital exists on the liability side of a central bank's balance sheet, only the items 'currency in circulation' and 'deposits held by private banks'. Therefore, one is not surprised to hear that a central bank's net worth, correctly defined as its total assets minus its total liabilities, is assumed to be zero, and that 'because changes in central bank net worth are not important to our analysis we will also ignore those'. This ignorance is also characteristic of Peter Bofinger's widely used text *Monetary Policy* (2001, pp. 41–3), where in a simplified balance sheet of the Eurosystem the items 'capital and reserves' are completely wiped out, although they appear in the official consolidated balance sheet of the Eurosystem on which Bofinger's simplification is based. In Oliver Blanchard's well-known textbook on *Macroeconomics* (2003, p. 76), not only is the central bank devoid of capital but so too are the commercial banks. While in Frederic Mishkin's classic on *Banking* (2001, pp. 214 f. and 392–4) the importance of 'bank capital, the bank's net worth which equals the difference between its total assets and liabilities', is correctly analyzed as a buffer for 'bad debts which have to be written off', such insights are missing in his discussion of the consolidated balance sheet of the Federal Reserve System.[5]

The myth of the unlimited capacity of the central bank to create money is most vehemently maintained by the Berlin School of Monetary Keynesianism, most prominently in the writings of the founder of the school, Hajo Riese (1993 and 2000). The theory of the Berlin School is interesting because it, not unlike those of Moore and Heinsohn and Steiger, does not analyse money as a means to facilitate barter but as a *means of payment* arising out of a credit contract. Riese's approach to central banking deserves particular attention, because he is the first central banking theorist who has recognized that Bagehot's discussion of the lender of last resort responsibility of the central bank manifests itself in 'the connection between the elasticity of the money supply . . . and the avoidance of the . . . form of *liquidity crisis*' that results, not from insolvency but '*from payment difficulties of the central bank*' (Riese, 1993, p. 5; emphasis added).

According to Riese, such an inability to pay cannot be avoided when, as in the case of the Bank of England in the wake of Peel's Bank Act of 1844, the money supply is restricted by a given amount of certain assets – in the case of the Bank of England: gold. The ability of the central bank to pay is not achieved, however, by simply suspending the restriction due to gold but through Bagehot's famous *open discount window*. This economic journalist was first to understand what the economics profession of his time had not grasped: it was 'only the opening of the discount window in 1866 which overcame the liquidity crises which had repeatedly shaken England since the pound became a world currency' (Riese, 1993, p. 11).

What is the meaning of an open discount window? According to Riese, it 'means that *every* demand for money resulting from a credit relationship is satisfied', and then only the question 'remains as to the *price* at which this is satisfied' (1993, p. 37; emphasis in the German original). In other words: the establishment of the central bank as lender of last resort leads to the suspension of the gold restriction for the issue of banknotes, thereby overcoming the payment difficulties of the central bank and '*securing the ability of the economy to function*' (Riese, 1993, p. 31; emphasis in the German original).

However, this praise of the beneficial effects of the role of the lender of last resort is bound to the assumption of its capacity to create money without limit. As we have seen, the founders of the theory of central banking did not adhere to this view, albeit not always on sufficient grounds. For them, on a generous interpretation, the capacity to create money is limited by a lack of good securities of its counterparties and the capacity of its own capital to absorb losses.

What has Monetary Keynesianism to say about good securities and own capital? More or less nothing! On the one side, Riese (1993, p. 35) mentions Baghehot's second rule of advancing money only against '"proper" security' without, however, discussing its meaning. On the other side, he dismisses the rule as a 'strictly conservative course . . . – a condition which, alongside a high interest rate which acts as a market barrier against the surge to liquidity, is able to avoid the domino effects of a liquidity crisis' (Riese, 1993, p. 38).

With Riese's dismissal of good securities in mind, it is not surprising that the central bank's own capital is not mentioned at all, not to speak of its being made a topic for discussion. This is revealed in his analysis of the interaction of the central bank (*Z*), its counterparties, the commercial banks (*B*) and the non-bank public (*P*). The interaction is demonstrated by numerical examples of the balance sheet structures of the three sectors. Out of eight differing cases of interaction analyzed by Riese (1993, p. 20; and see p. 24), we discuss (see Table 8.1) (1) the case of a sale of central bank money to the public and (2) the case of the results of a multiple process of credit creation.

In his analysis, Riese wants to demonstrate the '*bifurcation of monetary demand and credit demand*' by considering that holdings of money exist for the public – *C* – as well as for the commercial banks – *R* – which '*result from the risk of losses of assets*'. Riese regards such holdings as 'a market constellation of disequilibrium' allowing for the dissolving of 'the identification of money and credit' (1993, pp. 22 f.; emphasis in the German original). However, he does not understand that these holdings on the asset side of the balance sheets of both the commercial banks and the public only make sense as *reserves* with the corresponding contra entry *net worth of assets* or *own capital* on their liability side. In case (2), for example, the commercial banks cannot secure their claims on the public, $F_p = 3000$, by reserve holdings of $R = 200$ because the total of their assets, $R + F_p = 3200$, is equal to their liabilities, $V_z + D$. To write off bad debts, the banks need a *surplus* of their assets over their liabilities, that is, a net worth of assets.[6] And the same holds true, of course, for the money holdings of the public, $C = 1000$, to secure their claims on the banks, $D = 2000$.

Table 8.1 Balance sheet structures à la Riese

	Z		B		P
		(1)			
F_b 1200	M 1200	F_p 1200	V_z 1200	C 1200	V_b 1200
		(2)			
F_b 1200	M 1200	R 200	V_z 1200	C 1000	V_b 3000
		F_p 3000	D 2000	D 2000	

F_b = claims on commercial banks
M = money supply
F_p = claims on the public
V_z = liabilities to the central bank
C = holdings of money
V_b = liabilities to commercial banks
R = reserve holdings
D = deposit holdings, with $C/D = 0.5$

Source: Excerpt from Riese (1993, p. 20): 'Figure 1.1: Balance sheet structures', upper and lower case.

Needless to say the item own capital is also missing in Riese's balance sheet of the central bank. As distinct from the commercial banks and the public, the 'risk of loss of assets' of this institution never becomes a topic of discussion. On the contrary, Riese explicitly rules out such a risk. Why?

Unlike the commercial banks, Riese maintains, who 'in principle are faced with a liquidity problem because their liabilities, in one way or another, have to be transformed into central bank money' which they cannot create, the central bank is devoid of this problem (2000, p. 492). Why? Because that which is the essence of the inability to pay, not having enough money to discharge debts, can be created by the central bank itself without any difficulty and *without* making *commitments*. This can be verified by its balance sheet, he argues, where the money supply on the liability side, as contra entry to its claims to the commercial banks on the asset side, is assumed to express a 'production of liquidity', a 'creation of assets by the central bank' (Riese, 2000, p. 492). 'The money in circulation does not simply represent, as sometimes is still supposed, some kind of liability of the central bank. What should the central bank be obliged to do? To formulate it ironically, the central bank as producer of liquidity *ex definitione* can only transform, again and again, self-made liquidity into self-made liquidity' (Riese, 2000, p. 492).

However, Riese is not wholly convinced of this explanation *ex definitione*. Therefore, he provides an additional one. It is true that the central bank is a bank, he concedes, but unlike a '"normal"' commercial bank, the former is not subject to risk because its creation of money implies a production of assets. Therefore, Riese concludes that the banknotes created by the central bank in credit contracts with the commercial banks involve a transfer of assets to the commercial banks. The central bank 'as universal producer of liquidity is *not* subject to a *creditor's risk* and cannot, therefore, get into payment difficulties because of a bad loan. Being risk-free in its business, it is true that the central bank is forced to behave most carefully when granting a loan . . . . However, *the decisive point is that its holdings of money imply a production of assets* – which in matters of book-keeping says that a central bank books the issue of money as a liability. And in this, in analogy to a *net worth, the parting with the asset "money"* is expressed' (Riese, 2000, p. 493; emphasis added).

After all, Riese cannot avoid the term net worth, that is, own capital which he correctly localizes on the central bank's liability side, however, only for 'matters of bookkeeping'. Thereby, Riese reveals that he does not understand that notes issued by a central bank cannot represent a net worth for the bank, that is, a *surplus* of its assets over its liabilities. Central bank money is created as an asset for commercial banks only. It represents, therefore, a liability for the central bank, and not a net worth the disposal of which the latter has the option to give up (Heinsohn and Steiger, 2000b, p. 518; and see 2006b, pp. 77 f.). By simply looking at a real balance sheet of a central bank, Riese would have immediately recognized why its notes, as distinct from those of other central banks, do not appear on its asset side and why its net worth, *in addition* to its notes, is booked on its liability side as own capital: without this item, the central bank would be unable to withdraw notes from circulation not paid back in case of bad loans. Furthermore, central bank money is not an asset *per se* but '*a derivative of assets*' (Stadermann, 2000, p. 536; emphasis added). Money is a note which a commercial bank receives in an interest-charged credit contract from the central bank against an asset to be pledged to the latter. By redeeming the note, the commercial bank exercises its right to release the pledged asset from the central bank respectively forcing the latter to return it.

Unlike Riese, another leading Monetary Keynesian, Heinz-Peter Spahn, recognizes that a private bank of issue faces a liquidity problem, albeit for the wrong reasons. According to Spahn (2001, p. 62), such a problem is due to the redeemability of its notes. He does not understand that a private bank of issue, just like a central bank, can become illiquid because of a lack of own capital. 'Today nearly all currencies in the world are issued without the right of redemption of their bearers.' This is true, but does it rule out the liquidity problem? Spahn does not understand that the abandonment of the right of redemption results from today's watertight two-tier banking system, with relations only between the central bank and their counterparties the business banks on the one side and between the latter and the public on the other. Only the public no longer has the right of redemption, while it still exists – and has to exist – for the commercial banks. More importantly, if the business banks are unable to redeem the notes loaned, the central bank has to withdraw them from circulation by offering its own capital 'when the market value of the collateral is less than the amount of the loan or advance to the banks concerned' (Folkerts-Landau and Garber, 1992, p. 99). And when its reserve is exhausted, the central bank faces a liquidity problem like any private bank of issue.

The institution, which Spahn and Riese and even the aforementioned famous textbook authors have in mind when analysing the business of a bank of issue, is obviously not a genuine central bank but a mere State bank of issue. As distinct from the former, the latter can indeed issue notes by buying debt titles from their *issuers*. Such titles are more or less worthless, because they are reproducible in any number and non-marketable, while a true central bank has to buy the debt titles on the market from the commercial banks who, as *creditors* of the titles, have to consider their inherent risk when offering them to the central bank: in contrast to the case of a State bank of issue, the risk here is with the creditor, and not the debtor. Therefore, the State bank is an issuer of a *debtor's* money – and as such it needs no own capital either because it is obliged in no way whatsoever to redeem its notes.

The genuine central bank, on the other hand, needs own capital – last but not least to act as lender of last resort. However, as shown above, this role is at the same time restricted by the possible losses its own capital can absorb. Therefore, what even the strongest central bank deserves is the backing of another institution, the State. 'What stands behind the liabilities of the CB [central bank] is *not* the capital of the CB but the strength and taxing power of the State' (Goodhart 1999, p. 234). Therefore, 'the central bank's losses on acquired bank assets fall ultimately on the taxpayers. In effect, the taxpayer has assumed the credit risk inherent in bank assets that serve as collateral for central bank lending' (Folkerts-Landau and Garber, 1992, p. 100).

The message of this section is clear. The central bank has to control its money supply for the same reason as a commercial bank its credit supply. The latter cannot satisfy every demand from the non-bank public, and the former cannot respond either, like an automat, to the demand from the private banks. Both types of banks have to avoid the danger of bankruptcy and, therefore, to restrict their lending.[7] In the case of the central bank, of course, other considerations also make such 'credit rationing' necessary, first of all, its monetary policy goals. In the next section, it will be demonstrated how this is done in the Eurosystem.

HOW TO CONTROL THE SUPPLY OF CENTRAL BANK MONEY, OR: WHAT COULD BE LEARNED FROM THE EUROSYSTEM?

The Eurosystem is the de-centralized central banking managing the common currency of European Monetary Union (EMU), the euro. It consists of the 12 national central banks (NCBs) of EMU and the European Central Bank (ECB). The peculiarity of the System is that it does not have a central monetary authority. The ECB is not a bank of issue and, therefore, not the System's lender of last resort. Central bank money is issued exclusive by the NCBs, with the ECB as a form of intermediate agent between the NCBs and Council of Governors of the System, the body that determines monetary policy in EMU. The Council consists of the six Executive Directors of the ECB and the Presidents of the 12 NCBs.[8]

The decisions of the Council on the rate of interest and the amount of central bank money to be supplied are normally implemented by the NCBs, and not the ECB. This means that the ECB only coordinates the refinancing operations, while the transactions are carried out by the NCBs. Refinancing means the supplying by the NCBs of central bank money to those of their domestic commercial banks which are in need of liquidity. In what follows, the Eurosystem's main refinancing operations (MROs) and its longer-term refinancing operations (LTROs) are discussed to demonstrate whether these procedures confirm the thesis of a clearly horizontal supply function of money or not. Following a suggestion by Marc Lavoie (2004), the System's marginal lending facilities (MLFs) are also considered as a monetary policy instrument that could save the horizontal supply function.[9]

Before we present the MROs and LTROs of the Eurosystem, we will give a child's guide to the question: why do commercial banks go to the central bank at all? Is there not another source of getting central bank money? Yes, indeed there are other sources. The banks can go to other banks – this is what they regularly do at the money or interbank market – or they can go to the non-bank public – their business of attracting deposits, which means a withdrawal of banknotes out of circulation. While the first method leaves the liquidity of the banking system unchanged, the latter leads to its increase, because banknotes in circulation means liquidity absorbing liabilities for the banking system. Therefore, as long as banknotes circulate their *circulation creates a structural liquidity deficit*[10] in the banking system which forces the banks to go to the central bank. 'Banknotes in circulation absorb the banking system's liquidity because they have to be obtained from the central bank, and credit institutions have to borrow funds from the central bank because of this' (ECB, 2004b, p. 88). However, the necessity to go to go to the central bank does not mean that banknotes in circulation are 'under the control of the monetary authority' (ECB, 2004b, p. 87). They are clearly not because of the banks' possibility of attracting deposits respectively the public's preference of banknotes over deposits. And due to these factors, the *stock* of circulating banknotes normally is not a result of monetary policy operations and, therefore, in the Eurosystem labelled as one of the so-called 'autonomous factors'[11] determining liquidity in the banking system. Notwithstanding these considerations, they do not answer the question of whether the central bank has any power to restrict the forced demand of the private banks for the *flow* of new funds, that is, banknotes and banks' reserves at the central bank. An answer can only be given by looking in more detail at the main monetary policy operations of the Eurosystem, the MROs and the LTROs.

The MROs within the Eurosystem are conducted by the NCBs[12] as weekly reverse transactions with a maturity of one week.[13] The transactions are executed through standard tenders[14] in the form of variable rate tenders.[15] In this procedure, the Governing Council sets a minimum bid rate in order to signal its monetary policy stance, and the counterparties of the NCBs, their domestic business banks, bid both the amount of money they wish to transact and the interest rate at which they wish to enter into the transaction. In preparing their bids for the forthcoming MROs, the banks are assisted by a weekly announcement of the *estimated* liquidity needs of the banking system in EMU until the settlement day for the next MRO. However, this does *not* mean a pre-announcement of the quantity of central bank money the Council has decided to allot.

In the variable rate tender, the banks' bids with the highest rates are satisfied first, followed by bids with successively lower rates, until the total quantity of central bank money to be provided is exhausted. The lowest accepted rate is the so-called *marginal rate of interest*, that is, the rate at which the aggregate quantity of bids exceeds the remaining amount to be supplied. At this rate bids are *rationed* in line with the Council's 'decision on the total amount of liquidity to be allotted' (ECB, 2004b, p. 80). The allotment procedure follows a *multiple* (American) auction,[16] that is, the interest rate for *each* counterpart's allotment is equal to *its* interest bid.

It goes without saying that the Eurosystem's variable rate tenders imply a clearly horizontal supply function of central bank money – however, it has to be emphasized, only for the commercial banks' bids *above* the marginal rate of interest. For these rates the demands of the banks are fully satisfied, while the bids at the marginal rate are allotted only *pro rata*.

Therefore, the thesis of a clearly horizontal supply function of central bank money *in toto* cannot be confirmed with respect to the Eurosystem's MROs.[17]

A closer look at four MROs between 27 October and 11 November 2003 verifies my view. The amount of bids ranged from €113 to 136 billions and the amounts of allotment from €99 to 117 billions, with a bid–cover ratio of between 1.07 and 1.50, that is, in these MRO cases the banks' demand for central bank money was never fully satisfied (ECB, 2003, p. 26). However, on a few occasions each year – for example, in 2003 on 4 March and 4 June (ECB, 2003, p. 8*) – the problem of 'underbidding' arose, meaning that the aggregate of all bids was lower than the amount the Council wanted to supply.[18] Only in such cases, is the demand for money fully satisfied, and the amounts allotted equal to the amounts of the bids, that is, the money supply function is clearly horizontal. In other words, the central bank cannot determine its money supply exogenously by forcing the commercial banks to borrow the money they want to loan, as the mainstream naïve view of 'pumping liquidity into the economy' suggests. On the other hand, as verified by the overwhelming cases of MROs in the Eurosystem, the central bank clear has some power to restrict the demand for liquidity. In these cases no clear horizontal supply function exists, other than a horizontal function restricted by the central bank's rationing of or queuing for the demand for its funds.

The power of rationing the money supply is even greater when the central bank executes fixed rate tenders, which the Eurosystem did before 28 June 2000. In this case, the demand for money by the banks at the fixed interest rate will only be satisfied when it is equal to the quantity the central bank wants to supply. In the MROs of the Eurosystem until 21 June 2000, this never happened: on the contrary the bids greatly exceeded the amount allotted. The ECB's monetary statistics reveal a 'severe overbidding . . ., which resulted from the existence of a wide and persistent spread between money market interest rates and the fixed rate' (ECB, 2004b, p. 80). In the first half of 2000, the bid–cover ratio was ca 48.5 on average, on one occasion – 7 June – even as high as over 113 (ECB, 2000, p. 6*). 'The information given by the aggregate bids was . . . useless, and the sum of aggregate bids was higher than the value of all the available collateral', leading to unforeseeable allotment ratios and the (theoretical) risk of incurring penalties in the case of lack of collateral (Vento, 2004, p. 83). That's why the Eurosystem abandoned the fixed rate tenders and introduced variable rate operations.

The power of the Eurosystem to control the supply of central bank money can also be shown with respect to its longer-term refinancing operations (LTROs), which accounted on average for 26 per cent of the outstanding amount of open market operations from January 1999, the start of the Eurosystem, until June 2003. The LTROs are executed monthly by the NCBs, with a maturity of three months. They are conducted as pure[19] variable rate tenders with, as distinct from the MROs, a *pre-announcement* of the amounts to be supplied. 'The Governing Council indicates in advance the volume to be allotted in forthcoming tenders' (ECB, 2004b, p. 82). In the first half of 1999 the bid–cover ratio varied between 3 and 5; since mid-1999 it has stabilized around 2 (ECB, 2000, p. 7*, and 2004a, p. S 8). Therefore, even in the case of the LTROs, a clearly horizontal money supply function does not exist.

But what about the Eurosystem's monetary policy instrument of marginal lending facilities (MLFs)? Do they not indicate that central bank money is fully endogenous in the Eurosystem, after all? In support of this view, the ECB can be quoted as claiming that 'the decisions on the volumes of weekly tenders *are taken so as to ensure that these operations close the liquidity deficit* of the banking system' (ECB, 1999, p. 38; emphasis added). The reason that there are more bids than available central bank money in the MROs and LTROs could be that banks avoid being forced to go to the MLFs, which carry an interest or marginal lending rate that is much higher than the rate applied to the MROs or to the overnight rate (EONIA). However, as shown above, according to the ECB, 'overbidding' has to be explained by the wide spread between the money market rates and the fixed rate, as happened until 21 June 2000 in the case of MROs with fixed rate tenders, or by 'significant interest speculation' (counterparts are betting on a rate increase) due to the two weeks duration of the MROs, as happened in the case with variable rate tenders from 28 June 2000 until 3 March 2004 – a speculation which the Council hopes to avoid by shortening the duration to one week from 10 March 2004 onward.

Independently of whether these explanations are right or not, it has to be emphasized that the European banks did not turn to the MLFs for their unsatisfied demands for central bank money. On the contrary, these facilities were used to a larger extent only after the exceptional cases of *underbidding*, for example, after the auctions of 14 February and 10 April 2001 when banks used the MLFs for a total amount above €60 billions – nearly equivalent to the total underbidding amount of €52 billions (Vento, 2004, pp. 81 f.). The ECB's monetary statistics clearly show that MLFs are used regularly, and even in cases of overbidding, on a minor scale only. In the early days of the Eurosystem, in February 1999, they provided liquidity to the banks at an amount of €3.8 billions, while the MROs and LTROs provided €104.6 and 34.2 billions respectively (ECB, 1999, p. 8*). In 2003, the MLFs had decreased to even more negligible amounts – ranging between €0.1 and 0.6 billions, with a range of €179.5 to 235.5 billions for the MROs and €45 billions for the LTROs (ECB, 2004a, p. S 9).

The small figures are not surprising, because the banks only use the MLFs 'when there are no other alternatives' in the money market for overnight loans (ECB, 2004b, p. 74). They *cannot* use them as an alternative to their demands unsatisfied by the MROs and LTROs. If the banks turned to the MLFs, the Council would forcefully restrict such a demand. 'There is no limit on resources to the standing facilities, although the ECB [the Council] may impose *restrictions* or adapt the conditions connected to their use in particular circumstances. Moreover, in the case of the marginal facility, counterparties must post an adequate amount of collateral' (ECB, 1999, p. 31; emphasis added). In another document, the ECB explains more clearly when and why the use of the MLFs has to be restricted. Within the monetary policy framework of the Eurosystem, the MLFs form an instrument 'intended to satisfy counterparties temporary liquidity needs', however, *not* corresponding to *what the banking system* deems to be necessary to close a liquidity deficit *but* to *what the Eurosystem* deems to be necessary (ECB, 2004c, p. 23). The Council as the sovereign institution to decide on the amount of central bank money to be allotted clearly rules the roost, and not the wants of the banks. Therefore, in spite of the fact that 'there is no limit to the amount of funds that can be advanced under the marginal facility', the Council always has the power of '*suspension of the facility*' when it thinks that the banks' demand for liquidity is not in accordance with its monetary policy goals. 'Access to the facility is granted only in accordance with the objectives and general monetary policy considerations of the ECB [the Council]. The ECB may adapt the conditions of the facility or *suspend it at any time*' (ECB, 2004c, pp. 23 f.; last emphasis added).

A MODIFIED HORIZONTAL SUPPLY FUNCTION OF MONEY

The message of the preceding section is clear. The Eurosystem can restrict its supply of central bank money. Therefore, this contribution concludes that the money supply function cannot be clearly horizontal.

Basil Moore and the adherents of the endogenous money school are right in rejecting the view that the supply of money can be determined exogenously by the central bank, because it cannot force the banking system to demand funds it does not want. However, this thesis does not imply that central bank money is fully endogenous. Central banks do not supply cash reserves in each and every case to the banking system automatically on demand at the minimum lending rate. On the contrary, they have the power to control the supply by restricting the demand

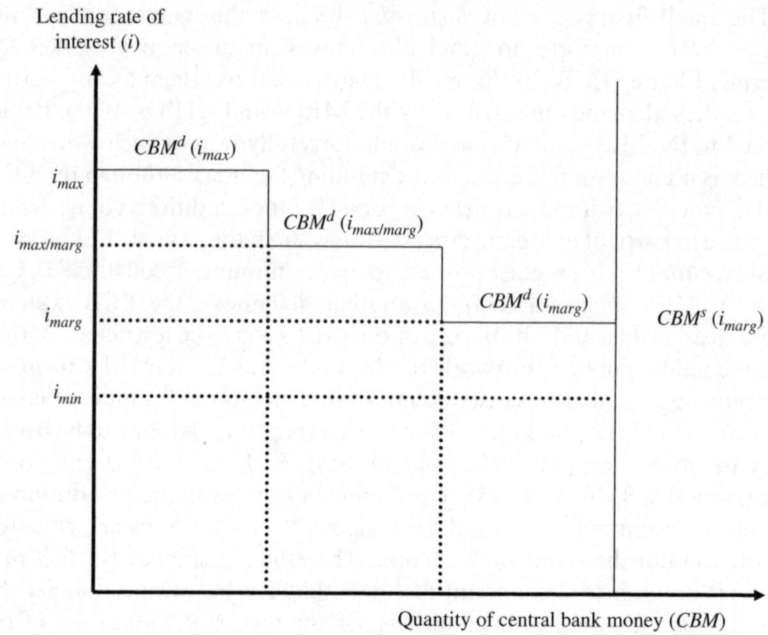

Figure 8.1 The modified horizontal or 'staircase' supply function of central bank money

through rationing or queuing when they deem the demand as endangering their capital[20] or interfering with their monetary policy goals if fully satisfied. Therefore, the endogenous money supply function is not clearly horizontal and has to be modified. But how?

I suggest a diagram for the MROs of the Eurosystem, with the different bid rates of interest on the vertical axis and the amount of central bank money allotted on the horizontal axis, in which a vertical line is inserted in that part of the horizontal supply function which is related to the accepted lowest rate, the marginal lending rate, i_{marg}. The vertical line indicates the amount of money the central bank supplies by restricting the demand for it at the marginal rate.

In Figure 8.1, the money supply function would start as a horizontal line at the highest bid rate, i_{max}, at which the demand for central bank money, CBM^d, is fully satisfied. It is followed successively by similar, but lower, horizontal lines for all bid rates, $i_{max/marg}$ below i_{max} and above i_{marg}, at which the demand, again, is fully satisfied. Next comes the again lower horizontal line corresponding to the marginal lending rate, i_{marg}, at which the demand is rationed. This is shown by a vertical line, cutting or, better: 'ending', the i_{marg}

line. The vertical line represents the supply of central bank money, CBM^s, and indicates the power of the central bank to restrict demand. It goes without saying that the horizontal line below i_{marg}, corresponding to the lowest bid rate, i_{min}, represents a virtual demand only because it is not satisfied at all. *In toto*, the money supply function looks like a descending staircase ending, not at the floor, but at a wall.[21]

NOTES

1. This chapter is a revised and extended version of section II of Steiger (2004). Fruitful discussions with Marc Lavoie of the University of Ottawa on the endogeneity of central bank money in the Eurosystem are acknowledged.
2. Basil Moore (1988, pp. 222 and 254) has acknowledged, with reference to my earlier writings with Gunnar Heinsohn between 1983 and 1986, that our private property approach to money implies an *endogenous* determination of the money supply. They 'have argued forcefully that modern money did not evolve from commodity money to replace barter as is conventionally believed, but rather was intrinsically related to the need for credit with the development of capitalism and private property' (p. 222). Due to a better understanding of the role of property as distinct from possession for the creation of money in our writings from 1996 onward, we have modified our view on the endogeneity of money as presented in this contribution.
3. To avoid the problem of 'fictitious assets', popular in Germany in the 1920s and decisively contributing to the destruction of its monetary system, so-called 'financial titles', that is, debt titles issued by a competing bank *D*, will also not be accepted for the refinancing of *A*.
4. However, Bagehot – in contrast to Steuart, Thornton and Hawtrey – did not comprehend the full meaning of such a loss. While the latter two unequivocally saw the loss of the bank's *own capital*, the former stressed the loss of the bank's *reserve* in the form of its own notes. The holding of such a reserve by the Bank of England was due to its particular division into an Issue and a Banking Department. Without this particularity, a central bank never holds its notes as a reserve because for a bank of issue they are not an asset but a liability. Therefore, it deletes them from its books the very moment they flow back against the return of the debt instruments which were conditional for their creation. At the Bank of England, this demonetization of the notes occurred at the Issue Department when it handed out gold against its notes. Therefore, the Banking Department, which could not create the notes, had to hold a reserve of banknotes equal to the amount deposited with it by the commercial banks, which themselves did not hold such a reserve; for more detail, see Steiger (2002, pp. 58 f.).
5. This verdict also holds for a prominent Post Keynesian, Marc Lavoie, who, in an analysis of a pure credit system, emphasizes that the 'unique bank could become insolvent . . . if the amount of defaulting loans were to exceed the amount of own funds of the bank, thus reducing the value of assets below the value of liabilities' (2003, p. 515). However, when it comes to the analysis of the two-stage banking system such insights are missing in Lavoie's discussion of the balance sheet of the central bank (2003, pp. 519–41).
6. In economic texts, the trivial necessity of double bookkeeping in the balance sheet to contra an entry on the asset side on the liability side and *vice versa*, with a surplus (deficit) assets over liabilities to be booked on the liability (asset) side, often leads to improper conclusions as to the character of these items, for example, in the popular view of own capital or net worth as 'a liability to oneself'. As a matter of course, positive (negative) own capital is no liability (claim) but an asset (liability), because it is booked on the liability (asset) side only to equilibrate the balance sheet. Correspondingly, in the profit and loss account the profit (loss) as surplus (deficit) of returns over costs does not mean that

profits are costs and losses returns, because the former have to be booked as contra entries on the cost and the latter on the return side. To avoid such confusions, the Bank for International Settlements has proposed to call the opposite of the asset side not simply the 'liability side' but the 'liability *and capital* side'; see Blenck et al. (2001, pp. 39–42; emphasis added).
7. For a further discussion of this conclusion see note 20 below.
8. For more detail on the Eurosystem, with emphasis on its missing lender of last resort, see Heinsohn and Steiger (2006a), Spethmann and Steiger (2005) and Steiger (forthcoming).
9. An alternative to injecting central bank money into the banking system are outright purchases of assets in foreign currency by the NCBs which would reduce the need for MROs and LTROs. However, although foreign assets in the Eurosystem provide nearly as much liquidity to the banking system of EMU as is absorbed by the circulation of banknotes – €331.3 billions compared to 373.2 daily average stocks between 24 May and 23 June 2003 (ECB, 2004b, p. 88) – additional purchases are not practiced because, unlike the case of repurchase transactions used in the MROs and LTROs (see below), the risk of holding assets purchased outright lies with the NCBs, and not with the private banks.
10. The other factor which has a liquidity-absorbing effect for the banking system are banks' reserve requirements. Unlike the stock of banknotes in circulation (see below), theirs is clearly reliant on monetary policy operations.
11. The other autonomous factors are government deposits and net foreign assets. While the former are liquidity absorbing liabilities and not under the control of the central bank, the latter are liquidity providing assets and can be controlled by the central bank.
12. The allocation of the MROs between the 12 NCBs and, therefore, of their share of euro banknotes is determined by the NCBs' paid-up share in the ECB's capital. (The ECB is owned by the NCBs.)
13. As of 10 March 2004; two weeks prior to that date.
14. 'Standard' means tender operations conducted according to a pre-announced schedule, which is completed within 24 hours from the tender's announcement to the communication of the results.
15. As of 28 June 2000; prior to that date in the form of fixed rate tenders.
16. The alternative to this procedure would be a *single* rate (Dutch) auction, that is, the interest rate for *all* counterpartis is equal to the marginal interest rate; see ECB (2004c, p. 63).
17. A rationing of its money supply was also practiced in the monetary policy operations of the Bundesbank before it became part of the Eurosystem. Until the mid-1980s the Bank's MROs consisted exclusively of discounting bills of exchange or trade bills which were allotted *pro rata* to the commercial banks, that is, the latter's demand for central bank money was never fully satisfied. With the rise of repurchase agreements in the mid-1980s, discounting survived on a minor scale. As the repo rate (the interest rate stipulated by the Bundesbank for repurchase agreements) was set above the discount rate, the acceptance of bills of exchange *had* to be rationed, of course.
18. From the beginning of single monetary policy in EMU until July 2003, underbidding has occurred nine times – once before and eight times after the adoption of variable rate tenders (Vento, 2004, p. 81). The ECB regards such cases as 'episodes' stemming from 'significant interest speculation' (counterparts are betting on a rate cut) triggered by the duration of the MROs' maturity of two weeks, which the Council hopes to overcome by shortening the maturity to one week as in the Federal Reserve System (ECB, 2004b, p. 82); see note 13 above. For a closer look at the Eurosystem's experience with under- and overbidding see Bindseil (2004, pp. 5–15).
19. Variable tenders without a minimum bid rate.
20. In defence of Moore's clearly horizontal money supply function, it could be argued that the central bank is usually backed by a State with the authority to tax and, therefore, the ability to top up the central bank's own capital in case of a loss. This was done during the 1990s in, for example, Chile (see Fry, 1997, p. 344), Brazil and Hungary (Dalton and Dziobek, 2005, pp. 8–10), but with the result that their central banks, and the currencies they issue, lost reputation, as most strikingly in the recent case of the Argentine central

bank during the peso crisis of 2001/02; see Steiger (2002, pp. 79 f.). In the Eurosystem such backing would be impossible because its NCBs – and also the ECB – are owned by the different member states of EMU, and the European Commission in Brussels disposes only of the tiny sum of about 2 per cent of the European Union's aggregate gross domestic product (GDP); see Spethmann and Steiger (2005, p. 63) and Steiger (forthcoming).

21. Corresponding diagrams for the LTROs and MLFs of the Eurosystem would in no way differ from that for the MROs.

REFERENCES

Bagehot, W. (1873) *Lombard Street: A Description of the Money Market*, New York: Scribner, Armstrong. Reprinted New York: John Wiley & Sons, 1999.

Bindseil, U. (2004) 'Over- and Underbidding in Central Bank Operations Conducted as Fixed Rate Tenders', in *ZEI Working Papers*, Universität Bonn: Center for European Integration Studies (ZEI), B 03, February.

Blanchard, O. (2003) *Macroeconomics*, 3rd edition, Upper Saddle River, NJ: Prentice Hall.

Blenck, D., H. Hasko, S. Hilton and K. Masaki (2001) 'The Main Features of the Monetary Policy Framework of the Bank of Japan, the Federal Reserve System and the Eurosystem', in Bank for International Settlements (BIS), *Comparing Monetary Policy Operating Procedures across the United States, Japan and the Euro Area: BIS Paper New Series*, 9, December, 23–56.

Bofinger, P., with J. Reischle and A. Schächter (2001) *Monetary Policy: Goals, Institutions, Strategies, and Instruments*, Oxford: Oxford University Press.

Dalton, J. and C. Dziobek (2005) 'Central Bank Losses and Experiences in Selected Countries', IMF Working Paper, WP/05/72, April.

ECB (1999) *Monthly Bulletin of the European Central Bank*, May.

ECB (2000) *Monthly Bulletin of the European Central Bank*, July.

ECB (2003) *Monthly Bulletin of the European Central Bank*, December.

ECB (2004a) *Monthly Bulletin of the European Central Bank*, January.

ECB (2004b) *The Monetary Policy of the ECB*, 2nd edition, Frankfurt am Main: European Central Bank, February.

ECB (2004c) *The Implementation of Monetary Policy in the Euro Area: General Documentation on Eurosystem Monetary Policy Instruments and Procedures*, Frankfurt am Main: European Central Bank, March.

Folkerts-Landau, D. and P.M. Garber (1992) 'The ECB: A Bank or a Monetary Policy Rule?', in: M.B. Canzonieri, V. Grilli and M. Masson (eds), *Establishing a Central Bank: Issues in Europe and Lessons from the US*, Cambridge: Cambridge University Press, 86–110.

Fry, M. (1997) 'The Fiscal Abuse of Central Banks', in M.I. Blejer and T. Ter-Minasian (eds), *Macroeconomic Dimensions of Central Banks: Essays in Honour of Vito Tanzi*, London: Routledge, 337–59.

Goodhart, C.A.E. (1999) 'Myths about the Lender of Last Resort', in C.A.E. Goodhart and G. Illing (2002), 227–45.

Goodhart, C.A.E. (ed.) (2000a) *Which Lender of Last Resort for Europe?*, London: Central Banking Publications.

Goodhart, C.A.E. (2000b) 'Introduction', in C.A.E. Goodhart (2000a), 3–12.

Goodhart, C.A.E. and G. Illig (eds) (2002) *Financial Crises, Contagion, and the Lender of Last Resort*, Oxford: Oxford University Press.

Hawtrey, R.G. (1932) *The Art of Central Banking*, London: Longmans; new impression, London: Frank Cass & Co., 1970.

Heinsohn, G. and O. Steiger (1996) *Eigentum, Zins und Geld: Ungelöste Rätsel der Wirtschaftswissenschaft*, Reinbek: Rowohlt; 3rd, reset and corrected edition, Marburg: Metropolis, 2004.

Heinsohn, G. and O. Steiger (2000a) 'The Property Theory of Interest and Money', in J. Smithin (ed.), *What Is Money?*, London: Routledge, pp. 67–100. Reprinted, with corrections and additions, in G. Hodgson (ed.), *Recent Developments in Institutional Economics*, Cheltenham, UK and Northampton, MA, USA: Edward Elgar, 2003, 486–517.

Heinsohn, G. and O. Steiger (2000b) 'Warum eine Zentralbank nicht über ihr Geld verfügen kann' (Comment on H. Riese (2000)), *Ethik und Sozialwissenschaften: Streitforum für Erwägungskultur*, 11(4) (December), 516–19.

Heinsohn, G. and O. Steiger (2006a) 'The European Central Bank and the Eurosystem: An Analysis of the Missing Central Monetary Institution in European Monetary Union', in D. Ehrig and O. Steiger (eds), *The Euro, the Eurosystem, and European Economic and Monetary Union*, Hamburg: LIT-Verlag.

Heinsohn, G. and O. Steiger (2006b) *Eigentumsökonomik*, Marburg: Metropolis.

Heinsohn, G. and O. Steiger (forthcoming), 'Interest and Money: The Property Explanation', in P. Arestis and M. Sawyer (eds), *A Handbook of Alternative Economics*, Cheltenham, UK and Northampton, MA, USA: Edward Elgar.

Krugman, P.R. and M. Obstfeld (2003, *International Economics: Theory and Policy*, 6th edition, Boston: Addison Wesley.

Lavoie, M. (2003) 'A Primer on Endogenous Credit-Money', in L.-P. Rochon and S. Rossi (eds), *Modern Theories of Money: The Nature and Role of Money in Capitalist Economies*, Cheltenham, UK and Northampton, MA, USA: Edward Elgar, 506–43.

Lavoie, M. (2004) E-mail to Otto Steiger, 17 February.

Lerrick A. (2001) 'A Way Out for Japan', *Financial Times*, 1 May, 13.

Mishkin, F.S. (2000) *The Economics of Money, Banking, and Financial Markets*, 6th edition, Boston: Addison Wesley.

Moore, B.J. (1988) *Horizontalists and Verticalists: The Macroeconomics of Credit Money*, Cambridge: Cambridge University Press.

Riese, H. (1993) 'Bagehot versus Goodhart: Why a Central Bank Needs Commercial Banks'; translated from the German original in J. Hölscher and H. Toman (eds), *Money, Development and Economic Transformation: Selected Essays by Hajo Riese*, London and New York: Palgrave Macmillan, 2004, 1–59.

Riese, H. (2000) 'Geld – die unverstandene Kategorie der Nationalökonomie', *Ethik und Sozialwissenschaften: Streitforum für Erwägungskultur*, 11(4) (December), 487–98.

Schoenmaker, D. (2000) 'What Kind of Financial Stability for Europe?', in C.A.E. Goodhart (2000a), 213–23.

Schwartz, A.J. (2002) 'Earmarks of a Lender of Last Resort', in C.A.E. Goodhart and G. Illig (2002), 449–60.

Spahn, H.-P. (2001) *From Gold to Euro: Monetary Theory and the History of Currency Systems*, Berlin: Springer.

Spethmann, D. and O. Steiger (2005) 'The Four Achilles' Heels of the Eurosystem: Missing Central Monetary Institution, Different Real Rates of Interest, Nonmarketable Securities, and Missing Lender of Last Report', *International Journal of Political Economy*, 34(2), Summer, 46–68.

Stadermann, H.-J. (2000) 'Aus Nichts wird Nichts' (Comment on H. Riese (2000)), *Ethik und Sozialwissenschaften: Streitforum für Erwägungskultur*, 11(4) (December), 534–7.

Steiger, O. (2002) 'Der Staat als "Lender of Last Resort" – oder: Die Achillesferse des Eurosystems', in I. Barens and M. Pickardt (eds), *Die Rolle des Staates in der Ökonomie – Finanzwissenschaftliche Perspektiven: Festschrift für Otto Roloff zum 65. Geburtstag*, Marburg: Metropolis, 51–84.

Steiger, O. (2004) 'Which Lender of Last Resort for the Eurosystem? A Contribution to the Theory of Central Banking', paper presented at Complexity, Endogenous Money and Exogenous Interest Rates: A Conference in Honour of Basil Moore, Universiteit van Stellenbosch, Stellenbosch, South Africa, 7–11 January.

Steiger, O. (forthcoming) 'Which Lender of Last Resort for the Eurosystem?', in V. Chick (ed.), *The Challenge of Endogenous Money: Theory and Policy*, London: Palgrave Macmillan. (Earlier version published in *ZEI Working Papers*, Universität Bonn: Center for European Integration Studies (ZEI), B23, September 2004.)

Steuart, J. (1767) *An Inquiry into the Principles of Political Oeconomy: Being an Essay on the Science of Domestic Policy in Free Nations*, London: A. Millar & T. Cadell. Reprinted Düsseldorf: Verlag Wirtschaft und Finanzen, 1993, vol. II.

Thornton, H. (1802) *An Enquiry into the Nature and Effects of the Paper Credit of Great Britain*, ed. with an introduction by F.A. Hayek, London: G. Allen & Unwin, 1939.

Vento, G.A. (2004) 'The Eurosystem Operational Framework, Use of Collateral, and Liquidity Distribution in the Euro Area: Towards a Single Interbank Market', *Banca Nazionale del Lavoro Quarterly Review*, 57(223) (March), 71–100.

9. Endogenous money, central banks and the banking system: Basil Moore and the supply of credit

Louis-Philippe Rochon[1]

> Credit is the pavement along which production travels; and bankers if they knew their duties, would provide the transport facilities to just the extent that is required in order that the productive powers of the community can be employed to their full capacity.
>
> Keynes, Treatise, II, 220

INTRODUCTION

Basil Moore is a central figure in post-Keynesian economics. His numerous contributions to monetary policy and theory have had over the years an enormous impact on an entire generation of post-Keynesians. It is therefore a true privilege, to say the very least, to contribute a chapter to Basil's Festschrift, and a pleasure to honor the man, the scholar and a friend whose views I not only respect, but which very much influenced the core of my thinking. Indeed, it is in part because of Basil's work that I am an unrepented horizontalist.

It was in the early 1980s, when I was a student at the University of Ottawa, that I was first introduced to Basil's ideas. I was a junior majoring in economics. Due to a lack of interesting courses, I signed up for an obscure course called *Introduction to Post-Keynesian Economics* taught by an equally obscure professor (at least for me, at the time) named Marc Lavoie. I had no idea of what I was getting myself into. Obviously the course had a profound impact on me, and two decades later, I remain a devoted horizontalist and a student of realism. Today, a number of post-Keynesians are devoted to the 'Moorian' or Kaldorian view of central bank policy (which we may also call the Eichnerian view).

The purpose of this chapter is to honor Basil, and to add to his body of research by offering a way of tying up some loose ends. The chapter begins with a quick review of the structuralist/horizontalist debates of the early

1990s. It looks at two very specific criticisms directed at Basil's views on endogenous money, namely that commercial banks and the central bank are both 'passive' players in the money creation process. I argue that this was never Basil's position.

The next section develops a more detailed theory of the supply of bank credit, based on Basil's insights. Although he rarely discussed the supply of credit, the theory developed here is wholly consistent with his views, and fills an important void in the horizontalist theory of bank lending. This approach rests on two core characteristics of Post Keynesian economics: uncertainty and endogenous money.

Indeed, it has been said that in horizontalism, commercial banks lend to all who demand credit. As I will argue here, this is not the case: there is ample room within the horizontalist view of endogenous money to recognize a 'fringe of unsatisfied customers' and the possible lack of accommodation from central banks (Lavoie, 1996). Once this is accomplished, it becomes clear that we should, in fact, all be horizontalists now!

THE STRUCTURALIST/HORIZONTALIST DEBATE REVISITED

Endogenous money is a central component of post-Keynesian theory. It is the foundation upon which the theories of effective demand, distribution and growth are built. Indeed, if credit is needed to finance production and investment, then there cannot be wages, effective demand or growth without bank credit. This is the essence of Keynes's 'monetary theory of production'.

Moore's seminal book, *Horizontalists and Verticalists*, published in 1988 – what King (2002, p. 175) calls the 'definitive . . . defence of horizontalism' – continued down the path well established in the post-Keynesian tradition by such luminaries as Alfred Eichner, Nicholas Kaldor, and Joan Robinson. It explored and presented clear ideas pertaining to the functioning of the banking system and in particular the central bank. The book quickly led to an important debate, with challenges from well-known structuralists like Palley (1991), Pollin (1991) and Wray (1992a, p. 297). For structuralists, horizontalism is an extreme version of endogenous money, and is a special case (Wray, 1992c, p. 172).

The debates focused immediately on two important arguments. The specific role of the central bank was front and center, but so was the ability of banks to lend to potential borrowers. Hence, structuralists directly criticized Moore, claiming that his approach to endogenous money was an extreme position.

For instance, Cottrell (1994, p. 599) argues that 'on the Kaldor–Moore view . . . the banks are mere ciphers in this process, passively accommodating whatever demands they happen to experience'. Minsky (1996, p. 77) refers to them as 'simpletons'. Rousseas (1992, p. 79) calls the horizontalist approach 'political, not economic'. Cottrell (1988, 1994) calls it 'radical endogeneity', while Wray (1992b, p. 1160) refers to it as an 'extreme' post-Keynesian theory of money.

At the heart of the matter is a particular interpretation of horizontalism, according to which banks grant credit to anyone who demands it; banks simply do not refuse credit. Dow and Dow (1989, p. 164, n. 12), for instance, claim that 'it surely cannot be suggested that credit is fully accommodating to the extent that no potential borrower is ever refused credit'. Wray (1992c, p. 172) interprets the horizontalist position in the same light:

> private banks passively supply credit money at any short-term interest rate established by the central bank's discount and open market policies. They are able to meet any level of credit demand since they can always obtain reserves from the central bank at the discount rate. . . . There is no room in [Moore's] model for liquidity preference, for entrepreneurial financial institutions, for market power, or for credit rationing and quantity restraints.

Yet, as I have carefully shown elsewhere (see Rochon, 1999, ch. 5) in trying to 'set the record straight', these accusations were groundless: Moore *never* claimed that banks passively supplied all loans demanded, nor for that matter did he claim that central banks passively accommodated the reserve needs of banks (on which, see below). On the contrary, Moore defended the notions that both the central bank and commercial banks are active in their lending activities and not 'passive' players in the money creation process. Banks do refuse credit to many borrowers, and central banks may not fully accommodate. But these acknowledgements never put into question his horizontalist believe in the exogeneity of the rate of interest, endogenous money or indeed the horizontal money supply curve. What Moore made amply clear is that banks will accept all those borrowers who meet the creditworthy criteria established by the banks themselves.

For instance, Moore (1996, p. 90) argues that 'provided borrowers have sufficient asset and/or income collateral, they will be granted formal lines of credit up to some predetermined amount', thereby specifically acknowledging that some borrowers will be refused credit if they do not meet the collateral requirements of the banks.

And neither is this an argument developed late in his writings. In fact, it runs through his work. In Moore (1994, p. 123, original emphasis), we find:

> This is not to deny that many small borrowers are effectively credit-constrained. New businesses and poor households in particular do not possess the income, assets, and credit record criteria that banks require in order to make profitable and financially sound loans (the banks' three C's: credit, collateral and character).

The argument is repeated in Moore (1995, p. 264, original emphasis):

> In an overdraft system, bank accommodation of increased demand for funds by credit-worthy borrowers is in no sense extreme. It is instead, completely normal, *so long as borrowers remain within their allocated credit limits.*

If these references to Moore were unique, then perhaps the structuralist criticism could be well taken. However, this is not the case, since Moore made the same argument as early as 1988, in *Horizontalists and Verticalists.* Here, Moore (1988) explicitly argues that:

> commercial bank loan officers must assure that loan requests meet the bank's income and asset collateral requirements. They must in general satisfy themselves as to the credit-worthiness of the project and the character of the borrower. It is precisely for these reasons that banks develop client relationships with their borrowers.

It is still unclear why debate centered on the alleged passivity of commercial banks since Moore's position was clear throughout his career. Moreover, what this shows is that Moore recognized early on the compatibility of the horizontalist position with Keynes's 'fringe of unsatisfied customers'. This has been confirmed by Lavoie (1993, p. 10) who writes that 'to argue that the money supply is horizontal is not to argue that there are no constraints on credit'. Lavoie (1996, p. 284) later writes clearly that 'the claim, quite legitimate, that banks have some restrictions on their lending does not call into question the validity of horizontalism. . . . Banks often choose not to lend.' Rochon (1999, p. 170) reiterates this point, arguing that 'horizontalists acknowledge and accept the notion that banks often *do* restrict credit. Banks do not meet all the demand for loans. Despite this, the slope of the money supply curve is unaffected.'

As for the role of the central bank, the debate was surely more intense, and certainly dominated the debates, leading Pollin (1991) to coin the expression 'accommodationist' to describe horizontalists. The debate centered not only on whether the central bank meets all the demand for bank reserves, but also on the implications of such policy actions. Structuralists argued that a lack of accommodation would automatically hinder the ability of banks to lend.

But this debate was again a misinterpretation of Moore's position, and that of horizontalists in general. It was always recognized, although perhaps not in as forthright a manner, that central banks do not always meet the demand for bank reserves. But the overall argument here was that central banks need to protect against the possibility of a banking crisis. This is why Moore (1979, p. 126) 'rank[s] the supportive responsibilities of central banks above their control duties'. This is certainly an argument with which all post-Keynesians agree.

Moreover, if horizontalists agree that central banks may not always accommodate all the reserve needs, this remains nonetheless rare, and is done only when the central bank wants to change the rate of interest. Indeed, a lack of accommodation would result in an increase in the rate of interest. Hence, the actions of the central bank affect the price, not the quantity of loans. It is for these reasons that Moore (1985, p. 12) argued repeatedly that central banks are 'impotent in their ability to restrict the rate of growth of the money stock' (Moore, 1985, p. 12).

But the lack of accommodation would also jeopardize the stability of financial markets. This is certainly a theme that runs through post-Keynesian theory. But this implies that non-accommodation cannot be done repeatedly. Hence, to guarantee the stability of markets and to prevent systemic risk, the central bank necessarily accommodates. Hence, rather than being an extreme position, it is a general rule. Even Wray (1999, p. 109), with his more recent conversion to the horizontalist cause, accepts the horizontalist doctrine, despite his earlier rejection of it.

This implies therefore that the supply of reserves is endogenous to economic activity. According to Eichner (1987, p. 850):

> The change in the Fed's holdings of government securities and thus its open market operations, instead of being strictly a policy variable, is for the most part endogenously determined by the need to maintain the liquidity of the banking system. Indeed, this is why it is an error to assume, as macroeconomic theory normally does, that the monetary base, or high-powered money . . . is an exogenously determined policy variable.

Eichner (1987, p. 847) identifies two types of reserve endogeneity behavior: defensive and accommodating behaviors. The accommodative behavior of the central bank is the traditional post-Keynesian role attributed to central banks. In this context, the central bank agrees to supply additional reserves incurred as a result of increases in commercial bank loans or credit, which create deposits and reserves. As a result, commercial banks are in need of reserves. Typically, they will turn to the central bank and borrow these reserves, which the central bank accommodates.

The post-Keynesian emphasis was necessarily on the reserve needs following an increase in bank *credit*. This was because of the overall emphasis on endogenous money, and the specific link between credit, the creation of bank deposits and endogenous money. Post-Keynesians also usually assume a single-bank system.

Yet, post-Keynesians largely ignored an important aspect of central bank operations, which has not gone unnoticed by some, including Moore, who unfortunately never developed this aspect of his theory.

Apart from changes in the supply of credit altering the liquidity position of banks, there are a multitude of daily operations that do the same thing. This is especially true in a multi-bank system where transactions take place between two agents each with accounts at different banks. Hence, a simple transaction between two agents implies the creation of interbank debts, which are settled on the accounts of the central bank. Each transaction modifies the liquidity position of each bank, leading to surplus and deficit banks. These transactions then place pressure on the rate of interest and the system as a whole. The central bank is therefore needed to offset and neutralize these flows of money. This is what Eichner (1987, p. 847) calls the defensive role of the central bank, which he defines as the 'component of the Fed's open market operations [consisting] of buying or selling government securities so that, on net balance, it offsets these flows into or out of the monetary-financial system'. Eichner gives an excellent account of this view, which has now been developed by others, including Lavoie (2006) and Rochon and Rossi (2004a, 2004b). This suggests that central banks are active not only in meeting the reserve needs of banks whenever a credit is created, but also in meeting the day-to-day needs of the banking system so as to both neutralize any unwanted pressures on interest rates and prevent systemic risk.

But Moore (1989, p. 26, emphasis added) made the exact same argument, which has never been recognized by other post-Keynesians (although see Rochon, 1999, ch. 5):

> Once it is recognised that loans are made at borrower initiative, and that loans create deposits, it logically follows that the money supply, bank reserves, and the high-powered base all vary endogenously in response to changes in the demand for *money* and *credit*.

Moore therefore recognizes the dual role of the central bank, both in terms of its accommodative role (the commercial banks' demand for reserves as a result of changes in the demand for *credit*), and its defensive role (resulting from changes in the demand for *money*).[2] I believe that had the defensive role – and thus the need of the central bank to intervene on a continuous basis – been highlighted, the horizontalist position would have been strengthened considerably. I would argue that it is the defensive role that is perhaps the most relevant role, as discussed at length by Eichner (1987), especially given the declining importance of reserves in recent years.

Like Eichner, Moore recognizes that the defensive role is by far the more important role. It is to say that the 'lender-of-last-resort' role of the central bank is not just of the fireman's type that rushes in to extinguish a crisis. Rather, it is ongoing. According to Moore (1988, p. 59):

> By far the bulk of the central bank's open-market operations involve continuously injecting into or withdrawing funds from the wholesale market defensively, in response to changes in net inflows and outflows of funds, as to maintain the depth of liquidity of these financial markets.

This suggests that Moore recognizes both short-run (changes in the composition of the money supply resulting from daily transactions) and long-run roles (resulting from changes or growth in the demand for credit) for the central bank. Indeed, the short-run role of the central bank is not only to set the rate of interest, but also to assure the smooth operation of the financial system on a daily basis and to prevent systemic risk from spreading. In the latter instance, the central bank accommodates the increasing demand for reserves to sustain the additional lending activities of banks. In the former, however, there are fluctuations in the commercial banks' need for reserves arising from the payments mechanism. The central bank responds to these needs in order to hit its interest rate target.

UNCERTAINTY AND THE BANKING SYSTEM

Having established that horizontalists and Moore in particular have clearly emphasized that banks do not always lend to all those who demand credit – that, indeed, many borrowers are credit constrained – how can we then develop a theory of credit supply from the post-Keynesian/horizontalist perspective? The challenge for horizontalists is to develop a theory of bank credit supply (and hence a theory of the transmission mechanism) that is consistent with some fundamental post-Keynesian arguments, namely endogenous money, the importance of aggregate demand and the existence of uncertainty.

As stated above, Moore did give some indications as to how to do all this, but his analysis remains largely undeveloped. The purpose of this section, therefore, is to suggest a possible extension of Moore's analysis, one that is consistent with the horizontalist perspective and post-Keynesian theory overall. In so doing, I will borrow some key insights from New Keynesians, but will incorporate them within a model of aggregate demand where banks always have the ability to lend, although they may choose not to do so. In this respect, it draws from Lavoie (1992, 1996), Moore (1988) and Wolfson (1996).

As the post-Keynesian theory of money emphasizes, banks create money in response to the demand for credit from the general public, generally but not exclusively from firms who wish to finance production. It is in this sense that the theory of output is simultaneously a theory of credit and money. Money creation results in the recording of borrowers' debts on the asset side of banks' balance sheets and deposits on the liability side. It is in this sense that loans create deposits. Obviously, banks cannot lend if there are no borrowers willing to enter into debt (Robinson, 1952, p. 29). The creation of money is thus proof of the existence of debt.

Banks therefore play a central role in economic activity (see Rochon, 1999 for how banks are important for an analysis of the multiplier). There is direct link between bank lending and output. A fall in the supply of credit can translate itself into an important drop in output. Hence, it is important to better understand the mechanisms behind the decisions of banks to grant credit. Yet, contrary to more orthodox or neoclassical theories, credit constraints in the post-Keynesian sense are not defined as a fall in the available supply of credit, as in the case of, for example, New Keynesianism, where a credit crunch is explained by a 'significant leftward shift in the supply curve for bank loans' (Bernanke and Lown, 1991, p. 207). By advocating a supply-determined theory of credit, their emphasis is naturally on credit *rationing*: there is a fixed amount of credit, determined by the liabilities of the banks, that must be rationed between those who demand credit.

For post-Keynesians, however, this is not the case. Emphasis is not on credit rationing, but rather on credit *constraints*: credit is not rationed in the sense of being in limited supply, but rather constrained by the limited number of creditworthy borrowers. Hence, any theory of credit supply must focus on the creditworthiness of borrowers, rather than the availability of credit. This is an important first difference. Yet, the behavior of commercial banks must also be taken into consideration. Indeed, banks set the norms and standards of creditworthiness. In this sense, a post-Keynesian theory of bank lending must focus simultaneously on the creditworthiness of borrowers, that is the 'financial profile' of borrowers (their income, assets, and credit history), as well as the behavior of banks, who are responsible for defining and redefining the conventions used to established the creditworthiness of would-be borrowers.

The problem now resides in how we translate this into a viable post-Keynesian theory of bank lending. To begin, we must acknowledge that banks have considerable discretionary powers to accept or deny a loan.

Loans are not automatic. The primary consideration of any bank in making lending decisions is whether the client is able to reimburse its loan in a timely fashion. Banks therefore face considerable uncertainty regarding the ability of firms to reimburse their existing and future debt. This necessarily implies that to be considered creditworthy, borrowers must prove their ability to reimburse their debt, either by providing sufficient collateral, or by showing they are capable of generating sufficient income in the future to reimburse their debt with interest. Banks must therefore take all of this into consideration: in other words, they must make sure that borrowers are creditworthy now and will remain creditworthy in the future. As Lavoie (1996, p. 284) writes, 'because of uncertainty and the complexities of decision making, bank lending depends on whether or not the potential borrower fulfils various norms and customs'.

Of course, all this can be found in Keynes's *Treatise on Money* (1971a, p. 212), in a now famous passage:

> There is apt to be an unsatisfied fringe of borrowers, the size of which can be expanded or contracted, so that banks can influence the volume of investment by expanding or contracting the volume of their loans, without there being necessarily any change in the level of the bank-rate, in the demand-schedule of borrowers, or in the volume of lending otherwise than through the banks. This phenomenon is capable, when it exists, of having great practical importance.

Let us then see how uncertainty affects the supply of bank credit. In this respect, banks will typically face two different sources of uncertainty, which can be labeled, respectively, microuncertainty and macrouncertainty. Microuncertainty will be defined as arising from the 'probability' (perhaps a poor choice of words) that a *particular* bank borrower will default, arising from insufficient sales receipts or the inability to generate sufficient profits to reimburse bank debt regardless of the business cycle. Macrouncertainty, on the other hand, is defined as ignorance regarding the future level of effective demand and the business cycle, and the unknown level of real interest rates set by the central bank. Macrouncertainty affects all firms. This analysis is similar to Keynes's lenders' risk, described in the *General Theory*. Recall that Keynes claimed that lender's risk resulted from 'either moral hazard, i.e., the voluntary default or other means of escape, possibly lawful, from the fulfillment of the obligation, or to the possible insufficiency of the margin of security, i.e., involuntary default due to the disappointment of expectation' (1973, p. 144). Here, there is no 'voluntary default'. Both micro and macrouncertainty affects the 'involuntary default' of the borrower, but in different ways.

Microuncertainty is present irrespective of the level of effective demand and hence of where we are in the business cycle. For instance, even if effective demand is strong and the economy is growing, inevitably some firms may still be unable to meet their contractual agreements with banks and will default, resulting from mismanagement or poor sales. This may be called a bad loan. In this sense, responsibility must be shared with the bank for failure to properly evaluate borrowers due to asymmetric information, which may arise for a number of reasons. Banks may not have all the relevant information about a firm, the competence of its managerial team or other pertinent issues. Whether this information is asymmetric or simply unknown to both parties is not the issue. From the bank's point of view, it may not be able to properly assess the potential of a firm to generate profits in the future. *Ex post* of course, it is always easy to identity the bad loans; *ex ante*, the bank must place a 'bet' despite its best efforts to evaluate the borrower.

Macrouncertainty will affect all firms equally. A general downturn in the cycle will pose a risk to all firms. This is the concept of uncertainty post-Keynesians often discuss: we 'simply do not know' the future course of the cycle and how it will affect firms. While post-Keynesians have emphasized uncertainty and incorporated it within their theories of investment and consumption, little has been done to incorporate it within a theory of banking (see Wolfson, 1996). Banks, just like firms and households, are unaware of the future, and how it will subsequently impact on overall firms. This is in fact a 'bet' on the future of the business cycle, or more accurately, on the future course of short-term real rates and their effect on effective demand. Indeed, for post-Keynesians (see Lavoie, 1992), interest rates are a distributive variable. Any increase in the rate of interest will favor rentiers and may therefore have a negative impact on effective demand.

Of course, an increase in the rate of interest may also have a microuncertainty effect. A rise in the rate may translate into higher costs of servicing loans, and affect the individual borrower's cash flow. Weak firms may not be able to survive this increase in the rate of interest. In Minskian terminology, borrowers may go first from hedge, to speculative and finally to Ponzi situations.

I believe that the New Keynesian 'financial accelerator' principle or the balance sheet channel is indicative of the microuncertainy environment of firms. As rates rise, some firms may face cash flow problems.

Of course, Moore (1988, p. 48) recognized all this. What I discuss here as the effects of microuncertainty and macrouncertainty, Moore refers to as 'credit risk' and 'interest rate risk' respectively, where, in the latter case, 'earnings may be dramatically reduced by a rise in short-term borrowing costs'.

As a result of the presence of two uncertainties, banks therefore place two bets. Banks must, in the first instance, place a bet on the borrower, and then place a second bet on their expectations of the business cycle. Both bets are related in a sense. If the economy slows down, revenues and profits fall, and firms may default. However, firms may default irrespective of the health of the economy. Lavoie (1992, p. 106) emphasizes these two sources of uncertainty facing banks, and writes that 'the uncertainty about the future, as well as the lack of relevant knowledge about the competence of the managerial team and about the profitability of the project, forces bankers to rely on the performance record of the past, that is the profits generated in the past by the firm'.

As Lavoie mentions in the above quote, faced with uncertainty, bankers will rely on a set of conventions to guide their lending activities, such as, for instance, the assumption that the very near future looks very much like the current state of effective demand. Moreover, the existing relationship between a bank and a borrower is an important convention as well. Maintaining a close relationship with the bank enables the borrower to keep the bank informed of his/her activities and to help build confidence in the borrower's ability to manage his/her debt and meet contractual obligations. Moore (1988, p. 24) emphasized this important point, as did Keynes before him (1971b, p. 365). It is therefore beneficial for borrowers to maintain good relations with the lender in order to prevent the possibility of being credit constrained.

It becomes clear, therefore, that in a proper theory of banking behavior, both borrowers and banks are under the influence of uncertainty (Wolfson, 1996, p. 450). Hence, the unknown future must affect all agents alike. A theory of banks should therefore include the role of uncertainty. But how best to represent uncertainty in banks' credit supply decision-making process? In particular, how do banks deal with uncertainty, and how do they turn their expectations of the future into banking policy?

Banks have at their disposal essentially two tools to deal with uncertainty: the rate of interest which they charge on bank loans, and creditworthiness ratings. We will deal with each of these issues in turn. I will argue that each of these tools is related to different uncertainties, that is, micro and macrouncertainties respectively.

UNCERTAINTY AND THE SUPPLY OF CREDIT: A HORIZONTALIST PERSPECTIVE

Banks do not meet all demand for credit, but rather meet all creditworthy demand for credit (Moore, 1988). To do so, banks establish minimum lending criteria that all potential borrowers must meet. These criteria depend on such factors as the client's collateral, business plan, payment history, expertise and knowledge of management, various measures of liquidity, and so forth. They constitute the minimum that banks require to meet their assurances that borrowers will be able to reimburse their debt. If these minimum criteria are met, banks are satisfied that given the general level of effective demand, borrowers are able to raise sufficient revenues in the future to reimburse their existing debt. As Wolfson (1996, p. 455) argues, 'Bankers accommodate all *creditworthy* demands for credit, and ration those demands not deemed creditworthy' – which the author calls the 'effective' demand for credit. Lavoie (1996) has called this demand, 'solvent demand', although perhaps a better term would simply be to call this the 'creditworthy demand'.

But these minimum standards are not exogenous to the unknown future. It is certainly reasonable to assume that if banks believe that the future will be worse than originally expected, that is if banks become pessimistic as to the future levels of effective demand, they may require borrowers to provide better proof of their ability to meet their debt obligations.

Lavoie (1984, p. 791) made this argument over two decades ago:

> when bankers begin losing some of their high 'animal spirits' though they are aware of the fact that their new behavior will harm the economy, they prefer to restrain the creation of credit-money. They know that those banks that are the least affected by the recession are those banks that show the most moderation. For this reason, it is quite possible for the banking system to start reducing its credit lines just when firms needs extended loans.

Therefore, in light of pessimism about the future, banks will raise their minimum creditworthiness criteria (lending standards), eliminating a number of potential borrowers in the process and thereby leading to credit constraints. Yet, banks will still extend credit to all those who meet their new, albeit stricter, guidelines. In the face of greater uncertainty, banks will require their borrowers to be more creditworthy. To ensure that their new credit demand is honored (or rolled over), borrowers must ensure that they meet these new, stricter guidelines. It is here that maintaining good lender/borrower relations is important. As Moore (1988, p. 24) explains:

> Commercial bank loan officers must ensure that loan requests meet the bank's income and asset collateral requirements. They must in general satisfy themselves as to the credit-worthiness of the project and the character of the borrower. It is precisely for these reasons that banks develop client relationships with their borrowers.

Through the cycle, then, creditworthiness criteria will vary. For instance, at the beginning of a cycle when animal spirits are high, creditworthiness criteria will be lower and banks will seek out potential borrowers. Banks generally relax their lending practices. As the economy grows, banks may fear an eventual downturn, and may become more pessimistic about the future, and raise the minimum required criteria. They may also fear that as the economy heats up, the central bank may raise the rate of interest to discourage economic expansion. We would therefore expect banks to tighten credit conditions at the height of the business cycle, and to relax them at its trough.

A credit crunch, in a post-Keynesian world, is therefore explained not by a decrease in central bank reserves and a corresponding leftward shift in the supply of bank credit. This implies a scarcity of available funds, and hence the need to ration supply in light of greater demand. For post-Keynesians, credit is constrained not because demand is greater than supply, but because banks become very pessimistic and they *choose* not to lend to certain borrowers. Of course, it *may* be possible to assume that even after becoming pessimistic, banks may not cut back on credit supply. It *may* be (although it is highly unlikely) that all existing and new borrowers meet the banks' stricter lending conditions. What is important to note is that for post-Keynesians, there is no such thing as a leftward shift in the supply of credit. Credit is not scarce in the neoclassical sense. Banks will still lend to any borrower that meets their new criteria.

It is in this sense that Wolfson (1996, p. 459) claims that 'Tighter standards imply a direct form of credit rationing'. This constitutes a non-price based theory of credit constraints.

In a similar vein, Setterfield (2004) develops a shifting equilibrium model of effective demand in which turning points in the business cycle can result from 'accommodationism with endogenous credit rationing'. In this model, commercial banks face notional demands for loans from firms and change the proportion of this notional loan demand that they render effective (by actually supplying loans) in response to changes in their 'animal spirits' over the business cycle. This model is broadly consistent with the discussion presented above.

Hence, banks' optimism and pessimism over the future course of the economy, that is, their macrouncertainty or what Keynes calls the 'macrofinancial environment', will determine the minimum lending standards that all firms must meet. In more pessimistic times, firms will therefore need to raise their own collateral in order to qualify for a new loan or the renewal of an old loan. This position is contrary to Crotty (1996, p. 352) who argues that fundamental uncertainty and 'credit rationing' are unrelated.

Once firms have met banks' minimum creditworthiness criteria, banks must then 'bet' on the individual borrower by determining the precise creditworthiness of the borrower himself. Provided the borrower's creditworthiness is greater than the minimum creditworthiness criteria then he is guaranteed a loan. The rate of interest charged on the loan, however, will depend on the robustness of the borrower's creditworthiness. This is in line with Kalecki's principle of increasing risk. Interest rates may change depending on the type of loan demanded (for instance, a new loan *versus* a renewal; working capital *versus* fixed capital). This concept was well articulated by Lavoie (1996, p. 285) who argues that

> the higher the debt to equity ratio, the more risky the borrower, and hence the less likely the borrower will remain credit-worthy. What we have here is a cross-section at a moment in time. If there are two otherwise identical firms, A and B, with different leverage ratios, one is expected to be charged a higher rate of interest than the other.

In other words, higher debt/equity ratios translate into weaker or less robust firms, and hence higher rates of interest on loans (call this a risk premium). Hence we can say that the minimum creditworthiness criteria are the banks' 'macrobet' and way of dealing with macrouncertainty, whereas Kalecki's principle of increasing risk and the rate of interest charged on individual loans are the banks' 'microbet' on individual firms and their way of dealing with microuncertainty.

One can find in the post-Keynesian literature some bits and pieces of the views presented above, although these are few and far between and not well developed. For instance, Dow (1996, p. 499) writes:

> The 'moods' of the financial institutions may become pessimistic, or display reduced confidence in prediction. Then borrowers who had previously been acceptable may find the value of their collateral and projections of future income streams reduced accordingly to the assessment by financial institutions. The borrowers themselves may perceive no change in their own assessment of their credit-worthiness.

Here, Dow speaks of several points: the role of banks in credit supply, their importance in terms of evaluating firms' creditworthiness, but also of the possibility of 'asymmetric expectations', a concept central to Wolfson's (1996) approach as well. Howells (1995, p. 90) argues that 'banks set their collateral standards and their lending rates . . . and then meet all loan requests that are forthcoming'.

This is in effect a long-standing horizontalist position, as Lavoie (1996) points out. Kaldor (1981, p. 15) held these same views:

> When trade prospects are good or when the money value of borrowers' assets (collateral) rises as a result of a rise of prices, the demand for bank credit rises but by the same token the credit-worthiness of potential borrowers also

improves, so that the demand for and the supply of credit move simultaneously in the same directions.

The argument presented here is that while remaining consistent with horizontalism, the supply of bank credit will vary according to the banks' own degree of optimism and pessimism about the future prospects of the economy or, in other words, with the expected future ability of firms to generate sufficient proceeds and profits to reimburse working capital and investment expenditures respectively. While credit-led and demand-determined, economic activity is limited by the willingness of banks to supply credit. And while microuncertainty can affect an individual firm's ability to raise proceeds, it is perhaps the macrouncertainty that banks fear most.

CONCLUSION

Basil Moore has had a long and distinguished career. His views on money, influenced greatly by Kaldor, are today the cornerstone of post-Keynesian monetary theory. Though at times misunderstood and misinterpreted by his critics, his views remain as true today as they were some two decades ago.

Despite his work on endogenous money, Basil nonetheless only paid lip service to the supply of credit, as did many post-Keynesians, in fact. The emphasis on endogenous money and its demand-determined nature led many to ignore the supply side. This created further confusion when critics began to argue that Moorian economics was equivalent to passive banks. Of course, this was not the case. Basil did talk of supply, but unfortunately did not develop his views sufficiently.

The purpose of this contribution has been to fill in this gap, relying on the works of other horizontalists, such as Lavoie and Wolfson, to argue that credit constraints are compatible with a horizontalist approach to endogenous money, thereby disproving the claim that horizontalism is an 'extreme post-Keynesian approach'. It makes the case that it is possible to develop a model of 'credit rationing without credit scarcity'. The main point that emerges is that in a post-Keynesian theory of credit rationing, emphasis must be placed on credit *constraints* rather than on any literal scarcity of funds.

NOTES

1. The author would like to thank Claude Gnos, Peter Howells, Marc Lavoie, Alain Parguez, Sergio Rossi, Mario Seccareccia, Mark Setterfield, John Smithin and Basil Moore for discussion over sections of this chapter, or previous versions of it. All usual disclaimers apply.
2. In his new book (Moore, 2006), this defensive behaviour is fully articulated.

REFERENCES

Bernanke, B. and C. Lown (1991) 'The Credit Crunch', *Brookings Papers on Economic Activity*, 2, 205–39.

Cottrell, A. (1988) 'The Endogeneity of Money: A Reply', *Scottish Journal of Political Economy*, 35(3) (August), 295–7.

Cottrell, A. (1994) 'Post-Keynesian Monetary Theory', *Cambridge Journal of Economics*, 18(6) (December), 587–605.

Crotty, J. (1996) 'Is New Keynesian Investment Theory Really "Keynesian"? Reflections on Fazzari and Variato', *Journal of Post Keynesian Economics*, 18(3) (Spring), 333–57.

Dow, A.C. and S.C. Dow (1989) 'Endogenous Money Creation and Idle Balances', in J. Pheby (ed.), *New Directions in Post-Keynesian Economics*, Aldershot, UK and Brookfield, USA: Edward Elgar.

Dow, S. (1996) 'Horizontalism: A Critique', *Cambridge Journal of Economics*, 20, 497–508.

Eichner, A. (1987) *The Macrodynamics of Advanced Market Economies*, Armonk, NY: M.E. Sharpe.

Howells, P.G.A. (1995) 'The Demand for Endogenous Money', *Journal of Post Keynesian Economics*, 18(1) Fall, 89–106.

Kaldor, N. (1981) *Origins of the New Monetarism*, Cardiff: University College Cardiff Press.

Keynes, J.M. (1971a) *The Collected Writings of John Maynard Keynes. Volume v: A Treatise on Money. The Pure Theory of Money*, D. Moggridge (ed.), London: Macmillan and Cambridge University Press.

Keynes, J.M. (1971b) *The Collected Writings of John Maynard Keynes. Volume vi: A Treatise on Money. The Applied Theory of Money*, D. Moggridge (ed.), London: Macmillan and Cambridge University Press.

Keynes, J.M. (1973) *The Collected Writings of John Maynard Keynes. Volume vii: The General Theory of Employment, Money and Interest*, D. Moggridge (ed.), London: Macmillan and St Martin's Press.

King, J. (2002) *A History of Post Keynesian Economics since 1936*, Cheltenham, UK and Northampton, MA, USA: Edward Elgar.

Lavoie, M. (1984) 'Un modèle post-keynésien d'économie monétaire fondé sur la théorie du circuit', *Économies et Sociétés*, 18(2), 233–58.

Lavoie, M. (1992) *Foundations of Post-Keynesian Economic Analysis*, Aldershot, UK and Brookfield, USA: Edward Elgar.

Lavoie, M. (1993) 'A Post-Classical View of Money, Interest, Growth and Distribution', in G. Mongiovi and C. Rühl (eds), *Macroeconomic Theory: Diversity and Convergence*, Aldershot, UK and Brookfield, USA: Edward Elgar.

Lavoie, M. (1996) 'The Endogenous Supply of Credit – Money, Liquidity Preference and the Principle of Increasing Risk: Horizontalism versus the Loanable Funds Approach', *Scottish Journal of Political Economy*, 43(3) (August), 275–300.

Lavoie, M. (2006) 'A Post-Keynesian Amendment to the New Consensus on Monetary Policy', *Metroeconomica*, 57, May.

Minsky, H. (1996) 'The Essential Characteristics of Post Keynesian Economics', in G. Deleplace and E. Nell (eds), *Money in Motion: The Post Keynesian and Circulation Approaches*, London: Macmillan, pp. 70–88.

Moore, B. (1979) 'Monetary Factors', in A. Eichner (ed.), *A Guide to Post Keynesian Economics*, White Plains, NY: M.E. Sharpe.

Moore, B. (1985) 'Contemporaneous Reserve Accounting: Can Reserves be Quantity Constrained?', *Journal of Post Keynesian Economics*, 7(1) (Fall), 103–13.
Moore, B. (1988) *Horizontalists and Verticalists: The Macroeconomics of Credit Money*, Cambridge: Cambridge University Press.
Moore, B. (1989) 'A Simple Model of Bank Intermediation', *Journal of Post Keynesian Economics*, 12(1) (Fall), 10–28.
Moore, B. (1994), 'The Demise of the Keynesian Multiplier: A Reply to Cottrell', *Journal of Post Keynesian Economics*, 17(1) (Fall), 121–33.
Moore, B. (1995) 'The Exogeneity of Short-Term Interest Rates: A Reply to Wray', *Journal of Economic Issues*, 29(1) (March), 258–66.
Moore, B. (1996) 'The Money Supply Process: A Historical Reinterpretation', in E. Nell and G. Deleplace (eds), *Money in Motion*, London: Macmillan.
Moore, B. (2006) *Shaking the Invisible Hand: Complexity, Endogenous Money and Exogenous Interest Rates*, London and New York: Palgrave Macmillan.
Palley, T. (1991) 'The Endogenous Money Supply: Consensus and Disagreement', *Journal of Post Keynesian Economics*, 13(3) (Spring), 397–403.
Palley, T. (1994) 'Competing Views of the Money Supply Process: Theory and Evidence', *Metroeconomica*, 45(1), 67–88.
Pollin, R. (1991) 'Two Theories of Money Supply Endogeneity: Some Empirical Evidence', *Journal of Post Keynesian Economics*, 13(3) (Spring), 366–95.
Robinson, J. (1952) *The Rate of Interest and Other Essays*, London: Macmillan.
Rochon, L.-P. (1999) *Credit, Money and Production: An Alternative Post-Keynesian Approach*, Cheltenham, UK and Northampton, MA, USA: Edward Elgar.
Rochon, L.-P. and S. Rossi (2004a) 'Endogenous Money: The Evolutionary versus Revolutionary Views', working paper.
Rochon, Louis-Philippe and Sergio Rossi (2004b) 'Central Banking in the Monetary Circuit', in Marc Lavoie and Mario Seccareccia (eds), *Central Banking in the Modern World: Alternative Perspectives*, Cheltenham, UK and Northampton, MA, USA: Edward Elgar, 144–63.
Rousseas, S. (1992), *Post Keynesian Monetary Economics*, 2nd edition, Armonk, NY: M.E. Sharpe.
Setterfield, M. (2004) Financial Fragility, Effective Demand and the Business Cycle', *Review of Political Economy*, 16, 207–23.
Wolfson, M.H. (1996) 'A Post Keynesian Theory of Credit Rationing', *Journal of Post Keynesian Economics*, 18(3) (Spring), 443–70.
Wray, R. (1992a) 'Commercial Banks, the Central Bank, and Endogenous Money', *Journal of Post Keynesian Economics*, 14(3) (Spring), 297–310.
Wray, R. (1992b) 'Alternative Approaches to Money and Interest Rates', *Journal of Economic Issues*, 26(4) (December), 1145–78.
Wray, R. (1992c) 'Minsky's Financial Instability Hypothesis and the Endogeneity of Money', in S. Fazzari and D. Papadimitriou (eds), *Financial Conditions and Macroeconomic Performance: Essays in Honor of Hyman P. Minsky*, Armonk, NY: M.E. Sharpe.
Wray, R. (1999) *Understanding Modern Money: The Key to Full Employment and Price Stability*, Cheltenham, UK and Northampton, MA, USA: Edward Elgar.

10. The demand for endogenous money: a lesson in institutional change

Peter Howells

INTRODUCTION

When Davidson and Weintraub (1973) first drew attention to the endogenous nature of the money creation process they were responding to a quantity theory analysis of inflation which was popular at the time. But although their paper was a landmark in the cogency with which it put the case (and in putting it forward in a leading 'mainstream' journal), it was not the first to argue that a country's money stock might be elastic with respect to the needs of trade. Traces of this view can be found in debates over the cause of inflation in Tudor and Stuart England and in the 'banking' and 'bullionist' controversies of the nineteenth century. Neither was it the last of course. In later years Chick (1986), Dow (1993), Howells (1995), Kaldor (1982, 1985), Lavoie (1984), Niggle (1991), Pollin (1991), Wray (1990) and others have all supported and refined this fundamental proposition. The greatest campaigner, however, has been Basil Moore whose 1988 book (1988a) took the argument (and the evidence) to unprecedented levels of detail. So secure have the fundamentals of the argument become, that the literature in recent years has been entirely preoccupied with refinements. Furthermore, as central banks have placed a growing premium on the 'transparency' of their operations, it has become clear beyond the slightest doubt that central bankers regard the money supply as endogenously determined and that they accept their own role in making it so. Charles Goodhart, whose work has for years combined the analytical insights of economics with a keen appreciation of the *practice* of central banking, has done as much as anyone to encourage a realistic approach to money supply analysis and has largely succeeded, in the UK at least, by frequently denouncing the 'misinstruction' inherent in the base-multiplier model (Goodhart, 1984, p. 188). Just ten years later he observed that 'Almost all those who have worked in a [central bank] believe that this view is totally mistaken; in particular, it ignores the implications of several of the crucial institutional features of a modern commercial banking system . . .' (Goodhart, 1994, p. 1424). Just what those institutional features are (and how far they penetrate to the core of the modern banking system) he showed more recently in describing the arrangements that lay behind the US Fed's adoption of the language of monetary base control in 1979–82 (Goodhart, 2002, pp. 16–17).

And there is nothing peculiar about the Fed. For the Bank of England we have the statement from the Bank's Deputy Governor (now Governor) with responsibility for monetary policy. 'In the United Kingdom, money is endogenous – the Bank supplies base money on demand at its prevailing interest rate, and broad money is created by the banking system' (King, 1994, p. 264). And Borio's (1997) survey of central bank operating procedures in industrial countries shows that they are all essentially similar: the central banks set a short-term 'official' rate of interest which forms the basis for the structure of commercial rates. At that rate, the central bank supplies whatever volume of reserves is required by banks to meet the demands of their clients.

So Basil, Paul Davidson and the other campaigners were right. The money supply in modern banking systems is endogenous. The central bank sets its official dealing rate. Banks add a mark-up and endeavor to meet all the creditworthy demand for loans that is forthcoming at that rate. At the going rate of interest, the strength of this demand depends upon factors elsewhere in the economy and the supply of new loans creates a corresponding flow of new deposits. In the rest of this chapter I wish to return to one of the debates which I described earlier as 'refining' the endogeneity theory. This concerns the demand for endogenous money or, more formally, the mechanism whereby the *ex ante* flow of loan-created deposits is matched, *ex post*, with an aggregate willingness to hold them. For five years, from 1994, Basil and I differed profoundly over this question. In addition to what we published in the journals, there is at least one substantial file of emails and faxes testifying to the care with which Basil read my criticisms and to the detail in which he (always patiently and courteously) responded. So far as theory is concerned, I still see no reason to change my original view but I do think that the last few years have seen dramatic changes in institutions, certainly in the UK, that should bring our positions closer together. This is a timely reminder of Sir John Hicks's adage that 'Monetary theory . . . cannot avoid a relation to reality . . . It belongs to monetary history in a way that economic theory does not always belong to economic history' (Hicks, 1967, p. 153).

In the next section I outline 'the problem', giving credit, I hope, to all those before me who have felt there is something lacking in the simple 'loans create deposits' principle. In the third section, I outline the recent changes which I think bear upon our problem and offer some concluding remarks in the fourth section.

LOANS CREATE DEPOSITS

It is an obvious criticism to make of base-multiplier models of money supply determination that they are fundamentally 'uneconomic'. The multiplier is based upon two key ratios – the public's cash ratio and the banks' reserve ratio – which are treated as fixed (in the simplest versions) or subject to very slow and predictable change (in more advanced versions). Both ratios, however, are the outcome of complex portfolio decisions which one might have expected mainstream economics, with its rational, maximizing calculus, to be able to recognize as subject to changes in relative interest rates, risk, regulations, technology etc. Cuthbertson (1985) is an exception.[1] Furthermore, the models completely ignore all questions of the demand for money (or the demand for its credit counterparts for that matter). An open market purchase (for example) of government bonds increases the base and the money supply increases by the amount of the purchase times the value of the multiplier, with no thought given to the fact that the additional money must be held by someone. So no portfolio preferences here either.

It has been my view for a number of years that Basil's exposition of the endogeneity argument makes the same mistake, albeit starting from the opposite – credit counterparts – end. It provides a detailed and (I am happy to accept)[2] accurate account of how banks determine the amount of lending which they wish to do, in response to the demand for credit which they face. But it contains no account of how the flow of loan-induced deposits is bound to be matched by a corresponding increase in the demand for those deposits, an increase, in other words in the demand for money. Let me say at once that Basil's account of endogeneity is not the only one to overlook this problem (and I was not the first to point it out). We return to this in a moment. But let us be clear first that there *is* a potential problem.

The problem begins with the fact that the demand for bank loans emanates from one set of agents with their own motives (for them it is an income–expenditure decision) while the demand for money emanates from another set with different motives (for them it is a portfolio decision). Granted, the two groups partially overlap but they are not identical. So long as this distinction exists, then there must be a question of how the flow of new deposits, created by a subset of agents with income–expenditure deficits, is to be matched with the population's desire to arrange their wealth in such a way that they are willing to hold the additional money. And hold it they must (a) in order to satisfy the banks' balance sheet identity in which loans equal deposits and (b) because money is defined exclusively as deposits *held* by the non-bank private sector – in Dennis Robertson's memorable phrase, 'All money which is anywhere, must be somewhere' (Robertson, 1963, p. 350).

So far as Basil's work was concerned, the first person to raise the question of what had become of the demand for money was Charles Goodhart (1989). The paper, in the *Journal of Post Keynesian Economics*, was titled 'Has Moore Become Too Horizontal' which, given the central argument, was perhaps less appropriate than the one that Basil adopted for his 1991 reply – 'Has the Demand for Money Been Mislaid?'. The issue that was debated in these two papers (and in Goodhart's (1991) rejoinder) was whether or not it made sense to talk of a demand for money, independent of the money supply, where credit money was concerned. If there was no sense in visualizing an independent demand function for money, then there was no sense in the idea of a disequilibirum. In Basil's words 'One cannot have a supply of credit money independent of the demand for credit money, any more than one can have a supply of haircuts independent of the demand for them' (1991, p. 126). His argument was that, like haircuts, credit money was produced 'to contract' and thus supplied by banks only in response to a demand for it. But this argument, as I pointed out subsequently (Howells, 1995 p. 91) contained two distinct errors. The first was that it confused 'money' and 'credit'. What banks were responding to was a demand for *credit*. 'Money' was in the nature of a joint good, a by-product almost of the supply of loans. It is true that banks will only supply credit (like haircuts) if they are confronted by a demand for credit but this tells us nothing about the demand for *money*. Secondly, even though it is true that credit is supplied 'to contract' so that without a demand it would not be created, this does not deny the existence of an independent demand schedule. There *is* an independent demand schedule for haircuts (that is, a schedule stating consumers' preferences at various prices). It just so happens that goods and services produced to contract are only ever produced where the supply and demand schedules intersect so that disequilibrium prices and quantities are unobservable.

The possibility that the endogenous production of deposits could differ (*ex ante*) from the demand for them had been raised in 1986 by Victoria Chick. In what she describes as 'stage 2 banking' it becomes possible for investment to precede saving because firms can borrow from banks whose loans create the new deposits with which to finance the new investment. Chick's immediate concern is how exactly to *describe* the extra deposits as a form of saving. But the reference to the demand for them is obvious.

> . . . though the deposits are willingly held there is no actual decision to save. The deposits represent a passive (and grateful) acceptance of means of payment by workers and traders. Some of it will doubtless be used for consumption, some of it saved . . . [However] while individuals quite happily accepted claims on deposits – acceptability after all is the hallmark of the means of payment – the point on which I wish to insist is that no one actually asks those who

subsequently have larger deposits whether the expansion of bank balance sheets was alright with them. (Chick, 1992, p. 200)

This 1986 paper precedes Basil's *Horizontalists and Vertcalists* by two years (though Chick acknowledges helpful comments from Basil, so he presumably knew of it before the publication of his book). Chick's target in 1986 was the 1981 paper by Kaldor and Trevithick. This had also ruled out any problem in connection with the demand for endogenous money, though not on the theoretical ground that an independent money demand curve made no logical sense that Basil was to adopt. The Kaldor and Trevithick argument was that there would be an *automatic* application of excess receipts of money to the repayment of overdrafts. Thus, the individual actions of borrowers taking out new loans (or extending existing ones) could threaten an 'excess' creation of deposits *ex ante*, but the moment 'excess' deposits were recognized they would be devoted by their holders to repaying existing debt. Thus limiting the deposit-creating process – *ex post* – to only those deposits which people were willing to hold.

Note that 'automatically' is the keyword. It is a reasonable assumption that those with overdrafts who have receipts in excess of payments will use the excess to reduce their debt and this will ('automatically') reduce the quantity of new deposits that are actually created. The problem is – not everyone has an overdraft. Chick again:

> Kaldor and Trevithick (1981) argue that a credit-based money supply can never be larger than people want to hold because an excess supply will result in repayment. However, the money might not fall into the hands of those with overdrafts in the first instance. The money may be spent and push up prices, after which the money may be willingly held. (Chick, 1992, pp. 204–5. See also Cottrell, 1986)

And it is not sufficient to argue that some people somewhere (for example, virtually all firms) do have overdrafts. Once it is accepted that the first round recipients of 'new' money may not wish to hold it, then the problems begin. Some *process* must be triggered by agents as they seek to adjust. And we can see from the last line of the Chick quotation the magnitude of the potential disaster that this adjustment process threatens for the pioneers of endogenous money. The main purpose in building such an overwhelming case for the endogeneity of money was to destroy the revival of the quantity theory and its crude explanation of inflation. But after all that effort, here was an argument that the money supply might be fully endogenous and *still* cause inflation.

Maybe it was because the stakes were so high that Basil's book and later exchanges with Goodhart (and with me) focused on the alternative strategy of denying the logical independence of a money demand schedule in a world of endogenous money.

In the 1991 reply to Goodhart, Basil based his rejection of a money demand schedule on the idea that the world is consequently changing and that 'equilibrium' is illusory. 'In the real world there is *no* unique "general equilibrium position" toward which the economy is tending' (Moore, 1991, p. 128). Moore's argument is that since there *is* money, there must be uncertainty; if there is uncertainty, then there is no general equilibrium; if there is no general equilibrium '. . . *there is no meaning to the notion of an "ultimate equilibrium" stock of money demanded*' (Moore, 1991, p. 130; emphasis in the original). This seems to be confusing necessary and sufficient conditions. In order to have an equilibrium position, it is true that one requires independent supply and demand schedules. But does it follow that the existence of these schedules means that we must be at equilibrium? Surely not. The whole idea of *disequilibrium* is built upon the existence of independent supply and demand schedules but agents constrained in their behavior from arriving at the point of intersection. They still have *preferences*.

This is one of two points which Goodhart makes in his 1991 rejoinder. We may all be sceptical about 'general equilibrium' but this need not entail the extreme position of rejecting all ideas that people have preferences to which they will seek to give expression. In trying to make the point that Goodhart would always accept whatever quantity of money was offered to him (and therefore that the demand for money was a redundant concept), Moore's contention had been that Goodhart would hardly refuse a gift from his aunt and since he would not refuse it then he must have a demand for it.

> Moore is, of course, absolutely correct that I will *accept* $10 000 . . . but I do not necessarily want to *hold* that sum as a money balance indefinitely. Given the *existing* pattern of expectations, prices, my wealth (now happily increased by $10 000), I do have an underlying *partial* equilibrium demand for money balances that does differ from the amount with which I have just been supplied, and that difference will cause me to rearrange my whole portfolio . . . (Goodhart, 1991, pp. 134–5; emphasis in original)

This little exchange reveals another problem in Basil's approach. This is the question of what we mean by the 'demand for money'. Look again at the quotation from Goodhart. His argument is that rejecting equilibrium does not mean rejecting preferences. If rejecting the idea of preferences is rather extreme, equating acceptance with demand is surely a step too far. Let us consider the case of a small trader who finds as the week goes on that business is better than he originally expected at the beginning of the week. Does he start to refuse deposits for payment, on Thursday say, because money balances threaten to become larger than planned? Surely not. Acceptability is simply the hallmark of money (see the Chick quotation above). If the payments were not accepted, we would not be discussing money at all. Acceptance proves nothing either way. It is at the end of the week that the 'demand for money' becomes relevant. It is the demand for money which determines whether the unplanned additions to deposits continue to be held or whether, unless other variables change, decisions are made to switch out of money and into other assets until the unplanned level of money balances reaches its original planned proportion of the portfolio.

However, if one persists with the idea that 'acceptance' is proof of 'demand' then one has to recognize that universal and unquestioning acceptance means in effect that people have a perfectly elastic demand and a perfectly elastic demand for any good is something of a novelty. To make such behavior plausible, Moore describes the action of sellers who passively accumulate the 'new' deposits created by lending, as 'convenience lending'. The idea is that all the deposits are held (for reasons we shall see in a moment) as a matter of 'convenience' because no special inducement is required to get people to accept them in exchange. Acquiring them involves no sacrifice. No consumption is deferred and no liquidity is surrendered. The new deposits act like a windfall. The 'lending' refers to the status of deposits as loans to the bank.

But it is difficult to see how the fact that people receive 'windfalls' entails no *subsequent* effect on behavior. The fact that something is acquired in greater quantity than was planned is surely likely to induce a reaction, regardless of whether or not effort was exerted in its acquisition. It still seems implausible that the unsolicited deposits will not at some point be exchanged for some other form of wealth. Indeed, we do not expect lottery winners to reject their prize because it would raise their money balances to unplanned levels, but no one expects the winners to hold their increased wealth, unchanged, as bank deposits. Indeed, Moore himself concedes, and this is significant in the light of what is to follow, that *individuals* may hold these deposits only for so long as it takes them to decide on future consumption and investment patterns but then crucially he says 'For the economy as a whole . . . such [convenience] lending is long term' (Moore, 1988b, p. 298). By this, of course, Moore means that *individuals* may decide periodically to sweep their growing deposits into higher earning non-bank liabilities but this only shuffles the ownership of the deposits, it does not change the quantity. (As we accepted in the last paragraph, the newly-created deposits *are* held.) Only actions which cause *repayment* of loans cause a reduction in deposits.

There are echoes of Kaldor and Trevithick in the last sentence, but what goes before is more significant. Firstly, we can all agree that people making payments to each other by trading money balances has no effect on the aggregate stock of deposits unless some loans are repaid or net payments are made to the public sector. Think of Chick again: 'The money may be spent and push up prices, after which the money may be willingly held'. Or, in a more Keynesian spirit, we might imagine the deposits being exchanged for financial assets with only small effects on prices and yields which *then* may have some effect upon real expenditure which in turn may increase real output if resources are underutilized. But one thing is for sure, *something* will happen. Agents will not individually build up money balances willy-nilly and the moment they act on a preference somewhere a price and a quantity will change. However uncomfortable it may be to admit it, the fact that money is endogenously determined does not exempt it from causing all sorts of mischief.

RECENT DEVELOPMENTS

In many expositions of endogenous money, the demand for loans (given the level of interest rates etc.) is said to be determined by the 'state of trade', that is, by movements in nominal income. If this is true, then we might think it unlikely that loans could create deposits at a rate which varied very much from the path of the demand for those deposits since this too would follow nominal GDP. But this supposes either (a) that the demand for loans is dominated by movements in nominal income, that is, that people borrow only to finance production or (b) that if the demand for loans is driven by other variables, then these are closely linked to nominal income.

But neither may be correct. Let us start with the latter. Nominal income, as we all know, refers to the current value of output. The measure of nominal income excludes transactions at intermediate stages of production, in secondhand goods and thus in existing assets, real and financial. For years it has been the practice in macro textbooks to gloss over any possible difficulty in moving from nominal income, PY, to *total* transactions, PT, on the grounds that we are usually interested in rates of change rather than absolute magnitudes and these move together. But figures from the UK's Association for Payments Clearing Systems (APACS) show that any such relationship has broken down in recent years. In the 1970s, total transactions (PT) were about 20 times the level of nominal income (PY). During the 1980s, the multiple increased rapidly to 50 by 1989. In 1990 and 1991 it fell back to 40 and has continued around that level until the present.

Turning our attention now to the demand for bank loans, with Khaled Hussein's help (Howells and Hussein, 1999), I was able to show that PT performed better than PY as an explanatory variable. In the light of our earlier discussion therefore, we have a situation where the demand for loans is creating *ex ante* deposits at a rate which considerably exceeds the requirements of trade and conjures up the prospect of substantial adjustment being required to bring the supply into line with demand *ex post*. Given our earlier discussion, this could have involved some combination of higher inflation, higher asset prices, lower real interest rates and higher real output. We could possibly make a case for the higher asset prices but lower real interest rates have not been forthcoming precisely because of the *fall* in inflation. It is not obvious, on a casual look at the evidence, that a major disparity has occurred between the *ex ante* and *ex post* growth in deposits. How can this be the case?

Firstly, it might be worth considering whether the rise in the *PT*/*PY* ratio has any relevance to the demand for money. The possibility that the demand for money has been driven in recent years by something other than gross domestic product (GDP) has some credibility. For example, Anderson (1993) showed that the boom in mortgage refinancing in the USA led to an increase in the volume and volatility of financial transactions relative to GDP transactions, and that this had measurable effects upon the demand for M1 deposits (it is worth bearing in mind that some of the rise in UK *PT* is the result of the increasingly speculative nature of housing transactions). More recently, Palley (1995) and Pollin and Schaberg (1998) have demonstrated that money demand estimates in the USA can be improved by recognizing a role for total transactions where the behavior of the latter is proxied by measures which refer to some part of the property market and to financial activity, two major categories of spending included in *total* transactions but excluded from conventional measures of GDP. Again with Khaled Hussein (Howells and Hussein, 1997) I showed that the APACS series itself gave better results than either GDP or wealth in an otherwise standard money demand equation.

The conclusion we must draw, therefore, is that although there has been a rapid creation of deposits by a demand for loans which contains a large element of borrowing for non-productive purposes, this has not necessarily generated a great *ex ante* surge in 'unwanted' deposits partly because the demand for deposits may itself have increased rapidly for similar reasons. What we inevitably observe is a sharp fall in the income velocity of M4 through the 1980s as *PT* surged ahead of *PY*, and a more stable figure since the mid-1990s.

But the tendency for the demand for money to be subject to influences similar to those governing the demand for loans, may not be the only reason why *ex ante* deposit creation may have followed demand quite closely. To see why, we need to return to Kaldor, Trevithick, Chick and Cottrell and to recall that the debate there was over the ability of *all* agents to adjust their money holdings by repaying existing debt. If this is the case, then its relevance to the present debate is that it effectively prevents 'excess' deposits coming into existence in the first place. In the past, the manifest weakness with the argument was that borrowers from banks were only a subset of holders of money ('not everyone has an overdraft') and thus the remaining subset were left with the reconciliation problem. It is worth noting that the Kaldor–Trevithick mechanism is quite demanding. It requires not only that virtually everyone who holds money is simultaneously in debt to a bank but also that the nature of the debt must be such that its size can be adjusted easily. Remember, for the mechanism to work, holders of 'excess' deposits must reduce their bank debt 'automatically'. This means *loan repayment must be the first choice* in the face of excess liquidity. In the UK this limits the relevant type of bank loan to the overdraft where borrowers are free to vary their borrowing on demand and at their own discretion, subject to an upper borrowing limit. It is no use pointing out that 60 per cent of UK households have a mortgage on their house. Paying off small slices of a mortgage loan with 'petty cash' involves punitive transaction costs. In many cases the early repayment of the whole mortgage involves an early-repayment penalty.[3] Similarly, personal loans are for a fixed amount for a fixed period and interest must be paid on that amount regardless of whether or not an agent's liquidity position requires the whole of the loan to be outstanding at a particular time. None of these (major lines of credit) will fit the argument. It *has* to be an overdraft and the problem for the Kaldor–Trevithick argument is that overdrafts are limited by banks to firms and wealthy individuals, some of whom even then may decide not to take up the facility.

In the last 20 years, however, we have seen the rapid expansion of personal credit in the UK, based upon the widespread use of credit cards (and to a small extent through the use of 'charge' cards which allow credit for the short periods between scheduled repayments). Indeed, anecdotes abound of people (even children) receiving unsolicited offers of credit through the mail. Notice that the cards we are discussing here are issued by banks (though which bank may not be immediately obvious from looking at the card itself).[4] This is important because it means that outstanding credit on these cards involves a loan from a bank. Furthermore, although most card companies impose the requirement of a fixed minimum monthly payment, this is usually a very small fraction of the total outstanding. Consequently, there is very considerable discretion about the size of the repayment and the outstanding stock of credit: this can be increased and decreased with no cost (other than the interest paid of course). The similarities with the overdraft arrangement are obvious.

Table 10.1 shows the increase in the number of these cards in absolute terms and in relation to the adult population. 'Adult' here is defined as anyone aged 16 or over.

Table 10.1 Credit/charge cards in the UK, 1992–2002

Year	Credit card (000s)	Charge card (000s)	As % of adult population
1992	26 277	2353	38
1994	26 151	2305	38
1996	31 336	2803	42
1998	38 299	3270	50
2000	47 080	3772	57
2002	58 794	4311	64

Source: APACS, *Yearbook of Payment Statistics, 2003*, tables 6.1, 8.8.

Table 10.1 shows the growth in the number of cards in issue in the UK. It also shows the percentage of the adult population with one or more of these cards. The latest figures are for 2002, but looking at the trend we can be confident that more than two-thirds of adults now have access to this flexible source of credit, compared with about one-third just over ten years ago.

Table 10.2 puts the magnitude of this form of credit into context. Remember that the point at issue is the ability of credit card borrowing to provide individuals with an easy and effective way of adjusting their total indebtedness to banks, bearing in mind fluctuations in their liquidity position. Column 5 shows the total amount of credit card borrowing, a figure which has more than tripled over ten years. As a percentage of their total borrowing from banks, individuals' credit card borrowing has increased from about 2.4 per cent to 3.8 per cent (column 6). Total borrowing is dominated by lending secured on property by means of a mortgage. Even so, it is notable that *un*secured lending has been increasing steadily as a fraction of the total, from 13 to 18 per cent in the last ten years or so (column 4). From column 7, we can see that some of this increase in unsecured lending is accounted for by the growing role of credit cards. As a fraction of total unsecured borrowing, the credit card contribution increases from 18.8 to 21 per cent. Finally, if we are going to argue that the increasing use of credit card debt provides a cheap and convenient method of adjustment to liquidity shocks, we should perhaps look at the magnitude of credit card borrowing in the light of holdings of money. The final column shows that individuals' credit card debt has almost doubled in relation to their holdings of broad money in the last ten years. 5.6 per cent may not look a particularly large figure, but that rather depends upon the magnitude of *ex ante* divergences in deposit creation and demand, and that, by definition, we cannot measure. We should also bear in mind, that column 2 shows holdings of *total* M4. This includes notes and coin and time deposits.

Table 10.2 Borrowing on credit card in relation to total borrowing and liquidity of persons

Date	Total sterling bank lending to individuals £m (1)	Individuals' holdings of M4, £m (2)	Unsecured sterling bank lending to individuals (consumer credit) £m (3)	(3) as % of (1) (4)	Individuals' sterling borrowing on credit card, £m (5)	(5) as % of (1) (6)	(5) as % of (3) (7)	(5) as % of (2) (8)
1993	410940	344670	53301	13.0	10030	2.4	18.8	2.9
1995	448552	378890	68202	15.2	13011	2.9	19.1	3.4
1997	519424	420690	88081	17.0	16612	3.2	18.9	3.9
1999	609897	476590	116155	19.0	23241	3.8	20.0	4.9
2001	732764	547782	141718	19.3	28731	3.9	20.3	5.2
2003	944653	645390	170546	18.0	35828	3.8	21.0	5.6

Source: www.bankofengland.co.uk Series nos. (1)VZQB; (2)VQSM; (3)VZRD; (4)VZQH.

Sight deposits, where unplanned fluctuations in liquidity would appear, are less than half of total M4. As a fraction of sight deposits, credit card borrowing is about 12 per cent.

CONCLUSION

Basil Moore has done more than most economists to persuade a reluctant profession, especially in the United States, that the money supply is endogenously determined. This is now widely accepted and the debate has moved on to a number of subsidiary issues. One (but only one) of these is how the flow of deposits, newly created by the demand for bank credit, is brought into line with the demand for money. This is an issue to which many people have contributed over the years. In the end, the truth is probably some combination of all the mechanisms that have been suggested – the use of money as a buffer stock, switches between money and financial assets, repayments of overdrafts, even (whisper it quietly) some real balance effects. But as always, the institutional framework is critical. Money is endogenous, fundamentally because money today is 'credit money'. It wasn't always so. In the last few years, we have seen a shift in the pattern of bank lending to individuals in the UK. Unsecured lending has increased as a fraction of the total and within that there has been a doubling of the role played by credit cards. One consequence is that the argument that the repayment of bank loans via the overdraft facility would 'automatically' prevent the emergence of excess deposits is now a good deal more plausible than it was when it was first floated, provided that we take credit cards and overdrafts together.

NOTES

1. Bain and Howells (2003, pp. 61–4) show that, at the very least, these portfolio decisions must result in the size of the multiplier varying positively with the rate of interest on non-money assets with the result that the money supply curve (drawn in interest–money stock space) must have a positive slope.
2. I am aware that others do not. Both the arguments over structural/accommodative endogeneity and the slope of the money supply curve reflect differing views of the lending process.
3. As an example of how rapidly institutional changes can modify arguments, this sentence was true when the first draft of this chapter was prepared. But starting in 2004 some UK banks began to offer 'smart' mortgages which were linked to checking accounts from which the surplus above a specified level could be automatically devoted to reducing the mortgage. As yet (2005) these remain highly unusual arrangements. However, as the editor has pointed out, such arrangements are quite common in the USA, and no doubt in other countries too. Both cases reinforce the broader argument of this section, namely, that when it comes to understanding how money works, institutional arrangements are crucial – not least because they change continuously.

4. The position with credit granted by stores, which may also take the form of discretionary borrowing involving a card is more complex. It depends upon how the store is financing the credit. If it is borrowing from a bank on overdraft terms then the amount of customer credit outstanding will be reflected directly in the size of this bank loan to the store and being a bank loan variations in its size must be matched by variations in deposits. In this situation, the store is effectively acting as an agent for the bank. But the credit may instead be financed by the store borrowing in the money markets. In granting credit to a customer it is then only lending someone else's money.

REFERENCES

Anderson R.G. (1993) 'The Effect of Mortgage Refinancing on Money Demand and the Monetary Aggregates', *Federal Reserve Bank of St Louis Review*, 75(4), 49–63.

Bain, K. and P.G.A. Howells (2003) *Monetary Economics*, Basingstoke: Palgrave.

Borio, C.E.V. (1997) 'Monetary Policy Operating Procedures in Industrial Countries', Basel: Bank for International Settlements, Working Paper no. 40.

Chick, V. (1986) 'The Evolution of the Banking System and the Theory of Saving, Investment and Interest', *Économies et Sociétés*, Série M P, no. 3.

Chick, V. (1992) 'Keynesians, Monetarists and Keynes', in P. Arestis and S.C. Dow (eds), *On Money, Method and Keynes: Selected Essays*, London: Macmillan.

Chick, V. (1993) 'The Evolution of the Banking System and the Theory of Monetary Policy', in S.F. Frowen (ed.), *Monetary Theory and Monetary Policy: New Tracks for the 1990s*, London: Macmillan, 79–92.

Cottrell, A. (1986) 'The Endogeneity of Money and Money–Income Causality', *Scottish Journal of Political Economy*, 33(1), 2–27.

Cuthbertson, K. (1985) *The Supply and Demand for Money*, Oxford: Blackwell.

Davidson, P. (1972) *Money and the Real World*, London: Macmillan.

Davidson, P. (1988) 'Endogenous Money, the Production Process and Inflation Analysis', *Economie Appliquée*, XLI(1), 151–69.

Davidson, P. and S. Weintraub (1973) 'Money as Cause and Effect', *Economic Journal*, 83(332), 1117–32.

Dow S.C. (1993) *Money and the Economic Process*, Aldershot, UK and Brookfield, USA: Edward Elgar.

Goodhart, C.A.E. (1984) *The Theory and Practice of Money*, London: Macmillan.

Goodhart, C.A.E. (1989) 'Has Moore Become Too Horizontal?' *Journal of Post Keynesian Economics*, 12(1), 29–34.

Goodhart, C.A.E. (1991) 'Is the Concept of an Equilibrium Demand for Money Meaningful?' *Journal of Post Keynesian Economics*, 14(1), 134–6.

Goodhart, C.A.E. (1994) 'What Should Central Banks Do? What Should Be their Macroeconomic Objectives and Operations?' *Economic Journal*, 104, 1424–36.

Goodhart, C.A.E. (2002) 'The Endogeneity of Money', in P. Arestis, M. Desai and S.C. Dow, *Money, Macroeconomics and Keynes: Essays in Honour of Victoria Chick*, vol. 1, London: Routledge.

Hicks, J.R. (1967), *Critical Essays in Monetary Theory*, Oxford: Oxford University Press.

Howells, P.G.A. (1995) 'The Demand for Endogenous Money', *Journal of Post Keynesian Economics*, 18(1) (Fall), 89–106.

Howells, P.G.A. (1997) 'The Demand for Endogenous Money: A Rejoinder', *Journal of Post Keynesian Economics* (Spring), 429–34.

Howells, P.G.A. and K.A. Hussein (1997) 'The Demand for Money in the UK: Transactions as the Scale Variable', *Economics Letters*, 55, 371–7.

Howells, P.G.A. and K.A. Hussein (1999) 'The Demand for Loans and "the State of Trade"', *Journal of Post Keynesian Economics*, 21(3).

Kaldor, N. (1982) *The Scourge of Monetarism*, Oxford: Oxford University Press.

Kaldor, N. (1985) 'How Monetarism Failed', *Challenge*, 28(2), 4–13.

Kaldor, N. and J. Trevithick (1981) 'A Keynesian Perspective on Money', *Lloyds Bank Review* (January).

King, M. (1994) 'The Transmission Mechanism of Monetary Policy', *Bank of England Quarterly Bulletin* (August), 261–7.

Lavoie, M. (1984) 'The Endogenous Credit Flow and the Post Keynesian Theory of Money', *Journal of Economic Issues*, 16(3), 771–97.

Moore, B.J. (1988a) *Horizontalists and Verticalists*, Cambridge: Cambridge University Press.

Moore, B.J. (1988b) 'The Endogenous Money Supply', *Journal of Post Keynesian Economics*, X(3), 372–85.

Moore, B.J. (1991) 'Has the Demand for Money Been Mislaid?' *Journal of Post Keynesian Economics*, 14(1), 125–33.

Niggle, C.J. (1991) 'The Endogenous Money Supply Theory: An Institutionalist Appraisal', *Journal of Economic Issues*, XXV(1), 137–51.

Palley, T.I. (1994) 'Competing Views of the Money Supply Process: Theory and Evidence', *Metroeconomica*, 45(1), 67–88.

Palley, T.I. (1995) 'The Demand for Money and non-GDP Transactions', *Economic Letters*, 48, 145–54.

Pollin, R. (1991) 'Two Theories of Money Supply Endogeneity: Some Empirical Evidence', *Journal of Post Keynesian Economics*, 13(3), 366–96.

Pollin, R. and M. Schaberg (1998) 'Asset Exchanges, Financial Market Trading and the M1 Income Velocity Puzzle', *Journal of Post Keynesian Economics*, XX1(1), 135–62.

Robertson, D.H. (1963) *Lectures on Economic Principles*, London: Fontana.

Weintraub, S. (1978) *Keynes, Keynesians and Monetarists*, Philadelphia: University of Philadelphia Press.

Wray, L.R. (1990) *Money and Credit in Capitalist Economies*, Aldershot, UK and Brookfield, USA: Edward Elgar.

11. Tax-driven money: additional evidence from the history of economic thought, economic history and economic policy[1]

Mathew Forstater

I arrived as a new graduate student in the Economics Department at the Graduate Faculty of the New School for Social Research in the autumn of 1987. Nicholas Kaldor had passed away in 1986, and the Department organized a conference in collaboration with the then-new Jerome Levy Economics Institute of Bard College, to celebrate Kaldor's life and contributions. I received a small grant from the Levy Institute to assist Edward Nell and Willi Semmler in assembling the papers and editing the conference volume, *Nicholas Kaldor and Mainstream Economics: Confrontation or Convergence?* (Nell and Semmler, 1991). The all-star line-up included a super-session on endogenous money and credit and exogenous interest rates with James Tobin, Paul Davidson, Hyman Minsky, Marc Lavoie, and Basil Moore (Moore, 1991). When Basil Moore's book, *Horizontalists and Verticalists* (1988), appeared the following year, it was all the rage. The notions of endogenous money and exogenous interest rates appealed not only to those working within the Post Keynesian framework, but to Sraffians, Marxists, and Institutionalists as well. Soon thereafter, I assisted Nell in organizing another conference at the Levy Institute focusing on money, bringing together the Post Keynesians and the French and other Europeans working on the theory of the monetary circuit. Once more, I assisted in the conference volume, *Money in Motion: The Post Keynesian and Circulation Approaches* (Deleplace and Nell, 1996). Again, Basil Moore attended the conference and contributed to the volume (Moore, 1996).

I met Basil and Sibs again at the Levy Institute in 1992, at the memorial conference for Tom Asimakopulos, and at the Fifth International Post Keynesian Summer Workshop in Knoxville, Tennessee in 1998. By that time, I was a Visiting Scholar at the Levy Institute, working with Randy Wray, another important contributor to the endogenous money approach, on the revival of the chartalist approach to money. Chartalism acknowledges the endogeneity of money and exogeneity of interest rates, but with a slight modification. Under a modern money system (no gold standard or fixed exchange rates), bank money comprises the horizontal component of the money supply process, and short-term interest rates are certainly exogenous, but the creation and destruction of money by the sovereign State constitutes the 'vertical' component of the money supply process (Mosler and Forstater, 1999; Wray, 1998).

The chartalist concept of 'tax-driven money' (TDM) refers to the idea that the power of the State (or other political authority) to impose a tax (or similar) liability payable in its own currency is sufficient to create a demand for that currency and give it value. The revival of TDM has inspired a number of authors to go back to the classic (and not so classic) texts in the history of economics to find evidence of the perspective. We now know that the list of those expressing something of the TDM view includes Adam Smith and John Maynard Keynes from the gallery of all-time greats (see Wray, 1998); Georg Friedrich Knapp of the German Historical School (Knapp, 1924 [1905]); a little-known author by the name of Mitchell Innes (1913, 1914; see also Wray, 2004); and, more recently, Abba Lerner (1947), Kenneth Kurihara (1950, pp. 34–9), Hyman Minsky (1986), Charles Goodhart (1998, 1989, p. 36; see also Bell and Nell, 2003), and James Tobin (1998, p. 27). This note intends to add to this list John Stuart Mill, Karl Marx, William Stanley Jevons, Philip H. Wicksteed, and Fred M. Taylor (plus an interesting titbit from Jean-Baptiste Say). A heretofore overlooked but important citation from Abba Lerner will also be introduced.

The chapter also reveals some instances of the TDM perspective from economic policy discussions in history, in particular from the speeches of John C. Calhoun, one-time US Senator and Vice President of the United States of America in the nineteenth century. Additional evidence in support of the view is offered from economic history, in particular from precolonial (and colonial) Africa. Finally, some newly discovered contemporary occurrences of the TDM view in conventional neoclassical economics, as well as from political science and history, are cited.

TAX-DRIVEN MONEY IN CLASSICAL ECONOMICS

One of the clearest and earliest references to the idea that a state-issued currency not tied to gold or any other commodity or currency can be managed through taxation and the declaration of public receivability is the now oft-quoted passage from Adam Smith's *An Inquiry into the Nature and Causes of the Wealth of Nations*:

> A prince, who should enact that a certain proportion of his taxes should be paid in a paper money of a certain kind, might thereby give a certain value to this paper money; even though the term of its final discharge and redemption should depend altogether on the will of the prince. (Smith, 1904 [1776], 312)

Cannan's 'sidebar' (his summary of each paragraph given in the margin) for this passage reads: 'A requirement that certain taxes should be paid in particular paper money might give that paper a certain value even if it was irredeemable' (ibid.; see Wray, 1998, for a discussion). We may now add to this a remark from J.B. Say's *A Treatise on Political Economy*, Book I, 'Of the Production of Wealth', Chapter XXII, 'Of Signs or Representatives of Money', Section IV, 'Of Paper-Money', to the effect that:

> In the first place, a paper, wherewith debts can be legally, though fraudulently, discharged, derives a kind of value from that single circumstance. Moreover, the paper-money may be made efficient to discharge the perpetually recurring claims of public taxation. (Say, 1803 [1964], p. 280)

We get a longer discussion of the subject from J.S. Mill's *Principles of Political Economy*, in Book III, Chapter XIII, paragraph III.13.1, 'Of an Inconvertible Paper Currency':

> 1. After experience had shown that pieces of paper, of no intrinsic value, by merely bearing upon them the written profession of being equivalent to a certain number of francs, dollars, or pounds, could be made to circulate as such, and to produce all the benefit to the issuers which could have been produced by the coins which they purported to represent; governments began to think that it would be a happy device if they could appropriate to themselves this benefit, free from the condition to which individuals issuing such paper substitutes for money were subject, of giving, when required, for the sign, the thing signified. They determined to try whether they could not emancipate themselves from this unpleasant obligation, and make a piece of paper issued by them pass for a pound, by merely calling it a pound, and *consenting to receive it in payment of the taxes*. And such is the influence of almost all established governments, that they have generally succeeded in attaining this object: I believe I might say they have always succeeded for a time, and the power has only been lost to them after they had compromised it by the most flagrant abuse.
>
> In the case supposed, the functions of money are performed by a thing which derives its power for performing them solely from convention; but convention is quite sufficient to confer the power; since nothing more is needful to make a person accept anything as money, and even at any arbitrary value, than the persuasion that it will be taken from him on the same terms by others. The only question is, what determines the value of such a currency; since it cannot be, as in the case of gold and silver (or paper exchangeable for them at pleasure), the cost of production.
>
> We have seen, however, that even in the case of a metallic currency, the immediate agency in determining its value is its quantity. If the quantity, instead of

depending on the ordinary mercantile motives of profit and loss, could be arbitrarily fixed by authority, the value would depend on the fiat of that authority, not on cost of production. The quantity of a paper currency not convertible into the metals at the option of the holder, can be arbitrarily fixed; especially if the issuer is the sovereign power of the state. The value, therefore, of such a currency is entirely arbitrary. (Mill, 1987 [1848], pp. 542–3; emphasis added)

Once again, we see that many authors understood the possibility of a tax-driven currency, under certain institutional arrangements. This is not to say that they viewed all money as such, or that they understood all the details. But one fact seems certain: many more authors than previously believed considered the workings of a tax-driven currency.

TAXES AND THE RISE AND DEVELOPMENT OF CAPITALISM: TAX-DRIVEN MONEY IN MARX

Marx is well-known to have commodity money in *Capital* and other writings. Like many other authors, Marx also considered tax-driven money, and it was a key to the development of wage-labor and therefore the rise and development of capitalism, particularly in the colonies (see Forstater, 2005). In the *Grundrisse*, Notebook I, 'The Chapter on Money', Marx recognized that 'Prussia has paper money of forced currency. (A reflux is secured by the obligation to pay a portion of taxes in paper.)': (Marx, 1973 [1857], p. 132). Furthermore, Marx viewed this as part of the larger transition associated with money and the role of the State:

(To be further developed, the influence of the transformation of all relations into money relations: taxes in kind into money taxes, rent in kind into money rent, military service into mercenary troops, all personal services in general into money services, of patriarchal, slave, serf and guild labour into pure wage labour.) (Marx, 1973 [1857], p. 146)

In the period of the rising absolute monarchy with its transformation of all taxes into money taxes, money indeed appears as the moloch to whom real wealth is sacrificed. (Marx, 1973 [1857], p. 199)

This same theme was brought out in *Capital*, where Marx discussed the 'primitive accumulation' necessary for capitalist development:

The different moments of primitive accumulation can be assigned in particular to Spain, Portugal, Holland, France, and England, in more or less chronological order. These moments are systematically combined together at the end of the seventeenth century in England; the combination embraces the colonies, the

> national debt, the modern tax system, and the system of protection. These methods depend in part on brute force, for instance the colonial system. But, they all employ the power of the state, the concentrated and organized force of society, to hasten, as in a hot-house, the process of transformation of the feudal mode of production into the capitalist mode, and to shorten the transition. Force is the midwife of every old society which is pregnant with a new one. It is itself an economic power. (Marx, 1990 [1867], pp. 915–16)

And again:

> The modern fiscal system, whose pivot is formed by taxes on the most necessary means of subsistence . . . thus contains within itself the germ of automatic progression. Over-taxation is not an accidental occurrence, but rather a principle. In Holland, therefore, where this system was first inaugurated, the great patriot, DeWitt, extolled it in his Maxims as the best system for making the wage-labourer submissive, frugal, industrious . . . and overburdened with work. Here, however, we are less concerned with the destructive influence it exercises on the situation of the wage-labourer than with the forcible expropriation, resulting from it, of peasants, artisans, in short, of all constituents of the lower middle-class. There are no two opinions about this, even among the bourgeois economists. Its effectiveness as an expropriating agent is heightened still further by the system of protection, which forms one of its integral parts. (Marx, 1990 [1867], p. 921)

Marx's understanding of the role of taxation in the creation of wage-labor expanded after 1861 during his study of the Russian peasantry and their proletarianization (White, 1996, p. 247). In particular, he was influenced by his reading of N. Flerovsky's *The Condition of the Working Class in Russia* (Flerovsky was the pseudonym of V.V. Bervi) (White, 1996, p. 247). Marx wrote to Engels that 'this is the most important book which has appeared since your *Condition of the Working Class*' (White, 1996, p. 248):

> Flerovsky made it plain that . . . not all Russian peasants were on the same economic level . . . While rich peasants . . . could earn their living entirely from the land, the poorer ones could not because 'the amount of taxes levied on the peasantry is so great that they cannot pay it without earning wages.' (White, 1996, p. 248)

According to Flerovsky, 'The main reason which compels the worker to resort to the capitalist is to pay his taxes' (White, 1996, p. 249). As White reports, 'Marx was delighted with Flerovsky's book and as he wrote to Engels: "What I like, among other things, in Flerovsky is his polemic against direct taxes exacted from the peasants"' (White, 1996, p. 249):

> Flerovsky's book had a lasting significance for Marx's studies of Russian economic development, because the picture it presented was not contradicted by any of the other sources which Marx used, and indeed, the statistical materials

> which he consulted served only to add substance to what Flerovsky had said. (White, 1996, p. 249)

Marx's extensive study of the *Reports of the Fiscal Commission* 'served to substantiate Flerovsky's opinion that the system of taxation in Russia . . . was responsible for turning workers into proletarians' (White, 1996, p. 249).

The influence of Flerovsky seems to be present in Engels' analysis, inserted in Chapter 43 of *Capital*, Volume 3, where he refers to 'Russian and Indian peasants succumbing to the screws of taxation':

> the lands of the Russian and Indian communistic communities, which had to sell a portion of their product, and an ever-growing one at that, to get money for the taxes exacted by a merciless state despotism – often enough by torture. These products were sold with no regard to their costs of production, sold at the price which the dealer offered, because the peasant absolutely had to have money at the payment date. (Marx, 1981 [1891], p. 860)

Later in Volume 3, in Chapter 47, Marx himself makes clear that taxes function to speed up the preconditions for capitalist development. In a discussion of the Mercantile system, Marx argues that the transformation from feudal society to capitalism was in no way 'natural', but was facilitated by the state:

> We have already noted how the Monetary System correctly proclaims that production for the world market and the transformation of the product into a commodity, hence into money, is the precondition and requirement for capitalist production . . . But it is also a characteristic feature of the self-interested merchants and manufacturers of that time, and belongs to the period of capitalist development that they represent, that the transformation of feudal agricultural societies into industrial societies, and the resulting industrial struggle of nations on the world market, involves an accelerated development of capital which cannot be attained in the so-called natural way but only by compulsion. It makes a substantial difference whether the national capital is transformed into industrial capital gradually and slowly, or whether this transformation is accelerated in time by the taxes they impose via protective duties, principally on the landowners, small and middle peasants and artisans, by the accelerated expropriation of independent direct producers, by the forcibly accelerated accumulation and concentration of capital, in short, by the accelerated production of the conditions of the capitalist mode of production. (Marx, 1991 [1891], p. 920)

While Marx's interest in the role of money taxes in primitive accumulation certainly deepened as a result of his reading of Flerovsky, there is evidence that this recognition was not new and that he had already understood the importance of these processes earlier. The entries in the *Grundrisse* have already been noted. In the *Urtext*, the original draft of *A Contribution to the Critique of Political Economy*, written in 1858, Marx emphasized 'the way that an absolute monarchy pressures for production for exchange simply by demanding money taxes' (Nelson, 1999, p. 102):

> The absolute monarchy, itself already a product of the development of bourgeois wealth to a level incompatible with old feudal relationships, is – in accordance with the uniform general power which it must be able to exercise at every point of the periphery – in need of a material instrument of that power: the *universal equivalent*, wealth in its constant battle-ready form in which it is completely independent of particular local, natural, individual relations. It needs wealth in the form of money. A system of services and deliveries in-kind tends to impart, in accordance with their specific character, a particular character to their use as well. Money is alone capable of being converted into any particular use value. So the absolute monarchy is actively engaged in converting money into the universal means of payment. That can be done only through forced circulation, which makes products circulate at below their value. For the absolute monarchy, the conversion of all taxes into money taxes is a vital matter. (Marx, 1987 [1858], pp. 430–31)

In Part III of *Theories of Surplus Value*, in a discussion of early capitalist development and the genesis of wage-labor, Marx again highlights the importance of 'the conversion of rent into money rent and generally of all payments in kind (taxes, etc., rent) into money payments' (Marx, 1971 [1863], p. 289).

Marx's TDM-related work is interesting because it focuses on the roles that taxation and the declaration of public receivability played, not only in monetization but also the creation of wage-labor and marketization, indeed, in the development of capitalism. The implications for the theory of the state and economic history are potentially quite significant.

TAX-DRIVEN MONEY IN EARLY NEOCLASSICAL ECONOMICS

Some of the early neoclassical authors also displayed an understanding of tax-driven money. One of the founders of the neoclassical approach, William Stanley Jevons, in Chapter XVIII of his *Money and the Mechanism of Exchange*, 'Methods of Regulating a Paper Currency', referred to the '*The Revenue Payments Method*': 'Inconvertible paper money may be freely issued, but an attempt may be made to keep up its value by receiving it in place of coin in the payment of taxes' (Jevons, 1892 [1875], p. 214).

The most elaborate discussion, however, is found in Chapter VII of Book II of Philip H. Wicksteed's *The Common Sense of Political Economy*, on 'BANKING. BILLS. CURRENCY':

The Government has, however, a further resource. It has the means of maintaining a perpetual recurrence of persons thus desiring money at its face value, for the Government itself has more or less defined powers of taking the possessions of its subjects for public purposes, that is to say, enforcing them to contribute thereto by paying taxes. Ultimately it requires food, clothing, shelter, and a certain amount of amusement and indulgence for its soldiers and all its officials; and it requires fire-arms, ammunition, and the like. And in proportion to its advance in civilization it may have other and humaner purposes to fulfil. Now, as long as gold has any application in the arts and sciences it exchanges at a certain rate with other commodities, just as oxen exchange at a certain rate against potatoes, pig-iron, or the privilege of listening, in a certain kind of seat, to a prima donna at a concert. The Government, then, levying taxes upon the community, may say: 'I shall take from you, in proportion to your resources, as a tribute to public expenses, the value of so much gold. You may pay it to me in actual metallic gold or you may pay it to me in anything which I choose to accept in lieu of the gold. If you do not give it me I shall take it from you, in gold or any other such articles as I can find, and which would serve my purpose, to the value of the gold. But if you can give me a piece of paper, of my own issue, to the face value of the gold that I am entitled to claim of you, I will accept that in payment.' Now, as these demands of the Government are recurrent, there will always be a set of persons to whom the Government paper stamped with a unit weight of gold is actually equivalent to that weight of gold itself, because it will secure immunity from requisitions to the exact extent to which the gold would secure it. This gives to the piece of paper an actual power of doing the work that gold to its face value could do, in the way of effecting exchanges; and therefore the Government will find that the persons of whom it has made purchases, or whom it has to pay for their services, will not only be obliged to accept the paper in lieu of payments already due, and which it chooses to say that these papers discharge, but will also be willing to enter into fresh bargains with it, to supply services or to surrender things for the paper, exactly as if it were gold; as long as it is easy to find persons who, being themselves under obligation to the Government, actually find the Government promise to relinquish their claim for gold as valuable as the gold itself. The persons who pay taxes constitute a very large portion of the community and the taxes they have to pay form a very appreciable fraction of their total expenditure, and consequently a very large number of easily accessible persons actually value the paper as much as the gold up to a certain determined point, the point, to wit, of their obligations to the Government. Thus it is that a limited demand for paper, at its face value in gold, constitutes a permanent market, and furnishes a basis on which a certain amount of other transactions will be entered into. The Government, in fact, is in a position very analogous to that of an issuing bank. An issuing bank promises to pay gold to any one who presents its notes, and to a certain extent that promise performs the functions of the gold itself, and a certain volume of notes can be floated as long as the credit of the bank is good. Because bank promises to pay are found to be convenient, as a means of conducting exchanges. After this number has been floated the notes begin to be presented at the bank, and presently it has to redeem its promises as quickly as it issues them. The limit then has been reached and the operation cannot be repeated. After this people will decline to accept the promises of the bank in lieu of the money, or, which is the same thing, they will instantly present the promise and require its fulfillment. The amount of notes in circulation may

> be maintained, but it cannot be increased. The issuing Government does not, without qualification, say that it will pay gold to any one who presents the note, but, in accepting its own notes instead of gold, it says, in effect, that it will give gold for its own notes to any *of its own debtors*; and as long as there is a sufficient body of these debtors to vivify the circulating fluid the Government can get its promises accepted at par. Any Government which, even for a short time, insists on paying in paper and receiving in gold, that is to say, any Government that does not honour its own issue when presented by its debtors, will find that its subjects decline to enter into voluntary contracts with it except on the gold basis; and if its paper still retains any value whatever, it will only be because of an expectation of a different state of things hereafter that gives a certain speculative value to the promise. In fact a Government which refuses to take its own money at par has no vivifying sources to rely on except the very disreputable and rapidly exhausted one of proclaiming to debtors, and persons under contract to pay periodic sums, that they need not do so if they hold a certificate of immunity from the Government. Such immunity will be purchased at a price determined, like all other market prices, by the stock available (qualified by the anticipations of the stock likely to be available presently) and the nature of the services it can render. The power, then, of Governments to make their issues do exchange work depends on their power to make a note of a certain face value do a definite amount of exchange work; and this they can effect by giving it a definite primary value to certain persons, and then keeping the issue within the corresponding limits. It does not consist in an anomalous, and, in fact, inconceivable, power of enabling an indefinite issue to perform a definite work, and arriving at the value of each individual unit by a division sum. (Wicksteed, 1910, pp. 620–22)

The pre-twentieth century history of economic doctrine is filled with references to and discussions of tax-driven money. Theorists as diverse as J.S. Mill, Marx, and Jevons all recognized the possibility of a state currency managed under certain institutional arrangements, that is, through taxation and declaration of public receivability (what Wray, 1998, calls 'twintopt': 'that which is necessary to pay taxes').

TAX-DRIVEN MONEY IN TWENTIETH CENTURY ECONOMIC THOUGHT

Chartalism in the twentieth century is associated most closely with Georg Friedrich Knapp and John Maynard Keynes (see Wray, 1998). Another important discussion of the idea can be found in Section 2 ('Principles') of Chapter 3 ('Monetary Principles') of Fred M. Taylor's, *Some Chapters on Money: Printed for the Use of Students in the University of Michigan*:

> Principle 1. Under modern conditions in most civilized countries the full and continuous circulation of any kind of money in any particular country

> commonly requires a measure of legal authorization from the government of that country. (Taylor, 1906, p. 86)

Here we have a statement that appears to be closer to a 'legal', rather than 'tax', brand of chartalism. Taylor continues, however, making it clear that legal tender laws may not be enough to drive a currency:

> Principle 2. Under modern conditions representative money which is not redeemable, directly or indirectly, in either standard money or goods, seems generally to require, as a condition of currency, that it should be a valid tender in some important relation, e.g., payments to government. (Taylor, 1906, p. 89)

It is the ability to settle the tax and other obligations to the State that drives the currency.

As the subtitle suggests, this work was specifically designed as a textbook for Taylor's students at the University of Michigan. The discussion contains some additional insights relevant to the present discussion. Taylor goes on to suggest that:

> standard coins which fall much short of legal requirements in respect to weight will not commonly remain in circulation, unless, though short in weight, they continue to be a valid tender in some important relation, particularly in payments to government. (Taylor, 1906, p. 90)

This insight supports the thesis that even metallic currency under certain conditions can be 'chartal' money. On the one hand, acceptance at government pay offices can keep up the value of underweight coin, while on the other refusal to accept can result in a money's termination:

> in repeated instances governments have found it easy to expel an obnoxious money from circulation by depriving it of all legal tender status, i.e., relieving creditors of the obligation to receive it in payment of debts, and refusing to accept it for public dues. (Taylor, 1906, p. 90)

The issue of acceptability was emphasized by another of the great twentieth century contributors to chartalist thought, Abba Lerner. While Lerner's contributions to chartalism and functional finance have been outlined elsewhere (see Forstater, 1999, 2003), his entry on 'Money' in the *Encyclopedia Britannica* has heretofore been overlooked:

> Any particular seller will accept as money what he can use for buying things himself or for settling his own obligations. This seems to say that a means of payment will be generally acceptable if it is already generally acceptable, and it looks like a circular argument. But it only means that general acceptability is not

> easily established. General acceptability may come about gradually. If a growing number of people are willing to accept payment in a particular form, this makes others willing to accept that kind of payment. General acceptability may be established rapidly if very important sellers or creditors are willing to accept payment in a particular form of money. For example if the government announces its readiness to accept a certain means of payment in settlement of taxes, taxpayers will be willing to accept this means of payment because they can use it to pay taxes. Everyone else will then be willing to accept it because they can use it to buy things from the taxpayers, or to pay debts to them, or to make payments to others who have to make payments to the taxpayers, and so on. (Lerner, 1946, p. 693)

Lerner's 1946 entry was subsequently replaced with one by Milton Friedman.

The chartalist notion that taxes-drive-money and related ideas such as the role of taxation and the declaration of public receivability in the creation of wage-labor can be found in Classical, Marxist, early Neoclassical, and twentieth century economic thought. The claim is not that this is the only or even the predominant theory of money, but rather simply that the ideas were put forward by many more economists (and of all theoretical persuasions) than was once commonly understood. Likewise, many more historical instances of tax-driven money can be identified. We now turn to one particularly fascinating case, the West African cowrie.

THE TAX-DRIVEN COWRIE

Chartalism forces a reconsideration of virtually all of the received wisdom coming out of traditional monetary theory and history. The cowrie currency used in parts of Africa and Asia, for example, is often cited as an example of 'primitive' money (see, for example, Friedman, 1972, p. 927). A brief examination of the history of the cowrie, however, shows it to be tax-driven. We would do well to take seriously Polanyi's admonition that 'A warning is in order against the ethnocentric bias that so easily takes hold of us on economic subjects that arise outside of our own Western culture' (1966, p. 177):

> We are used to ranging cowrie with the other shells as a sample of primitive money in a supposed evolutionary perspective of the 'origins and development of money.' Historical research removes this evolutionary bias. Cowrie currencies emerged on the Middle and Upper reaches of the Niger at a time when metal currencies and, indeed, coined money were long established in the Mediterranean heartlands. This is the background against which the emergence of a new nonmetallic currency in Islamic West Africa should be viewed. It will then not be erroneously regarded as part of a general evolution of money, but

> rather as a feature in the spread both of *centralized government* and of food markets in the early [African] empires which left its imprint on the local history of money. (Polanyi, 1966, p. 178; emphasis added)

The use of the cowrie as money in West Africa began between 1290 and 1352, and gold and metallic coin had long been in use prior to that time in the region (Polanyi, 1966, pp. 179–80). According to Polanyi, 'Dahomey's cowrie was definitely not primitive money' (1966, p. 189); rather, it is an example of 'the launching of a currency as an instrument of taxation' (1966, p. 186). Even the local legend regarding the cowrie's origin supports the thesis that cowrie money is a creature of the state (1966, p. 186):

> Cowrie money . . . appears in the legend as the innovation of an autochthonous king. And the result – 'people now found food to eat and no longer exchanged articles' – suggests a close connection between money and markets. Actually, as we know, Dahomean markets were food markets in which – notable fact – cowrie payment was enforced. The acting force that shaped and organized the economy was the state, in the person of the king. Food, money, and market are all statemade.' (Polanyi, 1966, p. 186)

Evidence from other areas and authorities now exists to support the thesis of the tax-driven cowrie. Lovejoy reports that in pre-colonial Nigeria:

> Dependencies of such emirates as Nupe paid their levies in cowries as well, so that the taxation system effectively assured that people participated in the market economy and used the currency, a policy remarkably similar to the one which the later colonial regimes pursued in their efforts to see their own currencies accepted. (Lovejoy, 1974, p. 581)

Law confirms the thesis for other areas of West Africa, such as Bornu in the nineteenth century:

> The apparent preference to the payment of taxes in money – cowries or gold – is especially interesting. It must be assumed that the spread of the use of cowry shells as money in West Africa depended upon state initiative – this was certainly the case with the introduction of the cowry currency in Bornu in the 1840s. (Law, 1978, p. 49)

One of the factors that sustained the widespread misunderstanding of the origins and nature of the cowrie was the myth that the cowrie was freely available in virtually unlimited quantities. On the contrary, the cowrie was not native to West Africa; the state 'guarded against its proliferation by preventing shiploads from being freely imported' (Polanyi, 1966, p. 189); and the *stringing* of cowries 'was a monopoly of the palace' (Law, 1978, p. 49;

see also Polanyi, 1966). This latter refers to strings of specific numbers of cowries, and specific numbers of strings collected in a 'head' (Law, 1977, p. 209).

The cowrie's geographical occurrence in West Africa supports the state money thesis and refutes any evolutionary explanation: 'cowrie using areas and areas where it was not accepted for payment were as if their boundaries were drawn by administrative authority' (Polanyi, 1966, p. 190):

> This was a place of multiple currencies, while Dahomey and Ashanti had succeeded in keeping their monetary systems separate in the face of what must appear to the modern mind as insuperable obstacles. Dahomey used cowrie exclusively, in elaborate, never-changing division, maintained at an unvarying exchange rate of 32,000 cowries to one ounce gold – an amazing feat. (Polanyi, 1966, p. 29)

The 'compulsory monetization of sale-purchase' meant that nothing was available for sale except in cowrie, and there was no barter whatsoever (Polanyi, 1966, p. 84). It now seems likely that the cowrie was also tax-driven in other areas of the world where it served as money. Elwin reported in 1942 that in parts of India, 'There are still many of the older generation who remember the days when the cowrie was used as currency and was accepted in the payment of taxes' (Elwin, 1942, p. 121).

The cowrie was clearly tax-driven over most if not all of pre-colonial West Africa, and elsewhere. Much more research is required, of course, but it appears that many more monies in history may have been tax-driven than was previously believed.

TAX-DRIVEN MONEY IN THE HISTORY OF ECONOMIC POLICY: THE CASE OF JOHN C. CALHOUN

In addition to tax-driven money in the history of economic thought and economic history, the idea can be found in the history of economic policy discussions. One interesting instance is the case of John C. Calhoun, a US Senator and Vice President of the United States of America in the nineteenth century. In several speeches in the US Senate in the 1830s, Calhoun spoke of the idea and made references to a number of additional historical cases.

In an 1838 speech in reply to Daniel Webster on the Subtreasury bill, Calhoun argued that:

> I now undertake to affirm positively, and without the least fear that I can be answered, what heretofore I have but suggested – that a paper issued by the

government, with the simple promise to receive it in all its dues . . . , would, to the extent that it would circulate, form a perfect paper-circulation. (1981 [1838], p. 220)

Earlier, in 1837, in a speech on a bill authorizing the issue of treasury notes, Calhoun cited the case of North Carolina in support of a tax-driven currency:

North Carolina, just after the Revolution, issued a large amount of paper, which was made receivable in dues to her. It was also made a legal tender; which, of course, was not obligatory after the adoption of the federal constitution. A large amount, say between four and five hundred thousand dollars, remained in circulation after that period, and continued to circulate for more than twenty years, at par with gold and silver the whole time, with no other advantage than being received in the revenue of the State, which was much less than one hundred thousand dollars per annum. (Calhoun, 1980a [1837], p. 566)

In a speech the next month on his amendment to separate the government and the banks, Calhoun added the case of Russia:

We are told there is no instance of a government paper that did not depreciate. In reply, I affirm that there is none assuming the form I propose [notes receivable by government in payment of dues] that ever did depreciate. Whenever a paper receivable in the dues of government had anything like a fair trial, it has succeeded. Instance the case of North Carolina referred to in my opening remarks. The drafts of the treasury at this moment, with all their incumbrance, are nearly par with gold and silver; and I might add the instance alluded to by the distinguished senator from Kentucky [Henry Clay], in which he admits, that as soon as the excess of the issues of the Commonwealth Bank of Kentucky were reduced to the proper point, its notes rose to par. The case of Russia might also be mentioned. In 1827 she had a fixed paper-circulation in the form of bank-notes, but which were inconvertible, of upward of $120,000,000, estimated in the metallic ruble, and which had for years remained without fluctuation; having nothing to sustain it but that it was received in the dues of government, and that, too, with a revenue of only about $90,000,000 annually. (Calhoun, 1980b [1837], p. 607)

Both Calhoun's ideas and the cases he identifies must be subject to further investigation. It is clear from his remarks, however, that he was speaking of the advantages of a tax-driven currency.

TAX-DRIVEN MONEY IN CONTEMPORARY THOUGHT: WALRASIAN NEOCLASSICAL AND INTERDISCIPLINARY OCCURRENCES

There are a number of interesting contemporary occurrences of the TDM view, in both orthodox neoclassical economics, as well as works in political science and history. In neoclassical economics, there has long been a question of the place of money within the modern Walrasian general equilibrium framework. In a 1974 paper in *Econometrica* that even cites Lerner's 1947 article, Starr investigates the 'possibility of the price of money being zero in equilibrium and the role of taxes (payable in money) in preventing a zero price' (1974, p. 45).

> How can we eliminate the possibility of the price of money being zero in equilibrium? In order to do this we must arrange that there be a positive excess demand for money when the price of money is zero. One way to achieve this is to guarantee that money can always be used in payment of taxes . . . Taxes can be used to create a demand for money independent of its usefulness as a medium of exchange, thereby ensuring that its price will not fall to zero. (1974, p. 46)

More recently, Starr has similarly argued that 'Government issued fiat money has a positive equilibrium value from its acceptability for tax payments' (2003, p. 455; see also, Starr, 2002a, 2002b). Dror Goldberg of Texas A & M University is currently working on a 'tax-foundation theory of money' within a neoclassical (search-theoretic) framework which recognizes that modern money is tax-driven (Goldberg, 2006).

Harvard University political scientist David Woodruff argues that a chartalist perspective assists in the understanding of recent economic events in Russia and Argentina. In *Money Unmade* (1999), Woodruff uses the chartalist framework to understand the ruble's decline. More recently, Woodruff employs his chartalist-inspired 'institutional-sociological' approach to money to look at the spread of 'monetary surrogates' in Argentina after going off the dollar-peg (Woodruff, 2005).

Recent work by University of California (UCLA) historian Richard Von Glahn discusses the chartalist (he uses 'cartalist') monetary theorists of early modern China. In *Fountain of Fortune* (1996), Von Glahn documents state monetary policies from the Song, Ming, and Qing dynasties, and the theoretical traditions that informed them and through which they may be understood. As Von Glahn's work makes clear, the debate between the chartalists and the metallists is not unique to the West.

CONCLUSION

The notion of tax-driven money can be found throughout the history of economic thought, in the works of a remarkable range of authors representing various time periods and schools of thought. The idea also appears in policy discussions and in fields outside economics, such as political science and history. Neither is the idea unique to the West, as Von Glahn's work demonstrates. It also appears that monies previously thought to be 'primitive', such as the cowrie, were actually tax-driven. Nevertheless, the idea is conspicuously absent from textbooks and works on monetary theory and history.

One possible explanation for the silence concerning the notion may have something to do with the implications of the TDM idea for the relation of the economy and the state. Orthodox and even many heterodox approaches view the economy as relatively 'autonomous' and theory often assumes a 'pure' economy with no government. The TDM perspective implies that not only is money a creature of the state, but that much else about the economy is as well. The traditional distinction between 'endogenous' and 'exogenous' factors may need to be re-examined, or even discarded. There may, then, also be important methodological implications of the TDM view. More research needs to be conducted in all these areas.

NOTE

1. Versions of this chapter were presented at the Eastern Economic Association annual meetings, Washington, DC, February 2004; the Conference in Honor of Basil Moore at Stellenbosch University, South Africa, January 2004; and the Money Seminar at the University of Missouri–Kansas City, Fall 2003. I want especially to thank Mark Peacock and Scott Fullwiler for insightful comments on earlier drafts.

REFERENCES

Bell, S.A. and E.J. Nell (2003) *The State, the Market, and the Euro: Chartalism versus Metallism in the Theory of Money*, Cheltenham, UK and Northampton, MA, USA: Edward Elgar.

Calhoun, J.C. (1980a) [1837] 'Speech on the Bill Authorizing an Issue of Treasury Notes', 18 September 1837, in C.N. Wilson (ed.), *The Papers of John C. Calhoun, Vol. XIII, 1835–1837*, Columbia, SC: University of South Carolina Press.

Calhoun, J.C. (1980b) [1837] 'Speech on His Amendment to Separate the Government and the Banks', 3 October 1837, in C.N. Wilson (ed.), *The Papers of John C. Calhoun, Vol. XIII, 1835–1837*, Columbia, SC: University of South Carolina Press.

Calhoun, J.C. (1981) [1838] 'Speech in Reply to Daniel Webster on the Sub-Treasury Bill', 22 March 1838, in C.N. Wilson (ed.), *The Papers of John C. Calhoun, Vol. XIV, 1837–1839*, Columbia, SC: University of South Carolina Press.

Deleplace, G. and E.J. Nell (eds) (1996) *Money in Motion: The Post Keynesian and Circulation Approaches*, New York: Macmillan.

Elwin, V. (1942) 'The Use of Cowries in Bastar State, India', *Man*, 42 (November–December), 121–4.

Forstater, M. (1999) 'Functional Finance and Full Employment: Lessons from Lerner for Today', *Journal of Economic Issues*, XXXIII (2), 475–82.

Forstater, M. (2003) 'Toward a New Instrumental Macroeconomics: Abba Lerner and Adolph Lowe on Economic Method, Theory, History, and Policy', in E.J. Nell and M. Forstater (eds), *Reinventing Functional Finance: Transformational Growth and Full Employment*, Cheltenham, UK and Northampton, MA, USA: Edward Elgar.

Forstater, M. (2005) 'Taxation and Primitive Accumulation: The Case of Colonial Africa', in P. Zarembka (ed.), *The Capitalist State and its Economy; Democracy in Socialism, Research in Political Economy*, vol. 22, New York: Elsevier.

Friedman, M. (1972) 'Comments on the Critics', *The Journal of Political Economy*, 80 (5) (September–October), 906–50.

Goldberg, D. (2006) 'The Tax-Foundation Theory of Money' Department of Economics, Texas A & M University, http://econweb.tamu.edu/dgoldberg/research/tax.pdf.

Goodhart, C.A.E. (1989) *Money, Information and Uncertainty*, Cambridge, MA: The MIT Press.

Goodhart, C. (1998) 'The Two Concepts of Money: Implications for the Analysis of Optimal Currency Areas', *European Journal of Political Economy*, 14, 407–32. Reprinted in S. Bell and E.J. Nell (eds), *The State, the Market, and the Euro: Chartalism versus Metallism in the Theory of Money*, Cheltenham, UK and Northampton, MA, USA: Edward Elgar, 2003.

Innes M.A. (1914) 'The Credit Theory of Money', *Banking Law Journal* (December/January), 151–68. Reprinted in L.R. Wray (ed.), *Credit and State Theories of Money*, Cheltenham, UK and Northampton, MA, USA: Edward Elgar, 2004.

Innes M.A. (1913) 'What is Money?', *Banking Law Journal* (May), 377–408. Reprinted in L.R. Wray (ed.), *Credit and State Theories of Money*, Cheltenham, UK and Northampton, MA, USA: Edward Elgar, 2004.

Jevons, W.S. (1892) [1875] *Money and the Mechanism of Exchange*, New York: D. Appleton.

Knapp, G.F. (1924) [1905] *The State Theory of Money*, New York: Augustus M. Kelley.

Kurihara, K. (1950) *Monetary Theory and Public Policy*, New York: Norton.

Law, R. (1977) *The Oyo Empire, c. 1600–c. 1836: A West African Imperialism in the Era of the Atlantic Slave Trade*, Oxford: Clarendon Press.

Law, R. (1978) 'Slaves, Trade, and Taxes: The Material Basis of Political Power in Precolonial West Africa', *Research in Economic Anthropology*, 1, 37–52.

Lerner, A.P. (1946) 'Money', in *Encyclopædia Britannica*, Chicago: Encyclopædia Britannica.

Lerner, A.P. (1947) 'Money as a Creature of the State', *American Economic Review*, 37 (2), 312–17.

Lovejoy, P.E. (1974) 'Interregional Monetary Flows in the Precolonial Trade of Nigeria', *Journal of African History*, XV (4), 563–85.

Marx, K. (1971) [1863] *Theories of Surplus Value*, Part III, Moscow: Progress Publishers.

Marx, K. (1973) [1857] *Grundrisse: Foundations of a Critique of Political Economy*, New York: Vintage.

Marx, K. (1987) [1858] 'The Original Text of the Second and the Beginning of the Third Chapter of *A Contribution to the Critique of Political Economy* [the

Urtext]', in Marx and Engels, *Collected Works*, Volume 29, *Karl Marx, 1857–61*, New York: International Publishers.
Marx, K. (1990) [1867] *Capital: A Critique of Political Economy*, vol. 1, New York: Penguin.
Marx, K. (1991) [1891] *Capital*, vol. 3, New York: Penguin.
Mill, J.S. (1987) [1848] *Principles of Political Economy*, London: Augustus M. Kelley.
Minsky, H.P. (1986) *Stabilizing an Unstable Economy*, New Haven, CT: Yale University Press.
Moore, B.J. (1988) *Horizontalists and Verticalists*, Cambridge: Cambridge University Press.
Moore, B.J. (1991) 'Marx, Keynes, Kalecki and Kaldor on the Rate of Interest as a Monetary Phenomenon', in E.J. Nell and W. Semmler (eds), *Nicholas Kaldor and Mainstream Economics: Confrontation or Convergence?*, New York: Macmillan.
Moore, B.J. (1996) 'The Money Supply Process: A Historical Reinterpretation', in G. Deleplace and E.J. Nell (eds), *Money in Motion: The Post Keynesian and Circulation Approaches*, New York: Macmillan.
Mosler, W. and M. Forstater (1999) 'A General Framework for the Analysis of Currencies and Commodities', in P. Davidson and J. Kregel (eds), *Full Employment and Price Stability in a Global Economy*, Cheltenham, UK and Northampton, MA, USA: Edward Elgar.
Nell, E.J. and W. Semmler (eds), (1991) *Nicholas Kaldor and Mainstream Economics: Confrontation or Convergence?*, New York: Macmillan.
Nelson, A. (1999) *Marx's Concept of Money*, London: Routledge.
Polanyi, K. (1966) *Dahomey and the Slave Trade; An Analysis of an Archaic Economy*, Seattle: University of Washington Press.
Say, J.B. (1964) [1880] *A Treatise on Political Economy*, 4th edition, New York: A.M. Kelley.
Smith, Adam (1904) [1776] *An Inquiry into the Nature and Causes of the Wealth of Nations*, ed. E. Cannan, New York: Modern Library.
Starr, R.M. (1974) 'The Price of Money in a Pure Exchange Economy', *Econometrica*, 42 (1), 45–54.
Starr, R.M. (2002a) 'Existence and Uniqueness of "Money" in General Equilibrium: Natural Monopoly in the Most Liquid Asset', UCSD Economics Department Discussion Paper No. 2002-20, University of California–San Diego, December.
Starr, R.M. (2002b) 'Monetary General Equilibrium with Transaction Costs', UCSD Economics Department Discussion Paper No. 2002-01R, University of California–San Diego, July.
Starr, R.M. (2003) 'Why is there Money? Endogenous Derivation of "Money" as the Most Liquid Asset: A Class of Examples', *Economic Theory*, 21, 455–74.
Taylor, F.M. (1906) *Some Chapters on Money: Printed for the Use of Students in the University of Michigan*, Ann Arbor: George Wahr.
Tobin, J. (with S. Golub) (1998) *Money, Credit, and Capital*, New York: McGraw-Hill.
Von Glahn, R. (1996) *Fountain of Fortune*, Berkeley: University of California Press.
White, J.D. (1996) *Karl Marx and the Intellectual Origins of Dialectical Materialism*, London: Macmillan.
Wicksteed, P.H. (1910) *The Common Sense of Political Economy*, London: Macmillan.

Woodruff, D. (1999) *Money Unmade*, Ithaca, NY: Cornell University Press.
Woodruff, D.M. (2005) 'Boom, Gloom, Doom: Balance Sheets, Monetary Fragmentation, and Financial Crisis in Argentina and Russia', *Politics & Society*, 33(4), 3–47.
Wray, L.R. (1998) *Understanding Modern Money*, Cheltenham, UK and Northampton, MA, USA: Edward Elgar.
Wray, L.R. (2004) *Credit and State Theories of Money*, Cheltenham, UK and Northampton, MA, USA: Edward Elgar.

12. Monetary policy when money is endogenous

Philip Arestis and Malcolm Sawyer

INTRODUCTION

Basil Moore is well known for his strong advocacy of the concept of endogenous money by way of contrast with exogenous money (or to draw on the title of Moore, 1988, a horizontalist view rather than a verticalist view of the supply of money), and for his many contributions to the analysis of endogenous money. His advocacy of the endogenous money view can be seen to have triumphed over the exogenous view in that few would now adhere to the monetarist view based on exogenous money: in policy terms monetary policy is now clearly operated through the setting of a key interest rate and not through a money supply target. With only slight overstatement it can be said that in macroeconomic analysis 'we are all endogenous money people now', which is very much reflected in the 'new consensus in macroeconomics' (outlined below) where money is treated as endogenous, with the interest rate as the key instrument of monetary policy. This view of the interest rate, rather than the stock of money, as the key focus of monetary policy represents a catching-up of the mainstream analysis with the position long taken by post Keynesians with Basil Moore as a leading exponent. But although money is largely treated as endogenous, there are two distinct approaches, and in this contribution we explore some of the differences. One approach arises from the work of Moore and other post Keynesians, whereas the other is that which has been labelled as the 'new consensus'.

This chapter considers the nature and role of monetary policy when money is envisaged as credit money endogenously created within the private sector (by the banking system). Monetary policy is now based in many countries on setting (or targeting) of a key interest rate, such as the Central Bank discount rate. The amount of money in existence then arises from the interaction of the private sector and the banks on the basis of the demand to hold money and the willingness of banks to provide loans. Monetary policy has become closely linked with the targeting of the rate of inflation.

In this contribution, we consider whether monetary policy is well equipped to act as a counter-inflation policy and discuss the more general role of monetary policy in the context of money being treated as endogenous.

In the next section we critically explore monetary policy in the context of the 'new consensus macroeconomics' approach. This is followed by the third section in which we ask whether monetary policy is effective in countering falls in aggregate demand. This is followed in the fourth section by a discussion of the post Keynesian view of endogenous money, and this is followed by a consideration of the role of monetary policy from that perspective.

THE 'NEW CONSENSUS MACROECONOMICS'

The term 'new consensus in macroeconomics' has been widely used to summarize what is seen as a new prevailing orthodoxy in macroeconomic analysis: and we draw on this new consensus to illustrate how money is now perceived and the nature of monetary policy. It has been summarized in terms of a simple model with the following three equations (drawn from Meyer, 2001; but see, also, McCallum, 2001, and Clarida et al., 1999):

$$Y_t^g = a_0 + a_1 Y_{t-1}^g + a_2 E_t(Y_{t+1}^g) - a_3[R_t - E_t(p_{t+1})] + s_1 \qquad (12.1)$$

$$p_t = b_1 Y_t^g + b_2 p_{t-1} + b_3 E_t(p_{t+1}) + s_2, \quad (\text{with } b_2 + b_3 = 1) \qquad (12.2)$$

$$R_t = RR^* + E_t(p_{t+1}) + c_1 Y_{t-1}^g + c_2(p_{t-1} - p^T) \qquad (12.3)$$

where Y^g is the output gap, R is the nominal rate of interest, p is the rate of inflation, p^T is the inflation rate target, RR^* is the 'equilibrium' real rate of interest, that is the rate of interest consistent with a zero output gap which implies, from equation (12.2), a constant rate of inflation, and s_i (with $i = 1, 2$) represents stochastic shocks and E_t refers to expectations held at time t. Equation (12.1) is the aggregate demand equation with the output gaps determined by past and expected future output gap and the real rate of interest. Equation (12.2) is a Phillips curve with inflation based on the current output gap and past and future inflation. Equation (12.3) is a monetary policy-operating rule (of the Taylor's rule form with sluggish adjustment) with the nominal interest rate based on expected inflation, the output gap, the deviation of inflation from target, and the 'equilibrium' real rate of interest. In some versions of the model a lagged interest rate is included to capture interest rate 'smoothing' undertaken by the monetary authorities (see, for example, McCallum, 2001). We omit it only for the simple reason that the analysis is not affected at all by this omission.

A fourth equation can be added which relates the stock of money to 'demand for money variables' such as income, prices and the rate of interest, which would reinforce the endogenous money nature of this approach with the stock of money being demand determined. Clearly, though, such an equation would be superfluous in that the stock of money thereby determined is akin to a residual and does not feed back to affect other variables in the model.

In this analysis, monetary policy (in the form of interest rates) is designed to control demand inflation, and not cost inflation. The position taken on cost inflation is that it should either be accommodated, or that supply shocks come and go – and on average are zero and do not affect the rate of inflation (see, for example, Clarida et al., 1999). The significance of the 'new consensus' is that it strongly suggests that inflation can be tamed through interest rate policy (using demand deflation) and that there is an equilibrium rate (or 'natural rate') of interest which can balance aggregate demand and aggregate supply and which is feasible, and leads to a zero gap between actual and capacity output.

In the context of the working of monetary policy, this focus on inflation as caused by demand raises three issues. First, how effective is monetary policy at influencing aggregate demand and thereby inflation. The evidence, which we have surveyed in Arestis and Sawyer (2002), suggests that it is rather ineffectual. Second, if inflation is a 'demand phenomenon', and not a cost phenomenon, as reflected in the Phillips curve relationship hypothesized in the 'new consensus' macroeconomic model, then the question arises as to whether monetary policy is the most effective (or least ineffective) way of influencing aggregate demand (and in Arestis and Sawyer, 2002, we concluded that it is not), and fiscal policy is a clear alternative policy instrument. Third, there is the question of whether the possibility of sustained cost-push and other non-demand-related inflation can be as lightly dismissed as the 'new consensus' appears to do. The version of the Phillips curve referred to above is a (heavily) reduced form that does not explicitly consider wages, material costs and imported prices. A sustained money wage push makes no appearance in the Phillips curve relationship and it would appear that there is no explicit representation of such pressures. An increase in, for example, wage aspirations on the part of workers or pressure for higher profit margins are not incorporated, though it could be argued that they would be reflected in the stochastic term. This may be acceptable if pressures for higher wages and profit margins varied in a stochastic fashion over time (and averaged to zero). But even a sequence of time periods in which wage or profit margin pressures were positive, reflected in positive stochastic terms in the Phillips curve equation, would have long-lasting effects as one period's inflation feeds through to subsequent periods' inflation (through the lagged inflation term in the Phillips curve). Similarly if expectations on inflation were to rise (for whatever reason), then inflation would rise according to the Phillips curve, and subsequent inflation would also be higher (than otherwise). In the event of a sustained increase in inflation (due to cost pressures, as would seem to have been the case during the 1970s), this could only be met, in this framework, by raising interest rates and grinding down inflation by low demand and unemployment.

Endogenous money suggests little role for monetary policy with respect to inflation, and the empirical evidence we have assembled supports this claim (Arestis and Sawyer, 2002). The worldwide decline in inflation in the past two decades or so has gone alongside an enhanced position for monetary policy often associated with an 'independent' Central Bank pursuing inflation targeting. We would argue that it has been low levels of demand and pressure on commodity prices which have produced the decline in inflation. Further, inflation has fallen, not just in inflation-targeting countries, but also in countries that pursue different economic policies. Still, the case for inflation targeting is based to a large extent on 'reputation' (Barro and Gordon, 1983a, 1983b; Barro, 1986), and on the inflationary bias of discretionary monetary policy (Kydland and Prescott, 1977). But recent history has not been supportive to this view, if it ever was; and to quote Blinder (1998),

> In fact, the history of much of the industrial world since roughly 1980 has been one of disinflation – sometimes sharp disinflation, and sometimes at high social cost. Furthermore, the monetary authorities of many countries, especially in Europe, have displayed a willingness to maintain their tough anti-inflation stances to this very day, despite low inflation and persistently high unemployment. Whether or not you applaud these policies, they hardly look like grabbing for short-term employment gains at the expense of inflation. (pp. 40–41)

In any case, the negative correlation between Central Bank Independence (CBI) and actual inflation is not robust at all, and does not imply causation either (Posen, 1993; Campillo and Miron, 1997). This is particularly the case in large samples that include developing countries; also, in the case where a variety of variables are included in a multivariate analysis, the results thereby obtained cast doubt on the robustness of the correlations between CBI indexes and inflation or inflation variability. Actually, 'the only significant correlations developed in the specifications examined here suggest a *negative* correlation between CBI and real growth, and a *positive* correlation between CBI and unemployment' (Fuhrer, 1997, p. 34).

MONETARY POLICY IN THE PRESENCE OF A FALL IN AUTONOMOUS DEMAND

The 'new consensus' approach views aggregate demand as stable subject to stochastic (and serially uncorrelated) shocks. Monetary policy responds to these variations in aggregate demand through the monetary policy rule that models the setting of the rate of interest by the Central Bank. But we can ask whether monetary policy would be able to deal with a significant and sustained change in the level of aggregate demand. We examine this question by taking the case of a fall in autonomous demand and examining the extent to which monetary policy can help to restore aggregate demand. In doing so we use the 'new consensus' model but modify equation (12.1) along the lines of Arestis and Sawyer (2003). We retain the closed economy nature of the model, explicitly include the capacity level of output labelled Y^*, and introduce a simple consumption function,

$$C_t = d_1 + d_2 Y_{t-1} - \alpha [R_t - E_t(p_{t+1})]$$

where Y represents output. An investment function is also introduced:

$$I_t = d_3 + d_4 E(Y_{t+1}) - \beta [R_t - E_t(p_{t+1})].$$

We then have:

$$Y_t = (d_1 + d_3) + d_2 Y_{t-1} - \alpha [R_t - E_t(p_{t+1})] + d_4 E(Y_{t+1}) - \beta [R_t - E_t(p_{t+1})]$$

and with the output gap incorporated, this can be written as:

$$\begin{aligned}(Y_t - Y^*) = {} & (d_1 + d_3) + (d_2 + d_4 - 1) Y^* + d_2 (Y_{t-1} - Y^*) \\ & + d_4 [E(Y_{t+1}) - Y^*] - (\alpha + \beta) [R_t - E_t(p_{t+1})] \quad (12.1')\end{aligned}$$

It is now evident that the 'equilibrium' rate of interest (for a zero output gap) is given by:

$$[R_t - E_t(p_{t+1})] = (d_1 + d_3)/(\alpha + \beta) + [(d_2 + d_4 - 1)/(\alpha + \beta)] Y^*$$

It is evident from this expression that there is not a unique 'natural rate' of interest.

The empirical investigation of the effectiveness of monetary policy is generally undertaken in the context of an econometric model that could be viewed as an elaboration of the 'new consensus' model. The econometric model is, of course, much larger and involves many leads and lags which do not appear in the 'new consensus' model, but the econometric models generally impose the existence of a supply-side equilibrium (say the non-accelerating inflation rate of unemployment (NAIRU)) which is equivalent to the zero output gap for which inflation is constant. With a policy regime which pushes the economy towards the supply-side equilibrium (reflected in Taylor's rule), there is little room for output to substantially diverge from the supply-side equilibrium. Consequently, starting from the 'new consensus' model (or its equivalent) provides little role for monetary policy. It is assumed that there is a feasible 'equilibrium rate' of interest which will secure a level of aggregate demand equal to the capacity level of output (which itself is compatible with constant inflation).[1]

It is pertinent to question the effectiveness of monetary policy in the context of a major shift in the coefficients of the model formed by equations (12.1′) and (12.2). Suppose, for example, there is a change in 'animal spirits' or technological opportunities for investment that leads to a reduction in d_3. For monetary policy to be able to offset that reduction (to maintain demand at Y^*) would require a change in the real rate of interest of $-\Delta d_3/(\alpha+\beta)$. The question then relates to whether there can be a feasible nominal interest rate change that is sufficient to do the job. We think the answer is likely to be no. Let us take some illustrative numbers: consider a reduction in investment expenditure, which is equivalent to 1 per cent of gross domestic product (GDP) (of Y^*). If $(\alpha+\beta)=0.2$ (as the semi-elasticity, that is percentage change in demand divided by change in interest rate), then this would require a change of five percentage points in the real rate of interest. Note that a fall in investment would have multiplier effects on the level of output, and a similar reduction in interest rates would have multiplier effects. In the simulations surveyed in Arestis and Sawyer (2002), the largest effect of interest rate on investment was that a one-percentage point change in the rate of interest generated a 3 per cent change in investment (and generally the numbers were very much lower). Investment is 15 to 20 per cent of GDP, and hence a one-percentage point change in rate of interest was associated with a 0.45 to 0.6 per cent change in GDP (at the most). Given the bounds within which interest rates can be changed, falls in the autonomous components of aggregate demand equivalent to say 2 per cent would require interest rate reductions of say six percentage points. Consequently, the normal rather small interest rate changes would have little impact in offsetting the fall in autonomous demand.

THE POST KEYNESIAN ENDOGENOUS MONEY ANALYSIS

A simple representation of the post Keynesian endogenous money approach treats the Central Bank rate of interest as given, with the Central Bank providing bank reserves which are required (at a price which it sets). Banks provide loans at a rate of interest that is a mark-up over the Central Bank rate, and meets all credit demanded (subject to credit-standard requirements). The mark-up may vary as banks' liquidity preference and position, market power and attitude to risk vary. The loans are created in response to the demand for loans, and bank deposits are thereby created. The repayment of loans destroys money, and the amount of money that remains in existence depends on the demand to hold money. Money is generated within the inflationary process, and the rate of inflation influences the rate of increase of the stock of money, but money itself does not in any sense *cause* inflation.

The Central Bank rate can be viewed as the key rate on which all other interest rates are based – often explicitly so as in the case of the interest rates charged by banks on loans and paid by banks on deposits. However, while that is a useful way to proceed in the short run (the period over which the Central Bank holds its interest rate constant), it clearly leaves open the question of the forces that influence or determine the Central Bank interest rate in the longer term. This should be seen as a key issue in the analysis of endogenous money, yet it has been generally neglected in the post Keynesian endogenous money literature. The discussion has usually pointed to the discretion possessed by the Central Bank and exchange rate considerations: 'A central bank's key decision variable throughout the business cycle, and its central control instrument of monetary policy, is the nominal supply price at which it provides additional reserves. Over a wide range the central bank can determine exogenously the supply price at which it provides liquidity to the financial system. The upper and lower limits of this range are set by the size and openness of the economy and by the exchange rate regime in force' (Moore, 1989, p. 27).

However, little has been said about the underlying determinants of the discount rate set by the Central Bank. But, if the Central Bank is able to set its discount rate at some 'equilibrium rate' (where savings and investment are equal at the target rate of output, as in the 'new consensus' approach above, or at a target level of employment such as full employment), any problem of demand deficiency appears to be effectively dispensed with. We can first consider the relationship between the discount rate set by the Central Bank and other interest rates, and then come to the question as to whether the discount rate can be used to overcome demand deficiency.

The Central Bank is perceived to be able to set a discount rate that generates a spectrum of interest rates (on bank deposits, loans, bonds etc.) that is compatible with a balance between savings and investment occurring at a level of employment corresponding to capacity output (at which it is assumed inflation would be constant). The post Keynesian endogenous money approach recognizes the significance of the Central Bank rate of interest for the general level of interest rates. Indeed it takes a strong stance on this in the sense that the Central Bank determines the key discount rate and can enforce that rate. This does not mean that there is some one-for-one correspondence between the Central Bank rate and some other specified rate of interest (and in particular the long-term rate of interest on bonds may vary only to a minor extent when the Central Bank rate changes). The relationship between any particular rate of interest and the Central Bank rate is likely to be influenced by a variety of factors including the degree of market power of the banking system and what may be termed liquidity preference.

The causal link that runs from investment expenditure to savings requires the availability of finance to enable the investment to occur, in effect ahead of the generation of savings. Savings are available *ex post* to fund investment, but are not available *ex ante*. The level of income is perceived to adjust following an increase in investment expenditure. The notion of endogenous (bank) money upon which banks are able to make loans for the financing of investment is key to the explanation of the process whereby investment enhancement leads to expansion in savings and income. Yet, the rate of interest on loans is closely linked with the rate of interest set by the Central Bank. The factors that influence the setting and changing of the interest rate by the Central Bank become crucial to the relationship between savings and investment. To take an extreme view, if the Central Bank could vary the rate of interest to ensure that savings and investment were continuously equated at levels that corresponded to a supply-side equilibrium (perhaps full employment), then there would be no deficient demand problem.

There are, however, (at least) four reasons to be skeptical of the conclusion that interest rate policy can guide the economy to equilibrium with demand and supply in balance and inflation on target. The first is that the 'equilibrium' rate of interest is either negative or positive but so low as to be unattainable.[2] In some respects this has overtones of the 'liquidity trap', but the mechanisms are different. In the case of the 'liquidity trap', it is presumed that the rate of interest on bonds is so low (and the price of bonds so high) that no one is willing be buy bonds in light of the possible capital losses in doing so. In the present case, a negative interest rate is ruled out on the basis that a zero rate of interest can also be obtained by holding cash.

The real rate of interest given by a_0/a_3 may be negative. This would be equivalent to saying that the savings and investment schedules do not intersect in the positive range of interest rates. The aggregate demand equation (equation 12.1) above clearly assumes that aggregate demand (and presumably investment) is interest rate sensitive (such that a_3 is greater than zero) and that there is a substantial autonomous component of demand (otherwise a_0 would be non-positive). The emphasis here would be on the failure of the equation $I(r, Y_f) = S(r, Y_f)$ to have an economically meaningful solution, where Y_f is the income level for which the output gap is zero.

Second, and not unrelated to the previous point, interest rates may have very little effect on the levels of investment and savings and hence variations in the rate of interest would be ineffectual in reconciling savings and investment. The arguments on the ambiguity of the sign of the relationship between savings and the rate of interest are well known. The empirical literature on investment has often cast doubt on the impact of interest rates on investment and stressed the roles of profitability and capacity utilization. 'In the investment literature, despite some recent rehabilitation of a role for neoclassical cost-of-capital effects . . . there remains considerable evidence for the view that cash flow, leverage, and other balance-sheet factors also have a major influence on spending' (Bernanke et al., 1999, p. 1344). In the same study it is further noted in a footnote that 'contemporary macroeconometric forecasting models, such as the MPS model used by the Federal Reserve, typically do incorporate factors such as borrowing constraints and cash-flow effects' (p. 1344, fn. 2).

Third, the domestic interest rate may be incompatible with those rates that are being set internationally or have severe implications for the capital account. Insofar as interest rate parity holds, then the difference between the domestic interest rate and the foreign interest rate will be equal to the (expected) rate of change of the exchange rate. The relevant domestic interest rate (for international capital movements) may be a rate such as that on bonds, but one assumed to be linked to the discount rate set by the Central Bank. Although the interest rate parity result appears often not to hold, it could still be expected that there is some relationship between domestic interest rates (relative to international rates) and movements in the exchange rate.

Fourth, the Central Bank cannot calculate and attain the 'equilibrium rate' of interest through reasons of lack of information, a moving target or incompetence. It can be seen in the equations given above that the 'equilibrium rate' depends on a_0/a_3 and these are parameters that can vary over time. The Central Bank has imperfect information on the equilibrium real rate of interest RR^* (assuming that such a rate exists), and may aim for a real rate of interest which is not equal to a_0/a_3. It can also be noted that it is assumed in equation (12.3) that there are no stochastic errors in decision-making, with accurate knowledge on the lagged output gap and inflation rate. These assumptions need not be sustained in the real world; in fact, it is almost certain that they would not be. Furthermore, shifts in the propensity to save (as observed, for example, during the 1990s in the UK and the USA), in the propensity to invest, in the demand for exports and in the fiscal stance, could all be expected to lead to a shift in the equivalent of a_0/a_3. Information on the 'equilibrium rate' is not exactly readily available. Indeed, the Central Bank (or the government) may not wish to attain the 'equilibrium rate' of interest as defined above. In other words, the Central Bank does not pursue a policy rule akin to Taylor's rule. The Central Bank may use its interest rate for objectives other than a target rate of inflation and/or zero output gap; indeed, these objectives may very well include the rate of growth of the stock of money or a target level of the exchange rate.

THE ROLE FOR MONETARY POLICY IN AN ENDOGENOUS MONEY ANALYSIS

The post Keynesian endogenous money approach is embedded in a different perception of the macroeconomy as compared with the 'new consensus'. First, while the 'new consensus' views inflation as driven by excess demand and inflationary expectations, the Keynesian endogenous money view is that inflation can arise from a variety of sources including cost-push pressures (from wages, imported prices etc.), from struggles over income shares and from inadequate productive capacity. Second, the macroeconomy is viewed as subject to shocks from both the demand side and the supply side, with substantial variations in the level of economic activity over the business cycle. Further, variations in the level of demand are often driven by variations in investment expenditure emanating from accelerator-type mechanisms as well as shifts in liquidity preference and in the state of expectations. The financial sector itself is intimately involved with the generation of business cycles through its ability to grant loans to finance expenditure, the fluctuations in the liquidity position of the banks and other financial institutions, and, more importantly, changes in their liquidity preference.

The rest of this section attempts to answer the question of the role of monetary policy in the Keynesian endogenous money analysis.

Objectives of Monetary Policy

The basic rationale for assigning monetary policy the sole objective of inflation targeting is the view that 'inflation is always and everywhere a monetary [policy] phenomenon' and that the classical dichotomy holds in the form that monetary policy does not have real effects. These propositions came to the fore with the revival of monetarism based on an exogenous and controllable money stock, but have been carried over to a monetary policy based on interest rates. However, when inflation is viewed as a 'demand phenomenon', then fiscal policy can be viewed as an alternative (or complementary) policy for targeting inflation. When monetary policy has an impact on real variables (which we would argue is the general case, and effects on investment and on the exchange rate are two significant examples), then at a minimum the setting of monetary policy should give consideration to those real side effects.[3]

In the 'new consensus' model outlined above, the rate of inflation converges on the target rate of inflation. Expectations that the rate of inflation will be around the target rate, and that the monetary authorities will respond to increases in the rate of inflation by lowering aggregate demand, ensure that the rate of inflation does indeed converge on the target rate. Thus, much of the 'work' of monetary policy is accomplished through a belief that the inflation target is credible. But there is nothing unique about monetary policy in that regard: any policy (and specifically fiscal policy) which sets a credible inflation target would have a similar effect.

We would argue that the objectives of monetary policy should broaden, or perhaps more accurately that the considerations which bear on interest rate decisions should broaden. In particular, the effects which interest rate changes may have on the exchange rate and on investment, and perhaps asset prices, should be fully incorporated into the decision-making process. The effects of monetary policy on the exchange rate and on investment may well have long-lasting consequences, and hence monetary policy should not be set solely with the immediate impact on inflation in mind, but rather with due consideration given to potentially long-lasting real side effects.

Credit Rationing and Monetary Policy

The effects of monetary policy work through a variety of channels. In the mainstream literature a number of channels have been identified. These channels, which include two credit channels (narrow and broad), are distinct but complementary ways whereby imperfections in financial markets might affect real magnitudes in the economy. They are concerned with how changes in the financial positions of lenders and borrowers can affect aggregate demand in the economy, on the assumption of credit market frictions. The *narrow credit channel* (also labelled as the *bank lending channel*; see Hall, 2001) concentrates on the role of banks as lenders

(Roosa, 1951; Bernanke and Blinder, 1988). The *broad credit channel* (also labelled as the *balance sheet channel*; see Hall, 2001) describes how the financial health of borrowers can affect the supply of finance and ultimately aggregate demand (Bernanke and Gertler, 1989, 1999; Bernanke et al., 1999). The next two are labelled the *interest rate channel* and the *monetarist channel* together. These two channels depend heavily on the assumption made about the degree of substitutability between money and other assets. Changes in asset prices are important in the case of the *wealth effect channel* too. The mechanism in this case works via consumer expenditure where the consumption function is hypothesized to depend on consumer wealth. The sixth channel of the impact of monetary policy is the *exchange rate channel*, operating through import prices and net external demand.

Some of the effects may be described as 'price effects' of a change in the interest rate, but others take the form of changes in the extent of credit rationing. But the extent of credit rationing which occurs depends on decisions made by banks (and other financial institutions) and depends on their attitudes towards risk and liquidity. This observation raises the question as to whether interest rate policy should be supplemented by explicit forms of credit control implemented by the Central Bank (or other government agencies). Financial institutions do, for example, vary the conditions under which mortgages are provided in terms of the permissible loan to income ratio etc. A policy which sought to impose limits on the loan to income ratio may be possible.

However, credit controls may affect the quality of intermediation thereby having adverse effects on investment. Shaw (1973) describes the negative aspects of credit controls and rationing as follows:

> 'Rationing is expensive to administer. It is vulnerable to corruption and conspiracy in dividing between borrowers and officers of the intermediary monopoly rent that arises from the difference between low, regulated loan rate and the market-clearing rate. It can be frustrated by borrowers who simply do not repay loans and keep their place in the ration queue by extending maturities. The rationing process discriminates poorly among investment opportunities . . . and the social cost of this misallocation is suggested by the high incremental ratios of investment to output that lagging economies report. (p. 86)

Credit controls can be ineffective and expensive, in view of the high degree of sophistication of their institutional arrangements. Under these circumstances, the ability of borrowers to get around credit restrictions might be effective. We would, therefore, accept the possibility of limited credit rationing for the reasons discussed earlier in this section, but accept that a permanent policy of credit rationing would not be effective (see also

Stiglitz and Weiss, 1981). An example of what we have in mind here is provided by situations, such as those during the late 1980s, which arise from the rapid growth of credit and that can generate a bubble. The bubble eventually bursts, but the possibility arises of preventing the bubble and thereby prolonging the boom through some form of control over the volume, and direction, of credit. Another example relates to the state of the UK economy at the time of writing (May 2004). Balance of payments considerations dictate a lower interest rate than otherwise. The booming housing market should involve a higher interest rate than otherwise. This conflict can be overcome by a lower interest rate and prudential credit controls to 'cool off' the housing market. This would not be a permanent state of affairs of course. Once the housing market returned to 'normal', credit controls could be eased and indeed abandoned. There are difficulties with this approach, as argued above, and it is for this very reason that we are not arguing that credit controls *per se* would stimulate the economy. We are, thus, not arguing for credit controls as a permanent tool of monetary policy. It is only under certain circumstances, as in the examples just cited, that such a policy might be helpful alongside the other policies for which we have argued in this chapter.

SUMMARY AND CONCLUSIONS

In the context of endogenous money, the key decision to be made by the Central Bank relates to the discount rate, with the general structure of interest rates resting on the discount rate and the stock of money endogenously determined outside the control of the Central Bank. The use of interest rates as the key element of monetary policy raises the issue of the effectiveness of monetary policy. It has to be recognized that there are clear limits on interest rates, notably that nominal interest rates cannot become negative, and the level of international interest rates constrains domestic interest rates. Another line along which we think monetary policy should be judged concerns the question of the ability of monetary policy to counter a major shock to the autonomous components of aggregate demand. We have suggested that interest rate changes necessary to combat a major shift in aggregate demand are so large as to be infeasible in practice.

We may, therefore, conclude by suggesting that fiscal policy to regulate aggregate demand is paramount, along with monetary policy to control the exchange rate. In addition, credit controls may be used in a supportive manner as necessary, but we are not convinced by their effectiveness. Clearly, the monetary policy implications of this school of thought are rather different from those of the 'new consensus'.

NOTES

1. We use the expression 'Feasible "equilibrium rate" of interest' in the sense of involving a positive nominal rate of interest that is also compatible with the prevailing level of the exchange rate.
2. This discussion is in terms of the Central Bank rate. It is assumed that the rate of interest on loans is above the Central Bank rate, and that it is the rate of interest on loans that is relevant for investment decisions. Given the risks for banks involved in extending loans, it can be assumed that there is a minimum level below which banks would not go in terms of the loan rate.
3. It may well be that those real side effects are (in some relevant size) rather small: but if that is so, then the effects on inflation are also likely to be rather small. If the effects of monetary policy on inflation are indeed rather small (as we would argue), then little regard should be paid to the use of monetary policy.

REFERENCES

Arestis, P. and M. Sawyer (2002) 'Can Monetary Policy Affect the Real Economy?' Levy Economics Institute of Bard College, Working Paper 355.

Arestis, P. and M. Sawyer (2003) 'On the Effectiveness of Monetary Policy and of Fiscal Policy', Levy Economics Institute of Bard College, Working Paper 369.

Barro, R.J. (1986) 'Reputation in a Model of Monetary Policy with Incomplete Information', *Journal of Monetary Economics*, 17(1), 3–20.

Barro, R.J. and R. Gordon (1983a) 'A Positive Theory of Monetary Policy in a Natural Rate Model', *Journal of Political Economy*, 91(4), 589–610.

Barro, R.J. and R. Gordon (1983b) 'Rules, Discretion and Reputation in a Model of Monetary Policy', *Journal of Monetary Economics*, 12(1), 101–21.

Bernanke, B.S. and A.S. Blinder (1988) 'Credit, Money and Aggregate Demand', *American Economic Review*, 78(2), 435–9.

Bernanke, B.S. and M. Gertler (1989) 'Agency Costs, Net Worth, and Business Fluctuations', *American Economic Review*, 79(1), 14–31.

Bernanke, B.S. and M. Gertler (1999) 'Monetary Policy and Asset Price Volatility', in *New Challenges for Monetary Policy*, proceedings of the Symposium Sponsored by the Federal Reserve Bank of Kansas City, Jackson Hole, Wyoming, 77–128, www.kc.frb.org. PUBLICAT/SYMPOS/1999/sym99prg.htm.

Bernanke, B.S., M. Gertler and S. Gilchrist (1999) 'The Financial Accelerator in a Quantitative Business Cycle Framework', in J. Taylor and M. Woodford (eds), *Handbook of Macroeconomics*, Volume 1, Amsterdam: North-Holland.

Blinder, A.S. (1998) *Central Banking in Theory and Practice*, Cambridge, MA and London, England: The MIT Press.

Campillo, M. and A. Miron (1997) 'Why does Inflation Differ Across Countries?' in C. Romer and D. Romer (eds), *Reducing Inflation: Motivation and Strategy*, Chicago: University of Chicago Press, 335–57.

Clarida, R., J. Galí and M. Gertler (1999) 'The Science of Monetary Policy: A New Keynesian Perspective', *Journal of Economic Literature*, 37(4), 1661–707.

Fuhrer, J.C. (1997) 'Central Bank Independence and Inflation Targeting: Monetary Policy Paradigms for the Next Millennium', *New England Economic Review* (January/February), 19–36.

Hall, S. (2001) 'Credit Channel Effects in the Monetary Transmission Mechanism', *Bank of England Quarterly Bulletin*, Winter, 442–8.

Kydland, F.E. and E.C. Prescott (1977) 'Rules rather than Discretion: The Inconsistency of Optimal Plans', *Journal of Political Economy*, 85(3), 473–92.

McCallum, B.T. (2001) 'Monetary Policy Analysis in Models without Money', *Federal Reserve Bank of St. Louis Review*, 83(4), 145–60.

Meyer, L.H. (2001) 'Does Money Matter?' *Federal Reserve Bank of St. Louis Review*, 83(5), 1–15.

Moore, B.J. (1988) *Horizontalists and Verticalists: The Macroeconomics of Credit Money*, Cambridge: Cambridge University Press.

Moore, B.J. (1989) 'A Model of Bank Intermediation', *Journal of Post Keynesian Economics*, 12(1), 10–29.

Posen, A.S. (1993) 'Why Central Bank Independence does Not Cause Low Inflation: There is No Institutional Fix for Politics', in R. O'Brien (ed.), *Finance and the International Economy*, Oxford: Oxford University Press, 40–65.

Roosa, R.V. (1951) 'Interest Rates and the Central Bank', in *Money, Trade and Economic Growth: Essays in Honour of John Henry Williams*, New York: Macmillan, 270–95.

Shaw, E.S. (1973) *Financial Deepening in Economic Development*, New York: Oxford University Press.

Stiglitz, J. and A. Weiss (1981) 'Credit Rationing in Markets with Imperfect Information', *American Economic Review*, 71(3), 393–410.

13. ICT, financial innovation and monetary policy: some critical considerations

Claudio Sardoni[1]

INTRODUCTION

This chapter is concerned with the effects of technological advances in the fields of communication and information on the monetary and financial sectors of advanced economies, where the impact of the so-called 'ICT revolution' has been stronger and more pervasive. More precisely, the chapter looks at the implications of ICT-related innovations for monetary policy. The discussion of this topic raises some analytical and theoretical issues that are at the core of post Keynesian economics, even though post Keynesian economists have not been particularly active in the debate on ICT innovations in relation to monetary analysis.[2]

The discussion of the policy implications of ICT innovations is carried out on two different levels. The following section focuses on the question of whether the development of new means of payment and new clearing systems, both favored by the 'ICT revolution', will impair the central banks' ability to implement effective monetary policies. The chapter then deals with the more general question of whether ICT innovations, which give rise to an increased availability and improved distribution of information, are leading markets closer to perfect competition, with agents perfectly informed and informational asymmetries eliminated or significantly reduced; that is, a world in which monetary policy – or, for that matter, policy in general – has no relevance for the workings of the economy. The final section contains some concluding remarks.

With respect to the first issue, the chapter argues that, although in principle a large diffusion of ICT-related innovations could lead to the displacement of conventional money and the weakening of the power of central banks, this is a highly unlikely outcome. The displacement of conventional money and the weakening of central banks could occur if the process of financial innovation goes far beyond its current state of advancement and gives rise to a new means of payment that is completely independent of conventional money and is administered by an institution other than the central bank. In particular, the new instrument would have to replace conventional money in its function as the economy's unit of account. Such a process of displacement meets with significant obstacles that ultimately derive from the nature of money itself. Money is a 'social relation' and the switching from one money to another can only take place through a complex economic, social and institutional process rather than through mere technological change.

The idea that an improved diffusion and distribution of information can lead to a perfectly competitive world in which there is no need for monetary policy is criticized in the penultimate section. It is contended that markets in the real world are characterized by the existence of uncertainties that ICT-related innovations cannot eliminate. On the contrary, in an inherently uncertain world with speculative markets, the adoption of technologies that favor a more rapid transmission of information can even imply a higher degree of instability and volatility of markets. It is for these reasons that monetary policy, or policy in general, may well become even more important in the future.

ICT INNOVATIONS, DEMAND FOR CONVENTIONAL MONEY AND THE CENTRAL BANKS' ABILITY TO CONTROL INTEREST RATES

In recent years, monetary economists have begun discussing whether ICT innovations may eventually imply the impossibility of central banks implementing effective monetary policies. Two different positions have emerged. There are those who take an essentially 'optimistic' position: ICT financial innovations may well reduce the demand for conventional money but they do not represent a serious threat to central banks. Others arrive at less optimistic conclusions: ICT innovations could imply a reduction of the central banks' ability to affect the economy through monetary policy.

One of the most evident effects of the ICT revolution is a significant growth in the number and value of electronic transactions in advanced economies. The diffusion of so-called electronic money (e-money) as a new means of payment is often associated with these developments.[3] Moreover, ICT innovations favor the development of new clearing systems that do not imply the holding of commercial banks' reserves at the central bank. More available information transmitted rapidly and at low cost can favor the creation of private clearing systems. Settlement payments could be made by banks by using what Freedman calls 'network money', that is, funds stored in some electronic form that can be transferred over communication networks (Freedman, 2000). If these transformations of the payment system become widely diffused, there would be a significant reduction in the demand for conventional money and, in particular, in the demand for base money in the form of banks' reserves at the central bank.

There is an almost universal consensus that the crucial issue at stake is the possibility of a significant reduction in the demand for banks' reserves at the central bank, that is, in the demand for base money.[4] However, even a large reduction in the banks' demand for reserves at the central bank does not necessarily mean that the central bank's power is consequently diminished. It has been argued, in particular by Woodford (2000, 2001, 2002, 2003), that, no matter how little is the demand for reserves, central banks can always affect the economy by influencing interest rates through monetary policy. Central banks can do so by paying interest on commercial banks' reserves.

Woodford considers an extreme case in which commercial banks do not clear through the central bank's settlement balances but adopt a different system of clearing.[5] In this situation, the banks' demand for balances with the central bank, which they regard as being as useful as any other equally riskless overnight investment, would be nil at any interest rate higher than the settlement cash rate and horizontal at any rate equal to or lower than the settlement cash rate. The central bank is still able to control interest rates by varying the rate it pays on its deposits. If the central bank changes its rate, the market rate has to change as well, because otherwise there would be an excess demand for (supply of) liquid assets, eliminated by arbitrage.

The central bank can always fix the interest rate on its liabilities because there is no inherent equilibrium value for a fiat unit of account like the 'dollar' (the central bank's liability), unless a particular value is determined through the monetary policy commitments of the central bank itself. The unit of account in a purely fiat system is defined in terms of the central bank's liabilities. A contract promising to deliver a certain amount of dollars at a certain date implies a payment in terms of settlement balances at the central bank, or in terms of some kind of payment that the payee is willing to accept as a suitable equivalent. In any case, settlement balances at the central bank define the value of whatever is contractually accepted as payment. Woodford (2001, p. 346) points out: 'Even in the technological utopia imagined by the enthusiasts of "electronic money" – where financial market participants are willing to accept as final settlement transfers made over electronic networks in which the central bank is not involved – if debts are contracted in units of a national currency, then clearing balances at the central bank will still define the thing to which these other claims are accepted as equivalent'. The value of a dollar deposit with the central bank cannot be anything other than a dollar. This is not true of the instruments of private financial institutions.[6]

Benjamin Friedman (1999, 2000) has a different opinion from Woodford. For Friedman, central banks, in the future, can lose their ability to implement monetary policy because ICT innovations produce what he calls 'decoupling at the margin', that is, changes in the variables controlled by central banks do not give rise to corresponding changes in the relevant variables for the economy as a whole. Although, even now, their open market operations are a very small proportion of total financial transactions, central banks can still affect interest rates because their transactions are fundamentally different from all the others: their purchases (sales) of securities always imply an increase (decrease) in the reserve account of the seller's (buyer's) bank. No other participant in the market has such power. The central bank is 'a monopoly supplier (and withdrawer) of reserves'. The central bank can affect interest rates without engaging in large transactions because market participants know that the central bank, if it wishes to do so, can engage in large transactions and, hence, bring interest rates to the level that it wants.

The present situation, however, could drastically change. Banks hold reserves at the central bank, but it does not have to be so for ever; competition can threaten this aspect of the central bank monopoly power. Competition can come from the creation and development of private clearing mechanisms favored by the ICT revolution. In such a new framework, the central bank would see its power wane: 'being a monopolist is of little value if no one needs, or even wants, to have whatever the monopoly is of' (Friedman, 1999, p. 327). The central bank could still fix the yield of its own liabilities, but this variable would no longer be connected to the interest rates and asset prices that are relevant for the economy. In particular, the central bank would not be able to exert its influence through 'moral suasion': 'with nothing to back up the central bank's expressions of intent . . ., in time, the market would cease to do the central bank's work for it. This prospect is ultimately what the threat posed to monetary policy by the electronic revolution is all about' (Friedman, 2000, p. 271).

Decoupling at the margin can be regarded as a possible outcome, but it requires more solid and thorough argumentation than that offered by Friedman. Decoupling can take place only if conventional money is displaced as the economy's unit of account and not only as a medium of exchange. In fact, it is possible to contemplate situations in which conventional money remains crucial even though alternative payment systems have developed far beyond what actual economies currently experience. Let us consider, for example, a world in which factors of production are directly remunerated in e-money issued by firms that do not belong to the banking system and that third parties are willing to accept balances on the non-bank firm's books in payment for the firm that issues e-money. In this situation, there is no need for the issuing firm(s) to have bank balances to back up in full its (their) corresponding liability. E-money has developed to the point where it is not merely a medium of exchange but also a means of settlement.[7] However, in such a world the crucial role of conventional money would not disappear. If the central bank's liability remains the economy's unit of account, it necessarily maintains a fundamental role in the working of the economy as a whole. Contracts are expressed and enforced by law in the unit of account and this fundamentally explains the crucial role of conventional money.

That the central bank's liability remains crucial can be expressed by saying that it is *fully money* whereas any other means of payment is *quasi-money* (Hicks, 1989). In other words, the instrument that is the economy's unit of account is also its ultimate means of payment. The economy's unit of account is not merely a *numeraire*, but there is a positive demand for it that, in some situations, can rise to significant levels. In the real world, there arise situations in which agents demand fully money rather than quasi-money. This happens, for example, when the degree of confidence and trust among agents declines drastically because of severe economic shocks. In such situations, agents regard the central bank's liability as the instrument that can be most trusted.[8]

In principle, however, the ICT revolution could push advanced economies toward the adoption of a new money, which functions both as medium of exchange and as unit of account. Once the new monetary instrument has reached a 'critical' level of diffusion, positive network effects can induce the whole economy to adopt it.[9] But there are several obstacles to this process of displacement. There may, for example, be 'inertia' that prevents the displacement of the 'old' money, even though it is less efficient than the new instrument. Such inertia can be due to a high 'switching cost' (the cost implied by moving from one money to another) or to problems of coordination: the new instrument is actually more efficient than the old only if it is adopted by a large number of agents in the economy, but no single agent knows when and if the others are going to switch to the new means, so that almost nobody adopts the new instrument. As a consequence, the degree of competition among different monetary instruments is not very strong. The introduction of potentially more efficient means is not necessarily conducive to the displacement (or 'quasi-displacement') of 'inferior' instruments.[10]

It is also likely that the displacement of central banks as the privileged locus of settlements for commercial banks' payment imbalances would meet with significant obstacles. Central banks are risk-free and can be lenders of last resort.[11] A private bank could act as settlement agent for all the others, but a private bank is not risk-free and, moreover, the other banks would be uncomfortable about its competitive advantages.[12] Finally, central banks do not 'sit back' and watch passively the spontaneous evolution of markets. On the contrary, in order to reduce the risk that innovations will give rise to a system in which their power is reduced, central banks have been keeping financial markets under close scrutiny and have taken several measures to control their evolution. Central banks, with the help of governments, can introduce new regulations, or adjust those already existing, to face the new situation.[13] Thus, the displacement of conventional money and the waning of central banking, though possible in principle, seem to represent remote possibilities.

The considerations above can be expressed in more general terms. Money essentially is a 'social relation' rather than a mere technical device to effect payments.[14] The emergence of money, as both unit of account and medium of exchange, is the result of complex social and economic processes and not of mere technological changes or of individuals' optimizing behavior, as in the Mengerian tradition. The existence and the functions of central banks can be explained along similar lines. Trust is a fundamental factor in the explanation of money and its origins. An instrument is accepted as money in so far as agents in the economy believe that this instrument will be accepted by everyone. Historically, the instrument universally accepted and used as the ultimate means of payment has become the central banks' liability. In fact, central banks can offer guarantees of universal acceptability that no other agent can.[15]

If the problem of the possible displacement of conventional money and central banks is considered from this theoretical perspective, the passage from what currently constitutes money to a new instrument cannot be simply seen as the outcome of technological advances or of individual agents' optimizing decisions. The adoption of a new money and the creation of new institutions for its administration are economic, social and institutional processes. A historical analysis of money and central banks shows the complex and multifaceted nature of the processes that led to the monetary systems of today's advanced economies.

THE ICT REVOLUTION: INFORMATION, UNCERTAINTY AND MONETARY POLICY

The growth of electronic transactions and the means of payment associated with them may be the most visible effect of the ICT revolution, but its impact on markets is broader and more general. The new technologies favor the growth of the volume of information available to economic agents, which is an important factor in the working of markets. This section looks at this aspect of the ICT revolution and its implications for monetary policy.

The neoclassical paradigm of perfect competition is contingent on the assumption of perfect information. Knight (1921) stressed this aspect very clearly. The Arrow–Debreu model of general equilibrium depicts a world in which agents are perfectly informed.[16] In the Arrow–Debreu world of perfect information and no uncertainty, there is no significant role for money and monetary policy would have no real effect.[17] Only when the hypotheses of perfect information and certainty are abandoned can money play a significant role. In particular, the impossibility of all agents knowing which state of the world will occur can justify a positive demand for money (Arrow and Hahn, 1971). Monetary policy can be effective, that is, produce real effects, only if information is imperfect. In the real world, even 'small' imperfections can have large effects and implications for the working of the economic system. A fundamental implication of imperfect information is that money and monetary policy matter (Stiglitz and Greenwald, 2003). Also for the New Classical Macroeconomics of the 1970s and 1980s, monetary policy can have real, though temporary, effects only to the extent that central banks take agents by surprise. In other words, monetary policy can be effective only if agents are not perfectly informed.

If the basic obstacle to the realization of the neoclassical paradigm is that the real world is characterized by imperfect information, can the ICT revolution be regarded as the solution to this problem? Technological advances, by favoring the production and availability of information about goods and reducing transaction costs, could be bringing markets closer to the 'textbook model' of perfect competition and information. Information about goods and assets can be exchanged more cheaply and more comprehensively so that all the information is embodied in prices. In this world, monetary policy would determine only the general price level (Berk, 2002), as it becomes more difficult for central banks to 'surprise' better informed agents. The ICT revolution might be interpreted as a sort of vindication of the neoclassical paradigm.[18]

That the new technologies imply a significant reduction in many transaction costs and a more rapid diffusion of information can be accepted without question, but the idea that this, *per se*, is leading advanced economies toward the realization of the neoclassical model is highly questionable. First of all, it is important to consider what information is about and about which events it is possible to produce information. Information is about present and past events; it cannot be about the future. This obvious fact should have an immediate implication. The increase in the available information and its better distribution among agents *cannot* imply that agents are able to know the economy's so-called 'fundamentals'. The possibility for agents to determine the fundamental values of assets is contingent on their ability to know *future* streams of value, which cannot be inferred with certainty from knowing the present or the past. Information about the current and past states of the world is used to form expectations about such future streams, but there is no way that such information can produce perfect information about them. Even if all agents had perfect access to all available information, they would not know the future. The real world is characterized by a sort of 'imperfect' knowledge that cannot be eliminated.

Several strands of economics try to cope with this difficulty by considering economic variables as random variables with their own probability distributions. Agents attach subjective probabilities to events and, through learning, such probabilities gradually adjust to conform to facts. This solution, however, can be regarded as satisfactory only under precise and very restrictive assumptions about the nature of the economy: a hypothesis of ergodicity must be made.[19] Under such a hypothesis the future can be considered as a random draw from the past and uncertainty is only about the variability of phenomena due to random errors.[20] In an ergodic world, an increased availability and improved distribution of information are necessarily associated with a better working of markets, in which prices embody all available information and are perfectly efficient allocators. Thus, any claim that ICT pushes actual markets toward the realization of the paradigm of perfect competition must be based on the hypothesis of an ergodic world.

The 'ergodic way of escape' has been criticized by Arrow himself. The Arrow–Debreu model copes with the fact that all decisions must be made with reference to the present and the future by dating commodities and considering the same commodity at two different dates as two different commodities. But this approach encounters a difficulty: 'The information about future commodities needed includes their prices. These prices must be those found on a suitable market, one in which future supply and future demand are equated. Unfortunately, no such markets exist' (Arrow, 1974, p. 5). The implication of the incompleteness of markets is that agents must rely on expectations, which may be wrong. Optimizing agents live in a 'world of uncertainty'.

Introducing expectations does not imply insuperable difficulties with a hypothesis of ergodicity, but such a hypothesis has no foundation in the real world.

> If indeed the economic world exhibited the same structure in some sense from period to period, and if everybody observed everything relevant, then the

> probabilities ascribed by different individuals to the same events might be expected gradually to converge to the correct values and therefore be the same for all. In fact, of course, the basic economic facts are changing, partly endogenously because of capital accumulation in its most general sense, partly exogenously with predictable and unpredictable changes in technology and tastes; equally if not more important, though, is the fact that the dispersion of information which is so economical implies that different economic agents do not have access to the same observations. Hence, it is reasonable to infer that they will never come into agreement as to probabilities of future prices. (Arrow, 1974, p. 6)[21]

Arrow's criticism of the hypothesis of structural invariance of the economy can be regarded as essentially similar to the criticism of ergodicity by economists who draw their inspiration from Keynes's approach to uncertainty and expectations, in particular Paul Davidson (1996).

The post Keynesian critique rests on Keynes's notion of 'intractable', or 'fundamental', uncertainty (Keynes, 1937). In Keynes's analysis, long-term expectations, which are about the prospective yields of assets, partly depend on the knowledge of the present and past situations (which may be more or less certain and distributed in a more or less symmetric way) and partly depend on future events that are very uncertain. Expectations, therefore, are formed on very precarious bases. It is this precariousness that leads to the formation of expectations that rely disproportionately on information about the present situation. It is 'foolish' to rely significantly on very uncertain factors, so that agents tend to be guided by facts about which they feel confident, even though these facts may be much less relevant than those that are very uncertain.

In financial markets, the disproportionate weight of the current situation means that investment decisions are determined by the average expectation of those who operate in the markets, which is revealed by the price of assets. This characterization of financial markets implies that decisions about the future are based on a convention, that is to say on the assumption that the 'existing market valuation, however arrived at, is uniquely *correct* in relation to our existing knowledge of the facts which will influence the yield of the investment, and that it will only change in proportion to changes in this knowledge' (Keynes, 1936, p. 152).

In so far as this convention is maintained, the system can experience a high degree of stability,[22] but this convention is characterized by a high degree of precariousness. Keynes singled out some of the factors responsible for the convention's precariousness: (i) the growing presence in the market of people who do not have any real informed knowledge of investments; (ii) daily fluctuations in the profits of existing investments tend to have an excessive influence on the market; (iii) conventional valuations, established as the outcome of the mass psychology of a large number of 'ignorant' people, can change dramatically, because of changes in factors that, in reality, are of little importance for the future yields of assets.

In Keynes's analysis, another factor plays a crucial role: speculation, which is 'largely concerned, not with making superior long-term forecasts of the probable yield of an investment over its whole life, but with foreseeing changes in the conventional basis of valuation a short time ahead of the general public' (Keynes, 1936, p. 154). Speculation does not necessarily dominate markets all the time, but as financial markets become more organized and sophisticated, the predominance of speculative behavior increases.[23] In a world in which speculation plays a crucial role, information is not simply about the so-called 'fundamentals'; it is also about factors that derive their importance from the fact that they are suggestive of possible changes in the behavior of other market participants. Information about financial phenomena has a dual nature: it is also used for speculative decisions (Glickman, 1994).

From this perspective, a faster and wider diffusion of information can accentuate the effects of speculative behavior as well as enhance the impact of behavior based on mass psychology. In a situation in which all information is rapidly transmitted through markets and access to it is easier and less costly, it is difficult to isolate single markets from events taking place somewhere else and it is increasingly difficult to limit the effects of speculative behavior. It is from this perspective that Keynes argued that a partial solution to the problems created by speculation could be to make financial markets less liquid and less perfect.[24]

Keynes's analysis does not provide support for the idea that advances in information technologies can guarantee that markets approach the neoclassical paradigm. ICT-related innovations cannot be regarded as implying a radical change in the functioning of markets. These innovations can eliminate or, at least, reduce a number of informational asymmetries and contribute to the faster diffusion of information through the market; but this does not mean that the future can be better inferred from knowledge of the present. Moreover, Keynes's analysis suggests that more and less costly available information can even accentuate speculative behavior and its effects.

If financial markets function in the way Keynes thought, monetary policy is far from being relevant only for the determination of the general price level. In a world in which conventions and speculation are key features, policy in general, and monetary policy in particular, can play a decisive role in making markets more stable by providing a sort of 'anchor' for conventions, which in turn contributes to reducing the impact of speculative behavior. In this sense, the ability of monetary authorities to influence directly the interest rate is less relevant than their ability to provide markets with credible information and indications concerning their targets and objectives as well as the state of the economy. In a world in which information is transmitted more broadly and rapidly, central banks can play a more crucial role than in the past by providing markets with detailed information on key determinants of the behavior of the economy, which agents can exploit. The existence of better informed agents does not imply less effective monetary policies (as New Classical Macroeconomists believe) but *greater* policy efficacy.[25]

CONCLUDING REMARKS

In the 1990s, when some believed that a 'new economy', free of most of the old economy's flaws, had arrived, the debate on the economic impact of the ICT revolution flourished. At present, many of the delusions about the new economy having disappeared, caution seems to prevail in the profession. None the less, the discussions on the effects of ICT have raised some general theoretical issues that remain relevant regardless of the actual current impact of ICT innovations on the economy.

With respect to the problem of the creation of new monetary instruments and their effect on the working of the economy, this chapter argues that, although in principle it is possible to switch from one means of payment to another and, more importantly, from one unit of account to another, there exist major obstacles to such transformation. These obstacles fundamentally derive from the complex nature of money itself. Money essentially is a social construction rather than the spontaneous outcome of the working of markets. What an economic and social system regards as money can change as the system itself changes over time; however, the passage from one money to another cannot take place simply because of technological change or because agents regard the new money as a more efficient instrument. Social and economic institutions as well as complex market relations stand in the way of the adoption of a new money.

As to the effects of more available information on the working of the economy, the chapter argues that a larger availability of information and its perhaps better distribution among agents cannot represent a solution to the inherent problems arising from the existence of uncertainty about the future. More information, more rapidly and cheaply distributed, may even exacerbate speculative phenomena and instability, rather than being conducive to the realization of a world in which there is no role for monetary policy (or for any other type of policy). At the same time, however, the existence of better informed economic agents can help to make policies more effective.

This chapter is an attempt to contribute to the debate on these topics from a perspective inspired by the Keynesian and post Keynesian traditions in monetary macroeconomics, to which Basil Moore has made such important contributions. Thanks to its deeper comprehension of money and its role in market economies, Keynesian economics can offer important contributions to the debate on central banking, especially when an increasing number of participants in the debate seem to become more aware of theoretical aspects that have always been at the core of the post Keynesian concerns. If the problem of information is considered more generally, the role that post Keynesian economics can play will likely be enhanced. When confronted with the conviction that a wider and faster diffusion of information is leading market economies toward a utopian neoclassical world in which there is no need for policy, the post Keynesian approach can represent a powerful critical response. It is the nature of uncertainty about the future in the real world that makes the diffusion of information a blunt weapon with which to solve the inherent difficulties of market economies. Policy remains of fundamental importance to make the economy work better.

NOTES

1. I would like to thank Andrea Attar, Jean Cartelier and Geoff Harcourt for their helpful comments and suggestions. The responsibility for any remaining mistakes is, of course, mine. Funding from Ministero dell' Istruzione dell' Università della Ricerca (MIUR) is gratefully acknowledged.
2. Exceptions are Palley (2001–2) and Baddeley and Fontana (2005).
3. The term e-money is often used in a loose sense as it encompasses both new electronic means of payment and the fact that traditional systems of payment increasingly resort to electronics. Solomon (1997, p. 64) points out that 'much of what is called e money really ought to bear another name. A number of e-innovations create ingenious new ways to move around the money we already keep in banks, but those ways don't create a new value form'. On this confusion, see also Weiner (1999). In this chapter, I adopt the definition of e-money given by the European Central Bank, which emphasizes the distinctive features of e-money with respect to other means of payment: it is a store of monetary value used to make payments to economic agents other than its issuer, without necessarily involving the banking system. E-money functions as a pre-paid bearer instrument (ECB, 1998, p. 7). This definition includes the notion of 'network money' as defined below.
4. As to the other component of the demand for base money, most agree that even a large reduction in the public's demand for currency would not produce relevant effects on central banking. Woodford (2000) argues that a significant reduction in, or the elimination of, the public's demand for currency would make the implementation of monetary policy even easier.
5. He also analyzes cases that are closer to the actual current situation in most advanced economies.
6. They can offer liabilities that promise to pay a certain amount of dollars in the future, but they also must accept the market's present evaluation of such liabilities. Even if these liabilities were not perfect substitutes for other financial instruments, private financial institutions could not determine both the value of the liabilities issued and their nominal yield, whereas the central bank can determine both the quantity of settlement balances in existence and the nominal yield on those balances.

7. In 1970, Kaldor contemplated the possibility of a world where a number of large firms issue 'chits', in which employees are remunerated, and set up their own clearing system (Kaldor, 1970).
8. Laidler (2004) points out that 'a panic arising from reasons endogenous to the workings of financial markets' could induce banks to demand a large volume of reserves at the central bank.
9. Money, both as a medium of exchange and as a unit of account, is characterized by the existence of significant externalities and network effects. On this see, for example, Holthausen and Monnet (2003, pp. 9–10).
10. See Dowd and Greenaway (1993). Their analysis is mostly concerned with switching from one currency to another, but it can be easily extended to the choice of competing means of payment. Krueger (1999) has pointed out that this type of obstacle to the displacement of a means of payment becomes significantly stronger in the case of switching from one unit of account to another. In this case, in fact, externalities and network effects are stronger.
11. Moreover, dating from the time when there were reserve requirements in all countries, banks are used to holding reserves with the central bank.
12. Banks could also settle payments by transferring risk-free instruments, but in this case there would be no lender of last resort in case of shortfalls, so that banks would be obliged to hold large amounts of the liquid instruments to guarantee that they could meet their obligations. On these aspects see Freedman (2000).
13. For example, the use of conventional money can be made compulsory for certain classes of transactions like the payment of taxes.
14. See Ingham (1996, 2004) for an approach to money based on its social nature.
15. Hicks (1989) briefly explains why. Giannini (2004) explains the emergence and the existence of central banks as being due to the need to support the economy's trust in the instrument that is adopted and used as money. On the origins and the evolution of central banks as a complex social, institutional and economic process, see also Goodhart (1988).
16. Even though the amount of required information is 'modest': what optimizing agents need to know is their utility functions, the production possibility sets and the prices of goods and services traded (Arrow, 1974).
17. For Hahn, the Arrow–Debreu model, 'the best developed model of the economy', cannot find room for money (Hahn, 1982). See also Arrow (1974) and Hahn (1982, 1984).
18. Shiller, for example, states: 'At the present time, an individual sometimes cannot effectively make a contract to do something in the distant future in exchange for a payment today because no one can ascertain whether the person has made the same contract with someone else. . . . A smart computer network system could keep track, in an intelligent way, of all contracts that individuals make so that the system ensures that the contracts do not conflict with one another' (Shiller, 2003, p. 81). King (1999) thinks that the ICT revolution could bring real economies closer to the Walrasian model in which there is no need for money.
19. In general terms, a process is said to be ergodic if any past state will recur in the future with a certain probability and can never recur with a zero probability.
20. In an ergodic world, events have objective probability distributions, with known moments; information about the past and the present allows agents to determine subjective probability distributions that estimate the objective distribution reliably. In this world, it is possible to insure against any risk inherent in the random variability of phenomena.
21. Arrow's conclusions derive from acknowledging that in the real world markets are incomplete. Stiglitz (2000) argues that the incompleteness of markets derives from the fact that knowledge is imperfect. Stiglitz's observation is correct if 'imperfect knowledge' means that knowledge *cannot* be 'complete' because the future cannot be known and not simply that information about present and past events is imperfect. In order that all contingent markets exist, agents need to know all the possible future states of the world, but this cannot be true for the same reasons why agents cannot form expectations that converge to the variables' 'correct values'.
22. In fact, if the convention holds, 'an investor can legitimately encourage himself with the idea that the only risk he runs is that of a genuine change in the news *over the near future*' (Keynes, 1936, pp. 152–3).

23. Financial markets in general, and stock markets in particular, contribute to making capital assets more liquid for individual investors and, in so doing, facilitate real investment. At the same time, however, the liquidity of financial markets favors speculation.
24. 'It is usually agreed that casinos should, in the public interest, be inaccessible and expensive. And perhaps the same is true of stock exchanges. That the sins of the London Stock Exchange are less than those of Wall Street may be due, not so much to differences in national character, as to the fact that to the average Englishman Throgmorton Street is, compared with Wall Street to the average American, inaccessible and very expensive. The jobber's "turn", the high brokerage charges and the heavy transfer tax payable to the Exchequer, which attend dealings on the London Stock Exchange, sufficiently diminish the liquidity of the market . . . to rule out a large proportion of the transactions characteristic of Wall Street' (Keynes, 1936, pp. 159–60).
25. Woodford criticizes the new classical idea of the ineffectiveness of monetary policy along similar lines. Better informed markets do not make monetary policy ineffective, but the opposite is true: '. . . in the information economy, there should be considerable scope for the effective use of the traditional instruments of monetary policy. . . . The more sophisticated markets become, the more scope there will be for communication about even subtle aspects of the bank's decisions and reasoning, and it will be desirable for central banks to take advantage of this opportunity' (Woodford, 2001, pp. 307 and 312).

REFERENCES

Arrow, K.J. (1974) 'Limited Knowledge and Economic Analysis', *American Economic Review*, 64, 1–10.

Arrow, K.J. and F.H. Hahn (1971) *General Competitive Analysis*, San Francisco: Holden-Day.

Baddeley, M. and G. Fontana (2005) 'Monetary Policy in the Information Economy: Old Problems and New Challenges', in P. Arestis et al. (eds), *The New Monetary Policy: Implications and Relevance*, Cheltenham, UK and Northampton, MA, USA: Edward Elgar.

Berk, J.M. (2002) 'Central Banking and Financial Innovation. A Survey of the Modern Literature', *Banca Nazionale Quarterly Review*, 55, 263–97.

Davidson, P. (1996) 'Reality and Economic Theory', *Journal of Post Keynesian Economics*, 18, 479–508.

Dowd, K. and D. Greenaway (1993) 'Currency Competition, Network Externalities and Switching Costs: Towards an Alternative View of Optimal Currency Areas', *Economic Journal*, 103, 1180–89.

ECB (1998) *Report on Electronic Money*, Frankfurt: European Central Bank.

Freedman, C. (2000) 'Monetary Policy Implementation: Past, Present and Future – Will Electronic Money Lead to the Eventual Demise of Central Banking?' *International Finance*, 3, 211–27.

Friedman, B. (1999) 'The Future of Monetary Policy: The Central Bank as an Army with Only a Signal Corps?' *International Finance*, 2, 321–38.

Friedman, B. (2000) 'Decoupling at the Margin: The Threat to Monetary Policy from the Electronic Revolution in Banking', *International Finance*, 3, 261–72.

Giannini, C. (2004) *L'età delle banche centrali*, Bologna: Il Mulino.

Glickman, M. (1994) 'The Concept of Information, Intractable Uncertainty, and the Current State of the "Efficient Markets" Theory: A Post Keynesian View', *Journal of Post Keynesian Economics*, 16, 325–49.

Goodhart, C.A.E. (1988) *The Evolution of Central Banks*, Cambridge, MA: MIT Press.
Hahn, F.H. (1982) *Money and Inflation*, Oxford: Basil Blackwell.
Hahn, F.H. (1984) *Equilibrium and Macroeconomics*, Oxford: Basil Blackwell.
Hicks, J.R. (1989) *A Market Theory of Money*, Oxford: Clarendon Press.
Holthausen, C. and C. Monnet (2003) 'Money and Payments: A Modern Perspective', Working Paper 245, European Central Bank.
Ingham, G. (1996) 'Money is a Social Relation', *Review of Social Economy*, 54, 507–29.
Ingham, G. (2004) *The Nature of Money*, Cambridge: Polity.
Kaldor, N. (1970) 'The New Monetarism', *Lloyds Bank Review*, 97, 1–18. Reprinted in *Further Essays on Applied Economics. Collected Economic Papers by Nicholas Kaldor*, London: Duckworth, 3–21.
Keynes, J.M. (1936) *The General Theory of Employment Interest and Money*, London: Macmillan.
Keynes, J.M. (1937) 'The General Theory of Employment', *Quarterly Journal of Economics*, 51, 209–23. Reprinted in *The Collected Writings of John Maynard Keynes*, Vol. 14, London: Macmillan, 1973, 109–23.
King, M. (1999) 'Challenges for Monetary Policy: New and Old', *Bank of England Quarterly Bulletin*, 39, 397–415.
Knight, F.H. (1921) *Risk, Uncertainty and Profit*, Chicago: University of Chicago Press.
Krueger, M. (1999) 'Towards a Moneyless World?' Working Papers, 9916, Durham: University of Durham, Department of Economics & Finance.
Laidler, D. (2004) 'Central Bank as the Lender of Last Resort – Trendy or Passé?' *Central Banking and the Financial System*, Vol. 1, Warsaw: National Bank of Poland.
Palley, T.I. (2001–02) 'The E-Money Revolution: Challenges and Implications for Monetary Policy', *Journal of Post Keynesian Economics*, 24, 217–33.
Shiller, R.J. (2003) *The New Financial Order*, Princeton and Oxford: Princeton University Press.
Solomon, E.H. (1997) *Virtual Money*, New York: Oxford University Press.
Stiglitz, J.E. (2000) 'The Contributions of the Economics of Information to Twentieth Century Economics', *Quarterly Journal of Economics*, 115, 1441–78.
Stiglitz, J.E. and B. Greenwald (2003) *Towards a New Paradigm in Monetary Economics*, Raffaele Mattioli Lectures, Cambridge: Cambridge University Press.
Weiner, S.E. (1999) 'Electronic Payments in the U.S. Economy: An Overview', *Economic Review (Federal Reserve Bank of Kansas City)*, 84, 53–64.
Woodford, M. (2000) 'Monetary Policy in a World without Money', *International Finance*, 2, 229–60.
Woodford, M. (2001) 'Monetary Policy in the Information Economy', in *Economic Policy for the Information Economy*, Kansas City: Federal Reserve Bank of Kansas City, 297–370.
Woodford, M. (2002) 'Financial Market Efficiency and the Effectiveness of Monetary Policy', *Economic Policy Review, Federal Reserve Bank of New York*, 8, 85–94.
Woodford, M. (2003) *Interest & Prices*, Princeton and Oxford: Princeton University Press.

14. Features of a realistic banking system within a Post-Keynesian stock-flow consistent model

Marc Lavoie and Wynne Godley[1]

INTRODUCTION

This chapter presents the work in progress which we are carrying out. More specifically, our purpose is to present the banking system block which is to be found in two chapters of the monograph that we are writing. The manuscript is provisionally called *Monetary Economics: An Integrated Approach to Money, Credit, Production, Income and Wealth*. As is clear from the title, the objective of the book is quite ambitious. We wish to integrate production into various aspects of monetary analysis, including income, credit, money and wealth. To do so, we need to link the aggregates with which standard macroeconomic analysis is concerned to the financial aggregates which are usually the purview of flow of funds analysis, including balance sheets.

Our analysis is based on a few principles: (i) All financial stocks held as assets by one sector must have a counterpart liability within some other sector; (ii) Transaction flows must take into account revenues, expenditures, as well as changes in financial stocks; (iii) All inflows and outflows (sources and uses of funds) must be accounted for within a matrix (the transactions flow matrix), and there cannot be any black holes; (iv) Changes in balance sheets (changes in the value of stocks) must be accounted for either by flows (from the transactions flow matrix), or by appreciation; (v) All sectors must fulfill their balance sheet constraint, in expected and in realized form; (vi) Inflation accounting must be right; (vii) Inventories accounting, if it exists, must be right; (viii) The quadruple entry principle must hold: any change generates a change in at least four cells of the transactions matrix. This gives rise to stock-flow consistent macroeconomics, with several sectors. This was also the goal of Tobin (1982a), as he presented it in his Nobel Prize lecture, but we believe that we go at least one step beyond him.

The two closed-economy models that constitute the most realistic part of our manuscript contain several blocks: there is a production block, tied to the behavior of firms; a consumer block, tied to the behavior of households; a government block, tied to the behavior of the government per se; there is also a central bank block, and finally a block that deals with private banks. For simplicity, other financial institutions are omitted. This is understandable. The first main model by itself contains 75 equations, while the second model is approximately twice as big.

In the first of the two main models, the private bank block is based on the approach which is to be found in the *Cambridge Journal of Economics* article of Godley (1999) and in Godley (1997). This block is very much under control, and its behavior is well understood. In the second of the main chapters, more realistic features are introduced, and this is the work which is still in progress.

The outline of the chapter is as follows. In the first section, we present what we believe to be the essential differences between the neoclassical approach to banking, as can be found in the work of Tobin, and what we consider to be a post-Keynesian approach to banking. This alternative theory of banking, along with the links between the banks and the central bank, is of course how the present chapter relates to the important work of Basil Moore (1988). In the next section, we go over the approach to banking taken in Godley (1999), along with the mechanisms that explain the behavior of the interest rates administered by banks. We then introduce more realistic features, and the difficulties and consequences of these are outlined.

POST-KEYNESIAN VERSUS NEOCLASSICAL VIEWS OF BANKING

At the heart of our model is a principle which is of great importance if any degree of realism is to be introduced. All economic sectors need buffers that provide an adjustment factor. This is because the expectations of agents are usually not being fulfilled, so that agents need to adapt to situations that were not correctly foreseen. In the real world, there needs to be an immediate automatic adjustment that precedes the reaction functions which provide the more gradual adjustment that takes time to fully operate. So all sectors must include some buffers that will provide an automatic and immediate response to disequilibria, when it is too late to do anything about them within the period; in addition, there need to be reaction functions that will provide the disequilibrium dynamics, and which will act from period to period, hopefully providing the dynamics that will get back the sector towards the levels or the rates which are being targeted.

In the case of production firms, inventories are one of these buffers, more specifically the unexpected fluctuations in inventories. In addition to this current account buffer, bank loans also provide a buffer on the capital account of firms. Banks thus play a key role in post-Keynesian stock-flow consistent models.

Households also have buffers. Households have expectations about revenues expenditures and wealth. It is assumed that money deposits act as the buffer whenever expectations are not met. If revenues are lower than expected, for instance, this will show in the banking deposit account of households.

Governments have a buffer as well. Whenever tax revenues are insufficient to cover government expenditures, governments issue securities – bills or bonds. The quantity of securities issued or retired constitutes the government buffer. On the other hand, central banks play the role of a buffer for the entire economy. Central banks are the residual purchasing sector of Treasury bills. They also provide advances to the private banking sector, on demand, when such advances are required, as is usually the case in Continental Europe and in most other economies of the world. At a more refined level, which will not be dealt with here, the central bank also acts as a buffer within the settlement system, by providing day overdrafts when banks complete their inter-bank transactions.

Finally, as can be inferred from the above, private banks also benefit from a buffer. In the anglo financial systems, the so-called asset-based financial systems, the quantity of Treasury bills held by private banks are the main buffer.[2] In Continental Europe, and in other so called overdraft economies, advances obtained from the central bank are still the main buffer.

The presence of buffers is a key feature of monetary production systems. They prevent gridlock. Buffers provide the flexibility which is required by any well-functioning capitalist system. This buffer role also helps to explain the purpose of banks within a post-Keynesian approach. By contrast, one could say that there is neither need nor place for buffers in the neoclassical world; indeed their presence destroys the equilibrium condition on which neoclassical economics critically depends.

Table 14.1 helps to explain the main differences between a post-Keynesian bank and a neoclassical bank. The post-Keynesian features either arise from what has been said above or will be explained in the next section. We leave to the reader to decide whether previous efforts to model post-Keynesian banks fit within the proposed table (Palley, 1987–8; Dymski, 1988; Moore, 1988, ch. 3; Heise, 1992; Wray, 1989, 1992; Screpanti, 1997; Chick and Dow, 2002). We also leave it to the reader to decide whether some eclectic neoclassical writers such as Tobin (1969, 1982b) fit better in one or the other category (depending on the specific paper or even specific paragraph being considered).

Table 14.1 Post-Keynesian versus neoclassical banks

Post-Keynesian banks	Neoclassical banks
The crucial role of the banking system is to provide loans, which are systemically required if production takes time and sales cannot be predicted; its secondary role is to provide a well-functioning payments system	Banks are intermediaries and asset allocators; they make asset and liability choices
Banks accept all deposits	Banks have supply functions of deposits
Banks provide all creditworthy loans	Banks provide loans based on some profit-maximizing function
Banks set deposit rates	Deposit rates clear the deposit market
Loan rates are marked up over deposit rates	Loan rates clear the loan market

A FIRST-STEP BANKING SECTOR

The Balance Sheet Constraints of the Banking Sector

To understand the behavior of post-Keynesian banks, it is best to start from the following balance sheet matrix. All elements with a positive sign are an asset of the sector; all negative signs are a liability of the sector. As in all such stock matrices, there is a residual balance which ensures by definition that the sum of each column is zero. Any financial asset must have a counterpart financial liability, so that all rows, except the one devoted to tangible capital (here *IN* for inventories), must sum to zero as well. In Table 14.2, for simplification, loans to consumers have been omitted, and so have the financial assets of firms. Table 14.2 describes a pure asset-based financial system, akin to the financial systems that can be found in the major anglo countries such as the UK or the US. There is a stock of high-powered money (HPM), divided into cash balances H_h held by households and the reserves H_b held by private banks. There are checking deposits $M1$ and time deposits $M2$ held by households. Treasury bills B are held by households, private banks and the central bank. Long-term securities, bonds BL, are assumed to be held by households only, and their price is p_{bL}. And finally, banks make loans L to firms. Since the profits of firms and private banks are all assumed to be redistributed to households, while the profits of the central bank are given back to the government, these three sectors have zero net wealth. The net wealth of households is V_h, while that of government is $-GD$; in other words, the debt of government is GD. The net wealth of

Table 14.2 The balance sheet of a closed economy with a simple asset-based banking system

	Households	Firms	Govt	Central bank	Banks	Σ
Inventories		$+IN$				$+IN$
HPM	$+H_h$			$-H$	$+H_b$	0
Checking deposits	$+M1_h$				$-M1$	0
Time deposits	$+M2_h$				$-M2$	0
Bills	$+B_h$		$-B$	$+B_{cb}$	$+B_b$	0
Bonds	$+BL_h . p_{bL}$		$-BL . p_{BL}$			0
Loans		$-L$			$+L$	0
Balance	$-V_h$	0	$+GD$	0	0	$-IN$
Σ	0	0	0	0	0	0

the entire economy is equal to the value of inventories IN since fixed capital is assumed away here.

We now focus on the balance sheet constraint of the banking sector. From Table 14.1, it can be written as:

$$B_{bd} = M1_s + M1_s - L_s - H_{bd} \qquad (14.1)$$

Banks are assumed to provide loans L_s and money deposits (current accounts $M1_s$, and time deposits $M2_s$) on demand. Banks also need to acquire reserves H_{bd} from the central bank (in general, *s* subscripts stand for supply and *d* subscripts stand for demand). Since banks have no capital of their own (no net wealth), there is only one free element, the amount of bills held by banks. This is the only element of the banks' balance sheet which is not predetermined. The amount of bills held by banks thus will normally fluctuate, depending on the evolution of the other elements of the balance sheet. These bills constitute what Tobin (1982b, p. 497) called the *defensive position* of banks.

A second possibility is to have an overdraft financial system, as in Continental Europe. In this case, the banks hold no Treasury bills.[3] On the contrary, they get advances A at cost r_a from the central bank, that is, the central bank provides loans to the private banks. This system is illustrated with the balance sheet matrix of Table 14.3. In this pure overdraft system, the balance sheet constraint of the banking sector becomes:

$$A_{bd} = L_s + H_{bd} - M1_s - M2_s \qquad (14.2)$$

In this case, the buffer of the banking system is made up of the advances A_{bd} being demanded by the banking system from the central bank. If the

Table 14.3 The balance sheet of a closed economy with a simple overdraft banking system

	Households	Firms	Govt	Central bank	Banks	Σ
Inventories		$+IN$				IN
HPM	$+H_h$			$-H$	$+H_b$	0
Demand deposits	$+M1_h$				$-M1$	0
Time deposits	$+M2_h$				$-M2$	0
Advances				$+A$	$-A_b$	0
Bills	$+B_h$		$-B$	$+B_{cb}$		0
Bonds	$+BL_h \cdot p_{bL}$		$-BL \cdot p_{BL}$			0
Loans		$-L$			$+L$	0
Balance	$-V_h$	0	$+GD$	0	0	$-IN$
Σ	0	0	0	0	0	0

system is to function well at all, the advances must be provided whenever they are needed. In addition, the banks need to accept going into debt vis-á-vis the central bank. Such a system may arise if households are holding a large proportion of their money holdings in the form of cash, or if reserve ratios on money deposits are high.

Naturally we can have a mix of the two systems, with banks possibly holding bills while simultaneously piling up advances as part of their liabilities. This could be the case if banks face a compulsory secondary reserve ratio, for instance, a required bills to deposits ratio.

Whatever is the case, in fully consistent systems, there is always a hidden equation in the model, an equation which is not to be found explicitly in the model, but which will always turn out to be true. In our model, taking into account all blocks, this hidden equation is:

$$H_{bs} = H_{bd} \tag{14.3}$$

Equation (14.3) simply says that the supply of reserves is equal to the demand for reserves. It implies that reserves are supplied on demand. The central bank is always fully responding to the demand for reserves of the banking system, as was underlined by Moore (1988). This requirement arises out of necessity from the conditions imposed on the rest of the model.

The Banking Liquidity Ratio

A certain number of post-Keynesians have recently emphasized the fact that while banks may provide loans on demand to creditworthy borrowers, or may provide deposits on demand, they may exhibit liquidity preference (for example, Bibow, 2000). What is meant by liquidity preference is not always clear, but here two meanings can be established. First, higher liquidity preference by banks may mean that banks set up tougher standards when granting loans. This, I believe, can best be reflected within the investment function of firms, by modifying the autonomous component or by raising the (absolute) value of the coefficient attached to interest payments or to the leverage ratio of firms. This is congruent with Wolfson's (1996, 2003) interpretation of credit rationing, whereby the creditworthy demand for credit is shifted downwards (also see Lavoie, 1992, p. 178). The second meaning of liquidity implies that banks wish to hold a certain proportion of their assets in the shape of safe Treasury bills. This is the meaning that will be entertained here. When the liquidity preference of banks is on the increase, they wish to hold a higher proportion of safe assets.

Let us assume then that banks target a certain bills to loans ratio ($B_{bd} = \alpha L_s$), or what almost comes to the same thing, a certain bills to money deposits ratio ($B_{bd} = \beta(M1_s + M2_s)$). Let us assume that such a ratio needs to be realized in all periods, with no adjustment lag. Then, clearly, from what has been said about equation (14.1), such a ratio could not be achieved in general. If banks have self-imposed bills to loans ratios that must be achieved instantaneously, there has to be some buffer variable that will absorb shocks. This buffer variable can only be advances from the central bank. Thus, in a world where the demand for bills by banks is predetermined by the other elements of the balance sheet (loans and deposits), advances must be the buffer element, and the balance sheet constraint of banks becomes:

$$A_{bd} = B_{bd} + L_s + H_{bd} - M1_s - M2_s \tag{14.4}$$

This is the mechanism adopted by Zezza and Dos Santos (2004). If banks wish to hold more bills, everything else being equal, they will need to borrow more from the central bank. Godley (1999), however, proposes another mechanism, which is based on a reaction function and takes time to fully operate, based on an endogenous deposit rate. In Godley's view, deposit and loan rates are not market clearing in any way; still they may be endogenous.

Godley considers that banks have a *target banking liquidity ratio* (*BLR* ratio). This ratio is given by the bills/deposits ratio (the β coefficient mentioned above). This is a kind of non-compulsory secondary reserve ratio. It is nearly the converse of Alfred Eichner's (1985) *degree of liquidity pressure*, which is a loans/deposits ratio. Godley's *BLR* ratio must be within a certain range, between *bottom* and *top*, within a medium time frame, but in the short run the actual banking liquidity ratio may turn out to be outside its normal range.

How do banks react when they find out the actual banking liquidity ratio is not on target? Banks can only act upon incentives. When banks have an insufficient amount of bills relative to their liquidity preference, they increase the interest rates on deposits, and so induce households to trade their Treasury bills for bank deposits (mostly time deposits). This allows banks to recover a proper bills to deposits ratio, by increasing both the numerator and the denominator of the banking liquidity ratio by the same amount (by increasing their overall balance sheet, with both bills and deposits rising). Since bills represent only a small percentage of deposits, the ratio will rise. Conversely, when banks consider that they hold excessive amounts of bills, they will reduce deposit rates.

In the simple model, it is assumed that interest rates on bank loans are marked up over deposit rates. This implies that any change in the deposit rate will be reflected in loan rates. Hence an increase in deposit rates, following an insufficient bills to deposits ratio or an insufficient bills to loans ratio, will give rise to an increase in lending rates, which in theory should reduce the demand for inventories and hence the demand for loans arising from the production sector. This should also help the proper banking liquidity ratio to recover.

Deposit rates (and lending rates) will rise as long as the actual banking liquidity ratio stays below the bottom of the target range; similarly, deposit rates (and lending rates) will diminish as long as the actual banking liquidity ratio stays above the top of the target range. These movements will occur under the following additional two conditions. When deposit rates are rising, they face a ceiling: they cannot be any higher than bill rates, otherwise there would not be any point in households to holding Treasury bills since they are less liquid than bank deposits. Also, there is a floor to falling lending rates: they cannot be any lower than the rate on bills, for otherwise there wouldn't be any reason to make loans, since such an asset is always more risky than a Treasury bill. There is thus a hierarchy of interest rates: the lowest is the deposit rate, the highest is the lending rate, while the Treasury bill rate ought to be in between (Godley and Cripps, 1983, p. 160; see also Chick and Dow, 2002, p. 596). As a result, with the central bank setting the Treasury bill rate, we can say that the monetary authorities have a fairly strong influence over the deposit and lending rates that will be charged by the private banking system.

What occurs when the deposit rates rise to the level of the Treasury bill rate, or when the lending rates fall to the level of the bill rate? In these conditions, we may say that the target banking liquidity ratio constitutes a convention that is inadequate system-wide. The convention just cannot be met, and hence will need to be changed. Thus we can say that the model incorporates a necessary evolutionary component. As the spread between the lending rate and the bill rate shrinks, the banks need to increase their target banking liquidity ratio. Similarly, as the spread between the bill rate and the deposit rate gets near zero, the banks need to reduce their target banking liquidity ratio. Indeed, this is what has been observed by Eichner (1985). In his empirical work, Eichner notes that the actual degree of liquidity pressure *relative to trend*, rather than the absolute level of this ratio, explains the evolution of interest rates.

There is another possible escape route from the fact that the target banking liquidity ratio is inadequate system-wide. When deposit and lending rates are rising, the private banks may decide instead to borrow funds from the central bank, if such advances are readily available. The advances will allow the banks to purchase the bills they long for. Indeed the bills will now be provided by the central bank, in what looks like a kind of open-market operation. In a pure asset-based financial system, where central bank advances are not so well tolerated, a market-based escape hatch will be provided by the presence of commercial paper. Whenever lending rates (and deposit rates) rise relative to Treasury bills, firms will start issuing commercial paper, which households will add to their portfolio. Conversely, when lending rates fall to low levels, firms will retire commercial paper. This additional market-based financial asset will add a degree of flexibility to the financial system, and will help the banking system to achieve its target liquidity ratio, generating a more horizontalist system.

An Experiment: The Effects of an Increase in the Compulsory Reserve Ratio

As a way of illustrating the functioning of the mechanisms associated with the target banking liquidity ratio, let us make an experiment with the first main model of the manuscript (other experiments are provided in Godley (1997, 1999) and Lavoie (2001); all simulations were carried out using MODLER software). This will also help us understand how a formal model based on endogenous money is different from the standard verticalist story questioned by Moore (1988). Let us see what happens when the central bank imposes an increase in the compulsory reserve ratio. In the model described in elementary textbooks and even in intermediate macroeconomics or in money and banking courses, such an increase in the compulsory reserve ratio is said to lead to a brisk decrease in the supply of money. This arises from two features of textbook neoclassical analysis: the stock of high-powered money is said to be under the control of the central

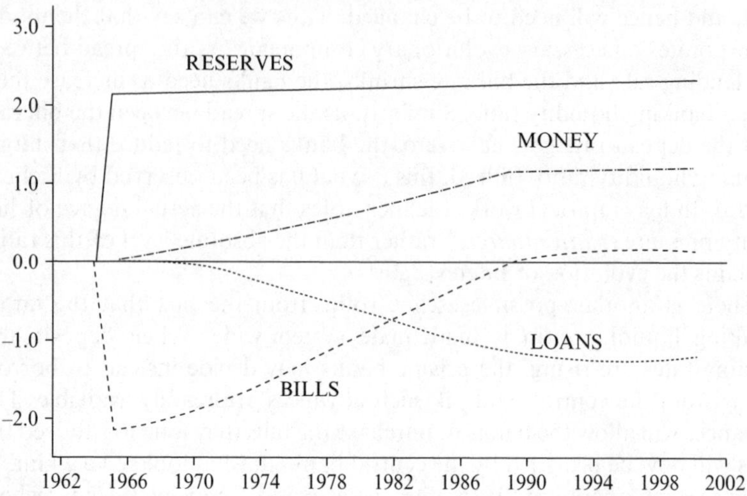

Figure 14.1 *Evolution of the balance sheet of banks, relative to the baseline, following an increase in the compulsory reserve ratio*

bank, and a stable relationship between high-powered money and money is presumed to exist. By contrast, in our model, the supply of high-powered money responds endogenously to demand, and the central bank sets the rate of return on Treasury bills.

In the experiment, the compulsory reserve ratio on all deposits is assumed to rise from 10 to 15 per cent – a 50 per cent change in that statutory ratio. Figure 14.1 shows that the immediate impact of the increase in the reserve ratio is an equivalent increase in the amount of reserves being held by private banks (all lines in Figure 14.1 measure differences compared with the original steady state). As argued in the second section, Treasury bills act as a buffer, and they absorb the shock on required reserves being inflicted by the central bank. Figure 14.1 shows that banks obtain the additional reserves by initially selling their Treasury bills to the central bank (which will then engage in accommodating open-market operations, if it wishes to keep the Treasury bill rate constant). There is no change whatsoever in the stock of money in the first period following the change in the reserve ratio, nor is there any change in the amount of loans.

In the following periods, the liquidity mechanism described above kicks in. Banks wind up with a banking liquidity ratio (called the bills ratio in Figure 14.2) which falls below the floor of the target range, the range being shown by the two fully horizontal lines of Figure 14.2. This mechanism generates rising deposit rates and lending rates. The rising deposit rates induce a portfolio change, with households gradually holding more bank

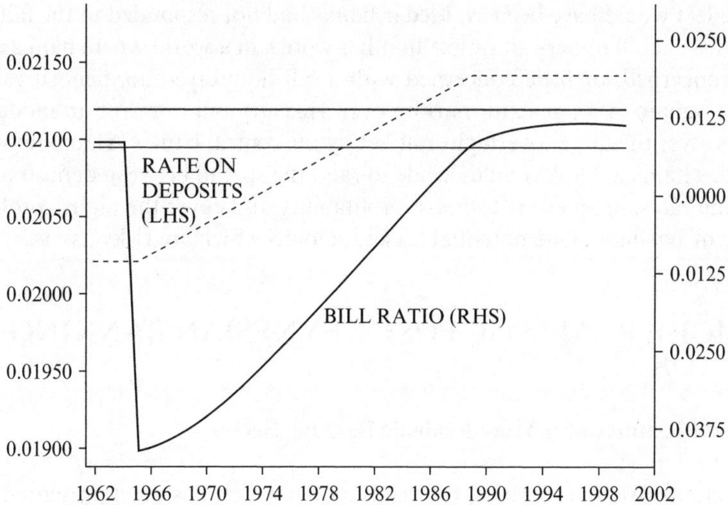

Figure 14.2 *Impact of an increase in the compulsory reserve ratio on the deposit interest rate and on the banking liquidity ratio (the bill ratio)*

deposits (tied to *M*2) and fewer Treasury bills, which are purchased by the banks. This leads to a slow rise in reserves held. On the other hand, the rising lending rates induce firms to reduce their target inventory to sales ratio, and as a result, their need for bank loans diminishes, which is illustrated in Figure 14.1 by a fall in the quantity of outstanding loans. There is thus a gradual change in the balance sheet of the banks. In the present case, there is a relative increase in term deposits and a relative fall in loans to the production sector. The increase in the compulsory reserve ratio has actually led to an *increase* in the (broadly defined) money supply (more precisely the sum of the current and time deposits), and not to a *reduction* of it as mainstream theory would have it!

The balance sheet of the banking sector is modified until finally deposit and lending rates stop rising. This occurs when the actual banking liquidity ratio is back within its target range. As can be seen in Figure 14.2, the actual banking liquidity ratio (the bill ratio) remains constant when it is to be found between the two horizontal lines representing the floor and the ceiling of the target liquidity ratio. At that stage, the deposit rate stops rising and remains constant.

In this model, the increase in the compulsory reserve ratio does not reduce the money supply; it only leads to higher deposit and lending rates, relative to the assumed constant Treasury bill rate. It should be pointed out that even this effect would have been avoided if banks had not responded to the fall in their actual bill to deposit ratio.[4] In other words, in a world where banks are not concerned, or little concerned with a bill liquidity ratio, deposit rates could remain at a constant markup over Treasury bill rates (or, in modern terms, over the target overnight rate set by the central bank). As an alternative mechanism, banks could decide to raise the spread between deposit and lending rates, in an effort to boost profitability and cover the higher probability of having to face potential losses on loans which are risky assets.[5]

A MORE REALISTIC POST-KEYNESIAN BANKING SECTOR

General Features of a More Realistic Banking Sector

Despite its original features, the bank model which has been presented in the previous section is still a long way from depicting the main features of an actual banking system. In the manuscript, we have tried to go beyond the banking sector that was described in the Godley (1999) model. This more realistic banking sector incorporates the following features:

- Banks issue equity
- Banks have retained earnings and net worth
- Banks may take advances from the central bank
- Banks face a BIS-imposed capital adequacy ratio (*CAR*)
- Banks have labor costs
- The markup that defines lending rates over deposit rates is endogenous
- Firms can issue commercial paper

While all these additional features would seem rather obvious, incorporating them into a fully coherent model is sometimes a daunting task, and it can generate instabilities.[6] In what follows, we identify some of the issues that we encountered as we added these realistic features.

The first issue is that of the balance sheet of the banking sector. Compared to Tables 14.2 and 14.3, things are now more complicated as a result of the role of the BIS-imposed capital adequacy ratio – the so-called Cooke ratio (named after Peter Cooke, the long-time Bank of England Chairman of the Basel Committee on Banking Supervision). One needs to keep track of the evolution of the own funds of the banking system. One has to devise two balance sheets for the banking system, rather than a single one. These two balance sheets are shown in Table 14.4. The balance sheet

Table 14.4 The two possible balance sheets of banks

Standard accounting		Macroeconomic accounting	
Assets	Liabilities	Assets	Liabilities
B_b	$M1$	B_b	$M1$
L	$M2$	L	$M2$
H_b	A_b	H_b	A_b
	OF_b		$eb.pe_b$
Total assets = Total liabilities		Assets – Liabilities = V_b	

on the right is in line with the overall macroeconomic balance sheet matrix, and ensures that all rows of financial assets sum to zero. The balancing item, termed V_b, ensures that the column of the banking sector, like all other columns, sums exactly to zero. This balancing item, which is the net worth of the banking system from a system-wide point of view, may be positive or negative. Indeed, it could be negative when the stock-market value of the shares issued by banks $eb.p_{eb}$ is high (eb is the outstanding number of shares issued by banks while p_{eb} is the price of each share). This balancing item plays no role in the behavioral equations.

Hence, we now need a second balance sheet, to be found on the left-hand side of Table 14.3, which corresponds to private accounting and which helps to keep track of the own funds of the private banks, termed OF_b. This other balance sheet provides the accounting constraint of the banks, a constraint which is similar in purpose to those described by equations (14.1), (14.2) and (14.4). With standard accounting, the value of the shares owned by households appears nowhere. Or rather, it is assumed that somehow the financial value of shares issued by banks is worth the residual item of the balance sheet, what accountants would call the net worth of banks, or what the BIS would call the capital of banks, and what we have called here the own funds of banks, OF_b. The own funds are the amount which, when added to liabilities, ensures that the asset total and the liability total are equalized.

To be viable, a firm or a bank must have assets that are larger than liabilities, and as a result, own funds are a positive number that is entered on the liability side. In the view of the accountant, if the firm or the bank were to be dissolved, this is the amount that would be left to shareholders. If own funds were to become negative, owners would get nothing back, but despite this the firm or the bank would be unable to pay back all of its liabilities. The business is thus not solvent anymore. In the case of banks, as already pointed out, such a situation could arise if borrowers were to default on their loans. If 100 million of these were to default, 100 million would need to be subtracted on both sides of the balance sheet, away from L and from OF_b. The bank would then need to act to achieve an adequate capital ratio, in other words it would need to find means to increase its own funds back to the required level relative to its loans. The own funds OF_b of banks are not the ultimate residual, since they are determined by the following equation:

$$OF_b = OF_{b-1} + FU_b + \Delta eb_s \cdot p_{eb} - NPL \quad (14.5)$$

This equation says that the change in the own funds of the banks is equal to the sum of their retained earnings FU_b and the proceeds of the new issues of shares, minus the amounts of non-performing loans NPL. As long as non-performing loans can be predicted, or if they are non-existent, banks will be able to achieve the level of own funds which is consistent with the capital adequacy ratio. The equation introduces historic time: the amount of own funds OF_b is historically dependent.

The logic of the banking sector is still essentially the same as it was in the simpler model. The amount of bills held by banks is still a residual (unless, as in Zezza and Dos Santos (2004), banks want to achieve a minimal bill to deposits ratio, in which case, bank advances become the residual item when the minimal ratio is under threat). In the asset-based case, the balance-sheet contraint of the private banks, equation (14.1), is only modified by the addition of own funds, and now becomes:

$$B_{bd} = M1_s + M2_s + OF_b - L_s - H_{bd} \quad (14.6)$$

An Endogenous Lending Rate Markup

In a world with explicit bank owners and compulsory capital adequacy ratios, banks need to make a definite amount of profits. They first need to cover the dividend payments which their household shareholders view as desirable; secondly they need to augment their own funds in line with the BIS rules on capital adequacy ratios. These two profitability requirements, which determine the required dividends and the required retained earnings, for given bank labor costs and given the interest rates administered by the central bank (the Treasury bill rate and the rate of central bank advances), determine the spread between the rate of interest on loans and the rate of interest on deposits. The deposit rate is determined as in the other main model, on the basis of the target banking liquidity ratio. The values targeted by banks are given by the following equations.

The total profit targeted by banks (F_b^T) is the sum of targeted dividends FD_b^T and retained earnings FU_b^T, the superscript T representing targets:

$$F_b^T = FD_b^T + FU_b^T \tag{14.7}$$

Targeted dividends depend on a conventional rate of return r_{bd}, which is applied either to own funds or more realistically to the stock-market value of bank shares (thus imposing a conventional price/earnings ratio):

$$FD_b^T = r_{bd} \cdot OF_{b-1} \tag{14.8a}$$

or

$$FD_b^T = r_{bd} \cdot eb_{s-1} \cdot p_{eb-1} \tag{14.8b}$$

Targeted retained earnings depend on whether capital adequacy requirements are being met. Banks need the following amount of own funds:

$$OF_b^T = CAR^T \,.\, L_{s-1} \tag{14.9}$$

where CAR^T is the targeted capital adequacy ratio, whereas the realized Cooke ratio is:

$$CAR = OF_b / L_s \tag{14.10}$$

To achieve the target amount of own funds OF_b^T, setting aside non-performing loans for now, firms need to achieve the following amount of retained earnings:

$$FU_b^T = \mu\{OF_b^T - (OF_{b-1} + \Delta eb_s \,.\, p_{eb-1})\} \tag{14.11}$$

We may assume that banks give themselves a certain flexibility in achieving the capital adequacy ratio. Thus in general the reaction coefficient μ will not be equal to unity. It also seems fair to assume that when actual own funds (OF_{b-1}) exceed the needed amount (OF_b^T), firms set μ to zero, thus avoiding the need to target negative retained earnings.

Equations (14.7) to (14.11) thus yield the amount of targeted bank profits. This can be compared with the actual amount of profits that banks make at given lending and deposit rates. Writing the lending rate r_l as a marked-up deposit rate r_m:

$$r_l = r_m + \xi \tag{14.12}$$

we thus obtain the value that the markup spread ξ must take for realized profits to equate targeted bank profits. That spread will depend on the targeted bank profit, the bank wage bill WB_b, on relative amounts of the various assets and liabilities and their rates of return (including the rate of interest on central bank advances, r_a), and on the absolute amount of loans.

$$\xi = (1/L_{-1})(F_b^T + WB_b + r_{a-1} \cdot A_{bd-1} - r_{b-1} \cdot B_{bd-1} + r_m \cdot (M2_{s-1} - L_{s-1})) \quad (14.13)$$

Preliminary work on this model shows that it is much more difficult to find a reference steady state and to conduct meaningful experiments. Falling loans may actually lead to rising spreads between lending and deposit rates, because the higher average fixed costs will tend to shrink the profit base, creating some cyclical behavior. For some parameter values, however, the more realistic model behaves in a way which is similar to that of the first model. For instance, shocked again with a drastic increase in the ratio of compulsory reserves, the deposit rate needs to be increase for a few periods, and the endogenously determined loan rate follows this upward trend, but in a more chaotic way, restoring profitability in the process.

The addition of consumer loans may create instabilities as well, because these loans could only very partially be absorbed by rising household deposits. As a result, the presence of commercial paper becomes essential in stabilizing interest rates. The addition of financial assets held by corporations may also provide a solution to this issue.

CONCLUSION

The main purpose of the present chapter was to show that it is possible to build a realistic and formal behavioral model of the banking system, based on severe accounting constraints, without relying on questionable neoclassical assumptions. This model yields results which are substantially different from those assumed in standard neoclassical textbooks. The purpose of this exercise is not to build a unique, canonical, post-Keynesian model of the bank, but rather to pave the way for further and more extensive research that uses the method advocated here. This hopefully will help heterodox authors to make some headway, and to provide firm answers to some of the controversies that have raged over the last decades.

NOTES

1. We wish to thank Charles Goodhart and Claudio Dos Santos for their useful comments on the first draft of this chapter. Comments by the participants at the conference also helped us to remove ambiguous sentences.

2. Certificates of deposits may be another.
3. Of course, even in an asset-based system, individual banks may need to borrow from other banks, as is the case with large city banks in the American financial system.
4. This is a point that was made to one of us by John Smithin, in a meeting in Berlin in March 2001.
5. This is a point that was made to one of us by email, by Charles Goodhart, in January 2004.
6. Ideally, firms should also hold financial assets, and consumers should be allowed to borrow. We have experimented successfully with the latter feature.

REFERENCES

Bibow, J. (2000) 'On Exogenous Money and Bank Behaviour: The Pandora's Box Kept Shut in Keynes' Theory of Liquidity Preference?' *Journal of History of Economic Thought*, 7(4), 532–68.

Chick, V. and S. Dow (2002) 'Monetary Policy with Endogenous Money and Liquidity Preference: A Nondualistic Treatment', *Journal of Post Keynesian Economics*, 24(4), 587–608.

Dymski, G. (1988) 'A Keynesian Theory of Bank Behavior', *Journal of Post Keynesian Economics*, 10(2), 499–526.

Eichner, A.S. (1985) 'The Demand Curve for Money Further Considered', in A.S. Eichner, *Toward a New Economics: Essays in Post-Keynesian and Institutionalist Theory*, Armonk: M.E. Sharpe, 98–112.

Godley, W. (1997) 'Macroeconomics Without Equilibrium or Disequilibrium', Jerome Levy Economics Institute at Bard College, Working Paper No. 205, August.

Godley, W. (1999) 'Money and Credit in a Keynesian Model of Income Determination', *Cambridge Journal of Economics*, 23(4), 393–411.

Godley, W. and F. Cripps (1983) *Macroeconomics*, London: Fontana.

Heise, A. (1992) 'Commercial Banks in Macroeconomic Theory', *Journal of Post Keynesian Economics*, 14(3), 285–96.

Lavoie, M. (1992) *Foundations of Post-Keynesian Economic Analysis*, Aldershot, UK and Brookfield, USA: Edward Elgar.

Lavoie, M. (2001) 'Endogenous Money in a Coherent Stock-flow Framework', Jerome Levy Economics Institute at Bard College, Working Paper No. 325.

Moore, B.J. (1988) *Horizontalists and Verticalists: The Macroeconomics of Credit Money*, Cambridge: Cambridge University Press.

Palley, T.I. (1987–8) 'Bank Lending, Discount Window Borrowing, and the Endogenous Money Supply: A Theoretical Framework', *Journal of Post Keynesian Economics*, 10(2), 282–303.

Screpanti, E. (1997) 'Banks, Increasing Risk, and the Endogenous Money Supply', *Economic Notes by Banca Monte dei Paschi di Siena*, 26(3), 567–88.

Tobin, J. (1969) 'A General Equilibrium Approach to Monetary Economics', *Journal of Money, Credit and Banking*, 1(1), 15–29.

Tobin, J. (1982a) 'Money and Finance in the Macroeconomic Process', *Journal of Money, Credit and Banking*, 14(2), 171–204.

Tobin, J. (1982b) 'The Commercial Banking Firm: A Simple Model', *Scandinavian Journal of Economics*, 84(4), 495–530.

Wolfson, M. (1996) 'A Post Keynesian Theory of Credit Rationing', *Journal of Post Keynesian Economics*, 18(3), 443–70.

Wolfson, M. (2003) 'Credit Rationing', in J. King (ed.), *The Elgar Companion to Post Keynesian Economics*, Cheltenham, UK and Northampton, MA, USA: Edward Elgar, 77–82.
Wray, L.R. (1989) 'A Keynesian Theory of Banking: A Comment', *Journal of Post Keynesian Economics*, 12(1), 152–6.
Wray, L.R. (1992) 'Commercial Banks, the Central Bank, and Endogenous Money', *Journal of Post Keynesian Economics*, 14(3), 297–310.
Zezza, G. and C. Dos Santos (2004) 'The Role of Monetary Policy in Post-Keynesian Stock-flow Consistent Macroeconomic Growth Models', in M. Lavoie and M. Seccareccia (eds), *Central Banking in the Modern World: Alternative Perspectives*, Cheltenham, UK and Northampton, MA, USA: Edward Elgar, 185–208.

PART IV

The macroeconomics of exogenous interest rates

15. When are interest rates exogenous?

L. Randall Wray

Perhaps the most important of Basil Moore's contributions to economic theory is the recognition that the money supply should be treated as an endogenous variable while the interest rate should be taken to be exogenous. The first proposition seems to have been accepted by virtually all Post Keynesians, while the second was – at least initially – seen as more problematic. Indeed, something of a controversy developed around the proposition that 'the' interest rate is exogenously administered by the central bank, briefly resulting in two 'rival' approaches: the 'horizontalist' approach developed by Moore and the 'structuralist' approach associated with Tom Palley and Bob Pollin (among some others). For the most part, I believe this particular debate was at best a result of misunderstanding, and I wish it had died a more timely death. The reader will be relieved that I am not going to dredge those murky waters – this will not be yet another attempt to explicate and synthesize horizontalism and structuralism.

Still, there are several issues surrounding interest rate exogeneity that are worth exploring. First there is the question of what we mean by the term exogeneity. I will dispense with that rather quickly by adopting the usual definition that identifies exogeneity with the ability of the monetary authorities to 'administer' 'the' interest rate – although I will explain why that is somewhat problematic. Second, and following directly from that question, we need to consider which interest rate(s) is(are) directly administered by policy. Third, we need to determine whether this interest rate exogeneity is in some sense 'natural', or, does it follow from particular institutional arrangements (including, perhaps, policy adopted by the central bank)? Relatedly, does interest rate exogeneity apply over all stages of the business cycle? Finally, we will examine implications arising from adoption of an exogenous interest rate for two theories that have traditionally played an important role in much Post Keynesian research: Keynes's liquidity preference theory, and Minsky's financial instability hypothesis.

EXOGENEITY

The term exogeneity is used in two or three quite different ways (Desai, 1989; Wray, 1992a; Cooley and LeRoy, 1981). The most common use (at least by Post Keynesians) is in the control sense: an exogenous variable is one whose value is set by government policy. Moore prefers to use the term 'administer' to indicate that policy makers change their interest rate target in reaction to economic outcomes and policy goals. The second sense in which the term is used is in the theoretical or causal sense: the exogenous variable in a model is assumed to cause changes in the endogenous variables. A strongly exogenous variable is independent of all endogenous variables in a model (including current and lagged values of these variables); a weakly exogenous variable can be defined as one whose value is independent of the contemporaneous values of the endogenous variables, but may depend on lagged values of these variables. Note that an exogenous variable in the control sense is not necessarily exogenous in the theoretical sense because policy makers may choose the target for that variable based on values of the endogenous variables. Indeed, any plausible theory of interest rate setting by the central bank would include a reaction function to make the interest rate at least weakly endogenous in the theoretical sense. Finally, we could define statistical exogeneity as a case in which the variable is independent of all the unobserved explanatory variables of a tested model – a condition that is required to generate unbiased estimates of coefficients. This is important for empirical tests, but is surely impossible to meet in the case of administration by the central bank of the interest rate(s). In what follows we will generally use the term in the control sense. However, we will note that this becomes problematic, particularly when we discuss exchange rate regimes.

WHICH INTEREST RATES ARE EXOGENOUS?

Moore convincingly argues that the central bank exogenously administers the overnight interbank lending rate (Fed funds rate in the USA). Once it sets a rate target, it has no choice but to accommodate 'horizontally' the demand for reserves. This has raised two objections. First, some have argued that this is no different from the usual orthodox exposition of monetary policy as a choice between targeting reserves or targeting the interest rate: if the central bank chooses an interest rate target, it loses control over reserves. However, it is supposed that the central bank *could* choose a reserve target and hence hit money targets. Moore's response has been that the central bank actually must accommodate the demand for reserves, but can choose a different interest rate target. Hence, *if* the central bank can indeed hit a reserve target, it does so only through its decision to raise or lower the interest rate to lower or raise the demand for reserves. Thus, the supply of reserves is best thought of as wholly accommodating the demand, but at the central bank's interest rate target.

This leads to the second question: why does the central bank accommodate the demand for reserves? We can identify at least four different answers that have been given. One of the earliest was provided by Moore's (1984) masterful analysis of lagged and contemporaneous reserve accounting. As it turns out, both methods result in a backward looking reserve requirement: the reserves that must be held today depend to a greater or lesser degree on deposits held in the fairly distant past. As banks cannot go backward in time, there is nothing they can do about historical deposits. Even if a short settlement period is provided to meet reserve requirements, the required portfolio adjustment could be too great – especially when one considers that many bank assets are not liquid. Hence, in practice, the central bank automatically provides an overdraft – the only question is over the 'price', that is, the discount rate charged on reserves. A second, less satisfying, answer is often given, which is that the central bank must operate as a lender of last resort, meaning that it provides reserves in order to preserve stability of the financial system. The problem with this explanation is that while it is undoubtedly true, it applies to a different time dimension. The central bank accommodates the demand for reserves day-by-day, even hour-by-hour. It would presumably take some time before refusal to accommodate the demand for reserves would be likely to generate the conditions in which bank runs and financial crises begin to occur. Once these occurred, the central bank would surely enter as a lender of last resort, but this is a different matter from the daily 'horizontal' accommodation. The third explanation is that the central bank accommodates reserve demand in order to ensure an orderly payments system. This might be seen as being closely related to the lender of last resort argument, but I think it can be more plausibly applied to the time frame over which accommodation takes place. Par clearing among banks, and more importantly par clearing with the government (see below), requires that banks have access to reserves for clearing. The final argument is that because the demand for reserves is highly inelastic, and because the private sector cannot increase the supply, the overnight interest rate would be highly unstable without central bank accommodation. Hence, relative stability of overnight rates requires 'horizontal' accommodation by the central bank. In practice, empirical evidence of relatively stable overnight interest rates over even very short periods of time supports the belief that the central bank *is* accommodating *horizontally*.

We can conclude decisively that the overnight rate is exogenously administered by the central bank. What about other rates? Short-term sovereign debt is a very good substitute asset for overnight reserve lending, hence, its interest rate will closely track the overnight interbank rate. Longer-term sovereign rates will depend on expectations of future short-term rates, largely determined by expectations of future monetary policy targets. Thus, we can take those as partly or largely exogenous in the control sense because the central bank could announce its intended targets far into the future and thereby affect the spectrum of rates on sovereign debt.

According to Moore (1988), the retail bank lending and deposit rates are determined by mark-ups and mark-downs. Given market power, banks set retail loan rates (as price-setters) as a mark-up over the central bank's interest rate target, and then satisfy all loan demand 'horizontally' at that rate (as quantity-takers). Similarly, they are price-setters and quantity-takers in retail deposit markets as they mark down the targeted overnight interest rate. Wholesale markets (brokered deposits) are competitive and are used by individual banks to compensate for any asymmetry in their ability to make loans or retain retail deposits. Here, banks are quantity-setters and price-takers. Finally, allowance is made for adjusting of interest rates to account for risk differentials. Once a bank has established risk weightings, it supplies loans 'horizontally' at an 'administered' loan rate that is itself a mark-up over the central bank's 'administered' overnight interbank lending rate target.

Whether retail loan rates and deposit rates should be considered 'exogenous' in the policy control sense depends on the behavior of the mark-up. If the mark-up does not vary with central bank policy itself, and is known, then the central bank could, trivially, raise the loan rate to hit any higher rate target (for a risk class) by raising the overnight rate target. If the mark-up varies through time – perhaps due to macro or micro conditions – then exogenous 'administration' of loan rates becomes more problematic, but might be managed with some slips 'twixt lip and cup'. There is also an obvious asymmetry: the central bank can raise loan rates, but its ability to lower them is limited by a zero overnight interbank lending rate (if banks want a mark-up of 400 basis points, the loan rate cannot be pushed below 4 per cent). In this case, the central bank's ability to exogenously 'administer' loan rates is limited because it cannot push them down once a zero overnight rate is reached.

At least some of the criticism of Moore's framework has been based on the argument that the mark-up depends on the state of the macroeconomy (for example, the stage of the business cycle) and also on the balance sheet positions of the lending bank and its borrower (which, again, may vary temporally). It is true that Moore does not deny that the mark-up might be variable – and I am sure he will agree that it can vary over the cycle – rising with pessimism and falling with optimism. This could even be seen as a reclassification of risks – borrowers that used to receive loans on the basis of a 200 basis point (bp) mark-up now are charged 400 bp because risks have risen. If I dared to venture into the horizontalist–structuralist debate, I would note that structuralists (wrongly) sought to refute a horizontal loan supply curve on the argument that over an expansion interest rates tend to rise because mark-ups rise as perceived risks grow. However, Moore's horizontal loan supply curve is at a point in time, while theirs is a plot of interest rates over time. Moore's horizontalism is not inconsistent with a rising mark-up over time as risks in the economy increase, and the structuralist concern with innovation and evolution of practice can be incorporated within Moore's framework. As we will see in the final section, the point that Hyman Minsky (1975) had tried to make is that over an expansion, and under some conditions, the balance sheets of both borrowers and lenders can become 'stretched' in such a way that loan rates tend to rise; this can be construed as either an upward sloping trend (structuralist) or as shifts due to rising risk (horizontalist).

What is somewhat more problematic is the vision of a perfectly elastic supply of credit at the marked-up loan rate. It is true that households hold credit cards with pre-approved lines of credit up to some limit at a fairly constant cost (fees and interest rate); utilization of these lines up to those limits would almost certainly impact rates and fees charged on additional borrowing, but this can be attributed to movement into a higher risk class. Firms also negotiate credit lines that typically trigger higher fees and rates as they are utilized, but this, too, can be seen as transition to riskier classes. Commercial loans (and mortgage loans) require individual negotiation, with loan quantities and uses carefully established at the time interest rates are quoted. The firm must meet very specific performance requirements to continue to draw upon the loan. Further, loan (and mortgage) rates can be partially or even mostly variable rate (depending on institutional arrangements). In these cases, it is difficult to see what it means to say that the supply of loans is 'horizontal', except that the lender will supply credit at the negotiated rate and up to the negotiated limit – with borrowing that might take place later and beyond that limit to be subject to another rate that will be either negotiated at that time, or fixed as some mark-up over a future prevailing rate (that is, LIBOR – London Interbank Overnight Rate) that is currently unknown.

Moore's important contribution was the recognition that loans are not reserve constrained and that they are made at a negotiated, or 'administered', rate. There is thus no *necessary* relation between the quantity of loans made and the interest rate charged. In that sense, the loan rate is 'exogenous', although this is not one of the usual definitions of the term. Further, any impact that the central bank might have on the loan rate comes through its overnight interest rate target and not through manipulation of the quantity of reserves. So, again, the rate is 'exogenous' of quantity, although it is not likely to be exogenous in the theoretical sense.

The claim that reserves are supplied 'horizontally' at the rate set by the central bank is, I think, beyond dispute. Reserves cannot be the 'raw material' from which loans are made, and it is more appropriate to see reserves as the result of loan-making activity. Because bank deposits are created with loans, they cannot be treated as part of the loan-making 'production function' either. Hence, both ISLM and loanable funds approaches to 'endogenous' interest rate determination must be abandoned. These are the critical insights that follow from Moore's work, regardless of how one interprets the exogeneity of interest rates.

WHEN ARE INTEREST RATES EXOGENOUS? IMPORTANCE OF THE EXCHANGE RATE REGIME

It is evident that Moore's exogenous interest rate approach relies on accommodative central bank behavior. From this, we can presume that interest rate exogeneity requires certain institutional arrangements. In this section we will explore the conditions in which (at least some) interest rates are exogenous.

Both Vicky Chick (1986) and Moore (1996) (as well as Chris Niggle, 1990) have advanced an 'evolutionary' or 'stages' approach to endogenous money, according to which money has become endogenous only relatively recently. For Chick, this depends on the level of development of the banking sector; for Moore it depends on the existence of a central bank that accommodates the demand for reserves. This has been called 'institutional endogeneity', contrasted with 'natural endogeneity' adopted by many circuitists (more properly called 'logical endogeneity'). I prefer to locate the origins of endogenous money in the distant past, probably some short time after the origins of 'state money' that Keynes dated to 2000 BC (but more recent historical research would probably push that date back another thousand years or more) (Wray, 1990, 1998, 2004). Similarly, and logically following from his views on the nature of the endogeneity of money, Moore would seem to locate the origins of exogenous interest rates in the rise of accommodative central banks. Again, I would want to push this much farther back: Michael Hudson has demonstrated to my satisfaction that interest rates were exogenously administered in ancient Mesopotamia (and the monumental work by Homer and Sylla (1991) would seem to confirm very long periods of stability of rates at other times and in other places that is consistent with the view that rates have long been exogenously 'administered'). (See Wray, 2004.) Paradoxically, I would not agree with Moore that interest rates have been exogenous in the US since the founding of the Fed in 1913 – rather, I would argue that US interest rates were endogenous from 1913 to the breakdown of Bretton Woods, and that the overnight rate has since been truly exogenous in the control sense. The key institution determining exogeneity that has been important since 1913 is the exchange rate regime.

In modern economies, the banking system operates as an agent of government, as almost all government payments and tax receipts flow through banks. In a floating rate regime, the government that issues the currency spends by crediting bank accounts. Tax payments result in debits to bank accounts. Deficit spending by government takes the form of net credits to bank accounts. Operationally, the entities receiving net payments from government hold banking system liabilities while banks hold reserves in the form of central bank liabilities (we can ignore leakages from deposits – and reserves – into cash held by the non-bank public as a simple complication that changes nothing of substance). While most Post Keynesian explications of horizontalism focus on central bank provision of reserves as part of monetary policy, actually net injections of reserves that accompany fiscal policy easily swamp this (for example, in the USA this year the treasury's operations will result in \$500 billion of net injections to bank deposits and to reserves held at the Fed). It is quite remarkable – at least to me – that \$500 billion of net injections of reserves by the treasury is routinely ignored by Post Keynesian monetary theorists, whose whole attention is absorbed by the relatively miniscule (and purposely temporary) operations of the central bank. Further, many economists (including Post Keynesians) find the coordinating activities between the central bank and the treasury quite confusing (Bell and Wray, 2003). I want to leave those issues mostly to the side and simply proceed from the logical point that deficit spending by the treasury results in net credits to banking system reserves, and that these fiscal operations can be huge.

If these net credits lead to excess reserve positions, overnight interest rates will be bid down by banks offering the excess in the overnight interbank lending market. Unless the central bank is operating with a zero interest rate target, declining overnight rates trigger open market bond sales to drain excess reserves. Hence, on a day-to-day basis, the central bank intervenes to offset undesired impacts of fiscal policy on reserves when they cause the overnight rate to move away from target. The process operates in reverse if the treasury runs a surplus, which results in net debits of reserves from the banking system and puts upward pressure on overnight rates – relieved by central bank open market purchases. If fiscal policy were biased to run deficits (or surpluses) on a sustained basis, the central bank would run out of bonds to sell (or would accumulate too many bonds, offset on its balance sheet by a treasury deposit exceeding operating limits). Hence, policy is coordinated between the central bank and the treasury to ensure that the treasury will begin to issue new securities as it runs deficits (or retire old issues in the case of a budget surplus). Again, these coordinating activities can be varied and complicated, but they are not important to our analysis here. When all is said and done, a budget deficit that creates excess reserves leads to bond sales by the central bank (open market) and the treasury (new issues) to drain all excess reserves; a budget surplus causes the reverse to take place when the banking system is short of reserves.

Bond sales (or purchases) by the treasury and central bank are, then, ultimately triggered by deviation of reserves from the position desired (or required) by the banking system, which causes the overnight rate to move away from target (if it is above zero). Bond sales by either the central bank or the treasury are properly seen as part of monetary policy designed to allow the central bank to hit its target. This target is exogenously 'administered' by the central bank. Obviously, the central bank sets its target as a result of its belief about the impact of this rate on a range of economic variables that are included in its policy objectives. In other words, setting of this rate 'exogenously' does not imply that the central bank is oblivious to the economic and political constraints it believes to reign (whether these constraints and relationships actually exist is a different matter). But, as Moore insists, the overnight rate can be taken as exogenous.

This discussion applies to nations in which the government issues a currency in a floating exchange rate regime. A country that pegs its currency to a foreign currency or precious metal operates in a quite different interest rate environment, however, generating constraints on both fiscal and monetary policy. If a government promises to redeem its currency for another currency, or for a precious metal, it must retain sufficient reserves of that currency or metal to meet all conceivable requests for conversion. This could require reserves equal to, or even greater than, the total stock of domestic high powered money (plus the portion of government bonds that is maturing in the near-term). Government budget deficits are then quite dangerous unless a trade surplus can keep the foreign currencies, or precious metals, flowing into official reserves. More relevantly for this chapter, interest rates become endogenous in the sense that monetary policy must discourage redemption of domestic currency assets for foreign currency or precious metal. Further, a looser fiscal policy must almost necessarily be offset by a tighter monetary policy (higher rate target) unless the country enjoys a sufficient trade surplus. If private banks offer convertible accounts, they must also retain sufficient reserves to meet conversions. Note also that central bank policy will tighten in crisis, just as the Bank of England used to raise rates and call in loans whenever there was a run on private banks during the nineteenth century (Wray, 1990). Accommodative behavior of the central bank operating in a fixed exchange rate regime is dangerous because it places the country's reserves of foreign currency or metal at risk. Thus, the Fed's timid response to the Great Depression, and its raising of rates in the accompanying financial crisis, were appropriate while the country was on the gold standard. While the Fed did still 'administer' the discount rate in a technical sense, it could not 'exogenously control' it because international financial markets dictated the domestic rate that would stem specie outflow.

Note that government bond sales by a nation operating on a fixed exchange rate can be thought of as something like a borrowing operation, a part of fiscal policy. If the government issues bonds denominated in the foreign currency reserve, it obtains reserves it can leverage in its deficit spending. If it borrows in its own currency, it destroys domestic currency that leveraged its foreign currency reserves and that could have been converted to drain those reserves (conversion would be postponed until the debt matured). By contrast, a sovereign government on a floating exchange rate simply credits bank accounts when it spends; bond sales merely drain excess reserves to maintain overnight rates on target. Much of the 'conventional wisdom' about fiscal policy applies only in the case of a fixed exchange rate regime. In such a regime, rising deficits will increase interest rates, not automatically as government borrowing 'competes' with private borrowing, but because the central bank will raise its target rate to protect reserves on a fixed exchange rate regime. In such a regime, government appears to face a 'government budget constraint': its spending is constrained by the sum of new debt issues, new money creation, and tax revenues. Taxes result in a currency drain that reduces leverage ratios on reserves of foreign currency or precious metal; while taxes don't really 'pay for' the government spending, they loosen the reserve constraint on spending. Issues of bonds also drain currency, substituting an interest-earning government liability with some time to maturity for non-earning reserves. At best, they simply push possible conversion of domestic currency to the reserve into the future. Hence, new issues will likely cause the central bank to raise interest rates to protect reserves. Finally, government spending financed by money emission increases leverage ratios on reserves, so will likely cause the central bank to raise rates for reasons just discussed. Thus, there is a reason to focus on the 'constraint' that governments face on fixed exchange rate regimes, and reason to believe that deficits raise interest rates and threaten the value of the currency. If the deficit causes exchange rates to depreciate, inflation would be a possible result. Thus government deficits are more-or-less correctly 'fought' by higher interest rates to protect reserves of foreign currency or metals.

By contrast, a sovereign government that issues a non-convertible currency on a floating exchange rate lives in a different environment. The 'government budget constraint' is nothing but an *ex post* identity that in no way constrains government spending. Government spends by crediting bank accounts; taxes drain bank accounts; deficits mean net credits to accounts. Even in this case, one can think of these net credits to bank accounts as a 'leverage' of reserves. However, because government does not promise to convert high powered money reserves to foreign currencies or metals, it can always supply domestic currency reserves 'horizontally' on demand. Bonds are still issued to drain excess reserves, but the interest rate target is exogenously set and that target rate *need not* be raised by the central bank in response to government deficits.

The argument that interest rates become endogenous on a fixed exchange rate is more than mere semantics, even though we have admitted earlier that central bank policy never completely ignores economic conditions, and that overnight rates must be 'administered' at least in the technical sense that the central bank sets them. Hence, it is true that even a central bank in a floating rate regime might pay attention to exchange rates and will take potential impacts on them into account when setting the overnight rate target. However, with a fixed exchange rate regime, the imperative of formulating policy to ensure exchange rate rigidity becomes overriding – the central bank simply cannot ignore forces that threaten the peg. Monetary policy is held hostage to the exchange rate such that the interest rate target can be considered to be endogenous – determined by what is thought necessary to protect reserves of foreign currency and metals. A central bank operating in a floating exchange rate regime might choose to raise target rates in response to treasury deficits, and it might even believe that this policy protects the exchange rate, but such behavior is not required in such a regime. The floating rate provides an additional degree of freedom to monetary policy that is not available in a fixed exchange rate system. In this sense, Moore's argument that the overnight rate is exogenous strictly applies only to a floating exchange rate regime.

KEYNES'S LIQUIDITY PREFERENCE THEORY

There have been a number of claims that Keynes's liquidity preference theory is inconsistent with both endogenous money and exogenous interest rate setting by the central bank. I believe that such claims result from a misinterpretation of Keynes's version of liquidity preference theory. While liquidity preference theory is often presented as a theory of demand for money (even occasionally by Keynes himself), the best expositions of Keynes's theory (in Chapter 17 of the *General Theory* (GT), in Keynes (1937) and in Townshend (1937) present it as a *general* theory of asset prices. When interpreted thus, liquidity preference theory is perfectly consistent with endogenous money and exogenous interest rate setting.

Let us take the most extreme form of horizontalism: the overnight rate as well as bank loan and deposit rates are all exogenously administered by central bank policy. Further, let us suppose that short-term government bond rates are similarly administered by the central bank while long-term government bond rates are simply set by expectations of future central bank policy. Does liquidity preference theory have any role to play in such a model of interest rate determination? Recall that in Chapter 17, Keynes argued that each asset has an expected return, comprising $q - c + l + a$, where q represents the expected yield of the asset, c is wastage or carrying cost, l stands for liquidity, and a is the expected appreciation/depreciation of the price of the asset in money terms. According to Keynes, most of the return to highly liquid assets comes from l (and c would be negligible), while for capital assets, most of the return would consist of the expected qs. As liquidity preference falls, the demand price for assets whose return consists primarily of l will fall relative to the value of assets whose return consists primarily of q. Under the assumptions of extreme horizontalism, this analysis does not apply to the overnight rate, to loan and deposit rates, and to government bond rates – whose rates and hence prices are all exogenously administered. Still, this leaves a great range of assets whose prices are in part determined by liquidity preference.

Note that Keynes did not mean to imply that liquidity preference is the *only* factor determining asset prices; indeed, it cannot be but one among a number of other factors. Among these factors we should include monetary policy and expected future interest rate targets. Keynes singled out for analysis liquidity preference because of the special role played by money, which has 'peculiar' properties – one of which is that it is usually the most liquid of assets. There are parts of Keynes's exposition that should be altered in recognition of abandonment of fixed exchange rates and (re)emergence of exogenous overnight interest rates. However, the argument that when uncertainty about economic prospects rises, demand prices of illiquid capital assets tend to fall relative to those of liquid financial assets surely applies even with floating rates and exogenous administration of some interest rates. There is thus no conflict between Keynes's liquidity preference approach and Moore's horizontalism.

MINSKY'S FINANCIAL INSTABILITY HYPOTHESIS AND EXOGENOUS RATE SETTING

Immediately after the GT was published, there were attempts to reconcile his liquidity preference approach with the loanable funds theory of orthodoxy, principally by Ohlin, Hicks, and Robertson. (See Wray, 1990 and 1992b.) Keynes vehemently rejected all such efforts, but after his death 'synthesizers' like Tsiang and Kohn continued to argue that saving and investment flows, and corresponding 'flows of finance', should be combined with demands for and supplies of stocks of money hoards to determine interest rates. (See Foley, 1975, for the more-or-less definitive explication of the relations between stocks and flows; also see Wray, 1990.) In recent years, some Post Keynesians have argued that the liquidity preference approach is close to – or perhaps is the same thing as – loanable funds theory. This has carried over into a critique of Hyman Minsky's work, which some followers of the circuit approach have argued is also based on a loanable funds approach. I think all of this results from a fundamental conflation of liquidity preference theory with traditional money demand theory, and from a misunderstanding of the impact of balance sheet positions on behavior.

The critique of Minsky begins with a few well-chosen quotes from his earliest writings in which he appears to confuse saving with finance and money; it is then claimed that Minsky held a loanable funds approach and hence that his financial instability hypothesis developed over the subsequent four decades is flawed. Some have also denied that it is even possible for balance sheets to become stretched or for income flows to be 'leveraged' in the manner Minsky described, instead advancing a sort of 'Say's Law' of finance (Lavoie and Seccareccia, 2001). In this view, no matter how hard economic units try to get themselves into debt, offsetting financial wealth is created along with the profits generated by their spending – hence, hedge units cannot become speculative or Ponzi, in Minsky's terminology. Because liquidity cannot be reduced, liquidity preference plays no role in determining interest rates/asset pricing, thus, Minsky's 'two price theory' of investment is as flawed as Keynes's liquidity preference theory. (See Papadimitriou and Wray, 2001.) However, as I will argue, this critique of Minsky appears to be based on two very 'un-Keynesian' arguments: (a) a 'financial Say's Law', and (b) a 'reverse fallacy of composition' in which whatever is true of the aggregate must also be true of individuals.

Using a very simple circuit model with no government and no foreign sector, and – importantly – with no money other than 'inside' credit (bank deposits created through loans), it is identically true that expansion of nonbank liabilities equals nonbank financial assets, hence, at any point in time, all loans and deposits can be retired. In such a simple model, it is not possible or even desirable to make a sharp distinction between stocks and flows – at the beginning of the circuit, loans advanced equal deposits created, equal the wage bill paid, equal income. Spending on output is counted as part of the reflux process, allowing firms to retire loans and extinguish deposits; any wage income not yet spent equals saving, equals deposits, equals money hoards, equals loans not retired. The circuit is closed when all income is finally spent, all deposits and loans are destroyed, and all saving and money hoards are eliminated. If the circuit is not closed, some saving in the form of deposits remains, but this exactly equals loans that were not repaid. Saving cannot be a net source of finance, for it simply represents income and deposits that did not reflux. Aggregate liquidity cannot be stretched since it is created with the payment of wages, thus equals income and remains only to the extent that there is positive savings – which can take place only in money form. There is no 'outside' money to leverage, and all 'inside' money 'leverages' actual production (equals income).

While the model is extremely useful for making these points, and for providing one possible avenue toward development of a monetary theory of production, it is not very useful for explaining the evolution of balance sheets through time in a more complicated economy with several sectors and with finance of long-lived capital equipment in an uncertain world. This was Minsky's central concern for some four decades, during which he developed an increasingly sophisticated model of the transformation of financial positions toward greater fragility. His earliest work focused on evolution of banking system balance sheets as innovations encouraged banks to shift portfolios toward more illiquid assets. One of the consequences was a nearly continual increase of the deposit (or loan) to reserve ratio – a leveraging of 'outside' money in a hierarchical money system – as well as a decrease of the loan (or deposit) to government bond ('secondary reserves') ratio. This is one aspect of the rising 'fragility' of the financial sector that Minsky continued to analyze as each new financial innovation brought new ways to stretch liquidity – a source of fragility that cannot be analyzed by Financial Say's Law circuitists, who operate with a severely truncated model that excludes outside money and bonds.

By the early 1960s, Minsky recognized that the impact of expansion on private nonbank balance sheets depends on the nature of the expansion. If the expansion is fueled mostly through government deficits, then private sector net indebtedness need not increase at all; however, a private-sector-led expansion could result in an increase of net indebtedness of that sector: 'During a protracted expansion dominated by household and business deficits the ratio of household and business financial commitments to income rises, whereas in an expansion dominated by government deficits the ratio of private commitments to income decreases' (Minsky, 1963, p. 412). Unlike the results from the simple circuit model, Minsky recognized that while it is true that at the global level, all debts and credits cancel, this is not true for individual sectors – which can be net creditors or net debtors. Many will recognize this as the sectoral analysis that is most closely associated with Wynne Godley today. Hence, an expansion can occur with the private sector running a surplus, a deficit, or a balance between its income and spending – and this is important for fragility. For a country like the USA, robust expansion almost automatically dictates that the private sector's balance will deteriorate as the government's budget moves toward balance (even to surplus during the Clinton years) and as a large balance of payments deficit opens up with the rest of the world. Hence, the Say's Law Post Keynesians have simply neglected to incorporate sectoral analysis into their model, and their critique of Minsky cannot hold. Further, Minsky recognized that economic agents incur debts to take positions in assets, and that purchase of assets need not generate a new income flow out of the productive sector. Such a possibility is not allowed in simple circuit models, in which loans and deposits are created only in conjunction with production. However, in the type of capitalism that Minsky modeled, a very large part of the financial superstructure is removed from production so that the volume of financial assets and liabilities can grow relatively to the underlying incomes generated in the production process – another kind of leveraging that increases fragility and that breaks the Say's Law of Finance.

In preparation for his *John Maynard Keynes* (JMK) book that eventually came out in 1975, Minsky very carefully re-read the *General Theory* (his detailed notes are archived at the Levy Economics Institute). This not only resulted in a reinterpretation of Keynes, but also in a major revision to Minsky's own exposition of his theory of investment and evolution of fragility. In his writings of the 1950s and through most of the 1960s, one can indeed find some passages that appear to indicate he had not fully incorporated Keynes's theory of the saving-investment relation within his own vision. In my view, his early work is still very valuable for the numerous insights into financial markets, and there is no doubt that he held an endogenous money view from the beginning. Still, one can see an obvious difference in his work after 1970. Further, shortly after writing the JMK book, Minsky 'discovered' Kalecki (he had almost certainly read Kalecki two decades earlier, although the profits equation does not appear in his earlier writing). Addition of Keynes and Kalecki led to a great improvement of the financial instability hypothesis.

Minsky termed his a 'financial theory of investment and an investment theory of the cycle' (Papadimitriou and Wray, 2001). Briefly, bank loans provide short-term financing of the production of investment goods and consumption goods; consumption out of the wage bill received by investment goods sector workers generates profit income flows in the consumption sector. Firms ordering the investment goods must obtain long-term finance for their position in these assets; they use a combination of internal funds (gross capital income flows, generated as above by consumption of investment sector workers) and external funds. The supply of internal funds is 'horizontal' (at the supply price of capital goods), but the supply of external funds is upward sloping due to lender's risk. This has nothing to do with loanable funds, but rather can be attributed to hesitation of lenders to take increasingly large positions in the liabilities of each particular firm – and in liabilities of firms in general. While Minsky uses the term 'risk', he does not mean this in the Knightian sense; rather the future is 'uncertain' in a Keynesian sense, but financial institutions (and their borrowers) operate conventionally, with rules of thumb, on whirlwinds of optimism and pessimism. Similarly, the prospective investment goods purchasers must estimate future returns from the capital goods; the demand price is horizontal so long as internal funds can cover the cost. When external funds are involved, borrower's risk is built-in, lowering the price the prospective borrower is willing to pay.

The intersection of demand price and supply price determines the quantity of investment undertaken, which in turn determines the amount of external finance required and the contracted commitments made. Rejecting the Financial Say's Law, Minsky argued that these investment decisions could result in rising fragility as greater portions of expected income flows became committed (in advance) to debt service. Further, as mentioned above, Minsky recognized that firms and other economic units take positions in assets by issuing liabilities and there is no necessary relation between the value of assets and the size of income flows generated in the production process. Over an expansion, balance sheets move from hedge to speculative and to Ponzi as the committed debt service rises relative to prospective income flows. If income flows turn out to be less than expected, or if finance costs rise, this normal and discretionary transformation to fragile positions would be hastened. Note also that if expansion tends to generate budget surpluses or balance of payments deficits, the aggregate budget situation of the private sector must (identically) worsen. In any case, because financial institutions live in the same expectational environment (more or less) inhabited by everyone else, a reversal of expectations about the future (regardless of current realized results) could indeed change perceptions of lenders' and borrowers' risk in such a way that external finance costs rise, investment spending falls, profits and other incomes fall, and a snowball of defaults could result. Again, this has nothing to do with 'lack of saving' but simply results from adoption of a more complex vision of capitalist finance than that incorporated in the simplest circuit models.

While Minsky's work causes us to reject simplistic Financial Say's Laws, is it necessarily inconsistent with horizontalism and exogenous interest rate administration by the central bank? Let us again take the most extreme form of horizontalism: the overnight rate as well as bank loan and deposit rates are all exogenously administered by central bank policy. Further, let us suppose that short-term government bond rates are similarly administered by the central bank while long-term government bond rates are simply set by expectations of future central bank policy. Those who advance a Financial Say's Law appear to want to go further, to deny any endogenous impacts on *any* interest rates or on *any* financial asset prices, but such a position is not inherent to the horizontalist approach, in which even the extreme position is simply that loan rates, deposit rates, and sovereign bond rates are exogenous. Note that Minsky's theory of investment finance really does not involve Moore's loan rates in any case, because the 'two price theory' of investment concerns long-term external finance supplied by investment banks, and not short-term lending by commercial banks. Commercial banks provide only the short-term working capital loans used during the production of investment goods, hence go into the 'current output' horizontal supply price, but do not play a role in formation of the 'lender's risk' that causes the supply price to rise. Hence, the process that Minsky describes really has nothing to do with the shape of the supply curve for commercial bank lending. The question is whether horizontalism necessarily rejects any process that can generate fragility.

Over the course of an expansion, the central bank normally begins to increase its administered target rate to prevent what it sees as 'overheating'. Other rates begin to rise, as short-term rates are marked up and as long-term rates rise on expectations of future rate hikes. This raises the costs of finance and can, as Minsky argued, lead to 'present value reversals' in the sense that projects that had been profitable at lower costs now become unprofitable. Firms must decide whether to continue production of projects already under way, absorbing sunk costs and taking a loss, or to abandon projects. The rate of spending on new investments declines, lowering profit flows and making it more difficult to service previously incurred debts. Financial problems arise even if the bank loan supply is horizontal at the new higher interest rates targeted by the central bank.

Increases to the central bank's target rate will be passed along to bank borrowers on new loans and on all adjustable rate loans. As discussed above, we do not even need a change of monetary policy to have rising finance costs, so long as an expansion pushes borrowers into higher risk classes. This can occur for micro reasons (larger outstanding loans to individual borrowers raise risks) and for macro reasons (bank loans as a percentage of total assets rise, especially relative to secondary reserves like government bonds – a necessary result if the expansion is led by the private sector; bank loans as a multiple of equity also rises, except in the simplest Financial Say's Law models). Thus, interest rates can tend to rise as the financial structure becomes more fragile. The supply price of investment goods rises, while demand prices fall as greater borrower's risk is recognized. Again, if an expansion is led by the domestic private sector, its spending must increase faster than its income, putting borrowers into increasingly precarious positions.

None of Minsky's analysis requires an exogenous money supply, or a loanable funds approach. The financial instability hypothesis survives even in the most extreme version of horizontalism. Indeed, if it did not, we would have to abandon horizontalism as being inconsistent with the real world, in which capitalist economies *do* exhibit the type of financial instability that absorbed much of Minsky's attention!

CONCLUSIONS

Moore's critical insight is that the supply of reserves should be modeled as horizontal at the administered overnight interest rate. The supply of bank money should be taken to be endogenous, with demand deposits created each time a bank makes a loan. If required or desired reserves rise in consequence, the central bank accommodates by providing more reserves. Loanable funds theory, according to which savings are the supply (or a portion of the supply) of the funds required to meet the demand for loans must be rejected. Just as investment spending creates an equivalent amount of saving flows, bank lending creates an equivalent amount of bank deposits. Similarly, ISLM analysis and the simultaneous determination of equilibrium interest rates and income must be rejected because it presumes an exogenously determined money supply. There cannot be any automatic and necessary impact of spending on interest rates because loans and deposits can and normally do increase as spending rises. The overnight rate will change only if and when the central bank decides to allow it to do so. Short-term loan and deposit retail rates can be taken as a somewhat variable mark-up and mark-down from the overnight rate.

None of this precludes a role for Keynes's version of liquidity preference as a theory of asset prices, with liquidity preference as one of the components that goes into determining interest rates that are not administered by central bank policy. Nor is this inconsistent with Minsky's financial instability hypothesis according to which expansions and evolution of financial practices tend to stretch liquidity and create a fragile financial structure more vulnerable to financial crises – even in a world of endogenous money, horizontally supplied reserves, and exogenously administered overnight rates.

Finally, insufficient attention has been paid to the importance of the exchange rate regime for the endogenous money approach and for exogenous interest rate setting by the central bank. Horizontalism really requires the assumption of floating exchange rates, for otherwise interest rate policy is severely constrained by international financial markets. In a fixed exchange rate regime, the overnight interest rate is best characterized as endogenous in the control sense because the central bank must choose its target so as to maintain sufficient reserves of foreign currency or gold to maintain convertibility. Many of the orthodox results regarding fiscal policy (such as that government deficits 'cause' interest rates to rise) then hold. By contrast, with a floating exchange rate, monetary and fiscal policy independence becomes possible.

REFERENCES

Bell, S. (2000) 'Do Taxes and Bonds Finance Government Spending?' *Journal of Economic Issues*, 34(3), 603–20.

Bell, S. and L.R. Wray (2002–3) 'Fiscal Effects on Reserves and the Independence of the Fed', *Journal of Post Keynesian Economics*, 25, 263–71.

Chick, V. (1986) 'The Evolution of the Banking System and the Theory of Saving, Investment and Interest', Department of Economics, University College of London, Discussion Paper No. 86-01.

Cooley, T. and S. LeRoy (1981) 'Identification and Estimation of Money Demand', *The American Economic Review*, 71, 825–44.

Desai, M. (1989) 'Endogenous and Exogenous Money', in John Eatwell, Murray Milgate and Peter Newman (eds), *The New Palgrave: Money*, New York and London: W.W. Norton.

Foley, D. (1975) 'On Two Specifications of Asset Equilibrium in Macroeconomic Models', *Journal of Political Economy*, 83, 303–24.

Homer, S. and R. Sylla (1991) *A History of Interest Rates*, 3rd edition, New Brunswick: Rutgers University Press.

Keynes, J.M. (1937) 'Alternative Theories of the Rate of Interest', *Economic Journal*, 47, 241–52.

Keynes, J.M. (1964) [1936] *The General Theory of Employment Interest and Money*, New York: Harcourt, Brace and Company.

Lavoie, M. and M. Seccareccia (2001) 'Minsky's Financial Fragility Hypothesis: A Missing Macroeconomic Link?' in Riccardo Bellofiore and Piero Ferri (eds), *Financial Fragility and Investment in the Capitalist Economy: The economic legacy of Hyman Minsky*, volume II, Cheltenham, UK and Northampton, MA, USA: Edward Elgar.

Meulendyke, A. (1988) 'Can the Federal Reserve Influence Whether the Money Supply is Endogenous? A Comment on Moore', *Journal of Post Keynesian Economics*, 10, 391–7.

Minsky, H.P. (1963) 'Discussion', *American Economic Review*, 53, 401–12.
Minsky, H.P. (1975) *John Maynard Keynes*, New York: Columbia University Press.
Moore, B. (1984) 'Contemporaneous Reserve Accounting: Can Reserves be Quantity-constrained?' *Journal of Post Keynesian Economics*, 7, 103–13.
Moore, B. (1988) *Horizontalists and Verticalists: The Macroeconomics of Credit Money*, Cambridge: Cambridge University Press.
Moore, B. (1991) 'Money Supply Endogeneity: "Reserve Price Setting" or "Reserve Quantity Setting"', *Journal of Post Keynesian Economics*, 13, 404–13.
Moore, B. (1996) 'The Money Supply Process: A Historical Reinterpretation', in Ghislain Deleplace and Edward J. Nell (eds), *Money in Motion: The Post Keynesian and Circulation Approaches*, New York: St Martin's Press, Inc.
Niggle, C. (1990) 'The Evolution of Money, Financial Institutions, and Monetary Economics', *Journal of Economic Issues*, 24, 443–50.
Palley, T. (1991) 'The Endogenous Money Supply: Consensus and Disagreement', *Journal of Post Keynesian Economics*, 13, 397–403.
Papadimitriou, D. and L.R. Wray (2001) 'Minsky's Analysis of Financial Capitalism', in Riccardo Bellofiore and Piero Ferri (eds), *Financial Keynesianism and Market Instability*, Cheltenham, UK and Northampton, MA, USA: Edward Elgar.
Pollin, R. (1991) 'Two Theories of Money Supply Endogeneity: Some Empirical Evidence', *Journal of Post Keynesian Economics*, 13, 366–96.
Townshend, H. (1937) 'Liquidity-premium and the Theory of Value', *The Economic Journal*, 47, 157–69.
Tsiang, S.C. (1956) 'Liquidity Preference and Loanable Funds Theories, Multiplier and Velocity Analysis: A Synthesis', *American Economic Review*, 46, 539–64.
Wray, L.R. (1992a) 'Alternative Approaches to Money and Interest Rates', *Journal of Economic Issues*, 24, 1145–78.
Wray, L.R. (1992b) 'Alternative Theories of the Rate of Interest', *Cambridge Journal of Economics*, 16, 69–89.
Wray, L.R. (1990) *Money and Credit in Capitalist Economies: The Endogenous Money Approach*, Aldershot, UK and Brookfield, USA: Edward Elgar.
Wray L.R. (1998) *Understanding Modern Money: The Key to Full Employment and Price Stability*, Cheltenham, UK and Lyme, USA: Edward Elgar.
Wray, L.R. (ed.) (2004) *Credit and State Theories of Money: The Contributions of A. Mitchell Innes*, Cheltenham, UK and Northampton, MA, USA: Edward Elgar.

16. Exogenous interest rates and modern monetary theory and policy: Moore in perspective

Colin Rogers

INTRODUCTION

As monetarism raged supreme in the early 1980s, Basil Moore (1988) was prominent among those post Keynesians who argued that attempting to run monetary policy by constraining the quantity of money (however defined) was a futile endeavor.[1] In his book, titled *Horizontalists and Verticalists: The Macroeconomics of Credit Money*, he went further and argued that the notion of some exogenous money supply was simply not applicable to an economy with a sophisticated financial system, and essentially neoclassical monetary economics needed to be completely rewritten. Today the landscape of monetary theory and policy has been transformed. At first glance, much of what has happened appears to be a vindication of Moore and the post Keynesians.

On the policy front, central bankers abandoned monetary targets in the mid 1980s in favor of an interest rate instrument. In the textbooks, monetarists have been consigned to those little boxes on the history of thought while core monetary theory is all about how to achieve price stability and other macroeconomic objectives using interest rate rules. Central bankers now explicitly acknowledge that 'bank rate' is the instrument of monetary policy and interest rates are adjusted to achieve macroeconomic objectives – Svensson (2003) presents flexible inflation targeting as the preferred framework. In the theoretical literature the *new Horizontalists*, Romer (2000) and DeLong (2000), have rejected the icon of the neoclassical synthesis, the IS-LM model.

The question I wish to examine in this chapter is whether this revolution in monetary theory and policy is in the spirit of Moore, or whether it is simply a restatement of the Real Analysis of the neoclassical synthesis with an interest rate rule. The essence of Moore's Monetary Analysis is the property that money and monetary policy are never neutral while neoclassical monetary theory holds that monetary policy is neutral in the long run, that is, monetary forces have no lasting influence on the forces of productivity, and growth.[2] Two factors that suggest there may be something missing from modern monetary theory and policy are the excessive concentration on the short run and the absence of any treatment of the principle of effective demand.

To investigate the relationship between Moore and modern monetary theory, the following section of the chapter examines Moore's critique of the *Verticalist* position on monetary theory and policy. The next section briefly outlines some key features of the modern or *new Horizontalist* analysis as developed by Romer (2000) and others. The chapter then compares Moore's views on monetary policy with some key developments in modern monetary policy presented by Svensson (2003) and Lavoie (2003). The final section concludes.

It will be argued that although the *new Horizontalists* have accepted that the quantity theoretic framework is a false description of how modern monetary systems work, and embraced part of Moore's *Horizontalism*, the core theoretical propositions of Real Analysis remain. The call by Moore for neoclassical monetary theorists to embrace Monetary Analysis remains unheeded.

MOORE'S HORIZONTALISM

In *Horizontalists and Verticalists* Moore makes the case that 'All models that treat money as exogenous – or virtually everything written in the monetary, macro, and growth literature – are either miss-specified or incomplete' (Moore, 1988, p. xiv). He goes on to outline 16 characteristics of the monetary literature of the time that he considered to be fundamentally false (Moore, 1988, pp. xiv–xv).[3] In terms of these 16 characteristics, the core of Moore's analysis is captured by points 6, 8 and 10, and I will focus on those.

Point 6 is the characteristic that money is neutral in the long run; point 8 refers to the independence of real and monetary forces as personified by the independence of the IS and LM curves. Point 10, a corollary of point 8, has the real rate of interest determined by the real forces of productivity and thrift. In addition to the negative features of received monetary theory Moore (1988, p. 19) goes on to sketch six essential positive features of what he calls a credit money economy (to distinguish it from commodity and fiat money systems – exogenous money systems).[4] The key element here is captured by point 3: 'The supply of credit money is also endogenous in the control sense. The exogenous variable is the price at which central banks supply base money on demand, which determines the general level of short term interest rates'. It is the exogenous nature of the interest rate under the control of a central bank and the perfectly elastic supply of base money at that rate which accounts for Moore's description of his analysis as *Horizontalist*. And although that was a useful description, and a neat way of contrasting his analysis with the dominant quantity theoretic tradition of the time, it is not sufficient to characterize Moore's monetary theory. The key element of Moore's monetary economics is not the *Horizontalist* feature, but the rejection of Real Analysis. From my perspective the key chapter in *Horizontalists and Verticalists* is chapter 10 and I would like to briefly consider the main points covered in chapter 10 to highlight the contrast with the *new Horizontalist* position considered in the next section.

The essence of chapter 10 is the argument that:

> Once it is recognized that in all credit money economies it is the level of nominal interest rates that is determined exogenously by the central bank, rather than the nominal money stock, monetary non-neutrality follows simply and directly. (Moore, 1988, p. 254)

What is at stake here? A reading of chapter 10 makes it abundantly clear, at least to me, that for Moore a credit money economy is one in which Say's Law fails and the principle of effective demand applies. This happens because the central bank can set a nominal (and an inflation-adjusted or real) rate of interest too high to ensure full employment. The argument reflects Keynes's (1936, p. 204) view that in a *laissez-faire* economy the rate of interest can fluctuate for decades about a level that is too high to ensure full employment, particularly if it is believed that the rate is somehow market determined rather than the outcome of 'policy'. Also, in Moore's chapter 10, as in Keynes (1936), the marginal efficiency of capital can adjust to the rate of interest. This is a crucial result of the principle of effective demand and amounts to a generalization and reversal of the relationship between the market and natural rates of interest found in the Real Analysis of Wicksell (1898).

In Real Analysis, the natural rate of interest is treated as a real rate, in the sense that the rate is determined by productivity and thrift as if saving and investment could be undertaken in kind, in a manner such that they are totally independent of any monetary influence (Moore's false propositions 8 and 10). The market or money rate of interest was presumed to gravitate to equality with this real natural rate in long-run equilibrium. In that sense money was treated as neutral in the long run even though it could cause problems in the short run (inflation or deflation) if the market rate of interest failed to follow the natural rate. I note in passing that Wicksell quite rightly always stressed that two rates of interest were involved – the cost of borrowing and the return on investing – but modern monetary theorists often conflate the two. By contrast, the principle of effective demand is the idea that the market rate of interest can rule the roost in the sense that the marginal efficiency of capital may adjust to the market rate of interest as determined by the monetary authorities. In that case Say's Law fails as firms face a limit to the profitable expansion of output; supply does not create its own demand because attempting to expand output beyond the point of effective demand will result in losses (it's all in the *General Theory*). In this world money and monetary policy are never neutral.

To sum up, Basil's *Horizontalist* position is more than the observation that the short-term interest rate is an exogenous variable and under the control of the central bank. In a credit money economy Moore (1988, ch. 10) argues that Real Analysis must be abandoned – money and monetary policy are never neutral, either in the short or the long run. The relevant analytical framework for monetary theory and policy is the Monetary Analysis of Keynes and the principle of effective demand.

NEW HORIZONTALISTS

Although interest rate rules were introduced in the early 1990s, their significance and *new Horizontalist* interpretation in the IS-LM context was first popularized by David Romer (2000) and later endorsed by DeLong (2000), among others. Romer sets out his position in terms of the 11 advantages he sees in abandoning the idea that the money supply is exogenous.[5] An inspection of this list reveals that it is motivated largely by considerations of realism and simplicity. In particular, Romer argues that assuming the central bank follows an interest rate rule is more realistic than the assumption that it targets the money supply. DeLong (2000) takes a stronger line and acknowledges that the assumption that central banks fix money stocks is simply false.

Romer (2000) therefore abandons the LM curve and replaces it with a horizontal monetary policy (MP) curve in (r, Y) space. Of the other advantages proposed by Romer and DeLong, most relate to the gains in terms of simplicity of the IS-MP structure over the IS-LM structure and the ease with which students can relate the model to what they read in the *Wall Street Journal*. Up to this point Moore and the *new Horizontalists* are in complete agreement. But that consensus breaks down when we examine Romer's MP curve in more detail.

Romer (2000, 2002) generalizes the horizontal MP curve on the grounds that central banks will raise the real rate of interest when real gross domestic product (GDP) increases. This specification allows for adjustments of the real rate of interest in response to both movements in real GDP (relative to its natural level) and inflation (relative to some target) as suggested by a simple Taylor Rule. Several features of this analysis require comment.

First it assumes that the central bank can control the real, inflation adjusted, cost of borrowing. This seems to me quite uncontroversial and quite consistent with Monetary Analysis. I think it is important to stress here, that although the central bank has control only of a nominal rate of interest, the manner in which it exercises that control determines what happens to the real or inflation adjusted rate of interest – the real cost of borrowing. And, through the term structure of interest rates, the central bank also influences, albeit indirectly, 'the' real long-term rate of interest.

However, even if we accept this aspect of the 'axiom of reals', that in itself is not sufficient to conclude that money is neutral in the long run. In Monetary Analysis, the real cost of borrowing may be too high, and result in insufficient effective demand to ensure full employment in the long run. Furthermore, even if wages and prices are flexible, that flexibility may not be sufficient to restore full employment in the long run (Moore's false propositions 12 and 13). For price and wage flexibility to eliminate unemployment, it must be such that wages (costs) fall faster than prices so as to raise the real marginal efficiency of capital relative to the real cost of borrowing in the long run and do so without destabilizing expectations and sufficiently to offset any reduction in consumption expenditures that result from the redistribution of income away from wages as the real wage falls. That is, for wage and price flexibility to restore full employment, the point of effective demand must shift so as to increase output and employment. As Keynes (1936) argued, there is no *a priori* reason why it should. Thus I see no reason why we can't accept that central bankers will attempt to adjust the real, inflation adjusted, cost of borrowing. What is significant is what happens to the point of effective demand when the real cost of borrowing is adjusted.

Second, Romer (2002) continues to argue that the central bank controls the nominal money supply directly. This is a false description of central bank behavior but can be treated as an innocuous simplification if it is interpreted to mean that, as a monopoly supplier of clearing balances (money), the central bank can always impose losses on the banks. The art of central banking is to keep the banks 'in the bank'. Without access to other sources of funds the banks rely on the central bank to provide clearing balances at minimum cost and disruption to the payments system. Modern electronic payments and clearing systems such as the real time gross settlements (RTGS) systems operated by the central banks of Australia, New Zealand and Canada, among others, are simply very efficient versions of the system described by Keynes in the *Treatise*. See Rogers and Rymes (2000, p. 261). In such systems the central bank exerts tight control over 'bank rate' and can adjust the rate efficiently by announcement, as all participants are aware of the losses that could be imposed on them by the bank so all rates adjust virtually immediately. Some new *Horizontalists* have modelled this feature of the monetary system (Woodford, 2000), so there is no disagreement here.

A more fundamental issue arises when we consider Romer's (2002) extension of the analysis to examine long-run issues in a model specified in inflation/output space. This model has all the properties of the neoclassical AD-AS (aggregate demand–aggregate supply) model – in particular the complete crowding out of fiscal policy in the long run and the long-run neutrality of money. The principle of effective demand is nowhere to be seen.

Romer (2002, p. 56) is explicit about the long-run properties of his analysis:

> Monetary policy does not affect either output or the real rate interest rate in the long run. Output equals its natural rate, and the real interest rate equals the value that brings the loan market into equilibrium when output is at that level. The inflation rate in the long run is therefore the inflation rate that causes the central bank to set the real rate to the level that equilibrates the loan market when output equals its natural rate.

All of this would no doubt be recognizable by Wicksell (1898) and it would be reasonable to describe Romer's analysis as Wicksellian. The technical limitations of that analysis have been well documented (Rogers, 1989), and it is not worth repeating them here. However, it is worth considering the historical context in which this analysis is presented.

The theoretical framework employed by Romer is based on the presumption that the sole function of the central bank is the maintenance of price stability. Apart from that, central banks have no real contribution to make to long-run stability or growth. Monetary policy, like money, is neutral in the long run. Maintaining price stability will allow the real relative price signals to operate effectively and maintain output at its natural level, and that is all monetary policy can be expected to deliver in the long run. However, the fact that many contracts are fixed in nominal terms and that indexation cannot protect against real 'shocks' means that sticky nominal values can generate a business cycle – positive serial correlation in output and inflation. Fiscal, and monetary, policy can then be employed to circumvent the need for a deflation of sticky nominal values in the face of a negative real shock and minimize the social costs of unemployment in the short run. This is the extent of the modern Keynesian vision. It is a caricature of both Keynes and modern monetary policy.

It is a caricature of Keynes (1936, p. 164) who advocated a fundamental change in the philosophy of economic policy to embrace a role for government in raising the marginal efficiency of capital.

> I expect to see the State, which is in a position to calculate the marginal efficiency of capital–goods on long views and on the basis of general social advantage, taking an ever greater responsibility for directly organising investment; since it seems likely that the fluctuations in the market estimation of the marginal efficiency of different types of capital, calculated on the principles I have described above, will be too great to be offset by any practicable changes in the rate of interest.

Keynes clearly intended to change the role of government so it could act as a stabilizing influence on the point of effective demand and improve the average level of output relative to its potential level (the potential level itself cannot be determined independently of government policy). In that sense Keynes was not proposing another theory of the business cycle, as many have erroneously concluded, but a change in the structure of the economy to involve a stabilizing role for government. In that respect the Keynes revolution has been an unparallelled success in the second half of the twentieth century. Government involvement in infrastructure investment has not only increased demand but has raised the marginal efficiency of capital as perceived by private investors. Government investment has successfully *crowded in* private investment. Inspection of the difference between the pre- and post-World War II business cycles should be sufficient to convince most, but apparently not all, sceptics. It's a pity the Keynesians haven't figured this out, leaving themselves exposed to silly arguments about *crowding out* when the world has just experienced the most effective 60 year period of *crowding in* since the pyramids!

In practical terms the inability of Keynesians, old and new, to see the issue is reflected in their treatment of investment and the capital stock. Misled, perhaps, by Keynes's treatment of the short run, Keynesians ignore the impact of investment on the capital stock. But this rules out the most effective mechanism through which monetary and fiscal policies influence real economic activity and growth. The principle of effective demand makes this clear because it highlights the roles and interdependence of the cost and return on capital. Neither of these two elements is independent of the policy regime. Keynes's (1936, p. 217) argument about these elements, generalized from Wicksell's insights, was very simple. Left to themselves in a *laissez-faire* economy, the mean and variance of the return on capital (the marginal efficiency of capital) would be too low relative to the average cost of capital (the rate of interest) to produce a level of output consistent with full employment. Keynes did, of course, flirt with the idea of a quasi-stationary state in which the marginal efficiency of capital was driven to zero. But like Malthus, he totally misjudged the role that technical progress could play in raising the marginal efficiency of capital once government took a more active role.

Keynes's Monetary Analysis therefore has a central role for government or what we today call fiscal policy. He doubted the ability of monetary policy alone to track the magnitude of the swings in the marginal efficiency of capital that would be generated in a *laissez-faire* economy. For Keynes, monetary policy would only be effective in an economy that had abandoned *laissez-faire* and stabilized the marginal efficiency of capital. Keynes intended the change in perspective about fiscal policy to bring about the structural change necessary to raise the marginal efficiency of capital relative to the cost of capital and in that endeavor governments have been largely successful over the last 60 years. Keynesians like Romer simply fail to recognize the real impact of this revolution in fiscal policy. Real GDP is a function of the economic policy regime so there is no sensible way in which we can assess economic policy by assuming that policy is somehow neutral in the long run.

THE NEW HORIZONTALISM AS A CARICATURE OF MODERN MONETARY POLICY

In a recent paper Svensson (2003) asks: 'What is wrong with Taylor Rules?' In answering this question he expresses dissatisfaction with interest rate rules such as the Taylor Rule on a number of grounds: they are not strictly applied and there are no rules to explain what to do when the rule is not followed; the behavior of the central bank is not treated in an optimizing fashion, and, in any event, no central bank has adopted an explicit interest rate rule. Thus although a Taylor-type interest rate rule may explain the movement of the interest rate controlled by the central bank reasonably well in particular historical periods (Taylor, 1998), these rules have the undesirable features sketched above.

To avoid these limitations Svensson (1997) has always advocated that optimal monetary policy can only be determined in the context of a well-specified macroeconomic model with a clearly specified loss function for the monetary authority. In that context it can then be shown (Romer, 2001, p. 507) that a Taylor Rule can be the optimal monetary policy. However, it is also apparent that the coefficients suggested by Taylor, and applied in most practical applications of the rule, are unlikely to satisfy the properties required by an optimal rule derived in the context of a contemporary version of the aggregate demand–aggregate supply model. Consequently, Svensson (2003) proposes moving beyond the interest rate rule and developing a simple and practical *targeting rule* (as opposed to an instrument rule) that equates the marginal rate of transformation between the policy 'bads', inflation and unemployment (or output gap), as measured by the

Phillips curve, and the marginal rate of substitution between them implied by a social loss function. In this way the authorities behave in an optimizing fashion just like all other agents that inhabit this world. Svensson (2003, p. 467) then proposes seven operational guidelines for the implementation of good monetary policy. The proposal is intended to be pragmatic and flexible (that is, operational), and incorporates judgment and discretion but supposedly not in the *ad hoc* fashion of the instrument rule approach. Despite the analytical rigor required to establish the operational optimum policy, everything is to be explained in transparent monetary policy reports of the type released by the Reserve Bank of New Zealand, the Bank of England and the Riksbank. Although there is much in Svensson's proposal with which all monetary economists may sympathize, it remains a misleading caricature of modern monetary policy.

To begin with, it is apparent that Svensson's (1997, 2003) analyses of optimal monetary policy are conducted in the context of models characterized by the natural rate hypothesis. In other words all these models have a unique natural rate of unemployment that is determined by real and not monetary factors. It is taken for granted by the *new Horizontalists* like Romer and Svensson that the supply side of any useful macroeconomic model is independent of monetary influence. The natural rate of unemployment, like Wicksell's natural rate of interest, is determined by real forces, such as productivity and the leisure choices of representative agents, independently of monetary policy. Consequently, the rate of inflation is unbounded if output and unemployment stray from their natural rates.

But as exponents of Monetary Analysis like Moore have always argued, this is a caricature of what monetary policy is about. In particular, optimal monetary policy cannot be considered in isolation from fiscal policy. As I have argued above, Keynes's revolution was premised on the view that a structural change to fiscal arrangements was required to stabilize a *laissez-faire* economy by increasing and stabilizing the marginal efficiency of capital (the real return on capital). Without the stabilization of the marginal efficiency of capital, its variability would be too great to be offset by monetary policy, that is, by any operational interest rate or targeting rule. Second, once Keynes's revolution is in place, monetary policy comes into its own but is never neutral in the long run. Monetary policy, by its impact on the real cost of capital, has a powerful influence on the pace of capital accumulation and the productivity of labor. This influence of policy on capital accumulation should link the aggregate demand and aggregate supply curves in any useful macroeconomic model. That link is missing in the models of the *new Horizontalists*.

Post Keynesians have acted to correct that limitation. Lavoie (2003) surveys the issues and develops a novel extension of *new Horizontalist* Real

Analysis to allow for the influence of monetary policy on real long-run equilibrium. Lavoie's model generates a continuum of stable but path-dependent long-run equilibria. Consequently, in Lavoie's model, inflation targeting can lead to a change in the 'natural' real rate of interest and 'natural' rate of growth. Increasing the real rate of interest (cost of borrowing) to bring inflation down results in a permanent rise in the 'natural' real rate of interest and a permanent fall in the 'natural' and actual growth rates. As Lavoie (2003, p. 21) observes, tight '[M]onetary policy has detrimental long-run effects on the real economy'.

For Svensson and Romer, by contrast, increasing the real rate of interest (real cost of borrowing) to bring inflation back into its target band results only in a temporary loss of output as a result of a temporary increase in the real cost of borrowing above the unchanged natural real return on capital. Once inflation falls, the model returns to the unique natural real rate of interest and real return on capital determined solely by the real forces of productivity and thrift.

So far the discussion of the monetary framework for monetary policy has dealt with questions of theory. What is the view of the practitioners? As usual, the position of central bankers is somewhat enigmatic. Central bankers have always paid lip service to the dominant fad in the academic literature while quietly getting on with the job. That was certainly true when monetarism was all the rage and is also true today as no central bankers have formally adopted a Taylor Rule or Svensson's targeting rules. Instead they have either adopted some form of inflation targeting[6] or just got on with the job without specifying any targets at all – what Romer (2001) describes as the 'just do it' approach of Alan Greenspan.

Nevertheless, whatever approach is adopted, it appears that some form of interest rate rule explains the adjustment of 'bank rate' by central banks (Taylor, 1998). Furthermore, it is apparent that the framework for inflation targeting is compatible with the analytical framework proposed by post Keynesians. The Australian case, which is comprehensively outlined by Stevens (2003), is a particularly good example of what has become known as flexible inflation targeting. It is a good example because it is clear that the Reserve Bank of Australia has a philosophy of monetary policy that aims to maximize the growth rate of the economy. To achieve that objective it aims to avoid significant movements in the real rate of interest (real cost of borrowing).

The inflation-targeting regime facilitates the creation of a low inflation environment within which the risks of real interest rate volatility are reduced. The inflation-targeting framework aims to achieve that outcome in several ways: (i) by providing an anchor for inflationary expectations to tie down wage claims and the bond market; (ii) by providing a coherent framework in which changes to interest rates can be explained (not always without tension); and (iii), by adopting a forward looking stance to monetary policy, acting in a pre-emptive fashion to moderate the business cycle and so head off excessive movements in the real cost of borrowing. Excessive volatility in the real rate of interest is thought to have a negative impact on growth.

That said, it is difficult to deduce from their actions what theoretical vision lies behind the actions of central bankers. Many no doubt accept the real-monetary dichotomy of the *new Horizontalists*. However, from examination of how decisions are taken within this framework, it appears to me that what is done has a lot more in common with the post Keynesian approach to monetary policy than the implementation of optimal monetary policy in the context of Real Analysis. Central bankers certainly do not apply a Taylor or other interest rate rule in mechanical fashion, and it was never intended that they should. Monetary policy will always require a lot of analysis and some element of discretion (Taylor, 1993). The challenge for post Keynesians is to grasp the opportunity presented by the use of interest rates as the instrument of monetary policy, and complete the old *Horizontalist* revolution by installing the long-run non-neutrality of money at the centre of monetary policy. Reducing the average rate of unemployment even by one or two percentage points would be a goal worth achieving.

CONCLUDING REMARKS

In this chapter I have argued that although Moore's *Horizontalist* analysis of the money supply process has been largely accepted by monetary theorists and practitioners, the theoretical framework in which the *new Horizontalist* money supply process is embedded remains the Real Analysis rejected by Moore. As many post Keynesians have stressed, money is neutral in the long run in the models of the *new Horizontalists*. In that respect little has changed from the days of the IS-LM model.

The IS-LM model was clearly akin to the Ptolemaic model of the solar system in the sense that it generated accurate (qualitative) predictions of the impact of changes in monetary policy on interest rates even though it is now acknowledged to be a false model, as DeLong (2000) has stressed. But the *new Horizontalists* have embraced an equally Ptolemaic IS-MP model because nothing of analytical substance has changed from the IS-LM model. Parts of the model are more descriptively realistic, but all other features of the model remain consistent with the Real Analysis rejected by Moore. The *new Horizontalists* have not embraced Monetary Analysis.

One consequence is that they fail to grasp the importance of the fundamental structural change that has occurred in the post-World War II economy that raised the marginal efficiency of capital relative to the rate of interest. The success of Keynes's revolution was necessary to create the environment for successful monetary policy. Instead, it seems that *new Horizontalists* now interpret this success as confirmation of the long-run neutrality of money!

On the question of the appropriate framework for the analysis of contemporary monetary policy, the model presented by Lavoie (2003) demonstrates that post Keynesians now have a golden opportunity to press home their analysis of monetary policy and install the long-run non-neutrality of money at the core of monetary policy and theory. That would be a fitting tribute to Basil and other post Keynesians who challenged conventional wisdom in the 1970s and 80s.

NOTES

1. Kaldor (1981) was another prominent critic of the *Verticalist* idea that the money supply was, or could be rendered, exogenous.
2. For a discussion of the distinction between Real and Monetary Analysis, see Rogers (1989).
3. For convenience, the complete list is reproduced in Appendix 1.
4. These points are reproduced in Appendix 2.
5. The list of advantages is presented in Appendix 3.
6. As Romer (2001, p. 509) shows, inflation targeting may be the optimal policy in the context of a suitably specified aggregate demand and supply model.

REFERENCES

DeLong B.J. (2000) 'How to Teach Monetary Policy: Do Central Banks Set the Interest Rate, or Do They Target the Money Stock?' http://www.j-bradford-delong.net/

Kaldor, N. (1981) *Origins of the New Monetarism*, Cardiff: University College of Cardiff Press.

Keynes, J.M. (1936) *The General Theory of Employment, Interest and Money*. Reprinted in *The Collected Writings of John Maynard Keynes*, vol. VII, London: Macmillan.

Lavoie, M. (2003) 'A Post-Keynesian alternative to the New Consensus on Monetary Policy', unpublished paper, University of Ottawa.

Moore, B.J. (1988) *Horizontalists and Verticalists: The Macroeconomics of Credit Money*, New York: Cambridge University Press.

Rogers, C. (1989) *Money, Interest and Capital, A Study in the Foundations of Monetary Theory*, Cambridge: Cambridge University Press.

Rogers, C. and T.K. Rymes (2000) 'The Disappearance of Keynes's Nascent Theory of Banking between the Treatise and the General Theory', in John Smithin (ed.), *What is Money?*, London: Routledge, 257–69.

Romer, D. (2000) 'Keynesian Macroeconomics without the LM Curve', *Journal of Economic Perspectives*, 14(2), 149–69.

Romer, D. (2001) *Advanced Macroeconomics*, 2nd edition, New York: McGraw-Hill.

Romer, D. (2002) 'Short-Run Fluctuations', unpublished manuscript, University of California, Berkeley. Available at: http://emlab.berkeley.edu/users/dromer/indexshtml

Stevens, G. (2003) 'Inflation Targeting: A Decade of Australian Experience', Reserve Bank of Australia.

Svensson, L.E.O. (1997) 'Inflation Forecast Targeting: Implementing and Monitoring Inflation Targets', *European Economic Review*, 41, 1111–46.

Svensson, L.E.O. (2003) 'What is Wrong with Taylor Rules?' *Journal of Economic Literature*, XLI(2), 426–77.

Taylor, J.B. (1993) 'Discretion versus Policy Rules in Practice', *Carnegie-Rochester Conference Series on Public Policy*, 39, 195–214.

Taylor, J.B. (1998) 'An Historical Analysis of Monetary Policy Rules', *National Bureau of Economic Research*, Working Paper 6768.

Wicksell K. (1898) *Interest and Prices*, translated by R.F. Kahn (1936), Macmillan: London.

Woodford, M. (2000) 'Monetary Policy in a World Without Money', National Bureau of Economic Research, Working Paper 7853.

APPENDIX 1: MOORE'S LIST OF 16 FUNDAMENTALLY FALSE PROPOSITIONS OF CONTEMPORARY MONETARY THEORY

1. Strong positive correlation between nominal money and nominal income is evidence for the quantity theory, even if prices fail to move proportionally to money 'in the short run'.
2. The central bank determines the nominal money stock but has no control over the real money stock.
3. The public chooses the real money stock but has no control over the nominal money stock.
4. The demand for money is a stable function of a few economic variables.
5. Observed changes in the nominal stock of money are best interpreted as nominal money 'shocks'.
6. Money is neutral in the long run. Agents care only about 'real' things such as goods, leisure, and effort, and have no money illusion ('the axiom of reals').
7. Government deficits are responsible for high interest rates.
8. Real and monetary forces (IS and LM relationships) are conceptually independent.
9. Income adjusts to equate planned investment and planned saving.
10. Real interest rates are determined in the long run by real forces of productivity and thrift.
11. Nominal interest rates have two components: a stable 'real' rate of interest and an inflation premium based on the expected rate of inflation.
12. The real balance (Pigou) effect operates to make aggregate demand inversely related to the price level.
13. Downward wage flexibility provides the economic system with a self-adjusting tendency towards full employment.
14. Inflation is caused by an excess supply of money.
15. Saving determines investment and so governs the rate of capital accumulation.
16. Inflation serves primarily to redistribute wealth between debtors and creditors.

APPENDIX 2: MOORE'S SIX ESSENTIAL FEATURES OF CREDIT MONEY SYSTEMS

1. There are fundamental differences between commodity, fiat and credit money.
2. The supply of credit money is endogenous in the statistical sense. It is invalid to regress income on credit money as if monetary changes were an exogenous variable.
3. The supply of credit money is also endogenous in the control sense. The exogenous variable is the price at which central banks supply base money on demand, which determines the general level of short-term interest rates.
4. The supply of credit money is credit driven, so that the money supply responds to changes in the demand for credit.
5. The supply of credit money is also demand determined. As a result an increase in the supply of credit money does not imply the existence of excess money balances. The notion of an independent supply and demand schedule is not applicable to a credit money economy. Demand and supply functions for credit money are not identifiable.
6. With regard to the definition of a particular credit money aggregate, the relevant magnitude for macroeconomic analysis, as will be shown, is the change in total credit granted by depository institutions. This corresponds loosely to the change in broad monetary aggregates.

APPENDIX 3: ROMER'S NEW HORIZONTALIST ANALYSIS – THE CLAIMED ADVANTAGES

1. The assumption that the central bank follows an interest rate rule is more realistic than the assumption that it targets the money supply.
2. The new approach describes monetary policy in terms of the real interest rate.
3. A real interest rate rule is simpler than the LM curve.
4. In the new approach, the aggregate demand curve relates inflation and output.
5. In the simplest version of the model there is no simultaneity.
6. The model's dynamics are straightforward and reasonable.
7. With the new approach, the correct concept of money to consider is unambiguous. [i.e. base money]
8. One can fully incorporate endogenous changes in expected inflation into the analysis of the aggregate demand side of the model.
9. The same framework can be used to analyze a closed economy, floating exchange rates, and fixed exchange rates.
10. With the new approach, one can show how a fixed exchange rate constrains monetary policy without adopting the unrealistic view that it completely determines it.
11. The new approach shows the asymmetry in a fixed exchange rate system; the central bank is free to pursue policies that create reserve gains, but beyond some point cannot pursue policies that create reserve losses.

17. Gradualism in the adjustment of official interest rates: some partial explanations

Charles Goodhart

CENTRAL BANK REACTION FUNCTIONS

After many decades during which mainstream economic theorists posited that Central Banks either did, or certainly should, fix the monetary base, with interest rates being subsequently determined endogenously (the famous IS/LM diagram), realism has finally triumphed (Bindseil, 2004; Goodhart, 2002). It is now accepted that, not only do Central Banks set official interest rates (which would be hard to deny given the publicity surrounding the meetings of FOMC (Federal Open Market Committee), MPC (Monetary Policy Committee) in the UK, ECB (European Central Bank), BoJ (Bank of Japan) for just that purpose), but that such procedures can be (nearly) optimal so long as Central Banks adjust interest rates appropriately and endogenously in response to foreseen developments in the economy (Woodford, 2003).

Most empirical research on the question of how Central Banks actually do, and also should, set official interest rates have been based on (what have become known as) Taylor-type reaction functions, whereby the Central Bank adjusts its interest rate in response to current deviations of inflation from target and of output from its estimated equilibrium, that is, the output gap (Taylor, 1993, 1999). Although the preference function is usually set out in quadratic form, the empirical studies have usually examined a linear equation of the form:

$$i_t = a + b_1(\pi_t - \pi^*) + b_2 x_t + \varepsilon_t \qquad (17.1)$$

where i_t is the current level of the interest rate, a is a constant equal to the equilibrium real rate of interest plus the target rate of inflation, π_t is current inflation, π^* is the target rate, x_t is the output gap, and ε_t a stochastic error term.

It was soon discovered, however, that such estimated equations did not fit well unless a lagged dependent variable was added, extending the equation to the following form:

$$i_t = a + b_1(\pi_t - \pi^*) + b_2 x_t + b_3 i_{t-1} + \varepsilon_t \qquad (17.2)$$

In such regressions the value of b_3 was usually found to be quite close to, but somewhat lower than, unity, often around 0.8 or 0.9. This was generally ascribed to a tendency for the short-run official response to a shock likely to affect the output gap and/or inflation to be much smaller than the ultimate long-run full equilibrium; such behavior was usually attributed to the reasons for cautious gradualism first identified by Brainard (1967).

Further work on the statistical characteristics of the time paths of official interest rates (see Sack, 1998, 2000; Sack and Wieland, 2000; Goodhart, 1999) revealed that their particular feature was long series of small interest rate changes of the same sign, continuations of similar signed (small) rate changes being far more, and strongly significantly so, likely than reversals.

It was, and remains, far from clear that such a gradualist time path is optimal. As I wrote in my 1999 paper (pp. 235–6),

> The key point is that the MPC should choose an appropriate future horizon at which to aim to return to the inflation target set by the Chancellor. By doing so, they should come close to minimising the variance of both output and inflation. Given that horizon, how then should the monetary authorities operate, according to the principles that flow from our models of the economy, always remembering, and I really want to emphasise this, that in most of these models the only uncertainty in the system is additive and stochastic?
>
> The answer to that conditional question is fairly clear. We should each month alter interest rates so that the expected value of our target, the forecast rate of inflation at the appropriate horizon about 18 months to two years hence, should exactly equal the desired rate of 2½%. Lars Svensson has written several papers (e.g. 1997a, 1997b, 1999) on the optimality of such a procedure. If we start from an initial position in which the predicted forecast value of inflation is already close to the objective, then as a first approximation we should expect interest rates to respond to the unanticipated element in the incoming news. Since this is by definition a martingale series, often somewhat loosely termed a 'random walk', then, on these assumptions, an optimally conducted interest rate path also ought to be nearly random walk. This is, broadly, what the generality of our economic models imply.

Neither I, nor I believe most of my colleagues, notably Willem Buiter, consciously aimed at gradualism, in the sense that we regularly voted to change interest rates by less than the amount we considered necessary to return inflation to target. Moreover my subsequent, and still continuing, work on the publicly available data on MPC forecasts supports the claim that the MPC's objectives were, indeed, to change interest rates so that inflation at the forecast horizon, two years, that is, eight quarters $t + 8$ ahead, would be driven back to the target level, RPIX (Retail Price Index excluding the direct effects of interest rates on the standard RPI) at 2.5 per cent. Thus in my paper 'What is the Monetary Policy Committee Attempting to Achieve?' (2004a), I conclude that, 'What I claim to have established is that the MPC has indeed aimed to drive the inflation forecast into line with target at a two-year horizon, with this latter horizon being well determined empirically'.

Subsequently I have been exploring how regressions, of the general form of equation (17.2), for Taylor-type reaction functions alter if these were run against the relevant *forecasts* (for inflation and output[1]) rather than actuals. The key result for me (readers can find all the results set out in Goodhart, 2004c), was that at a horizon of $t + 8$, the MPC appeared to act almost exactly so as to drive the forecast deviation of inflation from target[2] back into line with the 2.5 per cent target.

The key equation was:

$$i_t = -0.12 + \underset{(0.43)}{2.29}\,(\pi_{t+8} - 2.5\%) - \underset{(0.27)}{0.18}\,(dy_{t+8} - 2.25) + \underset{(0.09)}{1.01}\,i_{t-1}:$$

$$R^2 = 0.92,\ DW = 2.39 \qquad (17.3)$$

where dy_{t+8} is the rate of growth of output at $t + 8$ over the same quarter one year ago, that is, at $t + 4$, and 2.25 is the assumed sustainable trend rate of growth. Note that this suggests that the MPC changes the level of interest rates (NB the coefficient on the lagged dependent variable is exactly unity) by a large amount (2.29) for every unit of deviation of inflation from target. In the MPC's pamphlet on 'The Transmission Mechanism of Monetary Policy', the effect of a 1 per cent change of interest rates on inflation after eight quarters is close to 0.3 per cent. Multiply 0.3 by 2.29, and the implication is that the MPC acted *immediately* to offset almost all the foreseen deviation of inflation from target, that is, no hint of any evidence of any intended gradualism, or of long-run responses being a multiple of short-run responses.

Since the coefficient on the lagged dependent variable (at the horizon of $t + 8$) was almost exactly unity, this suggested that the proper specification would be in first difference; this had the advantage that we could test whether lagged (quarterly) changes in interest rates entered the reaction function. The results were:

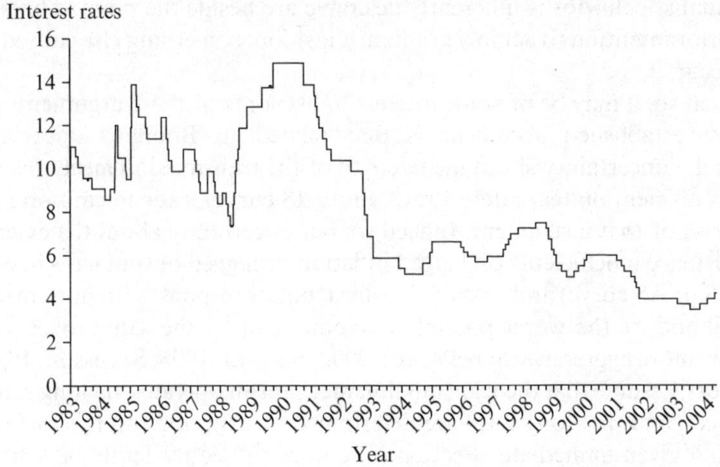

Figure 17.1 *The time path of official short-term interest rates*

$$di_t = \underset{(0.46)}{2.32}(\pi_{t+8} - 2.5) - \underset{(0.16)}{0.28}(dy_{t+8} - 2.25) + \underset{(0.19)}{0.02}di_{t-1} - \underset{(0.15)}{0.17}di_{t-2}:$$

$$R^2 = 0.74,\ DW = 2.45 \qquad (17.4)$$

Note that there is no sign of auto-correlation of interest rate changes, nor of gradualism, in this framework.

What, however, I find remarkable is that, although there is considerable evidence that the MPC was *not* behaving in a gradualist fashion, still the actual outcome for the time path of interest rates appears to have been just as auto-correlated, with similar long runs of continuations (and few reversals) in interest rate changes, as in earlier years or as in other countries. This can be seen in Figure 17.1, where the frequency of reversals is, if anything, lower, and the number of continuations higher, in recent years than before (whether you take the break date as occurring in 1993 with the adoption of Inflation Targetry, or in 1997 with the adoption of Operational Independence).

So what is going on?

ARGUMENTS FOR GRADUALIST BEHAVIOR

The central paradox of the first section is that the available evidence is that the MPC did *not* act in a gradualist fashion, and yet the outcome in the UK looked like gradualism. So on this reading of the evidence, arguments that gradualist behavior is inherently desirable are beside the point. There was no prior intention to act in a gradualist fashion; something else caused that to occur.

Even so, it may be of some interest to list some of these arguments. The oldest established argument is that related to Brainard uncertainty, whereby uncertainty about the strength of the transmission mechanism (of the coefficient on real interest rates in the IS curve) leads to caution in the exercise of that instrument. Indeed so, but uncertainty about the extent of persistence (coefficients on lagged inflation or lagged output gaps in either the IS or AS curve) and so-called 'robust' policy responses (to minimize the likelihood of the worst possible outcome) can by the same token make policy more aggressive (Schellekens, 2002; Sargent, 1998; Svensson, 1997c).

Next, assume that the transmission mechanism operates via long rates of interest, and that long rates are determined by expected future short rates. Then a given immediate effect on long rates can equivalently be achieved by an immediate spike in short rates, expected to last only a short period, or by a much smaller change in short rates expected to last for a long period (see Figure 17.2). If there are reasons to lessen the volatility of the level of short rates (for example, for reasons relating to the non-payment of interest on cash and hence an effect on the demand for money, or because of the

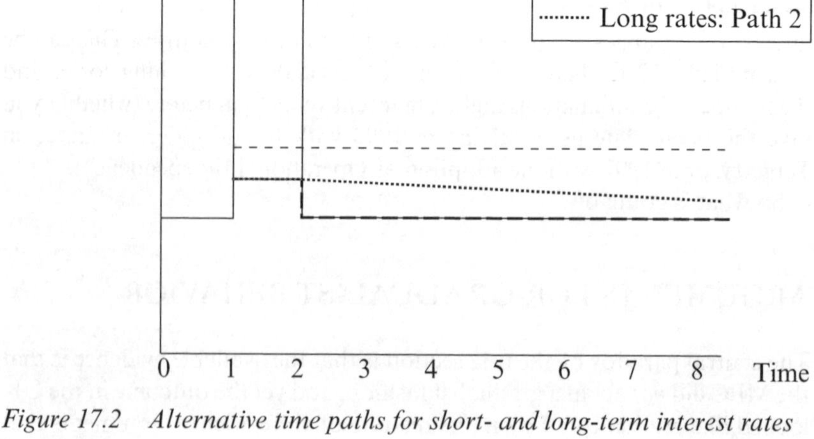

Figure 17.2 Alternative time paths for short- and long-term interest rates

zero bound on nominal interest rates; see Woodford, 2003, Chapter 4), then you want to keep the change in short rates, following some observed shock, small but persistent, as in Figure 17.2. Note, however, that there is only one change in interest rates there; the Woodford argument in its basic form is for persistence, not gradualism. The two are contrasted in Figure 17.3.

This example, however, relates only to a single shock. Assume, instead, that there is a sequence of shocks, and that the authorities can distinguish between major and minor shocks after they have hit. Then with large shocks hitting at A and B, and small shocks at intervening dates, a policy of a single step change (held for a long persistent period) gives a pattern with a lot of reversals as in Figure 17.4. It is difficult to see what the authorities are doing, so the response of long rates to any change in short rates may be muted. If, on the other hand, the authorities combine persistence with gradualism, as in Figure 17.5, then the longer-run policy stance of the authorities becomes far more easily discernible. Martin Ellison (2003) has written on 'The Learning Cost of Interest Rate Reversals' and this is, in some part, a diagrammatic exposition of that.

A related problem facing the authorities is that it is difficult, perhaps impossible, for outsiders to distinguish between a random walk path for policy that *perfectly* offsets the martingale path of shocks (and if 'shocks' do not follow such a martingale are they properly described as shocks?) and

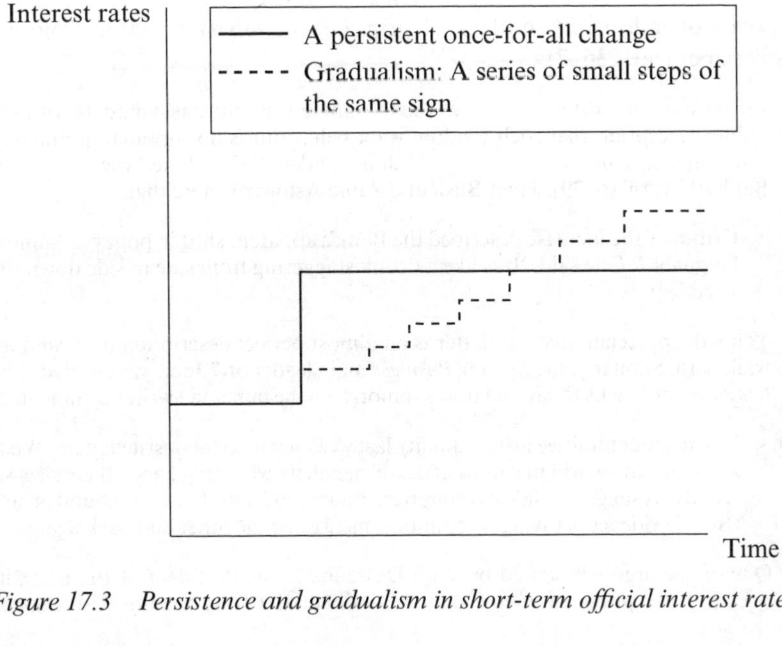

Figure 17.3 Persistence and gradualism in short-term official interest rates

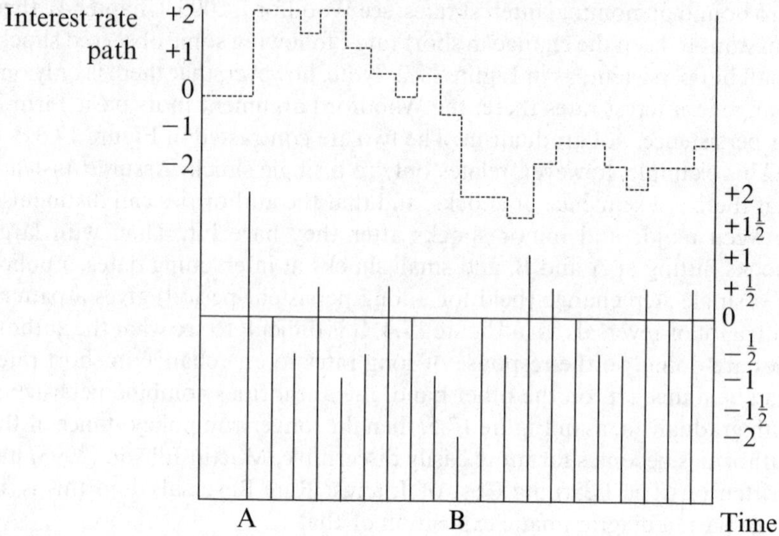

Notes: 0 is the neutral rate of (real) interest rates. This shows the reaction, left-hand side, of interest rates to expected inflation shocks. The bars at the bottom measure shocks to (expected) inflation, with scale on the right-hand side.

Figure 17.4 Time-varying shocks and reversals to interest rate changes

a policy of indecision and lack of grip. Let me repeat a section from my 1999 paper (pp. 236–7):

> I want to contrast the normative theory inherent in our basic models with the public perception that such random walk behaviour is not optimal in practice. Thus, in *The Times* on Thursday, 11 June, under the headline 'Anger grows at Bank's U-turn' (p. 29), Janet Bush and Anne Ashworth state that,
>
> > Critics of the increase described the Bank's apparent shift in policy as 'almost laughable'. One said: 'It is like a drunk staggering from side to side down the street'.
>
> You will appreciate that this latter is an almost perfect description of a random walk path. Similarly, the *Sunday Business* main leader of 7 June was entitled 'The fickleness of hawks today and doves tomorrow'; the unnamed writer commented,
>
> > Where the committee lost credibility last week lies in its inconsistency. . . . What is the outside world meant to make of members who can change their view so readily? It suggests a fickle committee, influenced by the latest anecdotal or statistical evidence, swaying its opinions one way or the other and back again.
>
> One of the arguments used by Wim Duisenberg, the President of the ECB, in rejecting the publication not only of individual voting records but also of

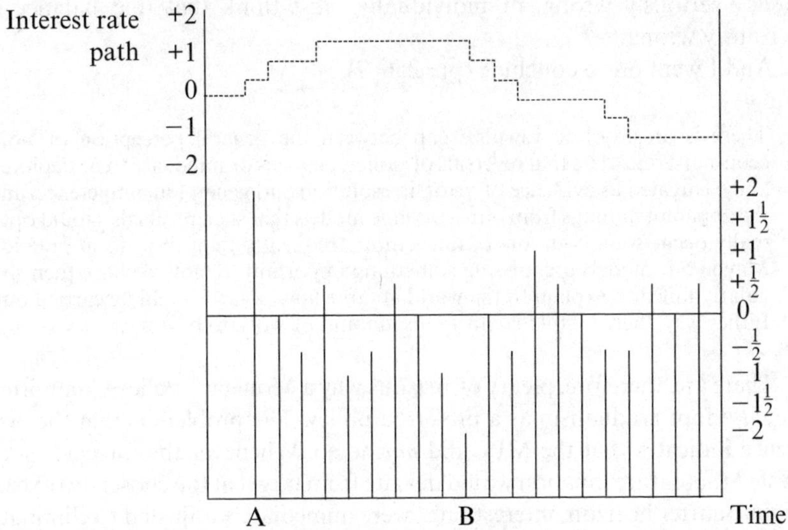

Notes: 0 is the neutral rate of (real) interest rates. This shows the reaction, left-hand side, of interest rates to expected inflation shocks. The bars at the bottom measure shocks to (expected) inflation, with scale on the right-hand side.

Figure 17.5 How gradualism can help to clarify the direction of policy

minutes for some long duration is apparently (and this passage is in direct quotes in Robert Chote's *Financial Times* article on 1 June (p. 10)) that:

> Publication of the minutes soon after decisions have been taken or meetings have taken place will – and this is only human – make it more difficult for individual participants in the discussion to change their minds and be convinced of the arguments of others.

Now this struck a particular chord with me; for example, yet another commentator, Jonathan Loynes, writing in *Greenwell Gilt Weekly* on 18 May, wrote,

> Of course, this does not mean that Professor Goodhart cannot switch *back* to the Hawks. If his change of heart was driven by recent softer earnings numbers then the latest pick-up could cause him to think again. But an immediate about-turn is most unlikely, if only for reasons of credibility.

Wim Duisenberg presumably now doubts my humanity, Jonathan Loynes my credibility. Yet let me reprise once again. If policy is roughly on course to deliver the desired objective, then policy should be finely balanced, and should react to incoming unanticipated news in an approximately random walk fashion. A committee, or an individual within that, who consistently votes the same way for month after month either has got the balance of policy seriously wrong, or individually must think that that balance is seriously wrong.

And I went on to conclude (pp. 256–7),

> There is an absolute yawning gap between the general perception of non-economist outsiders that reversals of policy, changes of mind, are to be deplored and castigated as evidence of error, irresolution and general incompetence, and the apparent findings from our economic models that such reversals should optimally occur some four, or so, times more frequently than they do in practice. Maybe our models are missing something important. If not, we have then singularly failed to explain to the world at large how policy should be carried out. Either way, there is still an enormous amount of work to be done.

There are, therefore, plenty of reasons why a Monetary Policy Committee *might* adopt gradualism as a preferred policy. The problem is that the evidence indicates that the MPC did *not* do so. Whenever the forecasts suggested that future inflation would deviate from target at the chosen two-year, eight-quarter horizon, interest rates were immediately adjusted to eliminate that deviation. So why were interest rate changes auto-correlated?

THE CONSTANT INTEREST RATE ASSUMPTION

One candidate explanation is that this arises quasi-automatically from the forecasting and decision-making procedures hitherto espoused by the MPC. Partly for historical reasons (owing to the unwillingness of the Bank to be thought to be infringing on the Chancellor's prerogative to set interest rates in the period 1993–7), the Bank has traditionally done its main forecast on the conditioning assumption that interest rates are to be held constant at the level set at the latest previous decision date. As is well known, constant nominal interest rates, beyond some horizon, will generate Wicksellian instability. Thus, except in rather rare cases, the trend (upwards or downwards) in the rate of inflation after the published horizon is likely to continue, and indeed often to become more exaggerated.[3] An example is given in Figure 17.6.

It is easy to see from this that simply rolling the forecast forward one quarter is likely to re-create the prior deviation of inflation from its target. Even if the MPC on each occasion thought that it was eliminating the deviation, a similar deviation was likely to recur at the next forecasting round. So auto-correlation of interest rate adjustments, whether for good or for ill, was, in a sense, built into the methods used by the MPC.

Undoubtedly there have been instances when the inflation forecast beyond the two-year horizon did show a continuing (occasionally even

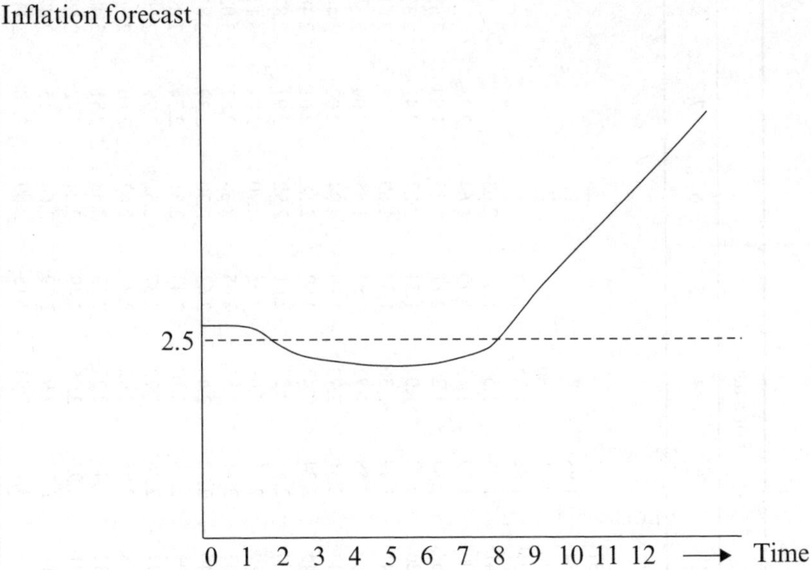

Figure 17.6 *How a constant interest rate assumption may lead to auto-correlated interest rate changes*

a worsening) trend. This might then well suggest a continuing future path of interest rate changes of the same sign. Although now an outsider to such decisions, my impression is that the forecast/decision-making round in February 2004 has been a case in point. This syndrome is one of the reasons why critics have criticized a constant-interest-rate (CIR) path as a conditioning assumption for the forecast, and would prefer instead some kind of explicit path, as done in New Zealand.[4]

Nevertheless the question of how far the CIR assumption necessarily induces auto-correlation into the MPC's decision-making process is, at least in part, an empirical issue. One way of trying to get a quantitative handle on this is to note that inflation at time t is associated with higher output (growth)[5] at time $t - 4$. Thus if it was the case that auto-correlations in interest rates were due to rolling forward trended inflation between $t + 8$ and $t + 12$, then one might expect to see that accompanied with above average growth in output forecasts from $t + 4$ to $t + 8$. In Table 17.1 we show the forecasts (modal) for output growth, compared in column 2 with contemporaneous estimates of output growth (see Goodhart, 2004b for derivation and detail).[6] This table is arranged so that consecutive forecasts for the same date are plotted horizontally. Thus for 2002 Q1, the contemporaneous estimate of output growth was 1.37 per cent. The fore-

Table 17.1 Bank forecast of GDP

	Output % growth 2003 estimate	Output % growth contemporaneous	Forecast t = 0	1	2	3	4	5	6	7	8
1997 Q3	3.19	3.89	3.39								
Q4	3.36	3.93	4.02	2.82							
1998 Q1	3.38	2.88	3.04	3.54	2.37						
Q2	2.79	2.47	2.41	2.33	2.84	1.85					
Q3	3.51	2.40	1.99	1.86	1.76	2.11	1.80				
Q4	2.82	2.02	1.95	1.66	1.71	1.64	1.33	1.83			
1999 Q1	2.72	1.70	1.16	1.28	1.41	1.76	1.59	1.41	2.03		
Q2	2.61	1.64	0.79	0.77	1.00	1.19	1.83	1.79	1.64	2.38	
Q3	2.60	2.30	1.32	0.99	0.68	0.84	1.29	2.11	2.15	1.93	2.63
Q4	3.26	2.75	2.50	1.90	1.20	0.83	1.01	1.54	2.27	2.41	2.33
2000 Q1	3.96	3.11	2.92	2.82	2.41	1.49	1.36	1.33	1.69	2.39	2.61
Q2	4.30	3.36	2.94	2.70	2.80	2.58	1.72	1.82	1.65	2.09	2.56
Q3	3.94	2.98	2.56	2.58	2.47	2.51	2.73	1.99	2.24	2.02	2.44
Q4	2.93	2.72	2.73	2.48	2.45	2.24	2.42	2.80	2.58	2.61	2.48
2001 Q1	2.56	3.01	2.86	2.76	2.50	2.57	2.27	2.61	2.92	2.97	2.83
Q2	2.23	2.65	2.25	2.30	2.39	2.51	2.61	2.35	2.70	3.01	3.11
Q3	1.80	2.24	1.62	2.03	2.07	2.31	2.53	2.65	2.38	2.82	3.02
Q4	1.95	1.71	2.09	1.82	2.46	2.22	2.40	2.63	2.70	2.39	2.83
2002 Q1	1.44	1.37	1.37	1.92	1.98	2.68	2.10	2.48	2.81	2.74	2.39
Q2	1.55	1.75	1.35	1.48	1.97	2.26	2.72	2.37	2.51	2.79	2.70
Q3	1.93	2.26	1.82	1.62	1.78	2.05	2.42	2.71	2.62	2.50	2.76
Q4	1.99	2.31	2.29	2.34	2.32	2.43	2.27	2.33	2.48	2.81	2.48
2003 Q1	1.84	2.10	2.53	3.06	2.91	2.95	2.76	2.49	2.24	2.42	2.89
Q2	1.98	1.84	2.38	2.58	3.18	2.75	2.95	2.79	2.66	2.15	2.42
Q3	1.89	1.89	1.59	2.00	2.33	3.17	2.94	3.15	2.69	2.70	2.11

cast of output growth made in February 2002 ($t = 0$) was also 1.37 per cent; the forecast made for 2002 Q1 in February 2001 ($t = 4$) was 2.10 per cent; and in February 2000 for 2002 Q1 ($t = 8$) was 2.39 per cent. This implies, however, that the forecasts for subsequent quarters at each quarterly decision date appear diagonally. Thus in 1998 Q1, the forecast in February for the contemporaneous quarter ($t = 0$) was 3.04 per cent, the forecast for 1998 Q2 was 2.33 per cent, for 1998 Q3 was 1.76 per cent, for 1998 Q4 was 1.64 per cent, and so on down diagonally. In order to show more clearly what the forecasts for output growth for subsequent quarters were at each quarter's date, we rotate this table, also showing in column 1 the interest rate decision.

This is shown in Table 17.2. The associated forecasts for inflation are shown in Tables 17.3 and 17.4.

These tables, however, reveal that there appears to be a common feature of the forecasts for output growth. At short horizons these forecasts tend to underestimate outcomes, even more so when one uses the latest available data rather than those estimated contemporaneously. The most pessimistic forecasts are those for $t + 0$ and $t + 1$. At longer horizons the forecasts have tended to become steadily more optimistic on average, so that by the longest horizon, $t + 7$, $t + 8$, growth has been generally expected to be slightly above trend (as contrasted with expectations of below trend growth around $t + 0$ till $t + 4$). Owing to the short sample, and the variance of the forecasts, such differences are, however, barely significant.

Nevertheless these, possibly systematic, tendencies for the output growth forecasts to change as the horizon lengthens raise the question whether one should compare each run of forecasts to the overall forecast average, or to the average forecast at each horizon. I have chosen to do the latter. Table 17.5 then reports the deviation of each forecast from actual *after* adjusting for the average bias in the forecast at that horizon (that is, the sum of deviations in each column adds to zero). Somewhat arbitrarily, we have given equal weight to each deviation between $t + 4$ and $t + 8$, and the resulting sum of these deviations is given in column 9.

The basic hypothesis is that strongly positive deviations (actual greater than forecast), implying low expected growth in the second year, would be associated with downwards trending inflation, and so under CIR would suggest a decline in interest rates in the next quarter, and vice versa for negative deviations. Again, somewhat arbitrarily, we assume that the sum of deviations is too low to influence a potential change in policy when it falls between $+1$ and -1. The resulting implied sign of interest rate effect is shown in column 10, and the actual sign of the change in the final column.

Table 17.2 GDP forecasts and associated interest rate changes

Date	IR	IR Change	GDP Actual	Forecast t =								
				0	1	2	3	4	5	6	7	8
1997 Q3	7	0.75	3.89	3.39	2.82	2.37	1.85	1.8	1.83	2.03	2.38	2.63
Q4	7.25	0.25	3.93	4.02	3.54	2.84	2.11	1.33	1.41	1.64	1.93	2.33
1998 Q1	7.25	0.00	2.88	3.04	2.33	1.76	1.64	1.59	1.79	2.15	2.41	2.61
Q2	7.25	0.00	2.47	2.41	1.86	1.71	1.76	1.83	2.11	2.27	2.39	2.56
Q3	7.50	0.25	2.4	1.99	1.66	1.41	1.19	1.29	1.54	1.69	2.09	2.44
Q4	6.75	−0.75	2.02	1.95	1.28	1	0.84	1.01	1.33	1.65	2.02	2.48
1999 Q1	5.50	−1.25	1.7	1.16	0.77	0.68	0.83	1.36	1.82	2.24	2.61	2.83
Q2	5.25	−0.25	1.64	0.79	0.99	1.2	1.49	1.72	1.99	2.58	2.97	3.11
Q3	5.00	−0.25	2.3	1.32	1.9	2.41	2.58	2.73	2.8	2.92	3.01	3.02
Q4	5.50	0.50	2.75	2.5	2.82	2.8	2.51	2.42	2.61	2.7	2.82	2.83
2000 Q1	6.00	0.50	3.11	2.92	2.7	2.47	2.24	2.27	2.35	2.38	2.39	2.39
Q2	6.00	0.00	3.36	2.94	2.58	2.45	2.57	2.61	2.65	2.7	2.74	2.7
Q3	6.00	0.00	2.98	2.56	2.48	2.5	2.51	2.53	2.63	2.81	2.79	2.76
Q4	6.00	0.00	2.72	2.73	2.76	2.39	2.31	2.4	2.48	2.51	2.5	2.48
2001 Q1	5.75	−0.25	3.01	2.86	2.3	2.07	2.22	2.1	2.37	2.62	2.81	2.89
Q2	5.25	−0.50	2.65	2.25	2.03	2.46	2.68	2.72	2.71	2.48	2.42	2.42
Q3	5.00	−0.25	2.24	1.62	1.82	1.98	2.26	2.42	2.33	2.24	2.15	2.11
Q4	4.00	−1.00	1.71	2.09	1.92	1.97	2.05	2.27	2.49	2.66	2.7	
2002 Q1	4.00	0.00	1.37	1.37	1.48	1.78	2.43	2.76	2.79	2.69		
Q2	4.00	0.00	1.75	1.35	1.62	2.32	2.95	2.95	3.15			
Q3	4.00	0.00	2.26	1.82	2.34	2.91	2.75	2.94				
Q4	4.00	0.00	2.31	2.29	3.06	3.18	3.17					
2003 Q1	3.75	−0.25	2.1	2.53	2.58	2.33						
Q2	3.75	0.00	1.84	2.38	2							
Q3	3.50	−0.25	1.89	1.59								

Table 17.3 Bank forecast of RPIX

	RPIX % change over 12 months	Forecast t =								
		0	1	2	3	4	5	6	7	8
1993 Q1	3.50	3.50								
Q2	2.80	3.40	3.40							
Q3	3.30	2.90	3.40	3.00						
Q4	2.70	3.30	3.00	3.20	3.10					
1994 Q1	2.40	2.80	3.60	3.20	3.20	3.40				
Q2	2.40	2.70	3.00	3.50	3.30	3.50	3.40			
Q3	2.00	2.30	2.90	3.10	3.50	3.30	3.60	3.40		
Q4	2.50	2.10	2.60	3.00	3.20	3.40	3.30	3.70	3.30	
1995 Q1	2.80	2.90	1.90	2.70	3.10	3.40	3.40	3.50		
Q2	2.80	2.70	2.80	2.00	3.00	3.40	3.30	3.40	3.60	
Q3	3.10	2.90	3.00	3.10	2.30	3.20	3.40	3.20		
Q4	3.00	3.20	3.00	3.10	3.20	2.40	3.20	3.30	3.20	
1996 Q1	2.90	2.80	3.30	3.20	3.40	2.70	2.80	3.40	3.30	
Q2	2.80	2.70	2.70	3.50	3.50	3.80	2.70	2.40	3.10	
Q3	2.90	2.70	2.50	2.40	3.20	3.40	3.70	2.60	2.40	
Q4	3.10	3.10	2.40	2.30	2.20	3.00	3.20	3.40	2.50	
1997 Q1	2.70	2.70	2.90	2.30	2.30	2.30	2.70	2.90	3.00	
Q2	2.70	2.60	2.40	2.80	2.30	2.20	2.30	2.70	2.80	
Q3	2.70	2.65	2.40	2.20	2.70	2.40	2.40	2.30	2.70	2.80
Q4	2.70	2.60	2.32	2.20	2.20	2.40	2.50	2.40	2.40	2.70
1998 Q1	2.60	2.60	2.51	2.19	2.20	2.30	2.40	2.60	2.40	2.40
Q2	2.80	2.83	2.63	2.42	2.06	2.20	2.50	2.50	2.70	2.50
Q3	2.50	2.51	2.35	2.42	2.27	1.99	2.30	2.70	2.60	2.80
Q4	2.60	2.54	2.56	2.35	2.41	2.19	2.08	2.50	2.80	2.70

Table 17.3 (continued)

	RPIX % change over 12 months	Forecast t =								
		0	1	2	3	4	5	6	7	8
1999 Q1	2.70	2.49	2.56	2.69	2.41	2.44	2.18	2.24	2.70	2.90
Q2	2.20	2.48	2.53	2.71	2.82	2.37	2.39	2.25	2.36	2.90
Q3	2.10	2.31	2.40	2.55	2.74	2.86	2.30	2.47	2.37	2.50
Q4	2.20	2.20	2.28	2.36	2.61	2.59	2.77	2.26	2.55	2.42
2000 Q1	2.00	1.93	2.12	2.09	2.20	2.52	2.56	2.69	2.27	2.64
Q2	2.20	1.88	1.98	2.06	1.99	2.23	2.49	2.51	2.56	2.35
Q3	2.20	2.38	1.93	1.95	2.02	1.88	2.25	2.47	2.48	2.47
Q4	2.00	2.36	2.28	2.10	2.05	1.84	1.92	2.23	2.47	2.45
2001 Q1	1.90	1.94	2.33	2.26	2.20	2.32	1.72	2.08	2.35	2.56
Q2	2.40	1.90	1.92	2.22	2.39	2.47	2.48	1.80	2.28	2.43
Q3	2.30	2.31	1.90	1.87	2.19	2.48	2.53	2.53	2.19	2.59
Q4	1.90	2.00	2.17	1.91	1.87	2.19	2.62	2.53	2.56	2.53
2002 Q1	2.30	2.14	2.03	2.17	1.91	2.09	2.18	2.68	2.53	2.58
Q2	1.50	2.02	1.87	1.85	1.91	1.94	2.18	2.37	2.70	2.56
Q3	2.10	1.84	2.08	1.96	2.06	1.96	2.03	2.27	2.46	2.72
Q4	2.70	2.64	2.25	2.24	2.11	2.06	2.13	2.16	2.42	2.56
2003 Q1	3.00	2.77	2.73	2.25	2.18	2.13	2.08	2.32	2.39	2.55
Q2	2.80	3.09	2.90	2.72	2.25	2.05	2.13	2.15	2.41	2.53
Q3	2.80	2.85	2.90	2.98	2.72	2.31	2.09	2.18	2.23	2.45

Table 17.4 Inflation forecasts

RPIX Actual	Forecast t = 0	1	2	3	4	5	6	7	8
2.70	2.65	2.32	2.19	2.06	1.99	2.08	2.24	2.36	2.50
2.70	2.60	2.51	2.42	2.27	2.19	2.18	2.25	2.37	2.42
2.60	2.60	2.63	2.42	2.41	2.44	2.39	2.47	2.55	2.64
2.80	2.83	2.35	2.35	2.41	2.37	2.30	2.26	2.27	2.35
2.50	2.51	2.56	2.69	2.82	2.86	2.77	2.69	2.56	2.47
2.60	2.54	2.56	2.71	2.74	2.59	2.56	2.51	2.48	2.45
2.70	2.49	2.53	2.55	2.61	2.52	2.49	2.47	2.47	2.56
2.20	2.48	2.40	2.36	2.20	2.23	2.25	2.23	2.35	2.43
2.10	2.31	2.28	2.09	1.99	1.88	1.92	2.08	2.28	2.59
2.20	2.20	2.12	2.06	2.02	1.84	1.72	1.80	2.19	2.53
2.00	1.93	1.98	1.95	2.05	2.32	2.48	2.53	2.56	2.58
2.20	1.88	1.93	2.10	2.20	2.47	2.53	2.53	2.53	2.56
2.20	2.38	2.28	2.26	2.39	2.48	2.62	2.68	2.70	2.72
2.00	2.36	2.33	2.22	2.19	2.19	2.18	2.37	2.46	2.56
1.90	1.94	1.92	1.87	1.87	2.09	2.18	2.27	2.42	2.55
2.40	1.90	1.90	1.91	1.91	1.94	2.03	2.16	2.39	2.53
2.30	2.31	2.17	2.17	1.91	1.96	2.13	2.32	2.41	2.45
1.90	2.00	2.03	1.85	2.06	2.06	2.08	2.15	2.23	
2.30	2.14	1.87	1.96	2.11	2.13	2.13	2.18		
1.50	2.02	2.08	2.24	2.18	2.05	2.09			
2.10	1.84	2.25	2.25	2.25	2.31				
2.70	2.64	2.73	2.72	2.72					
3.00	2.77	2.90	2.98						
2.80	3.09	2.90							
2.80	2.85								

There is a strong concordance between the implied signed direction of effect and the actual interest rate changes between Q3 1998 and Q2 1999. From Q3 1998 until 1999 Q2, the forecasts for output growth in the second year were consistently gloomy, and each subsequent quarter there were successive downwards adjustments in interest rates. Then in Q3 and Q4 1999 there were more buoyant forecasts for output growth in the second year, and upwards increases in interest rates in Q4 1999 and Q1 2000.

But for the rest of the period that can be examined in this way, the relationship is not strong. In eight cases, either there was no change in actuals when the deviation implied a change, or vice versa; in one case both indicated no change; and there were four instances when the output forecast

Table 17.5 Differential between GDP and forecast

	0	1	2	3	4	5	6	7	8	Sum of Cols 4–8	Sign of implied interest rate change	Sign of actual interest rate change
Q3	0.28	0.87	0.32	0.45	0.45	0.16	−0.26	−0.57	−0.08	−0.30	0	+
Q4	−0.31	−0.90	−0.56	0.12	0.54	0.26	0.07	0.54	0.67	2.08	–	0
1998 Q1	−0.38	−0.10	0.45	0.21	−0.04	−0.18	0.22	0.51	0.75	1.26	–	0
Q2	−0.16	0.30	0.12	−0.23	−0.34	0.16	0.55	0.89	1.05	2.31	–	+
Q3	0.19	0.12	0.10	0.28	0.86	1.18	1.49	1.44	0.79	5.76	–	–
Q4	−0.15	0.18	0.45	1.29	1.59	1.75	1.78	1.13	0.49	6.74	–	–
1999 Q1	0.32	0.63	1.43	1.75	1.60	1.51	0.81	0.28	0.43	4.63	–	–
Q2	0.63	1.07	1.36	1.45	1.49	0.96	0.21	0.21	−0.21	2.66	–	–
Q3	0.76	0.61	0.51	0.61	0.10	−0.11	0.16	−0.19	−0.53	0.57	0	+
Q4	0.03	0.05	0.37	0.30	0.15	0.37	0.02	−0.41	−0.87	−0.74	0	+
2000 Q1	−0.03	0.42	0.32	0.31	0.59	0.27	−0.07	−0.51	−0.77	−0.49	0	0
Q2	0.20	0.16	0.08	0.27	−0.11	−0.44	−0.92	−1.20	−0.70	−3.37	+	0
Q3	0.20	0.00	0.32	−0.03	−0.44	−0.95	−1.37	−0.87	−0.25	−3.88	+	0
Q4	−0.23	0.01	0.07	−0.24	−0.84	−1.14	−0.69	−0.07	0.08	−2.66	+	–
2001 Q1	−0.07	0.11	−0.02	−0.68	−0.88	−0.65	−0.29	−0.33	−0.54	−2.69	+	–
Q2	0.18	−0.03	−0.94	−1.48	−1.12	−0.48	−0.10	−0.15	−0.33	−2.18	+	–
Q3	0.40	−0.35	−0.80	−0.68	−0.31	−0.05	−0.07	−0.14	0.03	−0.54	0	–
Q4	−0.60	−0.79	−0.41	0.04	−0.11	−0.42	−0.75	−0.64				
2002 Q1	−0.22	0.03	0.29	−0.29	−0.81	−0.98	−0.73					
Q2	0.18	0.40	−0.20	−1.02	−1.26	−1.29						
Q3	0.22	−0.27	−1.00	−1.08	−1.20							
Q4	−0.20	−1.20	−1.53	−1.45								
2003 Q1	−0.65	−0.98	−0.63									
Q2	−0.76	−0.35										
Q3	0.08											
Average	0.22	0.24	0.19	0.17	0.15	0.03	−0.07	−0.17	−0.25			

suggested the opposite change to that undertaken, for example, low expected growth but an interest rate increase in Q3 1998, and the reverse combination at the start of 2001.

A further, and essentially, similar test is to take the difference between the forecasts for both output and inflation, between $t + 4$ and $t + 8$, at the time that the forecast was first made (that is, in 1997 Q3 for 1999 Q3), and compare it with the unanticipated changes in the inflation and output forecasts between $t + 8$ and $t + 0$ in successive forecasts. The question that this asks is whether the trends seen in output and inflation in the second year when the forecast was first made could be used to indicate the likely subsequent direction of forecast revisions on subsequent forecasting occasions. The data are shown in Table 17.6. We regress these subsequent revisions (for derivation, see Goodhart, 2004b) against the earlier perceived second year trends, columns 4 and 7.

The results in Table 17.7 show that the second year forecast trends in inflation and output had no relationship with subsequent revisions to the output forecast. However, there are signs that an upwards trend in inflation in the second year *was* positively associated with subsequent upwards revisions to the forecast for inflation. This latter is consistent with the quasi-automatic CIR hypothesis.

Thus the evidence provides *some* support for the CIR hypothesis, but the relationship appears sporadic rather than continual, and at best of moderate strength and explanatory power.

SYSTEMATIC FORECAST ERRORS

We turn next to the final potential cause of gradualism that we shall propose here (though we cannot rule out the possibility that we may have failed to consider other causes).[7] This is that the forecasters tended to make systematic, auto-correlated errors.[8]

On each forecasting occasion, as reported earlier and in more detail in Goodhart (2004c), the MPC normally acted to drive forecast inflation back close into line with target (NB *ex post* forecast inflation at $t + 8$ was throughout the period very close to 2.5 with little variance; see Goodhart, 2004a). Thereafter, however, the errors tended to be in same direction, that is, inflation (and output growth) was systematically under (over) predicted, despite successive changes (gradualism) to offset this. Similarly, if inflation (or output growth) at any particular horizon was under (over) predicted at any particular horizon, it would tend to be similarly under (over) predicted on the next occasion. This is shown in Tables 17.8 and 17.9 where we report the prediction errors for inflation and output growth (relative to

Table 17.6 Forecast at time of initial forecast

	Output		Diff	Inflation		Diff	Actual forecast change in output	Actual forecast change in inflation
	$t+4$	$t+8$		$t+4$	$t+8$			
1999 Q3	1.80	2.63	+0.83	1.99	2.50	+0.51	−1.67	−0.11
Q4	1.33	2.33	+1.00	2.19	2.42	+0.22	−0.87	−0.14
2000 Q1	1.59	2.61	+1.02	2.44	2.64	+0.20	−0.97	−0.94
Q2	1.83	2.56	+0.73	2.37	2.35	−0.02	−0.31	−0.84
Q3	1.29	2.44	+1.14	2.86	2.47	−0.39	−0.36	−0.70
Q4	1.01	2.48	+1.47	2.59	2.45	−0.09	0.10	−0.50
2001 Q1	1.36	2.83	+1.46	2.52	2.56	+0.04	0.25	−0.60
Q2	1.72	3.11	+1.39	2.23	2.43	+0.20	−0.65	−0.40
Q3	2.73	3.02	+0.29	1.88	2.59	+0.71	−0.26	0.00
Q4	2.42	2.83	+0.41	1.84	2.53	+0.69	−0.85	−0.38
2002 Q1	2.27	2.39	+0.12	2.32	2.58	+0.26	−1.42	−0.49
Q2	2.61	2.70	+0.09	2.47	2.56	+0.09	−1.90	−0.66
Q3	2.53	2.76	+0.23	2.48	2.72	+0.24	−1.58	−1.10
Q4	2.40	2.48	+0.08	2.19	2.56	+0.37	−0.86	−0.44
2003 Q1	2.10	2.89	+0.79	2.09	2.55	+0.46	−1.01	−0.18
Q2	2.72	2.42	−0.30	1.94	2.53	+0.59	−0.42	0.23
Q3	2.42	2.11	−0.31	1.96	2.45	+0.49	−0.83	0.08

Table 17.7 Regressions

Actual forecast change in Output = B*(difference in output) + C*(difference in RPIX)

B p-value St. Er.	C p-value St. Er.	R Sq.	DW
−0.33 0.14 0.21	−1.51 0.00 0.47	−0.40	0.85

Actual forecast change in Output = A + B*(difference in output) + C*(difference in RPIX)

A p-value St. Er.	B p-value St. Er.	C p-value St. Er.	R Sq.	DW
−1.08 0.00 0.33	0.45 0.15 0.30	0.01 0.98 0.60	0.18	1.25

Actual forecast change in Inflation = B*(difference in output) + C*(difference in RPIX)

B p-value St. Er.	C p-value St. Er.	R Sq.	DW
−0.45 0.00 0.12	−0.10 0.70 0.26	−0.18	0.78

Actual forecast change in Inflation = A + B*(difference in output) + C*(difference in RPIX)

A p-value St. Er.	B p-value St. Er.	C p-value St. Er.	R Sq.	DW
−0.65 0.00 0.17	0.02 0.87 0.15	0.82 0.01 0.31	0.40	1.51

Table 17.8 Autocorrelation in errors in forecasting GDP growth

	GDP % change over 12 months	Diffferential between GDP and forecast									Average	St. Dev.	1st. O. Autocorr.
		0	1	2	3	4	5	6	7	8			
Q3	3.89	0.5											
Q4	3.93	−0.09	1.11										
1998 Q1	2.88	−0.16	−0.66	0.51									
Q2	2.47	0.06	0.14	−0.37	0.62								
Q3	2.4	0.41	0.54	0.64	0.29	0.6							
Q4	2.02	0.07	0.36	0.31	0.38	0.69	0.19						
1999 Q1	1.7	0.54	0.42	0.29	−0.06	0.11	0.29	−0.33					
Q2	1.64	0.85	0.87	0.64	0.45	−0.19	−0.15	0	−0.74		0.22	0.58	0.48
Q3	2.3	0.98	1.31	1.62	1.46	1.01	0.19	0.15	0.37	−0.33	0.75	0.68	0.61
Q4	2.75	0.25	0.85	1.55	1.92	1.74	1.21	0.48	0.34	0.42	0.97	0.65	0.60
2000 Q1	3.11	0.19	0.29	0.7	1.62	1.75	1.78	1.42	0.72	0.5	1.00	0.64	0.60
Q2	3.36	0.42	0.66	0.56	0.78	1.64	1.54	1.71	1.27	0.8	1.04	0.50	0.56
Q3	2.98	0.42	0.4	0.51	0.47	0.25	0.99	0.74	0.96	0.54	0.59	0.26	0.11
Q4	2.72	−0.01	0.24	0.27	0.48	0.3	−0.08	0.14	0.11	0.24	0.19	0.17	0.14

2001 Q1	3.01	0.15	0.25	0.51	0.44	0.74	0.4	0.09	0.04	0.18	0.31	0.23	0.46
Q2	2.65	0.4	0.35	0.26	0.14	0.04	0.3	−0.05	−0.36	−0.46	0.07	0.31	0.52
Q3	2.24	0.62	0.21	0.17	−0.07	−0.29	−0.41	−0.14	−0.58	−0.78	−0.14	0.43	0.47
Q4	1.71	−0.38	−0.11	−0.75	−0.51	−0.69	−0.92	−0.99	−0.68	−1.12	−0.68	0.32	0.24
2002 Q1	1.37	0	−0.55	−0.61	−1.31	−0.73	−1.11	−1.44	−1.37	−1.02	−0.90	0.47	0.34
Q2	1.75	0.4	0.27	−0.22	−0.51	−0.97	−0.62	−0.76	−1.04	−0.95	−0.49	0.53	0.60
Q3	2.26	0.44	0.64	0.48	0.21	−0.16	−0.45	−0.36	−0.24	−0.5	0.01	0.44	0.71
Q4	2.31	0.02	−0.03	−0.01	−0.12	0.04	−0.02	−0.17	−0.5	−0.17	−0.11	0.17	0.31
2003 Q1	2.1	−0.43	−0.96	−0.81	−0.85	−0.66	−0.39	−0.14	−0.32	−0.79	−0.59	0.28	0.37
Q2	1.84	−0.54	−0.74	−1.34	−0.91	−1.11	−0.95	−0.82	−0.31	−0.58	−0.81	0.31	0.27
Q3	1.89	0.3	−0.11	−0.44	−1.28	−1.05	−1.26	−0.8	−0.81	−0.22	−0.63	0.55	0.44
Average	2.45	0.22	0.24	0.19	0.17	0.15	0.03	−0.07	−0.17	−0.25			
St. Deviation	0.68	0.37	0.57	0.70	0.86	0.89	0.35	0.78	0.70	0.60			
1st O. Autocorr.	0.71	0.34	0.39	0.63	0.74	0.73	0.75	0.76	0.70	0.79			

Table 17.9 *Autocorrelation in errors in forecasting inflation*

	RPIX % change over 12 months	Differential between RPIX and forecast									Average	St. Dev.	1st O. Autocorr.
		0	1	2	3	4	5	6	7	8			
1993 Q1	3.5	0											
Q2	2.8	−0.6	−0.6										
Q3	3.3	0.4	−0.1	0.3									
Q4	2.7	−0.6	−0.3	−0.5	−0.4								
1994 Q1	2.4	−0.4	−1.2	−0.8	−0.8	−1							
Q2	2.4	−0.3	−0.6	−1.1	−0.9	−1.1	−1						
Q3	2	−0.3	−0.9	−1.1	−1.5	−1.3	−1.6	−1.4					
Q4	2.5	0.4	−0.1	−0.5	−0.7	−0.9	−0.8	−1.2	−0.8		−0.58	0.51	0.49
1995 Q1	2.8	−0.1	0.9	0.1	−0.3	−0.6	−0.6	−0.7			−0.19	0.56	0.42
Q2	2.8	0.1	0	0.8	−0.2	−0.6	−0.5	−0.6	−0.8		−0.23	0.52	0.39
Q3	3.1	0.2	0.1	0	0.8	−0.1	−0.3	−0.1			0.09	0.35	−0.06
Q4	3	−0.2	0	−0.1	−0.2	0.6	−0.2	−0.3	−0.2		−0.08	0.29	−0.2
1996 Q1	2.9	0.1	−0.4	−0.3	−0.5	0.2	0.1	−0.5	−0.4		−0.21	0.29	−0.07
Q2	2.8	0.1	0.1	−0.7	−0.7	−1	0.1	0.4	−0.3		−0.25	0.50	0.24
Q3	2.9	0.2	0.4	0.5	−0.3	−0.5	−0.8	0.3	0.5		0.04	0.50	0.34
Q4	3.1	0	0.7	0.8	0.9	0.1	−0.1	−0.3	0.6		0.34	0.46	0.25
1997 Q1	2.7	0	−0.2	0.4	0.4	0.4	0	−0.2	−0.3		0.06	0.30	0.39
Q2	2.7	0.1	0.3	−0.1	0.4	0.5	0.4	0	−0.1		0.19	0.24	0.1
Q3	2.7	0.05	0.3	0.5	0	0.3	0.3	0.4	0	−0.1	0.19	0.21	−0.03
Q4	2.7	0.1	0.38	0.5	0.5	0.3	0.2	0.3	0.3	0	0.29	0.17	0.19

1998 Q1	2.6	0	0.09	0.41	0.4	0.3	0.2	0	0.2	0.2	0.20	0.15	0.32
Q2	2.8	−0.03	0.17	0.38	0.74	0.6	0.3	0.3	0.1	0.3	0.32	0.24	0.42
Q3	2.5	−0.01	0.15	0.08	0.23	0.51	0.2	−0.2	−0.1	−0.3	0.06	0.25	0.41
Q4	2.6	0.06	0.04	0.25	0.19	0.41	0.52	0.1	−0.2	−0.1	0.14	0.23	0.46
1999 Q1	2.7	0.21	0.14	0.01	0.29	0.26	0.52	0.46	0	−0.2	0.19	0.23	0.31
Q2	2.2	−0.28	−0.33	−0.51	−0.62	−0.17	−0.19	−0.05	−0.16	−0.7	−0.33	0.23	0.13
Q3	2.1	−0.21	−0.3	−0.45	−0.64	−0.76	−0.2	−0.37	−0.27	−0.4	−0.40	0.19	0.17
Q4	2.2	0	−0.08	−0.16	−0.41	−0.39	−0.57	−0.06	−0.35	−0.22	−0.25	0.19	0.09
2000 Q1	2	0.07	−0.12	−0.09	−0.2	−0.52	−0.56	−0.69	−0.27	−0.64	−0.34	0.27	0.37
Q2	2.2	0.32	0.22	0.14	0.21	−0.03	−0.29	−0.31	−0.36	−0.15	−0.03	0.26	0.69
Q3	2.2	−0.18	0.27	0.25	0.18	0.32	−0.05	−0.27	−0.28	−0.27	0.00	0.26	0.51
Q4	2	−0.36	−0.28	−0.1	−0.05	0.16	0.08	−0.23	−0.47	−0.45	−0.19	0.23	0.57
2001 Q1	1.9	−0.04	−0.43	−0.36	−0.3	−0.42	0.18	−0.18	−0.45	−0.66	−0.30	0.25	0.01
Q2	2.4	0.5	0.48	0.18	0.01	−0.07	−0.08	0.6	0.12	−0.03	0.19	0.27	0.14
Q3	2.3	−0.01	0.4	0.43	0.11	−0.18	−0.23	−0.23	0.11	−0.29	0.01	0.27	0.38
Q4	1.9	−0.1	−0.27	−0.01	0.03	−0.29	−0.72	−0.63	−0.66	−0.63	−0.36	0.30	0.62
2002 Q1	2.3	0.16	0.27	0.13	0.39	0.21	0.12	−0.38	−0.23	−0.28	0.04	0.27	0.54
Q2	1.5	−0.52	−0.37	−0.35	−0.41	−0.44	−0.68	−0.87	−1.2	−1.06	−0.66	0.32	0.73
Q3	2.1	0.26	0.02	0.14	0.04	0.14	0.07	−0.17	−0.36	−0.62	−0.05	0.28	0.46
Q4	2.7	0.06	0.45	0.46	0.59	0.64	0.57	0.54	0.28	0.14	0.41	0.21	0.32
2003 Q1	3	0.23	0.27	0.75	0.82	0.87	0.92	0.68	0.61	0.45	0.62	0.25	0.5
Q2	2.8	−0.29	−0.1	0.03	0.55	0.75	0.67	0.65	0.39	0.27	0.33	0.37	0.62
Q3	2.8	−0.05	−0.1	−0.13	0.08	0.49	0.71	0.62	0.57	0.35	0.28	0.34	0.75
Average	2.55	−0.02	−0.02	0.00	−0.03	−0.06	−0.09	−0.12	−0.13	−0.22			
St. Dev.	0.42	0.26	0.41	0.47	0.53	0.57	0.53	0.51	0.42	0.38			
1st. O. Autocorr.	0.61	−0.16	0.3	0.55	0.58	0.68	0.62	0.52	0.35	0.43			

contemporaneous actuals). The average values, standard errors and first order auto-correlations of the columns and rows of these deviations are also reported in these tables.

Let us now use these tables for a simple description of events. It is probably easiest to start with the forecasting errors in output growth (Table 17.8), (positive implying actual greater than forecast). Initially, in 1997 and early 1998, the forecasters predicted steady output growth, but this was increasingly overtaken by the arriving Asian crisis, which was not (unsurprisingly) foreseen, so that initially we see negative deviations in 1997/8. But the pessimism about that crisis shortly became overdone, and (again) the effects of the dot.com boom in 1999/2000 were not foreseen. So from end 1998 to early 2001, there are persistent strong positive deviations. By Q1 2001 the forecasters had caught up with the ongoing boom, just in time to miss the extent of decline caused by the bust of the bubble. So from 2001 Q3 to 2003 Q3 there is a sea of negative deviations, forecasts greater than outturn. The evidence from Table 17.8 is very clear; there is strong auto-correlation in the errors forecasters made in predicting output.

This picture, of auto-correlation in forecasting errors, is not quite so strong in the forecasts for inflation (Table 17.9). Here what seems to have happened in the initial years of our period is that the forecasters gave more weight to the presumptive effects of major exchange rate fluctuations on domestic inflation than was in practice justified. Thus there was a major devaluation of sterling in 1992, and inflation was overpredicted (negative deviations) in 1993 and 1994. From 1995 and 1997 Q2, there is no clear pattern of deviations. Then in 1997 (especially Q2 and Q3) there was a rapid, and historically large, appreciation of sterling. From 1997 Q3 until 1999 Q1 the forecasts systematically underpredict inflation. Perhaps because the forecasters initially failed to see the deflationary effects of the Asian crisis, inflation became overestimated in 1999 (negative residuals); but after that the patterns in the forecast errors are neither as clear, nor as auto-correlated, as with output growth.

In my earlier paper (Goodhart, 2004b), I decomposed the changes in the forecasts, for a particular end-date (and either inflation or output growth), for example, the forecast for Q3 2001, from the longest horizon forecast at $t + 8$ (for example, made in Q3 1999 for Q3 2001) to the shortest horizon forecast at $t = 0$ (for example, made in August 2001 for Q3 2001) into the unanticipated change in the forecast and the official response in the form of interest rate adjustments. This showed that policy, in the form of interest rate adjustments, was used systematically to offset such unanticipated changes to the forecasts.

So, what we have sought to establish is:

1. forecasting errors are auto-correlated, strongly so for output growth, less so for inflation;

2. interest rate adjustments are used to offset such auto-correlated errors.

Hence, in conclusion, the gradualism in interest rates derives in some large part from the auto-correlated errors of the forecasters. That this has been an important cause of gradualism, at least during this short sample period, seems patently clear.

CONCLUSION

The evidence, largely taken from Goodhart (2004c), indicates that the MPC was *not* seeking to behave in a gradualist fashion during our (short) data period, 1997–2003. So arguments in favor of such gradualist behavior being consciously undertaken, though of themselves interesting, are somewhat beside the point.

Yet, *ex post*, the actual path of interest rate changes did seem as gradual, with consecutive small steps, as previously or in other countries. Why? We examine two hypotheses. The first was that this was a quasi-automatic consequence of adopting the constant interest rate (CIR) forecasting method. There, almost certainly, have been occasions where this played a role (1998/9 and 2004 being cases in point), but the tests used here suggested that this effect was sporadic rather than regular and persistent.

What did, instead, seem systematic in this period was for forecasting errors to be auto-correlated, strongly so for output, weakly for inflation. We also document (primarily in Goodhart, 2004b) the tendency of policy-determined interest rate changes to be applied to offset such series of auto-correlated forecast errors, but only partially so. Hence I claim that gradualism, the auto-correlation in interest rate changes, has been, at least in this short time period, primarily a function of auto-correlated forecasting errors.

NOTES

1. Note, however, that, owing to data limitations, we had to use data on (forecasts and actuals of) output *growth*, rather than the output *gap*.
2. NB The Inflation Report forecasts are presented *after* the associated interest rate decisions have been taken. To assess what the *ex ante* forecasts would have looked like, we had to make adjustments to remove the effects on the *ex post* forecast of those interest rate changes themselves. We could do this by using the MPC's pamphlet (1999) on 'The Transmission Mechanism of Monetary Policy'. Details are given in Goodhart (2004b and 2004c).
3. Since such instability sets in seriously after this two-year horizon, simulations of longer-term outcomes using the Bank model are done after the inclusion of some equilibrating Taylor-type reaction function into the model to take effect after $t + 8$.

4. There is a set of further arguments for, and against, the CIR assumption. For criticisms, see Martijn and Samiei (1999), Meyer (2001), Svensson (2003). I have defended it (see Goodhart, 2001, 2004a).
5. Of course, it would be much better if I could use data on forecasts for the output gap. Alas we do not have these in the public domain.
6. Note that in this case it is correct to use the *ex post* forecast, published in the Inflation Report, rather than the *ex ante* forecast on which the MPC's immediately previous interest rate decision had been based. For a further analysis of this, see Goodhart (2004c).
7. Rudebusch and Wu (2004, p. 16) argue that,

> The persistence in S_t [a slope factor capturing the cyclical response of the Fed] reflects the fact that the Fed adjusts the short rate promptly to various determinants – output, inflation, and other influences in the residual u_t – that are themselves quite persistent (e.g., $\rho_u = .975$). Thus, our estimate of ρ_S decisively dismisses the interest rate smoothing or monetary policy inertia interpretation of the persistence in the short rate. The persistent deviations of slope from fitted slope . . . occur not because the Fed was slow to react to output and inflation but because the Fed responds to a variety of persistent determinants beyond current output and inflation.

But they never state explicitly what such other determinants may have been.

8. Such errors can also be due to failures to observe the correct current level of the output gap; see Rich (2003) and Orphanides (2001).

REFERENCES

Bindseil, U. (2004) 'Rise and Fall of Reserve Position Doctrine', European Central Bank, Directorate General Operations, Work in Progress.

Brainard, W. (1967) 'Uncertainty and the Effectiveness of Policy', *American Economic Review Papers and Proceedings*, 57, 411–25.

Bush, J. and A. Ashworth (1998) 'Anger Grows at Bank's U-turn', *The Times* (London), 11 June, 29.

Ellison, M. (2003) 'The Learning Cost of Interest Rate Reversals', Centre for Economic Policy Research (CEPR) Discussion Paper No. 4135, December.

Goodhart, C.A.E. (1999) 'Central Bankers and Uncertainty', Keynes Lecture in Economics (29 October 1998), reprinted in *Proceedings of the British Academy*, 101, 229–71.

Goodhart, C.A.E. (2001) 'Monetary Transmission Lags and the Formulation of the Policy Decision on Interest Rates', *Federal Reserve Bank of St Louis Review*, 83(4) (July/August), 165–81.

Goodhart, C.A.E. (2002) 'The Endogeneity of Money', Chapter 3 in P. Arestis, M. Desai and S. Dow (eds), *Money, Macroeconomics & Keynes: Essays in Honour of Vicky Chick*, London: Routledge, 14–24.

Goodhart, C.A.E. (2004a) 'What is the Monetary Policy Committee Attempting to Achieve?' paper presented at the Conference in Honour of C. Freedman, at the Bank of Canada, Ottawa (19/20 June 2003); subsequently published in Bank of Canada, *Macroeconomics, Monetary Policy and Financial Stability*, Ottawa: Bank of Canada.

Goodhart, C.A.E. (2004b) 'The Interaction between the Bank of England's Forecasts and Policy, and the Outturn', Financial Markets Group, London School of Economics, Discussion Paper 496, May; subsequently published in V.

Deville, J. von Landesberger, M. Muller, F. Schobert and A. Worms (eds) (2005), *Issues on Monetary Theory and Policy: Proceedings of a Colloquium in Honour of Wolfgang Gebauer*, Frankfurt: Bank-akademie Verlag GmbH, and *Atlantic Economic Journal* (2005), 33, 367–80.

Goodhart, C.A.E. (2004c) 'The Monetary Policy Committee's Reaction Function', Financial Markets Group, London School of Economics, Discussion Paper 495, May; subsequently published in Berkeley Electronic Journals in Macroeconomics (2005), manuscript 1240.

King, M.A. (2000) 'Monetary Policy: Theory in Practice', address to the joint luncheon of the American Economic Association and the American Finance Association, Boston Marriott Hotel (7 January 2000). See Bank of England website, http://194.129.36.50/speeches/speech67.htm.

Martijn, J.K. and H. Samiei (1999) 'Central Bank Independence and the Conduct of Monetary Policy in the United Kingdom', International Monetary Fund, Working Paper 99/170.

Meyer, L.H. (2001) 'Comment', *Federal Reserve Bank of St. Louis Review* (July/August), 183–6.

Monetary Policy Committee, Bank of England (1999) 'The Transmission Mechanism of Monetary Policy', pamphlet, Bank of England.

Orphanides, A. (2001) 'Monetary Policy Rules Based on Real-time Data', *American Economic Review*, 91, 964–85.

Rich, G. (2003) 'European Monetary Policy: Can the ECB Learn from the Fed?' paper initially presented to the 2 December 2003 meeting of the EMU Monitor.

Rudebusch, G.D. and T. Wu (2004) 'A Macro-finance Model of the Term Structure, Monetary Policy and the Economy', paper presented at the Federal Reserve Bank of San Francisco Conference on Interest Rates and Monetary Policy, 19–20 March.

Sack, B. (1998) 'Uncertainty, Learning and Gradual Monetary Policy', *Finance and Economics Discussion Series*, Board of Governors of the Federal Reserve System, July.

Sack, B. (2000) 'Does the Fed Act Gradually? A VAR Analysis', *Journal of Monetary Economics*, 46, 229–56.

Sack, B. and V. Wieland (2000) 'Interest-rate Smoothing and Optimal Monetary Policy: A Review of Recent Empirical Evidence', *Journal of Economics and Business*, 52, 205–28.

Sargent, T.J. (1998) 'Discussion of "Policy Rules for Open Economies" by Laurence Ball', Paper, University of Chicago (April).

Schellekens, P. (2002) 'Caution and Conservatism in the Making of Monetary Policy', *Journal of Money, Credit and Banking*, 34(1) (February), 160–77.

Svensson, L.E.O. (1997a) 'Inflation Forecast Targeting: Implementation and Monitoring Inflation Targets', *European Economic Review*, 41, 1111–46.

Svensson, L.E.O. (1997b) 'Inflation Targeting: Some Extensions', NBER Working Paper No. 5962.

Svensson, L.E.O. (1997c) 'Optimal Inflation Targets, "Conservative" Central Banks, and Linear Inflation Contracts', *American Economic Review*, 87 (March), 98–114(b).

Svensson, L.E.O. (1999) 'Inflation Targeting as a Monetary Policy Rule', *Journal of Monetary Economics*, 43, 607–54.

Svensson, L.E.O. (2003) 'The Inflation Forecast and the Loss Function', Chapter 4 in P. Mizen (ed.), *Central Banking, Monetary Theory and Practice*, Cheltenham, UK and Northampton, MA, USA: Edward Elgar.

Taylor, J.B. (1993) 'Discretion versus Policy Rules in Practice', *Carnegie-Rochester Conference Series on Public Policy*, 39, 195–214.

Taylor, J.B. (ed.) (1999) *Monetary Policy Rules*, Chicago: University of Chicago Press.

Woodford, M. (2003) *Interest and Prices*, Princeton, NJ: Princeton University Press.

PART V

Unemployment, inflation and the determination of aggregate income

18. Limitations to Keynesian demand management through monetary policy: whither Cartesian policy control?

Arne Heise

THE PROBLEM

Monetary policy as a stimulus to growth and employment has become increasingly popular again in the course of the past decade. On the one hand, it has been argued that monetary restriction, that is, a policy of zero inflation, does not come as a 'free lunch' but causes long term damage to growth and employment (see, for example, Akerlof et al., 1996; Wyplocz, 2001) – which in turn leaves room for cautious monetary expansion in order to grease economic growth. On the other hand, fiscal policy seems to lose effectiveness in a global world: according to the Fleming–Mundell model of open (integrated) economies, fiscal policy is less effective than monetary policy under the realistic assumption of a flexible exchange rate regime (see De Grauwe, 1997, p. 20). Furthermore, the degree of indebtedness of many public finances reduces considerably the room for maneuver through fiscal policies, leaving monetary policy as the principal tool of stabilization. Finally, in the European Monetary Union (EMU) fiscal policy has been completely 'neutralized' by the 'Stability and Growth pact' of public finances (see Arestis et al., 2001). Therefore, the European Central Bank (ECB) comes under mounting pressure to gear its monetary policy to demand management rather than purely guaranteeing price stability.

Due to its acceptance of the 'classical dichotomy', the traditional Walrasian economic model cannot consistently be taken as support for such a revival of monetary stabilization euphoria. Keynesian or Post Keynesian theorizing, however, allows for a long-term non-neutrality of monetary policy (see Moore, 1988a, pp. 366 ff.; Davidson, 1994, pp. 126 ff.) – which is often taken as a playground for hydraulic interventionist proposals.[1] In the following section, I will present a fresh model of a credit economy which allows for an exact analysis of the sometimes rather vague components of Post Keynesian model building.[2] I will then extend the basic model in order to introduce commercial banks as agents and to explore the interaction of the various economic agents (firms, wealth-owners, commercial banks) with the political actor (the central bank). In a next step, the impact of monetary policy on the decisions of the above-mentioned economic agents and, as a result, the process of income generation and employment will be elaborated. In a final section, I will answer the question whether or not monetary policy can be used in a hydraulic way for demand management and what this result implies for policy proposals.

THE BASIC MODEL

Although Post Keynesian model building is far from having established a unique, coherent set of equations and equilibrium conditions describing the functioning of markets (see Dunn, 2000), monetary endogeneity, the central position of (money) wealth-owners, the logical hierarchy of markets running from money and credit to commodity and labor markets and, as internal link, fundamental uncertainty, seem to be among the undisputed cornerstones of a constructive approach to Post Keynesianism (see, for example, Davidson, 1996; Minsky, 1996; Heine and Herr, 1999, p. 319).

Baisch and Kuhn (2001) have recently published a formally appealing model of a credit economy (*Risikowirtschaft* – risk economy), which bears many of the central features of Post Keynesianism and, in contrast to many other contributions to Post Keynesianism that remain vague with respect to the micro-foundations and functional relations of their reasoning (see Felderer and Homburg, 1992; Solow, 1979), allows for an in-depth analysis of the working of the model on the grounds of a portfolio-theoretic structure and a clear understanding of the interaction of the various economic agents.

At the outset, economic agents are separated according to their functions, that is, there are entrepreneurs whose function is simply to produce different types of commodities and services using capital and labor. In order to finance their production, they need to demand credit (or 'finance' as it had been termed by Keynes; see Keynes, 1937) from commercial banks. Entrepreneurs are the link between the credit and the commodity markets. Secondly, there are wealth-owners who are portrayed as risk-averse portfolio managers splitting their wealth into financial (that is, deposits at commercial banks) and real assets according to the principles of yield maximization under uncertainty. Thirdly, there are commercial banks providing credit to entrepreneurs, accepting deposits from wealth-owners and cash balances from the central bank. Fourthly, the central bank provides the unit of account (money or cash balances) to commercial banks and secures the stability of the banking system (lender of last resort). These different types of agents are often compounded in reality, that is, entrepreneurs may well additionally be wealth-owners, yet functional separation does not allow for the possibility of functional mixes. The labor and commodity markets (and, thus, the process of income generation) will not be modelled in detail.

Before presenting a full picture of the model, let us put forward some further preliminaries: (1) for the sake of simplicity, I shall concentrate on debt-financed production ignoring the possibility of equity finance or a mix of debt and equity. I shall do so under the assumption that this will not seriously alter the outcome of the principal focus of this chapter: the limitations of monetary policy (see Baisch and Kuhn, 2001, pp. 152 f.).[3] (2) Collateral requirements play a crucial role in a model which is based on debt and credit: commercial banks provide credit to entrepreneurs only under the provision of full collateral requirements which is the productive capital that entrepreneurs will have purchased with the credit given to them. This procedure reduces the default risk of commercial banks and links the monetary side of the economy (that is, the creation of real deposits and loans) to the real side of the economy (the creation of productive capital).[4] (3) The model is a static one-period model, in which the agents act in a forward-looking manner under conditions of fundamental uncertainty.

In Figure 18.1, the basic model of a credit economy of Post Keynesian orientation is presented. The first quadrant shows the relation between the interest rate on deposits and on financial credit given by commercial banks:

$$i_C = i_D + u \tag{18.1}$$

(with i_C = interest rate on financial credit; i_D = interest rate on deposits; u = risk premium).

The second quadrant depicts what Baisch and Kuhn call the 'transformation portfolio' (TP – *Überlassungsportfolio*) – the part of real wealth[5] (W/P) private wealth-owners are willing to give up in favor of real deposits (D/P). As the existing stock of real wealth (W/P[max]) includes all kinds of assets which are able to be transformed into a productive (that is, income generating) process (by the entrepreneurs), wealth-owners are willing to part with real wealth and transform it into deposits in relation to the rate of interest on deposits – the particular shape of the TP curve indicating risk aversion on the part of the wealth-owner. As any part of real wealth being given up must be invested, the fourth quadrant shows the 'investment portfolio' (IP – *Anlageportfolio*) as a function of the rate of interest on deposits.

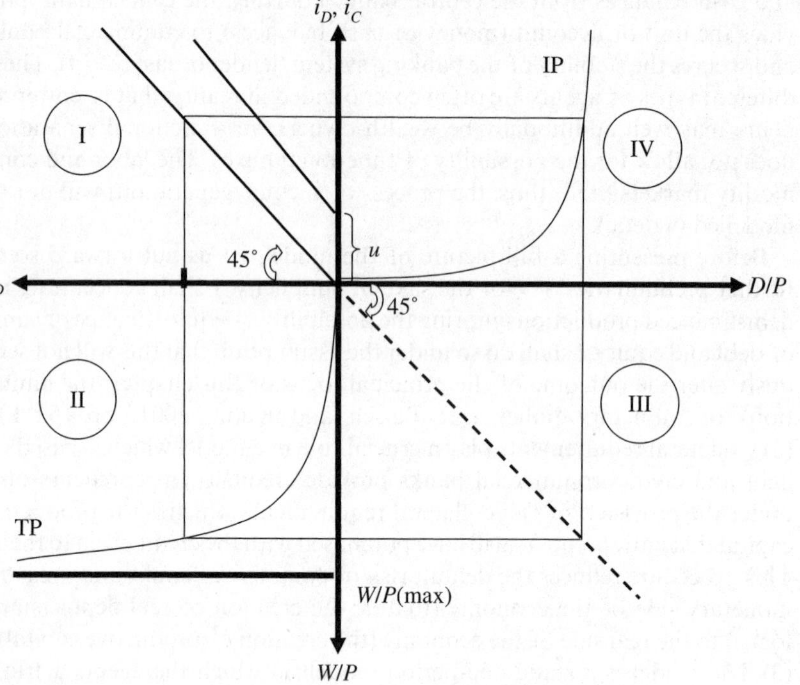

Figure 18.1 *The basic model*

Although the 'transformation portfolio' and the 'investment portfolio' are merely two sides of one and the same coin, the underlying incentives are logically different in the sense that the wealth-owner may be restricted in his effort to part with real wealth to the extent that he is (un)able to find investment – due to functional separation, wealth-owners only invest in bank deposits. The third quadrant, finally, simply joins financial and real wealth to secure the identity of $W/P \equiv D/P$.

This basic model, resting on the portfolio decisions of wealth-owners, must be extended in order to incorporate investors (entrepreneurs), commercial banks and the central bank.

REFINING THE MODEL

If we do not want to leave the rate of interest – on deposits and also on financial credit – hanging by its own bootstrap, we shall have to introduce the central bank as provider of cash balances (units of account or money in its narrowest definition), the commercial banks linking the creation of (long-term) credit to that of (short-term) deposits and cash balances and the entrepreneurial investors who demand real capital and provide jobs according to the principles of profit maximization.

At the beginning, we made the assumption of ignoring equity-based financing of productive investment. This establishes the identity of real deposits (D/P), the volume of real credit (Cr/P) and the stock of real capital (C/P) as shown in Figure 18.2A–D. Or, to put it differently, the portfolio decision of wealth-owners *uno actu* determines the supply of real credit and real capital in Figure 18.2D. In order to determine the volume of real investment and, assuming the complementarity of the real capital stock C/P and employment L (as in Figure 18.2F), the amount of employment demanded (with the amount of labor supplied as exogenously given), we simply have to introduce an ordinary Keynesian investment function comparing the marginal efficiency of capital (internal rate of interest) with the (external) rate of interest on financial credit (see Figure 18.2D).[6]

It may be noticed that Figure 18.2 includes yet another section, namely section G. This section is vital – and has been ignored by Baisch and Kuhn – because, on the one hand, it introduces the banking system as an actor in its own right into the model and on the other hand, it allows us to heal a slip in our argument: we have argued that the portfolio decision of wealth-owners *uno actu* determines the supply of real credit and real capital. This is not quite true as the 'transformation portfolio' (TP) may be rationed and the 'investment portfolio' (IP) cannot be established without the knowledge of the commercial bank's willingness to get indebted (or, in Keynesian terminology, the liquidity preference of commercial banks). This crucial element, establishing a truly endogenous money supply as the result of profit-maximizing commercial banks and entrepreneurs and price-setting central banks,[7] is depicted in Figure 18.2G.

Commercial banks transform short-term debts (deposits from wealth-owners and cash balances from the central bank) into long-term credit.[8] Profit maximization under conditions of uncertainty forces commercial banks to restrict lending according to their liquidity preference. Uncertainty in this context can be separated into two distinct categories: the uncertainty of redemption of outstanding debts associated with the borrower (investor) and the uncertainty of illiquidity associated with the transformation of the term structure of debts and loans. While the former uncertainty can be taken into account by the provision of collateral requirements (as we have assumed),[9] the latter forces commercial banks to keep a certain ratio of liquid cash balances (Ca/P) to less liquid deposits (D/P). This ratio depends on the credit multiplier m, which is no technical magnitude (as in most textbooks on money and credit) but a behavioral

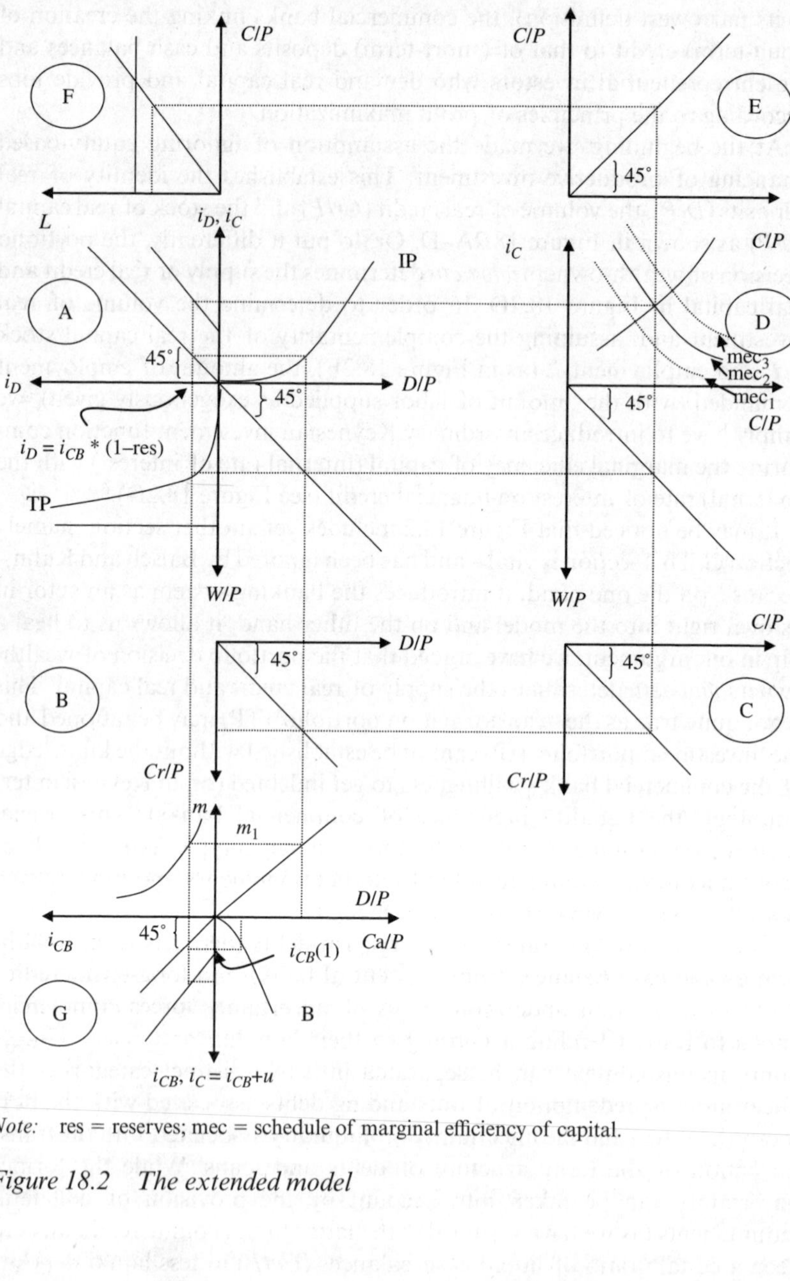

Note: res = reserves; mec = schedule of marginal efficiency of capital.

Figure 18.2 The extended model

one.[10] It depends on the central bank's prime rate (i_{CB}) as the cost of restoring liquidity, the interest rate on financial credit (i_C) as the yield of parting with liquidity and the liquidity preference of commercial banks as their perception of the uncertainty about price stability and future central bank behavior.[11] Given this liquidity preference of commercial banks, the higher the prime rate (i_{CB}) set by the central bank on a given reaction function (B), the lower will be the credit multiplier m simply due to the growing risk of entrepreneurs (as investors) falling into Domar's debt trap.[12] In order to close the monetary system, that is, to determine the volume of real debt and credit (and the capital stock), we need to know the investment demand curve as depicted in Figure 18.2D. Hence, the endogenous money supply does not merely follow investors' credit demand in a passive, hydraulic way as the 'horizontalist view' (which I have elsewhere dubbed the 'neo-banking school'; see Heise, 1992)[13] seems to argue, but is determined simultaneously by expected profitability and liquidity preference considerations.

MONETARY POLICY

At this stage, the ground is prepared for investigating the impact of monetary policy (that is, a change in the prime rate set by the central bank) on real magnitudes such as the volume of real investment and, finally and most important, employment or, as it is termed more technically, the transformation mechanism of monetary policy.

As a first step, a more restrictive policy stance by the central bank is portrayed in Figure 18.3G by a shift in the central bank's reaction function and an increase in the central bank's prime rate from $i_{CB}(1)$ to $i_{CB}(2)$. Clearly, a first immediate result will be an increase in the rate of interest on deposits and on financial credit (as in Figure 18.3A) and a fall in the credit multiplier m (as in 18.3G): commercial banks will hold fewer cash balances, yet will reduce the amount of outstanding real credit (as in 18.3B) and real deposits even further, thus reducing the 'credit margin' (that is, the ratio of real credit to real cash balances). Although wealth-owners are willing to transform more real wealth into financial wealth as the interest rate on deposits rises, the 'investment portfolio' indicates that they cannot succeed as long as entrepreneurs reduce the amount of real investment according to their schedule of marginal efficiency of capital (a movement from α to β in 18.3D). Finally, the result of a policy of monetary restriction will be a drop in employment due to capital shortages in Figure 18.3F.

In a few moments it will be apparent that the kind of hydraulic, deterministic policy control[14] which our example exhibits only works in one direction: by setting the cost of restoring liquidity, the central bank is able

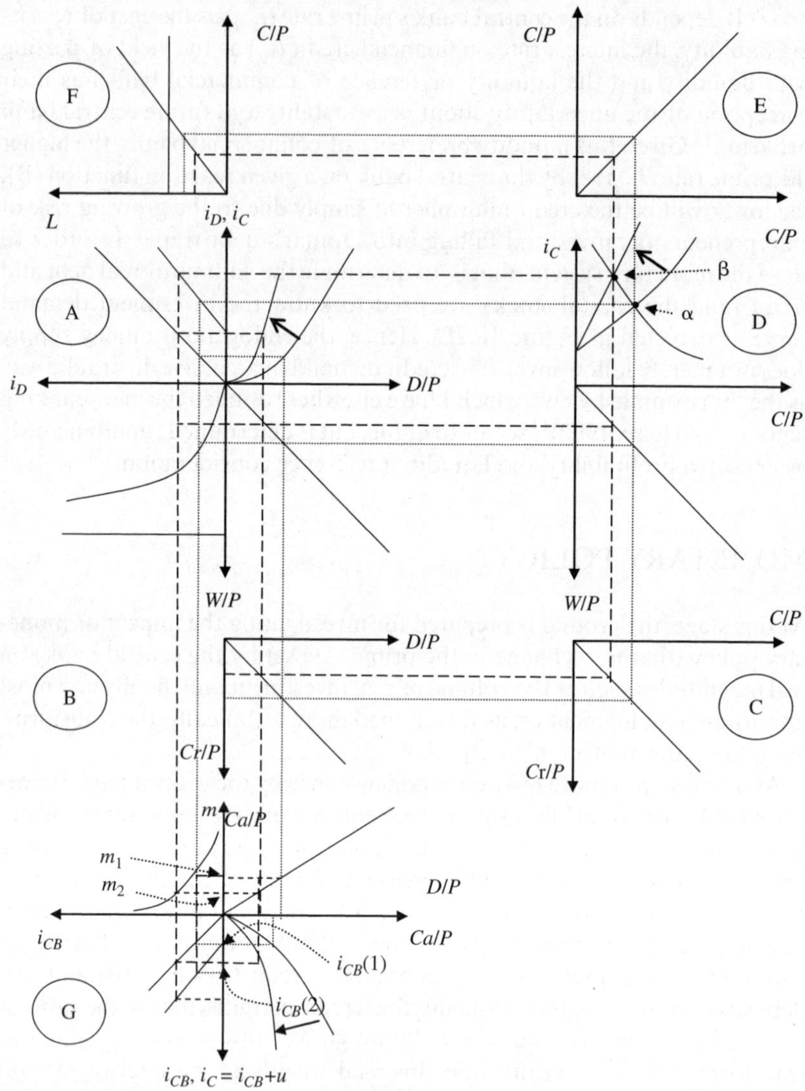

Figure 18.3 The extended model and restrictive monetary policy

to control monetary expansion in a restrictive way only. Let us assume that the central bank reduces its prime rate again from $i_{CB}(2)$ to $i_{CB}(1)$ in the next step. Of course, one would expect to regain the former macroeconomic position including a higher amount of employment as indicated by the light dotted lines in Figures 18.3 and 18.4. However, this is only one, and clearly

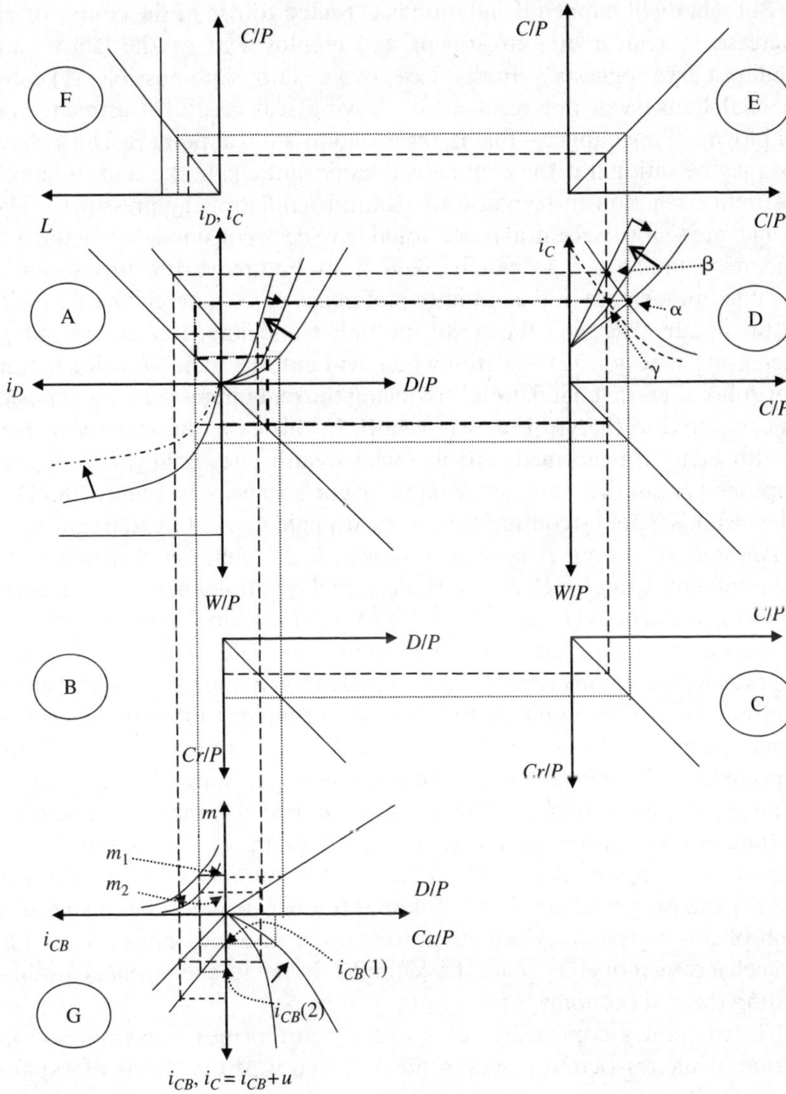

Figure 18.4 The extended model and expansionary monetary policy

the most optimistic, scenario that will come true only under the condition of stable inflation expectations correctly anticipated by wealth-owners, commercial bankers and investors alike. In this case, a drop in the bank rate will increase *m*, the volume of real deposits, real credit and real capital – hence a return from β to α in Figure 18.4D.

But what will happen if inflation is expected to rise in the course of an increase in real credit, investment and employment as the (short-run) Phillips curve suggests?[15] In that case, two reactions are possible: (1) commercial banks will not react at all, leaving real credit, investment and employment unchanged – that is, the economy stays at point β. This behavior may be rational if the commercial banks anticipate the central bank's restrictive reaction in response to mounting inflationary pressure.[16] The prime rate set by the central bank would have been considered to be too low and unsustainable.[17] As can be seen from Figure 18.4G, this scenario includes an increase in the liquidity preference of commercial banks (shift in the *m*-curve) leaving the credit multiplier unchanged at m_2 instead of increasing it to m_1. (2) Wealth-owners will enforce their 'transformation portfolio' if expected inflation is reducing the real interest rate on deposits as compared to the yield of real wealth. In this case, the scarcity of real wealth being transformed into financial wealth and, finally, real capital imposes yet another interactive equilibrium termed γ in Figure 18.4D.[18] The result is a policy contingency in the triangle marked by α, β and γ.

Another reasoning is needed, however, if we consider a deflationary environment. Under such circumstances, real wealth-owners would clearly like to transform as much real wealth as possible into financial wealth as long as commercial banks are considered to be safe. However, entrepreneurs as well as commercial banks will make their actions dependent on the central bank's ability and credibility to lower interest rates: if the central bank's prime rate has reached a lower limit – say zero per cent – or is not expected to fall any further for a period considered long enough to lower deposit rates accordingly, neither will commercial banks increase their lending nor will entrepreneurs increase their volume of real capital. This is a modern version of the standard Keynesian 'liquidity trap', which does not depend on 'speculative' cash holdings (money demand) but on a credit multiplier (that is, money supply) process which becomes interest-inelastic. In such a case, monetary policy has completely lost its effectiveness in stimulating the real economy.[19]

Clearly, policy control by the monetary authorities is asymmetric in nature: while restriction works in the intended way, the effects of expansionary monetary policy depend on its expected impact on prices and the overall inflationary or deflationary circumstances. In order to determine and predict such an impact, interactions of monetary and wage policy and the process of capital accumulation must be put in the picture. But before doing so, let us resume, and close, the consideration of a restrictive monetary policy by pointing out that the result reached above – that of deterministic policy control under a restrictive policy stance – rests on the implicit assumption of price rigidity in a downward direction.[20] If disinflationary or, rather, deflationary processes are allowed to occur in the aftermath of a restrictive increase in the central bank's prime rate, position β would not be sustainable as the real burden on debt-financed capital acquisition will increase (external rate of interest) and shift the investment-demand curve inward. If this prompts prices to fall even further, a destabilizing scenario may result and, as we have argued, monetary policy may become incapable of reflating the economy again. Hence Keynes's prominent verdict in book V of the *General Theory* that a stable price level and – as its foundation – a stable level of money-wages is the most advisable policy proposition (see Keynes, 1936, p. 270) and empirically documented price and money-wage rigidities[21] the proviso of stability in a monetary production economy.

ECONOMIC POLICY AFTER CARTESIAN POLICY CONTROL

The correct macroeconomic policy mix has always been an important tool of 'fine tuning' stabilization policy in Keynesian models since the famous IS-LM neoclassical synthesis.[22] However, 'policy mix' in a Post Keynesian understanding does not merely translate into implementing an exact dose of monetary and fiscal policy stimuli up until full employment has been established, but a coordinated effort among the quasi-autonomous policy actors, the central bank (monetary policy), the political actor (fiscal policy) and the social partners (wage and income policy) in order to create a 'macroeconomic constellation' that allows for economic growth without inflationary pressure and mounting fiscal debt (see, for example, Nordhaus, 1994; Rankin, 1998).[23] Inflationary pressure can be prevented only if the vicious circle of profit and income inflation in the case of output and employment growth is broken with the support of a concerted action, and the tax-wage-price spiral prevented due to the sustainability of public finances. These are necessary prerequisites for the economic agents (the commercial banks, investors, wealth-owners and consumers) to form systematic anticipations beyond the Phillips curve arithmetrics. Hence, economic policy can be best portrayed as 'coarse tuning' in the sense of creating a favorable 'macroeconomic constellation' rather than 'fine tuning' economic outcomes in order to reach certain predetermined policy goals.

This is not the place either to investigate the game-theoretic background and requirements of a coordinated policy strategy or to describe the exact contributions of the individual actors involved (see Heise, 2002), but rather the moment to summarize the findings: monetary policy cannot be used in a hydraulic way for 'fine tuning' demand management as in most textbook versions of Keynesian policy proposals. Its mechanics are asymmetric and particularly blurred in an expansionary direction. Therefore, to put all the weight of stabilization policy on the shoulders of the central bank would clearly overextend its potential and underestimate its difficult strategic position in a policy game.

However, that does not necessarily mean a nihilistic approach to policy control in general and monetary policy control in particular (see, for example, Fitzgibbons, 2000, pp. 103 ff.), but rather the confession of limited interventionist capabilities and the need for institutions that reduce the level of uncertainty about future policy stances and, therefore, macroeconomic outcomes important for the decisions of microeconomic units. And, of course, central banks may even refuse to utilize the small room for maneuver they actually have if they are uncertain about their signaling capacity and credibility in a non-cooperative environment. In that case, the central bank can at least be blamed for inflicting higher costs for providing price stability than are necessary (see, for example, Bibow, 2001).

NOTES

1. In a recent article Arestis and Glickman (1999, pp. 44 ff.) mention some political and external (due to the process of globalization) obstacles to and constraints on such hydraulic policy control but no internal ones.
2. In his most famous book – 'Horizontalists and Verticalists' – Basil Moore (1988a, p. xviii) expresses his hope to have set a new generation of economists on the way towards a reconstruction of economic theory beyond the (then and now) prevailing orthodoxy. I would be glad if Basil Moore accepted the following piece as a preliminary attempt to do so.
3. However, many interesting phenomena of the 'New Economy' – such as an asset inflation beyond the discounted value of (possibly expected) future yields – can only be analyzed once equity finance is brought into the picture.
4. In any case, commercial banks will prevent an overvaluation of real productive capital as it would jeopardize the monetization of collateral requirements in case of debt default. An under-valuation of productive capital cannot occur under the assumption of perfect competition. In the Baisch–Kuhn model the commercial banking system's sole function must be seen as securing a correct valuation of real wealth. We shall add another function of the banking system later.
5. The valuation of the stock of real wealth is done by wealth-owners alone in relation to its (non-pecuniary) yield (Baisch and Kuhn, 2001, pp. 70 ff.) – therefore, the value of real wealth is unrelated to the changing interest rate on deposits.
6. If we introduce an infinite number of different production techniques (that is, combinations of capital and labor) and allow for the possibility of re-switching, the negative interest rate elasticity of investment demand becomes obscure (as proven by the Cambridge capital controversy, see, for example, Harcourt, 1972). Yet, this assumption and the scenario of a re-switching point seem to be too unrealistic to be taken as a serious constraint in our argument. In any case, the Keynesian investment function argues in terms of 'capital widening' rather than 'capital deepening' categories; see Heise (1990). Although the determination of employment – and, hence, unemployment – is not a serious focus of this model, at first sight employment seems to be supply-driven (capital

stock). However, the capital stock (as the result of an investment process) depends on profit expectations and, implicitly, demand conditions. In a static model, where expectations are assumed to be fulfilled in equilibrium, the supply and demand orientations are only two sides of one and the same coin.

7. Central banks set a nominal price rather than a relative price – this is the conceptual link between the real and the monetary sides of the economy.
8. Of course, the sequence of action is exactly the opposite: by providing long-term credit to investors, the banking system as a whole is generating the complementary amount of deposits. Therefore, commercial banks can never be deposit-constrained but may be liquidity-constrained in the case of shifting deposits from one bank to another or demanding cash balances.
9. Reducing the risk premium on financial credit to transaction costs incurred in the course of monetizing collateral requirements.
10. As this ratio is crucial, the microeconomic behavior underlying its determination must be made more explicit: commercial banks are profit-driven enterprises. Therefore, they are tempted to expand loan creation to its extreme (which is only limited 'technically' by reserve requirements; labelled 'res' in Figure 18.2A). However, although loan creation *pari passu* generates deposits, commercial banks may become liquidity-constrained in the case of wealth-owners demanding cash balances for whatever reason. Or, as Dymski (1988, p. 516) puts it: 'The more credit banks create to satisfy loan demand, the fewer funds are available for redistribution to meet depositors' demands for liquidity'. The uncertainty of being forced to provide idle cash balances reflects the liquidity preference of commercial banks and explains why they do not necessarily expand loan creation to its technical extreme. They would only do so if they could expect to gain any amount of cash balances from the central bank at a fixed rate – which of course is the assumption of the 'accommodative endogeneity approach' to the money supply (see Pollin, 1991). Obviously, I do not subscribe to that view – neither do I accept central banks as pure price-setters and quantity-takers, nor would I agree with the idea that the cost of restoring liquidity can be accepted as constant (see Moore, 1991, p. 126). This cannot be so as the term structure of deposits is different from the term structure of loans, which results in an increasing marginal cost curve with growing loans (= deposits) to cash balances ratio. What will happen if commercial banks form wrong expectations about these costs can be studied with the savings and loan associations in the USA during the first half of the 1980s (see Stiglitz, 2003, pp. 36 ff.).
11. This is, as distinct from the transaction cost content of the risk premium described above, what Keynes called the 'liquidity premium' associated with cash-holdings according to the 'finance motive' (see Keynes, 1937, pp. 210 ff.) and must be included in u of equation (18.1).
12. Accepting the idea of a credit multiplier does not necessarily include the rejection of the money supply being demand-driven. Whether the money supply should be regarded as demand-driven or, rather, supply-determined depends on whether the amount of cash balances or the amount of loans (= deposits) in the 'credit margin' is predetermined. If it is the amount of loans – as the accommodative (horizontalist) view would suggest – we may speak of a demand-driven money endogeneity, and if it is the amount of cash balances – as the structuralist view would suggest – we may speak of a supply-driven money endogeneity.
13. The 'horizontalist view' may also be captured by making the central bank's reaction function (B) completely interest elastic (see Moore, 1988a and 1988b). However, this would raise questions about the stability of such a monetary economy – the system would be lacking a crucial constraint (see Heise, 1992, pp. 290 ff.). A positively sloping reaction function can better be brought in line with the 'structionalist view of endogeneity' (see Pollin, 1991) and may capture a 'leaning against the wind' policy stance (see Palley, 1991).
14. Accepting this kind of policy control implies that money supply becomes exogenous in a control sense although it is endogenous in a purely quantitative way.
15. This can be made plausible by assuming an ordinary price-setting function which equates the price level with nominal unit labor cost multiplied by a mark-up factor

representing market conditions in commodity markets. The nominal wage level, in turn, depends – among other factors – on the employment gap, that is, actual unemployment as compared to equilibrium unemployment. For an interesting model on the line of argument put forward here see Isaac (1991). The rationale for the implicit assumption of asymmetric inflation expectations will be put forward later.

16. This is particularly rational if the central bank is known for pursuing a policy of 'inflation targeting' as most independent central banks seem to do (see Bernanke and Woodford, 1997). Indeed, 'inflation targeting' may be a useful tool to increase the transparency of central bank behavior.
17. In this setting, commercial banks become the primary mover of the economy very much in line with Keynes's ideas: 'The control of finance is, indeed, a potent, though sometimes dangerous, method of regulating the rate of investment' (Keynes, 1937, pp. 210 f.).
18. In Figure 18.4 not all the consequences – such as for employment and credit creation – have been portrayed in order not to make the figure overly confusing. However, point γ can be an equilibrium point only if the expected profitability of investment suffers, that is, an inward shift of the investment-demand curve as indicated by the dotted line in 18.4D. This, of course, is quite plausible as the income-generating process has been harmed.
19. This seems to be what we have been experiencing in Japan since the late 1990s when the Bank of Japan reduced its bank rate to zero, yet commercial banks refrained from expanding their lending.
20. Obviously, we have simply assumed a fixed-price model in a restrictive direction and a flex-price model in an expansionary direction which explains the asymmetric results.
21. See, for example, Andersen (2001), Kahn (1997), Smith (2000).
22. When it comes to policy proposals, most Post Keynesian economists become quite traditional Keynesians or, at least, their demand-management proposals are difficult to distinguish from those of orthodox Keynesians; see for example, Arestis and Sawyer (1998), Epstein (1994/5); Epstein and Gintis (1995), Davidson (1991). This, of course, does not apply to those Post Keynesians in the tradition of George Shackle.
23. And, of course, the Post Keynesian paradigm, which allows for long-term interdependencies between monetary, fiscal and income policies, is best suited for inquiring into these interactions.

REFERENCES

Akerlof, G.A., W.T. Dickens and G.I. Perry (1996) 'The Macroeconomics of Low Inflation', *Brookings Papers on Economic Activity*, 1, 1–76.

Andersen, T. (2001) 'Can Inflation Be Too Low?' *Kyklos*, 54(4), 591–602.

Arestis, P. and M. Glickman (1999) 'Post Keynesian Economic Policy: Continuing Relevance', in S. Daniel, P. Arestis and J. Grahl (eds), *Money and Macroeconomic Policy*, Cheltenham, UK and Northampton, MA, USA: Edward Elgar, 34–51.

Arestis, P. and M. Sawyer (1998) 'Keynesian Policies for the New Millennium', *Economic Journal*, 108, 181–95.

Arestis, P., K. McCauley and M. Sawyer (2001) 'An Alternative Stability Pact for the European Union', *Cambridge Journal of Economics*, 25, 113–30.

Baisch, H. and W. Kuhn (2001) *Risikowirtschaft. Eigen- und Fremdfinanzierung im gesamtwirtschaftlichen Kontext*, Berlin: Duncker and Humbolt.

Bernanke, B.S. and M. Woodford (1997) 'Inflation Targets and Monetary Policy', *Journal of Money, Credit, and Banking*, 29(4), 653–84.

Bibow, J. (2001) 'The Monetary Policies of the European Central Bank and the Euro's (Mal)Functioning: A Stability-Oriented Assessment', Working Paper No. 338, Jerome Levy Institute of Bard College.

Davidson, P. (1991) *Controversies in Post Keynesian Economics*, Aldershot, UK and Brookfield, USA: Edward Elgar.

Davidson, P. (1994) *Post Keynesian Macroeconomic Theory*, Aldershot, UK and Brookfield, USA: Edward Elgar.

Davidson, P. (1996) 'What are the Essential Elements of Post Keynesian Monetary Theory?' in G. Deleplace and E.J. Nell (eds), *Money in Motion. The Post Keynesian and Circulation Approaches*, Houndsmill: Macmillan, 48–69.

De Grauwe, P. (1997) 'Paradigms of Macroeconomic Policy for the Open Economy', in M. Fratianni, D. Salvatore and J. von Hagen (eds), *Macroeconomic Policy in Open Economies*, Westport/London: Greenwood Press, 17–54.

Dunn, S. (2000) 'Whither Post Keynesian Economics?' *Journal of Post Keynesian Economics,* 20, 345–64.

Dymski, G.A. (1988) 'A Keynesian Theory of Bank Behaviour', *Journal of Post Keynesian Economics*, X(4), 499–526.

Epstein, G. (1994–5) 'Keynesian Demand Management is Alive and Ill', *Journal of Post Keynesian Economics*, 17, 2.

Epstein, G. and H. Gintis (1995) 'Macroeconomic Policies for Sustainable Growth', in G. Epstein and H. Gintis (eds), *Macroeconomic Policies after The Conservative Era: Studies in Investment, Savings and Finance*, Cambridge: Cambridge University Press, 3 ff.

Felderer, B. and S. Homburg (1992) *Macroeconomics and New Macroeconomics*, Berlin: Springer.

Fitzgibbons, A. (2000) *The Nature of Macroeconomics. Instability and Change in the Capitalist System*, Cheltenham, UK and Northampton, MA, USA: Edward Elgar.

Harcourt, G.C. (1972) *Some Cambridge Controversies in the Theory of Capital*, Cambridge: Cambridge University Press.

Heine, M. and H. Herr (1999) *Volkswirtschaftlehre*, Munich: Oldenbourg.

Heise, A. (1992) 'Commercial Banks in Macroeconomic Theory', *Journal of Post Keynesian Economics*, 14, 285–96.

Heise, A. (2002) 'Ein Loblied auf den kooperationsfreudigen Zentralbanker', in A. Heise (ed.), *Neues Geld – alte Geldpolitik? Die EZB im Makroökonomischen Interaktionsraum*, Marburg: Metropolis, 229–57.

Isaac, A.G. (1991) 'Money Supply Endogeneity in a Conflicting Claims Environment', *Journal of Post Keynesian Economics*, 14(1), 93–110.

Kahn, S. (1997) 'Evidence of Nominal Wage Stickiness from Microdata', *American Economic Review*, 87, 993–1008.

Keynes, J.M. (1936) *The General Theory of Employment, Interest and Money*, London: Macmillan. Quoted from D. Moggridge (ed.) (1973), *The Collected Writings of John Maynard Keynes*, Vol. VII, London: Macmillan.

Keynes, J.M. (1973) 'Alternative Theories of the Rate of Interest', *Economic Journal*, 47, 241–52. Quoted from D. Moggridge (ed.), *The Collected Writings of John Maynard Keynes, Vol. XIV: The General Theory and After, Part II: Defence and Development*, London/Basingstoke: Macmillan, 201–15.

Minsky, H.P. (1996) 'The Essential Characteristics of Post Keynesian Economics', in G. Deleplace and E.J. Nell (eds), *Money in Motion. The Post Keynesian and Circulation Approaches*, Houndsmill: Macmillan, 70–88.

Moore, B.J. (1988a) *Horizontalists and Verticalists: The Macroeconomics of Credit Money*, Cambridge: Cambridge University Press.

Moore, B.J. (1988b) 'Unpacking the Post-Keynesian Black Box: Wages, Bank Lending and the Money Supply', in P. Arestis (ed.), *Post-Keynesian Monetary Economics*, Aldershot, UK and Brookfield, USA: Edward Elgar, 122–51.

Moore, B.J. (1991) 'Has the Demand for Money been Mislaid? A Reply to "Has Moore become too horizontal"', *Journal of Post Keynesian Economics*, 14(1), 125–33.

Nordhaus, W.D. (1994) 'Policy Games: Coordination and Independence in Monetary and Fiscal Policies', *Brookings Papers in Economic Activity*, 2, 139–216.

Palley, T.I. (1991) 'The Endogenous Money Supply: Consensus and Disagreement', *Journal of Post Keynesian Economics*, 13(3), 397–403.

Pollin, R. (1991) 'Two Theories of Money Supply Endogeneity: Some Empirical Evidence', *Journal of Post Keynesian Economics*, 13(3), 366–96.

Rankin, N. (1998) 'Is Delegating Half of Demand Management Sensible?' *International Review of Applied Economics*, 12(3), 415–22.

Smith, J.C. (2000) 'Nominal Wage Rigidity in the UK', *Economic Journal*, 110, 176–95.

Stiglitz, J. (2003) *The Roaring Nineties. Seeds Of Destruction*, London: W.W. Norton.

Solow, R.M. (1979) 'Alternative Approaches to Macroeconomic Theory: A Partial View', *Canadian Journal of Economics*, 12, 339–54.

Wyplocz, C. (2001) 'Do We Know How Low Inflation Should be?' CEPR Discussion Paper, No. 2722, London.

19. Telling better stories in macroeconomic textbooks: monetary policy, endogenous money and aggregate demand[1]

Giuseppe Fontana

> When writing *Horizontalists and Verticalists*, after I had thoroughly persuaded myself of the correctness of the endogenous money hypothesis, I naively assumed that, after a short transition period, truth would soon – and surely – conquer. . . . Yet, twelve years after the publication of *Horizontalists and Verticalists*, to the best of my knowledge, none of the many mainstream introductory money and banking or macroeconomics textbooks have even referred to, let alone incorporated, endogenous money in their discussion of the money supply or the monetary transmission mechanism.
>
> (Moore, 2001)

INTRODUCTION

In a recent issue of the *Journal of Economic Perspectives*, David Romer (2000) discusses the use, for teaching purposes, of the *IS-LM* model as the basic aggregate demand model of short-run economic fluctuations. The thesis of the paper is indisputable. Most central banks no longer target monetary aggregates, but instead follow real interest rate rules (see also Blinder, 1997; Taylor, 1997; Walsh, 2002). Unfortunately, the former is one of the central assumptions of the *IS-LM* model. Could we then make the model more realistic and yet keep its simplicity and usefulness? Drawing on his expertise as a leading economist and textbook writer (for example, Romer 1996), Romer suggests replacing the *LM* (liquidity-money) curve with an *MP* (monetary policy) schedule.

A similar concern for a more realistic representation of the teaching of monetary economics and macroeconomics has been a long-standing interest of Basil Moore. In particular, as the quotation above suggests, he has been puzzled by the lack of attention in macroeconomic textbooks to the endogenous money hypothesis, namely, to the propositions that the stock of money in a country is determined by the demand for credit (that is, bank loans) by firms and consumers, and that the latter originates within the economic system to finance the purchase of inputs for the production process or durable goods.[2] With few recent exceptions (for example, Palacio-Vera, 2002; Dawson et al., 2003), no attempts have been made to amend the gap between academic research, policy making and macroeconomic textbooks.[3]

This chapter is an attempt to amend this situation and, in so doing, it takes on board Basil Moore's suggestion that every effort should be made to write clear and simple didactic presentations of the endogenous money hypothesis (Moore, 2001, p. 29, n. 1). The chapter builds on Romer's argument that modern central banks do not target monetary aggregates, but instead follow a real interest rate rule. However, it encompasses this mainstream plea for greater realism into a sounder analysis of the nature and origin of money. In effect, the mainstream argument does not have very solid theoretical foundations. It is based on William Poole's analysis that an interest rate policy is to be preferred to a monetary aggregate policy when, *ceteris paribus*, the variance of shocks to the money market is larger than that of shocks to the commodity market (Poole, 1970; see also Moore, 1972). Since the mid-to-late 1980s, these theoretical conditions have arisen in practice. As a result, one central bank after another has abandoned monetary aggregate policies in favor of interest rate policies. Thus, the mainstream position is that, under current historical circumstances, an interest rate policy is to be preferred to a monetary aggregate policy – but nothing precludes the possibility that, in the near future, things may change again and central banks may return to targeting monetary aggregates. However, for a monetary aggregate policy to be viable, at least two conditions must be met: (a) central banks need to have full control of the money supply, and (b) the relationship between the money supply and nominal income needs to be stable. Over his long career, Basil Moore has shown that *neither* of these two conditions holds in economies with modern financial systems (for example, Moore, 1988). Putting it differently, the variance of shocks to the economy is not independent of the policy choice of the central bank (Fontana and Palacio-Vera, 2004).

Drawing on Moore's work, this chapter attempts to present a simple, general endogenous money model. It is a general model because it starts with Romer's plea for more realism in the teaching of macroeconomic principles. However, it encompasses this crude empiricism into a sounder analysis of the money supply process that leads students toward an explicit consideration of the role of commercial banks, firms and consumers in the determination of the level of output and employment. At the same time, the model presented here is quite simple. It is based on a stylized version of the endogenous money model that provides solid theoretical foundations for the teaching of the aggregate demand model, but leaves out all sorts of unnecessary details and algebraic complications.[4] In short, the important pedagogical feature of the simple aggregate demand model presented here is that students will be naturally led to appreciate how economists base their theoretical arguments on, and draw their policy conclusions from, a sound and realistic economic model.

THE AGGREGATE DEMAND (*AD*) CURVE

The aggregate demand curve shows the quantity of goods and services (Y) that economic agents want to buy at each price level (P). Four major components of aggregate demand (AD) are usually identified, namely: consumption demand, investment demand, government demand and net foreign demand (that is, export demand minus import demand). The demand for consumption is the major component of total aggregate demand (usually around two-thirds of GDP). The standard assumption is that consumption demand (C) depends on the level of income (Y). As households experience increments in income, their consumption demand also increases. This basic relationship can be opportunely modified with the introduction of the real interest rate charged on loans (r_L). As will be explained in the next section, this is because individuals can borrow money from commercial banks in order to buy commodities like new cars or houses that they cannot (or choose not to) finance out of current income.

The demand for investment (I) is the most volatile component of aggregate demand. This volatility derives from the fact that investment decisions are always forward-looking. When firms make investment decisions they have to calculate what the flow of future income from a project will be. Whether based on guesses or forecasts, these expectations are inherently unstable and capable of sudden and sharp reversals. Thus, when a country experiences a boom or recession, these changes in the level of income are largely due to declines or recoveries in the demand for investment goods.

When firms plan their investments they are likely to consider two factors: (a) the real interest rate charged on bank loans, or the bank loans rate (r_L) for short; and (b) the expected returns from their projects. Most firms need to borrow money from banks in order to pay for investment goods. Thus, the bank loans rate (r_L) is the financial cost for firms of making additional investment. The link between the demand for investment and the bank loans rate can be expressed by saying that for a given expected return, an increase in (r_L) raises the financing cost of investment and thereby lowers the demand for investment.

The expected return on investment projects is the second factor that affects the investment decisions of firms. The expected returns from investment depend on many factors. Since these returns refer to expectations, when firms are more optimistic about the future, their expectations of future returns are likely to be higher than when firms are more pessimistic about the future. For instance, when the overall level of income is high and when there are prospects for that high level of income to continue, the expected returns from investment are likely to be greater (as compared with periods of low income). This process may be summarized by saying that investment will tend to be higher when income is higher because the prospects for expected returns are better. The level of income (Y) can then be used as a representative variable for the expected returns from investment projects. In algebraic form, the investment function (I) can be represented in the following way:

$$I = f\left(\underset{-}{r_L}, \underset{+}{Y}\right) \tag{19.1}$$

Government expenditure (G) is the third component of aggregate demand. For the sake of simplicity, the government expenditure can be taken to be an exogenous policy variable, that is, the value of this variable is taken to be determined outside the economic model. Finally, a closed economy is assumed. This means that the net foreign component of aggregate demand, namely export demand minus import demand, is ignored. The aggregate demand curve then shows, *ceteris paribus*, the total demand for goods and services by households, firms, and the government at any given price.

EXOGENOUS MONEY, ENDOGENOUS MONEY AND THE AGGREGATE DEMAND (*AD*) CURVE

Traditionally, the aggregate demand function is represented by a downward sloping (AD) curve in the price level (P)–income (Y) diagram, because of the effects of changes in the price level in an environment with an exogenous nominal money stock (M). In other words, the aggregate demand curve is derived from the *IS-LM* model by assuming an increase in the price level from P_0 to P_1 which produces a reduction of the supply of *real* money balances M/P and hence, via a shift upward of the LM curve, a reduction of the level of income from Y_0 to Y_1 (see, for instance, Mankiw, 2003, p. 292, Figure 11-5). Figure 19.1 reproduces the graphical derivation of the AD curve in traditional textbooks. However, the effect on the supply of real money balances of changes in the price level works through an *exogenous* supply of nominal money balances (M) controlled by the central bank. As

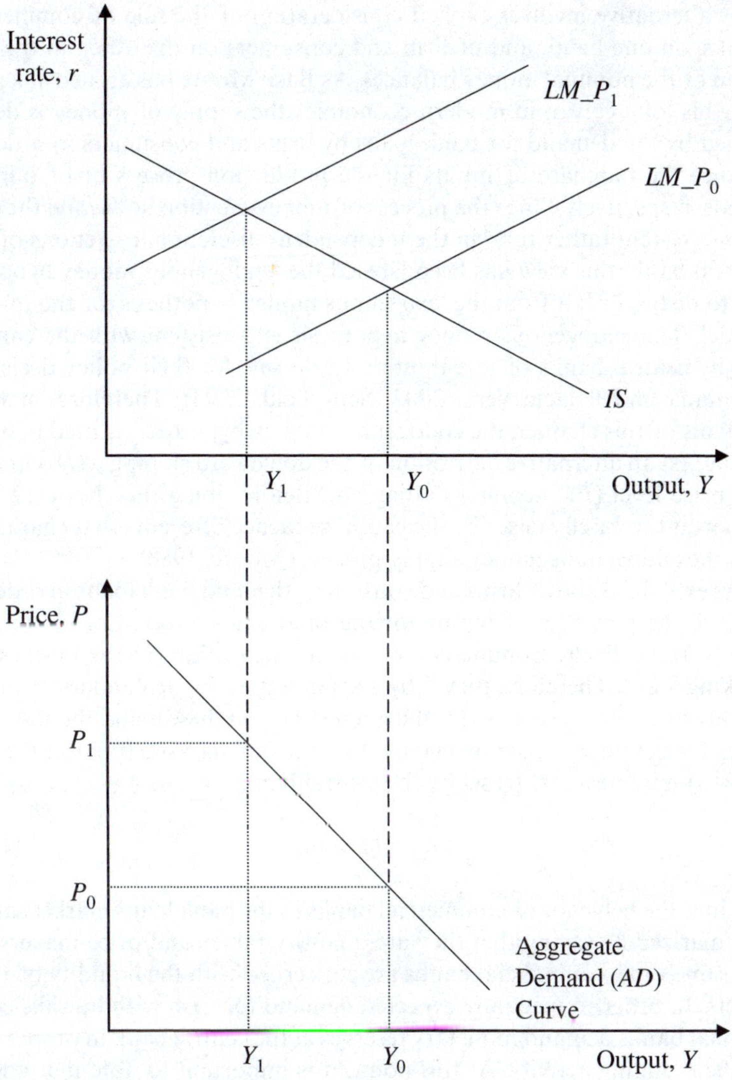

Figure 19.1 *The standard textbook derivation of the aggregate demand* (AD) *curve through the* IS-LM *model*

was argued above, this is an unrealistic assumption since central banks now manipulate the interest rate rather than the quantity of money.

In what follows, we do away with the *IS-LM* model and propose a more realistic alternative for explaining the slope of the aggregate demand curve.

This alternative involves explicit consideration of the role of commercial banks, on one hand, and of firm and consumers on the other, in the creation of the nominal money balances. As Basil Moore has argued at length over his long career, in modern economies the supply of money is determined by the demand for bank loans by firms and consumers in order to finance the purchase of inputs for the production process or of durable goods, respectively. Since the process of money creation lies *within* the economic system rather than in the independent discretionary actions of the central bank, this view has been labeled the 'endogenous money hypothesis' to distinguish it from the 'exogenous money hypothesis' of the *IS-LM* model. The endogenous money hypothesis is consistent with the current use by central banks of a real interest rate rule for their policy decisions (Fontana and Palacio-Vera, 2002; Setterfield, 2004). Therefore, in what remains of this chapter, the endogenous money hypothesis is used in order to suggest an alternative derivation of the downward sloping (*AD*) curve in the price level (*P*)–income (*Y*) diagram. Before doing this, however, it is important to briefly describe the causal sequence of events that characterizes the endogenous money supply process (Moore, 1988).

As explained above, firms and consumers demand bank loans in order to finance the purchase of inputs for the production process or of durable goods, respectively. Commercial banks are institutions in the business of making loans. Therefore, they fully accommodate the demand for loans by creditworthy borrowers. As for the interest rate on these loans, the so-called bank loans rate (r_L), commercial banks set it as a mark-up (m) over the real short-run interest rate (i) set by the central bank:

$$r_L = (1 + m)i \qquad (19.2)$$

Thus, the behavior of commercial banks in the bank loans market can be summarized by saying that they are quantity-takers and price-makers. At the same time, commercial banks are concerned with the liquidity of their assets. In order to meet any expected demand for cash withdrawals, commercial banks demand monetary reserves at the central bank in proportion to their lending activity. At this point, it is important to note that one of the major functions of the central bank is to safeguard the economic system from financial crises. Thus, as the ultimate supplier of liquidity, the central bank fully accommodates the demand for monetary reserves of commercial banks at a price of its own choice, the so-called real short-run interest rate (i). The four-panel diagram of Figure 19.2 illustrates the underlying sequential analysis that characterizes the endogenous money supply process.[5] The diagram should be read clockwise starting from the upper-right panel.

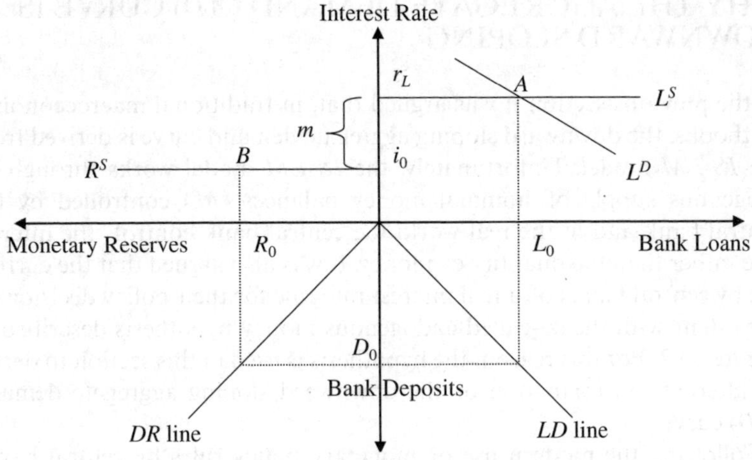

Figure 19.2 The endogenous money supply process

The upper-right panel shows the credit market where firms and consumers on one hand and commercial banks on the other negotiate their demand for and supply of bank loans, respectively. The supply curve of bank loans is represented by a perfectly elastic schedule at a bank loans rate (r_L) determined as a fixed mark-up over the short-term real interest rate (i_0) set by the central bank. The demand for bank loans (L^D) is a decreasing function of the bank loans rate (r_L) and, together with the supply of bank loans (L^S), determines the total volume of credit (L_0) (equilibrium point *A*).

The lower panels are used to describe the two main insights of the endogenous money hypothesis, namely that (a) bank loans create bank deposits (*LD* line) and (b) bank deposits make the demand for monetary reserves (*DR* line). Thus, the equilibrium in the credit market determines via the Loans–Deposits (*LD*) line the supply of new bank deposits (D_0) in the lower-right panel. Note that the *LD* line represents the balance sheet constraint of commercial banks and, for the sake of making the graphical exposition feasible, it is drawn on the assumption that banks hold their liabilities, like time or demand deposits, in fixed proportions.

Finally, the upper-left panel describes the monetary reserves market. The supply of reserves is represented by a horizontal line showing that the central bank accommodates the demand for monetary reserves by commercial banks at the short-term real interest rate (i_0). In fact, the supply of monetary reserves (R_0) associated with the new supply of bank deposits (D_0) is derived via the Deposits–Reserves (*DR*) line in the lower-left panel (equilibrium point *B*). The *DR* line represents the total demand for reserves.

WHY THE AGGREGATE DEMAND (*AD*) CURVE IS DOWNWARD SLOPING

In the previous section it was argued that, in traditional macroeconomic textbooks, the downward sloping aggregate demand curve is derived from the *IS-LM* model. Unfortunately, the *IS-LM* model works through an exogenous supply of nominal money balances (M) controlled by the central bank and in the real world the central bank controls the interest rate rather than the quantity of money. It was also argued that the current use by central banks of a real interest rate rule for their policy decisions is consistent with the so-called endogenous money hypothesis described in Figure 19.2. For this reason, the hypothesis is used in this section to derive an alternative explanation of the downward sloping aggregate demand (*AD*) curve.

Following the modern use of monetary policy rules by central banks around the world, a three-step approach is followed. Firstly, a positive relationship between changes in the price level (ΔP) and changes in the real interest rate (Δi) is derived. Secondly, it is shown that, *ceteris paribus*, there is a negative relationship between changes in the real interest rate (Δi) and changes in the level of investment (ΔI). Thirdly, a positive relationship between changes in the level of investment (ΔI) and changes in the level of output demanded (ΔY) is derived. In short, in the case of an increase in the price level, the three-step approach aims to show the following causal relationships:

$$(1)\ \uparrow P \Rightarrow \uparrow i;\ (2)\ \uparrow i \Rightarrow \downarrow I;\ (3)\ \downarrow I \Rightarrow \downarrow Y$$

The first relationship, between changes in the price level (ΔP) and changes in the real interest rate (Δi), is based on the operation of monetary policy. In many industrialized economies the central bank has been assigned the task of meeting an inflation objective, and to do so through changes in the real short-run interest rate (Δi).[6] The goal of controlling changes in the price level relies on a permanent positive relationship between changes in aggregate demand and changes in the price level. This implies a two-stage mechanism that relates firstly the price level (P) to the short-run real interest rate (i), and secondly the real interest rate (i) to the bank loans rate (r_L). This type of behavior of the central bank is called a *monetary policy rule* because it describes how much the real interest rate responds, as a rule, to changes in some measures of the state of the economy. Of course, there are several types of monetary policy rules. The central bank could target a single economic variable, like inflation, or a combination of variables, like output, employment and inflation. The simplest interest rate policy rule is to change the real interest rate (i) in response to variations of the price level (P).

Under the assumption that there is a constant mark-up (m) between the short-run interest rate (i) and the loan rate (r_L), equation (19.2) shows that an increase in (i) by the central bank would be translated by commercial banks into a proportional increase in (r_L). This means that the cost of financing investment is now higher and, for a given expected return, equation (19.1) tells us that the demand for investment goods (I) will now be lower. But investment is a component of aggregate demand. Therefore, *ceteris paribus*, a fall in investment (I) would negatively affect total output demanded (Y). A similar story can be told about the demand for consumption goods. An increase in the short-run interest rate (i) and hence in the bank loans rate (r_L) means that it is more expensive to borrow money from commercial banks in order to buy durable goods like homes and new cars. Thus, *ceteris paribus*, consumption (C) declines and hence total output demanded (Y) falls.[7]

In summary, by combining the results of the relationships discussed above, a downward sloping aggregate demand (AD) curve is easily derived. An increase in the price level (P) triggers an increase in the short run interest rate (i) by the central bank, which is passed on by commercial banks in the form of a higher bank loans rate (r_L). This negatively affects the demand for investment goods (I) and hence total output demanded (Y). In short, through the monetary policy rule, an increase in the price level (P) is linked to a reduction in total output demanded (Y). The next section demonstrates the graphical derivation of this downward sloping aggregate demand (AD) curve by examining the way in which the Bank of England sets the short-run interest rate and affects aggregate demand in the United Kingdom.

MONETARY POLICY AND THE SLOPE OF THE AGGREGATE DEMAND CURVE IN THE UNITED KINGDOM: A GRAPHICAL EXAMPLE

One of the major responsibilities of the Bank of England is to maintain price stability through the conduct of monetary policy. As explained in the previous sections, this involves the responsibility of deciding the level of the short-run interest rate necessary to meet the government's inflation target, currently set at 2 per cent. Thus, when the price level rises, the Bank of England increases the short-run interest rate in order to negatively affect the bank loans rate and, via the effects of the latter on investment spending, to reduce the level of aggregate demand. Conversely, when the price

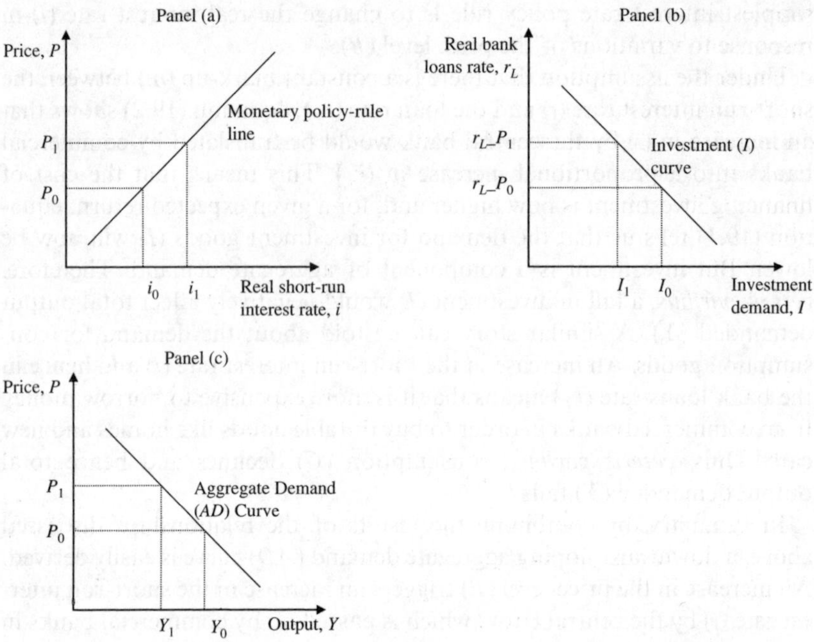

Figure 19.3 The alternative derivation of the aggregate demand (AD) *curve through the monetary policy rule*

level decreases, the Bank of England reduces the short-run interest rate in order to stimulate, via the bank loan rate, the levels of investment and aggregate demand (Bank of England, 1999). The case of the Bank of England is illustrative of the practice, common amongst modern central banks, of adopting price stability as the main objective of monetary policy.

In Figure 19.3, panel (a) illustrates a *monetary policy rule line* similar to that used by the Bank of England. When the price level increases from P_0 to P_1, the central bank increases the short-run real interest rate from (i_0) to (i_1). As a result of this change, the cost for commercial banks of getting monetary reserves is now higher. Thus, commercial banks pass on this cost increase to firms and consumers by raising the bank loans rate from (r_L–P_0) to (r_L–P_1) (see equation 19.2). Specifically, for a fixed mark-up (m), we can write that:

$$(r_L – P_0) = (1 + m)\, i_0 \text{ and } (r_L – P)_1 = (1 + m) i_1 \qquad (19.3)$$

The consequences of this are shown in panel (b), where the investment curve is represented. As panel (b) illustrates, the increase in the bank loans rate from $(r_L\_P_0)$ to $(r_L\_P)_1$ leads to a decrease of the level of investment from (I_0) to (I_1). But investment is a component of aggregate demand. Thus, *ceteris paribus*, total output demanded (Y) decreases from (Y_0) to (Y_1). Panel (c) shows the aggregate demand (AD) curve, summarizing this relationship between the output demanded (Y) and the price level (P): the higher the price level, the lower the output demanded.

SHIFTS IN THE AGGREGATE DEMAND (*AD*) CURVE

In the preceding sections it was argued that the bank loans rate (r_L) represents the cost of borrowing money from commercial banks, and as such it affects the demand for investment goods (I) and hence aggregate demand (AD). However, investment is also affected by another factor, namely, the expected return on investment projects, which, as was explained in the second section, can be approximated by the level of income (see equation (19.1)). Thus, for a given bank loans rate, an increase in the level of income is likely to produce an increase in the demand for investment, and hence in total output demanded. This case is illustrated in Figure 19.4.

As shown in Panel (a), any event that raises the expected returns from investment (Y) increases the profitability of investment and causes the investment curve to shift outward from $I(Y_0)$ to $I(Y_1)$. Panel (b) shows the positive effects of these changes on the aggregate demand curve. For any price level, an increase in the expected returns from investment shifts the aggregate demand (AD) curve from (AD_0) to (AD_1). More generally, any change in variables other than the bank loans rate that affect components of aggregate demand will shift the (AD) curve in Figure 19.4.

CONCLUDING REMARKS

In standard macroeconomic textbooks, the downward sloping aggregate demand curve is derived from the *IS-LM* model. Unfortunately, the *IS-LM* model works through an exogenous supply of nominal money balances (M) controlled by the central bank, whereas in the real world, the central bank controls the interest rate rather than the quantity of money. Could, then, the derivation of the downward sloping aggregate demand curve be made more realistic without necessarily sacrificing its simplicity and usefulness?

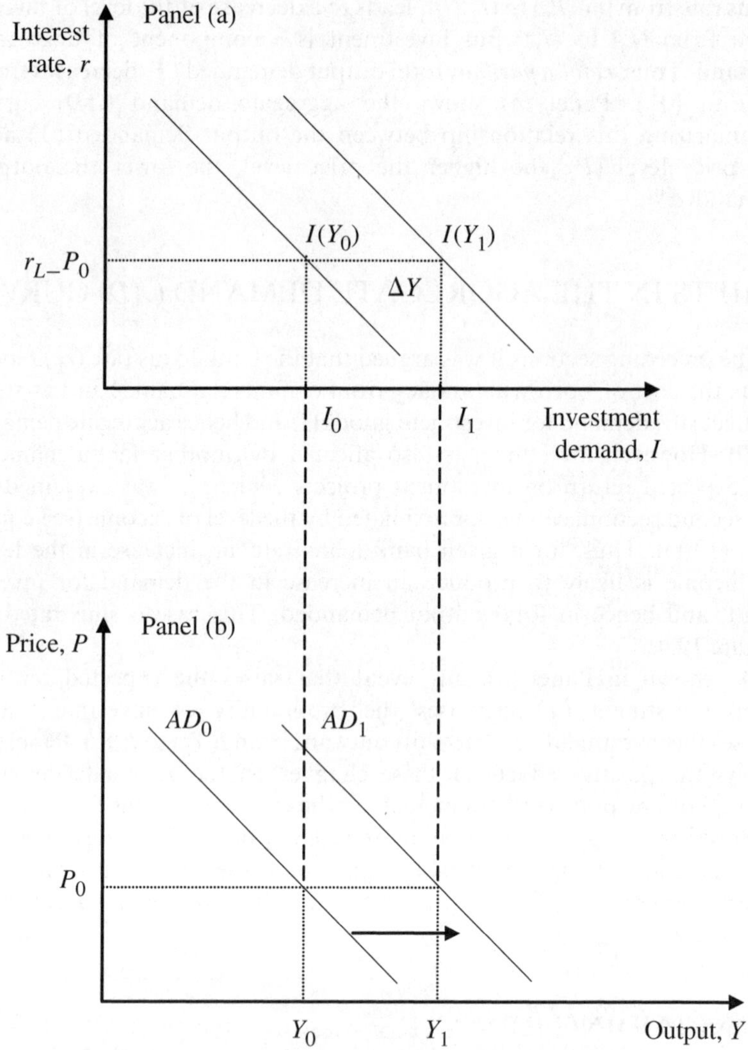

Figure 19.4 *Shifts of the aggregate demand* (AD) *curve through changes in the expected return on investment projects* (Y)

Drawing on the work of Basil Moore, this chapter has done away with the *IS-LM* model and its implicit exogenous money hypothesis. Rather, the alternative analysis of aggregate demand provided here explicitly considers the role of commercial banks on one hand, and of firm and consumers on the other, in the creation of the money supply. This is what has been labeled the endogenous money hypothesis. Using the investment demand curve and an interest rate monetary policy rule, the chapter then provides an alternative derivation of the downward sloping aggregate demand curve. In short, the simple lesson that emerges from this exercise is that a sound analysis of the endogenous money supply process adds greater realism to the teaching of macroeconomics without necessarily sacrificing the simplicity of the standard *IS-LM* model or any amended version of it.

NOTES

1. This chapter is part of an Open University project with Malcolm Sawyer on teaching modern macroeconomics. Drafts of the chapter were written when the author was Visiting Research Professor at the Economics Department and *C-FEPS* (Center for Full Employment and Price Stability), University of Missouri Kansas City (UMKC), Kansas City (USA) and Visiting Fellow at Clare Hall College and *CCEPP* (Cambridge Center for Economic and Public Policy), University of Cambridge, Cambridge (UK). I would like to express appreciation to members of those institutions for providing a stimulating and pleasant working environment. Last, but not least, I am grateful to two anonymous referees, David Colander, Geoff Harcourt, David Romer, Malcolm Sawyer, Pavlina Tcherneva, participants at the 2003 DEBE (Developments in Economics and Business Education) Conference, Heriot-Watt University, Edinburgh (UK), and especially to Mark Setterfield for comments and suggestions on previous drafts of the chapter. The usual disclaimer applies.
2. See Moore (1988) for an early discussion of this hypothesis, and Fontana (2003) and Fontana and Venturino (2003) for its modern interpretations.
3. A verdict only slightly more positive can be reached about the current state of intermediate and advanced textbooks on monetary economics. See, for instance, Handa (2000, ch. 10), Lewis and Mizen (2000, ch. 13, pp. 333–4, ch. 14, pp. 342–5), and especially Bain and Howells (2003, ch. 4, pp. 89–92, ch. 7, pp. 195–7).
4. More advanced students may find it useful to read, for instance, Graziani (2003), Lavoie (2003).
5. The four-panel diagram is derived from Fontana (2003, 2004) and is drawn on the assumption that the state of expectations of all agents involved in the money supply process is given and constant. This is what has been labeled a single period analysis of endogenous money.
6. In order to keep the analysis as simple as possible, two basic assumptions are made here. Firstly, it is assumed that the central bank controls directly the real short-run interest rate. In reality, the central bank can actually control only the nominal rather than real short-run interest rate, the difference between the two rates being the inflation rate. However, if, as is usually the case, some wage and price stickiness is assumed in the short run, then this assumption does not alter the conclusions of the analysis presented here. Secondly, it is assumed that the central bank responds to changes in the price level, whereas in reality modern central banks respond to changes in the inflation rate. Again, this assumption does not alter the conclusions of the analysis presented here.
7. Note that, for the sake of simplicity, the focus of the analysis in what follows is only on the effects of *changes* in the bank loans rate on investment spending.

REFERENCES

Bain, K. and P.G.A. Howells (2003) *Monetary Economics: Policy and its Theoretical Basis*, Basingstoke: Palgrave Macmillan.

Bank of England (1999) 'The Transmission Mechanism of Monetary Policy', *Bank of England Quarterly Bulletin*, 39, 1–12.

Blinder, A.S. (1997) 'What Central Bankers Could Learn from Academics – and Vice Versa', *Journal of Economic Perspectives*, 11, 3–19.

Dawson, G, S. Athreye, S. Himmelweit and M. Sawyer (eds) (2003) *Economics and Economic Change*, Milton Keynes, UK: The Open University.

Fontana, G. (2003) 'Post Keynesian Approaches to Endogenous Money: A Time Framework Explanation', *Review of Political Economy*, 15, 291–314.

Fontana, G. (2004) 'Rethinking Endogenous Money: A Constructive Interpretation of the Debate Between Horizontalists and Structuralists', *Metroeconomica*, 55, 367–85.

Fontana, G. and A. Palacio-Vera (2002) 'Monetary Policy Rules: What Are We Learning?' *Journal of Post Keynesian Economics*, 24, 547–68.

Fontana, G. and A. Palacio-Vera (2004) 'Monetary Policy Uncovered: Theory and Practice', *International Review of Applied Economics*, 18, 25–41.

Fontana, G. and E. Venturino (2003) 'Endogenous Money: An Analytical Approach', *Scottish Journal of Political Economy*, 50, 398–416.

Graziani, A. (2003) *The Monetary Theory of Production*, Cambridge: Cambridge University Press.

Handa, J. (2000) *Monetary Economics*, London: Routledge.

Lavoie, M. (2003) 'A Primer on Endogenous Credit-Money', in L.P. Rochon and S. Rossi (eds), *Modern Theories of Money: The Nature and Role of Money in Capitalist Economies*, Cheltenham, UK and Northampton, MA, USA: Edward Elgar, 506–43.

Lewis, M.K. and P.D. Mizen (2000) *Monetary Economics*, Oxford: Oxford University Press.

Mankiw, G. (2003) *Macroeconomics*, New York: Worth Publishers.

Moore, B.J. (1972) 'Optimal Monetary Policy', *Economic Journal*, 82(325), 116–39.

Moore, B.J. (1988) *Horizontalists and Verticalists: The Macroeconomics of Credit Money*, Cambridge: Cambridge University Press.

Moore, B.J. (2001) 'Some Reflections on Endogenous Money', in L.P. Rochon and M. Vernengo (eds), *Credit, Interest Rates and the Open Economy*, Cheltenham, UK and Northampton, MA, USA: Edward Elgar, 11–30.

Palacio-Vera, A. (2002) 'The "Modern" View of Macroeconomics: Some Critical Reflections', Working Paper No. 2002-17, Facultad de Ciencias Económicas y Empresariales, Universidad Complutense de Madrid, Spain.

Poole, W. (1970) 'Optimal Choice of Monetary Policy Instruments in a Simple Stochastic Macro Model', *Quarterly Journal of Economics*, 84(2), 197–216.

Romer, D. (1996) *Advanced Macroeconomics*, New York: McGraw-Hill.

Romer, D. (2000) 'Keynesian Macroeconomics without the *LM* Curve', *Journal of Economic Perspectives*, 14, 149–69.

Setterfield, M. (2004) 'Central Bank Behaviour and the Stability of Macroeconomic Equilibrium: A Critical Examination of the "New Consensus"', Paper presented at Economic and Econometric Seminar Series, LUBS, University of Leeds, UK, March.

Taylor, J.B. (1997) 'A Core of Practical Macroeconomics', *American Economic Review*, 87(2), 233–5.
Taylor, J.B. (2000) 'Teaching Macroeconomics at the Principles Level', *American Economic Review*, 90(2), 90–94.
Walsh, C.E. (2002) 'Teaching Inflation Targeting: An Analysis for Intermediate Macro', *Journal of Economic Education*, 33, 330–46.

20. Institutionalist-Post Keynesian economics and the Post Monetarist new consensus

Chris Niggle

This chapter interprets the history of macroeconomics over the last 30 years as a dialectical struggle between two opposing visions of the economy and the proper macroeconomic roles of the state. One vision is exemplified by New Classical Economics which sees the economy as essentially stable and tending toward an equilibrium characterized by high employment and an economic growth rate largely determined by the rate of technological change (the 'natural rate of unemployment' and the 'steady state' rate of growth). In sharp contrast, the work of Institutionalist and Post Keynesian economists such as Basil Moore begins with a vision of a very unstable economy, whose growth rate is the result of an open-ended transformational process taking place through economic fluctuations, characterized by excessive unemployment and inequality, and which is often threatened by incoherence and the possibility of breakdown. The first approach implies a noninterventionist role for the state in the economy; the second argues for a strong interventionist state. A third approach consisting of a synthesis of New Keynesian economics and New Endogenous Growth (NEG) theory acknowledges occasional episodes of instability and a limited role for the state in stabilization and the active promotion of growth; it forms the basis of an emerging 'new consensus' among mainstream macroeconomists.[1]

In the 1970s and 1980s, the macroeconomics done by Institutionalists and published in the movement's leading journal, the *Journal of Economic Issues*, merged with the macroeconomics found in the *Journal of Post Keynesian Economics*. Both came to hold similar views with respect to method and key theoretical concepts, including conceptions of time, uncertainty, money and contracts; both developed an understanding of economic institutions and systems as evolving through time; and their theoretical models and policy positions came to resemble each other closely (Keller, 1984; Hodgson, 1991 and 1999; Tymoigne, 2003). Throughout the

1980s, the Institutionalist-Post Keynesian macroeconomists (IPK below) turned their attention to the emerging New Classical economics (NCE) which had mounted a strong challenge to Keynesianism and came to dominate mainstream economics during that decade.[2] IPK criticized all aspects of NCE, including monetarism, rational expectations and real business cycle theory, criticizing and rejecting these approaches on methodological, theoretical and policy grounds.

As the influence of New Classical Economics began to wane and the 'new consensus' based upon New Keynesian (NK) and New Endogeneous Growth (NEG) theory emerged within the mainstream in the 1990s, the IPK economists turned their attention to the limitations of those aspects of modern macroeconomics (Fontana, 2002; Dalziel, 2002; Arestis and Sawyer, 2002a, b; Setterfield, 2002). This chapter attempts to compare and contrast IPK with the NK–NEG consensus; it argues that IPK presents a more radical departure from NCE and offers a more useful approach to macroeconomics than either New Classical or New Keynesian–New Economic Growth economics.[3]

OPPOSITION TO THE NEW CLASSICAL THEORY

Two strong currents questioning the validity and challenging the hegemony of NCE macroeconomics developed even as NCE emerged as a critique of Keynesian economics in the 1970s: the New Keynesians and the Institutionalist-post Keynesians. The New Keynesians operate within the mainstream, teaching at elite universities and publishing in the profession's highly ranked journals; many of them (Ben Bernanke, Alan Blinder, Stanley Fischer, Gregory Mankiw, Joseph Stiglitz, Lawrence Summers, John Taylor and Janet Yellen, for example) have held important policy-making positions in institutions such as the Federal Reserve, World Bank, Council of Economic Advisors, US Treasury and the International Monetary Fund (IMF).[4] Their research accepted some of the core of NCE economics, most importantly its individualist micro-foundations and Walrasian general equilibrium approach and method, while criticizing aspects of the theoretical structure erected upon those assumptions and techniques.

Meanwhile, outside the inner circle of mainstream economics and largely relegated to what Keynes termed the 'netherworld of economics', a radical critique of both NCE and NK economics based upon a different vision of the economy, a different set of assumptions about human behavior and economic reality, and perhaps a different set of social values and priorities, was developed by the IPK school.

NEW KEYNESIAN MACROECONOMICS

New Keynesians emerged in the late 1970s and early 1980s in reaction to the criticism of original IS-LM Keynesianism (termed 'bastard Keynesianism' by the IPK economists), mounted by the NCE school; the New Keynesian emphasis was on explaining the causes of business cycles.[5]

The New Keynesians retain Keynes's insistence that economic fluctuations can be caused by aggregate demand fluctuations as well as the aggregate supply shocks stressed by NCE, and they argue that aggregate demand fluctuations could be caused by factors other than monetary shocks. They retain the early consensus Keynesian approach which held that wages and prices were downwardly inflexible in the short run, and that recessions could be seen as the result of 'coordination failures' and 'quantity adjustments' to demand or supply shocks. Their textbooks continue to use the IS-LM model (for example, Andrew Abel and Ben Bernanke, 2001; Bradford DeLong, 2002; Mankiw, 2003; Stiglitz and Walsh, 2002), and they are skeptical of the Real Business Cycle theory explanation for business cycles (Mankiw, 1989). They retain the Keynesian view that recessions are inherent in capitalism, undesirable, socially expensive, and preventable with correct policy. But many of them accept the NCE micro-foundations argument that assuming rational utility-maximizing behavior by economic actors and some version of rational expectations was necessary and useful for economic analysis. They have produced a synthesis of original Keynesian and NCE economics, combining elements of each.

Although some NK economists have advocated the use of countercyclical fiscal policy in severe recessions or when the threat of deflation appears (Stiglitz, 2002; Auerbach, Blinder and Feldstein in FRB of Kansas City, 2002), most of them have argued that monetary policy is more efficient and generally sufficient to stabilize the economy. And although they advocate interventionist monetary policy to stabilize the economy (arguing that money isn't neutral in the short run), they generally express a preference for monetary policy rules as opposed to discretion (Taylor, 1999 and 2000). 'Rules' means setting targets for policy (the rate of inflation, or more often minimizing the gap between actual and potential gross domestic product (GDP), defined as the level of GDP consistent with the lowest sustainable level of unemployment without accelerating price inflation – the NAIRU), and designing a policy reaction function in which the central bank would increase or decrease interest rates (interest rates should be the operating instrument and intermediate target) by a given amount if GDP exceeds or falls below potential. Most of the New Keynesians see the money supply as endogeneous in the sense of its growth rate being the interaction of demand for credit and the central bank-determined level of short-term interest rates; and see money as neutral in the long run with respect to its influence over the growth path of the economy (De Long, 2000; Taylor, 2000).

Their primary focus and contribution with respect to understanding business cycles has been to demonstrate that (1) inflexible wages and prices could lead to quantity adjustments that were destabilizing (recessions could be understood as systemic coordination failures of the economy's markets since markets don't always quickly find prices that 'clear'), and (2) that rigid, sticky or slowly adjusting prices and wages could be seen as the result of rational responses by economic actors within the actual institutions of capitalist economies. Much of their research focused on the latter point; they found plausible explanations for sticky wages and prices, which challenged both the NCE argument that markets clear quickly (or would in a more nearly perfect world) and the NCE claim that the Walrasian equilibrium approach was useful as a description of reality. New Keynesian economics has been described as 'dis-equilibrium' economics, in that it explains why economies are usually not in equilibrium at the natural rate of unemployment and the potential level of output.

Inflexible wages and prices are explained by institutional factors such as monopolistic competition, menu costs, lengthy contracts, efficiency wage theory, wage and price staggering, markup pricing, bureaucratic inertia and marketing strategy (Blinder (1994) discusses 12 such factors mentioned in the NK literature). Other NK lines of attack on NCE involved skepticism regarding aspects of rational expectations, importantly including the assumption of inexpensive and complete information, the NCE assumption that workers, managers and owners actually think and behave like the NCE economists' models would have them, and propositions built upon rational expectations, such as the Ricardian equivalence story.

In summation, the New Keynesians argue that capitalism is often unstable due to the persistence of both demand and supply shocks, and to the ways in which the market system adjusts to such shocks. They also believe that it is both desirable and necessary to use interventionist policy to stabilize the economy; these positions put them in the Keynesian camp and in clear opposition to the views of the NCE economists. However, they prefer monetary policy over fiscal policy because (1) they think monetary policy by itself is usually effective, (2) they think that automatic stabilizers are more effective than discretionary policy due to the relatively small estimates for multipliers and the long time lags for fiscal policy, and (3) because of the political problems which make timely changes in fiscal policy difficult. This preference for monetary policy and for policy rules versus discretion differentiate them from the original Keynesians as well as the Post Keynesians (Arestis and Sawyer, 2002a, b).

The views of the New Keynesians appear to be currently hegemonic within mainstream academic macroeconomics in the US and UK from the perspective of who has been selected for policy advice by the Federal Reserve, the Bank of England, and recent governments in both countries; whose macroeconomics texts are most widely adopted and whose theoretical views are dominant in classrooms; and whose policy views are adhered to by the Federal Reserve. Taylor (1997, 2000) and Michael Parkin (2000) explore the way graduate and undergraduate macroeconomics is now taught; the core ideas emphasized are the New Keynesian views on stabilization policy, although NCE is also presented in intermediate and graduate-level courses.[6]

The articles by G. Fontana, G. Fontana and A. Palacio-Vera, P. Dalziel, and P. Arestis and M. Sawyer in the symposium on monetary economics in the *Journal of Post Keynesian Economics*, Summer 2002, discuss the 'new consensus' among central bankers (at least in Canada, the US, the UK and the European Union) and mainstream academic economists – most of whom are New Keynesians – regarding monetary policy: central banks should estimate the demand gap and adjust interest rates accordingly; the behavior of monetary aggregates is a residual with no causal importance. This appears to be the actual way central banks now behave (see Taylor, 1999; Bank of Canada, 2001; European Central Bank, 2002; Arestis and Sawyer, 2002a, 2002b; Volcker, 2002; Greenspan, 2003; and Meulendyke, 1988, 1998). Targeting interest rates, passively monitoring the behavior of monetary aggregates, and countercyclical monetary policy are antithetical to monetarism and much of the rest of New Classical Economics, although the central banks' adoption of this approach to monetary policy seems to have largely escaped notice within academic economics.

What remains of monetarism appears to be the high priority that most central banks give to low rates of inflation, which leads them to prefer tight monetary policy in spite of its effects on economic growth and unemployment (for example, the European Central Bank's strong preference for tight money). The other elements of NCE policy which still seem widely accepted within the mainstream are the arguments that fiscal policy can't and shouldn't be used for short-run stabilization, that governments should be small, and that government budget deficits and excessive government debt are bad because they reduce net saving and investment by the private sector. The lingering theoretical influence of other aspects of NCE within mainstream economics largely appears to be the understanding that expectations must be taken seriously in constructing economic models, and that modeling expectations is difficult. Some New Keynesians such as DeLong (2000) argue that the influence of these aspects of monetarism and NCE represents a 'triumph of monetarism'; Post Keynesians such as

Paul Dalziel (2002) disagree, arguing that the discredited quantity theory of money should be seen as the core concept defining monetarism so that the new consensus is 'post Monetarist'.[7]

NEW ECONOMIC GROWTH THEORY

Another interesting aspect of mainstream economics is the development of new approaches to economic growth which go beyond the once-dominant Solow growth models and lend support to arguments for government intervention in the economy. Solovian growth models are based upon neoclassical and New Classical assumptions such as perfect competition (and continuous market clearing), diminishing marginal returns to capital, the free flow of information and technological change, and equilibrium between aggregate demand and aggregate supply (so that the economy is assumed to be always at full employment). In these models, diminishing returns to capital leads to the counter-intuitive deduction that different rates of investment will have no effect on economic growth over the long run; 'conditional convergence' should obtain, in which countries with similar savings and population growth rates should converge to the same level of per capita national income and to the same rate of growth (the 'stationary state'), while countries with different characteristics would end up with different per capita income levels but the same growth rate. The common growth rate would be determined by the exogenous rate of technological change under the assumption that capital, technology and knowledge are mobile across countries (Solow, 1956); this leaves almost no role for the state in promoting economic growth (although countries with low capital/labor ratios might adopt policies to raise the saving rate to move toward a higher stationary state; during the transition toward the higher equilibrium, the country would temporarily have a higher growth rate).

The new economic growth theory (NEG) broadens the definition of capital to include knowledge (human capital), incorporates the spillover effects of investment in both human and fixed capital and the effects of increasing returns to scale, and introduces imperfect information and markets (Lucas, 1988; P. Romer, 1986, 1994). Under these conditions, countries with higher rates of savings and investment could have permanently higher rates of technological progress and economic growth. Since the growth rate of technological progress and output are influenced by the rate of investment – explained within the models – this approach is often termed 'endogenous growth theory'.

For present purposes, their importance is that the NEG models present another reason for state intervention in the economy: the state can encourage economic growth through its investment in human capital (education, research and development), in infrastructure (Aschauer, 1988), by developing appropriate institutions (competitive markets, well-regulated financial systems, stable money), and through policies which encourage saving and investment by the private sector.

POST KEYNESIAN ECONOMICS

Institutionalist and Post Keynesian economists have developed a radical critique of original IS-LM Keynesianism, New Classical Economics – especially its monetarist core – and New Keynesianism. Following the much admired Joan Robinson, the first generation of economists who referred to themselves as Post Keynesians such as Paul Davidson (1972) and Basil Moore (1988) used derogatory terms such as 'bastard Keynesianism', 'IS-LM Keynesianism', and 'textbook Keynesianism' to refer to what they saw as a much attenuated and misleading version of the master's views that had been developed in the 1940s and 1950s by the first generation of Keynesians. They argued that IS-LM Keynesianism ignores Keynes's stress on uncertainty and disequilibrium; it is another form of general equilibrium theory, describing a tendency towards equilibrium which doesn't exist in the real world (or in Keynes's theory). Besides Davidson's important book *Money and the Real World* (1972, revised edition 1978), other influential early contributions which focused on monetary-financial macroeconomics include books by Nicholas Kaldor (1960, 1970, 1982), Abba Lerner (1943, 1944), Hyman Minsky (1975, 1982 and 1986), Basil Moore (1984, 1988), Stephen Rousseas (1986), and Sidney Weintraub (1958, 1965); also important is John Hicks's later work in which he expressed reservations about the usefulness of his own IS-LM model (1967, 1980).[8]

These economists attempted go beyond Keynes's work ('post' Keynesian) by building on what they saw as Keynes's correct ideas and insights while rejecting what they found inadequate in his work. Included in the latter category are his *General Theory* assumption of a central bank-determined exogeneous money supply, his Marshallian price theory, and the lack of a theory of economic growth. The Post Keynesian project is to construct a realistic model of modern capitalism that would be useful in designing policy to encourage full employment, stability, growth and less inequality. A strong emphasis on finding practical solutions to economic policy problems is found throughout the work of this group, which has also been a hallmark of American Institutionalism. Many of the early Post Keynesians were (and some still are) sympathetic to some versions of democratic socialism; most advocate some form of incomes policy; and all advocate a powerful, interventionist state whose economic policies should give highest priority to encouraging full employment, economic growth and less inequality – the goals proposed by Keynes in the final chapter of his *General Theory of Employment, Interest and Money* (1936).

The core propositions of Post Keynesian economics (the first two form their 'pre-analytic vision' in Schumpeter's term) include (1) the recognition of 'fundamental or absolute uncertainty' as radically different from 'statistical' or 'probabilistic risk'; fundamental uncertainty does not allow us to make precise calculations of risk. Keynes observed that many of the most important economic decisions such as whether to invest in fixed capital, purchase a bond or hold money are made in situations in which the information necessary to evaluate risk probabilistically will always be absent. Davidson (1978, 1982–3) argues that the economy is 'non-ergodic' as it moves through time; from this perspective, rational expectations as a description of (or prescription for) behavior is nonsensical – we can't learn how to 'rationally' evaluate certain kinds of risk (or estimate future inflation) because the circumstances keep changing. Rules of thumb and conventions serve as useful guides for decisions, and since they are in fact widely used, economic models should incorporate them. The Post Keynesians' understanding of uncertainty is related to their stress on the importance of historical time and the irreversibility of many important decisions, and is antithetical to the NCE approach to knowledge and uncertainly.

(2) The economy is inherently unstable because of uncertainty and the instability of expectations, especially expectations regarding profit from investment and the future prices of assets. The classical and NCE equilibrating mechanism of flexible prices is weak (prices aren't very flexible downward) and it would actually increase instability if prices could somehow be made more flexible with institutional change, since falling prices in a recession would depress profit expectations and investment. Full employment is less likely than widespread unemployment. Financial speculation and financial instability are inherent in the structure of modern financial institutions and financial markets, and can be the cause of instability in the 'real' economy (see Minsky, 1975, 1982 and 1986 for discussions of the inherence and implications of financial instability). Society needs to impose stabilizing constraints on the economy, including institutions which stabilize prices, wages and interest rates. Most importantly, a large government sector whose expenditure can quickly increase in slumps is necessary to prevent downward instability (Minsky 1982); small state sectors reduce stability.

(3) Economic growth, economic fluctuations and income distribution are dialectically related and mutually reinforcing: inequality enhances instability;

instability (especially recessions) reduces investment and growth, while recessions and low growth increase inequality. This centrality of demand in Post Keynesian theory leads to the proposition of 'demand-led growth': the long-run growth path of the economy is determined by its short-run behavior.

(4) Economies are best understood as 'complex systems', which are 'self organizing' and exhibit 'emerging properties'. See Moore (1999) for a clear statement of this proposition and its implications; it is related to the Institutionalist economists' insistence that society's institutions evolve through time, so that theory must be institutionally specific to be useful. This means that we can't adequately understand an economy by observing just the behavior of a component and extrapolating that behavior to the system (this idea appears in Keynes's insight regarding the 'paradox of thrift' as an example of the fallacy of composition in classical macroeconomic analysis), and it is in sharp contrast to the NCE approach of building macroeconomics on the micro-foundations of individual rational choice under constraints. Post Keynesians emphasize the macro-foundations for individual behavior, such as risk, uncertainty and the possibility of instability.

If economies are complex systems with emerging properties which result from their history, this also implies that at best we may be able to understand aspects of their behavior for relatively brief periods of time before they fundamentally change, developing new laws of motion which require new institutions to improve their performance (Moore, 1999). Again, this is in sharp contrast to the mechanistic, timeless individual behavior and the equilibrium method and assumptions of NCE.

Moving to another core proposition on a lower level of abstraction, (5) the entry point into macroeconomics for the IPK school is a 'monetary theory of production' (Keynes, 1936). Money is created (by banks) to finance an increase in production which requires more fixed and circulating capital. Money is necessary for production to take place because production takes time and money is the social institution which transfers and stores purchasing power over time. Because of the existence of money, interruptions in the circular flow of income and expenditure can take place (by holding wealth in the form of money); such interruptions would be impossible in a barter economy or an economy in which money couldn't function as a store of value.

According to the IPK school, the NCE 'axiom of reals' (also held to a lesser extent by the NK school as well) – the assumed dichotomy between the monetary and real dimensions of the economy – is misleading; capitalism must be understood as a monetary economy, in which the circuit of money is as important as the physical flow of production and circulation of goods and services. Macroeconomics must begin with an analysis of money: its nature, origin, and functions; money is never neutral with respect to the real economy. The level of interest rates (the price of liquidity and the cost of credit) is a key price within the economy, since it influences both the willingness and ability of entrepreneurs to invest in real capital and of financial capitalists to hold non-monetary financial assets such as stocks and bonds. Keynes's and the Post Keynesians' concept of a monetary theory of production is similar to Marx's circuit of capital (which Keynes admired; see Dillard, 1948 for an early Institutionalist explanation of the Keynes–Marx correspondence), and his observation that the point of production and the motivation for the firm is the accumulation of capital in the form of money.

Another core proposition (6) is that the levels of prices, wages and interest rates should be understood as the result of distributional struggles which are determined by social institutions and complex processes, as opposed to their determination by the quantity theory of money as advanced by NCE. Rather than determining the level of wages and prices, the quantity of money in circulation is seen as the result of changes in the level of wages and prices, reversing the quantity theory's direction of causality. In IPK economics, changes in the level of wages lead to a change in the prices of goods, since firms practice markup pricing: prices are marked up over – primarily – labor costs of production, and estimates of average rather than marginal cost at normal output levels are used to set prices (Moore, 1988). Changes in the price level (inflation) lead *ceteris paribus* to an increase in the demand for working capital (credit), which banks accommodate. As more loans are made, the money supply increases (Moore, 1988).

A seventh core proposition is the endogeneous money supply theory, rigorously articulated by Moore (1988), which argues that anything that increases the demand for bank credit will increase the money supply; commercial banks must accommodate most of any increase in business or consumer loan demand, since most loans are made under predetermined lines of credit. Because central banks' first priority is an orderly payments system, they attempt to stabilize inter-bank loan rates: explicitly or implicitly they target the equivalent of the US federal funds rate and then adjust the level of bank reserves to meet that target (this is known as the 'accommodationist' explanation for endogenous money). This means that central banks determine the level of short-term interest rates (short rates are exogeneous) and the demand for bank credit determines the money supply (money is endogenous). Long rates and the maturity yield curve are complexly determined by expectations and perceptions of risk, as in Keynes's liquidity preference theory (Mott, 1985–6; Chick and Dow, 2002).

If central banks attempt to control the money supply or its growth by targeting monetary aggregates when the demand for credit is increasing, financial innovations allow bank lending and the monetary aggregates to increase even if interest rates rise (the 'structuralist' explanation for endogeneous money). Conversely, central banks can't expand the money supply if the demand for credit is contracting. Central banks can't control the money supply. For extended discussions of the various institutional factors and processes which determine the degree of money supply endogeneity and related issues, see Chick (1986), Evans (1984), Lavoie (1992), Moore (1988), Niggle (1991), Palley (1991, 1994), Pollin (1991), and Wray (1990, 1992 and 1998).

Finally, although IPK economists see the level of interest rates as important in influencing aggregate demand – especially business investment – their empirical work argues that spending and real output may not be very sensitive to interest rates in recessions, so that other demand-stimulating policies are necessary (Arestis and Sawyer, 2002a and 2002b; European Central Bank, 2002). Those same studies also provide evidence that interest rate changes are not very effective in reducing price inflation.

POST KEYNESIANS AND NEW KEYNESIANS

Although the IPK and New Keynesian economists agree on aspects of macroeconomics (the endogeneity of the money supply and the need for interventionist demand management for example), they disagree on many important points.[9]

(1) IPK economists see the economy as very unstable, requiring constraints stronger than discretionary monetary policy; New Keynesians assume strong equilibrating processes in the long run, pushing the economy toward equilibrium at a socially optimal natural rate of employment and the potential level of output.

(2) Following Keynes (1936), IPK argues that even if wages and prices were very flexible downward, capitalist economies wouldn't tend toward full employment; in fact most IPK economists see stable wage and price levels as a positive stabilizing factor – downwardly flexible prices would make things worse in a recession, since they would lower profits, asset prices and profit expectations, thus depressing investment. What is necessary to stabilize the economy is a large government sector whose automatic stabilizers and discretionary fiscal policy, coupled with stabilizing monetary policy, can keep the economy at full employment by balancing aggregate demand with potential supply (Minsky, 1982, 1986).

(3) IPK economists emphasize the problems associated with insufficient aggregate demand and excess industrial capacity – not just in the recession phase of business cycles but in the long run as well (Nell, 1988, 1992; Wray,

1990, 1998). From the IPK perspective, capitalist economies rarely fully utilize labor and capital; the economy is not supply or resource constrained but rather constrained by insufficient aggregate demand. They advocate inequality-reducing tax and transfer policies and a growing government share in aggregate output to keep the economy at full employment. Many (Wray, 1998) advocate government employer of last resort programs. Most also strongly favor public investment as a demand-creating and productivity-enhancing factor as well.

(4) IPK economics follows Keynes (and Kalecki) in arguing that savings does not finance investment as in the old classical, neoclassical, New Classical and New Keynesian models. Rather, investment is determined by profit expectations and the rate of interest, and it is financed by bank credit (and the growth in the money supply). The level of investment coupled with the variables that determine the Keynesian multiplier then determines the level of national income. National income moves toward the level that generates enough savings to equal the exogenously determined level of investment: investment determines savings, rather than savings determining investment.

This insight has powerful implications for many aspects of policy: most NCE and NK economists argue for policies (such as low marginal rates of taxation, high real interest rates, shrinking government, reducing the generosity of public pension systems) which should encourage higher net national savings (savings net of government budget deficits and depreciation), because in their models this would lead to higher private investment. From the IPK perspective this is wrong-headed: government spending – especially public investment – can increase productivity, private profits and profit expectations, thus encouraging private investment ('crowding in' rather than 'crowding out'). And the level of savings has little influence over either interest rates or investment, since interest rates are primarily determined by monetary policy and liquidity preference. In fact, *ceteris paribus*, a higher saving rate might depress investment and economic growth since it would lead to a lower level of consumption and aggregate demand growth.

(5) IPK economists put a higher priority on full employment than on price stability, and argue that the level of unemployment necessary to keep effective downward pressure on wages and prices entails unacceptable social costs. NK economists put a higher priority on low inflation than on full employment. On a more technical level, IPK economists don't think that we can accurately estimate the level of unemployment consistent with price and wage stability – the natural rate of unemployment or the NAIRU, which determines the potential level of national income in the NK model – and use that as a target for stabilization policy. In IPK theory, the level of

wages and prices is very complexly determined by a host of institutional and political factors reflecting the social and economic power of capital and labor which are more important in determining the rate of inflation than the level of unemployment. There is no natural rate of unemployment in either the sense of a 'strong attractor' that the economy tends toward or a predictable level consistent with price stability.

IPK economists argue that the important goals of full employment and both wage and price stability can only be reached by developing institutions which socially control wages, prices and the distribution of income across the social classes (the wage/profit ratio), and which link aggregate wage and profit increases to productivity gains: some form of incomes policy (Cornwall, 1985; Moore, 1988; Weintraub, 1971). Another approach to full employment and price stability advocated by IPK economists is a government employer of last resort strategy, coupled with expansionary fiscal policy (Wendell Gordon, 1997; Minsky, 1986; and Wray, 1998).

In contrast, New Keynesians argue that the NAIRU can be reliably estimated (although the range of estimates is seen by some as quite wide) and the estimates used as a target for stabilization policy; NK economists are willing to tolerate whatever levels of unemployment are necessary for price stability, disagreeing with the IPK view that 'non-traditional' forms of intervention such as incomes policy can be effective.[10]

(6) IPK economists propose a link between demand, cycles and growth: an economy that is well managed so as to avoid severe recessions and maintains a high level of employment will have higher levels of investment, technological change, productivity growth and output growth over the long run (John Cornwall, 1972, 1977, 1985, 1994; and Ed Nell, 1988, 1992). New Keynesians don't discuss this linkage.

(7) IPK economists agree with both Keynes and Kalecki (1939) that the distribution of income is important for business cycles and growth; they are interested in both the 'functional' or 'class' distribution between labor and capital and the 'personal' or 'size' distribution across individuals, households and families. One argument that Keynes and Post Keynesians make is that changes in the distribution of income can influence the composition and levels of aggregate demand (more profits means more investment; higher wages means more consumption). From this perspective, less inequality is preferred since it will stimulate production and employment in the short run, and thus stimulate investment and economic growth in the long run; lower interest rates both reduce inequality and stimulate investment (Keynes, 1936; Niggle, 1998 surveys and assesses some recent literature discussing the relationship between inequality and growth).

Followers of Kalecki observe that a declining wage share should be expected to reduce aggregate demand, capacity utilization and investment, and thus reduce both employment and economic growth. Proper macroeconomic policy implies paying attention to income distribution. Again, New Keynesians don't pay much attention to these issues.

(8) Propositions 4, 6 and 7 form parts of the IPK 'demand-led' approach to growth theory, in contrast to the NCE 'supply-side' approach which New Keynesians and New (endogenous) Economic Growth theories also stress. In the latter theories economic growth is seen as the result of increases in the quantity and quality of productive resources – natural resources, labor, capital and technology – which are analyzed as independent of the demand for output. IPK economists see the NEG as seriously flawed in assuming continuous market clearing, equilibrium at the natural rate and in assuming that savings finance investment, with causality flowing from savings to investment.[11]

(9) Many IPK economists advocate fixed exchange rate systems constructed around an international financial institution which could issue liquid financial assets as needed by deficit countries (Davidson, 1994); most New Keynesians accept flexible exchange rates with some important and influential exceptions such as Joseph Stiglitz (2002).

(10) IPK economists favor financial market regulation, and see unregulated financial markets as dangerous (Minsky, 1982, 1986; Isenberg, 2000); most New Keynesians are not in favor of financial market regulation.

SUMMARY AND CONCLUSIONS

In the 1970s and 1980s, New Classical economists developed and mainstream economics assimilated a set of propositions, models and theories which argued against both the need for and efficiency of Keynesian forms of state intervention in the economy to promote full employment, stability, equality and economic growth. Aspects of this economic philosophy – New Classical Economics, Monetarism, Real Business Cycle Theory, Supply Side Economics and Public Choice theory – offered theoretical support for neo-liberalism, and have been very influential both within economics and in the domains of policy and politics.

Modern Keynesian economists reject many aspects of the neo-liberal program based upon their competing 'New Keynesian' theoretical stance. Institutionalist and Post Keynesian economists present a more radical critique of NCE and offer a very different perspective on the economy. In the past decade, New Keynesian and New Growth Theory economics has become more influential within the mainstream. This phenomenon, coupled with the persistence of economic problems which seem intrinsic to unregulated global capitalism such as stagnation, increasing unemployment and inequality, and recurrent financial crises, opens up the possibility for IPK economics to be more seriously considered by mainstream economists, since IPK offers coherent explanations for those problems and plausible solutions to them.

NOTES

1. This chapter is taken from a longer paper prepared for the Basil Moore Festschrift in Stellenbosch, South Africa, 'A Short Course in Macroeconomics or Whatever Happened to Monetarism?' (January 2004, available upon request) which discusses original or 'first wave' Keynesian economics and both the Post Keynesian criticism and the New Classical counter-revolution to Keynesian economics in greater detail. Thanks to the Festschrift participants and editor Mark Setterfield for helpful comments and suggestions.
2. By 'mainstream' economics I mean the theoretical core and related policy proposals that are widely accepted as valid within academic economics, particularly as taught in elite graduate programs, which appear in the most widely adopted textbooks, and which support the worldview of those who become economic policy advisors. As a simplification, this might also be referred to as the 'orthodox' ideas of the academic, intellectual and political elites, as opposed to the 'heterodox' views critical of aspects of that orthodoxy. There are both scientific and political dimensions to the concept of 'orthodoxy', since the ideas of the dominant groups within a discipline are often privileged as scientifically correct.
3. The definition of Post Keynesian economics is problematic; this chapter accepts the 'big tent/broad church' definition advanced by Hamouda and Harcourt (1988), which includes followers of Kalecki and Sraffa as well as fundamentalist Keynesians. In sharp contrast Paul Davidson (2003) argues that the term should be reserved for those economists who stress the importance of fundamental uncertainty and rejection of the neoclassical axioms of ergodicity, gross substitutability and the neutrality of money. Davidson argues that Keynes's rejections of those 'special case' axioms allows the development of a 'general theory' based upon the smallest number of necessary axioms and interprets this as the most important distinguishing characteristic of Keynes's economics; Davidson's approach is often described as 'Keynesian Post Keynesianism'. Quite a few of the founders of the school were as strongly influenced by the Polish Marxist Michał Kalecki (for example, Joan Robinson and Nicholas Kaldor) and the Austrian Joseph Schumpeter (Hyman Minsky) as by Keynes; and many of them were sympathetic to or influenced by Marx as well (Minsky and Edward Nell for example). Piero Sraffa is also an influential figure for many of these economists. Perhaps 'post Keynesian, post Kaleckian, post Marxist', or 'post classical' would be more appropriate terms (Lavoie, 1992). Post Keynesian became a widely accepted term after the *Journal of Post Keynesian Economics* appeared in 1978. See Lavoie (1992) for an attempt at a synthesis of Post Keynesian micro and macroeconomics which a 'representative Post Keynesian' would find acceptable.
4. An informal survey of Federal Reserve Governors and CEA members in the 1970s, 1980s and 1990s didn't reveal any economists closely identified with NCE, except for a few monetarists on the Open Market Committee of the Fed. When asked what he would do if appointed to the CEA, NCE economist Robert Lucas replied that he would resign or abolish the Committee (Klamer, 1984).
5. Mankiw's 1990 article provides an overview of the rise of New Keynesianism and its opposition to elements of the new classical economics, especially real business cycle theory. See also Gordon (1990), Mankiw (1989), and the articles in Mankiw and Romer (1991). The interviews with Alan Blinder and John Taylor in Klamer (1984) discuss the views of two other prominent New Keynesians on new classical economics. Many of the

'old' Keynesians have also opposed aspects of NCE; see the interviews with Franco Modigliani, Robert Solow, and James Tobin in Klamer (1984), and Tobin (1980a, 1980b).

6. C. Romer and D. Romer's (2002) overview of the changes in stabilization policy over the post-World War II period presents evidence that the Federal Reserve and Council of Economic Advisors (CEA) have consistently practiced activist, interventionist policies to stabilize the economy. What changed over time was a shift toward attaching a higher priority to low inflation in the late 1970s, which resulted in higher real rates of interest, a movement away from discretionary fiscal policy as a stabilization tool, and their estimates of the natural rate or threshold rate for low unemployment which was consistent with low inflation. According to the Romers, the Fed and CEA's implied (and occasionally explicit) estimates for the natural rate were low in the 1960s, increased in the 1970s and 1980s, then decreased in the 1990s. In the Romers' story, neither the Fed nor the CEA ever undertook policy consistent with the NCE noninterventionist philosophy with respect to stabilization. The comments on their paper in *Rethinking Stabilization Policy*, a symposium sponsored by the FRB Kansas City (2002), are generally consistent with the Romers' position regarding activism.
7. Although a consensus regarding theory and policy appears to exist within the dominant elite, it may not exist within the broader population of professional economists. In an attempt to discover what economists believe, Fuller and Geide-Stevenson's (2003) survey of a sample of US economists finds 'strong consensus' on very few macroeconomic propositions, and only 'modest consensus' or 'none' on many critical propositions including the validity of rational expectations, the ability of central banks to control the money supply, the power of self-correcting mechanisms, and whether fiscal policy should be used to stabilize the economy.
8. Paul Davidson's (2003–4) review article of J. King (2002) provides a helpful history of the origins of Post Keynesian economics; see also King's book (2002). For a general introduction to Post Keynesian economics, see the entries on Post Keynesian economics by King, Lavoie and Wray in O'Hara (1999); also the introduction to Lavoie (1992). Eichner's *A Guide to Post Keynesian Economics* (1978) is regarded as an early 'manifesto' of the group; Holt and Pressman (2001) present a recent collection of articles.
9. Rotheim's (1998) book presents an interesting collection of articles by Post Keynesians, which attempt to differentiate New and Post Keynesian economics.
10. The articles by Stiglitz, Robert Gordon, Douglas Staiger, James Stock and Mark Watson, Olivier Blanchard and Lawrence Katz, Richard Rogerson, and James Galbraith in the Symposium on the Natural Rate of Unemployment, *Journal of Economic Perspectives* (1997) provide a good introduction to New Keynesian and Post Keynesian positions in the debates over the NAIRU. Robert Eisner (1997) also presents a Post Keynesian critique of NAIRU. C. Romer and D. Romer (2002) argue that mainstream economists rejected incomes policy, wage and price controls, and other 'non-traditional forms' of stabilization policy because they are ineffective and lead to inefficiency.
11. Setterfield (2002) presents articles which challenge the New Economic Growth theory's supply-side vision of economic growth from an IPK perspective; Setterfield's introductory chapter serves as a useful introduction and summary of the distinctions between the two approaches to economic growth. Moore (2003) also discusses the two approaches to growth theory.

REFERENCES

Abel, A. and B. Bernanke (2001) *Macroeconomics*, New York: Addison Wesley.
Arestis, R. (1988) *Post Keynesian Monetary Economics*, Aldershot, UK and Brookfield, USA: Edward Elgar.
Arestis, R. and A. Eichner (1989) 'The Post Keynesian Theory of Money and Credit', *Journal of Economic Issues*, 22, 1003–21.

Arestis, R. and M. Sawyer (2002a) 'The Bank of England Macroeconomic Model: Its Nature and Implications', *Journal of Post Keynesian Economics*, 24, 529–46.
Arestis, R. and M. Sawyer (2002b) 'Can Monetary Policy Affect the Real Economy?' Working Paper No. 355, Annandale-on-Hudson, Levy Economics Institute, available online at www.levy.org
Aschauer, D. (1989) 'Is Public Expenditure Productive?' *Journal of Monetary Economics*, 23, 177–200.
Bank of Canada (2001) 'A Primer on the Implementation of Monetary Policy in the LVTS Environment', available on the Bank of Canada website.
Bank of England (2000) *Economic Models of the Bank of England*, London: Bank of England.
Blanchard, O. and L. Katz (1994) 'On Sticky Prices: Academic Theories Meet the Real World', in G. Mankiw (ed.), *Monetary Policy*, Chicago: University of Chicago Press.
Blanchard, O. and L. Katz (1997) 'What We Know and Do Not Know About the Natural Rate of Unemployment', *Journal of Economic Perspectives*, 11, 51–72.
Blinder, A. (1994) 'On Sticky Prices: Academic Theories Meet the Real World', in G. Mankiw (ed.), *Monetary Policy*, Chicago: University of Chicago Press.
Blinder, A. and R. Solow (1973) 'Does Fiscal Policy Matter?' *Journal of Public Economics*, 2, 319–37.
Chick, V. (1986) 'The Evolution of the Banking System and the Theory of Saving, Investment and Interest', *Economie et Societés*, 3, 112–26.
Chick, V. and S. Dow (2002) 'Monetary Policy with Endogenous Money and Liquidity Preference: A Nondualistic Treatment', *Journal of Post Keynesian Economics*, 24, 587–608.
Cornwall, J. (1972) *Growth and Stability in a Mature Economy*, New York: John Wiley.
Cornwall, J. (1977) *Modern Capitalism: Its Growth and Transformation*, New York: St Martins.
Cornwall, J. (1985) *The Conditions for Economic Recovery: A Post-Keynesian Analysis*, White Plains, NY: M.E. Sharpe.
Cornwall, J. (1990) *The Theory of Economic Breakdown: An Institutional-Analytical Approach*, Oxford: Basil Blackwell.
Cornwall, J. (1994) *Economic Breakdown and Recovery*, Armonk, NY: M.E. Sharpe.
Dalziel, P. (2002) 'The Triumph of Keynes: What Now for Monetary Policy Research?' *Journal of Post Keynesian Economics*, 24, 511–28.
Davidson, P. (1972, 1978) *Money and the Real World*, 1st and 2nd editions, New York: Macmillan.
Davidson, P. (1974) 'A Keynesian View of Friedman's Theoretical Framework for Monetary Analysis', in R. Gordon (ed.) (1974).
Davidson, P. (1982–3) 'Rational Expectations: A Fallacious Foundation for Studying Crucial Decision-Making Processes', *Journal of Post Keynesian Economics*, 5, 182–98.
Davidson, P. (1994) *Post Keynesian Macroeconomic Theory*, Aldershot, UK and Brookfield, USA: Edward Elgar.
Davidson, P. (2003–4) 'Setting the Record Straight on John King's "A History of Post Keynesian Economics"', *Journal of Post Keynesian Economics*, 26, 1–32.
DeLong, B. (2000) 'The Triumph of Monetarism?' *Journal of Economic Perspectives*, 14, 83–94.
DeLong, B. (2002) *Macroeconomics*, New York: McGraw-Hill.

Dillard, D. (1948) *The Economics of John Maynard Keynes*, New York: Prentice-Hall.
Eichner, A. (ed.), (1978) *A Guide to Post Keynesian Economics*, White Plains, NY: M.E. Sharpe.
Eisner, R. (1997) 'A New View of the NAIRU', in P. Davidson and J. Kregel (eds), *Improving the Global Economy: Keynesianism and the Growth in Output and Employment*, Cheltenham, UK and Lyme, USA: Edward Elgar.
European Central Bank (2002) 'Recent Findings on Monetary Transmission in the Euro Area', *Monthly Bulletin* (October), 44–55.
Evans, G. (1984) 'The Long Run Endogeneous Money Supply', *Journal of Economic Issues*, 18, 66–74.
Federal Reserve Bank of New York (1990) *Intermediate Targets and Indicators for Monetary Policy: A Critical Survey*, New York: FRB of NY.
Federal Reserve Bank of Kansas City (2002) *Symposium: Rethinking Stabilization Policy*, available on FRBKC website http://www.kc.frb.org
Fontana, G. (2002) 'The Making of Monetary Policy in Endogenous Money Theory: An Introduction', *Journal of Post Keynesian Economics*, 24, 503–10.
Fontana, G. and A. Palacio-Vera (2002) 'Monetary Policy Rules: What Are We Learning?' *Journal of Post Keynesian Economics* 24, 547–68.
Fuller, D. and D. Geide-Stevenson (2003) 'Consensus among Economists: Revisited', *Journal of Economic Education*, 34, 369–87.
Galbraith, J. (1997) 'Time to Ditch the NAIRU', *Journal of Economic Perspectives*, 11, 93–108.
Gordon, R. (ed.) (1974) *Milton Friedman's Monetary Framework: A Debate With His Critics*, Chicago: University of Chicago.
Gordon, R. (1990) 'What is New-Keynesian Economics?' *Journal of Economic Literature*, 28, 1115–71.
Gordon, R. (1997) 'The Time-Varying NAIRU and its Implications for Economic Policy', *Journal of Economic Perspectives*, 11, 11–32.
Gordon, W. (1997) 'Job Assurance – The Job Guarantee Revisited', *Journal of Economic Issues*, 31, 826–34.
Greenspan, A. (2003) 'Monetary Policy under Uncertainty', Federal Reserve Bank of Kansas City Symposium, Jackson Hole, Wyoming (August), available online at the Federal Reserve home page (www.federalreserve.gov) under 'Speeches by Board Members'.
Haavelmo, T. (1945) 'The Multiplier Effects of Balanced Budget', *Econometrica*, 13, 311–18.
Hamouda, O.F. and G. Harcourt (1988) 'Post Keynesianism: From Critique to Coherency', *Bulletin of Economic Research*, 40.
Hicks, J. (1937) 'Mr. Keynes and the Classics: A Suggested Interpretation', *Econometrica*, 5, 144–59.
Hicks, J. (1967) 'Monetary Theory and History', *Critical Essays in Monetary Theory*, Oxford: Oxford University Press.
Hicks, J. (1980) 'IS-LM: An Explanation', *Journal of Post Keynesian Economics*, 3, 139–54.
Hodgson, G. (1991) *After Keynes and Marx: Essays in Political Economy*, New York: St Martin's Press.
Holt, R. and S. Pressman (ed.) (2001) *A New Guide to Post Keynesian Economics*, London and New York: Routledge.
Howard, D. (2001) 'A Primer on the Implementation of Monetary Policy in the LVTS Environment', Bank of Canada website.

Isenberg, D. (2000) 'The Political Economy of Financial Reform: The Origins of the U.S. Deregulation of the 1980s and 1990s', in R. Pollin (ed.), *Capitalism, Socialism, and Radical Political Economy*, Cheltenham, UK and Northampton, MA, USA: Edward Elgar.
Kaldor, N. (1960) 'The Radcliffe Report', *Review of Economics and Statistics*, 60, 127–38.
Kaldor, N. (1970) 'The New Monetarism', *Lloyds Bank Review*, 17, 1–18.
Kaldor, N. (1982) *The Scourge of Monetarism*, New York: Oxford University Press.
Kalecki, M. (1939) *Essays in the Theory of Economic Fluctuations*, London: Allen & Unwin.
Keller, R. (1983) 'Keynesian and Institutional Economics: Compatibility or Complementarity?' *Journal of Economic Issues*, 17, 1087–95.
Keynes, J. (1923) *A Tract on Monetary Reform*, Volume 4 in the *Collected Writings* (1971), New York: Macmillan.
Keynes, J. (1936) *The General Theory of Employment, Interest and Money*, Volume 7 in the *Collected Writings* (1971), New York: Macmillan.
King, J. (2002) *A History of Post Keynesian Economics*, Cheltenham, UK and Northampton, MA, USA: Edward Elgar.
Klamer, A. (1984) *Conversations with Economists*, Towota: Rowman & Allanheld.
Lavoie, M. (1992) *Foundations of Post-Keynesian Economic Analysis*, Aldershot, UK and Brookfield, USA: Edward Elgar.
Lerner, A. (1943) 'Functional Finance and the Federal Debt', *Social Research*, 10, 38–51.
Lerner, A. (1944) *The Economics of Control: Principles of Welfare Economics*, New York: Macmillan.
Lerner, A. and D. Colander (1980) *MAP: A Market Anti-Inflation Plan*, New York: Harcourt Brace Jovanovich.
Lucas, R. (1988) 'On the Mechanics of Economic Development', *Journal of Monetary Economics*, 22, 3–42.
Mankiw, G. (1989) 'Real Business Cycles: A New Keynesian Perspective', *Journal of Economic Perspectives*, 3, 79–90.
Mankiw, G. (1990) 'A Quick Refresher Course in Macroeconomics', *Journal of Economic Literature*, 28, 1645–60.
Mankiw, G. (2003), *Macroeconomics*, New York: Worth.
Mankiw, G. and D. Romer (eds) (1991) *New Keynesian Economics*, 2 volumes, Cambridge, MA: MIT Press.
Mariscal, I. and P. Howells (2002) 'Central Banks and Market Interest Rates', *Journal of Post Keynesian Economics*, 24, 569–86.
Meulendyke, A. (1988) 'Can the Federal Reserve Influence Whether the Money Supply is Endogeneous? A Comment on Moore', *Journal of Post Keynesian Economics*, 10, 390–97.
Meulendyke, A. (1998) *U.S. Monetary Policy and Financial Markets*, New York: Federal Reserve Bank of New York.
Minsky, H. (1957) 'Central Banking and Money Market Changes', *Quarterly Journal of Economics*, 82, 37–46.
Minsky, H. (1975) *John Maynard Keynes*, New York: Columbia University Press.
Minsky, H. (1982) *Can 'It' Happen Again?: Essays on Instability and Finance*, Armonk: M.E. Sharpe.
Minsky, H. (1986) *Stabilizing an Unstable Economy*, New Haven: Yale University Press.

Moore, B. (1984) 'The Endogeneous Money Stock', *Journal of Post Keynesian Economics*, 1, 49–70.
Moore, B. (1988) *Horizontalists and Verticalists: The Macroeconomics of Credit Money*, New York: Cambridge University Press.
Moore, B. (1999) 'Economics and Complexity', in M. Setterfield (ed.), *Growth, Employment and Inflation: Essays in Honor of John Cornwall*, New York: St Martins.
Moore, B. (2003) '*Shaking the Invisible Hand*', Manuscript, University of Stellenbosch.
Mott, T. (1985–6) 'Towards a Post-Keynesian Formulation of Liquidity Preference', *Journal of Post Keynesian Economics*, 8, 222–32.
Nell, E. (1988) *Prosperity and Public Spending: Transformational Growth and the Role of Government*, Boston: Unwin Hyman.
Nell, E. (1992) *Transformational Growth and Effective Demand*, New York: University Press.
Niggle, C. (1991) 'The Endogeneous Money Supply Theory: An Institutionalist Approach', *Journal of Economic Issues*, 25, 137–51.
Niggle, C. (1998) 'Equality, Democracy, Institutions and Growth', *Journal of Economic Issues*, 32, 523–30.
O'Hara, P. (ed.) (1999) *Encyclopedia of Political Economy*, New York and London: Routledge.
Palley, T. (1991) 'The Endogenous Money Supply: Consensus and Disagreement', *Journal of Post Keynesian Economics*, 13, 397–403.
Palley, T. (1994) 'Competing Views of the Money Supply Process: Theory and Evidence', *Metroeconomica*, 45, 67–88.
Parkin, M. (2000) 'The Principles of Macroeconomics at the Millenium', *American Economic Review*, 90, 85–9.
Pollin, R. (1991) 'Two Theories of Money Supply Endogeneity: Some Empirical Evidence', *Journal of Post Keynesian Economics*, 13, 366–96.
Rogerson, R. (1997) 'Theory Ahead of Language in the Economics of Unemployment', *Journal of Economic Perspectives*, 11, 73–92.
Romer, C. and D. Romer (2002) 'The Evolution of Economic Understanding and Postwar Stabilization Policy', in Federal Reserve Bank of Kansas City, *Symposium: Rethinking Stabilization Policy*, Kansas City: FRB of Kansas City.
Romer, P. (1986) 'Increasing Returns and Long-Run Growth', *Journal of Political Economy* (October), 1002–37.
Romer, P. (1994) 'The Origins of Endogenous Growth', *Journal of Economic Perspectives*, 8, 3–22.
Rotheim, R. (ed.) (1998) *New Keynesian Economics/Post Keynesian Alternatives*, London and New York: Routledge.
Rousseas, S. (1960) 'Velocity Changes and the Effectiveness of Monetary Policy', *Review of Economics and Statistics*, 42, 146–58.
Rousseas, S. (1986) *Post Keynesian Monetary Economics*, Armonk: M.E. Sharpe.
Setterfield, M. (ed.) (1999) *Growth, Employment and Inflation*, New York: Macmillan.
Setterfield, M. (ed.) (2002) *The Economics of Demand-Led Growth*, Cheltenham, UK and Northampton, MA, USA: Edward Elgar.
Solow, R. (1956) 'A Contribution to the Theory of Economic Growth', *Quarterly Journal of Economics*, 70, 65–94.
Staiger, D., J. Stock and M. Watson (1997a) 'The NAIRU, Unemployment and Monetary Policy', *Journal of Economic Perspectives*, 11, 33–50.

Staiger, D., J. Stock and M. Watson (1997b) 'Reflections on the Natural Rate Hypothesis', *Journal of Economic Perspectives*, 11, 3–10.
Stiglitz, J. (1997) 'Reflections on the Natural Rate Hypothesis', *Journal of Economic Perspectives*, 11, 3–10.
Stiglitz, J. (2002) *Globalization and its Discontents*, New York: W.W. Norton.
Stiglitz, J. and C. Walsh (2002) *Macroeconomics*, 3rd edition, New York: W.W. Norton.
Taylor, J. (1993) 'Discretion versus Policy Rules in Practice', *Carnegie-Rochester Conference Series on Public Policy*, 39, Amsterdam: North Holland, 195–214.
Taylor, J. (1997) 'A Core of Practical Macroeconomics', *American Economic Review*, 87, 233–35.
Taylor, J. (ed.) (1999) *Monetary Policy Rules*, Chicago: University of Chicago Press.
Taylor, J. (2000) 'Teaching Modern Macroeconomics at the Principles Level', *American Economic Review*, 90, 90–94.
Tobin, J. (1980a) 'Are New Classical Models Plausible Enough to Guide Policy?' *Journal of Money, Credit and Banking*, 12, 788–99.
Tobin, J. (1980b) *Asset Accumulation and Economic Activity: Reflections on Contemporary Macroeconomic Theory*, Chicago: University of Chicago Press.
Tobin, J. (1993) 'Price Flexibility and Output Stability: An Old Keynesian View', *Journal of Economic Perspectives*, 7, 45–65.
Tymoigne, E. (2003) 'Keynes and Commons on Money', *Journal of Economic Issues*, 37, 527–45.
Volcker, P. (2002) 'Monetary Policy Transmission: Past and Future Challenges', *Federal Reserve Bank of New York Economic Policy Review*, 7–11.
Weintraub, S. (1958) *Approach to the Theory of Income Distribution*, Philadelphia: Chilton.
Weintraub, S. (1965) *A Keynesian Theory of Employment, Growth and Income Distribution*, Philadelphia: Chilton.
Weintraub, S. and J. Wallich (1971) 'A Tax-Based Incomes Policy', *Journal of Economic Issues*, 5, 1–19.
Wray, L.R. (1990) *Money and Credit in Capitalist Economies: The Endogeneous Money Approach*, Aldershot, UK and Brookfield, USA: Edward Elgar.
Wray, L.R. (1992) 'Alternative Approaches to Money and Interest Rates', *Journal of Economic Issues*, 26, 1145–77.
Wray, L.R (1998) *Understanding Modern Money: The Key to Full Employment and Price Stability*, Cheltenham, UK and Lyme, USA: Edward Elgar.

21. A future for Keynesian macroeconomics[1]

Wendy Cornwall and John Cornwall

INTRODUCTION

This chapter is an overview of how Keynesian principles, originally developed to apply to the short run, can be extended to provide analytical tools applicable to the medium and long runs. The justification for the chapter is that such analytical tools have not been developed by others, despite the claims of New Keynesian (and New Consensus) macroeconomics. Given space limitations, we present only the core of our model; a detailed account is not relevant to our primary objective, which is to make a case for the wider application of Keynesian analysis. The interested reader will find detailed support for key theoretical points in the footnote references to other work by the authors. The extended model is applied to a group of OECD economies to explain changing unemployment performance over time, as well as differences among countries. The intent is to support our claim that extending the original Keynesian model beyond the short run produces a substantial increase in the applicability of Keynesian principles to analysis and macroeconomic policy.

Before introducing the model, we use the following two sections to distance our Keynesian analytical approach from current mainstream macroeconomics, which has New Keynesian economics at its centre. Examination of both its short-run and long-run features show it to lack essential Keynesian characteristics. More seriously, neither its short-run or long-run analyses are useful descriptive devices for real world macroeconomic processes; one consequence is that its continued wide acceptance, especially among academic economists, has reduced interest in macroeconomics. In the next two sections we outline our extension of the Keynesian model to the medium and long runs. We then consider two episodes in the development of mature capitalism – the prosperous Golden Age and the subsequent Age of Decline – to illustrate the explanatory value of our framework. In the concluding section it is argued that without a return to traditional Keynesian principles, macroeconomics will not regain the prestigious position that it held during the Golden Age.

NEW KEYNESIAN SHORT-RUN ANALYSIS

It has been claimed that the future of macroeconomics is New Keynesian, a claim bolstered by the status it is given in mainstream textbooks and journals. Its current ascendancy rests largely on research undertaken in the 1970s and 1980s to provide rigorous and realistic micro foundations for macroeconomics. Realism was provided by replacing the perfect competition framework of the New Classical model with imperfectly competitive markets. The introduction of imperfections abandons the frictionless price and wage adjustments of perfect competition. Following a shock, individual imperfectly competitive profit-maximizing firms make price and quantity decisions, an activity that slows down adjustment of the general price level; rigidity also stems from the possibility that the cost of changing price lists, catalogues, and so on. will exceed anticipated revenue gains. The existence of contracts, information asymmetries, and interdependent firms further complicates decision-making and hampers price adjustment, delaying the return to equilibrium. When aggregated, these imperfectly competitive markets would become the demand side of a short-run macroeconomic model along the lines of the familiar IS-LM model. To complete the model, a wage-price mechanism with real wage bargaining and the vertical Phillips curve comprise the supply side, together with adjustment mechanisms, for example, Pigou effects, that govern the system's response to shocks.

The shift to imperfect competition at the micro level distinguishes New Keynesian from New Classical economics. But does it make the model Keynesian? Imperfectly competitive micro markets allow the introduction of one Keynesian feature only: wage and price inflexibility. The consequence is that deviations from equilibrium are likely to be long-lived, and this provides an argument for monetary or fiscal policy, but only to speed up the return to equilibrium. Clearly the New Keynesian introduction of imperfectly competitive markets has not severed the tie with exogenous supply-determined equilibrium analysis. This fundamental characteristic is shared with the New Classical model. It does provide a more realistic explanation of the observed sluggish response of prices and wages to disturbances. Earlier explanations relied upon vaguely defined 'market imperfections' that caused short-run frictions, impeding the function of flexible prices in otherwise perfectly competitive market economies. New Keynesians have developed many variations of their model that rigorously illustrate these imperfections (Blanchard, 2000).

Despite this improvement, the core of New Keynesian economics is clearly non-Keynesian, at odds with Keynes's notion of an unemployment equilibrium determined by aggregate demand. But even on its own terms, serious problems arise from the New Keynesians having incorporated their new micro analysis into a short-run macroeconomic framework that assumes an exogenously determined, stable equilibrium. Three are worth citing. The first concerns the assumed exogeneity of the equilibrium; for example, if the equilibrium unemployment rate can be affected by economic variables (including the actual unemployment rate), it is not truly exogenous, and cannot function as an attractor of the system or as a fixed target for policy. Assuming the equilibrium to be exogenous, the second problem concerns the speed of adjustment when out of equilibrium. This must be rapid relative to the rate at which the exogenous determinants of equilibrium change. Even if this test is also passed, stability of the equilibrium requires the assumed adjustment mechanisms are able to counter not only the initial adverse shock, but also any additional induced cumulative adverse movements in aggregate demand, output and employment, for example, an accelerator-multiplier interaction. If they cannot, disturbances may be amplified, pushing the system further from equilibrium; that is, an equilibrium may exist, but it is unstable. In fact, there is no theoretical or empirical evidence to suggest that Keynes and Pigou effects are strong enough to perform this task (Tobin, 1993).[2] As a result, the New Keynesian short-run framework cannot explain movements in the actual unemployment rate. The economy would settle at this rate only by accident, and if disturbed would exhibit no tendency to return to it.

Thus while New Keynesian macroeconomics offers useful additions to micro analysis, its short-run equilibrium analysis, including its vertical Phillips curve component, is not useful. Therefore we reject the notion of a unique equilibrium unemployment rate (or output level), and substitute a downward sloping long-run Phillips curve with multiple equilibria as potential targets for policy makers. This restores the prominence of aggregate demand, an essential feature of Keynesian macroeconomics. We would add that concern over discarding equilibrium analysis in this context is unfounded. From a policy viewpoint, the important issue is whether shocks to an ongoing macroeconomic process have disturbance-amplifying tendencies. These possibilities are better understood by modelling short-run movements as the outcome of a Keynesian income-generating mechanism that incorporates the newly recognized wage and price inflexibilities.

NEW KEYNESIAN LONGER-RUN ANALYSIS

To formulate their core short-run model, New Keynesians have concentrated on the causes of wage and price rigidities and their impact on the economy. They have shown scant interest in developing its long-run properties. This neglect is consistent with their acceptance that, once disturbed, the system returns (no matter very slowly) to its short-run macroeconomic equilibrium at an exogenously determined NAIRU or natural rate of unemployment and output level. To construct their long-run framework, New Keynesians follow one of two approaches. The first simply fits a smoothly evolving trend line to an historical output or unemployment series, and designates this line as the long-run equilibrium path of the economy (Mankiw, 1994, figure 5.1 or CEPR, 1995, fn. 20). In effect, this approach assumes the moving equilibrium of the system can always be derived from the past history of the economy, whatever path this has taken. No theoretical or empirical evidence is provided to support this assumption.

The second approach treats the long-run equilibrium path of the economy as exogenous, but does so by attaching a neoclassical aggregate production function to the core short-run model (Solow, 2000). In this way, the moving equilibrium of the economy is assumed to be at the full employment rates of output growth and unemployment. In the absence of shocks the economic system moves along a steady state, full employment equilibrium path determined solely by exogenous supply-side factors. Alternatively, some New Keynesians combine this steady-state component with the core short-run model, but allow shocks. The result differs only in assuming mild, shock-induced cycles around a steady-state full employment growth path.

In either formulation the full employment assumption raises additional problems for the New Keynesian research program. First, there is the problem of internal inconsistency. By assuming the economy moves along a full employment growth path in the long run, markets are assumed neoclassical in the long run at the same time as they are Keynesian in the short run (Solow, 2000). Second, in assuming the economy moves along a full employment path, the New Keynesian long-run analysis also fails as a descriptive device. It describes a history of more or less continuous full employment, perhaps occasionally and briefly interrupted by shock-induced deviations from full employment. But the actual unemployment record of the developed capitalist economies reveals lengthy episodes of alternating low and high unemployment over a long-run period stretching from the end of World War I until the present.[3] This pattern is widely experienced by the developed economies, suggesting that such episodes are a common feature of capitalism. Unemployment rates were low in the 1920s (the unweighted average rate was 3.8 per cent),[4] followed by a long episode of high unemployment (9.2 per cent) and low growth in the Great Depression. Good performance returned in the episode following World War II (unemployment averaged 2.4 per cent), the so-called Golden Age of capitalism. This was to last less than a quarter of a century. The mid-1970s heralded an episode of high unemployment (6.2 per cent) and slow growth that still persists in most countries.

Further, while mild increases in unemployment rates within an episode might be caused by shocks, episodes of persistently high unemployment cannot be so explained. The unemployment has been too high and too widely dispersed across economies. Instead, these episodes draw attention to long periods of inadequate aggregate demand. The length of these high unemployment episodes varies, but their duration falls between the usual definitions of short run and long run. Each episode is therefore designated a medium run in our analysis (Solow, 2000; Blanchard, 1997). A sequence of such episodes defines our long run. In the previous section we questioned the usefulness of New Keynesian equilibrium analysis in modelling short-run movements of the unemployment rate. In our view it also lacks the analytical tools for explaining longer-run periods of unemployment. In the next section we present a political economy theory of aggregate demand that uses Keynesian principles to model the medium run.

MEDIUM-RUN KEYNESIAN MACROECONOMICS

The Demand for and Supply of Expansionary Policies

Our Keynesian alternative provides a theoretical framework that models the historical record for the medium and long runs. For our medium-run analysis, we outline an extension of a basic Keynesian principle. We start from the Keynesian assumption that capitalism is not self-regulating because the private sector cannot be relied upon to deliver continuous high aggregate demand. Without the use of stimulative fiscal policies, periods of high involuntary unemployment are therefore likely. We then extend the analysis by investigating *why* periods of insufficient aggregate demand are allowed to continue. For example, in periods of high unemployment such as the 1930s and the long episode since the Golden Age, when stimulative aggregate demand policies would have reduced unemployment, why did the authorities fail to provide full employment levels of aggregate demand.

To answer these questions, we model the *dominant* macroeconomic policy response of the authorities within any historical episode as the outcome of an interaction between the supply of and demand for full employment policies.[5] The strength of demand for full employment policies is determined by the distribution of political and economic power among organized interest groups. The policies supplied by the authorities depend upon whether there are constraints limiting their policy options, for example, because full employment levels of aggregate demand generate unacceptable inflation or external imbalance, or because there are laws that limit budget deficits. In this section we focus on the inflation constraint, a common problem facing high unemployment economies during these episodes, and use a theory of group preferences for our analysis.[6] The remainder of the chapter concentrates on the two post-World War II episodes.

The party control theory of economic policy is the most prominent of the models focusing on the demand side, offering a political explanation of policy choice and differences in unemployment rates across countries in terms of the relative strength of right-wing and left-wing political parties (for example, Kalecki, 1971; Hibbs, 1987; Alesina et al., 1997). This is assumed to depend upon the distribution of power between capital and labor. According to this theory, labor is more willing than capital to trade price stability for lower unemployment; this preference is registered at the ballot box through its choice of political parties. When these cross-country results are applied to intertemporal events, differences in aggregate demand policies and unemployment are traced to shifts in political power within an economy.

However, we contend that the impact of the distribution of political power on unemployment records can only be part of the story, accounting only for the strength of *demand* for expansionary policies. Even the most ardently pro-labor government must consider the costs of supplying a full employment policy, the most obvious among them the inflation cost. In this case, the determinant of the underlying costs and therefore the willingness to supply stimulative policies is the position of the Phillips curve, with a poorly placed Phillips curve acting as a constraint. For example, if the maximum politically acceptable rate of price inflation intersects the Phillips curve to the right of the full employment rate of unemployment, policy will target an unemployment rate greater than the full employment rate. In such an economy inflation costs constrain expansionary policy.

The Position of the Phillips Curve

The forces determining the position of the Phillips curve can be traced, both across economies and through time, to certain labor market institutions. In the period since World War II, the most important of these has been the strategy adopted by labor, business and government to institutionalize 'fairness' in labor markets. With some variations, there were two types of strategy. One permitted full employment with politically acceptable rates of inflation; the other failed to do so.[7] The latter describes the outcome of using a 'market power' strategy in which wage settlements were reached through unrestricted collective bargaining between labor and management. The adoption of this labor market strategy reflected, and helped to perpetuate, the conflict endemic to an adversarial industrial relations system, often manifested as a high strike volume. In these cases there were no institutions (other than the market) that would routinely coordinate wage settlements with national goals; governments had failed to exercise leadership in establishing such institutions. The lack of coordinating institutions resulted in a strong emphasis on the money wage as the target of bargaining. Maximizing increases in money wages, with the cost of living and wage settlements in other sectors as guides, was chosen by labor as the means to maximize real wage gains. Unfortunately efforts to maximize the rate of increase of money wages under full employment conditions led to politically unacceptable rates of wage and price inflation. The result was restrictive aggregate demand policies and lower output, leading to reduced growth rates of productivity and real wages.[8] More generally, since labor's market power rose when unemployment rates fell, this strategy generated a negatively sloped long-run Phillips curve with an unsatisfactory menu of inflation-unemployment choices.

In contrast, economies in which a 'social bargain' strategy was adopted in cooperation with capital and overseen by government, labor accepted the need for money wage restraint in order to achieve national goals such as wage and price stability and international competitiveness. In exchange, labor was promised full employment, the rising real wage that full employment generated through higher productivity growth, and welfare programs as a safety net. Variations in the institutional forms of the social bargain, including the generosity of welfare programs and employment protection measures, were largely the result of differences in the power of labor. In most of the developed capitalist economics, social bargain strategies were adopted and proved a success in restraining inflation at full employment during the Golden Age.

In summary, considering both the demand for and supply of policies allows us to offer an explanation of the dominant policy stance and macroeconomic outcomes, giving insight into the differences in macroeconomic performance between countries, a view supported in the penultimate section. In the next section we indicate its value in explaining differences in successive historical episodes. To anticipate our conclusions, the Golden Age was remarkable for its absence of constraints on full employment policies other than an unacceptable inflation cost, and even this was limited to a small number of economies. This enhanced the ability of the authorities to supply full employment. In the episode that followed the Golden Age new institutional constraints arose, as well as the spread of the inflation constraint to other countries, causing a proliferation of restrictive policies. There was also a shift in the distribution of power to capital in most economies, adversely affecting the demand for expansionary policies.

A LONG-RUN KEYNESIAN MODEL OF GROWTH AND DEVELOPMENT

Intertemporal Analysis

Our extension of the standard Keynesian framework deepens the analysis, incorporating Keynesian policy principles within a more formal political economy framework to derive a political economy theory of aggregate demand. Within each episode the overall macroeconomic outcome is modelled as the result of an interaction between political and economic processes. The former considers the authorities' policy response to the preferences of organized political interest groups responding to macroeconomic conditions. The latter considers the impact of government policy intervention on macroeconomic performance.

Since in our analysis the long run is essentially a sequence of medium-term episodes, the political economy theory of aggregate demand is easily extended over time to explain a sequence of alternating episodes of good or poor macroeconomic performance. Each episode is a medium-run in the economy's long-run development, beginning and ending with a marked change in unemployment rates and related performance variables.[9] Each episode is therefore characterized by its fixed institutional framework and its distribution of power. A sustained radical alteration in performance signals the arrival of a new episode, characterized by new institutions or a new power distribution or both, and a major shift in the dominant policy stance of the authorities. For example, the institutional shift from a social bargain to a market power strategy would lead to incompatibility of full employment with acceptable inflation rates and restrictive policies that would end the boom. A radical shift in the distribution in power is also a possible source of radical shift in macroeconomic policy and performance.[10]

Linkages between Episodes

To this point our long run is a sequence of seemingly disconnected episodes of alternating good and poor performance. It is of course possible that an episode might end because of one or more radical shocks. In this case, the long-run performance of the economy displays the characteristics stressed by complexity theorists such as Basil Moore. However, our contention is that even in the absence of such shocks the development of capitalist economies can generate its own change, creating links between successive episodes, yielding a path-dependent process. These links stem from the performance of the economy itself. In the medium run the institutions and

Distribution of power and institutional framework → AD policies adopted → Unemployment performance → New distribution of power and institutional framework

Figure 21.1 *Path dependence*

power distribution that define the episode are taken as exogenously given causes of economic performance. In the long run, that is, from one episode to the next, these institutions and the distribution of power are eventually subject to change induced by the medium-run performance of the economy, thus becoming endogenous effects of economic performance. In this way the long-run dynamics of the system are modelled as a path-dependent and evolutionary process with a negative feedback.[11] Although not found in Keynes's writings, this evolutionary feature is easily incorporated to formulate a long-run theory of growth and development in a Keynesian spirit.[12]

Figure 21.1 illustrates this dynamic interaction. Starting at some initial point in time, the prevailing institutional framework acts as a constraint limiting and shaping economic performance, including the set of policy options available to the authorities. However the policy chosen will also depend on the distribution of power, which influences the strength of demand for full employment policies. Moving across the diagram from left to right, the policies adopted then influence the actual unemployment performance of the economy. For example, if the distribution of political power in the first episode was strongly left-of-centre in an economy in which a social bargain had been adopted, we would expect expansionary policies to be in effect with low unemployment and rapid growth of productivity and living standards the result. As long as these institutional and power characteristics remain substantially unchanged, the episode of favorable macroeconomic performance would continue.

But the historical record is clear; good times come to an end and poor performance does not last forever. The right-most arrow in Figure 21.1 designates the endogenously induced impact of performance on the institutional framework and the distribution of power in what constitutes the *long run* in our analysis. For example, suppose the economy is experiencing a prolonged period of affluence, such as the Golden Age. As the episode lengthens, rising expectations and aspirations outpace the economy's capacity to meet them. Dissatisfaction with the income distribution enshrined in the social bargain increases, leading to their collapse and the adoption of a market power strategy. There is then a rightward shift of the Phillips curve, followed by accelerating inflation and a restrictive policy response. The new institutions and the reduced relative power of labor caused by the rising unemployment define a new episode, characterized by diminished macroeconomic performance; the new episode is causally linked to the previous one by endogenously induced institutional change.[13]

A CLOSER LOOK AT THE RECORD

The Golden Age

To illustrate the explanatory value of our evolutionary-Keynesian framework, we continue to focus on the second half of the twentieth century, comprising the years following World War II until the mid-1970s, and the period from the mid-1970s to the present. These two historical episodes, the Golden Age and the Age of Decline, are distinguished by markedly different macroeconomic performance, institutional frameworks and power structures. As we have outlined, they were endogenously linked, with performance in the second causally related to events in the first. Eighteen developed capitalist economies are included in our sample.

Table 21.1 allows a closer examination of the data for the post-World War II period. It shows unemployment and inflation rates for two short-run gross domestic product (GDP) cycles in the Golden Age episode and for three successive within-episode short-run GDP cycles in the Age of Decline.[14] Short-run cyclical movements occur within an episode because of wage and price rigidities. According to the arguments above, it is unlikely that in this succession of short-run cycles any short-run equilibrium was realized. Rather, each describes an example of a damped cyclical movement, generated by a Keynesian income-generating mechanism. In our analysis, markets are Keynesian in the short and medium runs. Moreover, as our long run consists of a series of medium runs, markets are Keynesian in the long run also. Hence, there is no internal inconsistency in our analysis.

Using a 3 per cent rate as the full employment rate of unemployment, in the Golden Age episode all but four of the eighteen countries in the table experienced full employment. Considering the entire post-World War II period, the economies fall into three groups: the 'low unemployment economies' with full employment in the Golden Age (1960–73) and in most of the subsequent short-run cycles; the 'high unemployment economies' with unemployment rates in excess of full employment both during and after the Golden Age; and the 'low-high unemployment economies' with full employment during the Golden Age followed by high unemployment.

It should also be noted that in the Golden Age the low unemployment economies did not experience appreciably higher rates of inflation, indicating that the inflation rate was not merely a politically acceptable trade-off; these economies did not pay a higher inflation cost for their full employment. According to the argument above, this remarkable development can be attributed to a combination of strong political demand for full employment and a willingness of the authorities to supply it, because there were no institutional constraints on aggregate demand. We trace the absence of constraints to the adoption of social bargains, which were designed to reconcile low unemployment with the containment of inflationary pressures.[15] There were such constraints in the high unemployment group. These economies performed badly because of weak demand for expansionary policies, or institutional constraints or from a combination of the two.

The Age of Decline

The Golden Age of capitalism lasted about a quarter of a century. Following the 'Great Inflation' of the late 1960s to early 1970s, a lengthy upward trend in unemployment rates began, without the compensation of lower inflation rates, signalling the start of a new episode of capitalist development. While the 'Great Inflation' is usually attributed to temporary disturbances, for example, oil price shocks, our analysis suggests the cause to have been a more lasting structural change linking this new episode with the Golden Age; social bargains collapsed as capital and labor adopted market power strategies in all but the few remaining low unemployment economies.[16] This institutional change, signalled by accelerating wage inflation, made it impossible to achieve low inflation at full employment in most countries. Indeed, inflation did not fall to Golden Age rates – the so-called 'victory over inflation' – until well into the 1990s. The persistence of high inflation reinforced the shift to low inflation as the overriding macroeconomic policy target and to restrictive aggregate demand as the preferred instrument. Table 21.1 records the near relentless rise in unemployment in all but five economies. Nevertheless, with the exception of Sweden in the 1990s, the five low unemployment economies maintained their commitment to social bargains and were able to maintain relatively low rates of unemployment.

The rising inflation cost of low unemployment was a severe constraint on aggregate demand, but now there were others. The widespread implementation of restrictive policies was itself an impediment to expansionary policies for any economy acting alone, thanks in part to changes in the international monetary system, which shifted to flexible exchange rates and increasing deregulation of financial capital movements. This threatens currency depreciation and accelerating inflation should any country attempt unilateral expansion. To this can be added the trend toward governments

Table 21.1 Annual average standardized unemployment rates (U) and rates of consumer price inflation ($\dot{p}$)** for 18 OECD countries (%)*

	1960–67		1968–73		1974–79		1980–89		1990–2000	
	U	$\dot{p}$	U	$\dot{p}$	U	$\dot{p}$	U	$\dot{p}$	U	$\dot{p}$
Low unemployment										
Austria	2.0	3.6	1.8	5.2	1.8	6.2	3.3	3.8	3.9	2.4
Japan	1.4	5.7	1.2	7.1	1.9	9.9	2.5	2.5	3.2	1.0
Norway	2.0	3.9	1.7	6.9	1.8	8.7	2.8	8.3	4.8	2.5
Sweden	1.6	3.8	2.2	6.0	1.9	9.8	2.6	7.9	7.1	3.3
Switzerland	0.0	3.4	0.0	5.6	0.4	4.0	0.6	3.3	3.1	2.3
Unweighted Average	1.4	4.1	1.4	6.2	1.6	7.7	2.4	5.2	4.4	2.3
High unemployment										
Canada	4.8	2.4	5.4	4.6	7.2	9.2	9.4	6.5	9.3	2.2
Ireland	4.9	4.0	5.6	8.9	7.9	14.9	14.3	9.2	11.3	2.6
Italy	4.8	4.0	5.7	5.8	6.6	16.1	8.0	11.1	10.6	4.0
United States	4.9	2.0	4.6	5.0	6.8	8.5	7.3	5.5	5.6	3.0
Unweighted Average	4.9	3.1	5.3	6.1	7.1	12.2	9.8	8.1	9.2	3.0

Low–high unemployment										
Australia	2.2	2.2	2.0	5.6	5.1	12.2	7.5	8.4	8.4	2.7
Belgium	2.0	2.8	2.5	4.9	7.1	8.4	9.8	4.9	8.5	2.2
Denmark	1.6	6.2	1.0	6.3	6.1	10.8	8.1	6.9	7.1	2.2
Finland	1.6	5.6	2.6	5.8	5.1	12.6	5.4	7.1	11.7	2.3
France	1.6	3.6	2.6	6.1	4.5	10.7	8.8	7.3	11.1	1.9
Germany	0.6	2.7	1.0	4.6	3.2	4.6	5.8	2.9	7.7	2.5
Netherlands	1.0	3.6	1.5	6.9	5.4	7.2	7.9	2.8	5.4	2.5
New Zealand	0.1	3.3	0.3	7.4	0.8	13.8	4.6	11.8	7.8	2.1
United Kingdom	2.7	3.6	3.3	7.5	4.7	15.6	9.8	7.4	8.0	3.6
Unweighted average	1.5	3.7	1.9	6.1	4.7	10.7	7.5	6.6	8.4	2.4
Overall Average	2.2	3.7	2.5	6.1	4.4	10.2	6.6	6.5	7.5	2.5

Notes:
* OECD, *Historical Statistics 1970–2000* and earlier issues, Table 2.19, Standardized Unemployment Rates. For 1960–64, unemployment rates were obtained from the LSE data set. For Austria, Denmark and Switzerland, and for New Zealand prior to 1974, standardized rates are not available; unemployment as a percentage of the total labor force is used instead.
** OECD, *Historical Statistics 1970–2000* and earlier issues, Table 7.10.

reducing their involvement in the economy by removing or assigning less importance to some policy targets by introducing formal political constraints. These include enacting constitutional amendments requiring balanced budgets, adherence to restrictive budgetary criteria required for membership in international agreements, for example, membership in the European Monetary System, Maastricht and later the Stability Pact, and making the central bank increasingly independent of government.[17] Each of these trends contributes to the rise in unemployment rates by placing the full employment goal beyond democratic control. Finally, there was wide acceptance by governments and capital that the demise of the Soviet Union had greatly reduced the political reasons for supporting social bargains.

Some Institutions are Better than Others

In summary, we maintain that during the Golden Age the economies that were able to reduce unemployment to low rates without experiencing serious inflation costs were those that did not leave wage settlements to market forces. As well, only economies that maintained their social bargains during the Age of Decline were able to limit increases in unemployment rates. In particular, cross-country studies brought new support to the view that social bargains, that is, institutions that 'interfere' with free labor market outcomes, were necessary for full employment because they kept inflation at acceptable rates. This coordinating function could not be performed by the market. Unrestricted collective bargaining was the order of the day in countries with the strongest attachment to *laissez-faire* principles such as Canada and the US. As a result their macroeconomic performance suffered.

The end of the Golden Age coincided with the widespread rejection of social bargains and the introduction of additional constraints on aggregate demand. Comparing cross-country differences in performance in the Age of Decline, the historical evidence points to social bargains as a necessary condition for superior performance. A conspicuous feature of Table 21.1 is the consistently poor post-war unemployment record of the United States, compared to the other economies; this situation prevailed until the mid-1990s. We attribute the relatively poor long-run unemployment performance of the United States to its sustained adversarial industrial relations system and its weak political demands for full employment.

A FUTURE FOR KEYNESIAN MACROECONOMICS

Whether the focus is on a historical period encompassing most of the twentieth century or the shorter period since World War II, episodes of high and prolonged unemployment have been an integral part of modern capitalism's historical development. It bears repeating: these episodes of high unemployment have been too long and too widely dispersed across economies to be attributed to shocks interrupting an otherwise full employment growth path. The record shows that capitalism is not self-regulating. From a Keynesian viewpoint a necessary condition for full employment (and indeed the faster growth of per capita incomes full employment brings) is strong, sustained and growing aggregate demand, achieved when necessary by stimulative policies.

We have argued that New Keynesian macroeconomics has limited Keynesian content, and that it cannot explain macroeconomic outcomes because it rests on a foundation of exogenous supply-determined equilibrium analysis. In its short-run analysis of the model, this foundation generates an equilibrium unemployment rate that fails to explain movements of the actual unemployment rate. The long-run version of this analysis typically adopts a steady-state full employment growth path, an assumption inconsistent with the historical record. As well, this kind of treatment of the long run leads to a model in which markets do not clear in the short run, but clear in the long run; the model is Keynesian in the short run and neoclassical in the long run. Our extended Keynesian framework has neither inconsistency. We model the long-run historical record of modern capitalism as a sequence of medium-run alternating episodes of favorable and unfavorable macroeconomic performance, each of which is composed of a sequence of Keynesian short runs.

New Keynesian macroeconomics suffers from another disability, related to the failure of its advocates to understand that capitalism comes in many different forms, and that the 'Anglo-Saxon' form is a rather special adversarial kind in which capital demands very special treatment and powers. Within this milieu New Keynesians have been prone to explain lengthy periods of high unemployment by government interventions that have limited capital's control and economic power. Their policy response is to reduce labour's power. But the cross-country comparisons in the last section show clearly that during the post-World War II period the best-performing economies were those in which the free play of market forces was restricted through interventions on behalf of labor.

If there is to be a future for macroeconomics it must be Keynesian, and the first step is to persuade macroeconomists that their theories should be free of internal inconsistencies and be consistent with the historical record. This will be a difficult task, requiring as it does the abandonment of a very large part of current macroeconomic research. Most important is the recognition that New Keynesian economics is trapped in an equilibrium framework that cannot provide an empirically respectable account of the stylized facts of the historical record. This we have traced to their insistence on adopting a framework in which aggregate demand merely adjusts passively to the dictates of a supply-determined equilibrium. This has prevented the development of a political economy theory of aggregate demand, a necessary condition for macroeconomics to provide an acceptable account of recent events. To escape, contemporary macroeconomics must reject its supply-determined equilibrium foundations. Our extended Keynesian framework offers an escape route.

NOTES

1. We are indebted to the Academic Vice-President's Office, the Faculty of Science and the Department of Economics, all of Dalhousie University for providing financial support for this research. We also wish to thank Myron Gordon and Mark Setterfield for their helpful comments and suggestions.
2. The ability of the monetary authorities to adjust aggregate demand by targeting interest rates is still untested.
3. See Table 2.1 in Cornwall and Cornwall (2001).
4. Figures based on data for 16 of the 18 OECD economies of Table 21.1 below; prior to the Golden Age, data are not available for Ireland and New Zealand.
5. See Gordon (1975) for an early explanation of policy outcomes stressing both demand and supply influences.
6. A fully specified version of this approach is tested econometrically in Chapter 5 of Cornwall and Cornwall (2001).
7. For greater detail see Cornwall (1994, Chapters 5–7).
8. Empirical work by the authors, reported in Chapter 11 of Cornwall and Cornwall (2001), shows a strong correlation between growth rates of output and labor productivity.
9. Compared with the Age of Decline, the Golden Age was an episode of rapid growth in *per capita* incomes and labor productivity.
10. Kalecki's (1971) famous model of the political business cycle offers an alternative explanation of the interruption of aggregate demand, that is, capital's ability to force governments to enact high unemployment policies.
11. In previous work (Cornwall and Cornwall, 2001) we have analyzed the entire period beginning in the 1920s as an evolutionary process consisting of the four episodes listed above. In this study we argued that the main cause of the Great Depression in the USA could be traced to basic changes in its industrial structure during the 1920s rather than in changes in institutions.
12. Kaldor's model of cumulative causation is an example of a path-dependent system in which outcomes depend upon initial conditions. Our model exhibits a path-dependent process that creates its own set of potential final outcomes in the course of its historical evolution (Setterfield, 1997, pp. 64–5).
13. Exogenous shocks could also lead to radical changes in institutions and the distribution of power. The impact of World War II is a clear example.
14. Comparable data are not available for all eighteen countries prior to 1960. The endpoints for the periods shown in the table are those published in *OECD Historical Statistics*.
15. See Cornwall (1994), Chapters 5–7.
16. See ibid., Chapter 7, for a detailed discussion and support.
17. For an estimate of the impact of these institutional changes on rising unemployment rates in the Age of Decline, see Cornwall and Cornwall (2001), Table 11.2.

REFERENCES

Alesina, A., N. Roubini and G. Cohen (1997) *Political Cycles and the Macroeconomy*, Cambridge, MA: The MIT Press.

Blanchard, O. (1997) 'Is There a Core of Usable Macroeconomics?' *Journal of Economic Perspectives*, 14, 244–6.

Blanchard, O. (2000) 'What do we Know about Macroeconomics that Fisher and Wicksell did Not?' *Quarterly Journal of Economics*, 115, 1375–409.

CEPR (1995) *Unemployment: Choices for Europe*, London: Centre for Economic Policy Research.

Cornwall, J. (1994) *Economic Breakdown and Recovery: Theory and Policy*, Armonk, NY: M.E. Sharpe.

Cornwall, J. and W. Cornwall (2001) *Capitalist Development in the Twentieth Century: An Evolutionary-Keynesian Analysis*, Cambridge: Cambridge University Press.

Gordon, R.J. (1975) 'The Demand for and Supply of Inflation', *Journal of Law and Economics*, 18, 807–36.

Hibbs, D. (1987) 'Political Parties and Macroeconomic Policy', in *The Political Economy of Industrial Democracies*, Cambridge, MA: Harvard University Press.

Kalecki, M. (1971) 'Political Aspects of Full Employment', chapter 12 in *Selected Essays on the Dynamics of the Capitalist Economy*, Cambridge: Cambridge University Press.

Mankiw, N.G. (1994) *Macroeconomics*, 2nd edition, New York: Worth Publishers.

OECD, *Historical Statistics 1970–2000*, Paris: OECD.

Solow, R. (2000) 'Towards a Macroeconomics of the Medium Run', *Journal of Economic Perspectives*, 14, 151–8.

Tobin, J. (1993) 'Price Flexibility and Output Stability: An Old Keynesian View', *Journal of Economic Perspectives*, 7, 45–65.

Selected works by Basil J. Moore

BOOKS

Shaking the Invisible Hand: Complexity, Endogenous Money and Exogenous Interest Rates, London and New York: Palgrave-Macmillan (2006).

Horizontalists and Verticalists: The Macroeconomics of Credit Money, Cambridge, New York and Melbourne: Cambridge University Press (1988).

An Introduction to Modern Economic Theory, London, Macmillan and New York: Free Press (1973). Spanish edition published 1974.

An Introduction to the Theory of Finance: Assetholder Behavior Under Uncertainty, New York: Free Press (1968). Japanese edition published 1971; Indian edition published 1971; Spanish edition published 1972.

ARTICLES IN JOURNALS AND CHAPTERS IN BOOKS

'The Post Keynesian Case for No Exchange Rates', in C. Gnos and L.P. Rochon (eds), *Post Keynesian Principles of Economic Policy*, Cheltenham, UK and Northampton, MA, USA: Edward Elgar (2006), 214–50.

'Saving and Investment: Keynes Revisited', in R. Arena and N. Salvadori (eds), *Money, Credit and the Role of the State: Essays in Honour of Augusto Graziani*, Aldershot: Ashgate (2004), 236–52.

'A Global Currency for a Global Economy', *Journal of Post Keynesian Economics*, 26(4) (Summer 2004), 631–53.

'L'endogénéité de l'offre de monnaie: fixe-t-on le "prix" ou la "quantité" des réserves?', in P. Piégay and L.P. Rochon (eds), *Théories monétaires post keynésiennes*, Paris: Economica (2003), 41–51.

'Saving is the Accounting Record of Investment', in P. Arestis, M. Baddeley and J.S.L. McCombie (eds), *Globalization, Regionalism and Economic Activity*, Cheltenham, UK and Northampton, MA, USA: Edward Elgar (2003), 245–65.

'Saving and Investment: The Theoretical Case for Lower Interest Rates', in P. Davidson (ed.), *A Post Keynesian Perspective on Twenty-First Century Economic Problems*, Cheltenham, UK and Northampton, MA, USA: Edward Elgar (2002), 137–57.

'Some Reflections on Endogenous Money', in L.P. Rochon and M. Vernengo (eds), *Credit, Interest Rates and the Open Economy: Essays on Horizontalism*, Cheltenham, UK and Northampton, MA, USA: Edward Elgar (2001), 11–30.

'Economics and Complexity', in M. Setterfield (ed.), *Growth, Employment and Inflation: Essays in Honour of John Cornwall*, London: Macmillan Press and New York: St Martin's Press (1999), 41–56.

'Why Wage and Price Flexibility is Destabilizing', in P. Arestis (ed.), *Essays in Honour of Paul Davidson, Volume 3: Method, Theory and Policy in Keynes*, Cheltenham, UK and Northampton, MA, USA: Edward Elgar (1998), 125–46.

'Money and Interest Rates in a Monetary Theory of Production', in R. Rotheim (ed.), *New Keynesian Economics/Post Keynesian Alternatives*, London and New York: Routledge (1998), 339–55.

'Accommodation to Accommodationism: A Note', *Journal of Post Keynesian Economics*, 21(1) (Fall 1998), 175–8.

'Reconciliation of the Supply and Demand for Endogenous Money', *Journal of Post Keynesian Economics*, 19(3) (Spring 1997), 423–8.

'The Money Supply Process: A Historical Reinterpretation', in G. Deleplace and E.J. Nell (eds), *Money in Motion: The Post Keynesian and Circulation Approaches*, London: Macmillan Press and New York: St Martin's Press (1996), 89–101.

'Sluggish Job Growth: Rising Productivity, Anemic Recovery, or Something Else?', *Journal of Post Keynesian Economics*, 17(3) (Spring 1995), 473–7.

'The Exogeneity of Short-Term Interest Rates: Reply', *Journal of Economic Issues*, 29(1) (March 1995), 258–66.

'The Demise of the Keynesian Multiplier: A Reply to Cottrell', *Journal of Post Keynesian Economics*, 17(1) (Fall 1994), 121–33.

'The Case for a Land Tax: From Entitlement to Restitution', *Indicator South Africa*, 9(2) (Autumn 1992), 25–9.

'Marx, Keynes, Kalecki and Kaldor on the Rate of Interest as a Monetary Phenomenon', in E.J. Nell and W. Semmler (eds), *Nicholas Kaldor and Mainstream Economics: Confrontation or Convergence?* New York: St Martin's Press (1991), 225–42.

'Has the Demand for Money Been Mislaid? A Reply', *Journal of Post Keynesian Economics*, 14(1) (Fall 1991), 125–33.

'Money Supply Endogeneity: "Reserve Price Setting" or "Reserve Quantity Setting"?', *Journal of Post Keynesian Economics*, 13(3) (Spring 1991), 404–13.

'Why Investment Determines Saving', *Challenge*, 33(3) (May–June 1990), 55–6.

'Money and Economic Activity, A Response to the Reserve Bank Comment', *South African Journal of Economics*, 58(3) (September 1990), 364–7.

'Inflation and Wealth Values', *Malaysian Journal of Economic Studies*, 26(1) (1989), 85–92.

'On the Endogeneity of Money Once More: Comment', *Journal of Post Keynesian Economics*, 11(3) (Spring 1989), 479–87.

'Does Money Supply Endogeneity Matter? A Comment', *South African Journal of Economics*, 57(2) (June 1989), 194–200.

'The Endogeneity of Credit Money', *Review of Political Economy*, 1(1) (Summer 1989), 65–93.

'A Simple Model of Bank Intermediation', *Journal of Post Keynesian Economics*, 12(1) (Fall 1989), 10–28.

'Money Supply Exogeneity/Endogeneity: A Historical Reconciliation', *Keizai Seminar*, No. 417, Nihonhyoronsha, Tokyo (September 1989), 58–65 (translated into Japanese by Toshio Ogata).

'Inflation and Financial Deepening: A Reply', *Journal of Development Economics*, 31(2) (October 1989), 397–401.

'The Effects of Monetary Policy on Income Distribution', in P. Davidson and J. Kregel (eds), *Macroeconomic Problems and Policies of Income Distribution:*

Functional, Personal, International, Aldershot, UK and Brookfield, USA: Edward Elgar (1989), 18–41.

'The Endogenous Money Supply: Concluding Comments', *Journal of Post Keynesian Economics*, 10(3) (Spring 1988), 398–400.

'The Endogenous Money Supply', *Journal of Post Keynesian Economics*, 10(3) (Spring 1988), 372–85.

'The Endogeneity of Money: A Comment', *Scottish Journal of Political Economy*, 35(3) (August 1988), 291–94.

'Keynes's Treatment of Interest', in O.F. Hamouda and J.N. Smithin (eds), *Keynes and Public Policy After Fifty Years, Volume 2: Theories and Method*, New York: New York University Press (1988), 121–9.

'Inflation and Financial Deepening', *Journal of Development Economics*, 20(1) (January–February 1986), 125–33.

'Wages, Money and Inflation', *South African Journal of Economics*, 54(1) (March 1986), 80–93 (with B. Smit).

'How Credit Drives the Money Supply: The Significance of Institutional Developments', *Journal of Economic Issues*, 20(2) (June 1986), 443–52.

'Wages, Bank Lending and the Endogeneity of Credit Money', in M. Jarsulic (ed.), *Money and Macro Policy*, Hingham, MA: Kluwer-Nijhoff (1985), 1–28. Reprinted as 'Desempaquetando La Caja Negra Postkeynesiana: Salarios, Credito Bancario Y La Oferta Monetaria', *Hacienda Publica Espanola* (1/1991).

'Corporate Bank Borrowing in the UK, 1965–1981', *Economica*, 52(25) (February 1985), 65–78 (with Andrew R. Threadgold).

'Unpacking the Post-Keynesian Black Box: Wages, Bank Lending and the Money Supply', *Thames Papers in Political Economy*, London: Thames Polytechnic (1984). Reprinted in P. Arestis (ed.), *Post-Keynesian Monetary Economics: New Approaches to Financial Modelling*, Aldershot, UK and Brookfield, USA: Edward Elgar (1988), 122–51.

'Keynes and the Endogeneity of the Money Stock', *Studi Economici*, 39(22) (1984), 23–69.

'A Causality Analysis of the Determinants of Money Growth', *British Review of Economic Issues*, 6(14) (Spring 1984), 1–25 (with Stephen L. Stuttman).

'Contemporaneous Reserve Accounting: Can Reserves be Quantity-constrained?', *Journal of Post Keynesian Economics*, 7(1) (Fall 1984), 103–13.

'Monetary Trends in the United States and the United Kingdom, A Review', *The Financial Review*, 18(2) (May 1983), 146–66.

'Unpacking the Post Keynesian Black Box: Bank Lending and the Money Supply', *Journal of Post Keynesian Economics*, 5(4) (Summer 1983), 537–56. Reprinted in M.C. Sawyer (ed.), *Post-Keynesian Economics*, Aldershot, UK and Brookfield, USA: Edward Elgar (1989), 120–39; and M. Musella and C. Panico (eds), *The Money Supply in the Economic Process: A Post Keynesian Perspective*, Cheltenham, UK and Brookfield, USA: Edward Elgar (1996), 365–84.

'A Monument to Monetarism', *Journal of Post Keynesian Economics*, 6(1) (Fall 1983), 118–21.

'In Praise of Markets: Wage Imitation and Price Stability', *Challenge*, 25(4) (September–October 1982), 52–6.

'The Importance of Dividends in Share Valuation (or Why the Dow Will Reach 3000 Before 1990)', in J. Boeckh and R. Coghlan (eds), *The Stock Market and Inflation*, Homewood, IL: Dow Jones-Irwin (1982), 119–36.

'The Endogenous Money Stock: A Reply', *Journal of Post Keynesian Economics*, 4(2) (Winter 1981–82), 306–9.

'Equity Values and Inflation: The Importance of Dividends', *Lloyds Bank Review*, 137(8) (July 1980), 1–15. Abridged in *Chartered Financial Analysts Digest* (1981).

'Is the Money Stock Really a Control Variable?', *Challenge*, 24(3) (July–August 1981), 43–6. Reprinted in R. Guttmann (ed.), *Reforming Money and Finance: Institutions and Markets in Flux*, Armonk, NY and London: M.E. Sharpe (1989), 58–61.

'The Difficulty of Controlling the Money Stock', *Journal of Portfolio Management*, 7(4) (Summer 1981), 7–14.

'Market Structure Versus Information Costs as the Determinants of Underwriters' Spreads on Municipal Bonds', *Journal of Financial and Quantitative Analysis*, XV(1) (March 1980), 85–97 (with W.W. Higgins).

'The Endogenous Money Stock', *Journal of Post Keynesian Economics*, 2(1) (Fall 1979), 49–70. Reprinted in M. Musella and C. Panico (eds), *The Money Supply in the Economic Process: A Post Keynesian Perspective*, Cheltenham, UK and Brookfield, USA: Edward Elgar (1996), 459–72.

'Monetary Factors', in A. Eichner (ed.), *A Guide to Post-Keynesian Economics*, New York: M.E. Sharpe (1979), 120–38.

'Life-Cycle Saving and Bequest Behavior', *Journal of Post Keynesian Economics*, 1(2) (Winter 1978–9), 79–99.

'The Economics of the Stock Market and the Great Depression', in J. Dreyer (ed.), *Breadth and Depth in Economics: Fritz Machlup – The Man and His Ideas*, Lexington, MA: Lexington Books (1978), 283–99.

'A Post-Keynesian Approach to Monetary Theory', *Challenge*, 21(4) (September–October 1978), 44–52.

'Equities, Capital Gains and the Role of Finance in Accumulation', *American Economic Review*, 65(5) (December 1975), 872–86. Reprinted in C. Panico and N. Salvadori (eds), *Post Keynesian Theory of Growth and Distribution*, Aldershot, UK and Brookfield, USA: Edward Elgar (1993), 287–301.

'The Pasinetti Paradox Revisited', *Review of Economic Studies*, 41(2) (April 1974), 297–99.

'Some Macroeconomic Consequences of Corporate Equities', *Canadian Journal of Economics*, 6(4) (November 1973), 529–44.

'Optimal Monetary Policy', *Economic Journal*, 82(325) (March 1972), 116–39.

'Asset Management and Monetary Policy: Discussion', *Journal of Finance*, 24(2) (May 1969), 242–4.

'Capitalization and Profitability in Canadian Banking', *Canadian Journal of Economics and Political Science*, XXVII(2) (May 1961), 192–204.

Index